America's 50 Fastest Growing Jobs

America's 50 Fastest Growing Jobs

J. Michael Farr
Includes information and data from various U.S. Department of Labor publications
Third Edition

This newly revised edition includes:

- Completely revised and updated job descriptions
- Latest growth projections for more than 250 jobs
- Revised information on important labor market trends
- Fastest growing jobs listed by education, industry, earnings, projected openings, and other criteria
- Expanded career planning and job search section
- Easier-to-use format in four complete sections
- New appendices providing details on employment projections for self-employed workers; more than 500 jobs organized by training and education required; plus projections, earnings, and education required for the 500 largest occupations

America's 50 Fastest Growing Jobs
Official Information on the Best Jobs in Our Economy
© 1995 by JIST Works, Inc.

Other Books by Mike Farr
- The Very Quick Job Search, 2nd Edition
- The Quick Resume & Cover Letter Book
- The Quick Interview & Salary Negotiation Book
- Getting the Job You Really Want, 3rd Edition

Other Books in the "Top Jobs" series include:
- *America's Top Federal Jobs*
- *America's Top Jobs for College Graduates*
- *America's Top Medical and Human Services Jobs*
- *America's Top Military Careers*
- *America's Top Office, Management, and Sales Jobs*
- *America's Top Technical and Trade Jobs*
- *America's Top 300 Jobs* (Based on the *Occupational Outlook Handbook*)
- *Career Guide to America's Top Industries*

Published by JIST Works, Inc.
720 North Park Avenue
Indianapolis, IN 46202-3431
Phone: 317-264-3720 Fax: 317-264-3709 E-mail: JISTWorks@AOL.com

Cover Design: LGN Graphics-Laura Nikiel

Printed in the United States of America

99 98 97 96   5 4 3 2

We have been careful to provide accurate information throughout this book, but it is possible that errors and omissions have been introduced. Please consider this in making any career plans or other important decisions. Trust your own judgment above all else and in all things.

ISBN 1-56370-199-5

ISSN 1070-8537

What This Book Is About

Preface

Please read this before you decide whether to buy this book.

What This Book Is About

Knowing more about the fastest growing jobs is an appealing concept. That's probably why you picked up this book, right? And this book will cover that subject very well. It provides lots of information on which occupations are the fastest growing—including thorough and up-to-date descriptions of the top 50.

But this book is really quite a bit more than *just* a book on the fastest growing jobs because it can also help you make good career decisions and find a good job. That's really what you were wondering about anyway, and I've provided a variety of information to help you with this task including:

- An overview of the labor market and its major trends
- A special section on career planning and job search skills
- Thorough descriptions of 50 of the fastest growing jobs
- Details on hundreds of the top jobs including projected growth, education required, earnings, and other data
- Appendixes that provide information on industry trends, self-employment, and more

Who Can Use This Book?

Everyone who is looking for a better job should find this book of interest including:

Those exploring career options: You will find information on the fastest growing jobs offering excellent opportunities and summary information on hundreds of additional jobs. A special career planning section is an added bonus that can help you identify career options.

Students and those considering more education or training: The thorough job descriptions can help you avoid costly career mistakes and increase your chances of planning a brighter future.

Job seekers: The information in this book will help you prepare for interviews. There is also a section providing job search advice proven to cut your job search time in half.

Counselors: *America's 50 Fastest Growing Jobs* is a valuable source of information on jobs and trends!

How This Book Is Organized-And Some Tips on How to Use It

You really don't need to *read* this book in a conventional front to back sense. (That should come as a great relief because there is a lot of information contained in these pages.) I've arranged it into four major sections so you can quickly get to the information that is of greatest interest to you.

Section 1—Labor Market Trends and the Fastest Growing Jobs: This section lists the fastest growing jobs and reviews important trends in the labor market.

Section 2—Up-to-Date Descriptions of the 50 Fastest Growing Jobs: This section provides thorough descriptions that include information on working conditions, skills required, future growth, earnings, education and training required, related jobs, and other details.

Section 3—Career Planning and Job Search Techniques: This section gives advice on career planning and on job search techniques. It's based on my many years of experience in finding ways to help people find a better job in less time.

Section 4—Appendices: This section includes various appendices that provide additional summary information on hundreds of additional jobs, industry trends, and other information I think you may find of interest.

Where Did All This Good Information Come From?

Most of the data I include in this book is based on information provided by the federal government. They really are the most reliable source of information on this topic, and we are all indebted to their hard work. This revision is primarily based on information published by the U.S. Department of Labor's Bureau of Labor Statistics in 1994 and 1995. Every two years the Bureau of Labor Statistics develops projections of the labor force, economic growth, industry output and employment, and occupational employment under three sets of alternative assumptions: low, moderate, and high. These projections cover a 10- to 15-year period in the future and provide the basis for much of the data in this book. Unless otherwise noted, the moderate alternative for each projection through the year 2005 was used. Let's hope that we are all around then to see if their projections were right...

Earlier editions of this book have been very well received. This is now the third edition and I hope that you find it useful, informative, and fun. I wish you well.

Mike Farr

Table of Contents

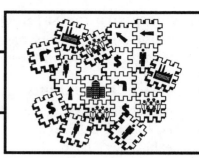

Labor Market Trends and the Fastest Growing Jobs

Section One

This section is divided into three major subsections. Because this book is about the fastest growing jobs, I figured that you would want to know which ones they are as soon as possible, so I've included lists of these jobs first.

Next comes information about the labor market. I assume that you are either considering various career alternatives or looking for a better job, so I've selected labor market details which I feel are most important for you to consider for these purposes. The third section includes a variety of charts and information which I felt might interest you. You don't have to read this entire section, although it will give you lots of good information about what is happening in the labor market.

The Fastest Growing Jobs

There are two ways to create a list of the fastest growing jobs in our economy. In previous editions of this book, I created a list beginning with the job with the highest percentage of projected growth and listing others in decreasing order. That list still makes sense and I have included such a list in this edition.

But one of the problems with such a list is that some occupations that were projected to create enormous numbers of openings were not among the fastest growing in terms of percentage growth. For example, the two jobs projected to have the largest number of job openings are retail salespeople and registered nurses, yet neither are among those with the highest percentage growth.

I've struggled with this issue for some time (believe it or not) because I wanted this book to be as helpful as possible to you in making career decisions. So, in this new edition, I have done something different: I've included two lists. The first one lists the fastest growing jobs in order of projected **percentage** growth and the second one lists the fastest growing jobs in order of the **number** of job openings they are projected to create.

Should I Consider Only the Fastest Growing Jobs?

With all the labor market change that is projected in the coming years, it would seem wise to consider those jobs that are growing most rapidly. Rapidly growing jobs are projected

to increase the numbers of people they employ and offer better-than-average opportunities for employment and job security. For this reason, you should certainly pay attention to jobs that are projected to grow rapidly. But you should also consider jobs that simply interest you, even if they are not among the fastest growing ones.

There will always be some openings for new people, even in slower-growing or declining jobs. Some of these jobs are numerous and will create many openings due to retirement, people leaving the field, and other reasons. Information on many of these jobs is provided in the appendices of this book. You should consider slower growing jobs if that is really what you want to do.

My Criteria for Selecting Jobs

Note that many jobs in each of the fastest growing jobs lists are in bold type and some are not. The jobs in bold have complete job descriptions provided in Section 2 of this book while the others do not.

I wanted to include thorough descriptions for 50 jobs in Section 2. To get to that number, I selected jobs I felt would be of the most interest to you: ones that have better earnings and/or potential for advancement and those that tend to require some formal training or education. That is why the job of cashier, for example, is not listed in bold, even though it is among the jobs expected to create the most openings. I also gave preference to jobs that were among the top 30 in percentage or numerical growth. The selection criteria I used in this edition made more sense to me and I hope it does to you as well.

The 50 Fastest Growing Jobs

While more than 12,000 different job titles are listed in the current *Dictionary of Occupational Titles*, about 500 of them account the job titles more than 85 percent of us actually hold.

Those 500 jobs are the most important ones for you to consider and I have used them in compiling the lists that follow. The projections are based on 1995 data provided by the U.S. Department of Labor (Bulletin 2451) and I have arranged them in order of their projected growth rates between now and the year 2005.

Jobs with an asterisk are also among those projected to have the greatest number of openings. I have provided a separate list of jobs projected to create the largest number of openings later in this section. Because some differences in job titles exist in various government listings (it's hard to explain why, trust me), some of the jobs are cross-referenced to the job title provided in Section 2.

Occupation	Percent growth projected
*Home health aides (see description "Homemaker—home health aides")	**138**
*Human services workers	136
Personal and home care aides (see description "Private household workers")	**130**
*Computer engineers and scientists (see description "Computer scientists and systems analysts")	**112**
*Systems analysts (see description "Computer scientists and systems analysts")	**110**
Physical and corrective therapy assistants and aides (see description "Medical assistants")	**93**
Physical therapists	88
Paralegals	86
*Teachers, special education (see description "School teachers—kindergarten, elementary and secondary")	**74**
Medical assistants	71
Correction officers	70
Detectives except public (see description "Police, detectives, and special agents")	**70**
*Childcare workers (see description "Preschool workers")	**66**
Travel agents	66
Radiologic technologists	63
Nursery workers	62
Medical records technicians	61
Operations research analysts	61
Occupational therapists	60
Legal secretaries (see description "Secretaries")	**57**
Manicurists (see description "Barbers and cosmetologists")	**54**
Producers, directors, actors, and entertainers (see description "Actors, directors and producers")	**54**
Teachers, kindergarten (see description, "School teachers—kindergarten, elementary and secondary")	**54**
Flight attendants	51
*Guards	51
Speech-language pathologists and audiologists	51
Insurance adjusters, examiners and investigators (see description "Adjusters, investigators and collectors")	**49**
Paving, surfacing, and tamping equipment operators	48

Occupation	Percent growth projected
Psychologists	48
Respiratory therapists	48
Bakers, bread and pastry (see description "Chefs, cooks, and other kitchen workers")	**47.3**
Amusement and recreation attendants	46.1
Laundry and dry-cleaning machine operators and tenders, except pressing	46.1
Baggage porters and bellhops	45.9
*Cooks, restaurant (see description "Chefs, cooks, and other restaurant workers")	**45.8**
Data processing equipment repairers (see description "Computer and office machine repairers")	**45.5**
*Nursing aides, orderlies, and attendants (see description "Nursing aides and psychiatric aides")	**45.4**
Bicycle repairers	45.3
Medical secretaries (see description "Secretaries")	**45.2**
Real estate clerks	44.1
All other health professionals and para-professionals	43.9
All other professional workers	43.8
Food services and lodging managers (see description "Restaurant and food service managers")	**43.5**
*Teacher aides and educational assistants (see description "Teacher aides")	**43.1**
Food preparation workers	42.9
Dental hygienists	42.7
Management analysts (see description "Management analysts and consultants")	42.7
Surgical technologists	42.4
Pharmacy assistants (see description "Medical assistants")	**41.9**
*Registered nurses	41.7

There, that is the list of the 50 fastest growing jobs, arranged by percentage. Because some did not meet my criteria for including their descriptions in Section 2, I needed a few more to get to the 50 descriptions that are included later in this book. They are:

Loan officers and counselors	**40.0**
Recreational therapists	**39.8**
Social workers	**39.5**
Dental assistants	**39.3**
Real estate appraisers (see description "Real estate agents, brokers, and appraisers")	**38.1**

The Fastest Growing Jobs Based on Number of Openings

As I mentioned earlier, I created this list by arranging jobs projected to have the largest numbers of openings between now and the year 2005. While some of the occupations in the previous list employ relatively few people, the ones on this list are all quite large, so even modest percentage growth can result in substantial numbers of new openings. Large occupations also may have many openings as a result of turnover, retirement, and other factors which result in many job openings even when their projections for percentage growth is low.

As with the list organized by percentage growth, many of these jobs also require education or training beyond high school, although some do not. While some jobs requiring less education are expected to have many openings, they tend to have lower pay or less-desirable hours or working conditions.

Note that a few jobs have asterisks in front of them. These are the ones that appear on both lists and are projected to be among those with the highest growth rates as well as large numbers of openings.

Occupation	Projected growth in thousands
Salespersons, retail (see description "Retail salesworkers")	**786**
*Registered nurses	765
Cashiers	670
General office clerks	654
Truckdrivers light and heavy (see description "Truckdrivers")	648
Waiters and waitresses	637
*Nursing aides, orderlies, and attendants (see description "Nursing aides and psychiatric aides")	**594**
Janitors and cleaners, including maids and housekeeping cleaners	548
Food preparation workers	524
*Systems analysts (see description "Computer scientists and systems analysts")	**501**

Occupation	Projected growth in thousands
*Home health aides (see description "Homemaker—home health aides")	**479**
Teachers, secondary school (see description "School teachers—kindergarten, elementary and secondary")	**462**
*Childcare workers (see description "Preschool workers")	**450**
*Guards	408
Marketing and sales worker supervisors (see description "Marketing, advertising, and public relations managers")	**407**
*Teacher aides and educational assistants (see description "Teacher aides")	**381**
General managers and top executives	380
Maintenance repairers, general utility (see description "General maintenance mechanics")	**319**
Gardeners and groundskeepers, except farm	311
Teachers, elementary (see description "School teachers—kindergarten, elementary, and secondary")	**311**
Food counter, fountain, and related workers	308
Receptionists and information clerks (see description "Information clerks")	**305**
Accountants and auditors	304
Clerical supervisors and managers	301
*Cooks, restaurant (see description "Chefs, cooks, and other restaurant workers")	**276**
*Teachers, special education (see description, "School teachers—kindergarten, elementary, and secondary")	**267**
Licensed practical nurses	261
Blue-collar worker supervisors	257
*Human services workers	256
*Computer engineers and scientists (see description "Computer scientists and system analysts")	**236**

Other Rapidly Growing Jobs

At the end of this section, I have provided a variety of listings of rapidly growing jobs by industry, education level, and other details. You may find it of interest to browse through those listings.

Jobs That Are Rapidly Declining

Following is a list of jobs that are projected to decline most rapidly. They are arranged by percentage of anticipated decline through the year 2005.

Compare this list to those jobs that are projected to grow most rapidly and you will notice several differences. First, most of the declining jobs do not require training or education beyond high school. If you look at the jobs that follow, only a few require training beyond what most people would learn on the job. The most rapidly declining jobs also tend to be in manufacturing and/or jobs that are being replaced by automation or other technological advances. While it is no consolation to those who lose their jobs in these occupations, more than enough new jobs are being created to replace them—although they often require different skills and additional education or training beyond high school.

Occupation	Percent decline
Frame wirers, central office (telephone)	-75
Peripheral electronic data processing equipment operators	-60
Directory assistance operators	-51
Central office operators	-50
Station installers and repairers, telephone	-50
Portable machine cutters	-40
Computer operators, except peripheral equipment	-39
Shoe sewing machine operators and tenders	-38
Central office and PBX installers and repairers (telephone)	-36
Childcare workers, private household	-35
Job printers	-35
Roustabouts	-33
Separating and still machine operators and tenders	-33
Cleaners and servants, private household	-32
Coil winders, tapers, and finishers	-32
Billing, posting, and calculation machine operators	-29
Sewing machine operators, garment	-29
Signal or track switch maintenance	-28
Compositors and typesetters, precision	-27
Data entry keyers, composing	-26
Drilling machine tool setters and set-up operators, metal and plastic	-26
Motion picture projectionists	-26
Boiler operators and tenders, low pressure	-25
Statement clerks	-24
Telephone and cable TV line installers and repairers	-24
Watchmakers	-23
Head sawyers and sawing machine operators and tenders	-22
Packaging and filling machine operators and tenders	-22
Tire building machine operators	-22
Farmers	-21

Important Labor Market Trends to Consider in Your Career Planning

The labor market is changing rapidly. About 20 million new jobs are projected to be added to our workforce over the next 10 years. That would increase our labor force to about 150 million people by the year 2005—a 20 percent increase. While many new jobs will be created, many more existing jobs will also be affected by changing technologies, new products and techniques, foreign trade, changing consumer preferences, and other factors.

Almost everyone will be affected by these changes and it is clear that some occupations will do better than others. Few jobs will remain the same and many people will need to upgrade their skills, change jobs, or even change careers.

No one can be sure of what will happen in the future but some trends in the labor market do give clues about what is likely to happen. When making decisions about your education or career, it is important to understand these trends and to make good choices based on this information. While a lot of labor market information is available, I have selected those issues that I believe are most important for you to consider. Spend a little time going over each one.

General Labor Market Trends

Without a doubt, the best information we have on the labor market comes from governmental sources. Thousands of pages of labor market information are published each year by various government agencies—entirely too much for most people. I've sifted through much of this information and selected a few things which I think will be of particular importance to you and present them here for you to ponder.

The Labor Market Will Continue to Grow

From 1950 through 1980, the labor market doubled from 45 million to 90 million nonfarm wage and hourly workers. More than half of this growth occurred in the 1970s, when 24 million new workers were absorbed by the labor market—a 29 percent increase. These were the years when baby boomers were entering the job market in large numbers. The 1980s saw rapid but more modest growth rates, adding about 20 million additional workers from 1980 through 1992.

Women also entered the labor force in much greater numbers during these years and stayed there longer. In 1950, only 39.1 percent of all women aged 35 to 44 were in the labor market but this had increased to 76.8 percent by 1992. Immigration during these years also increased the number of workers.

While it is not possible to know with certainty what the future holds, the projections by the US Department of Labor anticipate continuing increases in the size of our labor market. An additional 23 million more workers are expected between 1992 and the year 2005, an increase of about 19 percent. This is a very substantial growth rate which will result in many new jobs and opportunities for those prepared for them.

Some Jobs Will Grow More Rapidly Than Others

While there will be growth in most occupations, some will grow much more rapidly than others, and some will even decline. Obviously, occupations that are expected to grow quickly will offer many opportunities and these jobs are the focus of this book. Jobs with the fastest growth rates tend to require education and training beyond the high school level. This "upgrading" of skills is an important trend in our labor force because even entry-level jobs now typically require good academic skills as well as training beyond high school.

Most People Will Change Jobs and Careers

Young people tend to change jobs more frequently, but even workers older than 25 will change jobs an average of eight or more times during their working lives. Most people will also change their career—going from a truck driver to a teacher, for example—four or more times during their working lives. And the trend for changing jobs and careers more often is increasing. Sometimes, these changes will not be anticipated or will occur in unpredictable ways. For these reasons, preparing now for your next job or career change makes more sense than ever.

Most Jobs Require More Education

Back when factory jobs were plentiful, many people could get a good-paying factory job right out of high school. Today, intense competition exists for the few of these jobs that do come open.

While the labor market is projected to continue to grow rapidly, many of the new jobs it creates will differ from those in the past. You can clearly see this by reviewing the lists of rapidly growing jobs I included earlier. Those lists demonstrate that most of the rapidly growing jobs require more education and training than those created in years past.

This trend is likely to accelerate in the years ahead, with more and more jobs requiring technical training or advanced education. A big part of the reason for this is the increasing use of advanced technologies in many jobs including the widespread use of computers, automation, and other technologies. Even entry-level jobs typically held by high school graduates now often require some computer experience.

This upgrading of required skills to obtain the better jobs will continue. This means that those employed now will need to continue their education to keep up with the changing technology which affects their jobs, and entry-level workers will need more education to be considered for many of the better jobs.

The projected demand for college graduates will remain strong, though some fields will do better than others. College graduates, on the average, earn much more than workers with only a high school degree and this earnings gap has widened over the past 10 years. But a four-year college degree is not essential to do well in the labor market. Many of the rapidly growing jobs, for example, will require technical training which can be obtained in one or two years at a private vocational school or community college.

Recent studies have shown that the additional cost of education or training is often paid back quickly in higher earnings. And the increased earnings often last a lifetime, making a major difference in lifestyle. So consider investing in yourself and don't eliminate jobs that interest you if they require additional education. Instead, consider getting it.

Education and Earnings Are Related

While many of the fastest growing jobs require training beyond high school, the chart that follows indicates that there will be opportunities for people at all levels of education. The chart shows the projected growth rates for various major occupational clusters and includes details related to the education and earnings for these jobs. As you can see, while there is job growth projected in all major occupational groups, job growth will be fastest in groups requiring the highest levels of education—and these same groups have the highest earnings.

Projected Growth by Major Occupational Group and Educational Attainment					
		Educational attainment (percent)			
Occupational group	Projected growth 1992-2005 (percent)	High school or less	1 to 3 years of college	4 or more years of college	$ Median weekly earnings, 1992
Executives, administrators, and managers	26	25	27	48	652
Professional specialty workers	37	9	19	72	596
Technicians and related support workers	32	26	45	29	489
Marketing and sales workers	21	46	32	22	346
Administrative support workers, including clerical	14	50	37	13	341
Service workers	33	68	26	6	232
Agriculture, forestry, fishing, and related workers	4	75	17	8	258
Precision, production, craft, and repair workers	13	68	26	6	470
Operators, fabricators, and laborers	10	80	17	3	331
Totals	**22**	**50**	**27**	**23**	**$406**

As the chart shows, occupations that require more education will generally grow faster than occupations with lower educational requirements. Look over the lists of the fastest growing jobs found earlier in this chapter and you will notice that almost all of the fastest growing jobs require special training beyond high school. Only two occupational groups—health services and personal services—have approximately one-half of workers with a high school or less.

Three of the fastest growing occupational groups are executive, administrative, and managerial; professional specialty; and technicians and related support occupations. Not surprisingly, these occupations usually require the highest levels of education and skill. These three major occupational groups, which represent a little more than one-fourth of total employment, are expected to account for about 40 percent of the increase in employment through 2005.

In recent years, the educational attainment of the labor force has risen dramatically. Between 1975 and today, the proportion of the labor force aged 25 to 64 with at least one year of college increased from 33 percent to about 50 percent, while the proportion with four years of college or more increased from 18 percent to 26 percent. Even when workers with varying education levels are employed within the same occupation, those with higher education levels often earn considerably more than their less educated colleagues.

Many Openings Result from Turnover

While I have emphasized the increase in the size of the labor market and the many new jobs this will create, it is important to note that the majority of job openings result from the need to replace a worker. Replacement openings occur as people leave occupations. Some change careers, while others are promoted to other positions. Others stop working to return to school, assume household responsibilities, or retire.

Through 2005 most jobs will become available due to replacement needs. In some occupational groups, more openings are anticipated for replacement workers than from the creation of new positions. For example, marketing and sales positions will require an estimated 4.2 million replacement workers and another 2.3 million additional positions. This means that even in slow or no growth occupations, new people will still be hired to replace workers who leave.

Occupations with the most replacement openings tend to be large fields with low pay and status, low training requirements, and a high proportion of young and part-time workers. Cashiers, waiters and waitresses, and childcare workers are examples of jobs with high turnover rates.

Occupations with relatively few replacement openings usually have lengthy training requirements, a high proportion of prime working age, full-time workers, and provide high pay and status. Physical therapists, lawyers, and aircraft pilots are examples of workers who have generally spent several years acquiring training which may not be applicable to other occupations.

The Importance of Jobs in Small Business

In past years, most people worked for large employers and many people still conduct their career planning and job seeking as if this were still true. But according to government data, about 70 percent of private sector employment is in businesses with fewer than 500 workers. The largest employers now employ fewer workers than they did 10 years ago and most of the new jobs are being created by small employers. This means that you are now far more likely to work for a small employer than a large one.

Jobs with small employers tend to require more flexibility and more rapid adaptation to change. While large employers remain an important part of our economy, small employers have become increasingly important.

Additional Information on Labor Market Trends

I'm never sure just how much information to include on labor market trends, but the material that follows will provide you with additional details which you may find interesting. I've included more detailed information than what I included in the previous section or provided additional details.

Population and Regional Trends

Population trends affect employment opportunities in several ways. In the years to come, changes in the size and composition of the population will influence the demand for goods and services. For example, the population group aged 85 and over will grow about four times as fast as the total population, greatly increasing the demand for health services. Population changes also produce corresponding changes in the size and characteristics of the labor force.

The United States civilian noninstitutional population, aged 16 and over, is expected to increase from about 192 to 219 million through 2005, growing more slowly than it did during the period from 1979-1992. However, even slower population growth rates will increase the demand for goods and services, as well as the demand for workers in many occupations and industries.

The age distribution will shift toward relatively fewer children and teenagers and a growing proportion of middle-aged and older people into the 21st century. The decline in the proportion of teenagers reflects the lower birth rates during the 1980s; the impending large increase in the middle-aged population reflects the aging of baby boomers born between 1946 and 1964; and the very rapid growth in the number of elderly people is attributable to high birth rates prior to the 1930s combined with improvements in medical technology which have allowed many Americans to live longer.

Minorities and immigrants will constitute a larger share of the U.S. population in 2005 than they do today. Substantial increases in the number of Hispanics, Asians, and African Americans are anticipated, reflecting immigration and higher birth rates among African Americans and Hispanics. Substantial inflows of immigrants will continue to have significant implications for the labor force. Immigrants tend to be of working age but with different educational and occupational backgrounds than the U.S. population as a whole.

Population growth varies greatly among geographic regions, affecting the demand for goods and services and, in turn, workers in various occupations and industries. Between 1979 and 1992, the population of the Midwest and the Northeast grew by only 3 percent and 4 percent, respectively, compared with 19 percent in the South and 30 percent in the West. These differences reflect the movement of people seeking new jobs or retiring, as well as higher birth rates in some areas.

Projections by the Bureau of the Census indicate that the West and South will continue to be the fastest growing regions, increasing 24 percent and 16 percent, respectively, between 1992 and 2005. The Midwest population is expected to grow by 7 percent, while the number of people in the Northeast is projected to increase by only 3 percent.

The West and South will continue to be the fastest growing regions of the country.		
	Percent growth	
	1979-1992	**1992-2005**
West	30	24
South	19	16
Midwest	3	7
Northeast	4	3

Geographic shifts in the population alter the demand for and the supply of workers in local job markets. Moreover, in areas dominated by one or two industries, local job markets may be extremely sensitive to the economic conditions of those industries. For these and other reasons, local employment opportunities may differ substantially from the projections for the nation as a whole presented throughout this book.

The Labor Force Will Continue to Grow

Population is the single most important factor governing the size and composition of the labor force, which includes people who are working or looking for work. The civilian labor force, 127 million in 1992, is expected to reach 151 million by 2005. This projected 19 percent increase represents a slight slowdown in the rate of labor force growth, which is largely due to lower population growth.

An Increasingly Diverse Workforce

America's workers will be an increasingly diverse group as we move toward 2005. White nonHispanic men will make up a slightly smaller proportion of the labor force while women and minorities will comprise a larger share than in 1992. White nonHispanics have historically been the largest component of the labor force, but their share has been dropping, and is expected to fall from 78 percent in 1992 to 73 percent by 2005. White workers are projected to grow more slowly than African Americans, Asians, and others, but because of their size, whites will experience the largest numerical increase. Hispanics will add about 6.5 million workers to the labor force through 2005, an increase of 64 percent. Despite this dramatic growth, Hispanics' share of the labor force will increase from only 8 percent to 11 percent, as shown in chart 3. African Americans, Hispanics, Asians, and other racial groups will account for roughly 35 percent of all labor force entrants between 1992 and 2005.

Women Will Continue to Increase Their Participation in the Workforce

Women will continue to join the labor force in growing numbers. The percentage increase of women in the labor force between 1992 and 2005 will be larger than the percentage increase in the total labor force, but smaller than the percentage increase for women in the previous 13 years. In the late 1980s, the labor force participation of women under age 40 began to increase more slowly than in the past. Women accounted for 42 percent of the labor force in 1979; by 2005, they are expected to constitute 48 percent.

The Workforce Will Continue to Age

The changing age structure of the population will directly affect tomorrow's labor force. Compared to young, inexperienced workers, the pool of older, experienced workers will increase. In 1992, the median age of the labor force was 37.2 years; by 2005, it will be 40.5 years.

Between 1979 and 1992, the youth labor force (16 to 24 year olds) dropped by 5 million, a 20 percent decline. In contrast, the number of youths in the labor force will increase by 3.7 million over the 1992-2005 period, reflecting an increase of 18 percent, compared to 19 percent growth for the total labor force. As a result, young people are expected to comprise roughly the same percentage of the labor force in 2005 as in 1992. Among youths, the teenage labor force (16 to19 year olds) will increase by 31 percent over the 1992-2005 period, an increase of 2.1 million. The labor force of 20 to 24 year olds is projected to increase by 12 percent, an increase of 1.6 million workers. The total youth labor force accounted for 24 percent of the entire labor force in 1979, fell to 16 percent in 1992, and should stay about the same through 2005.

The scenario should be somewhat different for prime-age workers (25 to 54 year olds). The baby boom generation will continue to add members to the labor force but their share of the labor force peaked in 1985. These workers accounted for 62 percent of the labor force in 1979 and rose significantly to 72 percent in 1992, but should decline slightly to 70 percent by 2005. The proportion of workers in the 25-34 age range will decline dramatically, from 28 percent to 21 percent in 2005. On the other hand, the growing proportion of workers between the ages of 45 and 54 is equally striking. These workers should account for 24 percent of the labor force by the year 2005, up from 18 percent in 1992. Because workers in their mid-forties to mid-fifties usually have substantial work experience and tend to be more stable than younger workers, this could result in improved productivity and a larger pool of experienced applicants from which employers can choose.

The labor force will grow more slowly due to slower population growth.		
	Numerical change	**Percent change**
1979-1992	22 million	21
1992-2005	23.5 million	19

Source: 1994 OOH

The number of older workers, aged 55 and above, is projected to grow about twice as fast as the total labor force between 1992 and 2005, and about 15 times faster than they grew between 1979 and 1992. As the baby boomers grow older, the number of workers aged 55 to 64 will increase; they exhibit higher labor force participation than their older counterparts. By 2005, workers aged 55 and over will comprise 14 percent of the labor force, up from 12 percent in 1992.

The age distribution in the labor force will continue to shift.			
	Percent distribution		
Age	1979	1992	2005
55 and older	14	12	14
45 to 54	16	18	24
35 to 44	19	27	25
25 to 34	27	28	21
16 to 24	24	16	16

More Workers Have (and Will Need) More Education

In recent years, the level of educational attainment of the labor force has risen dramatically. In 1992, 27 percent of all workers age 25 and over had a bachelor's degree or higher, while only 12 percent did not possess a high school diploma. The trend toward higher educational attainment is expected to continue. Projected rates of employment growth are faster for occupations requiring higher levels of education or training than those requiring less.

Three out of the four fastest growing occupational groups will be executive, administrative, and managerial; professional specialty; and technicians and related support occupations. These occupations generally require the highest levels of education and skill, and will comprise an increasing proportion of new jobs. Office and factory automation, changes in consumer demand, and movement of production facilities to offshore locations are expected to cause employment to stagnate or decline in many occupations which require little formal education—apparel workers and textile machinery operators, for example. Opportunities for those who do not finish high school will be increasingly limited, and workers who are not literate may not even be considered for most jobs.

Those who do not complete high school and are employed are more likely to have low paying jobs with little advancement potential while workers in occupations requiring higher levels of education have higher incomes. In addition, many of the occupations projected to grow most rapidly between 1992 and 2005 are among those with higher earnings.

Nevertheless, even slower growing occupations that have a large number of workers will provide many job openings because the need to replace workers who leave the labor force or transfer to other occupations account for most job openings. Consequently, workers with all levels of education and training will continue to be in demand, although advancement opportunities will generally be best for those with the most education and training.

Employment Change

Total employment is expected to increase from 121.1 million in 1992 to 147.5 million in 2005, or by 22 percent. The 26.4 million jobs that will be added by 2005 will not be evenly distributed across major industrial and occupational groups, causing some restructuring of employment. Continued faster than average employment growth among occupations that require relatively high levels of education or training is expected.

(Note: You may remember this detail from earlier: "The civilian labor force, 127 million in 1992, is expected to reach 151 million by 2005. This projected 19 percent increase. . . ." This really isn't an error because people available to work and those actually working are two different things. That's why there appears to be a disagreement in these projections, although they really point to different data . . .)

Trends in Industries and Job Clusters

The following two sections examine projected employment change from both industrial and occupational perspectives. The industrial profile is discussed in terms of wage and salary employment, except for agriculture, forestry, and fishing, which includes self-employed and unpaid family workers. The occupational profile is viewed in terms of total employment including wage and salary workers as well as self-employed and unpaid family workers.

Industry Trends

While much of this book focuses on occupations, another way of looking at the labor market is from the perspective of various industries. I've selected information on trends in various industry sectors with an emphasis on those growing most rapidly.

The long-term shift from goods-producing to service-producing employment is expected to continue. For example, service-producing industries, including transportation, communications, and utilities; retail and wholesale trade; services; government; and finance, insurance, and real estate are expected to account for approximately 24.5 million of the 26.4 million jobs projected for the 1992-2005 period. In addition, the services division within this sector, which includes health, business, and educational services, contains 15 of the 20 fastest growing industries. Expansion of service sector employment is linked to a number of factors, including changes in consumer tastes and preferences, legal and regulatory changes, advances in science and technology, and changes in the way businesses are organized and managed. Specific factors responsible for varying growth prospects in major industry divisions are discussed below.

Service-producing industries will continue to account for most job growth.			
(Nonfarm wage and salary employment, in millions)			
Industry sector	1979	1992	2005
Goods-producing	26.5	23.1	23.7
Service-producing	63	84.7	109.2
Total	89.5	107.9	133

Source: 1995 OOH

Service-Producing Industries Are Increasingly Important

It is not true that we are becoming a service economy—we already are one and have been for some time. By the year 2005, projections indicate that nearly four out of five jobs will be in industries that provide services rather than in manufacturing. Expansion of service sector employment is linked to a number of different factors, including changes in consumer tastes and preferences, legal and regulatory changes, advances in science and technology, and changes in the organization and management of businesses. Contrary to popular belief, many of these jobs pay well.

Many people think of a service economy as one in which the workforce is dominated by retail sales workers, restaurant workers, and cashiers. In reality the fastest growing occupations will be those that require the most educational preparation. The two largest industries in this sector are health services and business services. Together, they account for 6.1 million of the projected jobs, or about one-fourth of the total increase.

The Difference between the Service Industry and Service Workers

Many people get confused about this difference and it is easy to understand why because the terminology is so similar. Data is collected by type of establishment (or industry) as well as type of occupation. For example, an accountant could work in auto manufacturing (a goods-producing industry) or a hospital (which does not produce goods and is, therefore, part of the service industry). Same occupation, different industries.

The government uses 12 clusters of related occupations and accountant falls under one called "Executive, Administrative and Managerial." One of those occupational clusters just happens to be called "Service Occupations" which includes jobs such as kitchen workers, flight attendants, dental assistants, and preschool workers. So, if you worked in the cafeteria of a hospital, you would be a service worker in a service industry. Well, yes, this is a bit confusing . . .

Trends within the Services Industry

Services is both the largest and fastest growing division within the service-producing sector. This division provided 38.6

million jobs in 1992. Employment is expected to rise 40 percent to 54.2 million by 2005, accounting for almost two-thirds of all new jobs. Jobs will be found in small firms and large corporations, and in industries as diverse as hospitals, data processing, and management consulting. Health services and business services are projected to continue to grow extremely fast. In addition, social, legal, and engineering and management services industries further illustrate this sector's strong growth.

Services will remain the fastest growing major industry division.		
Percent change in employment, 1992-2005		
	Goods	*Services*
Services		40
Construction	26	
Retail trade		23
Finance, insurance and real estate		21
Wholesale trade		19
Transportation and public utilities		14
Agriculture, forestry, and fishing	14	
Government		10
Manufacturing	-3	
Mining	-11	
Total, all industries 23		

Source: 1995 OOH

Health Services

Health services will continue to be one of the fastest growing industries in the economy with employment increasing from 9.6 to 13.8 million. Improvements in medical technology and a growing and aging population will increase the demand for health services. Employment in home health care services—the second fastest growing industry in the economy—nursing homes, and offices and clinics of physicians and other health practitioners is projected to increase rapidly. However, not all health industries will grow at the same rate. Despite being the largest health services industry, hospitals will grow more slowly than most other health services industries. Because of the rapid expansion, 6 of the 10 fastest growing occupations between now and 2005 will be health related.

Business Services

Demand for jobs which provide services to businesses are expected to increase rapidly. These jobs include many which require advanced training such as computer technicians and systems analysts as well as those requiring minimal training such as janitors. Jobs in accounting, marketing, engineering, finance, truck driving, and many others providing services to businesses are expected to increase.

Business services industries also will generate many jobs. Employment is expected to grow from 5.3 million in 1992 to 8.3 million in 2005. Personnel supply services, comprised primarily of temporary help agencies, is the largest sector in this group and will increase by 57 percent from 1.6 to 2.6 million jobs. However, due to a slowdown in labor force participation by young women and the proliferation of personnel supply firms in recent years, this industry will grow more slowly than during the 1979-92 period.

Business services also includes one of the fastest growing industries in the economy, computer, and data processing sector. This industry's rapid growth stems from advances in technology, worldwide trends toward office and factory automation, and increases in demand from business firms, government agencies, and individuals.

Education

Education is expected to add 2.8 million more jobs to the 9.7 million held in 1992. This increase reflects population growth and, in turn, rising enrollments projected for elementary, secondary, and postsecondary schools. The elementary school age population (ages 5-13) will rise by 2.8 million between 1992 and 2005, the secondary school age (14-17) by 3.4 million, and the traditional postsecondary school age (18-24) by 2.2 million. In addition, continued rising enrollment of older, foreign, and part-time students is expected to enhance employment in postsecondary education.

Not all of the increase in employment in education, however, will be for teachers; jobs for teacher aides, counselors, and administrative staff are also projected to increase.

Social Services

Employment in social services is expected to increase by 1.7 million bringing the total to 3.7 million by 2005, reflecting the growing elderly population. For example, residential care institutions, which provide around-the-clock assistance to older persons and others who have limited ability for self-care, is projected to be the fastest growing industry in the U.S. economy. Other social services industries that are projected to grow rapidly include child daycare services and individual and miscellaneous social services, which include elderly daycare and family social services.

Wholesale and Retail Trade

Employment in wholesale and retail trade is expected to rise by 19 and 23 percent, respectively, from 6 to 7.2 million in wholesale trade and from 19.3 to 23.8 million in retail trade. Spurred by higher levels of personal income, the fastest projected job growth in retail trade is in apparel and accessory stores, and appliance, radio, television, and music stores.

Substantial increases in retail employment are anticipated in large industries, including eating and drinking establishments, grocery stores, automotive dealers and service stations, and general merchandise stores.

Finance, Insurance, and Real Estate

Employment is expected to increase by 21 percent in these industries adding 1.4 million jobs to the 1992 level of 6.6 million. The strong demand for financial services is expected to continue. Bank mergers, consolidations, and closings resulting from overexpansion and competition from nonbank corporations which offer bank-like services are expected to limit job growth among commercial banks and savings and loan associations. The fastest growing industries within this sector are expected to be holding and investment offices and mortgage

bankers and brokers. Insurance agents, brokers, and services are expected to register the largest increases in jobs.

Transportation, Communications, and Public Utilities

Overall employment in these sectors will increase by 14 percent. Employment in the transportation sector is expected to increase by 24 percent from 3.5 to 4.3 million jobs. Truck transportation will account for 50 percent of all new jobs; air transportation will account for 29 percent. The projected gains in transportation jobs reflect the continued shift from rail to road freight transportation, rising personal incomes, and growth in foreign trade. In addition, deregulation in the transportation industry has increased personal and business travel options, spurring strong job growth in the passenger transportation arrangement industry, which includes travel agencies.

Employment in communications is projected to decline by 12 percent due to labor-saving technology and industry competition. Employment in utilities, however, is expected to grow with an additional 117,000 new jobs, driven by strong growth in water supply and sanitary services.

Government

By 2005, government employment, excluding public education and public hospitals, is expected to increase 10 percent from 9.5 to 10.5 million jobs. The growth will occur at state and local government levels only. Employment in the federal government and U.S. Postal Service is expected to decline by 113,000 and 41,000 jobs, respectively.

Goods-Producing Industries

While there are more jobs in the services industries, the goods-producing industries remain an important part or our labor market. Many service industry jobs, for example, provide support to or benefit from employment and income produced by the goods-producing sector of our economy.

Employment in this sector has not recovered from the recessionary period of the early 1980s and the trade imbalances that began in the mid-1980s. Although overall employment in goods-producing industries is expected to show little change, growth prospects within the sector vary considerably.

Construction

Construction is expected to increase by 26 percent from 4.5 to 5.6 million jobs. The need to improve the nation's infrastructure will result in increases in road, bridge, and tunnel construction. This will offset the decrease in demand for new housing which reflects the slowdown in population growth and the overexpansion of office building construction in recent years.

Agriculture, Forestry, and Fishing

After declining for many decades, overall employment in agriculture, forestry, and fishing is projected to grow by 14 percent from 1.7 to 2 million jobs. Strong growth in agricultural services will more than offset an expected continued decline in crops, livestock, and livestock products.

Manufacturing

Manufacturing jobs are expected to decline by 3 percent from the 1992 level of 18 million. The projected loss of manufacturing jobs reflects productivity gains achieved from increased investment in manufacturing technologies. The composition of manufacturing employment is expected to shift because most of the jobs that will disappear are production jobs. On the other hand, the number of professional positions in manufacturing firms will increase.

Mining

Mining employment is expected to decline 11 percent from 631,000 to 562,000 jobs. Underlying this projection is the assumption that domestic oil production will drop and oil imports will rise, reducing employment in the crude petroleum industry. In addition, employment in coal mining should continue to decline sharply due to the expanded use of labor-saving machinery.

Trends within Major Occupational Clusters

Continued expansion of the service-producing sector conjures up an image of a workforce dominated by cashiers, retail sales workers, and waiters. Although service sector growth will generate millions of these type jobs, it will also create jobs for financial managers, engineers, nurses, electrical and electronics technicians, and many other managerial, professional, and technical workers. As indicated earlier, the fastest growing occupations will be those that require the most education and training.

This section furnishes an overview of projected employment in 12 categories or clusters of occupations based on the Standard Occupational Classification (SOC). The SOC is used by all federal agencies that collect occupational employment data, and is the organizational framework for grouping jobs throughout this book.

In the discussion that follows, projected employment change is described as growing faster, slower, or same as the average for all occupations. While occupations that are growing fast generally offer good opportunities, the numerical change in employment is also important because large occupations, such as retail sales workers, may offer many more new jobs than a small, fast-growing occupation, such as paralegals.

Even though an occupation is expected to grow rapidly, it may provide fewer openings than a slower growing but larger occupation.		
Occupation	Percent change	Number change
Paralegals	88	81,000
Retail sales workers	21	786,000

Projected through 2005

Professional Specialty Occupations— The Fastest Growing Occupational Cluster

Workers in these occupations perform a wide variety of duties and are employed in almost every industry. Employment in this cluster is expected to grow by 37 percent, from 16.6 to 22.8 million jobs, making it the fastest growing occupational cluster in the economy. Human services workers, computer scientists and systems analysts, physical therapists, special education teachers, and operations research analysts are among the fastest growing professional specialty occupations.

Employment change will vary widely by broad occupational group.	
Occupational group	Percent change in employment through 2005
Professional specialty	37
Service	33
Technicians and related support	32
Executive, administrative, and managerial	26
Transportation and material moving	22
Construction trades and extractive	21
Marketing and sales	21
Helpers, laborers, and material movers	17
Mechanics, installers, and repairers	16
Administrative support, including clerical	14
Agriculture, forestry, fishing	3
Production	1
Total, all occupations	**22**

Service Occupations

This group includes a wide range of workers in protective services, food and beverage preparation, health services, cleaning, and personal services. Employment in these occupations is expected to grow by 33 percent, faster than average, from 19.4 to 25.8 million jobs. Service occupations that are expected to experience both fast growth and large job increases include homemaker-home health aides, nursing aides, child care workers, guards, and correction officers.

Technicians and Related Support Occupations

Workers in this group provide technical assistance to engineers, scientists, physicians, and other professional workers, as well as operate and program technical equipment. Employment in this cluster is expected to increase 32 percent, faster than average, from 4.3 to 5.7 million jobs. Employment of paralegals is expected to grow much faster than average as use of these workers in the rapidly expanding legal services industry increases. Health technicians and technologists, such as licensed practical nurses and radiological technologists, will add large numbers of jobs. Growth in other occupations, such as broadcast technicians, will be limited by labor-saving technological advances.

Executive, Administrative, and Managerial Occupations

Workers in this cluster establish policies, make plans, determine staffing requirements, and direct the activities of businesses, government agencies, and other organizations. Employment in this cluster is expected to increase by 26 percent, from 12.1 to 15.2 million jobs, reflecting average growth. Growth will be spurred by the increasing number and complexity of business operations and result in large employment gains, especially in the services industry division. However, many businesses will streamline operations by employing fewer managers, thus offsetting increases in employment.

Like other occupations, changes in managerial and administrative employment reflect industry growth and utilization of managers and administrators. For example, employment of health services managers will grow much faster than average, while wholesale and retail buyers are expected to grow more slowly than average.

Hiring requirements in many managerial and administrative jobs are becoming more stringent. Work experience, specialized training, or graduate study will become increasingly necessary. Familiarity with computers will continue to be important as a growing number of firms rely on computerized management information systems.

Transportation and Material Moving Occupations

Workers in this cluster operate the equipment used to move people and equipment. Employment in this group is expected to increase by 22 percent from 4.7 to 5.7 million jobs. Average growth is expected for bus drivers, reflecting rising school enrollments. Similar growth is expected for truck drivers and railroad transportation workers due to growing demand for transportation services. Technological improvements and automation should result in jobs for material moving equipment operators increasing more slowly than average. Water transportation workers are projected to show little change in employment as technological advances increase productivity.

Construction Trades and Extractive Occupations

Workers in this group construct, alter, and maintain buildings and other structures, and operate drilling and mining equipment. Overall employment in this group is expected to increase 21 percent, about as fast as average, from 3.7 to 4.5 million jobs. Virtually all of the new jobs will be in construction. Maintained by new projects and alterations to existing structures, average employment growth is expected in construction. On the other hand, increased automation, continued stagnation in the oil and gas industries, and slow growth in demand for coal, metal, and other materials will result in a decline in employment of extractive workers.

Marketing and Sales Occupations

Workers in this cluster sell goods and services, purchase commodities and property for resale, and stimulate consumer interest. Employment in this cluster is projected to increase by 21 percent, from 13 to 15.7 million jobs, about as fast as average. Demand for travel agents is expected to grow much faster than average. Due to strong growth in the industries that employ them, services sales representatives, securities and financial services sales workers, and real estate appraisers will experience faster than average growth. Many part- and full-time job openings are expected for retail sales workers and cashiers due to the large size and high turnover of these occupations. Opportunities for higher paying sales jobs, however, will tend to be more competitive.

Helpers, Laborers, and Material Movers

Workers in this group assist skilled workers and perform routine, unskilled tasks. Overall employment is expected to increase by 17 percent, about as fast as average, from 4.5 to 5.2 million jobs. Some routine tasks will become increasingly automated, limiting employment growth among machine feeders and offbearers. Employment of service station attendants will decline, reflecting the trend toward self-service gas stations. Employment of construction laborers, however, is expected to increase about as fast as average, reflecting growth in the construction industry.

Mechanics, Installers, and Repairers

These workers adjust, maintain, and repair automobiles, industrial equipment, computers, and many other types of equipment. Overall employment in these occupations is expected to grow by 16 percent, from 4.8 to 5.6 million jobs, due to increased use of mechanical and electronic equipment. The fastest growing occupation in this group is expected to be data processing equipment repairers, reflecting the increased use of these types of machines. In sharp contrast, communications equipment mechanics, installers, and repairers, and telephone and cable television line installers and repairers are expected to show a decline in employment due to labor-saving advances.

Administrative Support Occupations, including Clerical

Workers in this largest major occupational group perform a wide variety of administrative tasks necessary to keep organizations functioning smoothly. The group as a whole is expected to grow by 14 percent, from 22.3 to 25.4 million jobs, about as fast as average. Technological advances are projected to slow employment growth for stenographers, typists, and word processors. Receptionists and information clerks will grow faster than average, spurred by rapidly expanding industries such as business services. Because of their large size and substantial turnover, clerical occupations will offer abundant opportunities for qualified job seekers in the years ahead.

Agriculture, Forestry, Fishing, and Related Occupations

Workers in these occupations cultivate plants, breed and raise livestock, and catch animals. Although demand for food, fiber, and wood is expected to increase as the world's population grows, the use of more productive farming and forestry methods and the consolidation of smaller farms are expected to result in only a 3 percent increase in employment, from 3.5 to

3.6 million jobs. Employment of farm operators and farm workers is expected to rapidly decline, reflecting greater productivity. The need for skilled farm managers, on the other hand, should result in average employment growth.

Production Occupations

Workers in these occupations set up, install, adjust, operate, and tend machinery and equipment and use hand tools to fabricate and assemble products. Little change in the 1992 employment level of 12.2 million is expected due to increases in imports, overseas production, and automation. Compared to other occupations, employment in many production occupations is more sensitive to the business cycle and competition from imports.

Replacement Needs Result in Job Opportunities in All Areas of Our Economy

Most jobs through the year 2005 will become available as a result of replacement needs. Thus, even occupations with little or no employment growth or slower than average employment growth still may offer many job openings.

Replacement openings occur as people leave occupations. Some transfer to other occupations as a step up the career ladder or change careers. Others stop working in order to return to school, assume household responsibilities, or retire.

The number of replacement openings and the proportion of job openings made up by replacement needs varies by occupation. Occupations with the most replacement openings generally are large, with low pay and status, low training requirements, and a high proportion of young and part-time workers. Occupations with relatively few replacement openings tend to be associated with high pay and status, lengthy training requirements, and a high proportion of prime working age, full-time workers. Workers in these occupations generally acquire education or training that often is not applicable to other occupations. For example, among professional specialty occupations, only 38 percent of total job opportunities result from replacement needs, as opposed to 78 percent among production occupations .

Job openings arise from both occupational replacement needs and occupational growth.		
(Percent of job openings, 1992-2005)		
	Replacement	Growth
Production occupations	78	22
Professional specialty occupations	38	62

Career Planning and Job Seeking Skills Are More Important Than Ever

If you bought this book and have waded through all the information in this section, I have to figure that you are motivated to improve your lot in life. Assuming this is so, you need to keep one thing in your mind at all times: to succeed in today's labor market, you will need to spend more time on career planning and preparation.

Those who do spend this extra time are more likely to do better in the labor market—and are more likely to find a career that is satisfying to them. Good career planning includes more than just picking a job. It includes knowing what you want to accomplish, knowing which skills you enjoy using most, seeking a work environment that is satisfying to you, and (among other things) finding work that is meaningful to you.

A Few Words on Selecting a Career

A job is something you might take simply because it is available when you need one. A career is a longer-term decision to work within a certain area of expertise which may require special training or experience. When considering a longer-term career choice, it is important to understand that it is often better to prepare for or to select a job which you will really enjoy—and that will help you enter or prepare to enter a career which interests you. This increases your chances for long-term career satisfaction.

Most people will change jobs many times and careers several times during their working lives. When you are doing this, consider factors other than simply how fast that occupational group is growing. Even in careers that are projected to have slow or no growth, opportunities will remain. But if you are interested in a career within an occupation which is growing quickly, that can certainly work to your long-term advantage.

Because you are more likely to change jobs now than in the past, it is wise to learn how to conduct a more effective job search. Depending on unemployment rates, the average length of unemployment ranges from 12 to 16 weeks and can be much longer for some people. For example, older workers and those with higher earnings are two groups which take longer than average to find new jobs. Because of the major changes in the labor market, many people find that they are forced to look for work and don't know how to go about it effectively. The traditional job seeking techniques simply don't work very well and can lead to a frustrating and negative life experience.

I've spent the past 20 years researching ways to find jobs and have concluded that some job search methods work better than others. I have identified those that reduce the time it takes to find a job and increase your chances of getting more desirable ones. If you know more about looking for a job, this can make a big difference in your earnings and long-term career satisfaction.

I've included career planning and job search information in Section 3. It is enough to get you started but I encourage you to learn more about this than what is presented in one section. It makes sense to learn as much as you can about career planning and job seeking. In today's economy, knowledge of these techniques is becoming an essential economic survival skill. Those who do a thorough job in planning their careers will clearly do better than those who do not.

Additional Details and Charts of Interest

Education and Earnings

If you have been paying attention so far, it should come as no surprise to you that higher pay is related to higher educational attainment. Not always, of course, but on average. This chart provides a variety of information for major occupational groups. You can see the percent of people working in each cluster at various levels of education. Clusters that have higher average educational requirements tend to pay higher too.

Fastest Growing Jobs Requiring a College Degree

Here is a list of the fastest growing jobs typically requiring a four-year college degree. These are all based on projections through the year 2005. This might also be a good time to note that, ahem, I wrote another book titled *America's Top Jobs for College Graduates*.

Occupation	% Growth
Computer engineers and scientists	112
Systems analysts	110
Physical therapists	88
Teachers, special education	74
Operations research analysts	61
Occupational Therapists	60
Teachers, preschool and kindergarten	54
Psychologists	48
Speech-language pathologists and audiologists	48
Construction managers	47
Management analysts	43
Recreational therapists	40
Social workers	40
Recreation workers	38
Podiatrists	37
Teachers, secondary schools	37
Instructors and coaches, sports and physical training	36
Marketing, advertising, and public relations managers	36
Personnel training and labor relations specialists	36
Teachers and instructors, vocational education and training	36

Fastest Growing Jobs Requiring Some Postsecondary Training

Here is a list of jobs that don't require a four-year college degree but do require either formal training or education after high school or, in some cases, substantial on-the-job experience. Some of these jobs can pay pretty well, so it is not entirely true that a four-year college degree is required to do well.

Percent employment growth of occupations requiring some postsecondary or extensive employer training, projected 1992-2005	
Occupation	Percentage growth
Physical and corrective therapy assistants and aides	93
Paralegals	86
Occupation therapy assistants and aides	78
Medical assistants	71
Radiologic technologists and technicians	63
Medical records technicians	61
Legal secretaries	57
EEG technologists	54
Producers, directors, actors, and entertainers	54
Nuclear medicine technologists	50
Insurance adjusters, examiners, and investigators	49
Respiratory therapists	48
Cooks, restaurant	46
Data processing equipment repairers	45
Medical secretaries	45
Food service and lodging managers	44
Dental hygienists	43
Surgical technologists	42
Pharmacy assistants	42
Licensed practical nurses	40

Fastest Growing Jobs Requiring High School Education or Less

Here is a list of the fastest growing jobs that don't require education beyond the high school level. As you can see, some have very high growth rates projected through 2005. A few of these jobs pay pretty well, although those, like detectives, often require substantial on-the-job experience. You should also realize (should you be pondering this list for good jobs you can get without going to school) that high school graduates will often have to compete with those who have more education. For example, many detectives have college degrees and they will often be given a preference in hiring or promotion. I'm not saying you can't get ahead without an education, just that it is highly competitive for some jobs if you don't have the best credentials.

Fastest growing jobs requiring a high school education or less	
Occupation	**Percentage growth**
Home health aides	138
Human services workers	136
Personal and home health care aides	130
Electronic pagination systems workers	78
Corrections officers	70
Detectives, except public	70
Childcare workers	66
Travel agents	66
Nursery workers	62
Subway and streetcar operators	57
Manicurists	54
Flight attendants	51
Guards	51
Paving, surfacing, and tamping equipment operators	48
Bakers, bread and pastry	47
Amusement and recreation attendants	46
Baggage porters and bellhops	46
Laundry and drycleaning machine operators and tenders, except pressing	46
Bicycle repairers	45
Nursing aides, orderlies, and attendants	45

Manufacturing Industries with the Fastest Percentage Growth Rates

Manufacturing jobs are an important part of our economy and here is a list of manufacturing industries which are projected to grow the fastest, in terms of projected annual increases in employees.

Manufacturing industries with the fastest annual employment growth	
Industry	**Annual % change**
Aircraft and missile parts and equipment	3.2
Miscellaneous publishing	3
Railroad equipment	2.5
Medical instruments and supplies	2.4
Truck and bus bodies, trailers, and motor homes	2.4
Miscellaneous plastic products	2.4
Millwork and structural wood members	2.2
Boat building and repairing	2
Books	1.7
Metal services	1.7
Miscellaneous chemical products	1.5
X-ray and other electromedical apparatus	1.5
Industrial machinery	1.5
Partitions and fixtures	1.4
Periodicals	1.3

Source: BLS Occupational Outlook Quarterly, Vol. 38, No. 3

Manufacturing Industries Projected to Generate the Most Job Growth

This list shows you the industries that are creating the most jobs in numerical terms.

Industry	Thousands of jobs
Miscellaneous plastic products	224
Aircraft and missile parts and equipment	85
Medical instruments and supplies	79
Commercial printing and business forms	78
Metal products	62
Industrial machinery	61
Newspapers	61
Millwork and structural wood members	60
Drugs	41
Converted paper products, except containers	37
Miscellaneous publishing	37
Metalworking machinery	29
Books	28
Truck and bus bodies, trailers, and motor homes	28
Metal services	27

Fastest Growing Jobs in Manufacturing

Here are the fastest growing manufacturing jobs, arranged in projected percentage of growth through 2005.

Occupation	Percent employment growth
All other printing workers, precision	92.3
Electronic pagination system workers	77.9
Systems analysts	65.1
All other printing press setters and set up operators	51.1
Medical scientists	47.5
Computer engineers and scientists	41.8
Offset lithographic press operators	40.3
Cabinetmakers and bench carpenters	37
Screen printing machine setters and set up operators	36.7
Advertising clerks	34.3
Meat, poultry and fish cutters and trimmers	32.9
Biological scientists	31
All other printing, binding and related workers	30.3
Wood machinists	29.4
All other professional workers	29.2
Operations research analysts	28.4
Reporters and correspondents	26.9
All other precision woodworkers	26.7
Paper goods machine setters and set up operators	26.3
Personnel, training, and labor relations specialists	26.3

New and Replacement Openings by Occupational Group

The emphasis in this book is on jobs that are growing rapidly, but I have pointed out that some slower growing jobs will also have many openings. The following chart will give you some details by occupational group on where the openings will come from.

Job Openings due to Growth and Replacements Needs Projected 1992-2005 (millions)			
Occupation group	Replacement needs	Growth	Total
Service Workers	5.9	6.8	12.7
Professional specialty workers	3.6	6.2	9.8
Administrative support workers, including clerical	5.5	3.5	9.0
Operators, fabricators, and laborers	4.3	2.7	7.0
Marketing and sales workers	4.2	2.3	6.5
Precision production, craft, and repair workers	4.0	2.1	6.1
Executives, administrators, and managers	2.5	3.1	5.7
Technicians and related support workers	1.0	1.4	2.4
Agriculture, forestry, fishing, and related workers	.7	.5	1.2

*Source: **Occupational Outlook Quarterly**, Fall 1993*

More Than 300 Additional Jobs Listed in Order of Projected Growth

I've already provided a list of 50 fastest growing jobs in order of their projected percentage of growth. Here's a list that picks up from there, providing more than 300 additional jobs in order of their projected growth percentage. Because these jobs are the largest ones in our economy, they cover about 85 percent of the labor force. Occupations beginning with "All other . . ." refer to miscellaneous occupations within a category.

Because the labor market is expected to grow about 20 percent between now and the year 2005, occupations that are projected to grow at or below 20 percent or so are actually growing more slowly than average. That doesn't mean they are "bad," it's just something to consider when making your career plans.

Occupation	Percent growth projected
Hotel desk clerks	41.3
All other service workers	40.2
Bill and account collectors	40.0
Loan officers and counselors	40.0
Animal caretakers, except farm	39.8
Insulation workers	39.8
Recreational therapists	39.8
Licensed practical nurses	39.7
Social workers	39.5
Dental assistants	39.3
All other management support workers	39.0

Occupation	Percent growth projected
Recreation workers	38.1
Real estate appraisers	38.1
All other teachers and instructors	37.9
Paving, surfacing, and tamping equipment operators	37.7
Advertising clerks	37.5
Podiatrists	37.4
Offset lithographic press operators	37.2
Insurance claims clerks	37.0
Drywall installers and finishers	36.9
Electromedical and biomedical equipment repairers	36.8
Screen printing machine setters and set-up operators	36.7
Teachers, secondary school	36.6
Teachers and instructors, vocational education and training	36.5
Counter and rental clerks	36.3
Waiters and waitresses	36.3
All other food preparation and service workers	36.2
Instructors and coaches, sports and physical training	36.2
Marketing, advertising, and public relations managers	36.1

Occupation	Percent growth projected
Personnel, training, and labor relations specialists	36.1
Cooks, short order and fast food	36.0
Emergency medical technicians	35.9
Chiropractors	35.8
Opticians, dispensing and measuring	35.7
All other hand workers	35.7
Hosts and hostesses, restaurant, lounge, or coffee shop	35.6
Parking lot attendants	35.3
Aircraft pilots and flight engineers	35.2
Gardeners and groundskeepers, except farm	35.2
Cardiology technologists	35.0
Physicians	35.0
Property and real estate managers	35.0
All other managers and administrators	34.7
Hairdressers, hairstylists, and cosmetologists	34.7
Interviewing clerks, except personnel and social welfare	34.4
Physician assistants	33.8
Receptionists and information clerks	33.8
Institutional cleaning supervisors	33.7
Technicians, except health, engineering, and science	33.3
Meat, poultry, and fish cutters and trimmers, hand	32.9
Securities and financial services sales workers	32.8
Veterinarians and veterinary inspectors	32.7
Accountants and auditors	32.3
Counselors	32.2
Engineering, mathematical, and natural science managers	31.5
Lawyers	31.1
Medical scientists	30.8
Computer programmers	30.4
All other printing, binding, and related workers	30.3
Automotive body and related repairers	30.2
Reservation and transportation ticket agents and travel clerks	30.1
All other legal assistants, including law clerks	30.0
Directors, religious activities and education	29.9
Clergy	29.8
Construction and building inspectors	29.8
Cost estimators	29.8

Occupation	Percent growth projected
Dining room and cafeteria attendants and bar helpers	29.8
All other protective service workers	29.7
Heat, air conditioning, and refrigeration mechanics and installers	29.4
Ushers, lobby attendants, and ticket takers	29.3
All other agricultural, forestry, fishing, and related workers	29.2
Painters and paperhangers, construction and maintenance	29.2
Highway maintenance workers	29.0
Pharmacists	29.0
Wood machinists	28.7
Metallurgists and metallurgical, ceramic, and materials engineers	28.3
Painting, coating, and decorating workers, hand	28.0
Railroad conductors and yardmasters	27.9
Maintenance repairers, general utility	27.8
Bus drivers, school	27.6
Psychiatric aides	27.5
Truck drivers, light and heavy	27.1
Inspectors and compliance officers, except construction	27.0
Adjustment clerks	26.5
All other motor vehicle operators	26.5
Clinical lab technologists and technicians	26.5
College and university faculty	26.4
Paper goods, machine setters and set-up operators	26.4
Pipelayers and pipelaying fitters	26.4
All other construction trades workers	26.3
Architects, except landscape and marine	26.3
Dietitians and nutritionists	26.3
Landscape architects	26.3
Loan interviewers	26.3
Public relations specialists and publicity writers	26.3
All other helpers, laborers, and material movers, hand	26.1
Loan and credit clerks	26.1
Photographic process workers, precision	26.1
Reporters and correspondents	26.1
Psychiatric technicians	26.0
Bricklayers and stone masons	25.7
Instructors, adult (nonvocational) education	25.7

Occupation	Percent growth projected
Economists	25.3
Strippers, printing	25.3
Hard tile setters	25.2
Personnel clerks, except payroll and timekeeping	25.2
Personnel, training, and labor relations managers	25.2
Radio and TV announcers and newscasters	25.1
Biological scientists	25.0
Science and mathematics technicians	25.0
Technical assistants, library	25.0
Musicians	24.9
Photographers	24.9
Dancers and choreographers	24.8
Financial managers	24.8
Cabinetmakers and bench carpenters	24.5
Bus and truck mechanics and diesel engine specialists	24.4
Cashiers	24.4
Meteorologists	24.4
General office clerks	24.3
Electrical and electronics engineers	24.2
Shampooers	24.2
Credit authorizers	24.1
Underwriters	24.1
Combination machine tool setters, set-up operators, operators, and tenders	24.0
Court clerks	23.9
Clerical supervisors and managers	23.8
Vehicle washers and equipment cleaners	23.7
Civil engineers including traffic engineers	23.6
Dispatchers, except police, fire, and ambulance	23.3
All other material recording, schedule, and distribution workers	23.2
Urban and regional planners	23.2
Writers and editors, including technical writers	23.2
Camera operators, television, motion picture, video	23.0
Artists and commercial artists	22.9
Electrical and electronic technicians/technologists	22.8
Automotive mechanics	22.7
Forest and conservation workers	22.4
Structural and reinforcing metal workers	22.4
Geologists, geophysicists, and oceanographers	22.2
All other mechanics, installers, and repairers	22.1

Occupation	Percent growth projected
Employment interviewers, private or public employment service	21.8
Optical goods workers, precision	21.7
Roofers	21.7
Carpet installers	21.6
Salespersons, retail	21.5
Vehicle and mobile equipment mechanics and repairers	21.4
Farm managers	21.1
Teachers, elementary	21.3
Chemists	21.2
Brokerage clerks	20.9
Designers, except interior designers	20.6
Photoengravers	20.6
Grader, dozer, and scraper operators	20.5
Small engine specialists	20.5
Brokers, real estate	20.4
Crossing guards	20.4
All other social scientists	20.3
Mechanical engineers	20.3
Budget analysts	20.1
Excavation and loading machine operators	20.1
Marketing and sales worker supervisors	20.0
Numerical control machine tool operators and tenders, metal and plastic	19.9
Insurance policy processing clerks	19.8
Food counter, fountain, and related workers	19.7
Chemical engineers	19.4
Electricians	19.3
Cleaning and building service occupations, except private household	19.2
Data entry keyers, except composing	19.2
All other printing press setters and set-up operators	19.1
Customer service representatives, utilities	19.1
Janitors and cleaners, including maids and housekeeping cleaners	19.1
Jewelers and silversmiths	19.1
Tile examiners and searchers	19.1
File clerks	18.9
Photographics processing machine operators and tenders	18.8
Locksmiths and safe repairers	18.5
Water and liquid waste treatment plant and system operators	18.4

Occupation	Percent growth projected
Taxi drivers and chauffeurs	18.3
Tire repairers and changers	18.3
Curators, archivists, museum technicians, and restorers	18.2
All other precision woodworkers	18.1
Driver/sales workers	18.1
Elevator installers and repairers	18.1
Furniture finishers	18.0
Mail clerks, except mail machine operators and postal service	17.9
Library assistants and bookmobile drivers	17.8
Traffic, shipping, and receiving clerks	17.8
Funeral directors and morticians	17.6
Credit checkers	17.5
Sheet metal workers and duct installers	17.5
Helpers, construction trades	17.4
All other adjusters and investigators	17.2
Operating engineers	17.2
Industrial engineers, except safety engineers	16.8
Welfare eligibility workers and interviewers	16.8
Ambulance drivers and attendants except EMTs	16.7
Municipal clerks	16.7
Firefighters	16.6
Supervisors, farming, forestry, and agricultural related occupations	16.6
All other transportation and material moving equipment operators	16.4
Bindery machine operators and set-up operators	16.3
Dispatchers, police, fire, and ambulance	16.3
Plasterers	16.3
Tax examiners, collectors, and revenue agents	16.2
All other transportation and related workers	16.1
Fire fighting and prevention supervisors	16.1
Power generating and reactor plant operators	16.1
Crane and tower operators	16.0
All other engineering technicians and technologists	15.8
Order fillers, wholesale and retail sales	15.8
Cooks, institution or cafeteria	15.7
Optometrists	15.7
Camera and photographic equipment repairers	15.5
Welders and cutters	15.2
All other technicians	15.1

Occupation	Percent growth projected
All other plant and system operators	15.0
Insurance sales workers	15.0
Agricultural and food scientists	14.4
All other law enforcement occupations	14.4
All other sales and related workers	14.2
Aeronautical and astronautical engineers	14.1
Bookbinders	14.1
All other precision assemblers	14.0
Police patrol officers	13.9
Sheriffs and deputy sheriffs	13.9
Aircraft mechanics	13.8
Fire inspection occupations	13.2
Concrete and terrazzo finishers	13.4
Cooking and roasting machine operators and tenders, food and tobacco	13.4
Production, planning, and expediting clerks	13.4
Wholesale and retail buyers, except for products	13.3
General managers and top executives	13.2
Surveyors	13.2
All other extraction and related workers	13.1
Athletes, coaches, umpires, and related workers	13.1
Cannery workers	13.1
Duplicating, mail, and other office machine operators	13.1
Freight, stock, and material movers, hand	13.1
Farm equipment mechanics	12.8
Material recording, scheduling, dispatching, and distributing occupations	12.7
Police and detective supervisors	12.6
Billing, cost, and rate clerks	12.4
Blue-collar worker supervisors	12.4
Hand packers and packagers	12.4
All other cleaning and building service workers	12.3
Librarians, professional	12.3
Foresters and conservation scientists	12.2
Interior designers	12.2
Drafters	11.3
Sales agents, real estate	11.3
Upholsterers	11.2
Photoengraving and lithographic machine operators and tenders	10.7
Refuse collectors	10.5
Pressing machine operators and tenders, textile, garment, and related materials	10.3

Occupation	Percent growth projected
Communication, transportation, and utilities operations managers	10.0
Construction managers	10.0
Air traffic controllers	9.9
Electric power generating plant operators, distributors and dispatchers	9.9
All other precision workers	9.8
New accounts clerks banking	9.3
Statisticians	9.3
Musical instrument repairers and tuners	9.0
Dairy processing equipment operators, including setters	8.9
Stock clerks	8.8
Electrical powerline installers and repairers	8.5
Aircraft engine specialists	8.4
Locomotive engineers	8.3
Office machine and cash register servicers	8.1
Programmers, numerical, tool, and process control	8.1
Solderers and brazers	8.1
Police detectives and investigators	8.0
Plumbers, pipefitters, and steamfitters	7.8
Railroad brake, signal, and switch operators	7.7
Mathematicians and all other mathematical scientists	7.6
Captains and other officers, fishing vessels	7.4
Electronics repairers, commercial and industrial equipment	7.4
Printing press machine setters operators and tenders	7.3
Camera operators	7.2
Plastic molding machine operators and tenders setters and set-up operators	7.1
Correspondence clerks	7.0
Industrial truck and tractor operators	7.0
Platemakers	7.0
Precision instrument repairers	6.9
Railyard engineers, dinkey operators, and hostlers	6.3
Hoist and winch operators	6.2
Proofreaders and copy markers	6.2
All other precision food and tobacco workers	6.0
Bus drivers	5.9
Bakers, manufacturing	5.8
Dentists	5.2

Occupation	Percent growth projected
Stationary engineers	5.1
Fishers, hunters, and trappers	4.7
Pest controllers and assistants	4.6
Order clerks, materials, merchandise, and service	4.4
Electronic semiconductor processors	4.3
Secretaries, except legal and medical	4.3
Broadcast technicians	4.0
Logging tractor operators	4.0
Machine builders and other precision machine assemblers	4.0
Mobile heavy equipment mechanics	4.0
Credit analysts	3.7
Bookkeeping, accounting, and auditing clerks	3.5
Foundry mold assembly and shakeout workers	3.4
Dental lab technicians, precision	3.1
Government chief executives and legislators	3.1
Painters, transportation equipment	2.9
All other electrical and electronic equipment mechanics, installers, and repairers	2.5
All other clerical and administrative support workers	2.4
All other metal and plastic machine setters, operators, and related workers	2.4
Industrial production managers	2.4
Judges, magistrates, and other judicial workers	2.3
Mining engineers, including mine safety engineers	2.1
Extruding and forming machine setters, operators, and tenders	1.7
Messengers	1.7
Grinders and polishers, hand	1.6
All other precision metal workers	1.3
Riggers	1.1
Chemical plant and system operators	1.0
Postal mail carriers	0.9
Machine feeders and offbearers	0.7
Nuclear engineers	0.5
Coating, painting, and spraying machine operators, tenders, setters and set-up operators	0.4
Metal fabricators, structural metal products	0.4
Power distributors and dispatchers	0.2
Meter readers, utilities	0.3

Up-to-Date Descriptions of the 50 Fastest Growing Jobs

Section Two

The 50 job descriptions I've included in this section are very, very well done. They come directly from the 1994-95 edition of the *Occupational Outlook Handbook,* published by the U.S. Department of Labor. Each one includes information on:

- The Nature of the Work;
- Working Conditions;
- Employment
- Training, Other Qualifications, and Advancement;
- Job Outlook;
- Earnings;
- Related Occupations; and
- Sources of Additional Information.

I've arranged the 50 descriptions within clusters of related jobs. This approach allows you to easily explore similar occupations.

Note that this section only provides information regarding the fastest growing jobs—there are many other jobs that are not described here. Other sections of this book list additional occupations and include those that are not among the fastest growing ones. If you are interested in obtaining similar information on those jobs, you can find thorough descriptions for another 175 or so jobs in the current edition of the *Occupational Outlook Handbook,* published every two years by the U.S. Department of Labor. The same information is also available in a book titled *America's Top 300 Jobs,* published by JIST. Both books are available in most libraries and *America's Top 300 Jobs* can be ordered from most bookstores.

Listing of Descriptions of the 50 Fastest Growing Jobs Within Clusters of Related Jobs

Following is a list of all the jobs that have descriptions included in this section. If you are someone with an excellent memory for detail, you may realize that some of the job titles here differ from those listed among the fastest growing jobs list in Section 2. But, if you are such a person, you should also remember that I explained this back there. It is the government's fault really and relates to how they track information, but the lists I used in Section 2 cross-reference this all very nicely.

You will notice that some clusters include relatively few job descriptions. This is because few jobs within that cluster are projected to grow quickly through 2005. As I mentioned earlier, this does not mean that you should not consider other jobs within that cluster which are projected to grow more slowly. Openings will continue to exist in all occupations—even in those projected to decline—to replace workers who leave the fields for various reasons.

Executive, Administrative, Managerial Occupations

Accountants and Auditors
General Managers and Top Executives
Loan Officers and Counselors
Management Analysts and Consultants
Marketing, Advertising, and Public Relations Managers
Restaurant and Food Service Managers

Professional Specialty Occupations

Actors, Directors, and Producers
Computer Scientists and Systems Analysts
Human Services Workers
Occupational Therapists
Operations Research Analysts
Physical Therapists
Psychologists
Recreational Therapists
Registered Nurses
Respiratory Therapists
School Teachers—Kindergarten, Elementary,
   and Secondary
Social Workers
Speech-Language Pathologists and Audiologists

Technicians and Related Support Occupations

Dental Hygienists
Licensed Practical Nurses
Medical Records Technicians
Paralegals
Radiologic Technologists
Surgical Technologists

Marketing and Sales Occupations

Real Estate Agents, Brokers, and Appraisers
Retail Sales Workers
Travel Agents

Administrative Support Occupations, Including Clerical

Adjusters, Investigators, and Collectors
Clerical Supervisors and Managers
General Office Clerks
Information Clerks
Secretaries
Teacher Aides

Service Occupations

Barbers and Cosmetologists
Chefs, Cooks, and Other Kitchen Workers
Correction Officers
Dental Assistants
Flight Attendants
Guards
Homemaker-Home Health Aides
Medical Assistants
Nursing Aides and Psychiatric Aides
Police, Detectives, and Special Agents
Preschool Workers
Private Household Workers

Mechanics, Installers, and Repairers

Computer and Office Machine Repairers
General Maintenance Mechanics

Production Occupations

Blue-Collar Worker Supervisors

Transportation and Material Movers Occupations

Truckdrivers

Executive, Administrative, and Managerial Occupations

Accountants and Auditors

Nature of the Work

Managers must have up-to-date financial information in order to make important decisions. Accountants and auditors prepare, analyze, and verify financial reports and taxes, and monitor information systems that furnish this information to managers in all business, industrial, and government organizations.

Four major fields of accounting are public, management, government, and internal auditing. Public accountants have their own businesses or work for accounting firms. They perform a broad range of accounting, auditing, tax, and consulting activities for their clients who may be corporations, government agencies, nonprofit organizations, or individuals. Management accountants, also called industrial, corporate, or private accountants, record and analyze the financial information of the companies for which they work. Government accountants and auditors maintain and examine the records of government agencies and audit private businesses and individuals whose activities are subject to government regulations or taxation. Internal auditors verify the accuracy of their organization's records and check for mismanagement, waste, or fraud.

Within each field, accountants often concentrate on one phase of accounting. For example, many public accountants concentrate on tax matters, such as preparing an individual's income tax returns and advising companies of the tax advantages and disadvantages of certain business decisions. Others concentrate on consulting and offer advice on matters such as employee health care benefits and compensation; the design of companies' accounting and data processing systems; and controls to safeguard assets. Some specialize in forensic accounting which involves investigating and interpreting bankruptcies and other complex financial transactions. Still others work primarily in auditing, that is examining a client's financial statements and reporting to investors and authorities that they have been prepared and reported correctly. However, fewer accounting firms are performing this type of work because of potential liability.

Management accountants analyze and interpret the financial information corporate executives need to make sound business decisions. They also prepare financial reports for nonmanagement groups, including stock holders, creditors, regulatory agencies, and tax authorities. Within accounting departments, they may work in financial analysis, planning and budgeting, cost accounting, and other areas.

Internal auditing is rapidly growing in importance. As computer systems make information more timely and available, top management can base its decisions on actual data rather than personal observation. Internal auditors examine and evaluate their firms' financial and information systems, management procedures, and internal controls to ensure that records are accurate and controls are adequate to protect against fraud and waste. They also review company operations—evaluating their efficiency, effectiveness, and compliance with corporate policies and procedures, laws, and government regulations. There are many types of highly specialized auditors, such as electronic data processing auditors, environmental auditors, engineering auditors, legal auditors, insurance premium auditors, bank auditors, and health care auditors.

Accountants and auditors also work for federal, state, and local government agencies. Government accountants ensure that revenues are received and expenditures are made in accordance with laws and regulations. Many people with an accounting background work for the federal government as Internal Revenue Service agents or in financial management, financial institution examination, and budget analysis and administration.

In addition, a small number of people trained as accountants teach and conduct research at business and professional schools. Some work part-time as accountants or consultants.

Computers are widely used in accounting and auditing. With the aid of special computer software packages, accountants summarize transactions in standard formats for financial records or organize data in special formats for financial analysis. These accounting packages are easily learned and require few specialized computer skills, and greatly reduce the amount of tedious work associated with figures and records. Personal and laptop computers enable accountants and auditors in all fields—even those who work independently—to use their clients' computer systems and to extract information from large mainframe computers. Internal auditors may recommend controls for their organization's computer system to ensure the reliability of the system and the integrity of the data. A growing number of accountants and auditors have extensive computer skills and specialize in correcting problems with software or developing software to meet unique data needs.

Working Conditions

Accountants and auditors usually work in offices, but public accountants may frequently visit the offices of clients while conducting audits. Self-employed accountants may be able to do part of their work at home. Accountants and auditors employed by large firms and government agencies may travel frequently to perform audits at their clients' place of business, branches of their firm, or government facilities.

The majority of accountants and auditors generally work a standard 40 hour week, but many work longer, particularly if they are self-employed and free to take on the work of as many clients as they choose. For example, about 4 out of 10 self-employed accountants and auditors work more than 50 hours per week, compared to 1 of 4 wage and salary accountants and auditors. Tax specialists often work long hours during the tax season.

Employment

Accountants and auditors held about 939,000 jobs in 1992. They worked in all types of firms and industries, but nearly one-third worked for accounting, auditing, and bookkeeping firms, or were self-employed.

The majority of accountants and auditors were unlicensed management accountants, internal auditors, or government accountants and auditors. However, in 1992 there were more than 475,000 state-licensed Certified Public Accountants (CPAs), Public Accountants (PAs), Registered Public Accountants (RPAs), and Accounting Practitioners (APs). The vast majority of these—more than 400,000—were CPAs, but there may have been far fewer practicing CPAs in the country; many CPAs hold licenses in several states at once.

Most accountants and auditors work in urban areas where public accounting firms and central or regional offices of businesses are concentrated. Roughly 10 percent of all accountants were self-employed, and less than 10 percent worked part-time.

Some accountants and auditors teach full-time in junior colleges, colleges, and universities; others teach part-time while working for private industry or government or as self-employed accountants.

Training, Other Qualifications, and Advancement

Most public accounting and business firms require applicants for accountant and internal auditor positions to have at least a bachelor's degree in accounting or a related field. Those wishing to pursue a bachelor's degree in accounting should carefully research accounting curricula before enrolling. Many states will soon require CPA candidates to complete 150 semester hours of course work prior to taking the CPA exam, and many schools have altered their curricula accordingly. Some employers prefer those with a master's degree in accounting or a master's degree in business administration with a concentration in accounting. Most employers also prefer applicants who are familiar with computers and their applications in accounting and internal auditing. For beginning accounting and auditing positions in the federal government, four years of college (including 24 semester hours in accounting or auditing) or an equivalent combination of education and experience is required.

Previous experience in accounting or auditing can help an applicant get a job. Many colleges offer students an opportunity to gain experience through summer or part-time internship programs conducted by public accounting or business firms. Such training is invaluable to gaining permanent employment in the field. Professional recognition through certification or licensure is also helpful. In the majority of states, CPAs are the only accountants who are licensed and regulated. Anyone working as a CPA must have a certificate and a license issued by a state board of accountancy. The vast majority of states require CPA candi-

dates to be college graduates, but a few states substitute a certain number of years of public accounting experience in lieu of the educational requirement. Based on recommendations made by the American Institute of Certified Public Accountants and the National Association of State Boards of Accountancy, some states currently require that CPA candidates complete 150 semester hours of college coursework, and many other states are working toward adopting this law. This 150 hour rule requires an additional 30 hours of coursework beyond the usual four year bachelor's degree in accounting.

All states use the four-part Uniform CPA Examination prepared by the American Institute of Certified Public Accountants. The two day CPA examination is rigorous, and only about one-quarter of those who take it each year pass each part they attempt. Candidates are not required to pass all four parts at once, although most states require candidates to pass at least two parts for partial credit. Many states require all sections of the test to be passed within a certain period of time. Most states also require candidates for the CPA certificate to have some accounting experience.

The designations PA or RPA are also recognized by most states and several states continue to issue these licenses. With the growth in the number of CPAs, however, the majority of states are phasing out the PA, RAP, and other non-CPA designations by not issuing new licenses. Accountants who hold PA or RPA designations have similar legal rights, duties, and obligations as CPAs, but their qualifications for licensure are less stringent. The designation of Accounting Practitioner is also awarded by several states. It requires less formal training than a CPA license and covers a more limited scope of practice.

Nearly all states require both CPAs and PAs to complete a certain number of hours of continuing professional education before their licenses can be renewed. The professional associations representing accountants sponsor numerous courses, seminars, group study programs, and other forms of continuing education.

Professional societies bestow other forms of credentials on a voluntary basis. Voluntary certification can attest to professional competence in a specialized field of accounting or auditing. It can also certify that a recognized level of professional competence has been achieved by accountants and auditors who acquired some skills on the job, without the amount of formal education or public accounting work experience needed to meet the rigorous standards required to take the CPA examination. Increasingly, employers seek applicants with these credentials.

The Institute of Internal Auditors confers the designation of Certified Internal Auditor (CIA) on graduates from accredited colleges and universities who have completed two years of work in internal auditing and passed a four-part examination. The EDP Auditors Association confers the designation of Certified Information Systems Auditor (CISA) on candidates who pass an examination and have five years of experience in auditing electronic data processing systems. However, auditing or data processing experience and college education may be substituted for up to three years. Other organizations, such as the National Association of Certified Fraud Examiners and the Bank Administration Institute, confer other specialized auditing designations.

The Institute of Management Accountants (IMA), formerly the National Association of Accountants, confers the Certified Management Accountant (CMA) designation on college graduates who pass a four-part examination, agree to meet continuing education requirements, comply with standards of professional conduct, and have at least two years of work in management accounting. The CMA program is administered through an affiliate of the IMA, the Institute of Certified Management Accountants. The Accreditation Council for Accountancy and Taxation, a satellite organization of the National Society of Public Accountants, awards a Certificate of Accreditation in Accountancy to those who pass a comprehensive examination, and a Certificate of Accreditation in Taxation to those with appropriate experience and education. It is not uncommon for a practitioner to hold multiple licenses and designations. For instance, one internal auditor might be a CPA, CIA, and CISA.

People planning a career in accounting should have an aptitude for mathematics, be able to analyze, compare, and interpret facts and figures quickly, and make sound judgments based on this knowledge. They must be able to clearly communicate the results of their work, orally and in writing, to clients and management. Accountants and auditors must be good at working with people as well as with business systems and computers. Accuracy and the ability to handle responsibility with limited supervision are important. Perhaps most important, because millions of financial statement users rely on their services, accountants and auditors should have high standards of integrity.

Capable accountants and auditors should advance rapidly while those having inadequate academic preparation may be assigned routine jobs and find promotion difficult. Many graduates of junior colleges and business and correspondence schools, as well as bookkeepers and accounting clerks who meet the education and experience requirements set by their employers, can obtain junior accounting positions and advance to more responsible positions by demonstrating their skills on the job.

Beginning public accountants usually start by assisting with work for several clients. They may advance to positions with more responsibility in one or two years and to senior positions within another few years. Those who excel may become supervisors, managers, or partners, open their own public accounting firms, or transfer to executive positions in management accounting or internal auditing in private firms. Beginning management accountants often start as cost accountants, junior internal auditors, or as trainees for other accounting positions. As they rise through the organization, they may advance to accounting manager, chief cost accountant, budget director, or manager of internal auditing. Some become controllers, treasurers, financial vice presidents, chief financial officers, or corporation presidents. Many senior corporation executives have a background in accounting, internal auditing, or finance.

There is a large degree of mobility among public accountants, management accountants, and internal auditors. Practitioners often shift into management accounting or internal auditing from public accounting, or between internal auditing and management accounting. However, it is less common for accountants and auditors to move from either management accounting or internal auditing into public accounting.

Job Outlook

Employment of accountants and auditors is expected to grow faster than the average for all occupations through 2005. Qualified accountants and auditors should have good job opportunities. Although the profession is characterized by a relatively low rate of turnover, the occupation is very large and many openings will arise as accountants and auditors retire, die, or move into other occupations. CPAs should have the widest range of opportunities, especially as more states enact the 150 hour rule and certification as a CPA becomes more difficult.

As the economy grows, the number of businesses increases, requiring more accountants and auditors to set up their books, prepare their taxes, and provide management advice. As these businesses grow, the volume and complexity of information developed by accountants and auditors on costs, expenditures, and taxes will increase as well. More complex requirements for accountants and auditors also arise from changes in legislation related to taxes, financial reporting standards, business investments, mergers, and other financial matters. In addition, businesses will increasingly need quick, accurate, and individually tailored financial information due to the demands of growing international competition.

The changing role of public accountants, management accountants, and internal auditors will also spur job growth. Public accountants will perform less auditing work due to potential liability and less tax work due to growing competition from tax preparation firms, but they will assume an even greater management advisory role and expand their consulting services. These rapidly growing services will lead to increased demand for public accountants in the coming years. Management accountants also will take on a greater advisory role as they develop more sophisticated and flexible accounting systems, and focus more on analyzing operations rather than just providing financial data. Similarly, management will increasingly need internal auditors to develop new ways to discover and eliminate waste and fraud.

Despite growing opportunities for qualified accountants and auditors, competition for the most prestigious jobs—such as those with major accounting and business firms—will remain keen. Applicants with a master's degree in accounting, a master's degree in business administration with a concentration in accounting, or a broad base of computer experience will have an advantage. Moreover, computers now perform many simple accounting functions, allowing accountants and auditors to incorporate and analyze more information. This increasingly complex work requires greater knowledge of more specialized areas such as international business and current legislation, and expertise in specific industries.

Earnings

According to a College Placement Council Salary survey in 1993, bachelor's degree candidates in accounting received starting salary offers averaging $28,000 a year while master's degree candidates in accounting were offered more than $30,000. According to a survey of workplaces in 160 metropolitan areas, accountants with limited experience had median earnings of $24,700 in 1992, with the middle half earning between $22,200 and $27,500. The most experienced accountants had median earnings of $76,000, with the middle half earning between $68,500 and $84,600. Public accountants employed by public accounting firms with limited experience had median earnings of $28,000 in 1992, with the middle half earning between $26,500 and $29,400. The most experienced public accountants had median earnings of $42,400, with the middle half earning between $36,900 and $50,400. Many owners and partners of firms earned considerably more.

Based on a survey by the Institute of Management Accountants (IMA), the average salary of IMA members was about $55,100 a year in 1992. IMA members who were certified public accountants averaged $61,900, while members who were certified management accountants averaged $58,700. According to a survey by the Institute of Internal Auditors, salaries of internal auditors in 1992 ranged from $26,500 for those with less than two years of experience to $60,700 for those with more than 10 years of experience.

In the federal government, the starting annual salary for junior accountants and auditors was about $18,300 in 1993. Candidates who had a superior academic record could begin at about $22,700. Applicants with a master's degree or two years of professional experience began around $27,800. Accountants employed by the federal government in nonsupervisory, supervisory, and managerial positions averaged $46,300 a year in 1993; auditors averaged $48,200.

Related Occupations

Accountants and auditors design internal control systems and analyze financial data. Others for whom training in accounting is invaluable include appraisers, budget officers, loan officers, financial analysts and managers, bank officers, actuaries, underwriters, tax collectors and revenue agents, FBI special agents, securities sales workers, and purchasing agents.

Sources of Additional Information

Information about different accounting licenses and the standards for licensure in your state may be obtained from your state board of accountancy. A list of the addresses and chief executives of all state boards of accountancy is available from:

❏ National Association of State Boards of Accountancy, 380 Lexington Ave., Suite 200, New York, NY 10168-0002.

Information about careers in certified public accounting and about CPA standards and examinations may be obtained from:

❏ American Institute of Certified Public Accountants, 1211 Avenue of the Americas, New York, NY 10036-8775 or call 1-800-862-4272.

Information on management and other specialized fields of accounting and auditing and on the Certified Management Accountant program is available from:

❏ Institute of Management Accountants, 10 Paragon Dr., Montvale, NJ 07645-1760;

❏ National Society of Public Accountants and the Accreditation Council for Accountancy and Taxation, 1010 North Fairfax St., Alexandria, VA 22314;

❏ The Institute of Internal Auditors, 249 Maitland Ave., Altamonte Springs, FL 32701-4201; and

❏ The EDP Auditors Association, 455 Kehoe Blvd., Suite 106, Carol Stream, IL 60188-0180.

For information on accredited accounting programs and educational institutions offering a specialization in accounting or business management, contact:

❏ American Assembly of Collegiate Schools of Business, 605 Old Ballas Rd., Suite 220, St. Louis, MO 63141.

General Managers and Top Executives

Nature of the Work

Chief executive officer, executive vice president for marketing, department store manager, financial institution president, brokerage office manager, college president, school superintendent, police chief—these are examples of general managers and top executives who, at the upper end of the management hierarchy, formulate the policies and direct the operations of the nation's private firms and government agencies.

The fundamental objectives of private organizations are to maintain efficiency and profitability in the face of shifting consumer tastes and needs, accelerating technological complexity, economic interdependence, and domestic and foreign competition. Similarly, nonprofit organizations and government agencies must effectively implement programs subject to budgetary constraints and shifting public preferences. General managers and top executives try to ensure that their organizations meet these objectives.

An organization's general goals and policies are established by the chief executive officer in collaboration with other top executives—usually executive vice presidents and a board of directors. In a large corporation, a chief executive officer may frequently meet with top executives of other corporations, domestic or foreign governments, or outside consultants to discuss matters affecting the organization's policies. Although the chief executive officer retains ultimate authority and responsibility, the chief operating officer may be delegated the authority to oversee executive vice presidents who direct the activities of various departments and are responsible for implementing the organization's policies in these departments.

The scope of executive vice presidents' responsibilities depends greatly on the size of the organization. In large corporations, their duties may be highly specialized. For example, they may oversee general managers of marketing, sales promotion, purchasing, finance, personnel, training, industrial relations, administrative services, electronic data processing, property management, transportation, or legal services departments. In smaller firms, an executive vice president might be responsible for a number of these departments.

General managers, in turn, direct their individual department's activities within the framework of the organization's overall plan. With the help of supervisory managers and their staffs, general managers oversee and strive to motivate workers to achieve their department's goals as rapidly and economically as possible. In smaller organizations, such as independent retail stores or small manufacturers, a general manager may be responsible for purchasing, hiring, training, quality control, and all other day-to-day supervisory duties.

Working Conditions

General managers in large firms or government agencies are provided with offices close to the departments they direct and to the top executives to whom they report. Top executives may be provided with spacious offices and often meet and negotiate with top executives from other corporations, government agencies, or foreign countries. Long hours, including evenings and weekends, are the rule for most top executives and general managers, though their schedules may be flexible. Though still uncommon, more executives are accepting temporary positions, sometimes only working for the duration of one project or several months.

Substantial travel is often required. General managers may travel between national, regional, and local offices to monitor operations and meet with other executives. Top executives may travel to meet with their counterparts in other corporations in the country or overseas. Many attend meetings and conferences that are sponsored by industries and associations and provide invaluable opportunities to meet with peers and keep abreast of technological and other developments. Perquisites such as reimbursement of a spouse's travel expenses may help executives cope with frequent or extended periods away from home. In large corporations, job transfers between the parent company and its local offices or subsidiaries, here or abroad, are common.

With increasing domestic and international competition, general managers and top executives are under intense pressure to attain, for example, ever higher production and marketing goals. Executives in charge of poorly performing companies or departments often find that their jobs are in jeopardy.

Employment

General managers and top executives held nearly 2.9 million jobs in 1992. They are found in every industry, although wholesale and retail trade and services industries employ more than 6 out of every 10 general managers and top executives.

Training, Other Qualifications, and Advancement

The educational background of managers and top executives varies as widely as the nature of their diverse responsibilities. Many general managers and top executives have a bachelor's degree in liberal arts or business administration. Their major is often related to the departments they direct. For example, a general manager of finance may hold an accounting degree or a computer science major may be a general manager of information systems. Graduate and professional degrees are common. Many managers in administrative, marketing, financial, and manufacturing activities have a master's degree in business administration. Managers in highly technical manufacturing and research activities often have a master's or doctoral degree in an engineering or scientific discipline. A law degree is mandatory for general managers of corporate legal departments and hospital administrators generally have a master's degree in health services administration or business administration. College presidents and school superintendents generally have a doctorate, often in education administration, although some have a law degree. On the other hand, in some industries such as retail trade, competent individuals without a college degree may become general managers.

Many general managers in the public sector have a liberal arts degree in public administration or one of the social sciences such as economics, psychology, sociology, or urban studies. For others, experience is still the primary qualification. For park superintendents, a liberal arts degree also provides a suitable background. Police chiefs must be graduates of police academies, and a degree in police science or a related field is increasingly important. Similarly, fire chiefs are graduates of fire academies, and a degree in fire science is gaining in importance as well. For harbormasters, a high school education and experience as a harbor pilot are sufficient.

Most general manager and top executive positions are filled by promoting experienced, lower level managers. Some companies prefer that their top executives have specialized backgrounds, in finance or marketing, for example. However, certain qualities, including leadership, self-confidence, motivation, decisiveness, flexibility, the ability to communicate effectively, and sound business judgment are far more important. In small firms, where the number of positions is limited, advancement to a higher management position may come slowly. In large firms, promotions may occur more quickly.

Advancement may be accelerated by participation in company training programs to broaden knowledge of company policy and operations. Attendance at national or local training programs sponsored by numerous industry and trade associations and continuing education, normally at company expense, in colleges and universities can familiarize managers with the latest developments in management techniques. Every year, thousands of senior managers, who often have some experience in a particular field such as accounting, engineering, or science, attend executive development programs to facilitate their promotion from functional specialists to general managers. In addition, participation in interdisciplinary conferences and seminars can expand knowledge of national and international issues influencing the manager's firm.

People interested in becoming general managers and top executives must have highly developed personal skills. A highly analytical mind able to quickly assess large amounts of information and data is very important. The ability to consider and evaluate the interrelationships of numerous factors and to select the best course of action is imperative. In the absence of sufficient information, sound intuitive judgment is crucial for reaching favorable decisions. General managers and top executives must also be able to communicate clearly and persuasively with customers, subordinates, and other managers in their firm.

General managers may advance to top executive positions, such as executive or administrative vice president, in their own firm or to a corresponding general manager position in a larger firm. Similarly, top-level managers may advance to peak corporate positions—chief operating officer and, finally, chief executive officer. Chief executive officers and other top executives may also become members of the board of directors of one or more firms. Some general managers and top executives with sufficient capital and experience establish their own firms or become independent consultants.

Job Outlook

Employment of general managers and top executives is expected to grow more slowly than the average for all occupations through 2005 as companies restructure managerial hierarchies in an effort to cut costs. General managers and top executives may be more affected by these cost-cutting strategies than in the past, thus moderating employment growth.

Although this is a large occupation and many openings will occur each year as executives transfer to other positions, start their own businesses, or retire, competition for top managerial jobs will be keen. Many executives who leave their jobs transfer to other executive or managerial positions, limiting openings for new entrants, and large numbers of layoffs resulting from downsizing and restructuring will lead to an ample supply of competent managers. Moreover, the aging of the workforce will result in more senior middle managers vying for a limited number of top executive positions.

Projected employment growth of general managers and top executives varies widely among industries. For example, employment growth is expected to be faster than average in all services industries combined, but slower than average in all finance, insurance, and real estate industries combined. Employment of general managers and top executives is projected to decline in manufacturing industries overall.

Managers whose accomplishments reflect strong leadership qualities and the ability to improve the efficiency or competitive position of their organizations will have the best opportunities in all industries. In an increasingly global economy, certain types of experience, such as international economics, marketing, or information systems, or knowledge of several disciplines, will also be advantageous.

Earnings

General managers and top executives are among the highest paid workers in the nation. However, salary levels vary substantially depending on the level of managerial responsibility, length of service, and type, size, and location of the firm.

At the highest level, chief executive officers (CEOs) are extremely well-paid. According to a survey by *Fortune* magazine, CEOs at 200 major companies averaged $3.2 million in 1993, including bonuses and stock awards, which are often tied to performance. According to a similar survey of 365 companies by *Business Week* magazine, CEO salaries and bonuses averaged $1.1 million in 1992; total compensation, including stock options and dividends, averaged $3.8 million. Salaries are related to the size of the corporation, a top manager in a very large corporation can earn significantly more than a counterpart in a small firm.

Salaries also vary substantially by type and level of responsibilities and by industry. According to a salary survey by Robert Half International, a staffing services firm specializing in accounting and finance, senior vice presidents or heads of lending in banks with $1 billion and higher in assets earned about $200,000 in 1993. Based on a survey sponsored by the Society for Human Resource Management, the average base salary for top human resources managers was about $136,000 in 1993. A survey by *Network World* news weekly found that upper level computer network managers—including chief information officers, vice presidents, and directors—averaged $83,900 in 1993;

mid-level managers—including network, data communications, telecommunications, and technical support managers—averaged $59,400 that year. Among top network managers, those in the health care industry were the highest paid, averaging $142,500 in 1993, while those in wholesale/retail trade were the lowest paid, averaging $56,000. Among other industries, top network managers in manufacturing or finance and utilities were among the highest paid, while those in education and government were among the lowest paid.

Company-paid insurance premiums, physical examinations, executive dining rooms, use of company cars, paid country club memberships, and expense allowances are among the benefits enjoyed by some general managers and top executives in private industry.

Related Occupations

General managers and top executives plan, organize, direct, control, and coordinate the operations of an organization and its major departments or programs. The members of the board of directors and supervisory managers are also involved in these activities. Occupations in government with similar functions are governor, mayor, postmaster, commissioner, director, and office chief.

Sources of Additional Information

For a wide variety of information on general managers and top executives, including educational programs and job listings, contact:

❏ American Management Association, Management Information Service, 135 West 50th St., New York, NY 10020; or

❏ National Management Association, 2210 Arbor Blvd., Dayton, OH 45439.

Information about general managers and top executives in specific industries may be obtained from organizations listed under a number of headings—administration, administrators, directors, executives, management, managers, and superintendents—in various encyclopedias or directories of associations in public libraries.

Loan Officers and Counselors

Nature of work

Banks and other financial institutions need up-to-date information on companies and individuals applying for loans and credit. Customers and clients provide this information to the financial institution's loan officers and counselors, who are generally the first employees to be seen by them. Loan officers prepare, analyze, and verify loan applications, make decisions regarding the extension of credit, and help borrowers fill out loan applications. Loan counselors help consumers with low income or a poor credit history qualify for credit, usually a home mortgage.

Loan officers usually specialize in commercial, consumer, or mortgage loans. Commercial or business loans help companies pay for new equipment or expand operations. Consumer loans include home equity, automobile, and personal loans. Mortgage loans are made to purchase real estate or refinance an existing mortgage.

Loan officers represent lending institutions that provide funds for a variety of purposes. Personal loans can be made to consolidate bills, purchase expensive items such as an automobile or furniture, or finance a college education. Loan officers attempt to lower their firm's risk by receiving collateral—security pledged for the payment of a loan. For example, when lending money for a college education, the bank may insist that the borrower offer his or her home as collateral. If the borrower were ever unable to repay the loan, the borrower would have to sell the home to raise the necessary money. Loans backed by collateral are also beneficial to the customer because they usually carry a lower interest rate.

Loan officers and counselors must keep abreast of new financial products and services. To meet their customers' needs, for example, banks and other lenders now offer a variety of mortgage products, including reverse equity mortgages, shared equity mortgages, and adjustable rate mortgages. A reverse equity mortgage provides income to the owner of the property and is paid back through either a conventional mortgage or in a lump sum. A shared equity mortgage allows a group of people to jointly own and be responsible for payment of the mortgage. Adjustable rate mortgages have a fluctuating interest rate, commonly based on the interest rate paid on government bonds. A change in interest rates affects the borrower's monthly payment.

Loan officers meet with customers and gather basic information about the loan request. Often customers will not fully understand the information requested and will call the loan officer for assistance. Once the customer completes the financial forms, the loan officer begins to process them. The loan officer reviews the completed financial forms for accuracy and thoroughness, and requests additional information if necessary. For example, the loan officer verifies that the customer has correctly identified the type and purpose of the loan. The loan officer then requests a credit report from one or more of the major credit reporting agencies. This information, along with comments from the loan officer, is included in a loan file and compared to the lending institution's requirements. Banks and other lenders have established requirements for the maximum percentage of income that can safely go to repay loans. At this point, the loan officer, in consultation with company managers, decides whether or not to grant the loan. A loan that would otherwise be denied may be approved if the customer can provide the lender with appropriate collateral. Whether or not the loan request is approved, the loan officer informs the borrower of the lender's decision.

Loan counselors meet with consumers who are attempting to purchase a home or refinance debt, but who do not qualify for loans with banks. Often clients rely on income from self-employment or government assistance to prove that they can repay the loan. Counselors also help to psychologically prepare consumers to be homeowners and to pay their debts. Counselors frequently work with clients who have no experience with financial matters.

Loan counselors provide positive reinforcement along with the financial tools needed to qualify for a loan. This assistance may take several forms. Some clients simply need help to understand what information to give loan officers to complete a loan transaction. Most clients, however, need loans and grants for a down payment that sufficiently qualifies them for a bank-financed mortgage loan. Many clients have been renting for years and want to buy their own properties. While they have the desire to improve their lives through home ownership, they frequently have little or no resources for a down payment. Other clients want to move to a safer and more secure environment where, as owners, they can make decisions regarding the property. The loan counselor helps the client complete an application and researches federal, state, and local government programs which can provide the additional money needed for the client to purchase the home. Often several government programs are combined to provide the necessary money. Loan officers and counselors are particularly busy when interest rates are low, which results in a surge in loan applications.

Working Conditions

Loan officers and counselors work in offices, but mortgage loan officers frequently move from office to office and visit homes of clients while completing a loan request. Commercial loan officers employed by large firms may travel frequently to prepare complex loan agreements.

Most loan officers and counselors work a standard 40 hour week, but may work longer, particularly mortgage loan officers who are free to take on as many customers as they choose. Loan officers and counselors usually carry a heavy caseload and sometimes cannot accept new clients until they complete current cases. They are especially busy when interest rates are low.

Employment

Loan officers and counselors held about 172,000 jobs in 1992. About 7 out of 10 are employed by commercial banks, savings institutions, and credit unions. Others are employed by nonbank financial institutions, such as mortgage brokerage firms and personal credit firms. Most loan counselors work for state and local governments or for nonprofit organizations. Loan officers and counselors generally work in urban areas where large banks are concentrated.

Training, Other Qualifications, and Advancement

Most loan officer positions require a bachelor's degree in finance, economics, or a related field. Most employers also prefer applicants who are familiar with computers and their applications in banking. A mortgage loan officer is the exception, with training or experience in sales more crucial to potential employers. Many loan officers advance through the ranks in an organization, acquiring several years of work experience in various other occupations, such as teller or customer service representative.

Capable loan officers may advance to larger branches of the firm or to a managerial position, while less capable loan officers and those having inadequate academic preparation may be assigned to smaller branches and find promotion difficult. Advancement from a loan officer position usually includes becoming a supervisor over other loan officers and clerical staff.

Most loan counselors receive substantial on-the-job training, gaining a thorough understanding of the requirements and procedures for approval of loans. Some acquire this knowledge through work experience in a related field. In addition, accounting skills can be very helpful. Educational requirements vary. Some counselors are high school graduates while others have a college degree in economics, finance, or a related field. Like other workers, outstanding loan counselors can advance to supervisory positions. However, promotion potential is limited, and many loan counselors leave for better paying positions elsewhere.

People planning a career as a loan officer or counselor should have good mathematical and communications skills. Developing effective working relationships with different people—managers, clients, and the public—is essential to success as a loan officer or counselor. They also must be able to clearly communicate the results of their work, orally and in writing, to customers and management. Loan officers must enjoy public contact and be willing to attend community events as a representative of their employer.

People interested in counseling should have a strong interest in helping others and the ability to inspire trust, respect, and confidence. Because loan counselors frequently explain the complicated world of banking to clients who have never been exposed to it, patience and an understanding of mortgage banking is necessary to be an effective loan counselor. Counselors should be sensitive to their clients' needs and feelings. Clients want to improve their lives, and counselors must consider the importance and pride they attach to home ownership. Counselors should be able to work independently or as part of a team.

Job Outlook

Employment of loan officers and counselors is expected to grow faster than the average for all occupations through 2005. As the population and economy grow, applications for commercial, consumer, and mortgage loans will increase, spurring demand for loan officers and counselors. Growth in the variety and complexity of loans, and the importance of loan officers to the success of banks and other lending institutions, also should assure rapid employment growth. Although increased demand will generate many new jobs, most openings will result from the need to replace workers who leave the occupation or retire. College graduates and those with banking or lending experience should have the best job prospects.

Loan officers are less likely to lose their jobs than other workers in banks or lending institutions during difficult economic times. Because loans are the major source of income for banks, loan officers are central to the success of their organizations. Loan counselors typically have so many clients that a reduction in their numbers would lead to a decline in the services provided to the community. However, job security is influenced by the spending patterns of local governments. Budget reductions could result in less hiring or even layoffs of loan counselors.

Earnings

According to a salary survey conducted by Robert Half International, a staffing services firm specializing in accounting and finance, real estate mortgage loan officers earned between $25,000 and $45,000 in 1993; consumer loan officers, between $27,000 and $44,000. Larger banks generally paid higher salaries than smaller banks. Some mortgage loan officers who are paid on a commission basis, earn considerably more. Based on limited information, most loan counselors earned between $15,000 and $35,000 in 1993. Local government employees in large cities earned the highest salaries.

Banks and other lenders sometimes offer their loan officers free checking privileges and somewhat lower interest rates on personal loans. Loan counselors sometimes get awards for their service to the community.

Related Occupations

Loan officers and counselors help the public manage financial assets and secure loans. Occupations that involve similar functions include securities and financial services sales representatives, financial aid officers, real estate agents and brokers, and insurance agents and brokers.

Sources of Additional Information

For information on job opportunities as a loan officer or counselor, contact local employers such as banks, savings institutions, mortgage brokers, personal credit firms, or your municipal government, or the local state employment service office.

Information about a career as a loan officer may be obtained from:

❏ American Bankers Association, 1120 Connecticut Ave. NW., Washington, DC 20036.

Management Analysts and Consultants

Nature of the Work

A rapidly growing small company needs a better system of control over inventories and expenses. An established manufacturing company decides to relocate to another state and needs assistance planning the move. After acquiring a new division, a large company realizes that its corporate structure must be reorganized. A division chief of a government agency wants to know why the division's contracts are always going over budget. These are just a few of the many organizational problems that management analysts, as they are called in government agencies, and management consultants, as business firms refer to them, help solve. Although their job titles may differ, their job duties are essentially the same.

The work of management analysts and consultants varies from employer to employer and from project to project. For example, some projects require several consultants to work together, each specializing in one area, but at other times, they will work independently. In general, analysts and consultants collect, review, and analyze information; make recommendations; and often assist in the implementation of their proposal.

Both public and private organizations use consultants for a variety of reasons. Some don't have the internal resources needed to handle a project; others need a consultant's expertise to determine what resources will be required or problems encountered if they pursue a particular course of action. Still others want outside advice on how to resolve organizational problems that have already been identified or avoid troublesome problems that could arise.

Firms providing consulting services range in size from solo practitioners to large international organizations employing thousands of consultants. Some firms specialize by industry, others by type of business function, such as human resources or information systems. Consulting services are usually provided on a contract basis. A company first solicits proposals from consulting firms specializing in the area in which it needs assistance. These proposals include the estimated cost and scope of the project, staffing requirements, and deadline. The company then selects the proposal that best meets its needs.

When getting an assignment or contract, consultants define the nature and extent of the problem. During this phase of the job, they may analyze data such as annual revenues, employment, or expenditures; interview employees; or observe the operations of the organizational unit. Next, they use their knowledge of management systems and expertise in a particular area to develop solutions. In the course of preparing their recommendations, they must take into account the general nature of the business, the relationship the firm has with others in that industry, and the firm's internal organization, as well as information gained through data collection and analysis.

Once they have decided on a course of action, consultants usually report their findings and recommendations to the client, often in writing. In addition, they often make oral presentations regarding their findings. For some projects, this is all that is required; for others, consultants may assist in the implementation of their suggestions.

Management analysts in government agencies use the same skills as their private-sector colleagues to advise managers in government on many types of issues—most of which are similar to the problems faced by private firms. For example, if an agency is planning to purchase several personal computers, it first must determine which type to buy, given its budget and data processing needs. Management analysts would assess the various types of machines available and determine which best meets their department's needs.

Work Conditions

Management analysts and consultants usually divide their time between their offices and the client's operation. Although much of their time is spent indoors in clean, well-lighted offices, they may have to visit a client's production facility where conditions may not be so favorable. They must follow established safety procedures when making field visits to sites where they may encounter potentially hazardous conditions.

Typically, analysts and consultants work at least 40 hours a week. Overtime is common, especially when deadlines must be met. In addition, because they must spend a significant portion of time with clients, they may travel frequently.

Self-employed consultants can determine their own workload and hours and work at home. On the other hand, their livelihood depends on their ability to maintain and expand their client base, which can be difficult at times.

Employment

Management analysts and consultants held about 208,000 jobs in 1992. Four out of ten of these workers were self-employed. Most of the rest worked in management consulting firms and for federal, state, and local governments. The majority of those working for the federal government were found in the Department of Defense. Management analysts and consultants are found throughout the country, but employment is concentrated in metropolitan areas.

Training, Other Qualifications, and Advancement

No universal educational requirements exist for entry-level jobs in this field. However, employers in private industry prefer to hire those with a master's degree in business administration or a discipline related to their firm's area of specialization. Individuals hired directly from school with only a bachelor's degree are likely to work as research associates or junior consultants, rather than full-fledged management consultants. It is possible for research associates to climb the career ladder if they demonstrate a strong aptitude for consulting, but, more often, they need to acquire an advanced degree to do so.

Many entrants to this occupation have, in addition to the appropriate formal education, several years of experience in management or in another occupation. Most government agencies hire those with a bachelor's degree and no work experience as entry-level management analysts, and often provide formal classroom training in management analysis. Many fields of study provide a suitable formal educational background for this occupation because of the diversity of problem areas addressed by management analysts and consultants. These include most areas of business and management, as well as computer and information sciences and engineering.

Management analysts and consultants who are hired directly from school sometimes participate in formal company training programs. These programs may include instruction on policies and procedures, computer systems and software, research processes, and management practices and principles. Because of their previous industry experience, most who enter at middle levels do not participate in formal company training programs. However, regardless of background, analysts and consultants routinely attend conferences to keep abreast of current developments in their field. Additionally, some large firms offer in-house formal training programs for all levels of staff.

Management analysts and consultants often work under little or no supervision, so they should be independent and self-motivated. Analytical skills, strong oral and written communication skills, good judgment, the ability to manage time well, and creativity in developing solutions to problems are desirable qualities for prospective management analysts and consultants.

In large consulting firms, beginners usually start as members of a consulting team. The team is responsible for the entire project and each consultant is assigned to a particular area. As consultants gain experience, they may be assigned to work on one specific project full time, taking on more responsibility and managing their own hours. At the senior level, consultants may supervise entry-level workers and become increasingly involved in seeking out new business. Those with exceptional skills may eventually become a partner or principal in the firm. Others with entrepreneurial ambition may open their own firm.

A high percentage of management consultants are self-employed, partly because start-up costs are low. Little capital is required initially, and it is possible for self-employed consultants to share office space, administrative help, and other resources with other self-employed consultants or small consulting firms, thus reducing overhead costs.

The Institute of Management Consultants (a division of the Council of Consulting Organizations) offers the Certified Management Consultant (CMC) designation to those who pass an examination and meet minimum levels of education and experience. Certification is not mandatory for management consultants to practice, but it may give a job seeker a competitive advantage.

Job Outlook

Employment of management analysts and consultants is expected to grow much faster than the average for all occupations through 2005 as industry and government increasingly rely on outside expertise to improve the performance of their organizations. Growth is expected in large consulting firms, but also in small consulting firms whose consultants will specialize in highly specific areas of expertise. Although most job openings will result from employment growth of the occupation, additional opportunities will arise from the need to replace personnel who transfer to other fields or leave the labor force.

Increased competition has caused American industry to take a closer look at its operations. In more competitive international and domestic markets, firms cannot afford inefficiency and wasted resources or else they risk losing their share of the market. Management consultants are being increasingly relied on to help reduce costs, streamline operations, and develop marketing strategies. As businesses downsize and eliminate needed functions as well as permanent staff, consultants will be used to perform those functions on a contractual basis. On the other hand, businesses undergoing expansion, particularly into world markets, will also need the skills of management consultants to help with organizational, administrative, and other issues. Continuing changes in the business environment are also expected to lead to demand for management consultants:

Firms will use consultants' expertise to incorporate new technologies, cope with more numerous and complex government regulations, and adapt to a changing labor force. As businesses rely more on technology, there are increasing roles for consultants with a technical background, such as engineering or biotechnology, particularly when combined with an MBA.

Federal, state, and local agencies are also expected to expand their use of management analysts. In this era of budget deficits, analysts' skills at identifying problems and implementing cost reduction measures are expected to become increasingly important. However, because one-half of the management analysts employed by the federal government work for the Department of Defense, the pace of federal employment growth will vary with the defense budget.

In the private sector, job opportunities are expected to be best for those with a graduate degree and some industry expertise, while opportunities for those with only a bachelor's degree will be best in the federal government. Because many small consulting firms fail each year due to lack of managerial expertise and clients, those interested in opening their own firms should have good organizational and marketing skills, plus several years of consulting experience.

Despite projected rapid employment growth, competition for jobs as management consultants is expected to be keen in the private sector. Because management consultants can come from diverse educational backgrounds, the pool of applicants from which employers hire is quite large. Additionally, the independent and challenging nature of the work combined with high earnings potential make this occupation attractive to many.

Earnings

Salaries for management analysts and consultants vary widely by experience, education, and employer. In 1992, those who were wage and salary workers had median annual earnings of about $40,300. The middle 50 percent earned between $26,500 and $60,100.

In 1991, according to the Association of Management Consulting Firms (ACME), earnings—including bonuses and/or profit sharing—for research associates in ACME member firms averaged $31,300; for entry level consultants, $39,100; for management consultants, $56,300; for senior consultants, $76,700; for junior partners, $105,600; and for senior partners, $166,100.

Typical benefits for salaried analysts and consultants include health and life insurance, a retirement plan, vacation and sick leave, profit sharing, and bonuses for outstanding work. In addition, all travel expenses are usually reimbursed by the employer. Self-employed consultants usually have to maintain an office and do not receive employer-provided benefits.

Related Occupations

Management analysts and consultants collect, review, and analyze data; make recommendations; and assist in the implementation of their ideas. Others who use similar skills are managers, computer systems analysts, operations research analysts, economists, and financial analysts.

Sources of Additional Information

Information about career opportunities in management consulting is available from:

❏ ACME, The Association of Management Consulting Firms, 521 Fifth Ave., 35th Floor, New York, NY 10175-3598.

For information about a career as a state or local government management analyst, contact your state or local employment service.

People interested in a management analyst position in the federal government can obtain information from:

❏ U.S. Office of Personnel Management, 1900 E St. NW., Washington, DC 20415.

Marketing, Advertising, and Public Relations Managers

Nature of the Work

The fundamental objective of any firm is to market its products or services profitably. In small firms, all marketing responsibilities may be assumed by the owner or chief executive officer. In large firms that offer numerous products and services nationally or even worldwide, experienced marketing, advertising, and public relations managers coordinate these and related activities.

The executive vice president for marketing in large firms directs the overall marketing policy, including market research, marketing strategy, sales, advertising, promotion, pricing, product development, and public relations activities. (This occupation is included in the statement on general managers and top executives.) These activities are supervised by middle and supervisory managers who oversee staffs of professionals and technicians.

Marketing managers develop the firm's detailed marketing strategy. With the help of subordinates, including product development managers and market research managers, they determine the demand for products and services offered by the firm and its competitors and identify potential consumers—business firms, wholesalers, retailers, government, or the general public. Mass markets are further categorized according to various factors such as region, age, income, and lifestyle.

Marketing managers develop pricing strategy with an eye toward maximizing the firm's share of the market and its profits while ensuring that the firm's customers are satisfied. In collaboration with sales, product development, and other managers, they monitor trends that indicate the need for new products and services and oversee product development. Marketing managers work with advertising and promotion managers to best promote the firm's products and services and to attract potential consumers.

Sales managers direct the firm's sales program. They assign sales territories and goals and establish training programs for sales representatives. Managers advise sales representatives on ways to improve their sales performance. In large, multiproduct firms, they oversee regional and local sales managers and their staffs. Sales managers maintain contact with dealers and distributors. They analyze sales statistics gathered by their staffs to determine sales potential and inventory requirements and monitor the preferences of customers. Such information is vital to develop products and maximize profits.

Except in the largest firms, advertising and promotion staffs are generally small and serve as a liaison between the firm and the advertising or promotion agency to which many advertising or promotional functions are contracted. Advertising managers oversee the account services, creative services, and media services departments. The account services department is managed by account executives who assess the need for advertising and, in advertising agencies, maintain the accounts of clients. The creative services department develops the subject matter and presentation of advertising. This department is supervised by a creative director, who oversees the copy chief and art director and their staffs. The media services department is supervised by the media director who oversees planning groups that select the communication media—radio, television, newspapers, magazines, or signs—to disseminate the advertising.

Promotion managers supervise staffs of promotion specialists. They direct promotion programs combining advertising with purchase incentives to increase sales of products or services. In an effort to establish closer contact with purchasers—dealers, distributors, or consumers—promotion programs may involve direct mail, telemarketing, television or radio advertising, catalogs, exhibits, inserts in newspapers, in-store displays and product endorsements, and special events. Purchase incentives may include discounts, samples, gifts, rebates, coupons, sweepstakes, and contests.

Public relations managers supervise public relations specialists. These managers direct publicity programs to a targeted public. They use any necessary communication media in their effort to maintain the support of the specific group on whom their organization's success depends, such as consumers, stockholders, or the general public. For example, public relations managers may clarify or justify the firm's point of view on health or environmental issues to community or special interest groups. They may evaluate advertising and promotion programs for compatibility with public relations efforts.

Public relations managers, in effect, serve as the eyes and ears of top management. They observe social, economic, and political trends that might ultimately affect the firm and make recommendations to enhance the firm's public image in view of those trends. Public relations managers may confer with labor relations managers to produce internal company communications, such as news about employee-management relations, and with financial managers to produce company reports. They may assist company executives in drafting speeches, arranging interviews and other forms of public contact, overseeing company archives, and responding to information requests. In addition, public relations managers may handle special events such as sponsorship of races, parties introducing new products, or other activities the firm supports in order to gain public attention through the press without advertising directly.

Increasing competition in products and services will spur rapid employment growth among marketing, advertising, and public relations managers.

Working Conditions

Marketing, advertising, and public relations managers are provided with offices close to top managers. Long hours, including evenings and weekends, are common. Working under pressure is unavoidable as schedules change, problems arise, and deadlines and goals must be met. Marketing, advertising, and public relations managers meet frequently with other managers; some meet with the public and government officials.

Substantial travel may be involved. For example, attendance at meetings sponsored by associations or industries is often mandatory. Sales managers travel to national, regional, and local offices and to various dealers and distributors. Advertising and promotion managers may travel to meet with clients or representatives of communications media. Public relations managers may travel to meet with special interest groups or government officials. Job transfers between headquarters and regional offices are common, particularly among sales managers, and may disrupt family life.

Employment

Marketing, advertising, and public relations managers held about 432,000 jobs in 1992. These managers are found in virtually every industry. Industries employing them in significant numbers include motor vehicle dealers; printing and publishing firms; advertising agencies; department stores; computer and data processing services firms; and management and public relations firms.

Training, Advancement, and Other Qualifications

A wide range of educational backgrounds are suitable for entry into marketing, advertising, and public relations managerial jobs, but many employers prefer a broad liberal arts background. A bachelor's degree in sociology, psychology, literature, or philosophy, among other subjects, is acceptable. However, requirements vary depending on the particular job.

For marketing, sales, and promotion management positions, some employers prefer a bachelor's or master's degree in business administration with an emphasis on marketing. Courses in business law, economics, accounting, finance, mathematics, and statistics are also highly recommended. In technical industries, such as computer and electronics manufacturing, a bachelor's degree in engineering or science combined with a master's degree in business administration may be preferred.

For advertising management positions, some employers prefer a bachelor's degree in advertising or journalism. A course of study should include courses in marketing, consumer behavior, market research, sales, communications methods and technology, and visual arts.

For public relations management positions, some employers prefer a bachelor's or master's degree in public relations or journalism. The individual's curriculum should include courses in advertising, business administration, public affairs, political science, and creative and technical writing. For all these specialties, courses in management and completion of an internship while in school are highly recommended. Familiarity with computerized word processing and database applications are also important for many marketing, advertising, and public relations management positions.

Most marketing, advertising, and public relations management positions are filled by promoting experienced staff or related professional or technical personnel, such as sales representatives, purchasing agents, buyers, product or brand specialists, advertising specialists, promotion specialists, and public relations specialists. In small firms, where the number of positions is limited, advancement to a management position may come slowly. In large firms, promotion may occur more quickly.

Although experience, ability, and leadership are emphasized for promotion, advancement may be accelerated by participation in management training programs conducted by many large firms. Many firms also provide employees with continuing education opportunities, either in-house or at local colleges and universities, and encourage employee participation in seminars and conferences, frequently provided by professional societies. Numerous marketing and related associations sponsor national or local management training programs, often in collaboration with colleges and universities. Courses can include brand and product management, international marketing, sales management evaluation, telemarketing and direct sales, promotion, marketing communication, market research, organizational communication, and data processing systems procedures and management. Many firms pay all or part of the cost for employees who successfully complete courses.

Some associations (listed under sources of additional information) offer certification programs for marketing, advertising, and public relations managers. Certification is a sign of competence and achievement in this field that is particularly important in a competitive job market. While relatively few marketing, advertising, and public relations managers are currently certified, the number of managers who seek certification is expected to grow. For example, Sales and Marketing Executives International offers a management certification program

based on education and job performance. The Public Relations Society of America offers an accreditation program for public relations practitioners based on years of experience and an examination. The American Marketing Association is developing a certification program for marketing managers.

People interested in becoming marketing, advertising, and public relations managers should be mature, creative, highly motivated, resistant to stress, and flexible, yet decisive. The ability to communicate persuasively, both orally and in writing, with other managers, staff, and the public is vital. Marketing, advertising, and public relations managers also need tact, good judgment, and exceptional ability to establish and maintain effective personal relationships with supervisory and professional staff members and client firms.

Because of the importance and high visibility of their jobs, marketing, advertising, and public relations managers are often prime candidates for advancement. Well-trained, experienced, successful managers may be promoted to higher positions in their own or other firms. Some become top executives. Managers with extensive experience and sufficient capital may open their own businesses.

Job Outlook

Employment of marketing, advertising, and public relations managers is expected to increase faster than the average for all occupations through 2005. Increasingly intense domestic and global competition in products and services offered to consumers should require greater marketing, promotional, and public relations efforts. Management and public relations firms may experience particularly rapid growth as businesses increasingly hire contractors for these services rather than support additional full-time staff.

In addition to faster than average growth, many job openings will occur each year as a result of managers moving into top management positions, transferring to other jobs, or leaving the labor force. However, many of these highly coveted jobs will be sought by other managers or highly experienced professional and technical personnel, resulting in substantial job competition. College graduates with extensive experience, a high level of creativity, and strong communication skills should have the best job opportunities.

Projected employment growth varies by industry. For example, employment of marketing, advertising, and public relations managers is expected to grow much faster than average in most business services industries, such as computer and data processing, and management and public relations firms, while average growth is projected in manufacturing industries overall.

Earnings

According to a College Placement Council survey, starting salary offers to marketing majors graduating in 1993 averaged about $24,000; advertising majors averaged about $21,000. The median annual salary of marketing, advertising, and public relations managers was $41,000 in 1992. The lowest 10 percent earned $22,000 or less, while the top 10 percent earned $79,000 or more. Many earn bonuses equal to 10 percent or more of their salaries.

Surveys show that salary levels vary substantially depending on the level of managerial responsibility, length of service, education, and the employer's size, location, and industry. For example, manufacturing firms generally pay marketing, advertising, and public relations managers higher salaries than nonmanufacturing firms. For sales managers, the size of their sales territory is another important factor.

According to a 1992 survey by Abbot, Langer and Associates, of Crete, Illinois, annual incomes for sales and marketing managers varied greatly, from under $25,000 to more than $250,000, depending on the manager's level of education, experience, industry, and the number of employees he or she supervises. The median annual income for top advertising managers was $45,000; product/brand managers, $54,000; top market research managers, $55,000; regional sales managers, $64,000; and chief marketing executives, $67,000.

Related Occupations

Marketing, advertising, and public relations managers direct the sale of products and services offered by their firms and the communication of information about their firms' activities. Other personnel involved with marketing, advertising, and public relations include art directors, commercial and graphic artists, copy chiefs, copywriters, editors, lobbyists, marketing research analysts, public relations specialists, promotion specialists, sales representatives, and technical writers.

Sources of Additional Information

For information about careers in sales and marketing management, contact:

❏ American Marketing Association, 250 S. Wacker Dr., Chicago, IL 60606; or

❏ Sales and Marketing Executives International, 458 Statler Office Tower, Cleveland, OH 44115.

For information about careers in advertising management, contact:

❏ American Advertising Federation, Education Services Department, 1101 Vermont Ave. NW., Suite 500, Washington, DC 20005.

Information about careers in promotion management is available from:

❏ Council of Sales Promotion Agencies, 750 Summer St., Stamford, CT 06901; or

❏ Promotion Marketing Association of America, Inc., 322 Eighth Ave., Suite 1201, New York, NY 10001.

Information about careers in public relations management is available from:

❏ Public Relations Society of America, 33 Irving Place, New York, NY 10003-2376.

Restaurant and Food Service Managers

Nature of the Work

Food is consumed outside the home in a variety of settings. Eating places range from restaurants that serve fast food or emphasize elegant dining, to institutional dining in school and employee cafeterias, hospitals, and nursing facilities. The cuisine offered, its price, and the setting in which it is consumed vary greatly, but the managers of these diverse dining facilities have many responsibilities in common. Efficient and profitable operation of restaurants and institutional food service facilities requires that managers and assistant managers select and appropriately price interesting menu items, efficiently use food and other supplies, achieve consistent quality in food preparation and service, recruit and train adequate numbers of workers and supervise their work, and attend to the various administrative aspects of the business.

In most restaurants and institutional food service facilities, the manager is assisted by one or more assistant managers, depending on the size and business hours of the establishment. In large establishments, as well as in many others that offer fine dining, the management team consists of a general manager, one or more assistant managers, and an executive chef. The executive chef is responsible for the operation of the kitchen, while the assistant managers oversee service in the dining room and other areas of the operation. In some smaller restaurants, the executive chef may also be the general manager and sometimes the owner. In fast-food restaurants and other food service facilities that operate long hours, seven days a week, the manager is aided by several assistant managers, each of whom supervises a shift of workers. (For additional information, see the statements on general managers and top executives and chefs, cooks, and other kitchen workers.)

Many restaurants rarely change their menu, but other eating establishments change theirs frequently. Institutional food service facilities and some restaurants offer a new menu every day. Managers or executive chefs select menu items, taking into account the likely number of customers, the past popularity of various dishes, and considerations such as food left over from prior meals that should not be wasted, the need for variety on the menu, and the availability of foods due to seasonal and other factors. They analyze the recipes of the dishes to determine food, labor, and overhead costs and assign prices to the menu items. Menus must be developed far enough in advance that needed supplies are received in time.

Ordering supplies and dealing with suppliers are important aspects of the work of restaurant and food service managers. On a daily basis, managers estimate food consumption, place orders with suppliers, and schedule the delivery of fresh food and beverages. They receive and check the content of deliveries, evaluating the quality of meats, poultry, fish, fruits, vegetables, and baked goods. Managers meet or talk with sales representatives of restaurant suppliers to place orders to replenish stocks of tableware, linens, paper, cleaning supplies, cooking utensils, and furniture and fixtures. They also arrange for equipment maintenance and repairs, and for a variety of services such as waste removal and pest control.

Managers interview, hire, and, when necessary, discharge workers. They familiarize newly hired workers with the establishment's policies and practices and oversee their training. Managers schedule the work hours of employees, ensuring that there are enough workers present during busy periods, but not too many during slow periods.

Restaurant and food service managers supervise the kitchen and dining room. They oversee food preparation and cooking, checking the quality of the food and the sizes of portions to ensure that dishes are prepared and garnished correctly and in a timely manner. They also investigate and resolve customers' complaints about food quality or service. During busy periods, managers may roll up their sleeves and help with the cooking, clearing of tables, or other tasks. They direct the cleaning of the kitchen and dining areas and the washing of tableware, kitchen utensils, and equipment to maintain company and government sanitation standards. They continuously monitor workers and observe patrons to ensure compliance with health and safety standards and local liquor regulations.

Managers have a variety of administrative responsibilities. In larger establishments, much of this work is delegated to a bookkeeper, but in others, managers must keep accurate records of the hours and wages of employees, prepare the payroll, and do paperwork to comply with licensing laws and reporting requirements of tax, wage and hour, unemployment compensation, and Social Security laws. They must also maintain records of the costs of supplies and equipment purchased and ensure that accounts with suppliers are paid on a regular basis. In addition, managers record the number, type, and cost of items sold to weed out dishes that are unpopular or less profitable. Many managers are able to ease the burden of record-keeping and paperwork through the use of computers.

Managers are among the first to arrive and the last to leave at night. At the conclusion of each day, or sometimes each shift, managers must tally the cash and charge receipts received and balance them against the record of sales. They are responsible for depositing the day's income at the bank or securing it in a safe place. Managers are also responsible for locking up, checking that ovens, grills, and lights are off, and switching on alarm systems.

Working Conditions

Because evenings and weekends are popular dining periods, night and weekend work is common. However, many managers of institutional food service facilities work more conventional hours because factory and office cafeterias are often open only on weekdays for breakfast and lunch. Most restaurant and food service managers work 50 hours or more per week.

Managers often experience the pressure of simultaneously coordinating a wide range of activities. When problems occur, it is the responsibility of the manager to resolve them with minimal disruption to customers. The job can be hectic during peak dining hours, and dealing with irate customers or uncooperative employees can be particularly stressful.

Employment

Restaurant and food service managers held about 496,000 jobs in 1992. Most worked in restaurants or for contract institutional food service companies, but small numbers were also employed by educational institutions, hospitals, nursing and personal care facilities, and civic, social, and fraternal organizations. About two-fifths were self-employed. Jobs are located throughout the country, but are most plentiful in large cities and tourist areas.

Training, Other Qualifications, and Advancement

Many restaurant and food service manager positions are filled by promoting experienced food and beverage preparation and service workers. Waiters, waitresses, chefs, and fast-food workers who have demonstrated potential for handling increased responsibility sometimes advance to assistant manager or management trainee jobs when openings occur. Executive chefs need extensive experience working as a chef, and general managers need experience working as assistant manager. However, most food service management companies and national or regional restaurant chains also recruit management trainees from graduates of two-year and four-year college programs. Food service and restaurant chains prefer to hire people with degrees in restaurant and institutional food service management, but they often hire graduates with degrees in other fields who have demonstrated interest and aptitude.

A bachelor's degree in restaurant and food service management provides a particularly strong preparation for a career in this occupation. In 1992, more than 160 colleges and universities offered four year programs in restaurant and hotel management or institutional food service management. For people who do not want to pursue a four year degree, a good alternative is provided by the more than 800 community and junior colleges, technical institutes, and other institutions that offer programs in these fields leading to an associate degree or other formal award below the bachelor's degree. Both programs provide instruction in subjects such as accounting, business law and management, food planning and preparation, and nutrition. Some programs combine classroom and laboratory study with internships that provide on-the-job experience. In addition, many educational institutions offer culinary programs that provide food preparation training which can lead to a career as a cook or chef and provide a foundation for advancement to an executive chef position.

Most employers emphasize personal qualities. Restaurant and food service management can be demanding, so good health and stamina are important. Self-discipline, initiative, and leadership ability are essential. Managers must be able to solve problems and concentrate on details. They need good communication skills to deal with customers and suppliers as well as to motivate and direct their subordinates. A neat and clean appearance is also required because managers are often in close personal contact with the public.

Most restaurant chains and food service management companies have rigorous training programs for people hired for management jobs. Through a combination of classroom and on-the-job training, trainees receive instruction and gain work experience in all aspects of the operations of a restaurant or institutional food service facility, including food preparation, nutrition, sanitation, security, company policies and procedures, personnel management, recordkeeping, and preparation of reports. Usually after six months or a year, trainees receive their first permanent assignment as an assistant manager.

A measure of professional achievement for restaurant and food service managers is to earn the designation of certified Food service Management Professional (FMP). Although not a requirement for employment or advancement in the occupation, voluntary certification provides recognition of professional competence, particularly for managers who acquired their skills largely on the job. The Educational Foundation of the National Restaurant Association awards the FMP designation to managers who achieve a qualifying score on a written examination, complete a series of courses that cover a range of food service management topics, and meet standards of work experience in the field.

Willingness to relocate is often essential for advancement to positions with greater responsibility. Managers advance to larger establishments or regional management positions with restaurant chains. Some managers eventually open their own eating and drinking establishments. Others transfer to hotel management positions because management experience in their restaurant or institutional food service is a good background for food and beverage manager jobs at hotels and resorts.

Job Outlook

Employment of restaurant and food service managers is expected to increase much faster than the average for all occupations through 2005. In addition to growth in demand for these managers, the need to replace managers who transfer to other occupations or stop working will create many job openings. Job opportunities are expected to be best for people with bachelor's or associate degrees in restaurant and institutional food service management.

Employment growth is expected to vary by industry. Eating and drinking places will provide the most new jobs as the number of eating and drinking establishments increases and other industries continue to contract out their food services. Population growth, rising personal incomes, and increased leisure time will continue to produce growth in the number of meals consumed outside the home. To meet the demand for prepared food, more restaurants will be built, and more managers will be employed to supervise them. In addition, the number of manager jobs will increase in eating and drinking places as schools, hospitals, and other businesses contract out more of their food services to institutional food service companies located in the eating and drinking industry.

Employment of wage and salary managers in eating and drinking places is expected to increase more rapidly than self-employed managers. New restaurants are increasingly affiliated with national chains rather than being independently owned and operated. As this trend continues, fewer owners will manage restaurants themselves, and more restaurant managers will be employed to run the establishments.

Employment in eating and drinking establishments is not very sensitive to changes in economic conditions, so restaurant and food service managers are rarely laid off during hard times. However, competition among restaurants is always intense, and many restaurants do not survive.

Food service manager jobs are expected to increase in other industries, but growth will be slowed as contracting out becomes more common. Growth in the population of elderly people is expected to result in growth of food service manager jobs in nursing homes, residential care facilities, and other health care institutions. Likewise, growth in the population of young people enrolled in educational institutions should result in growth of food service manager jobs in school and college cafeterias.

Earnings

Median earnings for restaurant and food service managers were $418 a week in 1992. The middle 50 percent earned between about $300-$600 a week. The lowest paid 10 percent earned $225 a week or less, while the highest paid 10 percent earned more than $815 a week.

Earnings of restaurant and food service managers vary greatly according to their responsibilities and the type and size of establishment. Based on a survey conducted for the National Restaurant Association, the median base salary of managers in restaurants was estimated to be about $27,900 a year in early 1993, but managers of the largest restaurants and institutional food service facilities often had annual salaries in excess of $45,000. Managers of fast-food restaurants had an estimated median base salary of $24,900 a year; managers of full-menu restaurants with table service, almost $30,400; and managers of commercial and institutional cafeterias, nearly $29,300 a year in early 1993. Besides a salary, most managers received an annual bonus or incentive payment based on their performance. In 1993, most of these payments ranged between $2,000 and $8,000 a year.

Executive chefs had an estimated median base salary of about $33,600 a year in early 1993, but those employed in the largest restaurants and institutional food service facilities often had base salaries exceeding $49,000. Annual bonus or incentive payments for most executive chefs ranged between $2,000 and $4,000.

The estimated median base salary of assistant managers exceeded $23,400 a year in early 1993, but ranged from less than $19,800 in fast-food restaurants to more than $31,700 in some of the largest restaurants and food service facilities. Annual bonus or incentive payments of most assistant managers ranged between $1,000 and $4,000 a year.

Manager trainees had an estimated median base salary of about $20,200 a year in early 1993, but earned salaries of nearly $27,900 in some of the largest restaurants and food service facilities. Annual bonus or incentive payments of most trainees ranged between $1,000 and $3,000. Most salaried restaurant and food service managers received free meals, sick leave, health and life insurance, and one to three weeks of paid vacation a year, depending on length of service.

Related Occupations

Restaurant and food service managers direct the activities of business establishments that provide a service to customers. Other managers in service-oriented businesses include hotel managers and assistants, health services administrators, retail store managers, and bank managers.

Sources of Additional Information

Information about job opportunities may be obtained from local employers and local offices of the state employment service.

Career information about restaurant and food service managers, directories of two-year and four-year college programs in restaurant and food service management, and certification as a Food service Management Professional are available from:

❏ The Educational Foundation of the National Restaurant Association, Suite 1400, 250 South Wacker Dr., Chicago, IL 60606.

General information on hospitality careers may be obtained from:

❏ Council on Hotel, Restaurant, and Institutional Education, 1200 17th St. NW., Washington, DC 20036-3097.

Professional Specialty Occupations

Actors, Directors, and Producers

Nature of the Work

Actors, directors, and producers create a visual and aural image based on written words of a script in theaters, film, television, and radio. They make the words come alive for audiences.

Actors entertain and communicate with people through interpretation of dramatic roles. Actors read scripts and decide how they want to interpret their role. Then they discuss their ideas with directors and voice coaches on how to portray their characters. They rely on facial and verbal expression as well as body motion for creative effect. In some roles, they sing and dance. They also may use props and costumes to help communicate their ideas. Actors memorize lines and stage directions. Most actors also put on their own makeup.

Only a few actors achieve recognition as stars on the stage, in motion pictures, or on television. A somewhat larger number are well-known, experienced performers, who are frequently cast in supporting roles. Most actors struggle for a toehold in the profession and pick up parts wherever they can. Some actors employed by theater companies teach acting through courses offered to the public.

In addition to the actors with speaking parts, extras, who have small parts with no lines to deliver, are used in almost all motion pictures, many television shows, and some theater productions.

Directors interpret plays or scripts. In addition, they audition and select cast members, conduct rehearsals, and direct the work of the cast and crew. Directors use their knowledge of acting, voice, and movement to achieve the best possible performance and usually approve the scenery, costumes, choreography, and music.

Producers are entrepreneurs. They select plays or scripts, arrange financing, and decide on the size of the production and its budget. They hire directors, principal members of the cast, and key production staff members, and negotiate contracts with artistic personnel, often in accordance with collective bargaining agreements. Producers also coordinate the activities of writers, directors, managers, and other personnel.

Working Conditions

Acting demands patience and total commitment because actors must wait for parts or filming schedules, work long hours, and travel often. Evening work is a regular part of a stage actor's life. Flawless performances require tedious memorizing of lines and repetitive rehearsals. On television, actors must deliver a good performance with very little preparation. Actors need stamina to withstand the heat of stage or studio lights, heavy costumes, long, irregular hours, and adverse weather conditions that may exist on location. When plays are on the road, traveling is necessary. Actors often face the anxiety of intermittent employment and rejections when auditioning for work.

Directors and producers often work under stress as they try to meet schedules, stay within budgets, resolve personnel problems, and put together a production that will appeal enough to the public to succeed.

Employment

In 1992, actors, directors, and producers held an average of about 129,000 jobs in motion pictures, stage plays, television, and radio. Many others were between jobs, so that the total number of people actually employed as actors, directors, and producers over the course of the year was higher. In the winter, most employment opportunities on the stage are in New York and other large cities, many of which have established professional regional theaters. In the summer, stock companies in suburban and resort areas also provide employment. In addition, many cities have small nonprofit professional companies such as theaters, repertory companies, and dinner theaters, which provide opportunities for local amateur talent as well as for professional entertainers. Normally, casts are selected in New York City for shows that go on the road.

Employment in motion pictures and films for television is centered in Hollywood and New York City. However, studios are also located in Florida, Seattle, and other parts of the country. In addition, many films are shot on location and employ local professionals and nonprofessionals as day players and extras. In television, opportunities are at the network entertainment centers in New York and Los Angeles and local television stations around the country.

Training, Other Qualifications, and Advancement

Aspiring actors and directors should take part in high school and college plays or work with small theaters and other acting groups for experience. Formal dramatic training or acting experience is generally necessary, although some people enter the field without it. Many experienced actors get formal training to learn new skills and improve old ones. Training can be obtained at dramatic arts schools in New York and Los Angeles, and at colleges and universities throughout the country offering bachelor's degrees or higher in dramatic and theater arts. College drama curriculums usually include courses in liberal arts, stage speech and movement, directing, play writing, play production, design, and history of the drama, as well as practical courses in acting.

The best way to start is to use local opportunities and build on them. Local and regional theater experience may help in obtaining work in New York or Los Angeles. Modeling experience may also be helpful. Actors need talent, creative ability, and training that will enable them to portray different characters. Training in singing and dancing is especially useful. Actors must have poise, stage presence, and the ability to affect an audience, plus the ability to follow directions. Physical appearance is often a deciding factor in being selected for particular roles. Many professional actors rely on agents or managers to find them performing engagements, negotiate contracts, and plan their careers.

To become a movie extra, one must usually be listed by a casting agency, such as Central Casting, a no-fee agency that supplies all extras to the major movie studios in Hollywood. Applicants are accepted only when the number of people of a particular type on the list, for example, athletic young women, old men, or small children, is below the foreseeable need. In recent years, only a very small proportion of the applicants have succeeded in being listed.

There are no specific training requirements for directors and producers. Talent, experience, and business acumen are very important. Directors and producers come from different backgrounds. Actors, writers, film editors, and business managers often enter these fields. Formal training in directing and producing is available at some colleges and universities.

As the reputations of actors, directors, and producers grow, they work on larger productions or in more prestigious theaters. Actors also advance to lead roles. Some actors move into acting-related jobs as drama coaches or directors of stage, television, radio, or motion picture productions. A few teach drama in colleges and universities.

The length of a performer's working life depends largely on training, skill, versatility, and perseverance. Some actors, directors, and producers never retire, but many leave the occupation after a short time because they cannot find enough work to make a living.

Job Outlook

Employment of actors, directors, and producers is expected to grow much faster than the average for all occupations through 2005. In addition, workers leaving the field will create as many job openings as will growth. Nevertheless, the large number of people desiring acting careers and the lack of formal entry requirements should cause keen competition for actor, director, and producer jobs. Only the most talented should continue to find regular employment.

Rising foreign demand for American productions combined with a growing domestic market, which is fueled by the growth of cable television, home movie rentals, and television syndications, should stimulate demand for actors and other production personnel. Growth of opportunities in recorded media should be accompanied by increasing jobs in live productions. Growing numbers of people who enjoy live theatrical entertainment should continue to go to theaters for the excitement and aesthetic appreciation.

Earnings

Minimum salaries, working hours, and other conditions of employment are covered in collective bargaining agreements between producers of shows and unions representing workers in this field. The Actors' Equity Association represents stage actors; the Screen Actors Guild and the Screen Extras Guild cover actors in motion pictures, including television, commercials, and films; and the American Federation of Television and Radio Artists (AFTRA) represents television and radio performers. Most stage directors belong to the Society of Stage Directors and Choreographers, and film and television directors belong to the Directors Guild of America. Of course, each actor or director may negotiate for a salary higher than the minimum.

The minimum weekly salary for actors in Broadway stage productions was $950 in 1993. Those in small off-Broadway theaters received minimums ranging from $340 to $579 a week, depending on the seating capacity of the theater. For shows on the road, actors receive an additional $80 per day. Eight performances amount to a week's work on the stage, and additional performances are paid for as overtime. Actors usually work long hours during rehearsals. Once the show opens, they have more regular hours, working about 24 hours a week.

In 1993, motion picture and television actors with speaking parts earned a minimum daily rate of $485 or $1,685 for a five day week. Those without speaking parts—extras—earned a minimum daily rate of $99. In addition, actors receive contributions to their health and pension plans and additional compensation for reruns.

Earnings from acting are low because employment is so irregular. According to data from Actors' Equity Association, about 60 percent of their members had no earnings from acting in 1991, and only 918 members earned more than $35,000. The median earnings for stage acting in a course of a year was approximately $5,200. The Screen Actors Guild reported that the average income its members earned from acting was $1,400 a year, and 80 percent of its members earned less than $5,000 a year from acting. Therefore, many actors must supplement their incomes from acting by holding other jobs.

Some well-known actors have salary rates well above the minimums, and the salaries of the few top stars are many times the figures cited, creating a false impression that all actors are highly paid.

Many actors who earn more than a set minimum per year are covered by a union health, welfare, and pension fund, including hospitalization insurance, to which employers contribute. Under some employment conditions, Actors' Equity and AFTRA members have paid vacations and sick leave.

Earnings of stage directors vary greatly. The top money is on Broadway: $36,750 for a rehearsal period, which usually lasts five weeks. Regional theaters paid directors from $3,415 to $13,595 for a three to five week rehearsal period. Small dinner theaters and summer stock pay much less, $685 to $1,311 per week, but offer the most employment opportunities.

Producers seldom get a set fee, instead, they get a percentage of a show's earnings or ticket sales.

Related Occupations

People who work in occupations requiring acting skills include dancers, choreographers, disc jockeys, drama teachers or coaches, and radio and television announcers. Others working in occupations related to acting are playwrights, scriptwriters, stage managers, costume designers, makeup artists, hair stylists, lighting designers, and set designers. Workers in occupations involved with the business aspects of theater productions include managing directors, company managers, booking managers, publicists, and agents for actors, directors, and playwrights.

Sources of Additional Information

Information about opportunities in regional theaters may be obtained from:

❏ Theater Communications Group, Inc., 355 Lexington Ave., New York, NY 10017.

A directory of theatrical programs may be purchased from:

❏ National Association of Schools of Theater, 11250 Roger Bacon Dr., Suite 21, Reston, VA 22090.

Computer Scientists and Systems Analysts

Nature of the Work

The rapid spread of computers and computer-based technologies throughout the past two decades has generated a need for skilled, highly trained workers to design and develop hardware and software systems and to determine how to incorporate these advances into new or existing systems. Although many narrow specializations have developed and no uniform job titles exist, this professional specialty group is widely referred to as computer scientists and systems analysts.

Computer scientists, including computer engineers, conduct research, design computers, and discover and use principles of applying computers. Computer scientists and engineers may perform many of the same duties as other computer professionals throughout a normal workday, but their jobs are distinguished by the higher level of theoretical expertise they apply to complex problems and innovative ideas for the application or creation of new technology. Computer scientists employed by academic institutions work in areas from theory to hardware to language design, or on multidiscipline projects, for example, developing and advancing uses for artificial intelligence (AI). Their counterparts in private industry work in areas such as applying theory, developing specialized languages, or designing programming tools, knowledge-based systems, or computer games. Computer engineers often work as part of a team that designs new computing devices or computer-related equipment.

Far more numerous than scientists and engineers, systems analysts define business, scientific, or engineering problems and design their solutions using computers. This process may include planning and developing new computer systems or devising ways to apply existing systems to operations still completed manually or by some less efficient method. Systems analysts may design entirely new systems, including hardware and software, or add a single new software application to harness more of the computer's power.

Analysts begin an assignment by discussing the data processing problem with managers and users to determine its exact nature. Much time is devoted to clearly defining the goals of the system so that it can be broken down into separate programmable procedures. Analysts then use techniques such as structured analysis, data modeling, information engineering, mathematical model building, sampling, and cost accounting to plan the system. Once the design has been developed, systems analysts prepare charts and diagrams which describe it in terms that managers and other users can understand. They may prepare a cost-benefit and return-on-investment analysis to help management decide whether the proposed system will be satisfactory and financially feasible.

Analysts must specify the files and records to be accessed by the system, design the processing steps, and design the format for the output that will meet the users' needs. They must be sure that the system they design is user-friendly, so that it can be easily learned by the user and any problems encountered can be overcome quickly. Analysts also ensure security of the data by making it inaccessible to those who are not authorized to use it.

When the system is accepted, systems analysts may determine what computer hardware and software will be needed to set up the system or implement changes to it. They coordinate tests and observe initial use of the system to ensure it performs as planned. They prepare specifications, work diagrams, and structure charts for computer programmers to follow and then work with them to debug or eliminate errors from the system. Some organizations do not employ programmers; instead, a single worker called a programmer-analyst is responsible for both systems analysis and programming. This is becoming more common with the development of Computer Assisted Software Engineering (CASE) tools which automate much of the coding process, making programming functions easier to learn.

One of the biggest obstacles to wider computer use is the inability of different computers to communicate with each other. Many systems analysts are involved with connecting all the computers in an individual office, department, or establishment. This networking has many variations; it may be called local area network, wide area network, or multiuser system, for example. A primary goal of networking is to allow users of microcomputers (also known as personal computers or PC's) to retrieve data from a mainframe computer and use it on their machine. This connection also allows data to be entered into the mainframe from the PC.

Because up-to-date information such as accounting records, sales figures, or budget projections is so important in modern organizations, systems analysts may be instructed to make the computer systems in each department compatible with each other so facts and figures can be shared. Similarly, electronic mail requires open pathways to send messages, documents, and data from one computer mailbox to another across different equipment and program lines. Analysts must design the gates in the hardware and software to allow free exchange of data, custom applications, and the computer power to process it all. They study the seemingly incompatible pieces and create ways to link them so that users can access information from any part of the system.

Because the possible uses of computers are so varied and complex, analysts usually specialize in either business, scientific, engineering, or microcomputer applications. Previous experience or training in a particular area usually dictates the field in which they are most qualified to develop computer systems.

Working Conditions

Computer scientists and systems analysts work in offices or laboratories in comfortable surroundings. They usually work about 40 hours a week. Occasionally, however, evening or weekend work may be necessary to meet deadlines. Because computer scientists and systems analysts spend long periods of time in front of a computer terminal typing on a keyboard, they are susceptible to eye strain, back discomfort, and hand and wrist problems.

Employment

Computer scientists and systems analysts held about 666,000 jobs in 1992. Although they are found in most industries, the greatest concentration is in computer and data processing service firms. Many others work for government agencies, manufacturers of computer and related electronic equipment, insurance companies, and universities.

A small but growing number of these workers are employed on a temporary basis. For example, a company installing a new computer system may need the services of several systems analysts just to get the system running. Because not all of them would be needed once the system is functioning, the company might contract directly with the systems analysts themselves or with a temporary help agency or consulting firm. The company would contract for their services on a temporary basis; temporary jobs usually last for several months at least and some last for two years or more.

Training, Other Qualifications, and Advancement

There is no universally accepted way to prepare for a job as a computer professional because employers' preferences depend on the work being done. Prior work experience is very important. Many people develop an area of expertise in their jobs which tends to make them more marketable to employers. For example, people move into systems analyst jobs after working as computer programmers. Another example is the auditor in an accounting department who becomes a systems analyst specializing in accounting systems development.

College graduates are almost always sought for computer professional positions, and, for some of the more complex jobs, people with graduate degrees are preferred. Generally, a computer scientist working in a research lab or academic institution will hold a Ph.D. or master's degree in computer science or engineering. Some computer scientists are able to gain sufficient experience for this type of position with only a bachelor's degree, but this is more difficult. Computer engineers generally have a bachelor's degree in computer engineering, electrical engineering, or math.

Employers usually want systems analysts to have a background in business management or a closely related field for work in a business environment, while a background in the physical sciences, applied mathematics, or engineering is preferred for work in scientifically oriented organizations. Many employers seek applicants who have a bachelor's degree in computer science, information science, computer information systems, or data processing. Regardless of college major, employers look

for people who are familiar with programming languages and have a broad knowledge of computer systems and technologies. Courses in computer programming or systems design offer good preparation for a job in this field.

Systems analysts must be able to think logically, have good communication skills, and like working with ideas and people. They often deal with a number of tasks simultaneously. The ability to concentrate and pay close attention to detail is also important. Although systems analysts often work independently, they also work in teams on large projects. They must be able to communicate effectively with technical personnel, such as programmers and managers, as well as with other staff who have no technical computer background.

Technological advances occur so rapidly in the computer field that continuous study is necessary to keep skills current. Continuing education is usually offered by employers, hardware and software vendors, colleges and universities, or private training institutions. Additional training may come from professional development seminars offered by professional computing societies.

The Institute for Certification of Computer Professionals offers the designation of Certified Systems Professional (CSP) to those who have four years of experience and pass a core examination plus exams in two specialty areas. The Quality Assurance Institute awards the designation of Certified Quality Analyst (CQA) to those who meet education and experience requirements, pass an exam, and endorse a code of ethics. Neither designation is mandatory, but either may provide a job seeker a competitive advantage.

Systems analysts may be promoted to senior or lead systems analysts after several years of experience. Those who show leadership ability can also advance to management positions such as manager of information systems or chief information officer. Systems analysts with several years of experience may start their own computer consulting firms.

Computer engineers and scientists employed in industry can eventually move into managerial or project leader positions. Those employed in academic institutions can advance to become heads of research departments or published authorities in their field. Some start their own consulting firms.

Job Outlook

Computer scientists and systems analysts will be among the fastest growing occupations through 2005. In addition, tens of thousands of job openings will result annually from the need to replace workers who move into managerial positions or other occupations or leave the labor force.

The demand for computer scientists and engineers is expected to rise as organizations attempt to maximize the efficiency of their computer systems. As international and domestic competition increases, organizations will face growing pressure to use technological advances in areas such as office and factory automation, telecommunications technology, and scientific research. Computer scientists and engineers will be needed to develop this new technology. In addition, the complexity associated with designing new applications is growing. More computer scientists will be needed to develop innovative and increasingly sophisticated systems.

As users develop more sophisticated knowledge of computers, they become more aware of the machine's potential and are better able to suggest operations that will increase their own productivity and that of the organization. The need to design computer networks that facilitate the sharing of information will be a major factor in the rising demand for systems analysts. A greater emphasis on problem definition, analysis, and implementation will also guaranteed higher demand for systems analysts. In addition, falling prices of computer hardware and software are inducing more small businesses to computerize their operations, further stimulating demand for these workers.

Individuals with an advanced degree in computer science should enjoy very favorable employment prospects because the number of these degrees has not kept pace with the needs of employers. College graduates with a bachelor's degree in computer science, computer engineering, information science, or information systems should also experience good prospects for employment. College graduates with noncomputer science majors who have had courses in computer programming, systems analysis, and other data processing areas as well as training or experience in an applied field should be able to find jobs as systems analysts. Those who are familiar with CASE and other programming tools will have an even greater advantage. Employers will be more willing to hire someone who can combine programming skills with traditional systems analysis skills.

Earnings

Median annual earnings of systems analysts who worked full-time in 1992 were about $42,100. The middle 50 percent earned between $32,000 and $52,200. The lowest 10 percent earned less than $25,200 and the highest tenth, more than $65,500. Computer scientists with advanced degrees generally earn more than systems analysts. In the federal government, the entrance salary for recent college graduates with a bachelor's degree was about $18,300 a year in 1993; for those with a superior academic record, $22,700.

Related Occupations

Other workers who use research, logic, and creativity to solve business problems are computer programmers, financial analysts, urban planners, engineers, operations research analysts, management analysts, and actuaries.

Sources of Additional Information

Further information about computer careers is available from:

❏ Association for Computing Machinery, 1515 Broadway, New York, NY 10036.

Information about certification as a computer professional is available from:

❏ Institute for the Certification of Computer Professionals, 2200 East Devon Ave., Suite 268, Des Plaines, IL 60018.

Information about certification as a Certified Quality Analyst is available from:

❏ Quality Assurance Institute, 7575 Dr. Phillips Blvd., Suite 350, Orlando, FL 32819.

Human Services Workers

Nature of the Work

Human services worker is a generic term for people with various job titles, such as social service technician, case management aide, social work assistant, residential counselor, alcohol or drug abuse counselor, mental health technician, child abuse worker, community outreach worker, and gerontology aide. They generally work under the direction of social workers or, in some cases, psychologists. The amount of responsibility and supervision they are given varies a great deal. Some are on their own most of the time and have little direct supervision; others work under close direction.

Human services workers help clients obtain benefits or services. They assess the needs and establish the eligibility of clients for services. They examine financial documents such as rent receipts and tax returns to determine whether the client is eligible for food stamps, Medicaid, or other welfare programs, for example. They also inform clients how to obtain services; arrange for transportation and escorts, if necessary; and provide emotional support. Human services workers monitor and keep case records on clients and report progress to supervisors.

Human services workers may transport or accompany clients to group meal sites, adult daycare programs, or doctors' offices; telephone or visit clients' homes to make sure services are being received; or help resolve disagreements, such as those between tenants and landlords.

Human services workers play a variety of roles in community settings. They may organize and lead group activities, assist clients in need of counseling or crisis intervention, or administer a food bank or emergency fuel program. In halfway houses and group homes, they oversee adult residents who need some supervision or support on a daily basis, but who do not need to live in an institution. They review clients' records, talk with their families, and confer with medical personnel to gain better insight into their background and needs. Human services workers may teach residents to prepare their own meals and to do other housekeeping activities. They also provide emotional support and lead recreation activities.

In mental hospitals and psychiatric clinics, they may help clients master everyday living skills and teach them how to communicate more effectively and get along better with others. They also assist with music, art, and dance therapy and with individual and group counseling and lead recreational activities.

Working Conditions

Working conditions of human services workers vary. Many spend part of their time in an office or group residential facility and the rest in the field—visiting clients or taking them on trips or meeting with people who provide services to the clients. Most work a regular 40-hour week, although some work may be in the evening and on weekends. Human services workers in residential settings generally work in shifts because residents need supervision around the clock.

The work, while satisfying, can be emotionally draining. Understaffing and lack of equipment may add to the pressure. Turnover is reported to be high, especially among workers without academic preparation for this field.

Employment

Human services workers held about 189,000 jobs in 1992. About one-fourth were employed by state and local governments, primarily in public welfare agencies and facilities for the mentally retarded and developmentally disabled. Another fourth worked in private social services agencies offering a variety of services, including adult daycare, group meals, crisis intervention, and counseling. Still another fourth supervised residents of group homes and halfway houses. Human services workers also held jobs in clinics, community mental health centers, and psychiatric hospitals.

Training, Other Qualifications, and Advancement

While some employers hire high school graduates, most prefer applicants with some college preparation in human services, social work, or one of the social or behavioral sciences. Some prefer to hire people with a four year college degree. The level of formal education of human service workers often influences the kind of work they are assigned and the amount of responsibility entrusted to them. Workers with no more than a high school education are likely to perform clerical duties, while those with a college degree might be assigned to do direct counseling, coordinate program activities, or manage a group home. Employers may also look for experience in other occupations or leadership experience in school or in a youth group. Some enter the field on the basis of courses in social work, psychology, sociology, rehabilitation, or special education. Most employers provide in-service training such as seminars and workshops.

Because so many human services jobs involve direct contact with people who are vulnerable to exploitation or mistreatment, employers try to select applicants with appropriate personal qualifications. Relevant academic preparation is generally required, and volunteer or work experience is preferred. A strong desire to help others, patience, and understanding are highly valued characteristics. Other important personal traits include communication skills, a strong sense of responsibility, and the ability to manage time effectively. Hiring requirements in group homes tend to be more stringent than in other settings.

In 1992, 375 certificate and associate degree programs in human services or mental health were offered at community and junior colleges, vocational-technical institutes, and other post secondary institutions. In addition, 390 programs offered a bachelor's degree in human services. A small number of programs leading to master's degrees in human services administration were offered as well.

Generally, academic programs in this field educate students for specialized roles—work with developmentally disabled adults, for example. Students are exposed early and often to the kinds of situations they may encounter on the job. Programs typically include courses in psychology, sociology, crisis intervention, social work, family dynamics, therapeutic interviewing, rehabilitation, and gerontology. Through classroom-simulation internships, students learn interview, observation, and recordkeeping skills; individual and group counseling techniques; and program planning.

Formal education is almost always necessary for advancement. In group homes, completion of a one-year certificate in human services along with several years of experience may suffice for promotion to supervisor. In general, however, advancement requires a bachelor's or master's degree in counseling, rehabilitation, social work, or a related field.

Job Outlook

Opportunities for human services workers are expected to be excellent for qualified applicants. The number of human services workers is projected to more than double between 1992 and 2005, making it one of the most rapidly growing occupations. Also, the need to replace workers who retire or stop working for other reasons will create additional job opportunities. However, these jobs are not attractive to everyone because the work is responsible and emotionally draining and most offer relatively poor pay, so qualified applicants should have little difficulty finding employment.

Opportunities are expected to be best in job training programs, residential settings, and private social service agencies, which include such services as adult daycare and meal delivery programs. Demand for these services will expand with the growing number of older people, who are more likely to need services. In addition, human services workers will continue to be needed to provide services to the mentally impaired and developmentally disabled, those with substance abuse problems, and a wide variety of others. Faced with rapid growth in the demand for services, but slower growth in resources to provide the services, employers are expected to rely increasingly on human services workers rather than on other occupational workers who command higher pay.

Job training programs are expected to require additional human services workers as the economy grows and businesses change their mode of production and workers need to be retrained. Human services workers help determine workers' eligibility for public assistance programs and help them obtain services while unemployed.

Residential settings should also expand as pressures to respond to the needs of the chronically mentally ill persist. For many years, chronic mental patients have been reinstitutionalized and left to their own devices. Now, more community-based programs and group residences are expected to be established to house and assist the homeless and chronically mentally ill, and demand for human services workers will increase accordingly.

Although overall employment in state and local governments will grow only as fast as the average for all industries, jobs for human services workers will grow more rapidly. State and local governments employ most of their human services workers in correctional and public assistance departments. Correctional departments are growing faster than other areas of government, so human services workers should find their job opportunities increase along with other corrections jobs. Public assistance programs have been relatively stable within governments' budgets, but they have been employing more human services workers in an attempt to employ fewer social workers, who are more educated and higher paid.

Earnings

According to limited data available, starting salaries for human services workers ranged from about $12,000 to $20,000 a year in 1992. Experienced workers generally earned between

$15,000 and $25,000 annually, depending on their education, experience, and employer.

Related Occupations

Workers in other occupations that require skills similar to those of human services workers include social workers, community outreach workers, religious workers, occupational therapy assistants, physical therapy assistants and aides, psychiatric aides, and activity leaders.

Sources of Additional Information

Information on academic programs in human services may be found in most directories of two and four year colleges, available at libraries or career counseling centers.

For information on programs and careers in human services, contact:

❏ National Organization for Human Service Education, Brookdale Community College, Lyncroft, NJ 07738; or

❏ Council for Standards in Human Service Education, Montgomery Community College, 340 Dekalb Pike, Blue Bell, PA 19422.

Information on job openings may be available from state employment service offices or directly from city, county, or state departments of health, mental health and mental retardation, and human resources.

Occupational Therapists

Nature of the Work

Occupational therapists help individuals with mentally, physically, developmentally, or emotionally disabling conditions to develop, recover, or maintain daily living and work skills. They help patients improve basic motor functions and reasoning abilities and also to compensate for permanent loss of function. Their goal is to help patients have independent, productive, and satisfying lifestyles.

Occupational therapists use activities of all kinds ranging from using a computer to caring for daily needs, such as dressing, cooking, and eating. Practical activities increase strength and dexterity, while paper and pencil games may be used to improve visual acuity and the ability to discern patterns. A patient suffering short-term memory loss, for instance, might be encouraged to make lists to aid recall. One with coordination problems might be given extra tasks to improve eye-hand coordination. Computer programs have been designed to help patients improve decision making, abstract reasoning, problem solving, perceptual skills, memory, sequencing, and coordination, all of which are important for independent living.

For those with permanent functional disabilities, such as spinal cord injuries, cerebral palsy, or muscular dystrophy, therapists provide such adaptive equipment as wheelchairs, splints, and aids for eating and dressing. They also design or make special equipment needed at home or work. Therapists develop and teach patients to operate computer-aided adaptive equipment, such as microprocessing devices that permit individuals with severe limitations to communicate, walk, operate telephones and

television sets, and control other aspects of their environment.

Some occupational therapists, called industrial therapists, help patients find and hold a job. They arrange employment, plan work activities, and evaluate the patient's progress. Occupational therapists may work exclusively with individuals in a particular age group or with particular disabilities. In schools, for example, they evaluate children's abilities, recommend therapy, modify classroom equipment, and in general, help children participate as fully as possible in school programs and activities.

Occupational therapists in mental health settings treat mentally ill, mentally retarded, or emotionally disturbed individuals. To treat these problems, therapists choose activities that help people learn to cope with daily life. Activities include time management skills, budgeting, shopping, homemaking, and use of public transportation. They may also work with patients suffering from alcoholism, drug abuse, depression, eating disorders, and stress-related disorders.

Recording patients' activities and progress is an important part of an occupational therapist's job. Accurate records are essential for evaluating patients, billing, and reporting to physicians.

Working Conditions

Occupational therapists in hospitals and other health care settings generally work a regular 40-hour week. Those in schools may also participate in meetings and other activities, during and after the school day. In large rehabilitation centers, therapists may work in spacious rooms equipped with machines, tools, and other devices that may generate noise. The job can be tiring because therapists are on their feet much of the time. Those providing home health care may spend several hours a day driving from appointment to appointment. Therapists also face hazards such as backstrain from lifting and moving patients and equipment.

Employment

Occupational therapists held about 40,000 jobs in 1992. The largest number of jobs were in hospitals, including many in rehabilitation and psychiatric hospitals. School systems are the second largest employer of occupational therapists. Other major employers include offices of occupational therapists and other health practitioners, nursing homes, community mental health centers, adult daycare programs, job training services, and residential care facilities.

A small but rapidly growing number of occupational therapists are in private practice. Some are solo practitioners, while others are in group practices. They see patients referred by physicians or other health professionals, or provide contract or consulting services to nursing homes, adult daycare programs, and home health agencies.

Training, Other Qualifications, and Advancement

A bachelor's degree in occupational therapy is the minimal requirement for entry into this field. In addition, 36 states and the District of Columbia require a license to practice occupational therapy. To obtain a license, applicants must have a degree or a post-bachelor's certificate from an accredited educational program and pass a national certification examination given by the American Occupational Therapy Certification

Board. Those who pass the test are awarded the title of registered occupational therapist.

In 1992, entry-level education was offered in 67 bachelor's degree programs; 10 post-bachelor's certificate programs, for students with a degree other than occupational therapy; and 15 entry level-master's degree programs. Most schools have full-time programs, although a growing number also offer weekend or part-time programs.

Occupational therapy coursework includes physical, biological, and behavioral sciences and the application of occupational therapy theory and skills. Completion of six months of supervised clinical internship is also required.

People considering this profession should take high school courses in biology, chemistry, physics, health, art, and the social sciences. College admissions offices also look with favor on paid or volunteer experience in the health care field. Warmth and patience are needed to inspire both trust and respect. Ingenuity and imagination in adapting activities to individual needs are assets. Individuals working in home health care must be able to successfully adapt to a variety of settings.

Job Outlook

Employment of occupational therapists is expected to increase much faster than the average for all occupations through 2005 due to anticipated growth in demand for rehabilitation and long-term care services.

Several factors are increasing the need for rehabilitative services. Medical advances are now making it possible for more patients with critical problems to survive. These patients, however, may need extensive therapy. Also, there is the anticipated demand generated by the baby-boom generation's move into middle age, a period during which the incidence of heart attack and stroke increases. Additional services will also be demanded by the population 75 years of age and above, a rapidly growing age group that suffers from a very high incidence of disabling conditions. Finally, additional therapists will be needed to help prepare handicapped children to enter special education programs, as required by recent federal legislation.

Due to industry growth and more intensive care, hospitals will continue to employ the largest number of occupational therapists. Hospitals will also need occupational therapists to staff their growing home health care and outpatient rehabilitation programs. Moderate growth in schools will result from expansion of the school-age population and extended services for handicapped students.

The field of private practice will continue to provide opportunities for occupational therapists. Movement into private practice has been abetted by a legislative change which permits occupational therapists to bill Medicare directly for services provided. Previously, billings were submitted through a hospital, home health agency, or other Medicare-approved facility.

Employment of occupational therapists in the home health field is expected to grow very fast. The rapidly growing number of people age 75 and older who are more likely to need home health care, and the greater use of at-home follow-up care will encourage this growth.

Earnings

According to a national survey of hospitals and medical centers conducted by the University of Texas Medical Branch, the median annual salary for occupational therapists, based on a 40 hour week and excluding shift or area differentials, was $35,625 in October 1992. The average minimum was $30,470 and the average maximum was $44,958. Some states classify occupational therapists employed in public schools as teachers and pay accordingly. According to the National Education Association, elementary school teachers earned an average of about $34,777 during the 1992-93 school year, and secondary school teachers earned an average of about $36,509. Therapists in private practice generally earned more than salaried workers.

Related Occupations

Occupational therapists use specialized knowledge to help individuals perform daily living skills and achieve maximum independence. Other workers performing similar duties include orthotists, prosthetists, physical therapists, chiropractors, speech pathologists and audiologists, rehabilitation counselors, recreational therapists, art therapists, music therapists, dance therapists, horticultural therapists, and manual arts therapists.

Sources of Additional Information

For more information on occupational therapy as a career, a list of education programs, and requirements for certification, write to:

❏ American Occupational Therapy Association, P.O. Box 1725, 1383 Piccard Dr., Rockville, MD 20849-1725.

Operations Research Analysts

Nature of the Work

Efficiently running a complex organization or operation such as a large manufacturing plant, an airline, or a military deployment requires the precise coordination of materials, machines, and people. Operations research analysts help organizations coordinate and operate in the most efficient manner by applying scientific methods and mathematical principles to organizational problems. Managers can then evaluate alternatives and choose the course of action that best meets the organizational goals.

Operations research analysts, also called management science analysts, are problem solvers. The problems they tackle are usually those encountered in large business organizations: strategy, forecasting, resource allocation, facilities layout, inventory control, personnel schedules, and distribution systems. The methods they use generally revolve around a mathematical model or set of equations that explains how things happen within the organization. Models are simplified representations that enable the analyst to break down systems into their component parts, assign numerical values to each component, and examine the mathematical relationships between them. These values can be altered to determine what will happen to the system under different sets of circumstances. Types of models include simulation, linear optimization, networks, waiting lines, and game theory.

Operations research analysts use computers extensively in their work. They are typically highly proficient in database management, programming, and the development and use of sophisticated software programs. Most of the models built by operations research analysts are so complicated that only a computer can solve them efficiently.

The type of problem they usually handle varies by industry. For example, an analyst for an airline would coordinate flight and maintenance scheduling, passenger level estimates, and fuel consumption to produce a schedule that optimizes all of these factors to ensure safety and produce the most profits. An analyst employed by a hospital would concentrate on a different set of problems: scheduling admissions, managing patient flow, assigning shifts, monitoring use of pharmacy and laboratory services, or forecasting demand for new hospital services.

The role of the operations research analyst varies according to the structure and management philosophy of the firm. Some centralize operations research in one department; others disperse operations research personnel throughout all divisions. Some operations research analysts specialize in one type of application; others are generalists.

The degree of supervision varies by organizational structure and experience. In some organizations, analysts have a great deal of professional autonomy; in others, analysts are more closely supervised. Operations research analysts work closely with senior managers who have a wide variety of support needs. Analysts must adapt their work to reflect these requirements.

Regardless of the industry or structure of the organization, operations research entails a similar set of procedures. Managers begin the process by describing the symptoms of a problem to the analyst. The analyst then defines the problem, which is sometimes general in nature and at other times specific. For example, an operations research analyst for an auto manufacturer may be asked to determine the best inventory level for each of the materials for a new production line or, more specifically, to determine how many windshields should be kept in inventory.

After analysts define the problem, they learn everything they can about it. They study the problem, then break it into its component parts. Then they gather information about each of these parts. Usually this involves consulting a wide variety of people. To determine the most efficient amount of steel to be kept on hand, for example, operations research analysts might talk with engineers about production levels; discuss purchasing arrangements with industrial buyers; and examine data on storage costs provided by the accounting department.

With this information in hand, the operations research analyst is ready to select the most appropriate analytical technique. There may be several techniques that could be used, or there may be one standard model or technique that is used in all instances. In a few cases, the analyst must construct an original model to examine and explain the system. In almost all cases, the selected model must be modified to reflect the specific circumstances of the situation.

A model for airline flight scheduling, for example, might include variables for the amount of fuel required to fly the routes, several projected levels of passenger demand, varying ticket prices, pilot scheduling, and maintenance costs. The analyst chooses the values for these variables, enters them into a computer, which has already been programmed to make the calculations required, and runs the program to produce the best flight schedule consistent with several sets of assumptions. The analyst would probably design a model that would take into account wide variations in the different variables.

At this point, the operations research analyst presents the final work to management along with recommendations based on the results of the analysis. Additional runs based on different assumptions may be needed to help in making the final decision. Once a decision has been reached, the analyst works with others in the organization to ensure its successful implementation.

Working Conditions

Operations research analysts generally work regular hours in an office environment. Because they work on projects that are of immediate interest to management, analysts are often under pressure to meet deadlines and may work more than a 40-hour week.

Employment

Operations research analysts held about 45,000 jobs in 1992. They are employed in most industries. Major employers include computer and data processing services, commercial banks and savings institutions, insurance agencies, engineering and management services firms, manufacturers of transportation equipment, airlines, and the federal government. Some analysts work for management consulting agencies that conduct operations research for firms that do not have an in-house operations research staff.

Most analysts in the federal government work for the Armed Forces. In addition, many operations research analysts who work in private industry do work directly or indirectly related to national defense.

Training, Other Qualifications, and Advancement

Employers strongly prefer applicants with at least a master's degree in operations research or management science or other quantitative disciplines. A high level of computer skills is also required. Employers often sponsor skill-improvement training for experienced workers, helping them keep up with new developments in operations research techniques as well as advances in computer science. Some analysts attend advanced university classes on these subjects.

Operations research analysts must be able to think logically and work well with people, so employers prefer workers with good oral and written communication skills. The computer is the most important tool for quantitative analysis, and training or experience in programming is a must.

Beginning analysts usually do routine work under the supervision of experienced analysts. As they gain knowledge and experience, they are assigned more complex tasks, with greater autonomy to design models and solve problems. Operations research analysts advance by assuming positions as technical specialists or supervisors. The skills acquired by operations research analysts are useful for higher level jobs, and experienced analysts with leadership potential often leave the field altogether to assume nontechnical managerial or administrative positions.

Job Outlook

Organizations are increasingly using operations research and management science techniques to improve productivity and quality and to reduce costs. This reflects growing acceptance of a systematic approach to decision making as well as more affordable computers, which give even small firms access to operations research applications. The interplay of these two trends should greatly stimulate demand for these workers in the years ahead.

Those seeking employment as operations research or management science analysts who hold a master's or Ph.D. degree should find good opportunities through 2005. The number of openings generated each year as a result of employment growth and the need to replace those leaving the occupation is expected to exceed the number of people graduating with master's and Ph.D. degrees from management science or operations research programs. Graduates with only a bachelor's degree in operations research or management science should find good opportunities as research assistants or analyst assistants in a variety of related fields; only the most highly qualified are likely to find employment as operations research or management science analysts.

Employment of operations research analysts is expected to grow much faster than the average for all occupations through 2005 due to the increasing importance of quantitative analysis in decision making and the increasing availability of computing resources. Much of the job growth is expected to occur in the transportation, manufacturing, finance, and services sectors. Firms in these sectors recognize that quantitative analysis can achieve dramatic improvements in operating efficiency and profitability. More airlines, for example, are using operations research to determine the best flight and maintenance schedules, select the best routes to service, analyze customer characteristics, and control fuel consumption, among other things. Motel chains are beginning to use operations research to improve their efficiency by, for example, analyzing automobile traffic patterns and customer attitudes to determine location, size, and style of new motels. Like other management support functions, operations research grows by its own success. When one firm in an industry increases productivity by adopting a new procedure, its competitors usually follow. This competitive pressure will contribute to demand for operations research analysts.

Demand also should be strong in the manufacturing sector as firms expand existing operations research staff in the face of growing domestic and foreign competition. More manufacturers are using mathematical models to study the operations of the organization for the first time. For example, analysts will be needed to determine the best way to control product inventory, distribute finished products, and decide where sales offices should be based. In addition, increasing factory automation will require more operations research analysts to alter existing models or develop new ones for production layout, robotics installation, work schedules, and inventory control.

The Department of Defense and defense contractors employ many operations research analysts. For example, operations researchers helped plan the 1990 military deployment to Saudi Arabia. Not only did they determine the best air and water transport schedules to move the maximum number of personnel and amount of equipment in the shortest time, making optimal use of people, ships, aircraft, and fuel, but they were also central to the planning and command decisions made during combat. Because defense expenditures will be cut in the future, fewer jobs will be available in the military and defense-related industries for these workers. However, high demand outside the military should more than offset reductions in defense-related demand.

Earnings

According to recruiters and national operations research associations, operations research analysts with a master's degree generally earned starting salaries of about $30,000 to $35,000 a year in 1992. Experienced operations research analysts earned about $50,000 a year in 1992, with top salaries exceeding $90,000. The average annual salary for operations research analysts in the federal government in nonsupervisory, supervisory, and managerial positions was $57,419 in 1993.

Related Occupations

Operations research analysts apply mathematical principles to organizational problems. Workers in other occupations that stress quantitative analysis include computer scientists, applied mathematicians, statisticians, and economists. Operations research is closely allied to managerial occupations in that its goal is improved organizational efficiency.

Sources of Additional Information

Information on career opportunities for operations research analysts is available from:

❏ The Operations Research Society of America, 1314 Guilford Ave., Baltimore, MD 21202; or

❏ The Institute of Management Sciences, 290 Westminster St., Providence, RI 02903.

For information on careers in the Armed Forces and Department of Defense, contact:

❏ Military Operations Research Society, 101 South Whiting St., Suite 202, Alexandria, VA 22304.

Physical Therapists

Nature of the Work

Physical therapists improve the mobility, relieve the pain, and prevent or limit the permanent physical disabilities of patients suffering from injuries or disease. Their patients include accident victims and disabled individuals with conditions such as multiple sclerosis, cerebral palsy, nerve injuries, burns, amputations, head injuries, fractures, low back pain, arthritis, and heart disease.

Therapists evaluate patients' medical histories; test and measure their strength, range of motion, and ability to function; and develop written treatment plans. These plans, which may be based on physician's orders, describe the treatments to be provided, purpose, and anticipated outcomes. As treatment continues, they document progress, conduct periodic reevaluations, and modify treatments, if necessary.

Treatment often includes exercise for patients who have been immobilized and lack flexibility. Using a technique known as passive exercise, therapists increase the patient's flexibility by stretching and manipulating stiff joints and unused muscles. Later in the treatment, they encourage patients to use their own muscles to further increase flexibility and range of motion before finally advancing to weights and other exercises to improve strength, balance, coordination, and endurance.

Physical therapists also use electricity, heat, cold, or ultrasound to relieve pain or improve the condition of muscles or related tissues or to reduce swelling. They may use traction or deep-tissue massage to relieve pain and restore function. Therapists also teach and motivate patients to use crutches, prostheses, and wheelchairs to perform day-to-day activities and show them exercises to do at home.

Physical therapists document evaluations, daily progress, medical team conferences, and reports to referring practitioners and insurance companies. Such documentation is used to track the patient's progress, identify areas requiring more or less attention, justify billings, and for legal purposes. Some physical therapists treat a wide variety of problems; others specialize in such areas as pediatrics, geriatrics, orthopedics, sports physical therapy, neurology, and cardiopulmonary physical therapy.

Working Conditions

Physical therapists work in hospitals, clinics, and private offices that have specially equipped facilities, or they treat patients in hospital rooms, homes, or schools. Most physical therapists work a 40-hour week, which may include some evenings and weekends. The job can be physically demanding because therapists often have to stoop, kneel, crouch, lift, and stand for long periods of time. In addition, therapists move heavy equipment and lift patients or help them turn, stand, or walk.

Employment

Physical therapists held about 90,000 jobs in 1992; about one in four worked part-time. Hospitals employed one-third of all salaried physical therapists in 1992 and offices of other health practitioners, including those of physical therapists, employed one-quarter of them. Others held jobs in offices of physicians, home health agencies, nursing homes, and schools. Some physical therapists are in private practice, providing services to individual patients or contracting to provide services in hospitals, rehabilitation centers, nursing homes, home health agencies, adult daycare programs, and schools. These self-employed therapists may be in solo practice or part of a consulting group. Some physical therapists teach in academic institutions and conduct research.

Training, Other Qualifications, and Advancement

All states require physical therapists to pass a licensure exam after graduating from an accredited physical therapy program. Entry-level education in physical therapy is available in 70 bachelor's degree and 64 master's degree programs. The bachelor's degree curriculum usually starts with basic science courses such as biology, chemistry, and physics, and then introduces specialized courses such as biomechanics, neuroanatomy, human growth and development, manifestations of disease and trauma, evaluation and assessment techniques, research, and therapeutic procedures. Besides classroom and laboratory instruction, students receive supervised clinical experience in hospitals.

Individuals who have a four-year degree in a related field, such as genetics or biology, and want to be a physical therapist, should enroll in a master's level physical therapy program. A master's degree is also recommended for those with a bachelor's degree in physical therapy who are interested in promotion to an administrative position. For research and teaching jobs, a master's degree is required.

Competition for entry to physical therapy programs is keen, so interested students should attain superior grades in high school and college, especially in science courses. Courses useful when applying to physical therapy programs include anatomy, biology, chemistry, social science, mathematics, and physics. Many education programs also require experience as a volunteer in the physical therapy department of a hospital or clinic for admission.

Physical therapists should be patient, persuasive, resourceful, emotionally stable, and tactful to help patients understand the treatments and adjust to their disabilities. Similar traits are also needed to deal with the patient's family. Physical therapists should also have manual dexterity and physical stamina.

Physical therapists should expect to continue to develop professionally by participating in continuing education courses and workshops from time to time. A number of states require continuing education for maintaining licensure.

Job Outlook

Employment of physical therapists is expected to grow much faster than the average for all occupations through 2005. Growth will occur as new medical technologies save more people, who then need therapy; as new technologies permit more disabling conditions to be treated; and as the population grows and ages.

The rapidly growing elderly population is particularly vulnerable to chronic and debilitating conditions that will require more therapeutic services. At the same time, the baby-boom generation will enter the prime age for heart attack and strokes, increasing the demand for cardiac and physical rehabilitation. More young people will also need physical therapy as medical advances save the lives of a larger proportion of newborns with severe birth defects. Future medical developments will also permit a higher percentage of trauma victims to survive, creating additional demand for rehabilitative care.

Growth will also result from advances in medical technology which permit treatment of more disabling conditions. In the past, for example, the development of hip and knee replacements for those with arthritis gave rise to employment for physical therapists to improve flexibility and strengthen weak muscles.

The widespread interest in health promotion should also increase demand for physical therapy services. A growing number of employers are using physical therapists to evaluate worksites, develop exercise programs, and teach safe work habits to employees in the hope of reducing injuries.

Job prospects in physical therapy are expected to be excellent. There have been shortages of physical therapists in recent years. However, this situation may ease eventually as the number of physical therapy education programs increases and more students graduate.

Earnings

In 1992, median annual earnings of salaried physical therapists who usually work full-time were $35,464. The middle 50 percent earned between $26,624 and $43,628. The top 10 percent earned at least $52,468 and the bottom 10 percent earned less than $17,784. According to a University of Texas Medical Branch national survey of hospitals and medical centers, the median annual salary of physical therapists, based on a 40 hour week and excluding shift or area differentials, was $37,638 in October 1992. The average minimum salary was $31,887 and the average maximum salary was $47,288. Physical therapists in private practice tend to earn more than salaried workers.

Related Occupations

Physical therapists treat and rehabilitate people with physical or mental disabilities. Others who work in the rehabilitation field include occupational therapists, corrective therapists, recreational therapists, manual arts therapists, speech pathologists and audiologists, orthotists, prosthetists, respiratory therapists, chiropractors, acupuncturists, and athletic trainers.

Sources of Additional Information

Additional information on a career as a physical therapist and a list of accredited educational programs in physical therapy are available from:

❏ American Physical Therapy Association, 1111 North Fairfax St., Alexandria, VA 22314.

Psychologists

Nature of the Work

Psychologists study human behavior and mental processes to understand, explain, and change people's behavior. They may study the way a person thinks, feels, or behaves. Research psychologists investigate the physical, cognitive, emotional, or social aspects of human behavior. Psychologists in applied fields counsel and conduct training programs; do market research; apply psychological treatments to a variety of medical and surgical conditions; or provide mental health services in hospitals, clinics, or private settings.

Like other social scientists, psychologists formulate hypotheses and collect data to test their validity. Research methods depend on the topic under study. Psychologists may gather information through controlled laboratory experiments; personality, performance, aptitude, and intelligence tests; observation, interviews, and questionnaires; clinical studies; or surveys. Computers are widely used to record and analyze this information.

Because psychology deals with human behavior, psychologists apply their knowledge and techniques to a wide range of endeavors including human services, management, education, law, and sports. In addition to the variety of work settings, psychologists specialize in many different areas.

Clinical psychologists, who constitute the largest specialty, generally work in independent or group practice or in hospitals or clinics. They may help the mentally or emotionally disturbed adjust to life and are increasingly helping all kinds of medical and surgical patients deal with their illnesses or injuries. They may work in physical medicine and rehabilitation settings, treating patients with spinal cord injuries, chronic pain or illness, stroke, arthritis, and neurologic conditions, such as multiple sclerosis. Others help people deal with life stresses such as divorce or aging. Clinical psychologists interview patients; give diagnostic tests; provide individual, family, and group psychotherapy; and design and implement behavior modification programs. They may collaborate with physicians and other specialists in developing treatment programs and help patients understand and comply with the prescribed treatment. Some clinical psychologists work in universities, where they train graduate students in the delivery of mental health and behavioral medicine services. Others administer community mental health programs.

Counseling psychologists use several techniques, including interviewing and testing, to advise people on how to deal with problems of everyday living—personal, social, educational, or vocational. (Also see the statement on social workers elsewhere in this book.)

Developmental psychologists study the patterns and causes of behavioral change as people progress through life from infancy to adulthood. Some concern themselves with behavior during infancy, childhood, and adolescence, while others study changes that take place during maturity and old age. The study of developmental disabilities and how they affect a person and others is a new area within developmental psychology.

Educational psychologists evaluate student and teacher needs, and design and develop programs to enhance the educational setting.

Experimental psychologists study behavior processes and work with human beings and animals such as rats, monkeys, and pigeons. Prominent areas of experimental research include motivation, thinking, attention, learning and retention, sensory and perceptual processes, effects of substance use and abuse, and genetic and neurological factors in behavior.

Industrial and organizational psychologists apply psychological techniques to personnel administration, management, and marketing problems. They are involved in policy planning, applicant screening, training and development, psychological test research, counseling, and organizational development and analysis. For example, an industrial psychologist may work with management to develop better training programs and reorganize the work setting to improve worker productivity or quality of work life.

School psychologists work with students, teachers, parents, and administrators to resolve students' learning and behavior problems. Educational psychologists evaluate student and teacher needs, and design and develop programs to enhance the educational setting.

Social psychologists examine people's interactions with others and the social environment. Prominent areas of study include group behavior, leadership, attitudes, and interpersonal perception.

Some relatively new specialties include cognitive psychology, health psychology, neuropsychology, and geropsychology. *Cognitive psychologists* deal with the brain's role in memory, thinking, and perceptions; some are involved with research related to computer programming and artificial intelligence. *Health psychologists* promote good health through health maintenance counseling programs that are designed, for example, to help people stop smoking or lose weight. *Neuropsychologists* study the relation between the brain and behavior. They often work in stroke and head injury programs. *Geropsychologists* deal with the special problems faced by the elderly. The emergence and growth of these specialties reflects the increasing participation of psychologists in providing direct services to special patient populations.

Other areas of specialization include psychometrics, psychology and the arts, history of psychology, psychopharmacology, community, comparative, consumer, engineering, environmental, family, forensic, population, military, and rehabilitation psychology.

Working Conditions

A psychologist's specialty and place of employment determine working conditions. For example, clinical, school, and counseling psychologists in private practice have pleasant, comfortable offices and set their own hours. However, they often have evening hours to accommodate their clients. Some employed in hospitals, nursing homes, and other health facilities often work evenings and weekends, while others in schools and clinics work regular daytime hours. Psychologists employed by academic institutions divide their time among teaching, research, and administrative responsibilities. Some maintain part-time consulting practices as well.

In contrast to the many psychologists who have flexible work schedules, most in government and private industry have more structured schedules. They often work alone reading and writing research reports,. Many experience the pressures of deadlines, tight schedules, and overtime work. Their routine may be interrupted frequently. Travel may be required to attend conferences or conduct research.

Employment

Psychologists held about 144,000 jobs in 1992. Educational institutions employed nearly 4 out of every 10 salaried psychologists in positions involving counseling, testing, special education, research, and administration. Hospitals, mental health clinics, rehabilitation centers, nursing homes, and other health facilities employed 3 out of every 10 salaried psychologists, while government agencies at the federal, state, and local levels employed one-sixth of them. The Department of Veterans Affairs, the Department of Defense, and the Public Health Service employ the overwhelming majority of psychologists working for federal agencies. Governments employ psychologists in hospitals, clinics, correctional facilities, and other settings. Psychologists also work in social service organizations, research organizations, management consulting firms, marketing research firms, and other businesses.

After several years of experience, some psychologists—usually those with doctoral degrees—enter private practice or set up their own research or consulting firms. A growing proportion of psychologists are self-employed. Besides the jobs described above, many people held positions as psychology faculty at colleges and universities, and as high school psychology teachers. (See the statement on school teachers—kindergarten, elementary, and secondary elsewhere in this book.)

Training, Other Qualifications, and Advancement

A doctoral degree is generally required for employment as a psychologist. Psychologists with a Ph.D. qualify for a wide range of teaching, research, clinical, and counseling positions in universities, elementary and secondary schools, private industry, and government. Psychologists with a Psy.D.—Doctor of Psychology—qualify mainly for clinical positions.

People with a master's degree in psychology can administer tests as psychological assistants. Under the supervision of doctoral level psychologists, they can conduct research in laboratories, administer psychological evaluations, counsel patients, or perform administrative duties. They may teach in high schools or two-year colleges or work as school psychologists or counselors.

A bachelor's degree in psychology qualifies a person to assist psychologists and other professionals in community mental health centers, vocational rehabilitation offices, and correctional programs; to work as research or administrative assistants; and to take jobs as trainees in government or business. However, without additional academic training, their advancement opportunities in psychology are severely limited.

In the federal government, candidates having at least 24 semester hours in psychology and one course in statistics qualify for entry-level positions. Competition for these jobs is keen, however. Clinical psychologists generally must have completed the Ph.D. or Psy.D. requirements and served an internship; vocational and guidance counselors usually need two years of graduate study in counseling and one year of counseling experience.

In most cases, two years of full-time graduate study are needed to earn a master's degree in psychology. Requirements usually include practical experience in an applied setting or a master's thesis based on a research project. A master's degree in school psychology requires about two years of coursework and a one-year internship.

Five to seven years of graduate work are usually required for a doctoral degree. The Ph.D. degree culminates in a dissertation based on original research. Courses in quantitative research methods, which include the use of computers, are an integral part of graduate study and usually necessary to complete the dissertation. The Psy.D. is usually based on practical work and examinations rather than a dissertation. In clinical or counseling psychology, the requirements for the doctoral degree generally include a year or more of internship or supervised experience.

Competition for admission into most graduate programs is keen. Some universities require an undergraduate major in psychology. Others prefer only basic psychology with courses in the biological, physical, and social sciences, statistics, and mathematics.

Most colleges and universities offer a bachelor's degree program in psychology; several hundred offer a master's and/or a Ph.D. program. A relatively small number of professional schools of psychology, some affiliated with colleges or universities, offer the Psy.D. The American Psychological Association (APA) presently accredits doctoral training programs in clinical, counseling, and school psychology. The National Council for Accreditation of Teacher Education, with the assistance of the National Association of School Psychologists, is also involved in the accreditation of advanced degree programs in school psychology. APA also accredits institutions that provide internships for doctoral students in school, clinical, and counseling psychology.

Although financial aid is difficult to obtain, some universities award fellowships or scholarships or arrange for part-time employment. The Veterans Administration (VA) offers pre-doctoral traineeships to interns in VA hospitals, clinics, and related training agencies. The National Science Foundation, the Department of Health and Human Services, and many other organizations also provide grants to psychology departments to help fund student stipends.

Psychologists in independent practice or those who offer any type of patient care, including clinical, counseling, and school psychologists, must meet certification or licensing requirements. All states and the District of Columbia have such requirements. Licensing laws vary by state, but generally require a doctorate in psychology, completion of an approved internship, and one to two years of professional experience. In addition, most states require that applicants pass an examination. Most state boards administer a standardized test and, in many instances, additional oral or essay examinations. Very few states certify those with a master's degree as psychological assistants or associates. Some states require continuing education for license renewal. Most states require that licensed or certified psychologists limit their practice to those areas in which they have developed professional competence through training and experience.

The American Board of Professional Psychology recognizes professional achievement by awarding diplomas primarily in clinical psychology, clinical neuropsychology, and counseling, forensic, industrial and organizational, and school psychology. Candidates need a doctorate in psychology, five years of experience, and professional endorsements. They also must pass an examination.

Even more so than in other occupations, aspiring psychologists who are interested in direct patient care must be emotionally stable, mature, and able to deal effectively with people. Sensitivity, compassion, and the ability to lead and inspire others are particularly important for clinical work and counseling. Research psychologists should be able to do detailed work independently and as part of a team. Verbal and writing skills are necessary to communicate treatment and research findings. Patience and perseverance are vital qualities because results from psychological treatment of patients or research are often long in coming.

Job Outlook

Employment of psychologists is expected to grow much faster than the average for all occupations through 2005. Largely because of the substantial investment in training required to enter this specialized field, psychologists have a strong attachment to their occupation—only a relatively small proportion leave the profession each year. Nevertheless, replacement needs are expected to account for most job openings, similar to most occupations.

Programs to combat the increase in alcohol abuse, drug dependency, marital strife, family violence, crime, and other problems plaguing society should stimulate employment growth. Other factors spurring demand for psychologists include increased emphasis on mental health maintenance in conjunction with the treatment of physical illness; public concern for the development of human resources, including the growing elderly population; increased testing and counseling of children; and more interest in rehabilitation of prisoners. Changes in the level of government funding for these kinds of services could affect the demand for psychologists.

Job opportunities in health care should remain strong, particularly in health care provider networks, such as health maintenance and preferred provider organizations that specialize in mental health, and in nursing homes and alcohol and drug abuse rehabilitation programs. Job opportunities will arise in businesses, nonprofit organizations, and research and computer firms. Companies will use psychologists' expertise in survey design, analysis, and research to provide personnel testing, program evaluation, and statistical analysis. The increase in employee assistance programs—in which psychologists help people stop smoking, control weight, or alter other behaviors—should also spur job growth. The expected wave of retirements among college faculty, beginning in the late 1990s, should result in job openings for psychologists in colleges and universities.

Other openings are likely to occur as psychologists study the effectiveness of changes in health, education, military, law enforcement, and consumer protection programs. Psychologists are also increasingly studying the effects on people of technological advances in areas such as agriculture, energy, the conservation and use of natural resources, and industrial and office automation.

Opportunities are best for candidates with a doctoral degree. People holding doctorates from leading universities in applied areas such as school, clinical, counseling, health, industrial, and educational psychology should have particularly good prospects. Psychologists with extensive training in quantitative research methods and computer science may have a competitive edge over applicants without this background.

Graduates with a master's degree in psychology may encounter competition for the limited number of jobs for which they qualify. Graduates of master's degree programs in school psychology should have the best job prospects, as schools are expected to increase student counseling and mental health services. Some master's degree holders may find jobs as psychological assistants in community mental health centers, although these positions often require direct supervision by a licensed psychologist. Others may find jobs involving research and data collection and analysis in universities, government, or private companies.

Bachelor's degree holders can expect very few opportunities directly related to psychology. Some may find jobs as assistants in rehabilitation centers or in other jobs involving data collection and analysis. Those who meet state certification requirements may become high school psychology teachers.

Earnings

According to a 1991 survey by the American Psychological Association, the median annual salary of psychologists with a doctoral degree was $48,000 in counseling psychology; $50,000 in research positions; $53,000 in clinical psychology;

$55,000 in school psychology; and $76,000 in industrial/organizational psychology. In university psychology departments, median annual salaries ranged from $32,000 for assistant professors to $55,000 for full professors. The median annual salary of master's degree holders was $35,000 for faculty; $37,000 in counseling psychology; $40,000 in clinical psychology; $48,000 in research positions; $50,000 in industrial/organizational psychology; and $52,000 in school psychology. Some psychologists have much higher earnings, particularly those in private practice.

The federal government recognizes education and experience in certifying applicants for entry-level positions. In general, the average starting salary for psychologists having a bachelor's degree was about $18,300 a year in 1993; those with superior academic records could begin at $22,700. Counseling and school psychologists with a master's degree and one year of counseling experience could start at $27,800. Clinical psychologists having a Ph.D. or Psy.D. degree and one year of internship could start at $33,600; some individuals could start at $40,300. The average salary for psychologists in the federal government in nonsupervisory, supervisory, and managerial positions was about $54,400 a year in 1993.

Related Occupations

Psychologists are trained to conduct research and teach, evaluate, counsel, and advise individuals and groups with special needs. Others who do this kind of work include psychiatrists, social workers, sociologists, clergy, special education teachers, and counselors.

Sources of Additional Information

For information on careers, educational requirements, financial assistance, and licensing in all fields of psychology, contact:

❏ American Psychological Association, Education in Psychology and Accreditation Offices, Education Directorate, 750 1st St. NE., Washington, DC 20002.

For information on careers, educational requirements, and licensing of school psychologists, contact:

❏ National Association of School Psychologists, 8455 Colesville Rd., Suite 1000, Silver Spring, MD 20910.

Information about state licensing requirements is available from:

❏ Association of State and Provincial Psychology Boards, P.O. Box 4389, Montgomery, AL 36103.

Information on traineeships and fellowships is also available from colleges and universities that have graduate departments of psychology.

Recreational Therapists

Nature of the Work

Recreational therapists employ activities to treat or maintain the physical, mental, and emotional well-being of patients. Activities include sports, games, dance, drama, arts and crafts, and music, as well as field trips for sightseeing, ball games, or picnics. They help individuals build confidence, socialize effectively, and remediate the effects of illness or disability. Recreational therapists should not be confused with recreation workers, who organize recreational activities primarily for enjoyment.

In clinical settings, such as hospitals and rehabilitation centers, recreational therapists treat and rehabilitate individuals with specific medical problems, usually in cooperation with physicians, nurses, psychologists, social workers, and physical and occupational therapists. In nursing homes, residential facilities, and community recreation departments, they use leisure activities—mostly group oriented—to improve general health and well-being, but may also treat medical problems. In these settings they may be called activity directors or therapeutic recreation specialists.

Recreational therapists assess patients based on information from medical records, medical staff, family, and patients themselves. They then develop and carry out therapeutic activity programs consistent with patient needs and interests. For instance, patients having trouble socializing may be helped to play games with others or a right-handed person with a right-side paralysis may be helped to use his or her left arm to throw a ball or swing a racket. They may instruct patients in relaxation techniques to reduce stress and tension, in stretching and limbering exercises, and in individual and group sports.

Community based recreational therapists work in park and recreation departments, special education programs, or programs for the elderly or disabled. In these programs therapists help patients develop leisure activities and provide them with opportunities for exercise, mental stimulation, creativity, and fun.

Recreational therapists observe and record patients' participation, reactions, and progress. These records are used by the medical staff and others to monitor progress, to justify changes or end treatment, and for billing. Recreational therapists may prepare periodic reports on patients.

Working Conditions

Recreational therapists often plan events and keep records in offices and provide services in special activity rooms. In community settings they might also work with clients in a recreation room, on a playing field, or in a swimming pool. Therapists often lift and carry equipment as well as participate in activities. Recreational therapists generally work a 40-hour week, which may include some evenings, weekends, and holidays.

Employment

Recreational therapists held about 30,000 jobs in 1992. About one-half were in hospitals and one-third were in nursing homes. Others were in residential facilities, community mental health centers, adult day care programs, correctional facilities, community programs for people with disabilities, and substance abuse centers. Some therapists were self-employed, generally contracting with nursing homes or community agencies to develop and oversee programs.

Training, Other Qualifications, and Advancement

A bachelor's degree in therapeutic recreation (or in recreation with an option in therapeutic recreation) is the usual requirement for hospital and other clinical positions. An associate degree in recreational therapy; training in art, drama, or music therapy; or qualifying work experience may be sufficient for activity director positions in nursing homes.

The National Council for Therapeutic Recreation Certification certifies therapeutic recreation specialists. Specialists must have a bachelor's degree and pass a certification exam. Some employers require individuals to be certified; others prefer it. There are 105 programs that prepare recreational therapists. As of 1993, 54 programs were accredited by the National Council on Accreditation. Most offer bachelor's degrees, although some offer associate or master's degrees.

In addition to therapeutic recreation courses in clinical practice and helping skills, program design, management, and professional issues, students study human anatomy, physiology, abnormal psychology, medical and psychiatric terminology, characteristics of illnesses and disabilities, and the concepts of mainstreaming and normalization. Courses cover professional ethics, assessment and referral procedures, and the use of adaptive and medical equipment. In addition, 360 hours of internship under the supervision of a certified therapeutic recreation specialist are required.

Recreational therapists should be comfortable working with disabled people and be patient, tactful, and persuasive. Ingenuity and imagination are needed in adapting activities to individual needs and good physical coordination is necessary when demonstrating or participating in recreational events.

Job Outlook

Employment of recreational therapists is expected to grow faster than the average for all occupations through 2005 because of anticipated expansion in long-term care, physical and psychiatric rehabilitation, and services for the disabled. Hospitals will provide a large number of recreational therapy jobs through 2005. A growing number of these will be in hospital-based adult daycare and outpatient programs or in units offering short-term mental health and alcohol or drug abuse services. Long-term rehabilitation and psychiatric hospitals will provide additional jobs.

The rapidly growing number of older people is expected to spur job growth for activity directors in nursing homes, retirement communities, adult daycare programs, and social service agencies. Continued growth is expected in community residential facilities as well as daycare programs for people with disabilities. Job prospects are expected to be favorable for those with a strong clinical background.

Earnings

According to a survey of American Therapeutic Recreation Association members, the average salary for recreational therapists was $25,557 in 1991. According to limited data from a survey conducted by the National Association of Activity Professionals, the average salary of activity directors in nursing homes was between $15,000 and $25,000 a year in 1990. The average annual salary for all recreational therapists in the federal government in nonsupervisory, supervisory, and managerial positions was about $33,499 in 1993.

Related Occupations

Recreational therapists design activities to help people with disabilities lead more fulfilling and independent lives. Other workers who have similar jobs are orientation therapists for the blind, art therapists, drama therapists, dance therapists, music therapists, occupational therapists, and rehabilitation counselors.

Sources of Additional Information

For information on how to order materials describing careers and academic programs in recreational therapy, write to:

❑ American Therapeutic Recreation Association, C.O. Associated Management Systems, P.O. Box 15215, Hattiesburg, MS 39402-5215; or

❑ National Therapeutic Recreation Society, 2775 S. Quincy St., Suite 300, Arlington, VA 22206-2204.

Certification information may be obtained from:

❑ National Council for Therapeutic Recreation Certification, P.O. Box 479, Thiells, NY 10984-0479.

Registered Nurses

Nature of the Work

Registered nurses (R.N.'s) care for the sick and injured and help people stay well. They are typically concerned with the whole person, providing for the physical, mental, and emotional needs of their patients. They observe, assess, and record symptoms, reactions, and progress; assist physicians during treatments and examinations; administer medications; and assist in convalescence and rehabilitation. R.N.'s also develop and manage nursing care plans; instruct patients and their families in proper care; and help individuals and groups take steps to improve or maintain their health. While state laws govern the tasks R.N.'s may perform, it is usually the work setting which determines day-to-day job duties.

Hospital nurses form the largest group of nurses. Most are staff nurses, who provide bedside nursing care and carry out the medical regimen prescribed by physicians. They may also supervise licensed practical nurses and aides. Hospital nurses are usually assigned to one area such as surgery, maternity, pediatrics, emergency room, intensive care, or treatment of cancer patients, or may rotate among departments.

Nursing home nurses manage nursing care for residents with conditions ranging from a fracture to Alzheimer's disease. Although they generally spend most of their time on administrative and supervisory tasks, R.N.'s also assess residents' medical condition, develop treatment plans, supervise licensed practical nurses and nursing aides, and perform difficult procedures such as starting intravenous fluids. They also work in specialty-care departments, such as long-term rehabilitation for stroke and head-injury patients.

Public health nurses work in government and private agencies and clinics, schools, retirement communities and other community settings. They instruct individuals and families and other groups in health education, disease prevention, nutrition, child care, and home care of the sick or disabled. They arrange for immunizations, blood pressure testing, and other health screening. These nurses also work with community leaders, teachers, parents, and physicians in community health education. Some work in home health care, providing periodic services prescribed by a physician and instructing patients and families.

Private duty nurses care for patients needing constant attention. They work directly for families on a contract basis or for a nursing or temporary help agency which assigns them to patients. They provide services in homes, hospitals, nursing homes, and rehabilitation centers.

Office nurses assist physicians in private practice, clinics, surgicenters, emergency medical centers, and health maintenance organizations (HMO's). They prepare patients for and assist with examinations, administer injections and medications, dress wounds and incisions, assist with minor surgery, and maintain records. Some also perform routine laboratory and office work.

Occupational health or *industrial nurses* provide nursing care at worksites to employees, customers, and others with minor injuries and illnesses. They provide emergency care, prepare accident reports, and arrange for further care if necessary. They also offer health counseling, assist with health examinations and inoculations, and work on accident prevention programs.

Head nurses or *nurse supervisors* direct nursing activities. They plan work schedules and assign duties to nurses and aides, provide or arrange for training, and visit patients to observe nurses and to ensure that care is proper. They may also ensure that records are maintained and that equipment and supplies are ordered.

Working Conditions

Most nurses work in well-lighted, comfortable medical facilities. Public health nurses travel to patients' homes and to schools, community centers, and other sites. Nurses may spend considerable time walking and standing. They need emotional stability to cope with human suffering, emergencies, and other stresses. Because patients in hospitals and nursing homes require 24 hour care, nurses in these institutions may work nights, weekends, and holidays. Office, occupational health, and public health nurses are more likely to work regular business hours.

Nursing has its hazards, especially in hospitals and clinics where nurses may care for individuals with infectious diseases such as hepatitis and AIDS. Nurses must observe rigid guidelines to guard against these and other dangers such as radiation, chemicals used for sterilization of instruments, and anesthetics. In addition, nurses face back injury when moving patients, shocks from electrical equipment, and hazards posed by compressed gases.

Employment

Registered nurses held about 1,835,000 jobs in 1992. Approximately two out of three jobs were in hospitals. Others were in offices and clinics of physicians, nursing homes, home health care agencies, temporary help agencies, schools, and government agencies. About one-fourth of all R.N.'s worked part time.

Training, Other Qualifications, and Advancement

To obtain a nursing license, all states require graduation from an accredited nursing school and passing a national licensing examination. Nurses may be licensed in more than one state, either by examination or endorsement of a license issued by another state. Licenses must be periodically renewed, and continuing education is a requirement for renewal in some states.

In 1991, there were 1,470 entry-level R.N. programs. There are three major educational paths to nursing: Associate degree (A.D.N.), diploma, and bachelor of science degree in nursing (B.S.N.). A.D.N. programs, offered by community and junior colleges, take about two years to complete. More than 60 percent of graduates in 1991 were from A.D.N. programs. B.S.N. programs, offered by colleges and universities, take four or five years. More than 30 percent of graduates in 1991 were from these programs. Diploma programs, given in hospitals, last two to three years. A small and declining number of graduates come from these programs. Generally, licensed graduates of any of the three programs qualify for entry-level positions as staff nurses.

There have been attempts to raise the educational requirements for an R.N. license to a bachelor's degree and, possibly, create new job titles. However, such proposals have been around for years. These changes, should they occur, will be made state by state, through legislation or regulation. Changes in licensure requirements would not affect currently licensed R.N.'s, who would be grandfathered in, no matter what their educational preparation. However, individuals considering nursing should carefully weigh the pros and cons of enrolling in a B.S.N. program, since advancement opportunities are broader for those with a B.S.N. In fact, some career paths are open only to nurses with bachelor's or advanced degrees.

While A.D.N. or diploma preparation is enough for a nursing home nurse to advance to director of nursing, a bachelor's degree is generally necessary for administrative positions in hospitals and positions in community nursing. Moreover, the B.S.N. is a prerequisite for admission to graduate nursing programs. So individuals considering positions requiring graduate training, such as research, consulting, teaching, or clinical specialization should enroll in a B.S.N. program.

A growing number of A.D.N. and diploma-trained nurses are entering bachelor's programs to prepare for a broader scope of nursing practice. They can often find a hospital position and then take advantage of tuition reimbursement programs to get a B.S.N. Nursing education includes classroom instruction and supervised training in hospitals and other health facilities. Students take courses in anatomy, physiology, microbiology, chemistry, nutrition, psychology and other behavioral sciences, and nursing.

Supervised clinical experience is provided in hospital departments such as pediatrics, psychiatry, maternity, and surgery. A growing number of programs include courses in gerontological nursing and clinical practice in nursing homes. Some provide clinical training in public health departments and home health agencies.

Nurses should be caring and sympathetic. They must be able to accept responsibility, direct or supervise others, follow orders precisely, and determine when consultation is required. Experience and good performance can lead to promotion for increasingly more responsible positions. Nurses can advance, in management, to assistant head nurse or head nurse. From there, they can advance to assistant director, director, and vice president positions. Increasingly, management level nursing positions require a graduate degree in nursing or health services administration. They also require leadership, negotiation skills, and good judgment. Graduate programs preparing executive level nurses usually last one to two years.

Within patient care, nurses can advance to clinical nurse

specialist, nurse practitioner, nurse midwife, or nurse anesthetist. These positions require one or two years of graduate education, leading to a certificate or master's degree. Some nurses move into the business side of health care. Their nursing expertise and experience on a health care team equip them to manage ambulatory, acute, home health, and chronic care services. Some are employed by health care corporations in health planning and development, marketing, and quality assurance.

Job Outlook

Job prospects in nursing are good. Although employers in some parts of the country reported shortages of R.N.'s in the past, large wage increases have attracted more people to nursing and dampened demand. However, R.N. recruitment has long been a problem in rural areas, in some big city hospitals, and in specialty areas including intensive care, rehabilitation, geriatrics, and long-term care.

Employment of registered nurses is expected to grow much faster than the average for all occupations through 2005. Driving this growth will be technological advances in patient care, which permit a greater number of medical problems to be treated, and increasing emphasis on primary care. The number of older people, who are much more likely than younger people to need medical care, is projected to grow very rapidly. Many job openings will also result from the need to replace experienced nurses who leave the occupation, especially as the average age of the registered nurse population continues to rise.

Employment in hospitals, the largest sector, is expected to grow more slowly than in other health care sectors. While the intensity of nursing care is likely to increase, requiring more nurses per patient, the number of inpatients (those who remain overnight) is not likely to increase much. Also, patients are being released earlier and more procedures are being done on an outpatient basis, both in and outside hospitals. Most rapid growth is expected in hospitals' outpatient facilities.

Employment in physicians' offices and clinics, including HMO's, ambulatory surgicenters, and emergency medical centers is expected to grow very rapidly as health care in general expands. In addition, an increasing proportion of sophisticated procedures, which once were performed only in hospitals, are being performed here, thanks largely to advances in technology.

Employment in home health care is also expected to grow very rapidly. This is in response to a growing number of older people with functional disabilities, consumer preference for care in the home, and technological advances which make it possible to bring increasingly complex treatments into the home.

Employment in nursing homes is expected to grow very fast due to increases in the number of people in their eighties and nineties, many of whom will require long-term care. In addition, the financial pressure on hospitals to release patients as soon as possible should produce more nursing home admissions. Growth in units to provide specialized long-term rehabilitation for stroke and head injury patients or to treat Alzheimer's victims will also increase employment.

Earnings

Median annual earnings of full-time salaried registered nurses were $34,424 in 1992. The middle 50 percent earned between $27,820 and $41,600. The lowest 10 percent earned less than $21,944; the top 10 percent, more than $50,960. According to a University of Texas Medical Branch survey of hospitals and medical centers, the median annual salary of staff nurses, based on a 40 hour week and excluding shift or area differentials, was $33,278 in October 1992. The average minimum salary was $27,476 and the average maximum was $41,563. For head nurses, the median was $47,335; clinical nurse specialists, $44,845; professional nurse practitioners, $43,680; and nurse anesthetists, $66,622.

According to the Buck Survey conducted by the American Health Care Association, staff R.N.'s in chain nursing homes had median annual earnings of approximately $30,200 in January, 1993. The middle 50 percent earned between $27,200 and $33,400 a year. Many employers are offering flexible work schedules, child care, educational benefits, bonuses, and other incentives.

Related Occupations

Workers in other occupations with responsibilities and duties related to those of registered nurses are occupational therapists, paramedics, physical therapists, physician assistants, and respiratory therapists.

Sources of Additional Information

The National League for Nursing (NLN) publishes a variety of nursing and nursing education materials, including a list of nursing schools and information on student financial aid. For a complete list of NLN publications, write for a career information brochure. Send your request to:

❏ Communications Department, National League for Nursing, 350 Hudson St., New York, NY 10014.

For a list of B.S.N. and graduate programs, write to:

❏ American Association of Colleges of Nursing, 1 Dupont Circle, Suite 530, Washington, DC 20036.

Information on career opportunities as a registered nurse is available from:

❏ American Nurses' Association, 600 Maryland Ave. SW., Washington, DC 20024-2571.

Information about employment opportunities in Department of Veterans Affairs medical centers is available from local VA medical centers and also from:

❏ Title 38 Employment Division (054D), Department of Veterans Affairs, 810 Vermont Ave. NW., Washington, DC 20420.

For information on nursing careers in long-term care, write to:

❏ American Health Care Association, 1201 L St. NW., Washington, DC 20005-4014.

Respiratory Therapists

Nature of the Work

You are able to live without water for a few days and without food for a few weeks but without air, you will suffer brain damage within a few minutes and die after nine minutes or more. Respiratory therapists, also known as respiratory care practitioners, evaluate, treat, and care for patients with breathing disorders.

In evaluating patients, therapists test the capacity of the lungs and analyze the oxygen and carbon dioxide concentration and potential of hydrogen (pH), a measure of the acidity or alkalinity level of the blood. To measure lung capacity, therapists have patients breathe into an instrument that measures the volume and flow of air during inhalation and exhalation. By comparing the reading with the norm for the patient's age, height, weight, and sex, respiratory therapists can determine whether lung deficiencies exist. To analyze oxygen, carbon dioxide, and pH levels, therapists draw an arterial blood sample, place it in a blood gas analyzer, and relay the results to a physician.

Respiratory therapists treat all sorts of patients, from premature infants whose lungs are not fully developed to elderly people whose lungs are diseased. They provide temporary relief to patients with chronic asthma or emphysema and emergency care for heart failure, stroke, drowning, or shock victims. Respiratory therapists most commonly use oxygen or oxygen mixtures, chest physiotherapy, and aerosol medications. Therapists may place an oxygen mask or nasal cannula on a patient and set the oxygen flow at the level prescribed by a physician to increase a patient's concentration of oxygen. Therapists also connect patients who cannot breathe on their own to ventilators which deliver pressurized air into the lungs. They insert a tube into a patient's trachea or windpipe; connect the tube to the ventilator; and set the rate, volume, and oxygen concentration of the air entering the patient's lungs.

Therapists regularly check on patients and equipment. If a patient appears to be having difficulty or if the oxygen, carbon dioxide, or pH level of the blood is abnormal, they change the ventilator setting according to the doctor's order or check equipment for mechanical problems. In homecare, therapists teach patients and their families to use ventilators and other life support systems. They visit several times a month to inspect and clean equipment and ensure its proper use and make emergency visits if equipment problems arise.

Respiratory therapists perform chest physiotherapy on patients to remove mucus from their lungs to make it easier for them to breathe. For example, during surgery, anesthesia depresses respiration, so this treatment may be prescribed to help get the patient's lungs back to normal and prevent congestion. Chest physiotherapy is also used on patients suffering from lung diseases, such as cystic fibrosis, that cause mucus to collect in the lungs. Therapists place patients in positions to help drain mucus, thump and vibrate patients' rib cages, and instruct them to cough.

Respiratory therapists also administer aerosols—generally liquid medications suspended in a gas that forms a mist which is inhaled—and teach patients how to inhale the aerosol properly to assure its effectiveness. Other duties include keeping records of the materials used and charges to patients. Some therapists teach or supervise other respiratory therapy personnel. About 9 out of 10 respiratory therapists work in hospitals.

Working Conditions

Respiratory therapists generally work a 40-hour week. Because hospitals operate around the clock, therapists may work evenings, nights, or weekends. They spend long periods standing and walking between patients' rooms. In an emergency, they work under a great deal of stress. Gases used by respiratory therapists are potentially hazardous because they are used and stored under pressure. However, adherence to safety precautions and regular maintenance and testing of equipment minimize the risk of injury. As with many health occupations, respiratory therapists risk catching infectious diseases. Careful adherence to proper procedures minimizes the risk though.

Employment

Respiratory therapists held about 74,000 jobs in 1992. About 9 out of 10 jobs were located in hospitals in departments of respiratory care, anesthesiology, or pulmonary medicine. Durable medical equipment rental companies, home health agencies, and nursing homes accounted for most of the remaining jobs.

Training, Other Qualifications, and Advancement

Formal training is necessary for entry to this field. Training is offered at the postsecondary level by hospitals, medical schools, colleges and universities, trade schools, vocational-technical institutes, and the Armed Forces. Some programs prepare graduates for jobs as respiratory therapists; other, shorter programs lead to jobs as respiratory therapy technicians. In 1992, 283 programs for respiratory therapists were accredited by the Committee on Allied Health Education and Accreditation (CAHEA) of the American Medical Association (AMA). Another 187 programs offered CAHEA-accredited preparation for respiratory therapy technicians.

Formal training programs vary in length and in the credentials or degree awarded. Most of the CAHEA-accredited therapist programs last two years and lead to an associate degree. Some, however, are four-year bachelor's degree programs. Technician programs last about one year and award certificates. Areas of study for respiratory therapist programs include human anatomy and physiology, chemistry, physics, microbiology, and mathematics. Technical courses deal with procedures, equipment, and clinical tests.

Therapists should be sensitive to patients' physical and psychological needs. Respiratory care workers must pay attention to detail, follow instructions, and work as part of a team. Operating complicated respiratory therapy equipment requires mechanical ability and manual dexterity.

High school students interested in a career in respiratory care are encouraged to take courses in health, biology, mathematics, chemistry, and physics. Respiratory care involves basic mathematical problem-solving. An understanding of basic chemical and physical principles is also important. Computing medication dosages and calculating gas concentrations are just two examples of the need for knowledge of science and mathematics.

Thirty-seven states license respiratory care personnel. The National Board for Respiratory Care offers voluntary certification and registration to graduates of CAHEA-accredited programs. Two credentials are awarded to respiratory care practitioners who satisfy the requirements: Certified Respiratory Therapy Technician (CRTT) and Registered Respiratory

Therapist (RRT). All graduates—those from two- and four-year programs in respiratory therapy, as well as those from one year technician programs—may take the CRTT examination first. CRTT's who meet education and experience requirements can take a separate examination, leading to the award of the RRT.

Individuals who completed a four year program in a nonrespiratory field, but who have college level courses in anatomy, physiology, chemistry, biology, microbiology, physics, and mathematics, can become a CRTT after graduating from AMA accredited one or two year programs. After they receive two years of clinical experience, they are eligible to take the registry exam to become an RRT. Most employers require that applicants for entry-level or generalist positions hold the CRTT or are eligible to take the certification examination. Supervisory positions and those in intensive care specialties, usually require the RRT (or RRT eligibility).

Respiratory therapists advance in clinical practice by moving from care of general to critical patients, whom have significant problems in other organ systems such as the heart or kidneys. Respiratory therapists, especially those with four year degrees, may also advance to supervisory or managerial positions in a respiratory therapy department. Respiratory therapists in home care and equipment rental firms may become branch managers. Others leave the occupation to work as sales representatives or equipment designers for equipment manufacturers.

Job Outlook

Employment of respiratory therapists is expected to increase much faster than the average for all occupations through 2005 because of substantial growth of the middle-aged and elderly population, a development that will heighten the incidence of cardiopulmonary disease.

The elderly are the most common sufferers from respiratory ailments and cardiopulmonary diseases such as pneumonia, chronic bronchitis, emphysema, and heart disease. As their numbers increase, the need for respiratory therapists will increase as well. In addition, advances in treating victims of heart attacks, accident victims, and premature infants (many of whom may be dependent on a ventilator during part of their treatment) will require the services of respiratory care practitioners. Rapid growth in the number of patients with AIDS will also boost demand because lung disease often accompanies AIDS. Opportunities are expected to be highly favorable for respiratory therapists specializing in neonatal and cardiopulmonary care.

Very rapid growth is expected in home health agencies, equipment rental companies, and firms that provide respiratory care on a contract basis. As in other occupations, most job openings will result from the need to replace workers who transfer to other jobs or stop working altogether.

Earnings

Median annual earnings for respiratory therapists who worked full time in 1992 were $32,084. The middle 50 percent earned between $25,116 and $41,236. The lowest 10 percent earned less than $21,528; the top 10 percent earned more than $48,048. According to a national survey of hospitals and medical centers, conducted by the University of Texas Medical Branch, the median annual salary for respiratory therapists, based on a 40 hour week and excluding shift and area differentials, was $29,228 in October 1992. The average minimum annual salary was $24,770 and the average maximum was $36,553.

Related Occupations

Respiratory therapists, under the supervision of a physician, administer respiratory care and life support to patients with heart and lung difficulties. Other workers who care for, treat, or train people to improve their physical condition include dialysis technicians, registered nurses, occupational therapists, physical therapists, and radiation therapy technologists.

Sources of Additional Information

Information concerning a career in respiratory care is available from:

❏ American Association for Respiratory Care, 11030 Ables Ln., Dallas, TX 75229.

Information on gaining credentials as a respiratory therapy practitioner can be obtained from:

❏ The National Board for Respiratory Care, Inc., 8310 Nieman Rd., Lenexa, KS 66214.

For the current list of CAHEA-accredited educational programs for respiratory therapy occupations, write to:

❏ Joint Review Committee for Respiratory Therapy Education, 1701 W. Euless Blvd., Suite 300, Euless, TX 76040.

School Teachers—Kindergarten, Elementary, and Secondary

Nature of the Work

The role of a teacher is changing from that of a lecturer or presenter to one of a facilitator or coach. Interactive discussions and hands-on learning are replacing rote memorization. For example, rather than merely telling students about science, mathematics, or psychology, a teacher might ask students to help solve a mathematical problem or perform a laboratory experiment and discuss how these apply to the real world. Similarly, a teacher might arrange to bring three- and four-year-olds into the classroom to demonstrate certain concepts of child psychology.

As teachers move away from the traditional repetitive drill approaches, they are using more props or manipulatives to help children understand abstract concepts, solve problems, and develop critical thought processes. For example, young students may be taught the concept of numbers or adding and subtracting by playing board games. As children get older, they may use more sophisticated materials such as tape recorders, science apparatus, or cameras.

Classes are becoming less structured, and students are working in groups to discuss and solve problems together. Preparing students for the future workforce is the major stimulus generating the changes in education. To be prepared, students must be able to interact with others, adapt to new technology, and logically think through problems. Teachers provide the tools and environment for students to develop these skills.

Kindergarten and elementary school teachers play a vital role in the development of children. What children learn and experience during their early years can shape children's views of themselves and the world, and affect later success or failure in school, work, and their personal lives. Kindergarten and elementary school teachers introduce children to numbers, language, science, and social studies. They may use games, music, artwork, films, slides, computers, and other instructional technology to teach basic skills.

Most elementary school teachers instruct one class of children in several subjects. In some schools, two or more teachers teach as a team and are jointly responsible for a group of students in at least one subject. In other schools, a teacher may teach one special subject, usually music, art, reading, science, arithmetic, or physical education, to a number of classes. A small but growing number of teachers instruct multilevel classes—classrooms with students at several different learning levels.

Secondary school teachers help students delve more deeply into subjects introduced in elementary school and to learn more about the world and about themselves. They specialize in a specific subject, such as English, Spanish, mathematics, history, or biology, in middle school or high school. They may teach a variety of related courses—for example, American history, contemporary American problems, and world geography.

Special education teachers, who are found in lower grades and high schools, instruct students who have a variety of disabilities, such as visual and hearing impairments, learning disabilities, and physical disabilities. Special education teachers design and modify instruction to meet a student's special needs. Teachers also work with students who have other special instructional needs, such as those who are very bright or gifted or those who have limited English proficiency.

Teachers may use films, slides, overhead projectors, and the latest technology in teaching, such as computers, telecommunication systems, and video discs. Telecommunication technology can bring the real world into the classroom. Through telecommunications, American students can communicate with students in other countries to share personal experiences or research projects of interest to both groups. Computers are used in many classroom activities, from helping students solve math problems to learning English as a second language. Teachers must continually update their skills to use the latest technology in the classroom.

Teachers design their classroom presentations to meet student needs and abilities. They also may work with students individually. Teachers assign lessons, give tests, hear oral presentations, and maintain classroom discipline. Teachers observe and evaluate a student's performance and potential. Teachers are increasingly using new assessment methods, such as examining a portfolio of a student's artwork or writing to measure student achievement. Teachers assess the portfolio at the end of a learning period to judge a student's overall progress. They may then provide additional assistance in areas where a student may need help.

In addition to classroom activities, teachers plan and evaluate lessons, sometimes in collaboration with teachers of related subjects. They also prepare tests and report cards, grade papers, oversee study halls and homerooms, supervise extracurricular activities, and meet with parents and school staff to discuss a student's academic progress or personal problems. Secondary school teachers may assist a student in choosing courses, colleges, and careers. Special education teachers may help students with their transition into special vocational training programs, colleges, or a job. Teachers also participate in education conferences and workshops.

In recent years, site-based management, which allows teachers and parents to participate actively in management decisions, has gained popularity. In many schools, teachers help make decisions regarding the budget, personnel, textbook choices, curriculum design, and teaching methods.

Working Conditions

Seeing students develop new skills and gain an appreciation of the joy of learning can be very rewarding. However, teaching may be frustrating when dealing with unmotivated and disrespectful students.

Many teachers work more than 40 hours a week, including school duties performed outside the classroom. Most teachers work the traditional 10 month school year with a 2 month vacation during the summer. Teachers on the 10 month schedule may teach in summer sessions, take other jobs, travel, or pursue other personal interests. Many enroll in college courses or workshops in order to continue their education. Teachers in districts with a year-round schedule typically work eight weeks, are on vacation for one week, and have a five week midwinter break.

Most states have tenure laws that prevent teachers from being fired without just cause and due process. Teachers may obtain tenure after they have satisfactorily completed a probationary period of teaching, normally three years. Tenure is not a guarantee of a job, but it does provide some security.

Employment

Teachers held about 3,255,000 jobs in 1992; more than 9 out of every 10 teachers taught in public schools. Employment was distributed as follows: elementary—1,634,000; secondary—1,263,000, and special education—58,000. Employment is distributed geographically much the same as the population.

Training, Other Qualifications, and Advancement

All 50 states and the District of Columbia require public school teachers to be certified. Certification is generally for a specific subject or several related ones. Certification is usually granted by the state board of education or a certification advisory committee. Teachers may be certified to teach the early childhood grades (usually nursery school through grade 3); the elementary grades, (grades 1 through 6 or 8); or a special subject, such as reading or music. In most states, special education teachers receive a credential to teach kindergarten through grade 12. These teachers train in the specialty that they want, such as teaching children with learning disabilities or behavioral disorders.

Requirements for regular certificates vary by state. However, all states require a bachelor's degree and completion of an approved teacher training program with a prescribed number of subject and education credits and supervised practice teaching.

Traditional education programs for kindergarten and elementary school teachers include courses, designed specifically for those preparing to teach, in mathematics, physical science, social science, music, art, and literature, as well as prescribed professional education courses, such as philosophy of education, psychology of learning, and teaching methods. Aspiring secondary school teachers either major in the subject they plan to teach while also taking education courses or major in education and take subject courses. Some states require specific grade point averages for teacher certification.

Many states offer alternative teacher certification programs for people who have college training in the subject they want to teach but do not have the necessary education courses required for a regular certificate. Alternative certification programs were originally designed to ease teacher shortages in certain subjects, such as mathematics and science. The programs have expanded to attract other people into teaching, including recent college graduates and midcareer changers.

In some programs, individuals begin teaching immediately under provisional certification. After working under the close supervision of experienced educators for one or two years while taking education courses outside school hours, they receive regular certification if they have progressed satisfactorily. Under other programs, college graduates who do not meet certification requirements take only those courses they lack, and then become certified. This may take one or two semesters of full-time study. Aspiring teachers who need certification may also enter programs that grant a master's degree in education, as well as certification. States also issue emergency certificates to individuals who do not meet all requirements for a regular certificate when schools cannot hire enough teachers with regular certificates.

Almost all states require applicants for teacher certification to be tested for competency in basic skills such as reading and writing, teaching skills, or subject matter proficiency. Almost all require continuing education for renewal of the teacher's certificate, and some require a master's degree. Many states have reciprocity agreements that make it easier for teachers certified in one state to become certified in another. Teachers may become board certified by successfully completing the National Board for Professional Teaching Standards certification process. This certification is voluntary, but can result in a higher salary.

In addition to being knowledgeable in their subject, the ability to communicate, inspire trust and confidence, and motivate students, as well as understand their educational and emotional needs, is essential for teachers. They should also be organized, dependable, patient, and creative.

With additional preparation and certification, teachers may move into positions as school librarians, reading specialists, curriculum specialists, or guidance counselors. Teachers may become administrators or supervisors, although the number of positions is limited. In some systems, highly qualified, experienced teachers can become senior or mentor teachers, with higher pay and additional responsibilities. They guide and assist less experienced teachers while keeping most of their teaching responsibilities.

Job Outlook

Overall employment of kindergarten, elementary, and secondary school teachers is expected to increase faster than the average for all occupations through 2005, fueled by dramatic growth among special education teachers. However, projected employment growth varies among individual teaching occupations. Job openings for all teachers are expected to increase substantially by the end of the decade as the large number of teachers now in their forties and fifties reach retirement age.

Employment of special education teachers is expected to increase much faster than the average for all occupations through 2005 due to legislation emphasizing training and employment for individuals with disabilities; technological advances resulting in more survivors of accidents and illnesses; and growing public interest in individuals with special needs. Qualified people should have little trouble finding a job, due to increased demand for these workers combined with relatively high turnover among special education teachers. Many special education teachers switch to general education teaching or change careers altogether, often because of job stress associated with teaching special education, particularly excessive paperwork, and inadequate administrative support.

Employment of secondary school teachers is expected to grow faster than the average for all occupations through 2005, and average employment growth is projected for kindergarten and elementary school teachers. Assuming relatively little change in average class size, employment growth of teachers depends on the rates of population growth and corresponding student enrollments. The population of 14- to 17-year-olds is expected to experience relatively strong growth through 2005, spurring demand for secondary school teachers. The population of 5- to 13-year olds also is projected to increase, but at a

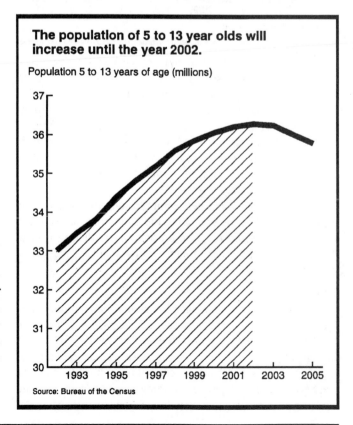

The population of 5 to 13 year olds will increase until the year 2002.

Population 5 to 13 years of age (millions)

Source: Bureau of the Census

slower rate, resulting in divergent growth rates for individual teaching occupations.

The supply of teachers is also expected to increase in response to reports of improved job prospects, more teacher involvement in school policy, greater public interest in education, and higher salaries. In fact, enrollments in teacher training programs have already increased in recent years. In addition, more teachers should be available from alternative certification programs.

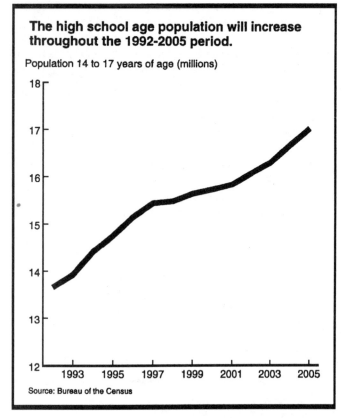

The high school age population will increase throughout the 1992-2005 period.

Population 14 to 17 years of age (millions)

Source: Bureau of the Census

Some central cities and rural areas have difficulty attracting enough teachers, so job prospects should continue to be better in these areas than in suburban districts. Mathematics, science, and special education teachers remain in short supply. Concerns over a future workforce that may not meet employers' needs could spur demand for teachers who specialize in basic skills instruction—reading, writing, and mathematics. With enrollments of minorities increasing, efforts to recruit minority teachers may intensify.

The number of teachers employed depends on state and local expenditures for education. Pressures from taxpayers to limit spending could result in fewer teachers than projected; pressures to spend more to improve the quality of education could mean more.

Earnings

According to the National Education Association, public secondary school teachers averaged about $36,000 a year in 1992-93; public elementary school teachers averaged $34,800. Earnings for special education teachers are comparable. Earnings in private schools are generally lower. In some schools, teachers receive extra pay for coaching sports and working with students in extracurricular activities. Some teachers earn extra

income during the summer working in the school system or in other jobs.

Many public school teachers belong to unions, such as the American Federation of Teachers and the National Education Association, that bargain with school systems over wages, hours, and the terms and conditions of employment.

Related Occupations

Kindergarten, elementary, and secondary school teaching requires a wide variety of skills and aptitudes, including a talent for working with children; organizational, administrative, and recordkeeping abilities; research and communication skills; the power to influence, motivate, and train others; patience; and creativity. Workers in other occupations requiring some of these aptitudes include college and university faculty, counselors, education administrators, employment interviewers, librarians, preschool workers, public relations specialists, sales representatives, social workers, and trainers and employee development specialists.

Special education teachers work with students with disabilities and special needs. Other occupations that help people with disabilities include school psychologists, speech pathologists, and occupational, physical, and recreational therapists.

Sources of Additional Information

Information on certification requirements and approved teacher training institutions is available from local school systems and state departments of education. Information on teachers' unions and education-related issues may be obtained from:

❑ American Federation of Teachers, 555 New Jersey Ave. NW., Washington, DC 20001; or

❑ National Education Association, 1201 16th St. NW., Washington, DC 20036.

A list of institutions with teacher education programs accredited by the National Council for Accreditation of Teacher Education can be obtained from:

❑ National Council for Accreditation of Teacher Education, 2010 Massachusetts Ave. NW., 2nd Floor, Washington, DC 20036.

For information on voluntary teacher certification requirements, contact:

❑ National Board for Professional Teaching Standards, 300 River Pl., Detroit, MI 48207.

A list of institutions offering training programs in special education may be obtained from:

❑ Council for Exceptional Children, 1920 Association Dr., Reston, VA 22091.

Social Workers

Nature of the Work

Social workers help people. They help individuals cope with problems such as inadequate housing, unemployment, lack of job skills, financial mismanagement, serious illness, disability, substance abuse, unwanted pregnancy, or antisocial behavior. They also work with families that have serious conflicts, including those involving child or spousal abuse.

Through direct counseling, social workers help clients identify their real concerns and help them consider solutions and find resources. Often, social workers provide concrete information such as: where to go for debt counseling; how to find child care or elder care; how to apply for public assistance or other benefits; or how to get an alcoholic or drug addict admitted to a rehabilitation program. Social workers may also arrange for services in consultation with clients and then follow through to assure the services are actually helpful. They may review eligibility requirements, fill out forms and applications, arrange for services, visit clients on a regular basis, and step in during emergencies.

Most social workers specialize in a clinical field such as child welfare and family services, mental health, medical social work, or school social work. Clinical social workers offer psychotherapy or counseling and a range of services in public agencies, clinics, as well as in private practice. Other social workers are employed in community organizations, administration, or research.

Social workers in child welfare or family services may counsel children and youths who have difficulty adjusting socially, advise parents on how to care for disabled children, or arrange for homemaker services during a parent's illness. If children have serious problems in school, child welfare workers may consult with parents, teachers, and counselors to identify underlying causes and develop plans for treatment. Some social workers assist single parents, arrange adoptions, and help find foster homes for neglected or abandoned children. Child welfare workers also work in residential institutions for children and adolescents.

Social workers in child or adult protective services investigate reports of abuse and neglect and intervene if necessary. They may institute legal action to remove children from homes and place them temporarily in an emergency shelter or with a foster family.

Mental health social workers provide services for people with mental or emotional problems, such as individual and group therapy, outreach, crisis intervention, social rehabilitation, and training in skills of everyday living. They may also help plan for supportive services to ease patients' return to the community. (Also see the statement on psychologists elsewhere in this book.)

Medical social workers help patients and their families cope with chronic, acute, or terminal illnesses and handle problems that may stand in the way of recovery or rehabilitation. They may organize support groups for families of patients suffering from cancer, AIDS, Alzheimer's disease, or other illnesses. They also advise family caregivers, and counsel patients and help plan for their needs after discharge by arranging for at-home services, such as meals-on-wheels to oxygen equipment. Some work on interdisciplinary teams that evaluate certain kinds of patients—geriatric or transplant patients, for example.

School social workers diagnose students' problems and arrange needed services, counsel children in trouble, and help integrate disabled students into the general school population. School social workers deal with problems such as student pregnancy, misbehavior in class, and excessive absences. They also advise teachers about how to deal with problem students.

Social workers in criminal justice make recommendations to courts, do pre-sentencing assessments, and provide services for prison inmates and their families. Probation and parole officers provide similar services to individuals on parole or sentenced by a court to probation.

Industrial or occupational social workers generally work in an employer's personnel department or health unit. Through employee assistance programs, they help workers cope with job-related pressures or personal problems that affect the quality of their work. They offer direct counseling to employees, often those whose performance is hindered by emotional or family problems or substance abuse. They also develop education programs and refer workers to specialized community programs.

Some social workers specialize in gerontological services. They run support groups for family caregivers or for the adult children of aging parents; advise elderly people or family members about the choices in such areas as housing, transportation, and long-term care; and coordinate and monitor services. Social workers should be emotionally mature, objective, and sensitive to people and their problems.

Working Conditions

Most social workers have a standard 40-hour week. However, they may work some evenings and weekends to meet with clients, attend community meetings, and handle emergencies. Some, particularly in voluntary nonprofit agencies, work part-time. They may spend most of their time in an office or residential facility, but may also travel locally to visit clients or meet with service providers. The work, while satisfying, can be emotionally draining. Understaffing and large caseloads add to the pressure in some agencies.

Employment

Social workers held about 484,000 jobs in 1992. Nearly 40 percent of the jobs were in state, county, or municipal government agencies, primarily in departments of human resources, social services, child welfare, mental health, health, housing, education, and corrections. Most in the private sector were in voluntary social service agencies, community and religious organizations, hospitals, nursing homes, or home health agencies. Although most social workers are employed in cities or suburbs, some work in rural areas.

Training, Other Qualifications, and Advancement

A bachelor's degree is the minimum requirement for most positions. Besides the bachelor's in social work (BSW), undergraduate majors in psychology, sociology, and related fields satisfy hiring requirements in some agencies, especially small community agencies. A master's degree in social work (MSW) is generally necessary for positions in health and mental health settings. Jobs in public agencies may also require an MSW. Supervisory, administrative, and staff training positions usually require at least an MSW. College and university teaching positions and most research appointments normally require a doctorate in social work.

In 1991, the Council on Social Work Education accredited 297 BSW programs and 103 MSW programs. There were 49 doctoral programs for Ph.D. in Social Work and for DSW (Doctor of Social Work). BSW programs prepare graduates for direct service positions such as caseworker or group worker.

They include courses in social work practice, social welfare policies, human behavior and the social environment, and social research methods. Accredited BSW programs require at least 400 hours of supervised field experience.

An MSW degree prepares graduates to perform assessments, manage cases, and supervise other workers. Master's degree programs usually last two years and include 900 hours of supervised field instruction or internship. Entry into an MSW program does not require a bachelor's in social work, but courses in psychology, biology, sociology, economics, political science, history, social anthropology, urban studies, and social work are recommended. Some schools offer an accelerated MSW program for those with a BSW.

Social workers may advance to supervisor, program manager, assistant director, and finally to executive director of an agency or department. Advancement generally requires an MSW, as well as experience. Other career options for social workers are teaching, research, and consulting. Some help formulate government policies by analyzing and advocating policy positions in government agencies, in research institutions, and on legislators' staffs.

Some social workers go into private practice. Most private practitioners are clinical social workers who provide psychotherapeutic counseling, usually paid through health insurance. Private practitioners must have completed an MSW and a period of supervised work experience. A network of contacts for referrals is also essential.

In 1993, all states and the District of Columbia had licensing, certification, or registration laws regarding social work practice and the use of professional titles. In addition, voluntary certification is offered by the National Association of Social Workers (NASW), which grants the titled ACSW (Academy of Certified Social Workers) or ACBSW (Academy of Certified Baccalaureate Social Workers) to those who qualify. For clinical social workers, professional credentials include listing in *the NASW Register of Clinical Social Workers* or in the *Directory of American Board of Examiners in Clinical Social Work*. These credentials are particularly important for those in private practice; some health insurance providers require them for reimbursement.

Social workers should be emotionally mature, objective, and sensitive to people and their problems. They must be able to handle responsibility, work independently, and maintain good working relationships with clients and coworkers. Volunteer or paid jobs as a social work aide offer ways of testing one's interest in this field.

Job Outlook

Employment of social workers is expected to increase faster than the average for all occupations through 2005. The number of older people, who are more likely to need social services, is growing rapidly. In addition, requirements for social workers will grow with increases in the need for and concern about services to the mentally ill, the mentally retarded, and individuals and families in crisis. Many job openings will also arise due to the need to replace social workers who leave the occupation.

Employment of social workers in hospitals is projected to grow much faster than the average for the economy as a whole

due to greater emphasis on discharge planning, which facilitates early discharge of patients by assuring that the necessary medical services and social supports are in place when individuals leave the hospital.

Employment of social workers in private social service agencies is projected to grow about as fast as the average. Although demand for their services is expected to increase rapidly, agencies will increasingly restructure services and hire more lower paid human services workers instead of social workers. Employment in government should also grow about as fast as the average in response to increasing needs for public welfare and family services.

Social worker employment in home health care services is growing, not only because hospitals are moving to release patients more quickly, but because a large and growing number of people have impairments or disabilities that make it difficult to live at home without some form of assistance.

Opportunities for social workers in private practice will expand because of the anticipated availability of funding from health insurance and public sector contracts. Also, with increasing affluence, people will be more willing to pay for professional help to deal with personal problems. The growing popularity of employee assistance programs is also expected to spur demand for private practitioners, some of whom provide social work services to corporations on a contract basis.

Employment of school social workers is expected to grow due to expanded efforts to respond to the adjustment problems of immigrants, children from single-parent families, and others in difficult situations. Moreover, continued emphasis on integrating disabled children into the general school population, a new requirement under the Education for All Handicapped Children Act, will probably lead to more jobs. The availability of state and local funding will dictate the actual increase in jobs in this setting, however.

Competition for social worker jobs is stronger in cities where training programs for social workers abound; rural areas often find it difficult to attract and retain qualified staff.

Earnings

The median earnings of social workers with MSW degrees were $30,000 in 1992, according to a membership survey of the National Association of Social Workers. For those with BSW degrees, median earnings were $20,000 according to the same survey. In hospitals, social workers who worked full-time averaged about $30,850 in 1993, according to a survey performed by the University of Texas Medical Branch. Salaries ranged from a minimum of about $25,600 to a maximum of nearly $38,700. Social workers employed by the federal government averaged $41,400 in 1993.

Related Occupations

Through direct counseling or referral to other services, social workers help people solve a range of personal problems. Workers in occupations with similar duties include the clergy, counselors, counseling psychologists, and vocational rehabilitation counselors.

Sources of Additional Information

For information about career opportunities in social work, contact:

❑ National Association of Social Workers, 750 First St. NE., Suite 700, Washington, DC 20002-4241; or

❑ National Network For Social Work Managers, Inc., 6501 North Federal Highway, Suite 5, Boca Raton, FL 33487.

An annual *Directory of Accredited BSW and MSW Programs* is available for $10 from:

❑ Council on Social Work Education, 1600 Duke St., Alexandria, VA 22314-3421.

Speech-Language Pathologists and Audiologists

Nature of the Work

Speech-language pathologists assess and treat people with speech, language, voice, and fluency disorders; audiologists assess and treat those with hearing and related disorders. Speech-language pathologists work with people who cannot make speech sounds, or cannot make them clearly; those with speech rhythm and fluency problems, such as stuttering; people with speech quality problems, such as inappropriate pitch or harsh voice; and those with problems understanding and producing language. They may also work with people who have oral motor problems that cause eating and swallowing difficulties.

Speech and language problems may result from causes such as hearing loss, brain injury or deterioration, cerebral palsy, stroke, cleft palate, voice pathology, mental retardation, or emotional problems. Speech-language pathologists use special instruments, as well as written and oral tests, to determine the nature and extent of impairment, and to record and analyze speech irregularities. For individuals with little or no speech, speech-language pathologists select alternative communication systems, including automated devices and sign language, and teach their use. They teach other patients how to make sounds, improve their voices, or increase their language skills.

Audiologists work with people who have hearing and related problems. They use audiometers and other testing devices to measure the loudness at which a person begins to hear sounds, the ability to distinguish between sounds, and the nature and extent of their hearing loss. Audiologists may coordinate these results with medical, educational, and psychological information, make a diagnosis, and determine a course of treatment. Treatment may include examining and cleaning the ear canal, the fitting of a hearing aid, auditory training, and instruction in speech or lip reading. They may recommend use of amplifiers and alerting devices. Audiologists also test noise levels in workplaces and conduct hearing protection programs.

Most speech-language pathologists and audiologists provide direct clinical services to individuals with communication disorders. In speech, language, and hearing clinics, they may independently develop and carry out a treatment program. In medical facilities, they may work with physicians, social workers, psychologists, and other therapists to develop and execute a treatment plan. Speech-language pathology and audiology personnel in schools also develop individual or group programs, counsel parents, and assist teachers with classroom activities to meet the needs of children with speech, language, or hearing disorders.

Speech-language pathologists and audiologists keep records on the initial evaluation, progress, and discharge of clients. This helps pinpoint problems, track client progress, and justify the cost of treatment when applying for reimbursement. They counsel individuals and their families about communication disorders and how to cope with the stress and misunderstanding that often accompany them. They also work with family members to recognize and change behavior patterns that impede communication and treatment, and show them communication-enhancing techniques to use at home.

Some speech-language pathologists and audiologists conduct research on how people speak and hear. Others design and develop equipment or techniques for diagnosing and treating problems. More than one-half of speech language pathologists and audiologists work in schools.

Working Conditions

Speech-language pathologists and audiologists usually work at a desk or table in clean comfortable surroundings. The job is not physically demanding, but does require attention to detail and intense concentration. The emotional needs of clients and their families may be demanding and there may be frustration when clients do not improve. Most full-time speech-language pathologists and audiologists work about 40 hours per week. Some work part time. Those who work on a contract basis may spend a substantial amount of time traveling between facilities.

Employment

Speech-language pathologists and audiologists held about 73,000 jobs in 1992. About one-half provided services in preschools, elementary and secondary schools, or colleges and universities. More than 10 percent were in hospitals. Others were in offices of physicians; offices of speech-language pathologists and audiologists; speech, language, and hearing centers; home health care agencies; and other facilities. Some were in private practice, working either as solo practitioners or in a group practice. Some experienced speech-language pathologists or audiologists contract to provide services in schools, hospitals, or nursing homes or work as consultants to industry.

Training, Other Qualifications, and Advancement

A master's degree in speech-language pathology or audiology is the standard credential in this field. Of the 43 states that regulate speech-language pathologists and/or audiologists, all require a master's degree or equivalent, 375 hours of supervised clinical experience, a passing score on a national examination and nine months of post-graduate professional experience. For licensure renewal, 23 states have continuing education requirements. Medicaid, Medicare, and private insurers generally require a license to qualify for reimbursement.

In some states, people with bachelor's degrees in speech-language pathology may work in schools with students who have communication problems. They may have to be certified by the state educational agency and may be classified as special education teachers rather than speech-language pathologists or audiologists. Recent federal legislation requires speech-language pathologists in school systems in almost every state to have a minimum of a master's degree or equivalent. All states require audiologists to hold a master's degree or equivalent.

About 230 colleges and universities offered master's programs in speech-language pathology and audiology in 1993. Courses cover anatomy and physiology of the areas involved in speech, language, and hearing; the development of normal speech, language, and hearing and the nature of disorders; acoustics; and psychological aspects of communication. Graduate students also learn to evaluate and treat speech, language, and hearing disorders and receive supervised clinical training in communication disorders.

Those with a master's degree can acquire the Certificate of Clinical Competence (CCC) offered by the American Speech-Language-Hearing Association. To earn the CCC, a person must hold a master's degree, have 375 hours of supervised clinical experience, complete a nine month post-graduate internship, and pass a national written examination.

Speech-language pathologists and audiologists should be able to effectively communicate test results, diagnoses, and proposed treatment in a manner easily understood by their clients. They also need to be able to approach problems objectively and provide support to clients and their families. Patience and compassion are important because a client's progress may be slow.

With experience, some salaried speech-language pathologists and audiologists enter private practice; others become directors or administrators of services in schools, hospitals, health departments, and clinics. Some become researchers.

Job Outlook

Employment of speech-language pathologists and audiologists is expected to increase much faster than the average for all occupations through 2005. Some job openings will also arise from the need to replace speech-language pathologists and audiologists who leave the occupation.

Employment in the health services industry will increase as a result of several factors. Because hearing loss is strongly associated with older age, rapid growth in the population aged 75 and over will cause the number of hearing-impaired people to increase markedly. In addition, baby boomers are now entering middle age, when the possibility of neurological disorders and their associated speech, language, and hearing impairments increases. Medical advances are also improving the survival rate of premature infants and trauma victims, who then need treatment.

The number of speech-language pathologists and audiologists in private practice, though small, is likely to rise sharply by 2005. Encouraging this growth is the increasing use of contract services by hospitals, schools, and nursing homes. Employment in schools will increase as elementary and secondary school enrollments grow. In 1986, federal legislation guaranteeing special education and related services to all eligible children with disabilities, while originally designed for school-age children, was extended to include children from three to five years of age. This legislation will also increase employment in day care centers, rehabilitation centers, and hospitals.

Earnings

Median annual earnings of full-time salaried speech-language pathologists and audiologists were $36,036 in 1992. The middle 50 percent earned between $27,404 and $42,120. According to a 1992 survey by the American Speech-Language-Hearing Association, the median annual salary for certified speech-language pathologists with one to three years experience was about $29,050; for certified audiologists, it was about $28,000. Speech-language pathologists with 16 years or more of experience earned a median annual salary of about $41,300, while experienced audiologists earned about $45,000. Salaries also vary according to geographic location. Speech-language pathologists and audiologists in hospitals earned a median annual salary of about $33,916, according to a 1992 survey conducted by the University of Texas Medical Branch.

Related Occupations

Speech-language pathologists and audiologists specialize in the prevention, diagnosis, and treatment of speech, language, and hearing problems. Workers in other rehabilitation occupations include occupational therapists, physical therapists, recreational therapists, and rehabilitation counselors.

Sources of Additional Information

State departments of education can supply information on certification requirements for those who wish to work in public schools. General information on speech-language pathology and audiology is available from:

❑ American Speech-Language-Hearing Association, 10801 Rockville Pike, Rockville, MD 20852.

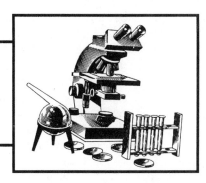

Technicians and Related Support Occupations

Dental hygienists

Nature of the Work

Dental hygienists provide preventive dental care and teach patients how to practice good oral hygiene. Hygienists examine patients' teeth and gums, recording the presence of diseases or abnormalities. They remove calculus, stain, and plaque from teeth; apply caries-preventive agents such as fluorides and pit and fissure sealants; take and develop dental x rays; place temporary fillings and periodontal dressings; remove sutures; and polish and recontour amalgam restorations. In some states, hygienists administer local anesthetics and nitrous oxide/oxygen analgesia, and place and carve filling materials.

Dental hygienists also help patients develop and maintain good oral health. For example, they may explain the relationship between diet and oral health, inform patients how to select toothbrushes, and show patients how to floss their teeth. Some hygienists develop and promote community dental health programs which may include teaching how to practice good oral hygiene.

Dental hygienists use hand and rotary instruments to clean teeth, x-ray machines to take dental pictures, syringes with needles to administer local anesthetics, and models of teeth to explain oral hygiene.

Working Conditions

Flexible scheduling is a distinctive feature of this job. Full-time, part-time, evening, and weekend work is widely available. Dentists frequently hire hygienists to work only two or three days a week, so hygienists may hold jobs in more than one dental office. Dental hygienists work in clean, well-lighted offices.

Important health safeguards include strict adherence to proper radiological procedures, compliance with recommended aseptic technique, and use of appropriate protective devices when administering nitrous oxide/oxygen analgesia. Dental hygienists also wear safety glasses, surgical masks and gloves to protect themselves from infectious diseases such as hepatitis and AIDS. The occupation is one of several covered by the Consumer-Patient Radiation Health and Safety Act of 1981, which encourages the states to adopt uniform standards for the training and certification of individuals who perform medical and dental radiological procedures.

Employment

Dental hygienists held about 108,000 jobs in 1992. Because multiple job holding is common in this field, the number of jobs greatly exceeds the number of hygienists. About half of all dental hygienists usually worked part-time—less than 35 hours a week. Almost all dental hygienists work in private dental offices. Some work in public health agencies, school systems, hospitals, and clinics.

Training, Other Qualifications, and Advancement

Dental hygienists must be licensed by the state in which they practice. To qualify for licensure, a candidate must graduate from an accredited dental hygiene school and pass both a written and a clinical examination. The American Dental Association Joint Commission on National Dental Examinations administers the written examination that is accepted by all states and the District of Columbia. State or regional testing agencies administer the clinical examination. In addition, examinations on legal aspects of dental hygiene practice are required by most states. Alabama also allows candidates to take its examination if they have been trained through a state-regulated on-the-job program in a dentist's office.

In 1993, 208 programs in dental hygiene were accredited by the Commission on Dental Accreditation. Although some programs lead to a bachelor's degree, most grant an associate degree. Five universities offer master's degree programs in dental hygiene. An associate degree is sufficient for practice in a private dental office. A bachelor's or master's degree is usually required for research, teaching, or clinical practice in public or school health programs.

About half of the dental hygiene programs prefer applicants who have completed at least one year of college. Some of the bachelor's degree programs require applicants to have completed two years. However, requirements vary from school to school. These schools offer laboratory, clinical, and classroom instruction in subjects such as anatomy, physiology, chemistry, microbiology, pharmacology, nutrition, radiography, histology (the study of tissue structure), periodontology (the study of gum diseases), pathology, dental materials, clinical dental hygiene, and social and behavioral sciences.

Dental hygienists should work well with others, particularly patients who may be under stress. Dental hygienists must have manual dexterity because they use dental instruments with little room for error within a patient's mouth. Recommended high school courses for aspiring dental hygienists include biology, chemistry, and mathematics.

Job Outlook

Employment of dental hygienists is expected to grow much faster than the average for all occupations through 2005 in response to increasing demand for dental care. Demand will be stimulated by population growth, greater retention of natural teeth by middle-aged and elderly people, and rising real incomes. Additional job openings will result from the need to replace workers who leave the occupation.

Also, dentists are likely to employ more hygienists, for several reasons. Older dentists, who are less likely to employ dental hygienists, will leave and be replaced by recent graduates, who are more likely to do so. In addition, as dentists' workloads increase, they are expected to hire more hygienists to perform preventive dental care such as cleaning, so they may use their own time more profitably.

Enrollments in dental hygiene programs have been on the rise recently after declining during the 1980s. Unless the number increases sharply, however, opportunities are expected to remain very good.

Earnings

Earnings of dental hygienists are affected by geographic location, employment setting, and education and experience. Dental hygienists who work in private dental offices may be paid on an hourly, daily, salary, or commission basis. According to the American Dental Association, dental hygienists who worked 32 hours a week or more averaged $609 a week in 1991; the average hourly earnings for all dental hygienists was $18.50.

Benefits vary substantially by practice setting, and may be contingent on full-time employment. Dental hygienists who work for school systems, public health agencies, the federal government, or state agencies usually have substantial benefits.

Related Occupations

Workers in other occupations supporting health practitioners in an office setting include dental assistants, ophthalmic medical assistants, podiatric assistants, office nurses, medical assistants, and physician assistants.

Sources of Additional Information

For information on a career in dental hygiene and the educational requirements to enter this occupation, contact:

❏ Division of Professional Development, American Dental Hygienists' Association, 444 N. Michigan Ave., Suite 3400, Chicago, IL 60611; or

❏ SELECT, American Dental Association, Department of Career Guidance, 211 E. Chicago Ave., Suite 1804, Chicago, IL 60611.

For information about accredited programs and educational requirements, contact:

❏ Commission on Dental Accreditation, American Dental Association, 211 E. Chicago Ave., Suite 1814, Chicago, IL 60611. The State Board of Dental Examiners in each state can supply information on licensing requirements.

Licensed Practical Nurses

Nature of the Work

Licensed practical nurses (L.P.N.'s), or licensed vocational nurses (L.V.N.'s) as they are called in Texas and California,

care for the sick, injured, convalescing, and handicapped, under the direction of physicians and registered nurses.

Most L.P.N.'s provide basic bedside care. They take vital signs such as temperature, blood pressure, pulse, and respiration. They also treat bedsores, prepare and give injections and enemas, apply dressings, give alcohol rubs and massages, apply ice packs and hot water bottles, and insert catheters. L.P.N.'s observe patients and report adverse reactions to medications or treatments. They may collect samples from patients for testing and perform routine laboratory tests. They help patients with bathing, dressing, and personal hygiene, feed them and record food and liquid intake and output, keep them comfortable, and care for their emotional needs. In states where the law allows, they may administer prescribed medicines or start intravenous fluids. Some L.P.N.'s help deliver, care for, and feed infants. Some experienced L.P.N.'s supervise nursing assistants and aides.

L.P.N.'s in nursing homes, in addition to providing routine bedside care, may also help evaluate residents' needs, develop care plans, and supervise nursing aides. In doctors' offices and clinics, including health maintenance organizations, they may also make appointments, keep records, and perform other clerical duties. L.P.N.'s who work in home health care may also prepare meals and teach family members simple nursing tasks.

Working Conditions

Most licensed practical nurses in hospitals and nursing homes work a 40-hour week, but because patients need round-the-clock care, some work nights, weekends, and holidays. They often stand for long periods and help patients move in bed, stand, or walk. They also face the stress of working with sick patients and their families. Hospital-based L.P.N.'s face hazards from caustic chemicals, radiation, and infectious diseases such as AIDS and hepatitis. L.P.N.'s are also subject to back injuries when moving patients and shock from electrical equipment.

L.P.N.'s employed in nursing homes often face heavy workloads. In addition, the people they take care of may be confused, irrational, agitated, or uncooperative.

In private homes, L.P.N.'s usually work 8 to 12 hours a day and go home at night. Private duty nurses can often set their own work hours.

Employment

Licensed practical nurses held about 659,000 jobs in 1992. About a quarter worked part-time. Two out of five L.P.N.'s worked in hospitals, almost one-quarter worked in nursing homes, and a tenth worked in doctors' offices and clinics. Others worked for temporary help agencies, home health care services, or government agencies.

Training, Other Qualifications, and Advancement

All states require L.P.N.'s to pass a licensing examination after completing a state-approved practical nursing program. A high school diploma is usually required for entry, but some programs accept people without a diploma. In 1991, approximately 1,200 state-approved programs provided practical nursing training. Trade, technical, or vocational schools offered almost half of these programs, while community and junior colleges provided more than a third. Some were offered in high schools, hospitals, and colleges and universities.

Most practical nursing programs last about a year and include both classroom study and supervised clinical practice (patient care). Classroom study covers basic nursing concepts and patient-care related subjects, including anatomy, physiology, medical-surgical nursing, pediatrics, obstetrics, psychiatric nursing, administration of drugs, nutrition, and first aid. Clinical practice is usually in a hospital, but sometimes includes other settings.

L.P.N.'s should have a caring, sympathetic nature. They should be emotionally stable because work with the sick and injured can be stressful. As part of a health care team, they must be able to follow orders and work under close supervision.

Job Outlook

Job prospects for L.P.N.'s are expected to be excellent, as employment grows much faster than it has in the past. Because of this growth, the number of new graduates needed will be well above the number graduated in recent years. As in most other occupations, replacement needs will be the main source of job openings. Employment of L.P.N.'s is expected to increase faster than the average for all occupations through 2005, in response to the long-term care needs of a rapidly growing population of older people and to the general growth of health care.

Nursing homes will offer the most new jobs for L.P.N.'s as the number of aged and disabled people in need of long-term care rises rapidly. In addition to caring for the aged, nursing homes may be called on to care for the increasing number of patients who have been released from the hospital and who have not yet recovered enough to return home. Very rapid growth is also expected in such residential care facilities as board and care homes, old age homes, and group homes for the mentally retarded, as well as in home health care services. Employment of L.P.N.'s in hospitals is not expected to increase much, largely because the number of inpatients, with whom most L.P.N.'s work, is not expected to increase much. Employment is projected to grow very rapidly in physicians' offices and clinics, including health maintenance organizations.

Earnings

Median annual earnings of full-time, salaried L.P.N.'s were $21,476 in 1992. The middle 50 percent earned between $18,148 and $25,948. The lowest 10 percent earned less than $15,392; the top 10 percent earned more than $31,668. According to a University of Texas Medical Branch survey of hospitals and medical centers, the median annual salary of L.P.N.'s, based on a 40 hour week and excluding shift or area differentials, was $22,360 in October 1992. The average minimum salary was $18,384 and the average maximum was $26,551. According to the Buck Survey conducted by the American Health Care Association, L.P.N.'s in chain nursing homes had median annual earnings of approximately $21,900 in January, 1993. The middle 50 percent earned between $19,800 and $24,900 a year.

Related Occupations

L.P.N.'s work closely with people while helping them. Emergency medical technicians, social service aides, human service workers, and teacher aides also perform similar work.

Sources of Additional Information

A list of state-approved training programs and information about practical nursing are available from:

❏ Communications Department, National League for Nursing, 350 Hudson St., New York, NY 10014; or

❏ National Association for Practical Nurse Education and Service, Inc., 1400 Spring St., Suite 310, Silver Spring, MD 20910.

For information about a career in practical nursing, contact:

❏ National Federation of Licensed Practical Nurses, Inc., P.O. Box 18088, Raleigh, NC 27619.

Information about employment opportunities in Department of Veterans Affairs medical centers is available from local VA medical centers and also from:

❏ Title 38 Employment Division, (054D), Department of Veterans Affairs, 810 Vermont Ave. NW., Washington, DC 20420.

For information on nursing careers in long-term care, write:

❏ American Health Care Association, 1201 L St. NW., Washington, DC 20005.

Medical Records Technicians

Nature of the Work

When you enter a hospital, you see a whirl of white coats of physicians, nurses, radiologic technologists, and others. Every time these health care personnel treat a patient, they record what they observed about and administered to the patient. This record includes information the patient provides about symptoms and medical history, and also the results of examinations, reports of X-ray and laboratory tests, and diagnoses and treatment plans. Medical records technicians organize and evaluate these records for completeness and accuracy.

When assembling a patient's medical records, technicians, who may also be called medical record technicians, first make sure that the medical chart is complete. They ensure that all forms are present and properly identified and signed, and that all necessary information is on a computer file. Sometimes, they talk to physicians or others to clarify diagnoses or get additional information.

Technicians assign a code to each diagnosis and procedure. They consult a classification manual and rely, too, on their knowledge of disease processes. Technicians may then use a software program to assign the patient to one of several hundred diagnosis-related groups, also called DRG's. The DRG determines the amount the hospital will be reimbursed if the patient is covered by Medicare or other insurance programs that use the DRG system. Technicians who specialize in coding are called medical record coders, coder/abstracters, or coding specialists.

Technicians may also tabulate and analyze data to help improve patient care, control costs, use in legal actions, or respond to surveys. Tumor registrars compile and maintain records of patients who have cancer to provide information to physicians and for research studies.

Medical records technicians' duties vary with the size of the facility. In large to medium facilities, technicians may specialize in one aspect of medical records or supervise medical record clerks and transcribers while a medical record administrator manages the department. In small facilities an accredited record technician may manage the department.

Working Conditions

Medical records technicians generally work a 40-hour week. Some overtime may be required. In hospitals where medical record departments are open 18-24 hours a day, 7 days a week, they may work day, evening, and night shifts. They work in pleasant and comfortable offices. Medical records technician is one of the few health occupations in which there is little or no contact with patients. Accuracy is essential, and this demands concentration and close attention to detail. Medical records technicians who work at video display terminals for prolonged periods may experience eyestrain and muscle pain.

Employment

Medical records technicians held about 76,000 jobs in 1992. About one half of jobs were in hospitals. Most of the remainder were in nursing homes, medical group practices, health maintenance organizations, and clinics. In addition, insurance, accounting, and law firms that deal in health matters employ medical records technicians to tabulate and analyze data from medical records. Public health departments hire technicians to supervise data collection from health care institutions and to assist in research. Some self-employed medical records technicians are consultants to nursing homes and physicians' offices.

Training, Other Qualifications, and Advancement

Medical records technicians entering the field usually have formal training in a two-year associate degree program offered at community and junior colleges. Courses include medical terminology and diseases, anatomy and physiology, legal aspects of medical records, coding and abstraction of data, statistics, databases, quality assurance methods, and computers as well as general education.

Technicians may also gain training through an Independent Study Program in Medical Record Technology offered by the American Health Information Management Association (AHIMA). Hospitals sometimes advance promising medical records clerks to jobs as medical records technicians, although this practice may be less common in the future. Advancement generally requires two to four years of job experience and completion of the hospital's in-house training program.

Most employers prefer to hire Accredited Record Technicians (ART). Accreditation is obtained by passing a written examination offered by the AHIMA. To take the examination, a person must be a graduate of a two year associate degree program accredited by the Committee on Allied Health Education and Accreditation (CAHEA) of the American Medical Association, or a graduate of the Independent Study Program in Medical Record Technology who has also obtained 30 semester hours of academic credit in prescribed areas. Technicians who have received training in nonCAHEA accredited programs or on the job are not eligible to take the examination. In 1992, CAHEA accredited 90 programs for medical records technicians.

Experienced medical records technicians generally advance in one of two ways—by specializing or managing. Many senior medical records technicians specialize in coding, particularly Medicare coding or in tumor registry. In large medical records departments, experienced technicians may become section supervisors, overseeing the work of the coding, correspondence, or discharge sections, for example. Senior technicians with ART credentials may become director or assistant director of a medical records department in a small facility. However, in larger institutions the director is a medical records administrator with a bachelor's degree in medical record administration.

Job Outlook

Hospitals will continue to employ the most technicians. Most job openings will occur because of replacement needs. The job prospects for formally trained technicians should be very good. Employment of medical records technicians is expected to grow much faster than the average for all occupations through 2005 due to rapid growth in the number of medical tests, treatments, and procedures and because medical records will be increasingly scrutinized by third party payers, courts, and consumers.

The need for detailed medical records in offices and clinics of doctors of medicine should translate into rapid growth in employment opportunities for medical records technicians in large group practices and offices of specialists. Rapid growth is also expected in health maintenance organizations, nursing homes, and home health agencies.

Earnings

According to a 1992 survey of AHIMA members, accredited records technicians who worked as coders averaged $11.30 an hour; unaccredited coders averaged $9.77 an hour; and accredited records technicians in supervisory positions averaged $29,599 a year. The average annual salary for medical records technicians in the federal government in nonsupervisory, supervisory, and managerial positions was $22,008 in 1993.

Related Occupations

Medical records technicians need a strong clinical background to analyze the contents of medical records. Other occupations that require a knowledge of medical terminology, anatomy, and physiology without directly touching the patient are medical secretaries, medical transcribers, medical writers, and medical illustrators.

Sources of Additional Information

Information on careers in medical records technology, including the Independent Study Program, is available from:

❏ American Health Information Management Association, 919 N. Michigan Ave., Suite 1400, Chicago, IL 60611.

A list of CAHEA-accredited programs for medical record technicians is available from:

❏ American Medical Association, Division of Allied Health Education and Accreditation, 515 N. State St., Chicago, IL 60610.

Paralegals

Nature of the Work

Not all legal work requires a law degree. Lawyers are often assisted in their work by paralegals—also called legal assistants—who perform many of the same tasks as lawyers, except for those tasks considered to be the practice of law. Paralegals work directly under the supervision of lawyers. Although the lawyers assume responsibility for the legal work, they often delegate many of the tasks they perform as lawyers to paralegals. Paralegals are prohibited from setting legal fees, giving legal advice, or presenting a case in court.

Paralegals generally do background work for lawyers. To help prepare cases for trial, paralegals investigate the facts of cases to make sure that all relevant information is uncovered. Paralegals may conduct legal research to identify the appropriate laws, judicial decisions, legal articles, and other materials that may be relevant to clients' cases. After organizing and analyzing all the information, paralegals may prepare written reports that attorneys use to decide how cases should be handled. Should attorneys decide to file lawsuits on behalf of clients, paralegals may help prepare the legal arguments, draft pleadings to be filed with the court, obtain affidavits, and assist the attorneys during trials. Paralegals also keep files of all documents and correspondence important to cases.

Besides litigation, paralegals may also work in areas such as bankruptcy, corporate law, criminal law, employee benefits, patent and copyright law, and real estate. They help draft documents such as contracts, mortgages, separation agreements, and trust instruments. They may help prepare tax returns and plan estates. Some paralegals coordinate the activities of the other law office employees and keep the financial records for the office.

Paralegals who work for corporations help attorneys with such matters as employee contracts, shareholder agreements, stock option plans, and employee benefit plans. They may help prepare and file annual financial reports, maintain corporate minute books and resolutions, and help secure loans for the corporation. Paralegals may also review government regulations to make sure that the corporation operates within the law.

The duties of paralegals who work in government vary depending on the type of agency that employs them. Generally, paralegals in government analyze legal material for internal use, maintain reference files, conduct research for attorneys, collect and analyze evidence for agency hearings, and prepare informative or explanatory material on the law, agency regulations, and agency policy for general use by the agency and the public.

Paralegals employed in community legal service projects help the poor, the aged, and other people in need of legal aid. They file forms, conduct research, and prepare documents. When authorized by law, they may represent clients at administrative hearings. Some paralegals, usually those in small and medium-sized law firms, have varied duties. One day the paralegal may do research on judicial decisions on improper police arrests and the next day may help prepare a mortgage contract. This requires a general knowledge of many areas of the law.

Some paralegals who work for large law firms, government agencies, and corporations, specialize in one area of the law. Some specialties are real estate, estate planning, family law, labor law, litigation, and corporate law. Even within specialties, functions are often broken down further so that paralegals may deal with one narrow area of the specialty. For example, paralegals who specialize in labor law may deal exclusively with employee benefits.

A growing number of paralegals are using computers in their work. Computer software packages are increasingly used to search legal literature stored in the computer and identify legal texts relevant to a specific subject. In litigation that involves many supporting documents, paralegals may use computers to organize and index the material. Paralegals may also use computer software packages to perform tax computations and explore the consequences of possible tax strategies for clients.

Working Conditions

Paralegals do most of their work at desks in offices and law libraries. Occasionally, they travel to gather information and perform other duties. Paralegals employed by corporations and government work a standard 40-hour week. Although most paralegals work year round, some are temporarily employed during busy times of the year then released when work diminishes. Paralegals who work for law firms sometimes work very long hours when they are under pressure to meet deadlines. Some law firms reward such loyalty with bonuses and additional time off.

Paralegals handle many routine assignments, particularly when they are inexperienced. Some find that these assignments offer little challenge and become frustrated with their duties. However, paralegals usually assume more responsible and varied tasks as they gain experience. Furthermore, as new laws and judicial interpretations emerge, paralegals are exposed to many new legal problems that make their work more interesting and challenging.

Employment

Paralegals held about 95,000 jobs in 1992. Private law firms employed the vast majority; most of the remainder worked for various levels of government. Paralegals are found in nearly every federal government agency; the Departments of Justice, Treasury, Interior, and Health and Human Services, and the General Services Administration are the largest employers. State and local governments and publicly funded legal service projects employ paralegals as well. Banks, real estate development companies, and insurance companies also employ small numbers of paralegals.

Training, Other Qualifications, and Advancement

There are several ways to enter the paralegal profession. Employers generally require formal paralegal training; several types of training programs are acceptable. However, some employers prefer to train their paralegals on the job, promoting experienced legal secretaries or hiring people with college education but no legal experience. Other entrants have experience in a technical field that is useful to law firms, such as a background in tax preparation for tax and estate practice or nursing or health administration for personal injury practice.

More than 600 formal paralegal training programs are offered by four-year colleges and universities, law schools, community and junior colleges, business schools, and proprietary schools. In 1993, 177 programs had been approved by the American Bar Association (ABA). Although this approval is neither required nor sought by many programs, graduation from an ABA-approved program can enhance one's employment opportunities. The requirements for admission to formal training programs vary widely. Some require some college courses or a bachelor's degree. Others accept high school graduates or people with legal experience. A few schools require standardized tests and personal interviews.

Most paralegal programs are completed in two years, although some take as long as four years and award a bachelor's degree on completion. Other programs take only a few months to complete, but require a bachelor's degree for admission. Programs typically include a combination of general courses on subjects such as the law and legal research techniques, and courses that cover specialized areas of the law, such as real estate, estate planning and probate, litigation, family law, contracts, and criminal law. Many employers prefer applicants with training in a specialized area of the law. Programs also increasingly include courses that introduce students to the legal applications of computers.

Many paralegal training programs include an internship in which students gain practical experience by working for several months in a law office, corporate legal department, or government agency. Experience gained in internships is an asset when seeking a job after graduation.

Depending on the program, graduates may receive a certificate, an associate degree, or, in some cases, a bachelor's degree. The quality of paralegal training programs varies; the better programs generally emphasize job placement. Prospective students should examine the experiences of recent graduates of programs in which they are considering enrolling.

Paralegals need not be certified, but the National Association of Legal Assistants has established standards for voluntary certification which require various combinations of education and experience. Paralegals who meet these standards are eligible to take a two day examination given each year at several regional testing centers by the Certifying Board of Legal Assistants of the National Association of Legal Assistants. People who pass this examination may use the designation Certified Legal Assistant (CLA). This designation is a sign of competence in the field and may enhance employment and advancement opportunities.

Paralegals must be able to handle legal problems logically and effectively communicate, both orally and in writing, their findings and opinions to their supervising attorney. They must understand legal terminology and have good research and investigative skills. Familiarity with the operation and applications of computers in legal research and litigation support is increasingly important. Paralegals must always stay abreast of new developments in the law that affect their area of practice. Because paralegals often deal with the public, they must be courteous and uphold the high ethical standards of the legal profession. A few states have established ethical guidelines that paralegals in the state must follow.

Experienced paralegals are usually given progressively more responsible duties and less supervision. In large law firms, corporate legal departments, and government agencies, experienced paralegals may supervise other paralegals and clerical staff and delegate work assigned by the attorneys. Advancement opportunities include promotion to managerial and other law-related positions within the firm or corporate legal department. However, some paralegals find it easier to move to another law firm when seeking increased responsibility or advancement.

Job Outlook

Employment of paralegals is expected to grow much faster than the average for all occupations through 2005. Job opportunities are expected to expand as more employers become aware that paralegals are able to do many legal tasks for lower salaries than lawyers. Both law firms and other employers with legal staffs should continue to emphasize hiring paralegals so that the cost, availability, and efficiency of legal services can be improved.

New jobs created by rapid employment growth will create most of the job openings for paralegals in the future. Other job openings will arise as people leave the occupation. Although the number of job openings for paralegals is expected to increase significantly through 2005, so will the number of people pursuing this career. Thus, keen competition for jobs should continue as the growing number of graduates from paralegal training programs keeps pace with employment growth. Still, job prospects are expected to be favorable for graduates of highly regarded formal programs.

Private law firms will continue to be the largest employers of paralegals as a growing population needs more legal services. The growth of prepaid legal plans should also contribute to the demand for the services of law firms. A growing array of other organizations, such as corporate legal departments, insurance companies, real estate and title insurance firms, and banks will also hire paralegals.

Job opportunities for paralegals will expand even in the public sector. Community legal service programs—which provide assistance to the poor, the aged, minorities, and middle-income families—operate on limited budgets and will employ more paralegals to keep expenses down and serve the most people. Federal, state, and local government agencies, consumer organizations, and the courts should also continue to hire paralegals in increasing numbers.

To a limited extent, paralegal jobs are affected by the business cycle. During recessions, demand declines for some discretionary legal services, such as planning estates, drafting wills, and handling real estate transactions. Corporations are less inclined to initiate litigation when falling sales and profits lead to fiscal belt tightening. As a result, full-time paralegals employed in offices adversely affected by a recession may be laid off or have their work hours reduced.

On the other hand, during recessions, corporations and individuals are more likely to face other legal problems, such as bankruptcies, foreclosures, and divorces, that require legal assistance. Furthermore, the continual emergence of new laws and judicial interpretations of existing laws creates new business for lawyers and paralegals without regard to the business cycle.

Earnings

Earnings of paralegals vary greatly. Salaries depend on the education, training, and experience the paralegal brings to the job; the type and size of employer; and the geographic location of the job. Generally, paralegals who work for large law firms or in large metropolitan areas earn more than those who work for smaller firms or in less populated regions.

Paralegals had an average annual salary of about $28,300 in 1993, according to a utilization and compensation survey by the National Association of Legal Assistants. Starting salaries of paralegals averaged $23,400, while paralegals with from 6 to 10 years of experience averaged $28,200 a year. Salaries of paralegals with 11 to 15 years of experience averaged $29,800 annually, according to the same survey. In addition to a salary, many paralegals received an annual bonus, which averaged $1,700 in 1993. Employers of the majority of paralegals provided life and health insurance benefits and contributed to a retirement plan on their behalf.

Paralegal specialists hired by the federal government in 1993 started at about $18,000 or $23,000 a year, depending on their training and experience. The average annual salary of paralegals who worked for the federal government in 1993 was about $37,600.

Related Occupations

Several other occupations also call for a specialized understanding of the law and the legal system but do not require the extensive training of a lawyer. Some of these are abstracters, claim examiners, compliance and enforcement inspectors, occupational safety and health workers, patent agents, police officers, and title examiners.

Sources of Additional Information

General information on a career as a paralegal and a list of paralegal training programs approved by the American Bar Association may be purchased for $5 from:

❑ Standing Committee on Legal Assistants, American Bar Association, 750 North Lake Shore Dr., Chicago, IL 60611.

For information on certification of paralegals, schools that offer training programs in specific states, and standards and guidelines for paralegals, contact:

❑ National Association of Legal Assistants, Inc., 1601 South Main St., Suite 300, Tulsa, OK 74119.

Information on a career as a paralegal, schools that offer training programs, and local paralegal associations can be obtained from:

❑ National Federation of Paralegal Associations, P.O. Box 33108, Kansas City, MO 64114.

Information on paralegal training programs may be obtained from:

❑ American Association for Paralegal Education, P.O. Box 40244, Overland Park, KS 66204.

Radiologic Technologists

Nature of the Work

Perhaps the most familiar use of the X ray is the diagnosis of broken bones. However, medical uses of radiation go far beyond that. Radiation is used not only to produce images of the interior of the body, but to treat cancer as well. At the same time, the use of imaging techniques that do not involve X rays, such as ultrasound and magnetic resonance scans, is growing rapidly. The term diagnostic imaging embraces these procedures as well as the familiar X ray.

Radiographers produce x-ray films (radiographs) of parts of the human body for use in diagnosing medical problems. They prepare patients for radiologic examinations by explaining the procedure, removing articles such as jewelry, through which X rays cannot pass, and positioning patients so that the correct parts of the body can be radiographed. To prevent unnecessary radiation exposure, technologists surround the exposed area with radiation protection devices, such as lead shields, or limit the size of the x-ray beam.

Radiographers position radiographic equipment at the correct angle and height over the appropriate area of a patient's body. Using instruments similar to a measuring tape, technologists may measure the thickness of the section to be radiographed and set controls on the machine to produce radiographs of the appropriate density, detail, and contrast. They place the x-ray film under the part of the patient's body to be examined and make the exposure. They then remove the film and develop it.

Experienced radiographers may perform more complex imaging tests. For fluoroscopies, radiographers prepare a solution of contrast medium for the patient to drink, allowing the radiologist, a physician who interprets X rays, to see soft tissues in the body. Some radiographers operate computed tomography scanners to produce cross-sectional views of patients and may be called CT technologists. Others operate machines using giant magnets and radiowaves rather than radiation to create an image and may be called magnetic resonance imaging (MRI) technologists.

Radiation therapy technologists, also known as radiation therapists, prepare cancer patients for treatment and administer prescribed doses of ionizing radiation to specific body parts. They operate many kinds of equipment, including high-energy linear accelerators with electron capabilities. They position patients under the equipment with absolute accuracy in order to expose affected body parts to treatment while protecting the rest of the body from radiation.

They also check the patients reactions for radiation side effects such as nausea, hair loss, and skin irritation. They give instructions and explanations to patients who are likely to be very ill and may be dying. Radiation therapists, in contrast to other radiologic technologists, are likely to see the same patient a number of times during the course of treatment.

Sonographers, also known as ultrasound technologists, induce nonionizing, high frequency sound waves into areas of the patient's body; the equipment then collects reflected echoes to form an image. The image is viewed onscreen and may be recorded on a printout strip or photographed for interpretation and diagnosis by physicians. Sonographers explain the procedure, record additional medical history, and then position the patient for testing. Viewing the screen as the scan takes place, sonographers look for subtle differences between healthy and pathological areas, and judge if the images are satisfactory for diagnostic purposes. Sonographers may specialize in neurosonography (the brain), vascular (blood flows), echocardiography (the heart), abdominal (the liver, kidneys, spleen, and pancreas), obstetrics/gynecology (the female reproductive system), and ophthalmology (the eye).

Radiologic technologists precisely follow physicians' instructions and regulations concerning use of radiation to ensure that themselves, patients, and coworkers are protected from overexposure. In addition to preparing patients and operating equipment, radiologic technologists keep patient records and adjust and maintain equipment. They may also prepare work schedules, evaluate equipment purchases, or manage a radiology department.

Working Conditions

Most full-time radiologic technologists work about 40 hours a week; they may have evening and weekend or on-call hours. Technologists are on their feet for long periods and may lift or turn disabled patients. They work at radiologic machines but may also do some procedures at patients' bedsides. Some radiologic technologists travel to patients in large vans equipped with sophisticated diagnostic equipment.

Radiation therapists are prone to emotional burnout because they regularly treat extremely ill and dying patients on a daily basis. Although potential radiation hazards exist in this occupation, they have been minimized by the use of lead aprons, gloves, and other shielding devices, as well as by instruments that measure radiation exposure. Technologists wear badges that measure radiation levels in the radiation area, and detailed records are kept on their cumulative lifetime dose.

Employment

Radiologic technologists held about 162,000 jobs in 1992. Most technologists were radiographers; some were sonographers and radiation therapists. About one radiologic technologist in every five worked part time. About three out of every five jobs are in hospitals. The rest are in physicians' offices and clinics, including diagnostic imaging centers.

Training, Other Qualifications, and Advancement

Preparation for this profession is offered in hospitals, colleges and universities, vocational-technical institutes, and the Armed Forces. Hospitals, which employ most radiologic technologists, prefer to hire those with formal training. Formal training is offered in radiography, radiation therapy, and diagnostic medical sonography (ultrasound). Programs range in length from one to four years and lead to a certificate, associate degree, or bachelor's degree. Two year programs are most prevalent.

Some one-year certificate programs are for individuals from other health occupations such as medical technologists and registered nurses who want to change fields or experienced radiographers who want to specialize in radiation therapy technology or sonography. A bachelor's or master's degree in one of the radiologic technologies is desirable for supervisory, administrative, or teaching positions.

The Committee on Allied Health Education and Accreditation (CAHEA) accredits most formal training programs for this field. CAHEA accredited 687 radiography programs, 120 radiation therapy programs, and 52 diagnostic medical sonography programs in 1992.

Radiography programs require, at a minimum, a high school diploma or the equivalent. High school courses in mathematics, physics, chemistry, and biology are helpful. The programs provide both classroom and clinical instruction in anatomy and physiology, patient care procedures, radiation physics, radiation protection, principles of imaging, medical terminology, positioning of patients, medical ethics, radiobiology, and pathology.

For training programs in radiation therapy and diagnostic medical sonography, applicants with a background in science or experience in one of the health professions are generally preferred. However, some programs consider applicants with liberal arts backgrounds as well as high school graduates with courses in math and science.

Radiographers and radiation therapists are covered by provisions of the Consumer-Patient Radiation Health and Safety Act of 1981, which aims to protect the public from the hazards of unnecessary exposure to medical and dental radiation by ensuring operators of radiologic equipment are properly trained. The act requires the federal government to set standards that the states, in turn, may use for accrediting training programs and certifying individuals who engage in medical or dental radiography. By 1992, 26 states required radiographers to be licensed, and 23 states required radiation therapists to be licensed. (Puerto Rico requires a license for the practice of either specialty.) One state, Utah, licenses diagnostic medical sonographers.

Voluntary registration is offered by the American Registry of Radiologic Technologists (ARRT) in both radiography and radiation therapy. The American Registry of Diagnostic Medical Sonographers (ARDMS) certifies the competence of sonographers. To become registered, technologists must be graduates of a CAHEA-accredited program or meet other prerequisites and have passed an examination. Many employers prefer to hire registered technologists.

With experience and additional training, staff technologists may become specialists, performing CT scanning, ultrasound, angiography, and magnetic resonance imaging. Experienced technologists may also be promoted to supervisor, chief radiologic technologist, and, ultimately, department administrator or director. Depending on the institution, courses or a master's degree in business or health administration may be necessary for the director's position. Some technologists progress by becoming instructors or directors in radiologic technology programs; others take jobs as sales representatives or instructors with equipment manufacturers.

With additional education available at major cancer centers, radiation therapy technologists can specialize as medical radiation dosimetrists. Dosimetrists work with health physicists and oncologists (physicians who specialize in the study and treatment of tumors) to develop treatment plans.

Job Outlook

Employment radiologic technologists is expected to grow much faster than the average for all occupations through 2005, as the health care industry grows, and because of the vast clinical potential of diagnostic imaging and therapeutic technology. Current as well as new uses of imaging equipment are virtually certain to sharply increase demand for radiologic technologists. Technology will continue to evolve. New generations of diagnostic imaging equipment are expected to give even better information to physicians and to be used more widely. Because ultrasound is noninvasive, it is also less risky and more comfortable for the patient than exploratory surgery.

Radiation therapy will continue to be used, alone or in combination with surgery or chemotherapy, to treat cancer. More treatment of cancer is anticipated due to the aging of the population, educational efforts aimed at early detection, and improved ability to detect malignancies through radiologic procedures such as mammography.

Although physicians are enthusiastic about the clinical benefits of new technologies, the extent to which they are adopted depends largely on cost and reimbursement considerations. Some promising new technologies may not come into widespread use because they are too expensive and third-party payers may not be willing to pay for their use. But on the whole, it appears that radiologic procedures will be used more widely.

Hospitals will remain the principal employer of radiologic technologists. However, employment is expected to grow most rapidly in offices and clinics of physicians, including diagnostic imaging centers. Health facilities such as these are expected to grow very rapidly through 2005 due to the strong shift toward outpatient care, encouraged by third-party payers and made possible by technological advances that permit more procedures to be performed outside the hospital. Some jobs will also come from the need to replace technologists who leave the occupation.

Earnings

In 1992, the median annual earnings for radiologic technologists who worked year round full time were $28,236. The middle 50 percent earned between $22,932 and $33,748 a week; 10 percent earned less than $19,708 a week; and 10 percent earned more than $40,456. According to a University of Texas Medical Branch national survey of hospitals and medical centers, the median annual salary for radiation technologists, based on a 40-hour week and excluding shift or area differentials, was $25,615 in October 1992. The average minimum salary was $22,250 and the average maximum was $32,553. For radiation therapy technologists, the median was $34,278 and for ultrasound technologists, $32,219.

Related Occupations

Radiologic technologists operate sophisticated equipment to help physicians, dentists, and other health practitioners diagnose and treat patients. Workers in related occupations include nuclear medicine technologists, cardiovascular technologists and technicians, perfusionists, respiratory therapists, clinical laboratory technologists, and electroencephalographic technologists.

Sources of Additional Information

For career information, enclose a stamped, self-addressed envelope with your request to:

❏ American Society of Radiologic Technologists, 15000 Central Ave. SE., Albuquerque, NM 87123-3917;

❏ Society of Diagnostic Medical Sonographers, 12770 Coit Rd., Suite 508, Dallas, TX 75251; or

❏ American Health Care Radiology Administrators, 111 Boston Post Rd., Suite 215, P.O. Box 334, Sudbury, MA 01776.

For the current list of accredited education programs in radiography, radiation therapy technology, or diagnostic medical sonography, write to:

❏ Division of Allied Health Education and Accreditation, American Medical Association, 515 N. State St., Chicago, IL 60610.

For information on certification in radiologic technology, contact:

❏ American Registry of Radiologic Technologists, 1255 Northland Dr., Mendota Heights, MN 55120.

For information on certification in sonography, contact:

❏ American Registry of Diagnostic Medical Sonographers, 2368 Victory Pky., Suite 510, Cincinnati, OH 45206.

Surgical Technologists

Nature of the Work

Surgical technologists, also called operating room technicians, assist in operations under the supervision of surgeons or registered nurses. Before an operation, surgical technologists help set up the operating room with surgical instruments, equipment, sterile linens, and fluids such as saline (a salt solution) or glucose (a sugar solution). They assemble, adjust, and check nonsterile equipment to ensure that it is in working order.

Technologists also prepare patients for surgery by washing, shaving, and disinfecting incision sites. They transport patients to the operating room, help position them on the operating table, and cover them with sterile surgical drapes. Technologists also observe patients' vital signs, check charts, and help the surgical team scrub and put on gloves, gowns, and masks.

During surgery, technologists pass instruments and other sterile supplies to surgeons and surgeon assistants. They may hold retractors, cut sutures, and help count sponges, needles, supplies, and instruments. Surgical technologists help prepare, care for, and dispose of specimens taken for laboratory analysis and may help apply dressings. They may operate sterilizers, lights, or suction machines, and help operate diagnostic equipment. Technologists may also maintain specified supplies of fluids such as plasma and blood. After an operation, surgical technologists may help transfer patients to the recovery room and clean and restock the operating room.

Working Conditions

Surgical technologists work in clean, well-lighted, cool environments. They must stand for long periods of time and remain alert during operations. Most surgical technologists work a regular 40-hour week, although they may be on call during weekends and evenings on a rotating basis.

Employment

Surgical technologists held about 44,000 jobs in 1992. Most surgical technologists are employed by hospitals. Others are employed in clinics and surgicenters, and in the offices of physicians and dentists who perform outpatient surgery. A few, known as private scrubs, are employed directly by surgeons who have special surgical teams like those for liver transplants.

Training, Other Qualifications, and Advancement

Surgical technologists receive their training in formal programs offered by community and junior colleges, vocational schools, universities, hospitals, and the military. In 1993, the Committee on Allied Health Education and Accreditation (CAHEA) of the American Medical Association recognized 130 accredited programs. High school graduation is normally required for admission. Programs last 9 to 24 months and lead to a certificate, diploma, or associate degree.

Programs provide classroom education and supervised clinical experience. Required study includes anatomy, physiology, microbiology, pharmacology, and medical terminology. Other studies cover care and safety of patients during surgery, aseptic techniques, and surgical procedures. Students also learn to sterilize instruments; prevent and control infection; and handle special drugs, solutions, supplies, and equipment.

Technologists may obtain voluntary professional certification from the Liaison Council on Certification for the Surgical Technologist by graduating from a formal program and passing a national certification examination. Continuing education or reexamination is required to maintain certification, which must be renewed every six years. Some employers prefer to hire certified technologists.

Surgical technologists need manual dexterity to handle instruments quickly. They must also be conscientious, orderly, and emotionally stable to handle the demands of surgeons. Technologists must respond quickly and know procedures well so that they can have instruments ready for surgeons without having to be told. They are expected to keep abreast of new developments in the field. Recommended high school courses include health, biology, chemistry, and mathematics.

Technologists may advance by specializing in a particular area of surgery, such as neurosurgery or open heart surgery. They may also work as circulating technologists. A circulating technologist is the unsterile member of the surgical team who prepares patients; helps with anesthesia; gets, opens, and holds packages for the sterile people during the procedure; interviews the patient before surgery; keeps a written account of the surgical procedure; and answers the surgeon's questions about the patient during the surgery. With additional training, some technologists advance to first assistants, who help with retracting, sponging, suturing, cauterizing bleeders, and closing and treating wounds. Surgical technologists may manage central supply departments in hospitals, or take positions with insurance companies, sterile supply services, and operating equipment firms.

Job Outlook

Employment of surgical technologists is expected to grow much faster than the average for all occupations through 2005, as the volume of surgery increases and operating room staffing patterns change. The number of surgical procedures is expected to rise as the population grows and ages. Older people require more surgical procedures. Technological advances, such as fiber optics and laser technology, will also permit new surgical procedures.

Some employers may seek to substitute surgical technologists for operating room nurses to reduce costs. However, because some facilities and states limit the work that surgical technologists can do, widespread displacement of operating room nurses is not likely to occur. Hospitals will continue to be the primary employer of surgical technologists. Nonetheless, the shift to outpatient or ambulatory surgery will create faster growth for technologists in offices and clinics of physicians, including surgicenters.

Earnings

According to a University of Texas Medical Branch survey of hospitals and medical centers, the median annual salary of surgical technologists, based on a 40-hour week and excluding shift or area differentials, was $21,741 in October 1992. The average minimum salary was $18,087 and the average maximum was $26,480.

Related Occupations

Other health occupations requiring approximately one year of training after high school are licensed practical nurses, respiratory therapy technicians, medical laboratory assistants, medical assistants, dental assistants, optometric assistants, and physical therapy aides.

Sources of Additional Information

For additional information on a career as a surgical technologist and a list of CAHEA-accredited programs, contact:

❏ Association of Surgical Technologists, 7108-C S. Alton Way, Englewood, CO 80112.

For information on certification, contact:

❏ Liaison Council on Certification for the Surgical Technologist, 7108-C S. Alton Way, Englewood, CO 80112.

Marketing and Sales Occupations

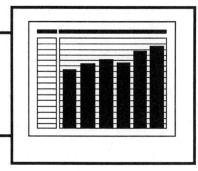

Real Estate Agents, Brokers, and Appraisers

Nature of the Work

The purchase or sale of a home, or an investment property, is not only one of the most important financial events in peoples' lives, but one of the most complex transactions as well. As a result, people generally seek the help of real estate agents, brokers, and appraisers when buying or selling real estate.

Real estate agents and brokers have a thorough knowledge of the housing market in their community. They know which neighborhoods will best fit their clients' needs and budgets. They are familiar with local zoning and tax laws, and know where to obtain financing. Agents and brokers also act as a medium for price negotiations between buyer and seller.

Brokers are independent business people who, for a fee, sell real estate owned by others and rent and manage properties. In closing sales, brokers often provide buyers with information on loans to finance their purchase. They also arrange for title searches and for meetings between buyers and sellers when details of the transactions are agreed upon and the new owners take possession. A broker's knowledge, resourcefulness, and creativity in arranging financing that is most favorable to the prospective buyer often mean the difference between success and failure in closing a sale. In some cases, agents assume the responsibilities in closing sales, but, in many areas, this is done by lawyers or lenders. Brokers also manage their own offices, advertise properties, and handle other business matters. Some combine other types of work, such as the sale of insurance or the practice of law, with their real estate business.

Real estate agents generally are independent sales workers who provide their services to a licensed broker on a contract basis. In return, the broker pays the agent a portion of the commission earned from property sold through the firm by the agent. Today, relatively few agents receive salaries as employees of a broker or realty firm. Instead, most derive their income solely from commissions.

Before showing properties to potential buyers, the broker or agent has an initial meeting with them to get a feeling for the type of home they would like and can afford. Then, they take them to see a number of homes that are likely to meet their needs and income. Because buying real estate is such an important part of the average person's life, agents may have to meet several times with a prospective buyer to discuss properties. In answering questions, agents emphasize those selling points that are likely to be most important to the buyer.

To a young family looking at a house, for example, they may point out the convenient floor plan and the fact that quality schools and shopping centers are close by. To a potential investor seeking the tax advantages of owning a rental property, they may point out the proximity to the city and the ease of finding a renter. If bargaining over price becomes necessary, agents must carefully follow the seller's instructions and may have to present counteroffers in order to get the best possible price.

Once the contract has been signed by both parties, the real estate broker or agent must see to it that all special terms of the contract are met before the closing date. For example, if the seller has agreed to a home inspection or a termite and radon inspection, the agent must make sure that this is done. Also, if the seller has agreed to any repairs, the broker or agent must see to it that they have been made, otherwise the sale cannot be completed. Increasingly, brokers and agents must handle environmental problems or make sure the property they are selling meets environmental regulations. For example, they may be responsible for dealing with problems such as lead paint on the walls. While many other details are handled by loan officers, attorneys, or other persons, the agent must check to make sure that they are completed.

There is more to agents' and brokers' jobs, however, than just making a sale. Because they must have properties to sell, they spend a significant amount of time obtaining "listings" (owner agreements to place properties for sale with the firm). They spend much time on the telephone exploring leads gathered from various sources, including personal contacts. When listing property for sale, agents and brokers make comparisons with similar properties that have been sold recently to determine its fair market value.

Most real estate agents and brokers sell residential property. A few, usually in large firms or specialized small firms, sell commercial, industrial, agricultural, or other types of real estate. Each specialty requires knowledge of that particular type of property and clientele. Selling or leasing business property, for example, requires an understanding of leasing practices, business trends, and location needs. Agents who sell or lease industrial properties must know about transportation, utilities, and labor supply. To sell residential properties, the agent must know the location of schools, religious institutions, shopping facilities, and public transportation, and be familiar with tax rates and insurance coverage. Agents and brokers increasingly use computers to generate lists of properties for sale, their location and description, and to identify available sources of financing.

Real estate transactions involve substantial financial commitments, so parties to the transactions usually seek the advice of real estate appraisers, objective experts who do not have a vested interest in the property. An appraisal is an unbiased estimate of the quality, value, and best use of a specific property. Appraisals may be used by prospective sellers to set a competitive price, by a lending institution to estimate the market value of a property as a condition for a mortgage loan, or by local governments to determine the assessed value of a property for tax purposes. Many real estate appraisers are independent fee appraisers or work for real estate appraisal firms while others are employees of banks, savings and loan associations, mortgage companies, and multi service real estate companies.

During an inspection, real estate appraisers evaluate the quality of the construction, the overall condition of the property, and its functional design. They gather information on properties by taking measurements, interviewing persons familiar with the properties history, and searching public records of sales, leases, assessments, and other transactions. They then estimate the present cost of reproducing any structures on the properties and how much the value of structures may have depreciated over time. Taking into consideration the location of the properties, current market conditions, and real estate trends or impending changes that could influence the future value of the properties, appraisers arrive at estimates of their value. Depending on the purpose of the appraisal, they may estimate the market value of the property, the insurable value, the investment value, or other kinds of value. Appraisers must prepare formal written reports of their findings that meet the standards of the Appraisal Foundation.

Real estate appraisers often specialize in certain types of properties. Most appraise only homes, but others specialize in appraising apartment or office buildings, shopping centers, or a variety of other types of commercial, industrial, or agricultural properties.

Working Conditions

Although real estate agents, brokers, and appraisers generally work in offices, much of their time is spent outside the office-showing properties to customers, analyzing properties for sale, meeting with prospective clients, researching the state of the market, inspecting properties for appraisal, and performing a wide range of other duties. Brokers provide office space, but agents generally furnish their own automobiles.

Agents, brokers, and appraisers often work more than a standard 40-hour week; 4 of every 10 worked 50 hours or more a week in 1992. They often work evenings and weekends to suit the convenience of their clients.

Employment

Real estate agents, brokers, and appraisers held about 397,000 jobs in 1992. Many worked part time, combining their real estate activities with other careers. Most were self-employed, working on a commission basis.

Most real estate and appraisal firms are relatively small; indeed, some are a one-person business. Some large real estate firms have several hundred real estate agents operating out of many branch offices. Many brokers have franchise agreements with national or regional real estate organizations. Under this type of arrangement, similar to many fast-food restaurant operations, the broker pays a fee in exchange for the privilege of using the more widely known name of the parent organization. Although franchised brokers often receive help in training salespeople and in running their offices, they bear the ultimate responsibility for the success or failure of the firm.

Real estate is sold and appraised in all areas, but employment is concentrated in large urban areas and in smaller but rapidly growing communities.

Training, Other Qualifications, and Advancement

Real estate agents and brokers must be licensed in every State and in the District of Columbia. All States require prospective agents to be a high school graduate, be at least 18 years old, and pass a written test. The examination-more comprehensive for brokers than for agents-includes questions on basic real estate transactions and on laws affecting the sale of property. Most States require candidates for the general sales license to complete at least 30 hours of classroom instruction and those seeking the broker's license to complete 90 hours of formal training in addition to a specified amount of experience in selling real estate (generally 1 to 3 years). Some States waive the experience requirements for the broker's license for applicants who have a bachelor's degree in real estate. A small but increasing number of States require that agents have 60 hours of college credit-roughly the equivalent of an associate degree. State licenses generally must be renewed every year or two, usually without reexamination. Many States, however, require continuing education for license renewal.

Federal law requires appraisers of most types of real estate (all property being financed by a Federally regulated lender) to be State certified. In some States, appraisers who are not involved with Federally regulated institutions do not have to be certified. State certification requirements for appraisers must meet Federal standards, but States are free to set more stringent requirements. Formal courses, appraisal experience, and a satisfactory score on an examination are needed to be certified, but college education may be substituted for a portion of the experience requirement. Requirements for licensure vary by State but are somewhat less stringent than for certification.

Individuals enter real estate appraisal from a variety of backgrounds. Traditionally, persons enter from real estate sales, management, and finance positions. However, a growing number of people are entering appraiser jobs directly from college. College courses in real estate, finance and business administration, economics, and English are helpful. Many junior and community colleges offer two-year degrees in real estate or appraisal. Trainee appraisers usually assist experienced appraisers until they become licensed.

Persons who take real estate agent, broker, and appraiser positions are older, on average, than entrants to most other occupations. Many homemakers and retired persons are attracted to real estate sales by the flexible and part-time work schedules characteristic of this field and may enter, leave, and later reenter the occupation, depending on the strength of the real estate market, family responsibilities, or other personal circumstances.

In addition to those who are entering or reentering the labor force, some transfer into real estate jobs from a wide range of occupations, including clerical and other sales jobs.

As real estate transactions have become more complex, involving complicated legal requirements, many firms have turned to college graduates to fill positions. A large number of agents, brokers, and appraisers have some college training, and the number of college graduates selling real estate has risen substantially in recent years. However, personality traits are fully as important as academic background. Brokers look for applicants who possess a pleasant personality, honesty, and a neat appearance. Maturity, tact, and enthusiasm for the job are required in order to motivate prospective customers in this keenly competitive field. Agents also should be well organized and detail oriented as well as have a good memory for names and faces and business details, such as taxes, zoning regulations, and local land-use laws.

People interested in beginning jobs as real estate agents often apply in their own communities, where their knowledge of local neighborhoods is an advantage. The beginner usually learns the practical aspects of the job, including the use of computers to locate or list available properties or identify sources of financing, under the direction of an experienced agent.

Many firms offer formal training programs for both beginners and experienced agents. Larger firms generally offer more extensive programs than smaller firms. Over 1,000 universities, colleges, and junior colleges offer courses in real estate. At some, a student can earn an associate or bachelor's degree with a major in real estate; several offer advanced degrees. Many local real estate boards that are members of the National Association of Realtors sponsor courses covering the fundamentals and legal aspects of the field. Advanced courses in appraisal, mortgage financing, property development and management, and other subjects also are available through various National Association of Realtor affiliates.

Many real estate appraisers voluntarily earn professional designations that represent formal recognition of their professional competence and achievements. A number of appraiser organizations have programs that, through a combination of experience, professional education, and examinations, lead to the award of such designations. These professional designations are desirable because requirements for them are more stringent than State standards. Among the more common are various designations awarded by the Appraisal Institute and the American Society of Appraisers.

Advancement opportunities for agents often take the form of higher commission rates and more and bigger sales, both of which increase compensation. This occurs as agents gain knowledge and expertise and become more efficient in closing a greater number of transactions. Experienced agents can advance in many large firms to sales or general manager. Persons who have received their broker's license may open their own offices. Others with experience and training in estimating property value may become real estate appraisers, and people familiar with operating and maintaining rental properties may become property or real estate managers. Agents, brokers, and appraisers who gain general experience in real estate and a thorough knowledge of business conditions and property values in their localities may enter mortgage financing or real estate investment counseling.

Job Outlook

Employment of real estate agents, brokers, and appraisers is expected to grow about as fast as the average for all occupations through the year 2005 as a result of the growing volume of sales of residential and commercial properties. Despite this rising demand, however, the large majority of job openings will be due to replacement needs. Each year, tens of thousands of jobs will become available as workers transfer to other occupations or leave the labor force. Because turnover is high, real estate sales positions should continue to be relatively easy to obtain. Not everyone is successful in this highly competitive field; many beginners become discouraged by their inability to get listings and to close a sufficient number of sales. Lacking financial sustenance and motivation, they subsequently leave the occupation. Well-trained, ambitious people who enjoy selling should have the best chance for success.

Employment growth in this field will stem primarily from increased demand for home purchases and rental units. Shifts in the age distribution of the population over the next decade Or so will result in a large number of persons in the prime working ages (25-54 years old) with careers and family responsibilities. This is the most geographically mobile group in our society and the one that traditionally makes most of the home purchases. As their incomes rise, they also may be expected to invest in additional real estate.

Increasing use of technology and electronic information may increase the productivity of realtors and brokers. More and more real estate companies are equipped with computers, faxes, modems, and databases. Some real estate companies are even using computer generated images to show houses to customers without even leaving the office. These devices enable one realtor to serve a greater number of customers. Use of this technology may eliminate some of the more marginal realtors such as those practicing real estate part time or between jobs. These workers will not be able to compete as easily with full-time realtors who have invested in this technology.

Employment of real estate agents, brokers, and appraisers is sensitive to swings in the economy. During periods of declining economic activity and tight credit, the volume of sales and the resulting demand for sales workers may decline. During these periods, the earnings of agents, brokers, and appraisers decline, and many work fewer hours or leave the occupation.

Earnings

Commissions on sales are the main source of earnings of real estate agents and brokers-few receive a salary. The rate of commission varies according to the type of property and its value; the percentage paid on the sale of farm and commercial properties or unimproved land usually is higher than that paid for selling a home.

Commissions may be divided among several agents and brokers. The broker and the agent in the firm that obtained the listing generally share their part of the commission when the property is sold; the broker and the agent in the firm that made the sale also generally share their part of the commission. Although an agent's share varies greatly from one firm to another, often it is about half of the total amount received by the firm. The agent who both lists and sells the property maximizes his or her commission.

Real estate agents, brokers, and appraisers who usually worked full time had median weekly earnings of $507 in 1992. The middle 50 percent earned between $323 and $802. The top 10 percent earned more than $1,247 and the lowest 10 percent earned less than $223.

Income usually increases as an agent gains experience, but individual ability, economic conditions, and the type and location of the property also affect earnings. Sales workers who are active in community organizations and local real estate boards can broaden their contacts and increase their earnings. A beginner's earnings often are irregular because a few weeks or even months may go by without a sale. Although some brokers allow an agent a drawing account against future earnings, this practice is not usual with new employees. The beginner, therefore, should have enough money to live on for about six months or until commissions increase.

Related Occupations

Selling expensive items such as homes requires maturity, tact, and a sense of responsibility. Other sales workers who find these character traits important in their work include automotive sales workers, securities and financial services sales workers, insurance agents and brokers, yacht brokers, travel agents, and manufacturers' representatives. Other appraisers specialize in performing many types of appraisals besides real estate, including aircraft, antiques and fine arts, business valuations, and yachts.

Sources of Additional Information

Details on licensing requirements for real estate agents, brokers, and appraisers are available from most local real estate and appraiser organizations or from the State real estate commission or board.

For more information about opportunities in real estate work, contact:

❏ National Association of Realtors, 777 14th St. NW, Washington, DC 20005.

Information on careers and licensing and certification requirements in real estate appraising is available from:

❏ Appraisal Institute, 875 North Michigan Ave., Suite 2400, Chicago, IL 60611-1980.

❏ American Society of Appraisers, P.O. Box 17265, Washington, DC 20041. (This organization may be called toll free at 1-800-ASA-VALU.)

Retail Sales Workers

Nature of the Work

Millions of dollars are spent each day on all types of merchandise—everything from sweaters and cosmetics to lumber and plumbing supplies. Sales workers are employed by many types of retailers to assist customers in the selection and purchase of these items. Whether selling shoes, computer equipment, or automobiles, a sales worker's primary job is to interest customers in the merchandise.

This may be done by describing the product's features, demonstrating its use, or showing various models and colors. For some jobs, particularly those selling expensive and complex items, special knowledge or skills are needed. For example, workers who sell personal computers must be able to explain to customers the features of various brands and models, the meaning of manufacturers' specifications, and the types of software that are available.

In addition to selling, most retail sales workers make out sales checks; receive cash, check, and charge payments; bag or package purchases; and give change and receipts. Depending on the hours they work, they may have to open or close the cash register. This may include counting the money in the cash register; separating charge slips, coupons, and exchange vouchers; and making deposits at the cash office. Sales workers are often held responsible for the contents of their register, and repeated shortages are cause for dismissal in many organizations.

Sales workers also handle returns and exchanges of merchandise, perform gift wrapping services, and keep their work areas neat. In addition, they may help stock shelves or racks, arrange for mailing or delivery of a purchase, mark price tags, take inventory, and prepare displays.

Sales workers must be aware of not only the promotions their store is sponsoring, but also those that are being sponsored by competitors. Also, they often must recognize possible security risks and know how to handle such situations.

Consumers often form their impressions of a store by its sales force. The retail industry is very competitive and, increasingly, employers are stressing the importance of providing courteous and efficient service. When a customer wants an item that is not on the sales floor, for example, the sales worker may check the stockroom and, if there are none there, place a special order or call another store to locate the item.

To provide better customer service, some firms employ personal shoppers. Some personal shoppers assist consumers in purchasing a particular item. For example, personal shoppers employed in department stores can assist customers in updating their wardrobes. Others actually choose the item for the client based on information provided. Those personal shoppers who work in food stores may buy groceries and arrange for their delivery for people confined to their homes.

Although most sales workers have many duties and responsibilities, in jobs selling standardized articles such as food, hardware, linens, and housewares, they often do little more than take payments and wrap purchases.

Working Conditions

Most sales workers in retail trade work in clean, comfortable, well-lighted stores. They often stand for long periods and may need supervisory approval when they want to leave the sales floor. The Monday through Friday, 9 to 5 work week is the exception rather than the rule in retail trade. Most salespersons can expect to work during some evening and weekend hours and longer than normal hours may be scheduled during Christmas and other peak periods. In addition, most retailers restrict the use of vacation time from Thanksgiving until early January.

This job can be rewarding for those who enjoy working with people. Patience is required, however, when the work is repetitive and the customers demanding.

Employment

Retail sales workers held about 4,086,000 jobs in 1992. They worked in stores ranging from small specialty shops employing several workers to the giant department store with hundreds of salespersons. In addition, some were self- employed representatives of direct sales companies and mail-order houses. The largest employers of retail sales workers, however, are department stores, apparel and accessories stores, grocery stores, and car dealers.

This occupation offers many opportunities for part-time work and is especially appealing to students, retirees and others looking to supplement their income. However, most of those selling "big ticket" items, such as cars, furniture, and electronic equipment, work full time and have substantial experience.

Because retail stores are found in every city and town, employment is distributed geographically in much the same way as the population.

Training, Other Qualifications, and Advancement

There usually are no formal education requirements for this type of work. Employers look for persons who enjoy working with people and have the tact and patience to deal with difficult customers. Among other desirable characteristics are an interest in sales work, a neat appearance, and the ability to communicate clearly and effectively. Before hiring, some employers may conduct a background check, especially for jobs in selling high-priced items.

In most small stores, an experienced employee or the proprietor instructs newly hired sales personnel in making out sales checks and operating the cash register. In larger stores, training programs are more formal and usually are conducted over several days. Topics usually discussed are customer service, security, the store's policies and procedures, and how to work the cash register. Depending on the type of product they are selling, they may be given additional specialized training. For example, those working in cosmetics receive instruction on the types of products available and for whom they would be most beneficial. This training is often provided by a manufacturer's representative.

As salespersons gain experience and seniority, they usually move to positions of greater responsibility and are given their choice of departments. This often means moving to areas with potentially higher earnings and commissions. The highest earnings potential is usually found in selling big-ticket items. This work often requires the most knowledge of the product and the greatest talent for persuasion.

Traditionally, capable sales workers without a college degree could advance to management positions, but today, large retail businesses generally prefer to hire college graduates as management trainees, making a college education increasingly important. Despite this trend, capable employees without a college degree should still be able to advance to administrative or supervisory work in large stores.

Opportunities for advancement vary in small stores. In some establishments, advancement opportunities are limited because one person, often the owner, does most of the managerial work. In others, however, some sales workers are promoted to assistant managers.

Retail selling experience may be an asset when applying for sales positions with larger retailers or in other industries, such as financial services, wholesale trade, or manufacturing.

Job Outlook

Employment of retail sales workers is expected to increase about as fast as the average for all workers through the year 2005 due to anticipated growth in retail sales. In addition, numerous job openings will be created as sales workers transfer to other occupations or leave the labor force. As in the past, replacement needs will generate an exceptionally large number of sales jobs because the occupation is large and turnover is much higher than average. There will continue to be many opportunities for part-time workers, and demand will be strong for temporary workers during peak selling periods such as the Christmas season.

During recessions, sales volume and the resulting demand for sales workers generally decline. Purchases of costly items such as cars, appliances, and furniture tend to be postponed during difficult economic times. In areas of high unemployment, sales of all types of goods may decline. However, since turnover of sales workers is usually very high, employers often can control employment simply by not replacing all those who leave.

In some geographic areas, employers face a shortage of qualified applicants. As a result, employers can be expected to improve efforts to attract and retain workers by offering higher wages, more generous benefits, and more flexible schedules.

Earnings

The starting wage for many part-time retail sales positions is the Federal minimum wage, $4.25 an hour. In some areas where employers are having difficulty attracting and retaining workers, wages are much higher than the established minimum. The following tabulation shows median weekly earnings by class of sales worker in several industries.

Motor vehicle and boats	$479
Radio, television, hi-fi, and appliances	415
Furniture and home furnishings	354
Hardware and building supplies	323
Parts	319
Other commodities	269
Apparel	255

Compensation systems vary by type of establishment and merchandise sold. Some sales workers receive an hourly wage. Others receive a commission or a combination of wages and commissions. Under a commission system, salespersons receive a percentage of the sales that they make. These systems offer sales workers the opportunity to increase significantly their earnings, but they may find their earnings depend on their ability to sell their product and the ups and downs in the economy.

Benefits may be limited in smaller stores, but in large establishments they are usually comparable to those offered by other employers. In addition, nearly all sales workers are able to buy their store's merchandise at a discount, often from 10 to 40 percent below regular prices. In some cases, this privilege is extended to the employee's family as well.

Related Occupations

Sales workers use sales techniques coupled with their knowledge of merchandise to assist customers and encourage purchases. These skills are used by people in a number of other occupations, including manufacturers' and wholesale trade sales workers, service sales representatives, counter and rental clerks, real estate sales agents, wholesale and retail buyers, insurance sales workers, and cashiers.

Sources of Additional Information

Information on careers in retail sales may be obtained from the personnel offices of local stores; from State merchants' associations; or from local unions of the United Food and Commercial Workers International Union.

In addition, general information about retailing is available from:

❏ National Retail Federation, 701 Pennsylvania Ave. NW., Washington, DC 20004-2608.

Travel Agents

Nature of the Work

Constantly changing air fares and schedules, a proliferation of vacation packages, and business/pleasure trip combinations make travel planning frustrating and time consuming. Many travelers, therefore, turn to travel agents, who can make the best possible travel arrangements for them.

Depending on the needs of the client, travel agents give advice on destinations, make arrangements for transportation, hotel accommodations, car rentals, tours, and recreation, or plan the right vacation package or business/pleasure trip combination. They may also advise on weather conditions, restaurants, and tourist attractions and recreation. For international travel, agents also provide information on customs regulations, required papers (passports, visas, and certificates of vaccination), and currency exchange rates. Travel agents may also plan conventions and other meetings; they are usually referred to as meeting planners.

Travel agents consult a variety of published and computer-based sources for information on departure and arrival times, fares, and hotel ratings and accommodations. They often base recommendations on their own travel experiences or those of colleagues or clients. Travel agents may visit hotels, resorts, and restaurants to judge, firsthand, their comfort, cleanliness, and quality of food and service.

Travel agents also promote their services. They present slides or movies to social and special interest groups, arrange advertising displays, and suggest company-sponsored trips to business managers.

Working Conditions

Travel agents spend most of their time behind a desk conferring with clients, completing paperwork, contacting airlines and hotels for travel arrangements, and promoting group tours. They may be under a great deal of pressure during vacation seasons. Many agents, especially those who are self-employed, frequently work long hours.

Employment

Travel agents held about 115,000 jobs in 1992 and are found in every part of the country. More than 9 out of 10 salaries agents worked for travel agencies; some worked for membership organizations. Many travel agents are self-employed. Nearly one-half of the travel agencies are in suburban areas; about 40 percent are in large cities; and the rest, in small towns and rural areas.

Training, Other Qualifications, and Advancement

Formal or specialized training is becoming increasingly important for travel agents since few agencies are willing to train people on the job. Many vocational schools offer 3- to 12-week full-time programs, as well as evening and Saturday programs. Travel courses are also offered in public adult education programs and in community and four-year colleges. A few colleges offer a bachelor's and a master's degree in travel and tourism. Although few college courses relate directly to the travel industry, a college education is sometimes desired by employers. Courses in computer science, geography, foreign languages, and history are most useful. Courses in accounting and business management also are important, especially for those who expect to manage or start their own travel agencies. Several home-study courses provide a basic understanding of the travel industry. The American Society of Travel Agents (ASTA) and the Institute of Certified Travel Agents offer a travel correspondence course. Travel agencies also provide on-the-job training for their employees a significant part of which consists of computer instruction. These computer skills are required by employers to operate airline reservation systems.

Travel experience is an asset since personal knowledge about a city or foreign country often helps to influence clients travel plans. Experience as an airline reservation agent also is a good background for a travel agent. Travel agents need good selling skills—they must be pleasant and patient and able to gain the confidence of clients.

Some employees start as reservation clerks or receptionists in travel agencies. With experience and some formal training, they can take on greater responsibilities and eventually assume travel agent duties. In agencies with many offices, travel agents may advance to office manager or to other managerial positions.

Experienced travel agents can take an advanced course, leading to the designation of Certified Travel Counselor, offered by the Institute of Certified Travel Agents. The institute awards a certificate to those completing an 18- month part-time course. It also offers certification, called designation of competence, in North American, Western European, Caribbean, or South Pacific tours. Those who plan meetings also may be designated as Certified Meeting Professional (CMP). The CMP exam is administered by the Convention Liaison Council. To qualify to take the exam, a candidate must be employed in a meeting management position and have at least three years of meeting planning experience.

Those who start their own agencies generally have experience in an established agency. They must generally gain formal supplier or corporation approval before they can receive commissions. Suppliers or corporations are organizations of airlines, ship lines, or rail lines. The Airlines Reporting Corporation, for example, is the approving body for airlines. To gain approval, an agency must be in operation, be financially sound, and employ at least one experienced manager/travel agent.

There are no Federal licensing requirements for travel agents. However, Rhode Island requires licensing, and Ohio, Hawaii, and California require registration. In California, travel agents not approved by a corporation are required to have a license.

Job Outlook

Employment of travel agents is expected to grow much faster than the average for all occupations through the year 2005. Many job openings will arise as new agencies open and existing agencies expand, but most will occur as experienced agents transfer to other occupations or leave the labor force.

Spending on travel is expected to increase significantly through the year 2005. As business activity expands, so will business-related travel. Employment of managerial, professional specialty, and sales representative occupations—those who do most business travel—is projected to grow rapidly. Also, with rising incomes, more people are expected to travel on vacation—and to do so more frequently—than in the past. In fact, many people take more than one vacation a year.

Charter flights and larger, more efficient planes have brought air transportation within the budgets of more people. So has the easing of Government regulation of air fares and routes, by fostering greater competition among airlines to offer better and more affordable service. In addition, American travel agents organize tours for the growing number of foreign visitors. Although most travel agencies now have automated reservation systems, this has not weakened demand for travel agents.

The travel industry generally is sensitive to economic downturns and political crises, when travel plans are likely to be deferred. Therefore, the number of job opportunities fluctuates.

Earnings

Experience, sales ability, and the size and location of the agency determine the salary of a travel agent. According to a Louis Harris survey, conducted for the Travel Weekly Magazine, the 1992 annual earnings of travel agents with less than 1 year experience were $12,428, from 1 to 3 years, $15,610; from 3 to 5 years, $17,975; from 5 to 10 years, $20,775; and more than 10 years, $25,007. Salaried agents usually have standard benefits, such as insurance coverage and paid vacations, that self-employed agents must provide for themselves.

Earnings of travel agents who own their agencies depend mainly on commissions from airlines and other carriers, cruise lines, tour operators, and lodging places. Commissions for domestic travel arrangements, cruises, hotels, sightseeing tours, and car rentals are about 10 percent of the total sale; and for international travel, about 11 percent. They may also charge clients a service fee for the time and expense involved in planning a trip.

During the first year of business or while awaiting corporation approval, self-employed travel agents generally have low earnings. Their income is generally limited to commissions from hotels, cruises, and tour operators and to nominal fees for making complicated arrangements. Even established agents have lower profits during economic downturns.

When they travel, agents usually get substantially reduced rates for transportation and accommodations.

Related Occupations

Travel agents organize and schedule business, educational, or recreational travel or activities. Other workers with similar responsibilities include secretaries, tour guides, airline reservation agents, rental car agents, and travel counselors.

Sources of Additional Information

For further information on training opportunities, contact:

❑ American Society of Travel Agents, Education Department, 1101 King St. Alexandria, VA 22314.

For certification information, contact:

❑ The Institute of Certified Travel Agents, 148 Lindon St., P.O. Box 82-56, Wellesley, MA 02181-0012, or phone toll free 1-800-542-4282.

For information on Certified Meeting Professionals (CMP's), contact:

❑ The Convention Liaison Council, 1575 Eye St. NW., Suite 1190, Washington, DC 20005.

Administrative Support Occupations, Including Clerical

Adjusters, Investigators, and Collectors

Nature of the Work

Handling complaints, interpreting and explaining policies or regulations, resolving billing disputes, collecting delinquent accounts, and determining eligibility for governmental assistance are examples of everyday situations that organizations must deal with smoothly and efficiently in order to maintain good relations with customers and clients. Organizations like insurance companies, department stores, banks, and government social services agencies employ adjusters, investigators, and collectors to act as intermediaries with the public in these kinds of situations. Following is a discussion of occupations that make up this group of workers.

Claim Representatives. Claim representatives at insurance companies investigate claims, negotiate settlements, and authorize payments to claimants. When a policyholder files a claim for damage or a loss, the *claim adjuster*, *claim examiner*, or *claim investigator* must initially determine whether the customer's insurance policy covers it and the amount of the loss.

Minor claims filed by automobile or homeowner policyholders are usually handled by inside adjusters or telephone adjusters. These workers contact claimants by telephone or mail to get information on repair costs, medical expenses, or other details the company needs. Many companies centralize this operation in a drive-in claims center, where the cost of repair is determined and a check is issued immediately.

More complex cases are referred to an independent adjuster or outside adjuster. Claim adjusters plan and schedule the work required to process a claim. They investigate claims by interviewing the claimant and witnesses, consulting police and hospital records, and inspecting property damage to determine the extent of the company's liability. They keep photographs, written or taped statements, or computer files of information obtained from witnesses and prepare reports of their findings. When the policy holder's claim is legitimate, the claim adjuster negotiates with the claimant and settles the claim. When claims are contested, adjusters may testify in court.

Some adjusters work with all lines of insurance. Others specialize in claims associated with fire damage, marine loss, automotive damage, product liability, or workers' compensation. Material damage adjusters inspect automobile damage and use the latest computerized estimating equipment to prepare estimates of the damage.

In life and health insurance companies, the counterpart of the claim adjuster is the claim examiner. In property and casualty insurance companies, the claim examiner may supervise claim adjusters. In both cases, they investigate questionable claims or authorize payment for those exceeding a designated amount. Larger claims are referred to senior examiners. Examiners may check claim applications for completeness and accuracy, interview medical specialists, consult policy files to verify information on a claim, or calculate benefit payments. They also maintain records of settled claims and prepare reports to be submitted to their company's data processing department.

Claim representatives are making greater use of computers to keep records of clients and actions taken in various claims. Many have computer terminals on their desks, and a growing number use portable lap-top computers to enter or access information when they are on assignment outside the office.

Insurance Processing Clerks. Policy processing clerks process new insurance policies, modifications to existing policies, and claims. They begin the new policy process by reviewing the insurance application to ensure that all the questions have been answered. After an application has been reviewed by underwriters and the company determines that it will issue a policy, a policy processing clerk prepares the necessary forms and informs the insurance sales agent of an application's processing status. Policy processing clerks also update existing policies, such as a change in beneficiary, amount of coverage, or type of insurance, and recalculate premiums. They mail correspondence notices regarding changes to the sales agent and to the policyholder. Policy processing clerks maintain files for each policyholder including policies that are to be reinstated or canceled.

Claim clerks, also called *claim interviewers*, obtain information from policyholders regarding claims like automobile accidents. They prepare reports and review insurance claim forms and related documents for completeness. They call or write insured or other involved people for missing information and update claim files. They may transmit routine claims for payment or advise the claim supervisor if further investigation is needed.

Like claim representatives, insurance processing clerks use computers extensively in their work. Most spend a large part of their time creating and updating records at a personal computer or terminal.

Adjustment Clerks. Adjustment clerks investigate and resolve customers' complaints about merchandise, service, billing, or credit rating. They may work for banks, department stores, utility companies, and other large organizations selling products and services to the public. Sometimes they are called customer service representatives, customer complaint clerks, or adjustment correspondents.

Adjustment clerks examine all pertinent information to determine the validity of a customer's complaint. In a department store, this may mean checking sales slips or warranties, as well as the merchandise in question. In a bank, it could mean reviewing records and videotapes of automated teller machine transactions. In a utility company, they review meter books, microfilm, computer printouts, and machine accounting records. Regardless of the setting, these clerks also get information—in person, by telephone, or through written correspondence—from the various parties involved, such as the customer and company personnel.

After an investigation and evaluation of the facts, adjustment clerks report their findings, adjustments, and recommendations. These may include exchanging merchandise, refunding money, crediting customers' accounts, or adjusting customers' bills. Adjustment clerks also ensure that the appropriate changes are set in motion and follow-up on the recommendations to ensure customer satisfaction. To prevent similar complaints in the future, they may recommend improvements in product, packaging, shipping methods, service, or billing methods and procedures to management. Adjustment clerks keep records of all relevant matters, using them to prepare reports for their supervisors.

Adjustment clerks also respond to inquiries from customers. Clerks frequently can answer these inquiries with a form letter, but other times they must compose a letter themselves. On request, adjustment clerks also issue duplicate or additional credit cards for banks and department stores.

Bill and Account Collectors. Bill and account collectors, sometimes called collection correspondents, are responsible for ensuring that customers pay their overdue accounts. Some collectors are employed by collection agencies; others, known as inside collectors, work directly for the original creditors, like department stores, hospitals, or banks.

Many companies automatically notify customers by mail if their account is overdue. When customers do not respond, collectors are called on to locate and notify them of the delinquent account, usually over the telephone, sometimes by letter. When customers move without leaving a forwarding address, collectors may check with the post office, telephone companies, credit bureaus, or former neighbors to obtain their new address. This is called skip-tracing.

Once collectors find the debtor, they inform them of the overdue account and solicit payment. If necessary, they review the terms of the sale, service, or credit contract with the customer. Collectors also may attempt to learn the cause of the delay in payment. Where feasible, they offer the customer advice and counsel on how to pay off the debts, such as through a bill consolidation loan. However, the collector's objective is always to ensure that the customer first pays the debt in question.

If customers agree to pay, collectors note that for the record and check later to verify that the payment was indeed made. Collectors may have authority to grant an extension of time if customers ask for one. If customers fail to respond at all, collectors prepare a statement to that effect for the credit department of the establishment. In more extreme cases, collectors may initiate repossession proceedings or service disconnections, or hand the account over to an attorney for legal action.

Most collectors handle other administrative functions for the accounts assigned to them, such as recording changes of address. Bill and account collectors keep records of the amounts collected and the status of the accounts. Some fill out daily reports to keep their supervisors apprised of their progress. In some organizations, inside collectors receive payments and post the amounts to the customers' accounts. In most operations, however, the posting and receiving are done by other clerical workers. Collectors employed by collection agencies do not receive payments; rather, their primary responsibility is to get customers to pay their obligation.

Increasingly, collectors use computers and a variety of automated systems to keep track of overdue accounts. Typically, collectors work at video display terminals that are linked to computers. In the most sophisticated systems, the computer dials the phone automatically and the collector begins to speak only when a connection has been made. Such systems eliminate time spent calling busy or nonanswering numbers. Many collectors use regular telephones; some wear headsets like those used by telephone operators. From time to time, supervisors may listen in on collectors' conversations with customers to evaluate their job performance.

Welfare Eligibility Workers and Interviewers. Welfare eligibility workers and interviewers, sometimes referred to as *intake workers, eligibility determination workers, eligibility specialists,* or *income maintenance specialists,* determine who can receive welfare and other types of social assistance. They do so by interviewing and investigating applicants and recipients to see who is eligible. Based on the personal and financial information they obtain and the rules and regulations of each program, they initiate procedures to grant, modify, deny, or terminate individuals' eligibility for various aid programs. This information is recorded and evaluated to determine the amounts of the grants.

Welfare eligibility workers and interviewers work with various kinds of public assistance programs. The most well-known are Aid to Families with Dependent Children, Medicaid, Food Stamps, and the Work Incentive Program. Depending on local circumstances, there may be other programs, such as those for public housing, refugee assistance, and fuel assistance.

Most welfare eligibility workers and interviewers specialize in a specific area, such as housing, but some are responsible for several areas. They may assist social workers by informing them of pertinent information they have gathered during their interviews with applicants. In some areas, particularly rural ones, eligibility workers may also perform other kinds of welfare duties.

These workers also provide information to applicants and current recipients. For example, they may explain and interpret eligibility rules and regulations or identify other resources available in the community for financial or social welfare assistance. More experienced workers may help train new workers. In addition, they may be assigned to special units whose responsibility is to detect fraud.

An increasing number of jurisdictions are using computers to increase worker productivity and to reduce the incidence of welfare fraud. In these settings, welfare eligibility workers and interviewers sit in front of computer terminals when they interview applicants and recipients. Welfare eligibility workers then enter the information provided. In the most advanced systems, the computer terminal prompts them with questions.

Although these workers usually interview applicants and recipients who visit their offices, they may make occasional home visits, especially if the applicant or recipient is elderly or disabled. They may also check with employers or other references to verify answers and get further information.

The authority of welfare eligibility workers and interviewers varies from one jurisdiction to another. In some places, these workers are authorized to decide on an applicant's eligibility, subject to review by their supervisor. In other places, however, they can only make recommendations to their supervisors, who in turn make the ultimate decision.

Working Conditions

Most claim examiners have desk jobs that require no unusual physical activity. They typically work a standard 40-hour week. Claim examiners may work longer hours during peak periods or when quarterly and annual statements are prepared. They may also travel from time to time to obtain information by personal interview.

Many claim adjusters work outside the office, visiting and inspecting damaged buildings, for example. Occasionally, experienced adjusters may be away from home for days when they travel to the scene of a disaster such as a tornado, hurricane, or flood to work with local adjusters and government officials. Some adjusters may be on emergency call in case of such incidents. Material damage adjusters work at local claim centers where policy holders may take their cars for estimates of damage.

Adjusters generally have the flexibility to arrange their work schedule to accommodate evening and weekend appointments with clients. Some report to the office every morning to get their assignments while others simply call from home and spend their days traveling to claim sites. This enables some adjusters to work independently.

Most insurance processing clerks work 40 hours per week in offices. Much of the work is routine and requires remaining at work stations for extended periods of time. Because most insurance information is stored on computers, many of these workers sit at video display terminals and enter or access information while the customer is on the phone. Because most companies provide 24-hour claim service to their policyholders, some claim clerks work evenings and weekends. Many claim clerks work part-time.

Adjustment clerks, bill and account collectors, and welfare eligibility workers and interviewers work in offices, usually during regular business hours. Some work part time. A few bill and account collectors work as temporaries. From their offices, they deal with customers, clients, or applicants, either by telephone or in person. Dealing with upset or angry clients can be part of the daily routine in these jobs, so the work can be stressful. Adjusters, investigators, and collectors who spend a lot of time working at video display terminals may experience musculoskeletal strain and eyestrain.

Some welfare eligibility workers and interviewers may be hired on a seasonal basis to help administer a specific program. For example, some states hire these workers for the winter to help run emergency fuel assistance programs.

Employment

Adjusters, investigators, and collectors held about 1,185,000 jobs in 1992. The following tabulation presents their employment distribution by detailed occupation:

Total (percent)	100
Adjustment clerks	30
Bill and account collectors	20
Insurance policy processing clerks	14
Insurance adjusters, examiners, and investigators	12
Insurance claims clerks	10
Welfare eligibility workers and interviewers	8
Claims examiners, property and casualty insurance	3
All other adjusters and investigators	3

Insurance companies employ the vast majority of claim adjusters, examiners, and investigators; property and casualty insurance claim examiners; policy processing clerks; and claim clerks. Real estate firms and government agencies employ most of the rest.

About one-fifth of all adjustment clerks are employed by department stores, grocery stores, or catalog and mail-order houses. Manufacturing firms, banks and other financial institutions, and telephone companies are other major employers of these workers.

One in six bill and account collectors works for a credit reporting and collection agency. Many others work in banks, department stores, and other institutions that extend credit.

Nine of every ten welfare eligibility workers and interviewers work for state or local government agencies. In 37 states, these workers are employed exclusively by the state government. In the remainder, they are employed by the county or municipal government. Most of those not employed by government work for private social service agencies.

Training, Other Qualifications, and Advancement

Most companies prefer to hire college graduates for claim representative positions. However, people may be hired without college training if they have specialized experience. For example, people with knowledge of automobile mechanics may qualify as material damage adjusters and those with extensive clerical experience might be hired as inside adjusters.

No specific college major is recommended as the best preparation to enter these positions. Although courses in insurance, economics, or other business subjects are helpful, a degree in almost any field is adequate. An adjuster who has a business or an accounting background might specialize in financial loss due to strikes, breakdowns in equipment, or damage to merchandise. College training in engineering is helpful in adjusting industrial claims, such as damage from fires and other accidents. A legal background is most helpful to those handling workers' compensation and product liability cases. Knowledge of computer applications is increasingly important.

Most large insurance companies provide on-the-job training and home-study courses to beginning claim adjusters and examiners. For example, material damage adjusters would learn about automobile body construction, analysis of collision data, and repair cost estimation, including computerized estimating equipment. They also learn how to deal with customers.

In smaller firms, workers may receive their training through courses offered by the Insurance Institute of America (IIA), a nonprofit organization offering educational programs and professional certification to workers in the property-liability insurance industry. The IIA offers an Associate in Claims (AIC) designation after successful completion of an essay examination. Adjusters can prepare for the examination by independent home study or through company or public classes.

The International Claim Association (ICA) offers a program on life and health insurance claim administration. Completion of the six-examination program leads to the professional designation, Associate, Life and Health Claims (ALHC).

The Life Office Management Association (LOMA) offers a comprehensive 10 course life and health insurance educational program that leads to the professional designation, Fellow, Life Management Institute (FLMI). LOMA also offers the Master Fellow Program (FLMI/M) that is designed specifically to meet the continuing education needs of life and health insurance professionals. Students can prepare for FLMI exams through independent home study or through insurance company or FLMI Society classes.

Most states require adjusters to be licensed. Applicants must usually comply with one or more of the following: pass a written examination covering the fundamentals of adjusting; complete an approved course in insurance or loss adjusting; furnish character references; be at least 20 or 21 years of age and a resident of the state; and file a surety bond.

Because they often work closely with claimants, witnesses, and other insurance professionals, claim representatives must be able to communicate effectively and gain the respect and cooperation of others. Some companies require applicants to pass a battery of written aptitude tests designed to measure communication, analytical, and general mathematical skills. Examiners must understand federal and state insurance laws and regulations. Both adjusters and examiners should be observant and enjoy working with details.

Beginning adjusters and examiners work on small claims under the supervision of an experienced worker. As they learn more about claim investigation and settlement, they are assigned larger, more complex claims. Trainees are promoted as they demonstrate competence in handling assignments and as they progress in their coursework. Because of the complexity of insurance regulations and claim procedures, workers who lack formal academic training may advance more slowly than those with more education. Employees who demonstrate competence in claim work or administrative skills may be promoted to department supervisor in a field office or to a managerial position in the home office.

High school graduation is considered adequate preparation for most insurance processing clerk positions. Courses in typing and word processing, and business arithmetic are desirable. Employers favorably view previous office experience and familiarity with computers. Most new workers begin as file clerks and move into insurance processing positions as they demonstrate their ability. However, people with considerable clerical experience may begin processing insurance policies immediately.

Some experienced insurance processing clerks may be promoted to a clerical supervisor position. Advancement to a claim representative or an underwriting technician position is possible for clerks who demonstrate potential, are college trained, or who have taken specialized courses in insurance. Many companies offer home-study courses that allow their employees to gain the necessary knowledge to advance.

Many employers do not require any formal education for adjustment clerk positions. Instead, they look for people who can read and write and who possess good communications and interpersonal skills. Typing ability is also viewed favorably.

Adjustment clerk is an entry-level position in some, but not all, organizations. Depending on their assignment, new adjustment clerks may receive training on the job from a supervisor or an experienced coworker, or they may enter a formal training course offered by the organization. Training covers such topics as how to use computers, what standard forms to use, whom to contact in other departments of the organization, and how to deal with customers. Some employers provide more advanced training for experienced adjustment clerks. This training may be offered in-house or from trade associations or local colleges.

While high school graduation is sometimes required by employers when they hire bill and account collectors, formal education beyond high school is not stressed. Previous work experience as a collector is particularly valuable, however. Experience in the field of telemarketing or as a telephone operator is also helpful, as is knowledge of the billing process. Employers seek individuals who speak well and who are persistent and detail-oriented.

Employers normally provide training to new bill and account collectors. This training, which may last up to a couple of months, is usually conducted in a classroom or on the job. It may use lectures, videotapes, computer programs, role-playing, and hands-on experience. In addition to learning about skip-tracing and the firm's billing procedure, new collectors learn communications and negotiating skills. Learning to use the firm's computer and telephone systems is an integral part of such training. Successful bill and account collectors may become supervisors. Some even start their own collection agencies.

Hiring requirements for welfare eligibility workers and interviewers vary widely. Depending on the jurisdiction, applicants may need a high school diploma, some post-secondary training, or a bachelor's degree. In some jurisdictions, especially rural ones, graduation from high school is not required. Previous work experience may be substituted for education in some places, particularly if it is in a closely related field like employment interviewing, social work, or insurance claims. Fluency in a foreign language may be an advantage in parts of the country with a high concentration of nonEnglish speaking people.

After they are hired, eligibility workers are given training, sometimes in a formal classroom setting, other times in a more informal manner. They are taught the policies, procedures, and program regulations that they are expected to use to determine eligibility. If a formal training program is selected, it generally is followed by on-the-job training provided by the supervisor.

Because they deal with people who are in difficult economic circumstances, welfare eligibility workers and interviewers should be compassionate and empathetic. Attention to detail is important because there are many policies, procedures, and regulations that must be observed. Advancement to the job of social worker is possible, although additional formal education, such as a bachelor's or master's degree, is usually needed.

Because a significant and growing proportion of adjusters, investigators, and collectors use computers, courses in typing or word processing are recommended. Employers increasingly view experience with computers as an asset.

Job Outlook

Overall employment of adjusters, investigators, and collectors is expected to grow about as fast as the average for all occupations through 2005. Most job openings will result from the need to replace workers who transfer to other occupations or leave the labor force.

Growth rates will vary considerably by occupation. Employment of insurance claim examiners is expected to grow about as fast as the average as the increasing volume of insurance results in more insurance claims. Shifts in the age distribution of the population will result in a large increase in the number of people who assume career and family responsibilities. People in this group have the greatest need for life and health insurance, as well as protection for homes, automobiles, and other possessions. A growing demand for insurance coverage for working women is also expected. New or expanding businesses will need protection for new plants and equipment and for insurance covering their employees' health and safety. Opportunities should be particularly good for claim representatives who specialize in complex business insurance such as marine cargo, workers' compensation, and product and pollution liability.

Employment of insurance processing clerks is expected to grow faster than average as computerization increases their importance in providing customer service to the increasing number of policyholders. Within this group, employment of adjusters and claim clerks will increase more rapidly than employment of policy processing clerks because they have much more interpersonal contact, which cannot be automated.

The number of job openings for workers in the insurance industry should not fluctuate greatly from year to year. This industry, particularly the health insurance component, is less sensitive to cyclical swings in the economy than most industries.

Employment of adjustment clerks is expected to grow about as fast as average as business establishments seek to maintain good customer relations. An important aspect of good customer service is resolving customers' complaints in a friendly and timely fashion. Because much of their work involves direct communication with customers, demand for adjustment clerks is expected to keep pace with the growth in the number of customers.

Bill and account collector jobs are expected to grow much faster than average as the level of consumer debt rises. As the economy expands, firms will strive to increase the efficiency of their debt collection to keep losses at a minimum. Contrary to the pattern in most occupations, employment of bill and account collectors tends to rise during recessions. This is due primarily to the difficulty that many individuals have in meeting their financial obligations.

Employment of welfare eligibility workers and interviewers is expected to grow about as fast as average as state and local governments respond to the growing need for public assistance among their constituents. The Family Support Act of 1988, a reform of the welfare system, aims to get people off the welfare rolls by helping them get back to work. At the same time, it increasingly involves welfare departments in such areas as job training, child care, and medical assistance. Over the long run, this legislation will probably increase the demand for counseling and other services provided by welfare eligibility workers and interviewers.

Earnings

Earnings of adjusters, investigators, and collectors vary significantly. For adjusters and investigators, the median weekly earnings in 1992 were about $400. The middle 50 percent earned between $310 and $510 a week. Adjusters are also furnished a company car or are reimbursed for use of their own vehicle for business purposes. Insurance claim representatives had median weekly earnings of $430 in 1992. The middle 50 percent earned between $340 and $580 a week. Specific information on earnings of insurance processing clerks is not available. However, median weekly earnings for records clerks, a category that includes policy processing clerks, were $350 in 1992. Interviewers, whose work is similar to that of claim clerks, also had median weekly earnings of $350.

Adjustment clerks had median weekly earnings of about $390 in 1992; the middle 50 percent earned between about $300 and $510 a week. The lowest paid 10 percent earned less than $250 a week, and the highest paid 10 percent earned more than $690 a week.

Median weekly earnings of full-time bill and account collectors were about $370 in 1992; the middle 50 percent earned between $290 and $450 a week. Ten percent earned less than $230 and ten percent earned more than $570. Some bill and account collectors receive a base salary and work on commission beyond that salary.

Median weekly earnings of full-time welfare eligibility workers and interviewers were about $390 in 1992; the middle 50 percent earned between $300 and $500 a week. The lowest 10 percent earned less than $270 and the top 10 percent earned more than $640.

Many welfare eligibility workers and interviewers belong to unions. The two principal unions representing these workers are the American Federation of State, County, and Municipal Employees and the Service Employees International Union.

Related Occupations

Insurance adjusters and examiners investigate, analyze, and determine the validity of their firm's liability concerning personal, casualty, or property loss or damages and effect settlement with claimants. Workers in other occupations that require similar skills include cost estimators, budget analysts, and private investigators.

The work of insurance processing clerks and adjustment clerks is similar to that of other workers who compile, review, or maintain records, including coding, contract, auditing, and reservation clerks and title searchers.

The work of bill and account collectors is related to that of customer service representatives, telemarketers, telephone interviewers, and other workers who deal with the public over the telephone.

The work of welfare eligibility workers is similar to that of human services workers, financial aid counselors, loan counselors, credit counselors, probation officers, and other workers who interview customers or clients.

Sources of Additional Information

General information about careers as a claim representative or an insurance processing clerk is available from the home offices of many life and property and liability insurance companies. Information about career opportunities in these occupations may be obtained from:

❏ Insurance Information Institute, 110 William St., New York, NY 10038.

Information about licensing requirements for claim adjusters may be obtained from the department of insurance in each state. For more information on claim representatives, contact:

❏ Alliance of American Insurers, 1501 Woodfield Rd., Suite 400 West, Schaumburg, IL 60173-4980.

For information about public insurance adjusting and independent insurance adjusting, contact respectively:

❏ Insurance Institute of America, 720 Providence Rd., P.O. Box 3016, Malvern, PA 19355-0716; or

❏ National Association of Independent Insurance Adjusters, 300 West Washington St., Room 845, Chicago, IL 60606.

Information on the Associate, Life and Health Claims (ALHC) and the Fellow, Life Management Institute (FLMI) designations can be obtained from:

❏ Life Office Management Association, 5770 Powers Ferry Rd., Atlanta, GA 30327-4308.

Career information on bill and account collectors is available from:

❏ American Collectors Association, Inc., P.O. Box 39106, Minneapolis, MN 55439-0106.

Employment information on welfare eligibility workers and interviewers is available at social service offices of municipal, county, and state governments.

Clerical Supervisors and Managers

Nature of the Work

All organizations need timely and effective clerical and administrative support to operate efficiently. Coordinating this support is the responsibility of clerical supervisors and managers. They can be found in nearly every sector of the economy, working in positions as varied as office manager, customer services supervisor, or chief telephone operator. Although some functions may vary considerably, many duties are common to all.

Supervisors perform administrative tasks to ensure that their staffs can work efficiently. For example, equipment and machinery used in their departments must be in good working order. If the computer system goes down or a photocopier malfunctions, they must try to correct the problem or alert repair personnel. They also request new equipment or supplies for their department when necessary.

Planning and supervising the work of their staff is another key function of this job. To do this effectively, the supervisor must know the strengths and weaknesses of each member of the staff as well as the required level of quality and time allotted to each job. They must make allowances for unexpected absences and other disruptions and adjust assignments or perform the work themselves if the situation requires it.

After allocating work assignments and issuing deadlines, clerical supervisors oversee the work to ensure that it is proceeding on schedule and meets established quality standards. This may involve reviewing each person's work on a computer, as in the case of accounting clerks, or, in the case of cashiers, listening to how they deal with customers. When supervising long-term projects, the supervisor may establish regular meetings with staff members to discuss their progress.

Another part of a clerical supervisor's job is to conduct performance evaluations. If a worker has done a good job, the supervisor records it in the employee's personnel file and may recommend a promotion or other award. Alternatively, if a worker is performing poorly, the supervisor discusses the problem with the employee to determine the cause and help the worker improve his or her performance. This might entail sending the employee to a training course or arranging personal counseling. If the situation does not improve, the supervisor may recommend a transfer, demotion, or dismissal.

Clerical supervisors and managers generally interview and evaluate prospective clerical employees. Some may be actively involved in recruiting new workers by performing functions like making presentations at high schools and business colleges. When new workers arrive on the job, supervisors greet them and provide orientation to acquaint them with the organization and its operating routines.

Supervisors also help train new employees in organization and office procedures. They may teach them to use the telephone system and to operate office equipment. Because much clerical work is computerized, they must also teach new employees to use the organization's computer system. When new office equipment or updated computer software is introduced, supervisors retrain experienced employees to use it efficiently. They may also arrange for special outside training for their employees if necessary.

Clerical supervisors often act as liaisons between the clerical staff and the professional, technical, and managerial staff. This may involve implementing new company policies or restructuring the work flow in their departments. They must also keep their superiors informed of their progress and abreast of any potential problems. Oftentimes this communication takes the form of research projects and progress reports. Because they have access to information like their department's performance records, they may compile and present this data for use in planning or designing new policies.

Clerical supervisors may be called on to resolve interpersonal conflicts among the staff. In organizations covered by union contracts, supervisors must know the provisions of labor-management agreements and run their departments accordingly. They may meet with union representatives to discuss work problems or grievances.

Working Conditions

Clerical supervisors and managers are employed in a wide variety of work settings, but most work in offices that are clean, well-lighted, and generally comfortable. Most work a standard 40 hour week. Because some organizations operate around the clock, however, clerical supervisors may have to work nights, weekends, and holidays. In some cases, supervisors rotate among the three shifts. In others, shifts are assigned on the basis of seniority.

Employment

Clerical supervisors and managers held about 1,267,000 jobs in 1992. Although jobs for clerical supervisors are found in practically every industry, the largest number are found in organizations with a large clerical workforce such as government agencies, retail establishments, wholesalers, business service firms, banks, and insurance companies. Due to the need in most organizations for continuity of supervision, few clerical supervisors and managers work on a temporary or part-time basis.

Training, Other Qualifications, and Advancement

Most people entering this occupation transfer from other occupations within the organization, very often from the ranks of those they subsequently supervise. To be promoted to a supervisory position, clerical or administrative support workers must prove that they are capable of handling additional responsibilities. When evaluating candidates, superiors look for strong teamwork skills, determination, loyalty, poise, and confidence. They also look for more specific supervisory attributes, such as the ability to organize and coordinate work efficiently, set priorities, and motivate others. Increasingly, supervisors need a broad base of office skills coupled with personal flexibility to adapt to changes in organizational structure and move among departments when necessary.

In addition, supervisors must pay close attention to detail in order to identify and correct errors made by subordinates. Good working knowledge of the organization's computer system is also an advantage. Many employers require some post secondary training. An associate degree is sufficient in many cases, but some organizations prefer candidates to hold bachelor's degrees.

A clerk with potential supervisory abilities may be given occasional supervisory assignments. To prepare for full-time supervisory duties, he or she may attend in-house training or take courses in time management, personal relations, or other management skills at a local community college or vocational school.

Some clerical supervisors are hired from outside the organization for positions with more managerial duties. These positions may serve as entry-level training for potential higher level managers. New college graduates may rotate through departments of an organization at this level to learn the work of the entire organization.

Job Outlook

Employment of clerical supervisors and managers is expected to grow about as fast as the average for all occupations through 2005. Although growth in the demand for clerical supervisors will generate many job openings, most openings will result from the need to replace experienced supervisors who transfer to other occupations or leave the labor force. Because the occupation is so large, replacement needs will create a large number of job openings.

Employment of clerical supervisors is tied somewhat to the demand for clerical workers. More clerical work will be generated as organizations and the economy grow, especially the business and service sectors. As the amount of clerical work to be done continues to increase, more managers will be needed to coordinate this rising volume of work. As office automation causes employment in some clerical occupations to slow or even decline, supervisors may have smaller staffs and perform more professional tasks. In other areas, fewer supervisors may be needed.

Earnings

Median annual earnings of full-time clerical supervisors were about $28,000 in 1992; the middle 50 percent earned between $21,100 and $39,400 a year. Ten percent earned less than $16,200 and ten percent more than $51,300. As is the case in most fields, large employers tend to pay higher salaries than small ones. In addition, employers in major metropolitan areas tend to pay higher salaries than those in rural areas.

Depending on their employer, clerical supervisors may receive a variety of benefits. These may include health and life insurance, paid vacations, tuition assistance, and a pension plan. Some clerical supervisors in the private sector may receive additional compensation in the form of bonuses and stock options.

Related Occupations

Clerical supervisors and managers must understand and sometimes perform the work of people whom they oversee, including accounting clerks, cashiers, bank tellers, and telephone operators. Their supervisory and administrative duties are similar to those of other managers.

Sources of Additional Information

State employment service offices can provide information about earnings, hours, and employment opportunities in this and other clerical jobs.

General Office Clerks

Nature of the Work

The duties of general office clerks are too varied and diverse for them to be classified in any specific administrative support occupation. Rather than specialize in a single primary task, general office clerks have duties that are as diverse as the needs of the employer. Some days may be spent filing or typing; others may be spent entering data at a computer terminal. They may also operate photocopiers, fax machines, or other office equipment; prepare mailings; proofread copy; and answer telephones and deliver messages.

A general office clerk in a doctor's office may not perform the same tasks as a clerk in a large financial institution or in the office of an auto parts wholesaler. Although they all may sort checks, keep payroll records, take inventory, or access information, they may also perform duties specific to their employer such as organizing medications, making transparencies for a presentation, or filling orders received by fax.

Duties also vary by level of experience. Inexperienced employees may transcribe data, operate calculators, or record inquiries while more experienced workers may handle greater responsibilities. They might maintain financial or other records, verify statistical reports for accuracy and completeness, handle and adjust customer complaints, take inventory of equipment and supplies, answer questions on departmental services and functions, and help prepare budgetary requests. Senior general office clerks may be expected to oversee and direct the work of lower level clerks.

Working Conditions

For the most part, working conditions for general office clerks are the same as those for other office employees in the same company. Those on a full-time schedule usually work a standard 40 hour week. Some may work shifts or overtime during busy periods and one in four works part-time. In addition, many general office clerks work as temporaries.

Employment

General office clerks held about 2,688,000 jobs in 1992. They work in every sector of the economy. Most general office clerks are employed in relatively small businesses, with more than 50 percent working in the services or wholesale and retail trade industries.

Training, Other Qualifications, and Advancement

Many general office clerk jobs are entry-level and do not require office or business experience. Employers usually require a high school diploma, and some require typing, word processing, and other general office skills. In addition, basic computer skills are becoming increasingly important. Training for this occupation is available in business education programs offered in high schools, community and junior colleges, and post secondary vocational schools. Courses in keyboarding, microcomputer applications, and office practices are particularly helpful.

General office clerks usually work with others. Therefore, they should be cooperative and able to work as part of a team.

They must also be willing to change to meet the unexpected requirements of the job. General office clerks who exhibit strong communication, interpersonal, and analytical skills may be promoted to supervisory positions. Others move into different clerical jobs, such as receptionist, typist, or secretary. Advancement to professional occupations in the establishment usually requires more formal education such as a college degree.

Job Outlook

Opportunities for people interested in becoming general office clerks should be quite favorable. The large size and high turnover of this occupation should produce a significant number of job openings. Job seekers who have typing and other secretarial skills, basic computer skills, and knowledge of office machine operation such as fax machines and copiers should have the best opportunities. General office clerks should find many opportunities for part-time or temporary work, especially during peak business periods.

Because they are so versatile, general office clerks find work in virtually every kind of industry. Therefore, employment is not dependent on the fortunes of any single sector of the economy. Similarly, because they perform a wide variety of office duties using many types of equipment, their employment is not necessarily dependent on any particular technological development.

Employment of general office clerks is expected to grow about as fast as the average for all occupations through 2005 as more small businesses place a single office worker—frequently a general office clerk—in charge of all clerical work.

Earnings

Median annual earnings of full-time general office clerks were about $18,500 in 1992; the middle 50 percent earned between $14,300 and $24,100 annually. Ten percent earned less than $11,400, and ten percent more than $29,500. According to a survey of workplaces in 160 metropolitan areas, beginning general office clerks had median annual earnings of $12,700 in 1992, with the middle half earning about $11,400 to $14,600 a year. The most experienced general office clerks had median annual earnings of about $23,800, with the middle half earning between about $20,800 and $26,900 a year.

General office clerks' salaries vary by industry. They tend to be highest in public utilities and mining and lowest in construction and finance, insurance, and real estate. In 1993, the federal government paid general office clerks a starting salary of between $13,382 and $16,393 a year, depending on education and experience. In 1993, general office clerks in the federal government earned an average annual salary of $22,791.

Related Occupations

General office clerk is usually an entry-level office job. Entry-level jobs in other settings include cashier, medical assistant, teacher aide, and food and beverage service worker.

Sources of Additional Information

State employment service offices and agencies that specialize in placing administrative support personnel can provide information about job openings for general office clerks.

Information Clerks

Nature of the Work

Information clerks gather information from and provide information to the public. Depending on the organization, they may be known as hotel and motel desk clerks, interviewing clerks, new accounts clerks, receptionists, reservation agents, transportation ticket agents, or travel clerks.

Although their day-to-day duties vary widely, many information clerks greet customers, guests, or other visitors, determine their needs, and either assist them or refer them to someone who can help. Other clerks answer telephones or elicit information from the public. Most information clerks use automated office equipment, such as multiline telephones, fax machines, and personal computers, in the course of their work. While this equipment allows them to process more information, it does not alter the basic requirements of their job—communication and human interaction.

Working Conditions

Those information clerks who greet customers and visitors usually work in areas that are highly visible and carefully designed and furnished to make a good impression. Working conditions are usually pleasant; work stations are clean, well-lighted, and relatively quiet. Reservation agents generally work away from the public, in a space that a number of agents share, and as a result it may be crowded and noisy.

Although most information clerks work a standard 40 hour week, some work irregular schedules. Some jobs—those in the transportation industry, hospitals, and hotels, in particular—may require working evenings, late night shifts, weekends, and holidays. Employees with the least seniority may be assigned the least desirable shifts.

The work of information clerks may be tiring, repetitious, and stressful. For example, receptionists may spend all day answering a continuously ringing telephone. Reservation agents and travel clerks use computer systems which may be electronically monitored by management. These workers may also have their telephone calls monitored or tape recorded by management, and may be subject to limitations on the time that they can spend on each call and quotas on the number of reservations which are made. Such practices can make stress-related complaints more common. Prolonged exposure to a video display terminal may lead to eye and musculoskeletal strain as well as complications in pregnancy.

Both hotel and motel desk clerks and ticket agents may be on their feet most of the time, and ticket agents may have to lift heavy baggage. During holidays and other busy periods, these clerks may find the work hectic due to the large number of people to be served. When service does not flow smoothly, because of canceled flights or mishandled reservations, for example, these clerks act as a buffer between the establishment and its customers. Trying to serve the needs of difficult or angry customers can be emotionally draining.

Employment

Information clerks held more than 1.3 million jobs in 1992. The following tabulation shows 1992 employment for the indi-

vidual occupations.

Receptionists and information clerks	904,000
Interviewing and new accounts clerks	175,000
Reservation and transportation ticket agents and travel clerks	131,000
Hotel desk clerks	122,000

These workers are employed throughout the economy, but are concentrated in hotels and motels, the health services industry, banks and savings institutions, firms providing business or real estate services, and the transportation industry. This type of work lends itself to part-time schedules, more so for receptionists, interviewing and new accounts clerks, and hotel and motel desk clerks than for reservation and transportation ticket agents. About 3 out of every 10 information clerks work part-time.

Training, Other Qualifications, and Advancement

Although hiring requirements vary from industry to industry, a high school diploma or its equivalent is often required. However, not all jobs require a high school diploma. Some high school and college students work part-time as information clerks outside of school hours. For some jobs, such as airline reservation and ticket agents, some college education is preferred.

With the exception of airline reservation and transportation ticket agents, orientation and training for information clerks are generally given on the job. Hotel and motel desk clerk job orientation is usually brief, and includes an explanation of the job duties and information about the establishment, such as room location and available services. They learn job tasks through on-the-job training under the guidance of a supervisor or an experienced clerk. They often need additional training to use computerized reservation, room assignment, and billing equipment systems.

Receptionists generally receive on-the-job training. They learn how to operate the telephone system and personal computers, and the proper procedures for greeting visitors, and distributing mail, fax, and parcel deliveries.

Most airline reservation agents learn their skills through formal company training programs. They spend some time in a classroom setting, learning company and industry policies, computer systems, and ticketing procedures. They learn to use a computer to obtain information on schedules, seat availability, and fares; to reserve space for passengers; and to plan passenger itineraries. They must learn airport and airline code designations, and are tested on this knowledge. Because reservation agents are expected to limit the time spent on each call without alienating customers, learning how to carry on a conversation in an organized, yet pleasant manner is an important part of their training.

After completing classroom instruction, new agents work with supervisors or experienced agents for a period of time. During this period, monitoring of telephone conversations may serve as a training device to improve the quality of customer service. In contrast, automobile clubs, bus lines, and railroads either train their travel clerks on the job, without formal classes, or conduct short in-house classes that can last several days. Most information clerks continue to receive instruction on new procedures and company policies after their initial training ends.

Because many information clerks deal directly with the public, a good appearance and pleasant personality are imperative, as are problem-solving abilities and good interpersonal skills. A clear speaking voice and fluency in the English language are essential because these employees frequently use the telephone or public address system. Courses useful to people wanting to enter these occupations include basic math, English, geography, U.S. history, psychology, communications, and public speaking. Good spelling, typing ability, and computer literacy are often needed. Some employers may require applicants to take a typing and spelling test to gauge their skills, with a minimum typing speed of 35 to 50 words per minute often required for employment. It is increasingly helpful for those wishing to enter the hotel and motel industry to learn a foreign language.

Advancement for information clerks generally comes about either by transfer to a more responsible occupation or by promotion to a supervisory position. For example, receptionists, interviewers, and new accounts clerks with typing or other clerical skills may advance to a better paying job as a secretary or administrative assistant. In the airline industry, a ticket agent may advance to lead worker on the shift.

Additional training is frequently helpful in preparing information clerks for promotion. In the lodging industry, for example, clerks can improve their chances for advancement by taking home or group study courses in lodging management, such as those sponsored by the Educational Institute of the American Hotel and Motel Association. In some industries, such as lodging, workers are commonly promoted through the ranks. In many industries, a college degree may be required for advancement to management ranks.

Job Outlook

Overall employment of information clerks is expected to increase faster than the average for all occupations through 2005. In addition to the many openings that will occur as businesses and organizations expand, numerous jobs for information clerks will result from the need to replace experienced workers who transfer to other occupations or leave the labor force. Replacement needs will create large numbers of job openings, reflecting relatively high turnover. Many young people work as information clerks for a few years before switching to other, better paying jobs. This work is well suited to flexible work schedules, and many opportunities for part-time work will continue to be available.

Economic growth and general business expansion are expected to stimulate demand for these workers. Employment of receptionists, hotel and motel desk clerks, hospital admitting clerks, and reservation and transportation ticket agents and travel clerks should grow more rapidly than that of new accounts clerks. The slower growth projected for new accounts clerks reflects slow growth among commercial banks and savings institutions, where employment is heavily concentrated.

Earnings

In 1992, median weekly earnings of full-time information clerks were about $320. The middle 50 percent earned between $260 and $420. The bottom 10 percent earned less than $210, while the top 10 percent earned more than $580. Earnings vary widely by occupation and experience. For example, weekly earnings ranged from less than $180 for the lowest paid hotel clerks to more than $775 for the highest paid reservation agents. Salaries of reservation and ticket agents tend to be significantly higher than for other information clerks, while hotel and motel desk clerks tend to earn quite a bit less, as the following tabulation of median weekly earnings shows:

Reservation and transportation ticket agents and travel clerks	$400
Interviewing and new accounts clerks	$350
Receptionists	$310
Hotel and motel clerks	$250

In 1993, the federal government commonly paid beginning receptionists with a high school diploma or six months of experience salaries ranging from $11,900 to $14,600 a year. The average salary for all receptionists employed by the federal government was $18,600 a year in 1993.

Earnings of hotel and motel desk clerks depend on the location, size, and type of establishment in which they work. Large luxury hotels and those located in metropolitan and resort areas generally pay clerks more than less expensive properties and those located in less populated areas. In general, hotels pay higher salaries than motels or other types of lodging establishments.

In addition to their hourly wage, full-time information clerks who work evenings, nights, weekends, or holidays may receive shift differential pay. Some employers offer educational assistance to their employees. Reservation and transportation ticket agents and travel clerks receive free or very low cost travel on their company's carriers for themselves and their immediate family and, in some companies, free uniforms. Relatively few information clerks belong to unions.

Related Occupations

A number of other workers deal with the public, receive and provide information, or direct people to others who can assist them. Among these are dispatchers, security guards, bank tellers, guides, and telephone operators.

Sources of Additional Information

State employment service offices and agencies that specialize in placing administrative support personnel can provide information about job openings for information clerks.

Secretaries

Nature of the Work

Most organizations employ secretaries to perform and coordinate office activities and to ensure that information gets disseminated in a timely fashion to staff and clients. Managers, professionals, and other support staff rely on them to keep administrative operations under control. Their specific duties depend on their level of responsibility and the type of firm in which they are employed.

Secretaries are responsible for a variety of administrative and clerical duties that are necessary to run and maintain organizations efficiently. They schedule appointments, give information to callers, organize and maintain files, fill out forms, and take dictation. They may also type letters, make travel arrangements, or contact clients. In addition, secretaries operate office equipment like fax machines, photocopiers, and telephones with voice mail capabilities.

In today's automated offices, secretaries increasingly use personal computers to run spreadsheet, word processing, database management, desktop publishing, and graphics programs—tasks previously handled by managers and professionals. Because they are often relieved from dictation and typing, they can support several members of the professional staff. Secretaries sometimes work in clusters of three or four so that they can work more flexibly and share their expertise.

Executive secretaries or administrative assistants perform fewer clerical tasks than lower level secretaries. As well as receiving visitors, arranging conference calls, and answering letters, they may handle more complex responsibilities like conducting research, preparing statistical reports, training employees, and supervising other clerical staff.

In addition to general administrative duties, some secretaries do highly specialized work that requires a knowledge of technical terminology and procedures. Further specialization in various types of law is common among legal secretaries. They prepare correspondence and legal papers such as summonses, complaints, motions, and subpoenas under the supervision of an attorney. They may also review legal journals and assist in other ways with legal research.

Medical secretaries transcribe dictation, prepare correspondence, and assist physicians or medical scientists with reports, speeches, articles, and conference proceedings. They record simple medical histories, arrange for patients to be hospitalized, or order supplies. They may also need to know insurance rules, billing practices, and be familiar with hospital or laboratory procedures. Other technical secretaries assist engineers or scientists. They may prepare correspondence, maintain the technical library, and gather and edit materials for scientific papers. Secretaries are increasingly taking on new responsibilities.

Working Conditions

Secretaries usually work in offices with other professionals or in schools, hospitals, or doctors' offices. Their jobs often involve sitting for long periods. If they spend a lot of time typing, particularly at a video display terminal, they may encounter problems of eyestrain or stress and repetitive motion problems such as carpal tunnel syndrome. Secretaries generally work a standard 40-hour week. In some cities, especially in the Northeast, the scheduled workweek is 37 hours or less.

Office work lends itself to alternative or flexible working arrangements, like telecommuting, and one secretary in every six works part time. In addition, a significant number of secretaries work as temporaries. A few participate in job-sharing arrangements in which two people divide responsibility for a single job.

Employment

Secretaries held 3,324,000 jobs in 1992, making this one of the largest occupations in the U.S. economy. The following tabulation shows the distribution of employment by secretarial specialty.

Legal secretaries	280,000
Medical secretaries	234,000
All other secretaries	2,810,000

Secretaries are employed in organizations of every description. About one-half of all secretaries are employed in firms providing services, ranging from education and health to legal and business services. Others work for firms that engage in manufacturing, construction, wholesale and retail trade, transportation, and communications. Banks, insurance companies, investment firms, and real estate firms are important employers, as are federal, state, and local government agencies.

Training, Other Qualifications, and Advancement

High school graduates may qualify for secretarial positions provided they have basic office skills. Today, however, knowledge of word processing, spreadsheet, and database management programs is increasingly important, and most employers require it. Secretaries must be proficient in keyboarding and good at spelling, punctuation, grammar, and oral communication. Shorthand is necessary for some positions. Employers also look for communication and interpersonal skills because secretaries must be tactful in their dealings with many different people. Discretion, judgment, organizational ability, and initiative are important for higher level secretarial positions.

As office automation continues to evolve, retraining and continuing education will remain an integral part of many jobs. Continuing changes in the office environment, for instance, have increased the demand for secretaries who are adaptable and versatile. Secretaries may have to attend classes to learn to operate new office equipment such as word processing equipment, information storage systems, personal computers, or new updated software packages.

The skills needed for a secretarial job can be acquired in various ways. Formal training, especially for computer skills, may lead to higher paying jobs. Secretarial training ranges from high school vocational education programs that teach office practices, shorthand, and keyboarding skills to one or two year programs in secretarial science offered by business schools, vocational-technical institutes, and community colleges. Many temporary service agencies provide training in computer and keyboarding skills. These skills are most often acquired, however, through instruction offered at the workplace by other employees or by equipment and software vendors. In addition, specialized training programs are available for students planning to become medical or legal secretaries or office automation specialists.

Testing and certification for entry-level office skills is available through the Office Proficiency Assessment and Certification (OPAC) program offered by Professional Secretaries International (PSI). As secretaries gain experience, they can earn the designation Certified Professional Secretary (CPS) by passing a series of examinations given by the Institute for Certifying Secretaries, a department of PSI. This designation is recognized by a growing number of employers as the mark of excellence for senior-level office professionals.

Similarly, those without experience who want to be certified as a legal support professional may be certified as an Accredited Legal Secretary (ALS) by the Certifying Board of the National Association of Legal Secretaries. They also administer an examination to certify a legal secretary with three years of experience as a Professional Legal Secretary (PLS).

Advancement for secretaries generally comes about by promotion to a secretarial position with more responsibilities. Qualified secretaries who broaden their knowledge of the company's operations may be promoted to other positions such as senior or executive secretary, clerical supervisor, or office manager. Secretaries with word processing experience can advance to jobs as word processing trainers, supervisors, or managers within their own firms or in a secretarial or word processing service bureau. They can also get jobs with manufacturers of word processing or computer equipment in positions such as instructors or sales representatives.

Job Outlook

Employment of secretaries is expected to grow more slowly than the average for all occupations through 2005. Nevertheless, employment opportunities should be quite plentiful, especially for well-qualified and experienced secretaries, who, according to many employers, are in short supply. The very large size of the occupation, coupled with moderate turnover, generates several hundred thousand secretarial positions each year as experienced workers transfer to other occupations or leave the labor force. Demand for secretaries will rise as the economy grows and as more workers are employed in offices. The trend toward secretaries assuming more responsibilities traditionally reserved for managers and professionals should also stimulate demand.

Increased productivity resulting from new office technologies, however, will offset this demand somewhat. In firms that have invested in electronic typewriters, word processors, or personal computers, secretaries can produce significantly more work than when they used electric or manual typewriters. New office technologies such as electronic mail, fax machines, and voice message systems are used in a growing number of organizations. These and other sophisticated computer software capabilities are expected to be used more widely in the years ahead.

Widespread use of automated equipment is already changing the workflow in many offices. Administrative duties are being reassigned and the functions of entire departments are being restructured. Large firms are experimenting with different methods of staffing their administrative support operations. In some cases, such traditional secretarial duties as typing or keyboarding, filing, copying, and accounting are being assigned to workers in other units or departments. In some law offices and physicians' offices, for example, paralegals and medical assistants are taking over some tasks formerly done by secretaries.

Professionals and managers increasingly do their own word processing rather than submit the work to secretaries and other support staff. In addition, there is a trend in many offices for groups of professionals and managers to share secretaries, allowing secretaries to assume new responsibilities. The traditional arrangement of one secretary per manager is becoming less prevalent; instead, secretaries increasingly support systems or units.

Developments in office technology are certain to continue, and they will bring about further changes in the secretary's work environment. However, many secretarial job duties are of a personal, interactive nature and hence, not easily automated. Duties such as planning conferences, receiving clients, and transmitting staff instructions require tact and communication skills. Because automated equipment cannot substitute for these personal skills, secretaries will continue to play a key role in the office activities of most organizations.

Earnings

The average annual salary for all secretaries was $26,700 in 1992. Salaries vary a great deal, however, ranging from $20,000 to $36,000, reflecting differences in skill, experience, and level of responsibility. The starting salary for inexperienced secretaries in the federal government was $16,400 a year in 1993. All secretaries employed by the federal government in 1993 averaged about $24,000.

Related Occupations

A number of other workers type, record information, and process paperwork. Among these are bookkeepers, receptionists, stenographers, personnel clerks, typists and word processors, legal assistants, medical assistants, and medical record technicians. A growing number of secretaries share in managerial and human resource responsibilities. Occupations using these skills include clerical supervisor, systems manager, office manager, and human resource officer.

Sources of Additional Information

For career information, write:

❏ Professional Secretaries International, 10502 NW. Ambassador Dr., Kansas City, MO 64195-0404 or call 816-891-6600.

People interested in careers as legal secretaries can request information from:

❏ National Association of Legal Secretaries (International), 2250 East 73rd St., Suite 550, Tulsa, OK 74136.

State employment offices can also provide information about job openings for secretaries.

Teacher Aides

Nature of the Work

Teacher aides, also called paraprofessionals or paraeducators, provide instructional and clerical support for classroom teachers, allowing teachers more time for lesson planning and teaching. Aides assist and supervise students in the classroom, cafeteria, schoolyard, or on field trips. They record grades, set up equipment, or help prepare materials for instruction. They also tutor and assist children in learning class material.

Aides' responsibilities vary greatly. Some teacher aides handle only routine nonteaching and clerical tasks. They grade tests and papers, check homework, keep health and attendance records, type, file, and duplicate materials. They also may stock supplies, operate audiovisual equipment, and keep classroom equipment in order.

Other aides instruct children, under the direction and guidance of teachers. They work with students individually or in small groups, listening while students read, reviewing or reinforcing class work, or helping them find information for reports. They may supervise independent study or help students in vocational or work-study programs find jobs. Teacher aides may also provide personal attention to at-risk students—those whose families live in poverty, for example—or students with special needs—those who speak English as a second language, for example. Aides help assess a student's progress by observing a student's performance and recording relevant data.

Many aides have a combination of instructional and clerical duties, designed to most effectively assist classroom teachers. Sometimes, aides take charge of special projects and prepare equipment or exhibits—for a science demonstration, for example.

Working Conditions

About half of all teacher aides work part-time during the school year. Most aides who provide educational instruction work the traditional 9-10 month school year, usually in a classroom setting. Aides also may work outdoors supervising recess when weather allows, and spend much of their time standing, walking, or kneeling. Seeing students develop and gain appreciation of the joy of learning can be very rewarding. However, working closely with students can be both physically and emotionally tiring.

Employment

Teacher aides held about 885,000 jobs in 1992. About 8 out of every 10 aides worked in elementary and secondary schools, mostly in the lower grades. A significant number assisted special education teachers in working with children who have disabilities. Most of the others worked in child daycare centers and religious organizations.

Training, Other Qualifications, and Advancement

Educational requirements for teacher aides range from a high school diploma to some college training. Those aides with teaching responsibilities usually require more training than those who don't have teaching tasks. Increasingly, employers prefer aides who have some college training. Many schools require previous experience in working with children.

A number of two-year and community colleges offer associate degree programs that prepare graduates to work as teacher aides. However, most teacher aides receive on-the-job training. Aides who tutor and review lessons with students must have a thorough understanding of class materials and instructional methods, and must be familiar with the organization and operation of a school. Aides also must know how to operate audiovisual equipment, keep records, and prepare instructional materials.

Teacher aides should enjoy working with children and be able to handle classroom situations with fairness and patience. Aides must also demonstrate initiative and willingness to follow a teacher's directions. They must have good oral and writing skills and be able to communicate effectively with students and teachers. Some aides must be able to speak a second language to help children whose primary language is not English. Clerical and computer skills may also be necessary.

Some states have established certification and training requirements for general teacher aides. To qualify, an individual may need a high school diploma or general equivalency degree (G.E.D.), or even some college training.

Advancement for teacher aides, usually in the form of higher earnings or increased responsibility, comes primarily with experience or additional education. Some school districts provide time away from the job so that aides may take college courses. Aides who earn bachelor's degrees may become certified teachers.

Job Outlook

Employment of teacher aides is expected to grow much faster than the average for all occupations through 2005. The increasing number of special education classes, restructuring of schools, and the rising number of students who speak English as a second language will spur rapid growth of teacher aides. Numerous job openings will also arise as workers transfer to other occupations or leave the labor force for family responsibilities, to return to school, or for other reasons—a characteristic of occupations that require limited formal education and offer relatively low pay.

Because many teacher aides work in special education—a field that is expected to experience rapid growth through 2005—strong demand is expected for teacher aides. The number of special education programs is rising in response to federal legislation which mandates appropriate education for all children with disabilities. Children with special needs require a lot of personal attention, and special education teachers rely heavily on teacher aides.

In addition, school reforms that call for more individual instruction should further enhance employment opportunities for teacher aides. More paraprofessionals are being employed to provide students with the personal instruction and remedial education they need; most students greatly benefit from additional attention, individual instruction, and positive feedback.

Teacher aide employment is sensitive to changes in state and local expenditures for education. Pressures on education budgets are greater in some states and localities than others. A number of teacher aide positions, such as Head Start assistant teachers, are financed through federal programs, which may also be affected by budget constraints.

Earnings

According to the National Survey of Salaries and Wages in Public Schools, conducted by the Educational Research Service, aides involved in teaching activities averaged $8.31 an hour in 1992-93; those performing only nonteaching activities averaged $7.82 an hour. Earnings varied by region, work experience, and academic qualifications. Many aides are covered by collective bargaining agreements and have benefits similar to those of the teachers in their schools.

Related Occupations

Teacher aides who instruct children have similar duties to those of preschool, elementary, and secondary school teachers and librarians. However, teacher aides do not have the same level of responsibility or training. The support activities of teacher aides and their educational backgrounds are similar to those of child-care workers, family daycare providers, library technicians, and library assistants.

Sources of Additional Information

Information on teacher aides and on a wide range of education-related subjects, including teacher aide unionization, can be obtained from:

❏ American Federation of Teachers, Organizing Department, 555 New Jersey Ave. NW., Washington, DC 20001.

For information on a career as a teacher aide in special education, contact:

❏ National Resource Center for Paraprofessionals in Special Education, 25 West 43rd St., Room 620, New York, NY 10036.

School superintendents and state departments of education can provide details about employment requirements.

Service Occupations

Barbers and Cosmetologists

Nature of the Work

Acquiring the right look has never been easy. It requires that perfect hairstyle, exquisite nails, a neatly trimmed beard, or the proper make-up to accent your coloring. As people increasingly demand styles that are better suited to their individual characteristics, they rely on barbers and cosmetologists more and more. Although tastes and fashions change from year to year, the basic job of barbers and cosmetologists remains the same: help people look their best.

Barbers cut, trim, shampoo, and style hair. Many people still go to a barber for just a haircut, but an increasing number seek more personalized hairstyling services. Barbers trained in these areas work in barber shops and styling salons, many of which are considered to be unisex because they serve both men and women. It is not uncommon for a barber to color or perm a customer's hair. In addition, barbers may fit hairpieces, provide hair and scalp treatments, shave male customers, or give facial massages. In most states, barbers are licensed to perform all the duties of cosmetologists except skin care and nail treatment.

Cosmetologists primarily shampoo, cut, and style hair. These workers, who are often called hairstylists, may also advise patrons on how to care for their hair. Frequently, they straighten or permanent wave a customer's hair to keep the style in shape. Cosmetologists may also lighten or darken hair color. In addition, most cosmetologists are trained to give manicures and scalp and facial treatments, provide makeup analysis for women, and clean and style wigs and hairpieces. Related workers include manicurists, who clean, shape, and polish customer's fingernails and toenails; makeup artists, who apply makeup; electrologists, who remove hair from skin by electrolysis; and estheticians, who cleanse and beautify the skin. Cosmetologists offer all of the services that barbers do except shaving men.

In addition to their work with customers, barbers and cosmetologists are expected to keep their work area clean and their hairdressing implements sanitized. They may make appointments and keep records of hair color and permanent wave formulas used by their regular patrons. Some sell hair products and other cosmetic supplies. Barbers and cosmetologists who operate their own salons also have managerial duties that include hiring, supervising, and firing workers, as well as keeping records and ordering supplies.

Working Conditions

Barbers and cosmetologists generally work in clean, pleasant surroundings with good lighting and ventilation. Good health and stamina are important because these workers must stand a great deal. Prolonged exposure to some hair and nail chemicals may be hazardous and cause irritation, so special care must be taken when working with these chemicals. Full-time barbers and cosmetologists may work more than 40 hours a week. This often includes evenings and weekends, when beauty and barber shops and salons are busiest. Although weekends and lunch periods are generally very busy, barbers and cosmetologists may have some time off during slack periods.

Employment

Barbers and cosmetologists held about 746,000 jobs in 1992; 9 of every 10 were cosmetologists. Most worked in beauty salons, barber shops, or department stores, and a few were employed by hospitals, hotels, and prisons. About four out of every five barbers and about half of all cosmetologists are self-employed. Cosmetologists work in a variety of settings to help people look their best.

Almost all cities and towns have barbershops and hair salons, but employment is concentrated in the most populous cities and states. Hairstylists usually work in cities and suburbs, where the greatest demand for their services exists. Stylists who set fashion trends with their hairstyles usually work in New York City, Los Angeles, and other centers of fashion and the performing arts.

One of every three barbers and cosmetologists works part-time. The abundance of part-time jobs attracts many people who want to combine a job with family, school, or other responsibilities.

Training, Other Qualifications, and Advancement

Although all states require barbers and cosmetologists to be licensed, the qualifications necessary to obtain a license vary. Generally, a person must have graduated from a state-licensed barber or cosmetology school, passed a physical examination, and be at least 16 years old. In addition, education requirements vary from state to state, some require graduation from high school while others require as little as an eighth grade education. In a few states, completion of an apprenticeship can substitute for graduation from a school, but very few barbers or cosmetologists learn their skills this way. Applicants for a license are usually required to pass a written test and demonstrate an ability to perform basic barbering or cosmetology services.

Some states have reciprocity agreements that allow licensed barbers and cosmetologists to practice in a different state without additional formal training. Other states do not recognize training or licenses obtained in another state; consequently, people who wish to become a barber or a cosmetologist should review the laws of the state in which they want to work before entering a training program.

Public and private vocational schools offer daytime or evening classes in barbering and cosmetology. These programs usually last 6 to 12 months. An apprenticeship program can last from one to two years. Formal training programs include classroom study, demonstrations, and practical work. Students study the basic services—haircutting, shaving, facial massaging, and hair and scalp treatments—and, under supervision, practice on customers in school clinics. Most schools also teach unisex hairstyling and chemical styling. Students attend lectures on barber services, the use and care of instruments, sanitation and hygiene, and recognition of certain skin ailments. Instruction is also given in selling and general business practices. There are also advanced courses for experienced barbers in hairstyling, coloring, and the sale and service of hairpieces. Most schools teach hairstyling of men's as well as women's hair.

After graduating from a training program, students can take the state licensing examination. The examination consists of a written test and, in some cases, a practical test of cosmetology skills. A few states include an oral examination in which the applicant is asked to explain the procedures he or she is following while taking the practical test. In some states, a separate examination is given for people who want only a manicurist license or a facial care license.

People who want to become barbers or cosmetologists must have finger dexterity and a sense of form and artistry. They should enjoy dealing with the public and be willing and able to follow patrons' instructions. Because hairstyles are constantly changing, barbers and cosmetologists must keep abreast of the latest fashions and beauty techniques. Business skills are important for those who plan to operate their own salons.

Many schools help their graduates find jobs. During their first months on the job, new workers are given relatively simple tasks, such as giving shampoos, or are assigned to perform the simpler hairstyling patterns. Once they have demonstrated their skills, they are gradually permitted to perform the more complicated tasks such as giving shaves, coloring hair, or applying a permanent.

Advancement is usually in the form of higher earnings as barbers and cosmetologists gain experience and build a steady clientele. Some barbers and cosmetologists manage large salons or open their own after several years of experience. Some teach in barber or cosmetology schools. Others become sales representatives for cosmetics firms, open businesses as beauty or fashion consultants, or work as examiners for state licensing boards.

Job Outlook

Overall employment of barbers and cosmetologists is expected to grow faster than the average for all occupations through 2005. Population growth, rising incomes, and a growing demand for the services that they provide will stimulate demand for these workers. Within this occupation, however, different employment trends are expected. Cosmetologists will account for virtually all of the employment growth, reflecting the continuing shifts in consumer preferences to more personalized services and in salons to full-service, unisex establishments. Demand for manicurists and cosmetologists who are trained in nail care will be particularly strong. Employment of barbers is expected to decline slightly.

The annual number of job openings in cosmetology should be quite large due to the large size of the occupation and expected rapid employment growth. However, there appears to be a large reserve pool of licensed cosmetologists who move in and out of the occupation. Consequently, newly licensed job seekers in this field are likely to compete for openings with an experienced pool of workers who choose to reenter the labor force.

Despite a projected employment decline, a significant number of active barbers should soon retire and need to be replaced. Those who receive training to perform a wide range of services, as most currently do, will improve their chances of finding employment in the growing number of full-service salons. Opportunities for people seeking part-time barbering and cosmetology positions should continue to be good.

Earnings

Barbers and cosmetologists receive income either from commissions or wages and tips. According to limited information, most full-time barbers and cosmetologists earned between $20,000 and $30,000 in 1992, including tips. Earnings depend on the size and location of the shop, the number of hours worked, customers' tipping habits, competition from other barbershops and salons, and the barber's or cosmetologist's ability to attract and hold regular customers.

Related Occupations

Other workers whose main activity consists of improving a patron's personal appearance include beauty consultants, make-up and wig specialists, and salon and health club managers. Other workers are employed in the cosmetology industry as instructors and beauty supply distributors.

Sources of Additional Information

Lists of barber schools, by state, are available from:

❏ National Association of Barber Schools, Inc., 304 South 11th St., Lincoln, NE 68502.

A list of licensed training schools and licensing requirements for cosmetologists can be obtained from:

❏ National Accrediting Commission of Cosmetology Arts and Sciences, 901 North Stuart St., Suite 900, Arlington, VA 22203; or

❏ Association of Accredited Cosmetology Schools, Inc., 5201 Leesburg Pike, Falls Church, VA 22041.

Information about barber and cosmetology schools is also available from:

❏ Accrediting Commission of Career Schools/Colleges of Technology, 750 1st St. NE., Suite 905, Washington, DC 20002.

For details on state licensing requirements and approved barber or cosmetology schools, contact the state board of barber examiners or the state board of cosmetology in your state capital.

Chefs, Cooks, and Other Kitchen Workers

Nature of the Work

A reputation for serving good food is essential to any restaurant, whether it prides itself on hamburgers and French fries or exotic foreign cuisine. Chefs, cooks, and other kitchen workers are largely responsible for the reputation a restaurant acquires. Some restaurants offer a varied menu featuring meals that are time-consuming and difficult to prepare, requiring a highly skilled cook or chef. Other restaurants emphasize fast service, offering hamburgers and sandwiches that can be prepared in advance or in a few minutes by a fast-food or short-order cook with only limited cooking skills.

Chefs and cooks are responsible for preparing meals that are tasty and attractively presented. Chefs are the most highly skilled, trained, and experienced kitchen workers. Although the terms chef and cook are still sometimes used interchangeably, cooks generally have more limited skills. Many chefs have earned fame for both themselves and the restaurants, hotels, and institutions where they work because of their skill in artfully preparing the traditional favorites and in creating new dishes and improving familiar ones. (For information on executive chefs, see the statement on restaurant and food service managers.)

Institutional chefs and cooks work in the kitchens of schools, industrial cafeterias, hospitals, and other institutions. For each meal, they prepare a small selection of entrees, vegetables, and desserts, but in large quantities.

Restaurant chefs and cooks generally prepare a wider selection of dishes for each meal, cooking most individual servings to order. Whether in institutions or restaurants, chefs and cooks measure, mix, and cook ingredients according to recipes. In the course of their work they use a variety of pots, pans, cutlery, and equipment, including ovens, broilers, grills, slicers, grinders, and blenders. They are often responsible for directing the work of other kitchen workers, estimating food requirements, and ordering food supplies. Some chefs and cooks also help plan meals and develop menus.

Bread and pastry bakers, called pastry chefs in some kitchens, produce baked goods for restaurants, institutions, and retail bakery shops. Unlike bakers who work at large, automated industrial bakeries, bread and pastry bakers need only supply the customers who visit their establishment. They bake smaller quantities of breads, rolls, pastries, pies, and cakes, doing most of the work by hand. They measure and mix ingredients, shape and bake the dough, and apply fillings and decorations.

Short-order cooks prepare foods to order in restaurants and coffee shops that emphasize fast service. They grill and garnish hamburgers, prepare sandwiches, fry eggs, and cook French fried potatoes, often working on several orders at the same time. Prior to busy periods, they may slice meats and cheeses or prepare coleslaw or potato salad. During slow periods, they may clean the grill, food preparation surfaces, counters, and floors.

Specialty fast-food cooks prepare a limited selection of menu items in fast-food restaurants. They cook and package batches of food such as hamburgers and fried chicken, which are prepared to order or kept warm until sold.

Other kitchen workers, under the direction of chefs and cooks, perform tasks requiring less skill. They weigh and measure ingredients, fetch pots and pans, and stir and strain soups and sauces. They clean, peel, and slice potatoes, other vegetables and fruits and make salads. They may also cut and grind meats, poultry, and seafood in preparation for cooking. Their responsibilities also include cleaning work areas, equipment and utensils, and dishes and silverware.

The number and types of workers employed in kitchens depend partly on the type of restaurant. For example, fast-food outlets offer only a few items, which are prepared by fast-food cooks. Smaller, full-service restaurants that offer casual dining often feature a limited number of easy-to-prepare items, supplemented by short-order specialties and ready-made desserts. Typically, one cook prepares all of the food with the help of a short-order cook and one or two other kitchen workers.

Large eating establishments may have more varied menus and prepare, from start to finish, more of the food they serve. Kitchen staffs often include several chefs and cooks, sometimes called assistant or apprentice chefs or cooks, a bread and pastry baker, and many less skilled kitchen workers. Each chef or cook usually has a special assignment and often a special job title—vegetable, fry, or sauce cook, for example. Executive chefs coordinate the work of the kitchen staff and often direct certain kinds of food preparation. They decide the size of servings, sometimes plan menus, and buy food supplies. Work hours in restaurants may include late evening, holiday, and weekend work.

Working Conditions

Many restaurant and institutional kitchens have modern equipment, convenient work areas, and air-conditioning; but others, particularly in older and smaller eating places, are frequently not as well-equipped. Other variations in working conditions depend on the type and quantity of food being prepared and the local laws governing food service operations. Workers generally must withstand the pressure and strain of working in close quarters during busy periods, stand for hours at a time, lift heavy pots and kettles, and work near hot ovens and grills. Job hazards include falls, cuts, and burns, but injuries are seldom serious.

Work hours in restaurants may include late evening, holiday, and weekend work, while hours in cafeterias in factories, schools, or other institutions may be more regular. Half of all short-order and fast-food cooks and other kitchen workers worked part-time; a third of all bakers and restaurant and institutional cooks worked part-time. Kitchen workers employed by public and private schools may work during the school year only, usually for 9 or 10 months. Vacation resorts may offer only seasonal employment.

Employment

Chefs, cooks, and other kitchen workers held nearly 3.1 million jobs in 1992. Short-order and fast-food cooks held 714,000 of the jobs; restaurant cooks, 602,000; institutional cooks, 406,000; bread and pastry bakers, 146,000; and other kitchen workers, 1,233,000. About three-fifths of all chefs, cooks, and other kitchen workers worked in restaurants and other retail eating and drinking places. One-fifth worked in institutions such as schools, universities, hospitals, and nursing homes. The remainder were employed by grocery stores, hotels, and many other organizations.

Training, Other Qualifications, and Advancement

Most kitchen workers start as fast-food or short-order cooks, or in one of the other less skilled kitchen positions that require little education or training and that allow them to acquire their skills on the job. After acquiring some basic food handling, preparation, and cooking skills, they may be able to advance to an assistant cook or short-order cook position, but many years of training and experience are necessary to achieve the level of skill required of an executive chef or cook in a fine restaurant. Even though a high school diploma is not required for beginning jobs, it is recommended for those planning a career as a cook or chef. High school or vocational school courses in business arithmetic and business administration are particularly helpful.

Many school districts, in cooperation with state departments of education, provide on-the-job training and sometimes summer workshops for cafeteria kitchen workers who wish to become cooks. Employees who have participated in these training programs are often selected for jobs as cooks. An increasing number of chefs and cooks are obtaining their training through high school or post-high school vocational programs and two or four year colleges. Chefs and cooks may also be trained in apprenticeship programs offered by professional culinary institutes, industry associations, and trade unions. An example is the three year apprenticeship program administered by local chapters of the American Culinary Federation in cooperation with local employers and junior colleges or vocational education institutions. In addition, some large hotels and restaurants operate their own training programs for cooks and chefs.

People who have had courses in commercial food preparation may be able to start in a cook or chef job without having to spend time in a lower skilled kitchen job, and they may have an advantage when looking for jobs in better restaurants and hotels, where hiring standards are often high. Some vocational programs in high schools offer this kind of training, but these courses are usually given by trade schools, vocational centers, colleges, professional associations, and trade unions. Postsecondary courses range from a few months to two years or more and are open in some cases only to high school graduates. The Armed Forces are also a good source of training and experience.

Although curricula may vary, students usually spend most of their time learning to prepare food through actual practice. They learn to bake, broil, and otherwise prepare food, and to use and care for kitchen equipment. Training programs often include courses in menu planning, determination of portion size and food cost control, purchasing food supplies in quantity, selection and storage of food, and use of leftover food to minimize waste. Students also learn hotel and restaurant sanitation and public health rules for handling food. Training in supervisory and management skills is sometimes emphasized in courses offered by private vocational schools, professional associations, and university programs.

Culinary courses are given by 550 schools across the nation. The American Culinary Federation accredited 70 of these programs in 1993. Accreditation is an indication that a culinary program meets recognized standards regarding course content, facilities, and quality of instruction. The American Culinary Federation has only been accrediting culinary programs for a relatively short time, however, and many programs have not yet sought accreditation.

Certification provides valuable formal recognition of the skills of a chef or cook. The American Culinary Federation certifies chefs and cooks at the levels of cook, working chef, executive chef, and master chef. It also certifies pastry professionals and culinary educators. Certification standards are based primarily on experience and formal training.

The ability to work as part of a team, a keen sense of taste and smell, and personal cleanliness are important qualifications for chefs, cooks, and other kitchen workers. Most states require health certificates indicating that these workers are free from contagious diseases.

Advancement opportunities for chefs and cooks are better than for most other food and beverage preparation and service occupations. Many acquire higher paying positions and new cooking skills by moving from one job to another. Besides culinary skills, advancement also depends on the ability to supervise lesser skilled workers and limit food costs by minimizing waste and accurately anticipating the amount of perishable supplies needed. Some cooks and chefs gradually advance to executive chef positions or supervisory or management positions, particularly in hotels, clubs, or larger, more elegant restaurants. Some eventually go into business as caterers or restaurant owners; others may become instructors in vocational programs in high schools, junior and community colleges, and other academic institutions.

Job Outlook

Job openings for chefs, cooks, and other kitchen workers are expected to be excellent through 2005. Growth in demand for these workers will create many new jobs, but most openings will arise from the need to replace the relatively high proportion of workers who leave this very large occupation each year. There is substantial turnover in many of these jobs because their limited requirements for formal education and training allow easy entry, and the many part-time positions are attractive to people seeking a short-term source of income rather than a career. Many of the workers who leave these jobs transfer to other occupations, while others stop working to assume household responsibilities or to attend school full-time.

Workers under the age of 25 have traditionally filled a significant proportion of the lesser skilled jobs in this occupation. The pool of young workers is expected to continue to shrink through the 1990s, but then begin to grow. Many employers will be forced to offer higher wages, better benefits, and more training to attract and retain workers in these jobs.

Employment of chefs, cooks, and other kitchen workers is expected to increase faster than the average for all occupations through 2005. Because a significant proportion of food and beverage sales by eating and drinking establishments is associated with the overall level of economic activity—workers' lunches and entertainment of clients, for example—sales and employment will increase with the growth of the economy. Other factors contributing to employment growth will be population growth, rising family and personal incomes, and more leisure time that will allow people to dine out and take vacations more often. Also, as more women join the workforce, families increasingly may find dining out a welcome convenience.

Employment in restaurants is expected to grow rapidly. As the average age of the population increases, demand will grow for restaurants that offer table service and more varied menus, which will require more highly skilled cooks and chefs. The popularity of fresh baked breads and pastries in fine dining establishments should ensure continued rapid growth in the employment of bakers. However, employment of short-order and specialty fast-food cooks is expected to increase more slowly than other occupations in this group because most hold jobs in fast-food restaurants, which are expected to have slower growth than in the past.

Employment of institutional and cafeteria chefs and cooks will grow about as fast as the average. Their employment is concentrated in the educational and health services sectors. Although employment in both sectors is expected to increase rapidly, growth of institutional and cafeteria cooks will not keep pace. Many high schools and hospitals are trying to make institutional food more attractive to students, staff, visitors, and patients. While some are employing more highly trained chefs and cooks to prepare more appealing meals, others are contracting out their food services. Many of the contracted companies emphasize fast-food chains and employ short-order and fast- food cooks instead of institutional and cafeteria cooks.

Earnings

Wages of chefs, cooks, and other kitchen workers vary depending on the part of the country and, especially, the type of establishment in which they work. Wages are generally highest in elegant restaurants and hotels, and many executive chefs earn more than $40,000 annually. According to a survey conducted by the National Restaurant Association, median hourly earnings of cooks were $6.57, with most earning between $6 and $8 in 1992. Assistant cooks had median hourly earnings of $6, with most earning between $5.50 and $6.50.

According to the same survey, short-order cooks had median hourly earnings of $5.99 in 1992; most earned between $5 and $6.75. Median hourly earnings of bread and pastry bakers were $6.25; most earned within the range of $6 to $7. Salad preparation workers generally earned less, with median hourly earnings of $5.90; most earned between $5 and $6. Food preparation workers in fast-food restaurants had median hourly earnings of $4.68, with most earning between $4.25 and $5.30 per hour.

Some employers provide uniforms and free meals, but federal law permits employers to deduct from wages the cost, or fair value, of any meals or lodging provided, and some employers exercise this right. Chefs, cooks, and other kitchen workers who work full-time often receive paid vacation and sick leave and health insurance, but part-time workers generally do not receive such benefits.

In some large hotels and restaurants, kitchen workers belong to unions. The principal unions are the Hotel Employees and Restaurant Employees International Union and the Service Employees International Union.

Related Occupations

Workers who perform tasks similar to those of chefs, cooks, and other kitchen workers include butchers and meatcutters, cannery workers, and industrial bakers.

Sources of Additional Information

Information about job opportunities may be obtained from local employers and local offices of the state employment service. Career information about chefs, cooks, and other kitchen workers, as well as a directory of two and four year colleges that offer courses or programs that prepare people for food service careers, is available from:

❏ The Educational Foundation of the National Restaurant Association, 250 South Wacker Dr., Suite 1400, Chicago, IL 60606.

For information on the American Culinary Federation's apprenticeship and certification programs for cooks, as well as a list of accredited culinary programs, write to:

❏ American Culinary Federation, P.O. Box 3466, St. Augustine, FL 32085.

For general information on hospitality careers, write to:

❏ Council on Hotel, Restaurant, and Institutional Education, 1200 17th St. NW., Washington, DC 20036-3097.

Correction Officers

Nature of the Work

Correction officers are charged with the security and safety of people who have been arrested, are awaiting trial or other hearing, or who have been convicted of a crime and sentenced to serve time in a correctional institution. Many correction officers guard prisoners in small municipal jails or precinct station houses where their responsibilities are wide ranging, while others control inmates in large state and federal prisons where job duties are more specialized. A relatively small number guard aliens being held by the Immigration and Naturalization Service before being released or deported. Regardless of the setting, correction officers maintain order within the institution, enforce rules and regulations, and often supplement the counseling that inmates receive from psychologists, social workers, and other mental health professionals.

To make sure inmates are orderly and obey rules, correction officers monitor inmates' activities, including working, exercising, eating, and bathing. They assign and supervise inmates' work assignments, as well as instruct and help them on specific tasks. Sometimes it is necessary to search inmates and their living quarters for weapons or drugs, to settle disputes between inmates, and to enforce discipline. Correction officers cannot show favoritism and must report any inmate who violates the rules. To prevent escapes, officers staff security positions in towers and at gates. They count inmates periodically to make sure all are present.

Correction officers inspect the facilities to assure the safety and security of the prisoners. For example, they check cells and other areas of the institution for unsanitary conditions, fire hazards, and evidence of infractions of rules by inmates. In addition, they routinely inspect locks, window bars, grille doors, and gates for signs of tampering.

Correction officers report orally and in writing on inmate conduct and on the quality and quantity of work done by inmates. Officers also report disturbances, violations of rules, and any unusual occurrences. They usually keep a daily record of their activities. In some modern facilities, correction officers monitor the activities of prisoners from a centralized control center with the aid of closed circuit television cameras and a computer tracking system.

Within the institution, correction officers escort inmates to and from cells and other areas and admit and accompany authorized visitors. They also escort prisoners between the institution and courtrooms, medical facilities, and other points. From time to time, they may inspect mail for contraband (prohibited items), administer first aid, or assist police authorities by investigating crimes committed within the institution and by searching for escaped inmates.

Counseling and helping inmates with problems are increasingly important parts of the correction officer's job. Correctional institutions usually employ psychologists and social workers to counsel inmates, but correction officers informally supplement the work of the professionals. They may arrange a change in a daily schedule so that an inmate can visit the library, help inmates get news of their families, talk over personal problems that may have led to committing a crime, or suggest where to look for a job after release from prison. In some institutions, officers receive specialized training and have a more formal counseling role and may lead or participate in group counseling sessions.

Correction sergeants directly supervise correction officers. They are usually responsible for maintaining security and directing the activities of a group of inmates during an assigned watch or in an assigned area.

Working Conditions

Correction officers may work indoors or outdoors, depending on their specific duties. Some indoor areas are well-lighted, heated, and ventilated, but others are overcrowded, hot, and noisy. Outdoors, weather conditions may be disagreeable, such as when standing watch on a guard tower in cold weather. Working in a correctional institution can be stressful and hazardous; correction officers occasionally have been injured or killed during inmate disturbances.

Correction officers usually work an eight hour day, five days a week. Prison security must be provided around the clock, which means some officers work weekends, holidays, and nights. In addition, officers may frequently be required to work overtime.

Employment

Correction officers held about 282,000 jobs in 1992. Six of every ten worked at state correctional institutions such as prisons, prison camps, and reformatories. Most of the remainder worked at city and county jails or other institutions run by local governments. A few thousand correction officers worked at federal correctional institutions. Most correction officers work in relatively large institutions located in rural areas, although a significant number work in jails and other smaller facilities located in cities and towns.

Training, Other Qualifications, and Advancement

Most institutions require that correction officers meet an 18 or 21 year age minimum, have a high school education or its equivalent, and be a United States citizen. In addition, correctional institutions increasingly seek correction officers with postsecondary education in psychology, criminology, and related fields, reflecting a continuing emphasis on personal counseling and rehabilitation of inmates.

Correction officers must be in good health. Many states require candidates to meet formal standards of physical fitness, eyesight, and hearing. Strength, good judgment, and the ability to think and act quickly are assets. Other common requirements include a driver's license, work experience that demonstrates reliability, and no felony convictions. Some states screen applicants for drug abuse and require candidates to pass a written or oral examination.

Federal, state, and local departments of correction provide training for correction officers based on guidelines established by the American Correctional Association, the American Jail Association, and other professional organizations. Some states have special training academies. All states and local departments of correction provide informal on-the-job training and advanced training as well.

Academy trainees generally receive several weeks or months of instruction on institutional policies, regulations, and operations; counseling psychology, crisis intervention, inmate behavior, and contraband control; custody and security procedures; fire and safety; inmate rules and rights; administrative responsibilities; written and oral communication, including preparation of reports; self-defense, including the use of firearms; cardiopulmonary resuscitation; and physical fitness training. New federal correction officers undergo two weeks of training at their assigned institutions followed by three weeks of basic correctional instruction at the Federal Bureau of Prisons training center in Glynco, Georgia. On-the-job trainees receive several weeks or months of similar training in an actual job setting under an experienced officer. Experienced officers receive inservice training to keep abreast of new ideas and procedures. Some complete home-study courses.

Correction officers employed in Michigan must be certified. The criteria for certification are 340 hours of academy training and 15 hours of more advanced training that includes the law regarding corrections; human growth and development; and prison organization. Officers in Pennsylvania's two year apprenticeship program, which provides 4 weeks of orientation, 4 weeks of training at its academy, and 20 months of on-the-job training, receive certification from the U.S. Department of Labor.

With additional education, experience, or training, qualified officers may advance to correction sergeant or other supervisory, administrative, or counseling positions. Many correctional institutions require experience as a correction officer for other corrections positions. Officers sometimes transfer to related areas, such as probation and parole.

Job Outlook

Job opportunities for correction officers are expected to be plentiful through 2005. The need to replace correction officers who transfer to other occupations or leave the labor force, coupled with rising employment demand, will generate several tens of thousands of job openings each year. Correctional institutions have traditionally experienced some difficulty in attracting qualified applicants, and this situation is expected to continue, ensuring highly favorable job prospects.

Employment of correction officers is expected to increase much faster than the average for all occupations through 2005 as additional officers are hired to supervise and counsel a growing inmate population. Expansion and new construction of correctional facilities are also expected to create many new jobs for correction officers, although state and local government budgetary constraints could affect the rate at which new facilities are built. Increasing public concern about the spread of illegal drugs which should result in more convictions, and the adoption of mandatory sentencing guidelines calling for longer sentences and reduced parole for inmates will also spur demand for correction officers. Layoffs of correction officers are rare because security must be maintained in correctional institutions at all times.

Earnings

According to a survey by CONTAC, Inc., starting salaries of state correction officers averaged about $18,600 a year in 1992, ranging from $12,000 in Arkansas to $30,500 in New Jersey. Salaries, overall, averaged about $23,200 and ranged from $15,500 in Tennessee to $38,600 in California. Salaries generally were comparable for correction officers working in jails and other county and municipal correctional institutions. At the federal level, the starting salary was about $18,300 a year in 1993; supervisory correction officers started at about $40,300 a year. The 1993 average salary for all federal nonsupervisory correction officers was about $30,000; for supervisors, about $53,000.

Correction officers are usually provided uniforms or an allowance to purchase their own. Most are provided or can participate in hospitalization or major medical insurance plans; many officers can get disability and life insurance at group rates. They also receive vacation, sick leave, and pension benefits. Officers employed by the federal government and most state governments are covered by civil service systems or merit boards. In more than half of the states, correction officers are represented by labor unions.

Related Occupations

A number of related careers are open to high school graduates who are interested in the protective services and the field of security. Bailiffs guard offenders and maintain order in courtrooms during proceedings. Bodyguards escort people and protect them from injury or invasion of privacy. House or store detectives patrol business establishments to protect against theft and vandalism and to enforce standards of good behavior. Security guards protect government, commercial, and industrial property against theft, vandalism, illegal entry, and fire. Police officers and deputy sheriffs maintain law and order, prevent crime, and arrest offenders.

Other corrections careers are open to people interested in working with offenders. Probation and parole officers counsel offenders, process their release from correctional institutions,

and evaluate their progress in becoming productive members of society. Recreation leaders organize and instruct offenders in sports, games, arts, and crafts.

Sources of Additional Information

Information about entrance requirements, training, and career opportunities for correction officers may be obtained from the Federal Office of Personnel Management, Federal Bureau of Prisons, state civil service commissions, state departments of correction, or nearby correctional institutions and facilities. Information on corrections careers, as well as information about schools that offer criminal justice education, financial assistance, and where to find jobs, is available from:

❏ CEGA Services, Inc., P.O. Box 81826, Lincoln, NE 68501-1826.

Additional information on careers in corrections is available from:

❏ The American Correctional Association, 8025 Laurel Lakes Ct., Laurel, MD 20707;

❏ The American Probation and Parole Association, P.O. Box 201, Lexington, KY 40584; or

❏ The International Association of Correctional Officers, Box 53, 1333 South Wabash Ave., Chicago, IL 60605.

Dental Assistants

Nature of the Work

Dental assistants perform a variety of patient care, office, and laboratory duties. They work chairside as dentists examine and treat patients. They make patients as comfortable as possible in the dental chair, prepare them for treatment, and obtain dental records. Assistants hand dentists instruments and materials and keep patients' mouths dry and clear by using suction or other devices. Assistants also sterilize and disinfect instruments and equipment; prepare tray setups for dental procedures; provide postoperative instruction; and instruct patients in oral health care.

Some dental assistants prepare materials for making impressions and restorations, expose radiographs, and process dental x-ray film as directed by a dentist. They may also remove sutures, apply anesthetic and preventive agents to teeth and gums, remove excess cement used in the filling process, and place rubber dams on the teeth to isolate them for individual treatment.

Those with laboratory duties make casts of the teeth and mouth from impressions taken by dentists, clean and polish removable appliances, and make temporary crowns. Dental assistants with office duties arrange and confirm appointments, receive patients, keep treatment records, send bills, receive payments, and order dental supplies and materials.

Dental assistants should not be confused with dental hygienists, who are licensed to perform a wider variety of clinical tasks. (See the statement on dental hygienists elsewhere in this book.)

Working Conditions

Dental assistants work in a well-lighted, clean environment. Handling radiographic equipment poses dangers, but they can be minimized with safety procedures. Likewise, dental assistants wear gloves and masks to protect themselves from infectious diseases like hepatitis. Dental assistants, like dentists, work either standing or sitting. Their work area is usually near the dental chair, so that they can arrange instruments, materials, and medication, and hand them to the dentist when needed. Most dental assistants have a 32- to 40-hour workweek which may include work on Saturday or evenings.

Employment

Dental assistants held about 183,000 jobs in 1992. Almost one out of every three worked part-time, sometimes in more than one dentist's office. Almost all dental assistants work in private dental offices. Some work in dental schools, private and government hospitals, state and local public health departments, or in clinics.

Training, Other Qualifications, and Advancement

Most assistants learn their skills on the job, although many are trained in dental assisting programs offered by community and junior colleges, trade schools, and technical institutes. Some assistants are trained in Armed Forces schools. Assistants must be a dentist's third hand; therefore, dentists look for people who are reliable, can work well with others, and have manual dexterity. High school students interested in careers as dental assistants should take courses in biology, chemistry, health, and office practices.

The American Dental Association's Commission on Dental Accreditation approved 232 training programs in 1993. Programs include classroom, laboratory, and preclinical instruction in dental assisting skills and related theory. In addition, students gain practical experience in dental schools, clinics, or dental offices. Most programs take one year or less to complete and lead to a certificate or diploma. Two-year programs offered in community and junior colleges lead to an associate degree. All programs require a high school diploma or its equivalent, and some require typing or a science course for admission. Some private vocational schools offer four- to six-month courses in dental assisting, but these are not accredited by the Commission on Dental Accreditation.

Certification is available through the Dental Assisting National Board. Certification is an acknowledgment of an assistant's qualifications and professional competence, but is usually not required for employment. In several states that have adopted standards for dental assistants who perform radiologic procedures, completion of the certification examination meets those standards. Candidates may qualify to take the certification examination by graduating from an accredited training program or by having two years of full-time experience as a dental assistant. In addition, applicants must have taken a course in cardiopulmonary resuscitation.

Without further education, advancement opportunities are limited. Some dental assistants working the front office become office managers. Others, working chairside, go back to school to become dental hygienists.

Job Outlook

Employment of dental assistants is expected to grow faster than the average for all occupations through 2005. Population growth, higher incomes, and greater retention of natural teeth by middle-aged and older people will fuel demand for dental services. Also, dentists are likely to employ more assistants for several reasons. Older dentists, who are less likely to employ assistants, will leave and be replaced by recent graduates, who are more likely to use one or even two. In addition, as dentists' workloads increase, they are expected to hire more assistants to perform routine tasks, so they may use their own time more profitably.

Most job openings for dental assistants will arise from the need to replace assistants who leave the occupation. Many assistants leave the job to take on family responsibilities, return to school, or transfer to another occupation.

Earnings

In 1992, median weekly earnings for dental assistants working full-time were about $332. The middle 50 percent earned between $284 and $420 a week. According to the American Dental Association, dental assistants who worked 32 hours a week or more averaged $332 a week in 1991; the average hourly earnings for all dental assistants were $9.20.

Related Occupations

Workers in other occupations supporting health practitioners include medical assistants, physical therapy assistants, occupational therapy assistants, pharmacy assistants, and veterinary technicians.

Sources of Additional Information

Information about career opportunities, scholarships, accredited dental assistant programs, and requirements for certification is available from:

- ❏ American Dental Assistants Association, 203 N. Lasalle, Suite 1320, Chicago, IL 60601-1225;

- ❏ Commission on Dental Accreditation, American Dental Association, 211 E. Chicago Ave., Suite 1814, Chicago, IL 60611; or

- ❏ Dental Assisting National Board, Inc., 216 E. Ontario St., Chicago, IL 60611.

Flight Attendants

Nature of the Work

It is the job of the flight attendant to see that all passengers have a safe, comfortable, and enjoyable flight. At least one hour before each flight, attendants are briefed by the captain on such things as expected weather conditions and special passenger problems. The attendants see that the passenger cabin is in order, that supplies of food, beverages, blankets, and reading material are adequate, and that first aid kits and other emergency equipment are aboard and in working order. As passengers board the plane, attendants greet them, check their tickets, and assist them in storing coats and carry-on luggage.

Before the plane takes off, attendants instruct passengers in the use of emergency equipment and check to see that all passengers have their seat belts fastened and seat backs forward. In the air, they answer questions about the flight; distribute reading material, pillows, and blankets; and help care for small children, elderly, and disabled people. They may administer first aid to passengers who become ill. Attendants also serve cocktails and other refreshments and, on many flights, heat and distribute precooked meals. After the plane has landed, flight attendants assist passengers as they leave the plane. They then prepare reports on medications given to passengers, lost and found articles, and cabin equipment conditions. Some flight attendants straighten up the plane's cabin.

Helping passengers in the event of an emergency is the most important responsibility of the flight attendant. This may range from reassuring passengers during occasional encounters with strong turbulence to directing passengers in evacuating a plane following an emergency landing.

Lead or first flight attendants aboard planes oversee the work of the other attendants while performing most of the same duties.

Working Conditions

Because airlines operate around the clock year-round, attendants may work at night and on holidays and weekends. They usually fly 75 to 85 hours a month. In addition, they generally spend about 75 to 85 hours a month on the ground preparing planes for flight, writing reports following completed flights, and waiting for planes that arrive late. Because of variations in scheduling and limitations on flying time, many attendants have 11 or more days off each month. Attendants may be away from their home base at least one-third of the time. During this period, the airlines provide hotel accommodations and an allowance for meal expenses.

The combination of free time and discount air fares provides flight attendants the opportunity to travel and see new places. However, the work can be strenuous and trying. Short flights require speedy service if meals are served. A rough flight can make serving drinks and meals difficult. Attendants stand during much of the flight and must remain pleasant and efficient regardless of how tired they are or how demanding passengers may be. Flight attendants are susceptible to injury because of the job demands in a moving aircraft.

Employment

Flight attendants held about 93,000 jobs in 1992. Commercial airlines employed the vast majority of all flight attendants, most of whom were stationed in major cities at the airlines' home bases. A small number of flight attendants worked for large companies that operate their own aircraft for business purposes.

Training, Other Qualifications, and Advancement

The airlines prefer to hire poised, tactful, and resourceful people who can deal comfortably with strangers. Applicants usually must be at least 19 to 21 years old, but some airlines have higher minimum age requirements. Flight attendants must fall into a specific weight range depending on their height and must have excellent health, good vision, and the ability to speak clearly.

Applicants must be high school graduates. Those having several years of college or experience in dealing with the public are preferred. More and more attendants being hired are college graduates. Flight attendants for international airlines generally must speak an appropriate foreign language fluently.

Most large airlines require that newly hired flight attendants complete four to six weeks of intensive training in their own schools. The airlines that do not operate schools generally send new employees to the school of another airline. Transportation to the training centers and an allowance for board, room, and school supplies may be provided. Trainees learn emergency procedures such as evacuating an airplane, operating an oxygen system, and giving first aid. Attendants also are taught flight regulations and duties, and company operations and policies. Trainees receive instruction on personal grooming and weight control. Trainees for the international routes get additional instruction in passport and customs regulations and dealing with terrorism. Toward the end of their training, students go on practice flights. Attendants must receive 12 to 14 hours of training in emergency procedures and passenger relations annually.

After completing initial training, flight attendants are assigned to one of their airline's bases. New attendants are placed in reserve status and are called on either to staff extra flights or fill in for attendants who are sick or on vacation. Reserve attendants on duty must be available on short notice. Attendants usually remain on reserve for at least one year; in some cities, it may take five years or longer to advance from reserve status. Advancement takes longer today than in the past because experienced attendants are remaining in this career for more years than they previously did. Attendants who are no longer on reserve bid for regular assignments. Because these assignments are based on seniority, usually only the most experienced attendants get their choice of base and flights. Some attendants transfer to flight service instructor, customer service director, recruiting representative, or various other administrative positions.

Job Outlook

As more career-minded people have entered this occupation, turnover—which traditionally has been very high—has declined. Still, most job openings through 2005 should flow from replacement needs. Thousands of job openings will arise each year to replace flight attendants who transfer to another occupation or who leave the labor force.

Employment of flight attendants is expected to grow much faster than the average for all occupations through 2005. Growth in population and income is expected to increase the number of airline passengers. Airlines enlarge their capacity by increasing the number and size of planes in operation. Because Federal Aviation Administration safety rules require one attendant for every 50 seats, more flight attendants will be needed.

Competition for jobs as flight attendants is expected to remain very keen because the number of applicants is expected to greatly exceed the number of job openings. The glamour of the airline industry and the opportunity to travel and meet people attract many applicants. Those with at least two years of college and experience in dealing with the public have the best chance of being hired.

Employment of flight attendants is sensitive to cyclical swings in the economy. During recessions, when the demand for air travel declines, many flight attendants are put on part-time status or laid off. Until demand increases, few new attendants are hired.

Earnings

Beginning flight attendants had median earnings of about $13,000 a year in 1992, according to data from the Association of Flight Attendants. Flight attendants with six years of flying experience had median annual earnings of about $20,000, while some senior flight attendants earned as much as $40,000 a year. Flight attendants receive extra compensation for overtime and night and international flights. In addition, flight attendants and their immediate families are entitled to reduced fares on their own and most other airlines.

Flight attendants are required to buy uniforms and wear them while on duty. Uniform replacement items are usually paid for by the company. The airlines generally provide a small allowance to cover cleaning and upkeep of the uniforms.

Many flight attendants belong to the Association of Flight Attendants. Others are members of the Transport Workers Union of America, The International Brotherhood of Teamsters, or other unions.

Related Occupations

Other jobs that involve helping people as a safety professional and require the ability to be pleasant even under trying circumstances include emergency medical technician, firefighter, maritime crew or camp counselor.

Sources of Additional Information

Information about job opportunities in a particular airline and the qualifications required may be obtained by writing to the personnel manager of the company. For addresses of airline companies and information about job opportunities and salaries, contact:

❏ Future Aviation Professionals of America, 4959 Massachusetts Blvd., Atlanta, GA 30337. This organization may be called toll free at 1-800-Jet-Jobs.

Guards

Nature of the Work

Guards, also called security officers, patrol and inspect property to protect against fire, theft, vandalism, and illegal entry. Their duties vary with the size, type, and location of their employer.

In office buildings, banks, hospitals, and department stores, guards protect records, merchandise, money, and equipment. In department stores, they often work with undercover detectives to watch for theft by customers or store employees.

At ports, airports, and railroads, guards protect merchandise being shipped as well as property and equipment. They screen passengers and visitors for weapons, explosives, and other contraband. They ensure that nothing is stolen while being loaded or unloaded, and watch for fires, prowlers, and trouble among work crews. Sometimes they direct traffic.

Guards who work in public buildings, such as museums or art galleries, protect paintings and exhibits. They also answer routine questions from visitors and sometimes guide tours.

In factories, laboratories, government buildings, data processing centers, and military bases where valuable property or information—such as information on new products, computer codes, or defense secrets—must be protected, guards check the credentials of people and vehicles entering and leaving the premises. University, park, or recreation guards perform similar duties and may also issue parking permits and direct traffic. Golf course patrollers prevent unauthorized people from using the facility and help keep play running smoothly.

At social affairs, sports events, conventions, and other public gatherings, guards provide information, assist in crowd control, and watch for people who may cause trouble. Some guards work as bouncers and patrol places of entertainment such as nightclubs to preserve order among customers and to protect property. Armored car guards protect money and valuables during transit. Bodyguards protect individuals from bodily injury, kidnapping, or invasion of privacy.

In a large organization, a security officer is often in charge of the guard force; in a small organization, a single worker may be responsible for all security measures. Patrolling is usually done on foot, but if the property is large, guards may make their rounds by car or motor scooter. As more businesses purchase advanced electronic security systems to protect their property, more guards are being assigned to stations where they monitor perimeter security, environmental functions, communications, and other systems. In many cases, these guards maintain radio contact with other guards patrolling on foot or in motor vehicles. Some guards use computers to store information on matters relevant to security—such as visitors or suspicious occurrences—during their hours on duty.

As they make their rounds, guards check all doors and windows, ensure that no unauthorized people remain after working hours, and confirm that fire extinguishers, alarms, sprinkler systems, furnaces, and various electrical and plumbing systems are working properly. They sometimes set thermostats or turn on lights for janitorial workers.

Guards are usually uniformed and may carry a nightstick and gun, although the bearing of guns is decreasing. They may also carry a flashlight, whistle, two-way radio, and a watch clock—a device that indicates the time at which they reach various checkpoints.

Working Conditions

Guards work indoors and outdoors patrolling buildings, industrial plants, and grounds. Indoors, they may be stationed at a guard desk to monitor electronic security and surveillance devices or to check the credentials of people entering or leaving the premises. They can also be stationed at gate shelters and may patrol grounds in all weather.

Because guards often work alone, there may be no one nearby to help if an accident or injury occurs. Some large firms, therefore, use a reporting service that enables guards to be in constant contact with a central station outside the plant. If they fail to transmit an expected signal, the central station investigates. Guard work is usually routine, but guards must be constantly alert for threats to themselves and to the property that they are protecting. Guards who work during the day may have a great deal of contact with other employees and members of the public.

Many guards work alone at night; the usual shift lasts eight hours. Some employers have three shifts, and guards rotate to divide daytime, weekend, and holiday work equally. Guards usually eat on the job instead of taking a regular break.

Employment

Guards held about 803,000 jobs in 1992. Industrial security firms and guard agencies employed more than one-half of all guards. These organizations provide security services on contract, assigning their guards to buildings and other sites as needed. The remainder were in-house guards, employed in large numbers by banks; building management companies; hotels; hospitals; retail stores; restaurants and bars; schools, colleges, and universities; and federal, state, and local governments. Although guard jobs are found throughout the country, most are located in metropolitan areas.

Training, Other Qualifications, and Advancement

Most employers prefer guards who are high school graduates. Applicants with less than a high school education can also qualify if they pass reading and writing tests and demonstrate competence in following written and oral instructions. Some jobs require a driver's license. Employers also seek people who have had experience in the military police or in state and local police departments. Most people who enter guard jobs have prior work experience, although it is usually unrelated. Because of limited formal training requirements and flexible hours, this occupation attracts some people seeking a second job. For some entrants, retired from military careers or other protective services, guard employment is a second career.

Applicants are expected to have good character references, no police record, good health—especially in hearing and vision—and good personal habits such as neatness and dependability. They should be mentally alert, emotionally stable, and physically fit in order to cope with emergencies. Guards who have frequent contact with the public should be friendly and personable. Some employers require applicants to take a polygraph examination or a written test of honesty, attitudes, and other personal qualities. Most employers require applicants and experienced workers to submit to drug screening tests as a condition of employment.

Virtually all states and the District of Columbia have licensing or registration requirements for guards who work for contract security agencies. Registration generally requires that employment of an individual as a guard be reported to the licensing authorities—the state police department or other state licensing commission. To be granted a license as a guard, individuals generally must be 18 years old, have no convictions for perjury or acts of violence, pass a background examination, and complete classroom training in such subjects as property rights, emergency procedures, and seizure of suspected criminals. In 1990, only about five states and the District of Columbia had licensing requirements for in-house guards.

Candidates for guard jobs in the federal government must have some experience as a guard and pass a written examination. Armed Forces experience is also an asset. For most federal guard positions, applicants must qualify in the use of firearms.

The amount of training guards receive varies. Training requirements are generally increasing as modern, highly sophisticated security systems become more commonplace. Many employers give newly hired guards instruction before they start the job and also provide several weeks of on-the-job training. More and more states are making ongoing training a legal requirement. For example, New York now requires guards to complete 40 hours of training after starting work. Guards receive training in protection, public relations, report writing, crisis deterrence, first aid, drug control, and specialized training relevant to their particular assignment.

Guards employed at establishments that place a heavy emphasis on security usually receive extensive formal training. For example, guards at nuclear power plants may undergo several months of training before being placed on duty under close supervision. Guards may be taught to use firearms, administer first aid, operate alarm systems and electronic security equipment, and spot and deal with security problems. Guards who are authorized to carry firearms may be periodically tested in their use according to state or local laws. Some guards are periodically tested for strength and endurance.

Although guards in small companies receive periodic salary increases, advancement is likely to be limited. However, most large organizations use a military type of ranking that offers advancement in position and salary. Higher level guard experience may enable individuals to transfer to police jobs that offer higher pay and greater opportunities for advancement. Guards with some college education may advance to jobs that involve administrative duties or the prevention of espionage and sabotage. A few guards with management skills open their own contract security guard agencies.

Job Outlook

Job openings for people seeking work as guards are expected to be plentiful through 2005. High turnover and this occupation's large size rank it among those providing the greatest number of job openings in the entire economy. Many opportunities are expected for people seeking full-time employment, as well as for those seeking part-time or second jobs at night or on weekends. However, some competition is expected for the higher paying in-house guard positions. Compared to contract security guards, in-house guards enjoy higher earnings and benefits, greater job security, and more advancement potential, and are usually given more training and responsibility.

Employment of guards is expected to grow much faster than the average for all occupations through 2005. Increased concern about crime, vandalism, and terrorism will heighten the need for security in and around plants, stores, offices, and recreation areas. The level of business investment in increasingly expensive plant and equipment is expected to rise, resulting in growth in the number of guard jobs. Demand for guards will also grow as private security firms increasingly perform duties formerly handled by government police officers and marshals, such as monitoring crowds at airports and providing security in courts. Because engaging the services of a security guard firm is easier and less costly than assuming direct responsibility for hiring, training, and managing a security guard force, job growth is expected to be concentrated among contract security guard agencies.

Guards employed by industrial security and guard agencies are occasionally laid off when the firm at which they work does not renew its contract with their agency. Most are able to find employment with other agencies, however. Guards employed directly by the firm at which they work are seldom laid off because a plant or factory must still be protected even when economic conditions force it to close temporarily.

Earnings

According to a survey of workplaces in 160 metropolitan areas, guards with less responsibility and training had median hourly earnings of $6 in 1992. The middle half earned between $5 and $7.35 an hour. Guards with more specialized training and experience had median hourly earnings of $11.15, with the middle half earning between $9.05 and $13.34 an hour. Guards employed by industrial security and guard agencies generally started at or slightly above the minimum wage, which was $4.25 an hour in 1993.

Depending on their experience, newly hired guards in the federal government earned between $14,600 and $16,400 a year in 1993. Experienced guards employed by the federal government averaged about $21,700 a year in 1993. These workers usually receive overtime pay as well as a wage differential for the second and third shifts.

Unionized in-house guards tend to earn more than the average. Many guards are represented by the United Plant Guard Workers Of America. Other guards belong to the International Union of Guards or the International Union Of Security Officers.

Related Occupations

Guards protect property, maintain security, and enforce regulations for entry and conduct in the establishments at which they work. Related security and protective service occupations include: bailiffs, border guards, correction officers, deputy sheriffs, fish and game wardens, house or store detectives, police officers, and private investigators.

Sources of Additional Information

Further information about work opportunities for guards is available from local employers and the nearest state employment service office. Information about registration and licensing requirements for guards may be obtained from the state licensing commission or the state police department. In states where local jurisdictions establish licensing requirements, contact a local government authority such as the sheriff, county executive, or city manager.

Homemaker-Home Health Aides

Nature of the Work

Homemaker-home health aides help elderly, disabled, and ill people live in their own homes instead of in a health facility. Most work with elderly or disabled clients who require more extensive care than spouse, family, or friends can provide. Some homemaker-home health aides work with families in which a parent is incapacitated and small children need care. Others help discharged hospital patients who have relatively short-term needs. These workers are sometimes called home care aides and personal care attendants.

Homemaker-home health aides provide housekeeping services, personal care, and emotional support for their clients. They clean clients' houses, do laundry, and change bed linens. Aides may also plan meals (including special diets), shop for food, and cook.

Home health aides provide personal care services, also known as hands-on care because they physically touch the patient. These aides may help clients move from bed, bathe, dress, and groom. They may also check pulse, temperature, and respiration; help with simple prescribed exercises; and assist with medication routines. Occasionally, they may change nonsterile dressings, use special equipment such as a hydraulic lift, give massages and alcohol rubs, or assist with braces and artificial limbs. Some accompany clients outside the home, serving as guide, companion, and aide.

Homemaker-home health aides also provide instruction and psychological support. For example, they may assist in toilet training a severely mentally handicapped child or just listen to clients talk about their problems. Aides keep records of services performed and of the client's condition and progress.

In home care agencies, homemaker-home health aides are supervised by a registered nurse, a physical therapist, or a social worker, who assigns them specific duties. Aides report changes in the client's condition to the supervisor or case manager. Homemaker-home health aides also participate in case reviews, consulting with the team caring for the client, which includes registered nurses, therapists, and other health professionals.

Working Conditions

The homemaker-home health aide's daily routine may vary. Aides may go to the same home every day for months or even years. More commonly, however, aides work with a number of different clients, each job lasting a few hours, days, or weeks. Aides often visit four or five clients on the same day. Surroundings differ from case to case. Some homes are neat and pleasant, while others are untidy or depressing. Some clients are angry, abusive, depressed, or otherwise difficult; others are pleasant and cooperative.

Homemaker-home health aides generally work on their own with periodic visits by their supervisor. They have detailed instructions explaining when to visit clients and what services to perform. Many aides work part-time, and weekend hours are common. Most aides generally travel by public transportation, but some need an automobile. In any event, they are responsible for getting to the client's home. Aides may spend a good portion of the working day traveling from one client to another.

Employment

Homemaker-home health aides held about 475,000 jobs in 1992. Most aides are employed by homemaker-home health agencies, home health agencies, visiting nurse associations, residential care facilities with home health departments, hospitals, public health and welfare departments, community volunteer agencies, and temporary help firms. Self-employed aides have no agency affiliation or supervision, and accordingly accept clients, set fees, and arrange work schedules on their own.

Training, Other Qualifications, and Advancement

The federal government has enacted guidelines for home health aides whose employers receive reimbursement from Medicare. The federal law requires home health aides to pass a competency test covering 12 areas: communication skills; observation, reporting, and documentation of patient status and the care or services furnished; reading and recording vital signs; basic infection control procedures; basic elements of body function and changes; maintenance of a clean, safe, and healthy environment; recognition of and procedures for emergencies; the physical, emotional, and developmental characteristics of the patients served; personal hygiene and grooming; safe transfer techniques; normal range of motion and positioning; and basic nutrition.

A home health aide may also receive training before taking the competency test. The federal law requires at least 75 hours of classroom and practical training supervised by a registered nurse. Training and testing programs may be offered by the employing agency, but they must meet the standards of the Health Care Financing Administration. Training programs may vary depending on state regulations. Thirteen states have specific laws on personal care services. The Foundation for Hospice and Home Care offers a National Homemaker-Home Health Aide certification. The certification is a voluntary demonstration that the individual has met industry standards.

Successful homemaker-home health aides like to help people and do not mind hard work. They have a sense of responsibility, compassion, emotional stability, and a cheerful disposition. Aides should be tactful, honest, and discreet because they work in private homes. Homemaker-home health aides must be in good health. A physical examination including state regulated tests such as those for tuberculosis may be required.

Advancement is limited. In some agencies, workers start out performing homemaker duties, such as cleaning. With experience and training, they may take on personal care duties. The most experienced aides may assist with medical equipment such as ventilators, which help patients breathe.

Job Outlook

A large number of job openings is expected for homemaker-home health aides, due to very rapid growth and very high turnover. Homemaker-home health aides is expected to be one of the fastest growing occupations through 2005—more than doubling in employment size.

The number of people in their seventies and beyond is projected to rise substantially. This age group is characterized by mounting health problems that require some assistance. Also, there will be an increasing reliance on home care for patients of all ages. This trend reflects several developments: efforts to contain costs by moving patients out of hospitals and nursing facilities as quickly as possible; the realization that treatment can be more effective in familiar surroundings rather than clinical surroundings; and the development of portable medical equipment for in-home treatment.

In addition to jobs created by the increase in demand for these workers, replacement needs are expected to produce numerous openings. Turnover is high, a reflection of the relatively low skill requirements, low pay, and high emotional demands of the work. For these same reasons, many people are unwilling to do this kind of work. Therefore, people who are interested in this work and suited for it should have excellent job opportunities, particularly those with experience or training as homemaker-home health aides or nursing aides.

Earnings

Earnings for homemaker-home health aides vary considerably. According to the National Association for Home Care, home health aides' average starting hourly wage in July 1992 was $6.31, and the average maximum hourly wage was $8.28. Wages were somewhat higher than these national averages in the Northeast and West and somewhat lower in the Midwest and South. Some aides were paid on a salary or per-visit basis.

Most employers give slight pay increases with experience and added responsibility. Aides are usually paid only for the time worked in the home. They are not normally paid for travel time between jobs. Some employers offer a full package of vacation and sick leave, health and life insurance, and a retirement plan. Others hire only on-call hourly workers, with no benefits.

Related Occupations

Homemaker-home health aide is a service occupation that combines duties of health workers and social service workers. Workers in related occupations that involve personal contact to help or instruct others include attendants in children's institutions, childcare attendants in schools, child monitors, companions, nursing aides, nursery school attendants, occupational therapy aides, nursing aides, physical therapy aides, playroom attendants, and psychiatric aides.

Sources of Additional Information

General information about training and referrals to state and local agencies about opportunities for homemaker-home health aides, a list of relevant publications, and information on national certification are available from:

❏ Foundation for Hospice and Homecare/National Certification Program, 519 C St. NE., Washington, DC 20002.

Medical Assistants

Nature of the Work

Medical assistants perform routine clinical and clerical tasks to keep offices of physicians, podiatrists, chiropractors, and optometrists running smoothly. Medical assistants should not be confused with physician assistants, who examine, diagnose, and treat patients, under the direct supervision of a physician.

The duties of medical assistants vary from office to office, depending on office location, size, and specialty. In small practices, medical assistants are usually generalists, handling both clerical and clinical duties and reporting directly to an office manager, physician, or other health practitioner. Those in large practices tend to specialize in a particular area under the supervision of department administrators.

Medical assistants perform many clerical duties. They answer telephones, greet patients, update and file patient medical records, fill out insurance forms, handle correspondence, schedule appointments, arrange for hospital admission and laboratory services, and handle billing and bookkeeping.

Clinical duties vary according to state law and include taking medical histories and recording vital signs; explaining treatment procedures to patients; preparing patients for examination; and assisting during the examination. Medical assistants collect and prepare laboratory specimens or perform basic laboratory tests on the premises; dispose of contaminated supplies; and sterilize medical instruments. They instruct patients about medication and special diets, prepare and administer medications as directed by a physician, authorize drug refills as directed, telephone prescriptions to a pharmacy, draw blood, prepare patients for X rays, take electrocardiograms, remove sutures, and change dressings. Medical assistants may also arrange examining room instruments and equipment, purchase and maintain supplies and equipment, and keep waiting and examining rooms neat and clean.

Assistants who specialize have additional duties. *Podiatric medical assistants* make castings of feet, expose and develop X rays, and assist podiatrists in surgery. *Ophthalmic medical assistants* help ophthalmologists provide medical eye care. They use precision instruments to administer diagnostic tests, measure and record vision, and test the functioning of eyes and eye muscles. They also show patients how to use eye dressings, protective shields, and safety glasses, and insert, remove, and care for contact lenses. Under the direction of the physician, they may administer medications, including eye drops. They also maintain optical and surgical instruments and assist the ophthalmologist in surgery.

Working Conditions

Medical assistants work in a well-lighted, clean environment. They constantly interact with other people, and may have to handle several responsibilities at once. Most full-time medical assistants work a regular 40-hour week. Some work evenings and weekends.

Employment

Medical assistants held about 181,000 jobs in 1992. More than 70 percent were employed in physicians' offices, and about 12 percent worked in offices of other health practitioners such as chiropractors, optometrists, and podiatrists. Others worked in hospitals, nursing homes, and other health care facilities.

Training, Other Qualifications, and Advancement

Medical assisting is one of the few health occupations open to individuals with no formal training. Although formal training in medical assisting is available, such training—while generally preferred—is not always required. Some medical assistants are trained on the job. Applicants usually need a high school diploma or the equivalent. High school courses in mathematics, health, biology, typing, bookkeeping, computers, and office skills are helpful. Volunteer experience in the health care field may also be helpful.

Formal programs in medical assisting are offered in vocational-technical high schools, postsecondary vocational schools, community and junior colleges, and in colleges and universities. College-level programs usually last either one year, resulting in a certificate or diploma, or two years, resulting in an associate degree. Vocational programs can take up to one year and lead to a diploma or certificate. Courses cover anatomy, physiology, and medical terminology as well as typing, transcription, recordkeeping, accounting, and insurance processing.

Students learn laboratory techniques, clinical and diagnostic procedures, pharmaceutical principles and medication administration, and first aid. They are also instructed in office practices, patient relations, and medical law and ethics. Accredited programs may include an externship that provides practical experience in physicians' offices, hospitals, or other health care facilities.

Two agencies recognized by the U.S. Department of Education accredit programs in medical assisting: The American Medical Association's Committee on Allied Health Education and Accreditation (CAHEA) and the Accrediting Bureau of Health Education Schools (ABHES). In 1993, there were 207 medical assisting programs accredited by CAHEA and 136 accredited by ABHES. The Joint Review Committee for Opthalmic Medical Personnel has approved 13 programs in ophthalmic medical assisting.

Although there is no licensing for medical assistants, some states require them to take a test or a short course before they can take X rays, draw blood, or give injections. Employers prefer to hire experienced workers or certified applicants who have passed a national examination, indicating that the medical assistant meets certain standards of competence. The American Association of Medical Assistants awards the Certified Medical Assistant credential; the American Medical Technologists awards the Registered Medical Assistant credential; the American Society of Podiatric Medical Assistants awards the Podiatric Medical Assistant Certified credential; and the Joint Commission on Allied Health Personnel in Ophthalmology awards the Ophthalmic Medical Assistant credential at three levels—Certified Ophthalmic Assistant, Certified Ophthalmic Technician, and Certified Ophthalmic Medical Technologist.

Because medical assistants deal with the public, they need a neat, well-groomed appearance and a courteous, pleasant manner. Medical assistants must be able to put patients at ease and explain physicians' instructions. They must respect the confidential nature of medical information. Clinical duties require a reasonable level of manual dexterity and visual acuity.

Medical assistants may be able to advance to office manager or become ward clerks, medical record clerks, phlebotomists, or EKG technicians in hospitals. Medical assistants may qualify for a wide variety of administrative support occupations, or may teach medical assisting. Some, with additional schooling, enter other health occupations such as nursing and medical technology.

Job Outlook

Employment of medical assistants is expected to grow much faster than the average for all occupations through 2005 as the health services industry expands. Employment growth will be driven by growth in the number of group and other health care practices that use support personnel. Medical assistants work primarily in outpatient settings, where fast growth is expected. Most job openings, however, will result from the need to replace experienced assistants who leave the occupation.

In view of the high turnover as well as the preference of many physicians for trained personnel, job prospects should be excellent for medical assistants with formal training or experience, particularly those with certification.

Earnings

The earnings of medical assistants vary widely, depending on experience, skill level, and location. According to a survey conducted by the Committee on Allied Health Education and Accreditation, the average starting salary for graduates of the medical assistant programs they accredit was about $15,059 a year in 1992. According to a 1991 survey by the American Association of Medical Assistants, the average annual salary for medical assistants was $18,334. Medical assistants with two years of experience or less averaged $13,715, while those with 11 years of experience or more averaged $20,885.

Related Occupations

Workers in other medical support occupations include medical secretaries, hospital admitting clerks, pharmacy helpers, medical record clerks, dental assistants, occupational therapy aides, and physical therapy aides.

Sources of Additional Information

Information about career opportunities, CAHEA-accredited educational programs in medical assisting, and the Certified Medical Assistant exam is available from:

❑ The American Association of Medical Assistants, 20 North Wacker Dr., Suite 1575, Chicago, IL 60606-2903.

Information about career opportunities and the Registered Medical Assistant certification exam is available from:

❑ Registered Medical Assistants of American Medical Technologists, 710 Higgins Rd., Park Ridge, IL 60068-5765.

For a list of ABHES-accredited educational programs in medical assisting, write:

❑ Accrediting Bureau of Health Education Schools, Oak Manor Office, 29089 U.S. 20 West, Elkhart, IN 46514.

Information about career opportunities, training programs, and the Certified Ophthalmic Assistant exam is available from:

❑ Joint Commission on Allied Health Personnel in Ophthalmology, 2025 Woodlane Dr., St. Paul, MN 55125-2995.

Information about careers for podiatric assistants is available from:

❑ American Society of Podiatric Medical Assistants, 2124 S. Austin Blvd., Cicero, IL 60650.

Nursing Aides and Psychiatric Aides

Nature of the Work

Nursing aides and psychiatric aides help care for physically or mentally ill, injured, disabled, or infirm individuals confined to hospitals, nursing or residential care facilities, and mental health settings. (Homemaker-home health aids, whose duties are similar but who work in clients' homes, are discussed elsewhere in this book.)

Nursing aides, also known as nursing assistants or hospital attendants, work under the supervision of nursing and medical staff. They answer patients' call bells, deliver messages, serve meals, make beds, and feed, dress, and bathe patients. Aides may also give massages, provide skin care to patients who cannot move, take temperatures, pulse, respiration, and blood pressure, and help patients get in and out of bed and walk. They may also escort patients to operating and examining rooms, keep patients' rooms neat, set up equipment, or store and move supplies. Aides observe patients' physical, mental, and emotional conditions and report any change to the nursing or medical staff.

Nursing aides employed in nursing homes are sometimes called geriatric aides. They are often the principal caregivers, having far more contact with residents than other members of the staff do. Because residents may stay in a nursing home for months or even years, aides are expected to develop ongoing relationships with them and respond to them in a positive, caring way.

Psychiatric aides are also known as mental health assistants, psychiatric nursing assistants, or ward attendants. They care for mentally impaired or emotionally disturbed individuals. They work under a team that may include psychiatrists, psychologists, psychiatric nurses, social workers, and therapists. In addition to helping patients dress, bathe, groom, and eat, psychiatric aides socialize with them and lead them in educational and recreational activities. Psychiatric aides may play games such as cards with the patients, watch television with them, or participate in group activities such as sports or field trips. They observe patients and report any signs which might be important for the professional staff to know. If necessary, they help restrain unruly patients and accompany patients to and from wards for examination and treatment. Because they have the closest contact with patients, psychiatric aides have a great deal of influence on patients' outlook and treatment.

Working Conditions

Most full-time aides work about 40 hours a week, but because patients need care 24 hours a day, some aides work evenings, nights, weekends, and holidays. Many work part-time. Aides spend many hours standing. Because they may have to move partially paralyzed patients in and out of bed or help them stand or walk, aides must guard against back injury.

Nursing aides often have unpleasant duties; they empty bed pans, change soiled bed linens, and care for disoriented and irritable patients. One-half of nursing aides work in nursing homes. Psychiatric aides are often confronted with violent patients. While their work can be emotionally draining, many aides gain satisfaction from assisting those in need.

Employment

Nursing aides held about 1,308,000 jobs in 1992, and psychiatric aides held about 81,000 jobs. About one-half of all nursing aides worked in nursing homes, and about one-fourth worked in hospitals. Some worked in residential care facilities, such as halfway houses and homes for the aged or disabled, or in private households. Most psychiatric aides worked in state and county mental institutions, psychiatric units of general hospitals, private psychiatric facilities, and community mental health centers.

Training, Other Qualifications, and Advancement

In many cases, neither a high school diploma nor previous work experience is necessary for a job as a nursing or psychiatric aide. A few employers, however, require some training or experience. Hospitals may require experience as a nursing aide or home health aide. Nursing homes often hire inexperienced workers who must complete a minimum of 75 hours of mandatory training and pass a competency evaluation program within 4 months of employment. Aides who complete the program are placed on the state registry of nursing aides. Some states require psychiatric aides to complete a formal training program.

These occupations can offer individuals an entry into the world of work. The flexibility of night and weekend hours also provides high school and college students a chance to work during the school year. The work is also open to middle-aged and older men and women.

Nursing aide training is offered in high schools, vocational-technical centers, many nursing homes, and community colleges. Courses cover body mechanics, nutrition, anatomy and physiology, infection control, and communication skills. Personal care skills such as the bathing, feeding, and grooming of patients are also taught. Some facilities, other than nursing homes, provide classroom instruction for newly hired aides, while others rely exclusively on informal on-the-job instruction from a licensed nurse or an experienced aide. Such training may last several days to a few months. From time to time, aides may also attend lectures, workshops, and in-service training.

Applicants should be healthy, tactful, patient, understanding, emotionally stable, dependable, and have a desire to help people. They should also be able to work as part of a team, and be willing to perform repetitive, routine tasks.

Opportunities for advancement within these occupations are limited. To enter other health occupations, aides generally need additional formal training. Some employers and unions provide opportunities by simplifying the educational paths to advancement. Experience as an aide can also help individuals decide whether to pursue a career in the health care field.

Job Outlook

Job prospects for nursing aides should be very good through 2005. Employment of nursing aides is expected to grow much faster than the average for all occupations in response to an emphasis on rehabilitation and the long-term care needs of a rapidly growing population of those 75 years and older. Employment will increase as a result of the expansion of nursing homes and other long-term care facilities for people with chronic illnesses and disabling conditions, many of whom are elderly. Also increasing employment of nursing aides will be modern medical technology which, while saving more lives, increases the need for the extended care provided by aides. As a result, nursing and personal care facilities are expected to grow very rapidly and to provide most of the new jobs for nursing aides. Employment is also expected to grow very rapidly in residential care facilities.

Employment of psychiatric aides is expected to grow faster than the average for all occupations. Employment will rise in response to the sharp increase in the number of older people—many of whom will require mental health services. Employment of aides in private psychiatric facilities and community mental health centers is likely to grow because of increasing public acceptance of formal treatment for drug abuse and alcoholism, and a lessening of the stigma attached to those receiving mental health care. While employment in private psychiatric facilities may grow, employment in public mental hospitals is likely to be stagnant due to constraints on public spending.

Replacement needs will constitute the major source of openings for aides. Turnover is high, a reflection of modest entry requirements, low pay, and lack of advancement opportunities.

Earnings

Median annual earnings of nursing and psychiatric aides who worked full-time in 1992 were about $13,800. The middle 50 percent earned between $11,000 and $17,900. The lowest 10 percent earned less than $9,500; the top 10 percent earned more than $23,900. According to a University of Texas Medical Branch survey of hospitals and medical centers, the median annual salary of nursing aides, based on a 40-hour week and excluding shift or area differentials, was $15,121 in October 1992. According to the Buck Survey conducted by the American Health Care Association, nursing aides in chain nursing homes had median annual earnings of approximately $11,600 in January, 1993. The middle 50 percent earned between $10,400 and $13,200 a year.

Aides in hospitals generally receive at least one week's paid vacation after one year of service. Paid holidays and sick leave, hospital and medical benefits, extra pay for late-shift work, and pension plans are also available to many hospital and some nursing home employees.

Related Occupations

Nursing aides and psychiatric aides help people who need routine care or treatment. Homemaker-home health aides, childcare attendants, companions, occupational therapy aides, and physical therapy aides perform similar duties.

Sources of Additional Information

For information on nursing careers in long-term care, write:

❏ American Health Care Association, 1201 L St. NW., Washington, DC 20005.

Information about employment also may be obtained from local hospitals, nursing homes, psychiatric facilities, and state boards of nursing.

Police, Detectives, and Special Agents

Nature of the Work

The safety of our nation's cities, towns, and highways greatly depends on the work of police officers, detectives, and special agents, whose responsibilities range from controlling traffic to preventing and investigating crimes. In most jurisdictions, whether on or off duty, these officers are expected to exercise their authority whenever necessary.

As civilian police department employees and private security personnel increasingly assume routine police duties, police and detectives are able to spend more time fighting serious crime. Police and detectives are also becoming more involved in community relations, which increases public confidence in the police and mobilizes the public to help the police fight crime.

Police officers and detectives who work in small communities and rural areas have many duties. In the course of a day's work, they may direct traffic at the scene of a fire, investigate a burglary, or give first aid to an accident victim. In a large police department, by contrast, officers are usually assigned to a specific type of duty. Most officers are detailed either to patrol or traffic duty; smaller numbers are assigned to special work such as accident prevention. Others are experts in chemical and microscopic analysis, firearms identification, and handwriting and fingerprint identification. In very large cities, a few officers may work with special units such as mounted and motorcycle police, harbor patrols, helicopter patrols, canine corps, mobile rescue teams, and youth aid services.

Sheriffs and deputy sheriffs generally enforce the law in rural areas or those places where there is no local police department. *Bailiffs* are responsible for keeping order in the courtroom. *U.S. marshals* serve civil writs and criminal warrants issued by federal judges and are responsible for the safety and transportation of jurors and prisoners.

Detectives and special agents are plainclothes investigators who gather facts and collect evidence for criminal cases. They conduct interviews, examine records, observe the activities of suspects, and participate in raids or arrests.

Federal Bureau of Investigation (FBI) special agents investigate violations of federal laws in connection with bank robberies, theft of government property, organized crime, espionage, sabotage, kidnapping, and terrorism. Agents with specialized training usually work on cases related to their background. For example, agents with an accounting background may investigate white-collar crimes such as bank embezzlements or fraudulent bankruptcies and land deals. Frequently, agents must testify in court about cases that they investigate.

Special agents employed by the U.S. Department of Treasury work for the U.S. Customs Service; the Bureau of Alcohol, Tobacco, and Firearms; the U.S. Secret Service; and the Internal Revenue Service. *Customs agents* enforce laws to prevent smuggling of goods across U.S. borders. *Alcohol, Tobacco, and Firearms agents* might investigate suspected illegal sales of guns or the underpayment of taxes by a liquor or cigarette manufacturer. *U.S. Secret Service agents* protect the president, vice president, and their immediate families; presidential candidates; former presidents; and foreign dignitaries visiting the United States. Secret Service agents also investigate counterfeiting, the forgery of government checks or bonds, and the fraudulent use of credit cards. *Internal Revenue Service special agents* collect evidence against individuals and companies that evade the payment of federal taxes.

Federal drug enforcement agents conduct criminal investigations of illicit drug activity. They compile evidence and arrest individuals who violate federal drug laws. They may prepare reports that are used in criminal proceedings, give testimony in court, and develop evidence that justifies the seizure of financial assets gained from illegal activity.

State police officers (sometimes called state troopers or highway patrol officers) patrol highways and enforce laws and regulations that govern their use. They issue traffic citations to motorists who violate the law. At the scene of an accident, they direct traffic, give first aid, and call for emergency equipment including ambulances. They also write reports that may be used to determine the cause of the accident. In addition, state police officers provide services to motorists on the highways. For example, they may radio for road service for drivers with mechanical trouble, direct tourists to their destination, or give information about lodging, restaurants, and tourist attractions. State police officers also provide traffic assistance and control during road repairs, fires, and other emergencies, as well as during special occurrences such as parades and sports events. They sometimes check the weight of commercial vehicles, conduct driver examinations, and give information on highway safety to the public.

In addition to highway responsibilities, state police in the majority of states also enforce criminal laws. In communities and counties that do not have a local police force or a large sheriff's department, the state police are the primary law enforcement agency, investigating crimes such as burglary or assault. They may also help city or county police catch lawbreakers and control civil disturbances.

Most new police recruits begin on patrol duty, riding in a police vehicle or walking on foot patrol. They work alone or with experienced officers in such varied areas as congested business districts or outlying residential neighborhoods. Officers attempt to become thoroughly familiar with conditions throughout their area and, while on patrol, remain alert for anything unusual. They note suspicious circumstances, such as open windows or lights in vacant buildings, as well as hazards to public safety such as burned-out street lights or fallen trees. Officers enforce traffic regulations and also watch for stolen vehicles. At regular intervals, officers report to police headquarters from call boxes, radios, or telephones.

Regardless of where they work, police, detectives, and special agents must write reports and maintain police records. They may be called to testify in court when their arrests result in legal action. Some officers, such as division or bureau chiefs, are responsible for training or certain kinds of criminal investigations, and those who command police operations in an assigned area have administrative and supervisory duties. Responsibilities of police officers range from controlling traffic and preventing and investigating crimes.

Working Conditions

Police, detectives, and special agents usually work 40 hours a week, but paid overtime work is common. Because police protection must be provided around the clock in all but the smallest communities, some officers work weekends, holidays, and nights. Police officers, detectives, and special agents are subject to call any time their services are needed and may work overtime, particularly during criminal investigations. The jobs of some special agents such as U.S. Secret Service agents require extensive travel.

Police, detectives, and special agents may have to work outdoors for long periods in all kinds of weather. The injury rate among these law officers is higher than in many occupations and reflects the risks taken in pursuing speeding motorists, apprehending criminals, and dealing with public disorders.

Police work can be very dangerous, and this can be very stressful for the officer as well as for his or her family.

Employment

Police, detectives, and special agents held about 700,000 jobs in 1992. Most were employed by local governments, primarily in cities with more than 25,000 inhabitants. Some cities have very large police forces, while hundreds of small communities employ fewer than 25 officers each. State police agencies employed about 12 percent of all police, detectives, and special agents; various federal agencies, particularly the Treasury Department and the Federal Bureau of Investigation, employed an additional 5 percent. There are about 17,000 state and local police departments in the nation.

Training, Other Qualifications, and Advancement

Civil service regulations govern the appointment of police and detectives in practically all states and large cities and in many small ones. Candidates must be U.S. citizens, usually at least 20 years of age, and must meet rigorous physical and personal qualifications. Eligibility for appointment depends on performance in competitive written examinations as well as on education and experience. Physical examinations often include tests of vision, strength, and agility.

Because personal characteristics such as honesty, good judgment, and a sense of responsibility are especially important in police and detective work, candidates are interviewed by a senior officer at police headquarters, and their character traits and background are investigated. In some police departments, candidates may also be interviewed by a psychiatrist or a psychologist, or be given a personality test. Most applicants are subjected to lie detector examinations and drug testing. Some police departments subject police officers in sensitive positions to drug testing as a condition of continuing employment. Although police and detectives often work independently, they must perform their duties in accordance with laws and departmental rules. They should enjoy working with people and serving the public.

In large police departments, where most jobs are found, applicants must usually have a high school education. An increasing number of cities and states require some college training, and some hire law enforcement students as police interns. Some departments require a college degree. A few police departments accept applicants as recruits who have less than a high school education, particularly if they have worked in a field related to law enforcement.

To be considered for appointment as an FBI special agent, an applicant either must be a graduate of an accredited law school; be a college graduate with a major in either accounting, engineering, or computer science; or be a college graduate with either fluency in a foreign language or three years of full-time work experience. Applicants must be U.S. citizens, between 23 and 35 years of age at the time of appointment, and willing to accept an assignment anywhere in the United States. They must also be in excellent physical condition with at least 20/200 vision corrected to 20/40 in one eye and 20/20 in the other eye. All new agents undergo 15 weeks of training at the FBI academy at the U.S. Marine Corps base in Quantico, Virginia.

Applicants for special agent jobs with the U.S. Department of Treasury must have a bachelor's degree, or a minimum of three years of work experience of which at least two are in criminal investigation. Candidates must be in excellent physical condition and be less than 35 years of age at the time they enter duty. Treasury agents undergo eight weeks of training at the Federal Law Enforcement Training Center in Glynco, Georgia, and another eight weeks of specialized training with their particular bureau.

Applicants for special agent jobs with the U.S. Drug Enforcement Administration must have a college degree in any field and either one year of experience conducting criminal investigations or have achieved a record of scholastic excellence while in college. The minimum age for entry is 21 and the maximum age is 36. Drug enforcement agents undergo 14 weeks of specialized training at the FBI Academy in Quantico, Virginia.

More and more, police departments are encouraging applicants to take post high school training in law enforcement. Many entrants to police and detective jobs have completed some formal postsecondary education and a significant number are college graduates. Many junior colleges, colleges, and universities offer programs in law enforcement or administration of justice. Other courses helpful in preparing for a police career include psychology, counseling, English, American history, public administration, public relations, sociology, business law, chemistry, and physics. Participation in physical education and sports is especially helpful in developing the stamina and agility needed for police work. Knowledge of a foreign language is an asset in areas that have concentrations of ethnic populations.

Some large cities hire high school graduates who are still in their teens as civilian police cadets or trainees. They do clerical work and attend classes and are appointed to the regular force at age 21 if qualified. Before their first assignments, officers usually go through a period of training. In small communities, recruits work for a short time with experienced officers. In state and large city police departments, they get more formal training that may last a number of weeks or months. This training includes classroom instruction in constitutional law and civil rights, state laws and local ordinances, and accident investigation. Recruits also receive training and supervised experience in patrol, traffic control, use of firearms, self-defense, first aid, and handling emergencies.

Police officers usually become eligible for promotion after a probationary period ranging from six months to three years. In a large department, promotion may enable an officer to become a detective or specialize in one type of police work such as laboratory analysis of evidence, traffic control, communications, or working with juveniles. Promotions to sergeant, lieutenant, and captain are usually made according to a candidate's position on a promotion list, as determined by scores on a written examination and on-the-job performance.

Many types of training help police officers and detectives improve their job performance. Through training given at police department academies—required annually in many states—and colleges, officers keep abreast of crowd-control techniques, civil defense, legal developments that affect their work, and advances in law enforcement equipment. Many police departments pay all or part of the tuition for officers to work toward associate and bachelor's degrees in law enforcement, police science, administration of justice, or public administration, and pay higher salaries to those who earn a degree.

Job Outlook

Employment of police officers, detectives, and special agents is expected to increase more slowly than the average for all occupations through 2005. A more security-conscious society and growing concern about drug-related crimes should contribute to the increasing demand for police services. However, employment growth will be tempered somewhat by continuing budgetary constraints faced by law enforcement agencies. In addition, private security firms may increasingly assume some routine police duties such as crowd surveillance at airports and other public places. Although turnover in police, detective, and special agent jobs is among the lowest of all occupations, the need to replace workers who retire, transfer to other occupations, or stop working for other reasons will be the source of most job openings.

The opportunity for public service through police work is attractive to many. The job is frequently challenging and involves much responsibility. Furthermore, in many communities, police officers may retire with a pension to pursue a second career while still in their 40's. Because of attractive salaries and benefits, the number of qualified candidates generally exceeds the number of job openings in many federal agencies and some state and local police departments—resulting in increased hiring standards and selectivity by employers. Competition is expected to remain keen for higher paying jobs in larger police departments. People having college training in law enforcement should have the best opportunities. Opportunities will be best in those communities with expanding departments that are having difficulty attracting an adequate supply of police officers. Competition is expected to be extremely keen for special agent positions with the FBI, Treasury Department, and Drug Enforcement Administration as these prestigious jobs tend to attract a far greater number of applicants than the number of job openings. Consequently, only the most highly qualified candidates will obtain jobs.

The level of government spending influences the employment of police officers, detectives, and special agents. The number of job opportunities, therefore, can vary from year to year and from place to place. Layoffs, on the other hand, are rare because early retirements enable most staffing cuts to be handled through attrition. Police officers who lose their jobs from budget cuts usually have little difficulty finding jobs with other police departments.

Earnings

In 1992, the median salary of nonsupervisory police officers and detectives was about $32,000 a year. The middle 50 percent earned between about $24,500 and $41,200; the lowest paid 10 percent were paid less than $18,400, while the highest paid 10 percent earned more than $51,200 a year. Generally, salaries tend to be higher in larger, more urban jurisdictions that usually have bigger police departments. Also in 1992, police officers and detectives in supervisory positions had a median salary of about $38,100 a year,. The middle 50 percent earned between $28,300 and $49,800; the lowest paid 10 percent were paid less than $23,200, while the highest paid 10 percent earned more than $58,400 annually.

Sheriffs, bailiffs, and other law enforcement officers had a median annual salary of about $25,800 in 1992. The middle 50 percent earned between $20,500 and $30,900; the lowest paid 10 percent earned less than $15,600, while the highest paid 10 percent earned more than $38,800.

In 1993, FBI agents started at about $30,600 a year, while Treasury Department agents started at about $18,300 or $22,700 a year, and DEA agents started at either $22,700 or $27,800 a year, depending on their qualifications. Salaries of experienced FBI agents started at around $47,900, while supervisory agents started at around $56,600 a year. Salaries of experienced Treasury Department and DEA agents started at $40,200, while supervisory agents started at $47,900. Federal agents, however, may be eligible for a special law enforcement compensation and retirement plans; applicants should ask their recruiter for more information.

Total earnings frequently exceed the stated salary due to payments for overtime, which can be significant, especially during criminal investigations or when police are needed for crowd control during sporting events or political rallies. In addition to the common fringe benefits—paid vacation, sick leave, and medical and life insurance—most police departments and federal agencies provide officers with special allowances for uniforms and furnish revolvers, nightsticks, handcuffs, and other required equipment. In addition, because police officers are generally covered by liberal pension plans, many retire at half-pay after 20 or 25 years of service.

Related Occupations

Police officers maintain law and order in the nation's cities, towns, and rural areas. Workers in related law enforcement occupations include guards, bailiffs, correction officers, deputy sheriffs, fire marshals, fish and game wardens, and U.S. marshals.

Sources of Additional Information

Information about entrance requirements may be obtained from federal, state, and local civil service commissions or police departments.

Contact any Office of Personnel Management Job Information Center for pamphlets providing general information and instructions for submitting an application for jobs as Treasury special agents, drug enforcement agents, FBI special agents, or U.S. marshals. Look under U.S. Government, Office of Personnel Management, in your telephone directory to obtain a local telephone number.

Information about law enforcement careers in general may be obtained from:

❏ International Union of Police Associations, 1016 Duke St., Alexandria, VA 22314.

Preschool Workers

Nature of the Work

Nurturing and teaching preschool children—those who are five years old or younger—is the job of preschool workers. Found in daycare centers, nursery schools, preschools, and family daycare homes, preschool workers play an important role in shaping the kind of adolescent a child will become by caring for the child when the parents are at work or away for other reasons. Some parents enroll their child in a nursery school primarily to provide him or her with the opportunity to interact with other children. In addition to attending to children's basic needs, these workers organize activities that stimulate the children's physical, emotional, intellectual, and social growth. They help children explore their interests, develop their talents and independence, build self-esteem, and learn how to behave with others.

Preschool workers must work in two different worlds—the child's and the parents'. At the same time that they create a safe, comfortable environment in which children can grow and learn, they must also keep records of each child's progress and discuss the children's progress and needs with the parents.

Depending on their experience and educational background, some preschool workers—often called preschool teachers—are responsible only for children's educational activities. Other workers—sometimes called child-care workers—provide only basic care to children. However, even by providing basic care, workers teach the children; the children learn trust and gain a sense of security. Most preschool workers perform a combination of basic care and teaching duties. For example, a worker who shows a child how to tie a shoe teaches the child and also provides for that child's basic care needs.

Young children cannot be taught in the same manner as older students because they are less physically, emotionally, and mentally developed. Children at this age learn mainly through play. What results is a less structured approach to teaching preschool children, including small group lessons, one-on-one instruction, and learning through creative activities, such as art, dance, and music.

Preschool workers greet children as they arrive, help them remove outer garments, and teach them how to dress and undress. When caring for infants, they feed and change them. In order to ensure a well-balanced program, preschool workers prepare daily and long-term schedules of activities. Each day's activities must balance individual and group play with quiet and active time. Recognizing the importance of play, preschool workers build their program around it. They capitalize on children's play to further language development (storytelling and acting games), improve social skills (working together to build a neighborhood in a sandbox), and introduce scientific and mathematical concepts (balancing and counting blocks when building a bridge or mixing colors when painting). (A statement on teacher aides—who assist classroom teachers—appears elsewhere in this book.)

Helping to keep children healthy is an important part of the job. Preschool workers serve nutritious meals and snacks and teach good eating habits and personal hygiene. They see to it that children have proper rest periods. They spot children who may not feel well or show signs of emotional or developmental problems and discuss these matters with their supervisor and the child's parents.

Early identification of children with special needs, such as those with behavioral, emotional, physical, or learning disabilities, is important to improve their future learning ability. Special education teachers often work with these preschool children to provide the individual attention they need. (Special education teachers are covered in the statement on school teachers found elsewhere in this book.)

Working Conditions

Preschool care facilities may be in private homes, schools, religious institutions, workplaces where employers provide care for employees' children, or private buildings. Individuals who provide care in their own homes are generally called family daycare providers.

Watching children grow, enjoy learning, and gain new skills can be very rewarding. The work, however, can be physically and emotionally taxing, as workers constantly stand, walk, bend, stoop, and lift to attend to each child's interests and problems. Preschool workers must be enthusiastic and constantly alert, anticipate and prevent problems, deal with disruptive children, and provide fair but firm discipline. They must be able to communicate effectively with the children and parents.

To ensure that children receive proper supervision, State regulations require certain ratios of workers to children. The ratio varies with the age of the children. Child development experts generally recommend that a single caregiver be responsible for no more than 3 or 4 infants (less than 1 year old), 5 or 6 toddlers (1 to 2 years old), or 10 preschool-age children (between 2 and 5 years old).

The working hours of preschool workers vary widely. Daycare centers are generally open year round with long hours so that parents can drop off and pick up their children before and after work. Daycare centers employ full-time and part-time staff with staggered shifts in order to cover the entire day. Public and many private preschool programs operate during the typical 9 or 10 month school year, employing both full-time and part-time workers. Family daycare providers have flexible hours and daily routines, but may work long or unusual hours to fit parents' work schedules. (Child-care workers who work in the child's home are covered in the statement on private household workers found elsewhere in this book.)

Employment

Preschool workers held about 941,000 jobs in 1992; many worked part-time. About half of all preschool workers are self-employed, most of whom are family daycare providers. About half of all salaried preschool workers are found in child daycare centers and preschools, and nearly one in four works for a religious institution. The rest work in other service organizations and government. Some employers run for-profit operations; many are affiliated with a local or national chain. Other employers, such as religious institutions, community agencies, school systems, and state and local governments, are nonprofit. A growing number of business firms operate daycare centers for the children of their employees.

Training, Other Qualifications, and Advancement

The training and qualifications required of preschool workers vary widely. Many states have licensing requirements that regulate caregiver training, which generally range from a high school diploma to college courses or a college degree in child development or early childhood education. Some states require continuing education for workers in this field. For instance, Virginia requires that all workers in daycare centers receive eight hours of courses related to child care each year. Formal education requirements in some private preschools and daycare centers exceed state requirements.

Many states require a Child Development Associate (CDA) credential, which is offered by the Council for Early Childhood Professional Recognition. The CDA credential is recognized as a qualification for teachers and directors in 49 states and the District of Columbia. There are two ways to become a CDA: through direct assessment or by completing a one-year training program. Direct assessment is appropriate for people who already have some background and experience in early childhood education, while the training program is designed for people with little or no child development education or experience. To receive the credential, the applicant must demonstrate the knowledge and skills that meet certain nationally recognized standards for working with young children to a team of child-care professionals from the Council for Early Childhood Professional Recognition. These skills can be acquired through formal training or experience.

Some employers may not require a CDA credential, but may require secondary or postsecondary courses in child development and early childhood education, and possibly work experience in a child-care setting. Other schools require their own specialized training. For example, Montessori preschool teachers must complete an additional year of training after receiving their bachelor's degree in early childhood education or a related field. Public schools typically require a bachelor's degree and state teacher certification. Teacher training programs include a variety of liberal arts courses, student teaching, and prescribed professional courses, including instruction in teaching gifted, disadvantaged, and other children with special needs.

Preschool workers should be mature, patient, understanding, articulate, and have energy and physical stamina. Skills in music, art, drama, and storytelling are also important. Those who work for themselves must have business sense and management abilities.

As preschool workers gain experience, they may advance to supervisory or administrative positions in large child-care centers or preschools. Often, however, these positions require additional training, such as a bachelor's degree. With a bachelor's degree, preschool workers may become certified to teach in public schools at the kindergarten, elementary, and secondary school levels. Some workers set up their own child-care businesses.

Job Outlook

Employment of preschool workers is projected to increase much faster than the average for all occupations through 2005. Job openings should be plentiful as many preschool workers leave the occupation each year for better paying jobs, family responsibilities, or other reasons. The relatively high turnover, combined with an increased demand for preschool workers, is expected to create many openings. Qualified people who are interested in this work should have little trouble finding and keeping a job.

Despite a slight decline in the number of children age five and under, the proportion of youngsters in daycare and preschool is expected to increase, reflecting a shift in the type of child-care arrangements parents choose. Many parents turn to formal child-care arrangements for a variety of reasons: they may need two incomes; they may find it too difficult to set up a satisfactory arrangement with a relative, babysitter, or live-in worker; or they may prefer the formal arrangements for personal reasons, such as a more structured learning and social environment.

Rising labor force participation among women age 20-44, though increasing more slowly than during the 1980s, will also contribute to the growth of employment among preschool workers. Currently, mothers of very young children are almost as likely to work as other women, and this pattern is not expected to change. Moreover, women are returning to work sooner after childbirth.

Earnings

Pay depends on the employer and educational attainment of the worker. Although the pay is generally low, more education means higher earnings in some cases. In 1992, median weekly earnings of full-time, salaried child-care workers were $260; for early childhood teacher assistants, $220. The middle 50 percent of child-care workers earned between $210 and $320; assistants, between $190 and $300. The top 10 percent of child-care workers earned at least $460; assistants, at least $420. The bottom 10 percent of child-care workers earned less than $140; teacher assistants, less than $150.

The small number of preschool workers in public schools who have state teacher certification generally have salaries and benefits comparable to kindergarten and elementary school teachers. According to the National Education Association, kindergarten and elementary school teachers earned an average salary of $34,800 in 1992.

Earnings of self-employed child-care workers vary depending on the hours worked, number and ages of the children, and the location.

Benefits for preschool workers also vary. Many employers offer free or discounted child care to employees. Some offer a full benefits package, including health insurance and paid vacations, but others offer no benefits at all. Some employers offer seminars and workshops to help workers improve on or learn new skills. A few are willing to cover the cost of courses taken at community colleges or technical schools.

Related Occupations

Child-care work requires patience; creativity; an ability to nurture, motivate, teach, and influence children; and leadership, organizational, and administrative abilities. Others who work with children and need these aptitudes include teacher aides, children's tutors, kindergarten and elementary school teachers, early childhood program directors, and child psychologists.

Sources of Additional Information

For information on careers in educating children and issues affecting preschool workers, contact:

❑ National Association for the Education of Young Children, 1509 16th St. N.W., Washington, DC 20036; or

❑ Association for Childhood Education International, 11141 Georgia Ave., Suite 200, Wheaton, MD 20902.

For information on the federally-sponsored Head Start program, contact:

❏ Head Start Bureau, Chief, Education Service Branch, P.O. Box 1182, Washington, DC 20013.

For eligibility requirements and a description of the Child Development Associate credential, write to:

❏ Council for Early Childhood Professional Recognition, 1341 G St. NW., Suite 400, Washington, DC 20005.

For information on salaries and efforts to improve compensation in child care, contact:

❏ Child Care Employee Project, 6536 Telegraph Ave., A201, Oakland, CA 94618. State Departments of Human Services or Social Services can supply state regulations and training requirements for child-care workers.

Private Household Workers

Nature of the Work

Private household workers clean homes, care for children, plan and cook meals, do laundry, administer the household, and perform numerous other duties. Private household workers are employed by many types of households of various income levels. Although wealthy families may employ a large staff, it is much more common for one worker to be employed in a household where both parents work. Many workers are employed in households having one parent. A number of household workers work for two or more employers. Private household child-care workers are often employed only while children are young.

Most household workers are *general houseworkers* and are usually the only worker employed in the home. They dust and polish furniture; sweep, mop, and wax floors; vacuum; and clean ovens, refrigerators, and bathrooms. They also wash dishes, polish silver, and change and make beds. Some wash, fold, and iron clothes. A few wash windows. Other duties may include looking after a child or an elderly person, cooking, feeding pets, answering the telephone and doorbell, and calling and waiting for repair workers. General houseworkers may also take clothes and laundry to the cleaners, buy groceries, and do other errands.

Household workers whose primary responsibility is taking care of children are called *child-care workers*. Those employed on an hourly basis are usually called *baby-sitters*. Child-care workers bathe, dress, and feed children; supervise their play, wash their clothes, and clean their rooms. They may also waken them and put them to bed, read to them, involve them in educational games, take them for doctors' visits, and discipline them. Those who are in charge of infants, sometimes called *infant nurses*, also prepare bottles and change diapers.

Nannies generally take care of children from birth to age 10 or 12, tending to the child's early education, nutrition, health, and other needs. *Governess'* look after children in addition to other household duties. They may help them with schoolwork, teach them a foreign language, and guide them in their general upbringing. (Child-care workers who work outside the child's home are covered in the statement on preschool workers elsewhere in this book.)

Those who assist elderly, handicapped, or convalescent people are called *companions* or *personal attendants*. Depending on the employers' needs, a companion or attendant might help with bathing and dressing, preparing and serving meals, and keeping the house tidy. They may also read to their employers, write letters for them, play cards or games, and go with them on walks and outings. Companions may also accompany their employers to medical appointments and handle their social and business affairs.

Households with a large staff may include a housekeeper or a butler, a cook, a caretaker, and a launderer. *Housekeepers* and *butlers* hire, supervise, and coordinate the household staff to keep the household running smoothly. Butlers also receive and announce guests, answer telephones, deliver messages, serve food and drinks, chauffeur, or act as a personal attendant. *Cooks* plan and prepare meals, clean the kitchen, order groceries and supplies, and may also serve meals. *Caretakers* do heavy housework and general home maintenance. They wash windows, wax floors, and hang draperies. They maintain heating and other equipment and do light carpentry, painting, and odd jobs. They may also mow the lawn and do some gardening if the household does not have a gardener.

Working Conditions

Private household workers usually work in pleasant and comfortable homes or apartments. Most are dayworkers who live in their own homes and travel to work. Some live in the home of their employer, generally with their own room and bath. Live-ins usually work longer hours. However, if they work evenings or weekends, they may get other time off. Living in may isolate them from family and friends. On the other hand, they often become part of their employer's family and may derive satisfaction from caring for them. Being a general houseworker can also be isolating because work is usually done alone. Housekeeping is hard work. Both dayworkers and live-ins are on their feet most of the day and do much walking, lifting, bending, stooping, and reaching. In addition, some employers can be very demanding.

Employment

Private household workers held about 869,000 jobs in 1992. More than half were general houseworkers, mostly dayworkers. About 40 percent were child-care workers, including baby-sitters. About four percent were housekeepers, butlers, cooks, and launderers. Most jobs are in big cities and the cities' affluent suburbs. Some are on large estates or in resorts away from cities.

Training, Other Qualifications, and Advancement

Private household workers generally do not need any special training. Individuals who cannot find other work because of limited language or other skills often turn to this work. Most jobs require the ability to clean well, cook, or take care of children. These skills are generally learned by young people while helping with housework at home.

Some training takes place on the job. Employers show the household workers what they want done and how. For child-care workers and companions, general education, background, and ability to get along with the person they will care for are most important. Private household workers must be honest, discreet, dependable, courteous, and neat. They need physical stamina.

Home economics courses in high schools and vocational and adult education schools offer training in cooking and child care. Courses in child development, first aid, and nursing in postsecondary schools are also useful. Special schools for butlers, nannies, and governesses teach household administration, early childhood education, nutrition, child care, and bookkeeping.

Opportunities for advancement within this occupation are very limited. There are very few large households with big staffs where general houseworkers can advance to cook, executive housekeeper, or butler, and these jobs may require specialized training. Advancement usually consists of better pay and working conditions. Workers may move to similar jobs in hotels, hospitals, and restaurants, where the pay and fringe benefits are usually better. Others transfer into better paying unrelated jobs.

Job Outlook

Job opportunities for people wishing to become private household workers are expected to be excellent through 2005, as the demand for these services continues to far outpace the supply of workers willing to provide them. For many years, demand for household help has outstripped the supply of workers willing to take domestic jobs. The imbalance is expected to persist, and possibly worsen, through 2005. Demand is expected to grow as more women join the labor force and need help running their households. Demand for companions and personal attendants is also expected to rise due to projected rapid growth in the elderly population.

The supply situation is not likely to improve. Unattractiveness of the work, low status, low pay, lack of fringe benefits, and limited advancement potential deter many prospective household workers. In addition, demographic factors will continue to aggravate the supply situation. Teenagers and young adults, the age group from which many child-care workers and baby-sitters come, will rebound in absolute terms, but continue to slip further as a share of the workforce.

Due to the limited supply of household workers, many employers have turned to domestic cleaning firms, child-care centers, and temporary help firms to meet their needs for household help. This trend is expected to continue.

Although employment of private household workers is expected to decline through 2005, many jobs will be available because of the need to replace the large number of workers who leave these occupations every year. People who are interested in this work and suited for it should have no trouble finding and keeping jobs.

Earnings

Earnings of private household workers depend on the type of work, the number of hours, household and staff size, geographic location, training, and experience. Nearly two out of three private household workers work part time, or less than 35 hours a week. Some work only two or three days a week, while others may work half a day four or five days a week. Earnings vary from about $10 an hour or more in a big city to less than the federal minimum wage in some rural areas (some domestic workers are not covered by minimum wage laws). Those covered by the federal minimum wage receive $4.25 an hour. In addition, dayworkers often get carfare and a free meal. Live-in domestics usually earn more than dayworkers and also get free room and board. However, they often work longer hours. Baby-sitters usually have the lowest earnings.

In 1992, median earnings for full-time private household workers were about $179 a week. The median for cleaners was about $191 and for child-care workers, about $154 a week. Some full-time live-in housekeepers or butlers, nannies, and governesses earn much higher wages than these. In New York City, for example, an experienced cook may earn up to $900 a week. Trained nannies start at $300-$375 per week, and with experience may earn up to $800 per week. A major domo, or senior butler, who runs a large household and supervises a staff of six people or more can expect to start at $20,000 and with experience earn more than $35,000 per year. Private household workers who live with their employers may be given room and board, medical benefits, a car, vacation days, and other benefits. However, most private household workers receive very limited or no benefits.

Related Occupations

Other workers with similar duties are building custodians, hotel and restaurant cleaners, child-care workers in day care centers, home health aides, cooks, kitchen workers, waiters and waitresses, and bartenders.

Sources of Additional Information

Information about job opportunities for private household workers is available from local private employment agencies and state employment service offices.

Mechanics, Installers, and Repairers

Computer and Office Machine Repairers

(Note: The information on the job titled "Computer and office machine repairers" occurs within the occupational cluster, "Electronic equipment repairers." Information not specific to the computer and office machine repairer job title is taken from the general electronic equipment repairers cluster.)

Nature of the Work

Computer and office machine repairers install equipment, do preventive maintenance, and correct problems. Computer repairers work on computers (mainframes, minis, and micros), peripheral equipment, and word processing systems, while office machine repairers work on photocopiers, cash registers, mail processing equipment, and typewriters. Some repairers service both computer and office equipment. They make cable and wiring connections when installing equipment, and work closely with electricians, who install the wiring.

Even with preventive maintenance, computers and other machines do break down. Repairers run diagnostic programs to locate malfunctions. Although some of the most modern and sophisticated computers have a self-diagnosing capacity that identifies problems, computer repairers must know enough about systems software to determine if the malfunction is in the hardware or software.

Electronic equipment repairers, also called service technicians or field service representatives, install, maintain, and repair electronic equipment used in offices, factories, homes, hospitals, aircraft, and other places. Equipment includes televisions, radar, industrial equipment controls, computers, telephone systems, and medical diagnosing equipment. Repairers have numerous job titles, which often refer to the kind of equipment they work with. Electronic repairers install, test, repair, and calibrate equipment to ensure that it functions properly. They keep detailed records on each piece of equipment to provide a history of tests, performance problems, and repairs.

When equipment breaks down, repairers first examine work orders, which indicate problems, or talk to equipment operators. Then they check for common causes of trouble such as loose connections or obviously defective components. If routine checks do not locate the trouble, repairers may refer to blueprints and manufacturers' specifications that show connections and provide instruction on how to locate problems. They use voltmeters, ohmmeters, signal generators, ammeters, and oscil-

loscopes and run diagnostic programs to pinpoint malfunctions. It may take several hours to locate a problem but only a few minutes to fix it. However, more equipment now has self-diagnosing features, which greatly simplifies the work. To fix equipment, repairers may replace defective components, circuit boards, or wiring, or adjust and calibrate equipment, using small handtools such as pliers, screwdrivers, and soldering irons.

Field repairers visit worksites in their assigned area on a regular basis to do preventive maintenance according to manufacturers' recommended schedules, and whenever emergencies arise. During these calls, repairers may also advise customers on how to use equipment more efficiently and how to spot problems in their early stages. They also listen to customers' complaints and answer questions, promoting customer satisfaction and good will. Some field repairers work full-time at installations of clients with a lot of equipment.

Working Conditions

Some electronic equipment repairers work shifts, including weekends and holidays, to service equipment in computer centers, manufacturing plants, hospitals, and telephone companies which operate round the clock. Shifts are generally assigned on the basis of seniority. Repairers may also be on call at any time to handle equipment failure.

Repairers generally work in clean, well-lighted, air-conditioned surroundings—an electronic repair shop or service center, hospital, military installation, or a telephone company's central office. However, some, such as commercial and industrial electronic equipment repairers, may be exposed to heat, grease, and noise on factory floors. Some may have to work in cramped spaces. Telephone installers and repairers may work on rooftops, ladders, and telephone poles.

The work of most repairers involves lifting, reaching, stooping, crouching, and crawling. Adherence to safety precautions is essential to guard against work hazards such as minor burns and electrical shock.

Employment

Computer and office machine repairers held about 143,000 jobs in 1992. Approximately 83,000 worked mainly on computer equipment, and the other 60,000 repaired mainly office machines. Three of every five were employed by wholesalers of computers and other office equipment, including the wholesaling divisions of equipment manufacturers, and by firms that provide maintenance services for a fee. Others worked for retail establishments and some with organizations that serviced their own equipment. Repairers work throughout the country, even in relatively small communities. Most repairers, however, work in large cities, where computer and office equipment is concentrated.

Electronic equipment repairers held about 398,000 jobs in 1992. Many worked for telephone companies. Others worked for electronic and transportation equipment manufacturers, machinery and equipment wholesalers, hospitals, electronic repair shops, and firms that provide maintenance under contract (called third-party maintenance firms). The distribution of employment in each occupation is presented in the following tabulation:

Computer and office machine repairers	143,000
Communications equipment repairers	108,000
Commercial and industrial electronic equipment repairers	68,000
Telephone installers and repairers	40,000
Electronic home entertainment equipment repairers	9,000

Training, Other Qualifications, and Advancement

Training in electronics, whether acquired formally or on the job, is required for entry-level jobs. Formal training is offered by public postsecondary vocational-technical schools, private vocational schools and technical institutes, junior and community colleges, and some high schools and correspondence schools. Programs last one to two years. The military services also offer formal training and work experience.

Training includes general courses in mathematics, physics, electricity, electronics, schematic reading, and troubleshooting. Students also choose courses which prepare them for a specialty, such as computers, commercial and industrial equipment, or home entertainment equipment. A few repairers complete formal apprenticeship programs sponsored jointly by employers and locals of the International Brotherhood of Electrical Workers.

Applicants for entry-level jobs may have to pass tests that measure mechanical aptitude, knowledge of electricity or electronics, manual dexterity, and general intelligence. Newly hired repairers, even those with formal training, usually receive some training from their employer. They may study electronic and circuit theory and math. They also get hands-on experience with equipment, doing basic maintenance, and using diagnostic programs to locate malfunctions. Training may be in a classroom or it may be self-instruction, consisting of videotapes, programmed computer software, or workbooks that allow trainees to learn at their own pace.

Experienced technicians attend training sessions and read manuals to keep up with design changes and revised service procedures. Many technicians also take advanced training in a particular system or type of repair.

Good eyesight and color vision are needed to inspect and work on small, delicate parts and good hearing is needed to detect malfunctions revealed by sound. Because field repairers usually handle jobs alone, they must be able to work without close supervision. For those who have frequent contact with customers, a pleasant personality, neat appearance, and good communications skills are important. Repairers must also be trustworthy because they may be exposed to money and other valuables in places like banks and securities offices, and some employers require that they be bonded. A security clearance may be required for technicians who repair equipment or service machines in areas where people are engaged in activities related to national security.

The International Society of Certified Electronics Technicians and the Electronics Technicians Association each administers a voluntary certification program. In both, an electronics repairer with four years of experience may become a Certified Electronics Technician. Certification, which is by examination, is offered in computer, radio-TV, industrial and commercial equipment, audio, and radar systems repair. An Associate Level Test, covering basic electronics, is offered for students or repairers with less than four years of experience. Those who test and repair radio transmitting equipment, other than business and land mobile radios, need a General Operators License from the Federal Communications Commission.

Experienced repairers with advanced training may become specialists or troubleshooters who help other repairers diagnose difficult problems, or work with engineers in designing equipment and developing maintenance procedures.

Because of their familiarity with equipment, repairers are particularly well qualified to become manufacturers' sales workers. Workers with leadership ability may also become maintenance supervisors or service managers. Some experienced workers open their own repair services or shops, or become wholesalers or retailers of electronic equipment.

Job Outlook

Employment of computer and office machine repairers is expected to grow faster than the average for all occupations through 2005. However, employment of repairers will grow less rapidly than the anticipated increase in the amount of equipment because of the improved reliability of computer and office machines and ease of repair.

Employment of those who repair computers is expected to grow much faster than the average for all occupations. Demand for computer repairers will increase as the amount of computer equipment increases—organizations throughout the economy should continue to automate in search of greater productivity and improved service. The development of new computer applications and lower computer prices, will also spur demand. More repairers will be needed to install, maintain, and repair these machines.

Overall, employment of electronic equipment repairers is expected to decline through 2005. Although the amount of electronic equipment in use will grow very rapidly, improvements in product reliability and ease of service and lower equipment prices will cause a decline in the need for repairers. The following tabulation presents the expected job growth for the various electronic equipment repairer occupations:

Earnings

In 1992, median weekly earnings of full-time electronic equipment repairers were $521. The middle 50 percent earned between $406 and $629. The bottom 10 percent earned less than $312, while the top 10 percent earned more than $729. Earnings vary widely by occupation and the type of equipment repaired, as shown in the following tabulations:

Telephone installers and repairers $626

Data processing equipment repairers 619

Electronic repairers, communications and
  industrial equipment 484

Office machine repairers 476

Central office installers, central office technicians, PBX installers, and telephone installers and repairers employed by AT&T and the Bell Operating Companies and represented by the Communications Workers of America earned between $752 and $824 a week in 1992.

According to a survey of workplaces in 160 metropolitan areas, beginning maintenance electronics technicians had median earnings of $12.34 an hour in 1992, with the middle half earning between $11.22 and $13.52 an hour. The most experienced repairers had median earnings of $18.28 an hour, with the middle half earning between $14.98 and $20.79 an hour.

Related Occupations

Workers in other occupations who repair and maintain the circuits and mechanical parts of electronic equipment include appliance and powertool repairers, automotive electricians, broadcast technicians, electronic organ technicians, and vending machine repairers. Electronics engineering technicians may also repair electronic equipment as part of their duties.

Sources of Additional Information

For career and certification information, contact:

❏ The International Society of Certified Electronics Technicians, 2708 West Berry St., Fort Worth, TX 76109.

For certification, career, and placement information, contact:

❏ Electronics Technicians Association, 604 North Jackson, Greencastle, IN 46135.

For information about the general radiotelephone operator license, write to:

❏ Federal Communications Commission, 1919 M St. NW., Washington, DC 20554.

For information on the telephone industry and career opportunities in it, request copies of *Phonefacts* from:

❏ United States Telephone Association, Small Companies Division, 900 19th St. NW., Suite 800, Washington, DC 20006.

For information on electronic equipment repairers in the telephone industry, write to:

❏ Communications Workers of America, 501 3rd St. NW., Washington, DC 20001.

General Maintenance Mechanics

Nature of the Work

Most craft workers specialize in one kind of work such as plumbing or carpentry. General maintenance mechanics use the skills of many different crafts. They repair and maintain machines, mechanical equipment, and buildings, and work on plumbing, electrical, and air-conditioning and heating systems. They build partitions, make plaster or drywall repairs, and fix or paint roofs, windows, doors, floors, woodwork, and other parts of building structures. They also maintain and repair specialized equipment and machinery found in cafeterias, laundries, hospitals, stores, offices, and factories. Typical duties include troubleshooting and fixing faulty electrical switches, repairing air-conditioning motors, and unclogging drains.

Those in small establishments, where they are often the only maintenance worker, do all repairs except for very large or difficult jobs. In larger establishments, their duties may be limited to the general maintenance of everything in a workshop or a particular area.

General maintenance mechanics inspect and diagnose problems and determine the best way to correct them, often checking blueprints, repair manuals, and parts catalogs. They obtain supplies and repair parts from distributors or storerooms. They use common hand and power tools such as screwdrivers, saws, drills, wrenches, and hammers as well as specialized equipment and electronic test devices. They replace or fix worn or broken parts, where necessary, or make adjustments.

These mechanics also do routine preventive maintenance and ensure that machinery continues to run smoothly, building systems operate efficiently, and the physical condition of buildings does not deteriorate. Following a checklist, they may inspect drives, motors, and belts, check fluid levels, replace filters, and so forth. Maintenance mechanics keep records of maintenance and repair work. A general maintenance mechanic is often responsible for the maintenance of all the systems in a building, such as a rooftop air conditioning unit.

Working Conditions

General maintenance mechanics often do a variety of tasks in a single day, generally at a number of different locations in a building, or in several buildings. They may have to stand for long periods, lift heavy objects, and work in uncomfortably hot or cold environments. Like other maintenance craft workers, they may work in awkward and cramped positions or on ladders. They are subject to electrical shock, burns, falls, and cuts and bruises. Most general maintenance workers work a 40-hour week. Some work evening, night, or weekend shifts, or may be on call for emergency repairs.

Those employed in small establishments, where they may be the only maintenance worker, often operate with only limited supervision. Those working in larger establishments may work under the direct supervision of an experienced craft worker.

Employment

General maintenance mechanics held about 1,145,000 jobs in 1992. They worked in almost every industry. More than one-third worked in service industries; most of these worked for elementary and secondary schools, colleges and universities, hospitals and nursing homes, and hotels. About 18 percent were employed in manufacturing industries. Others worked for real estate firms that operate office and apartment buildings or for wholesale and retail firms, government agencies, or gas and electric companies.

Training, Other Qualifications, and Advancement

Most general maintenance mechanics learn their skills informally on the job. They start as helpers, watching and learning from skilled maintenance workers. Helpers begin by doing simple jobs such as fixing leaky faucets and replacing light bulbs and progress to more difficult tasks such as overhauling machinery or building walls.

Others learn their skills by working as helpers for other repair or construction workers such as carpenters, electricians, or machinery repairers. Necessary skills can also be learned in high school shop classes and postsecondary trade or vocational schools. It generally takes from one to four years of on-the-job training or school, or a combination of both, to become fully qualified, depending on the skill level required.

Graduation from high school is preferred, but not always required, for entry into this occupation. High school courses in mechanical drawing, electricity, woodworking, blueprint reading, science, and mathematics are useful. Mechanical aptitude, ability to use shop math, and manual dexterity are important. Good health is necessary because the job involves much walking, standing, reaching, and heavy lifting. Difficult jobs require problem-solving ability, and many positions require the ability to work without direct supervision. A growing proportion of new buildings rely on computers to control building systems, so familiarity with computers may be helpful.

Many general maintenance mechanics in large organizations advance to maintenance supervisor or to one of the crafts such as electrician, heating/air-conditioning mechanic, or plumber. In small organizations, promotion opportunities are limited.

Job Outlook

Job opportunities for people who want to be general maintenance mechanics should be plentiful through 2005. Employment is related to the number of buildings and amount of equipment needing maintenance and repair. Employment growth, which is expected to be faster than the average for all occupations through 2005, will occur as the number of office and apartment buildings, stores, schools, hospitals, hotels, and factories increases. Although the pace of construction of these facilities is expected to be slower than in the past, many opportunities arise because this is a large occupation with significant turnover, and many replacements are needed for those who leave the occupation.

General maintenance mechanics who work in manufacturing industries may be laid off during recessions. Most mechanics, however, work in relatively stable nonmanufacturing industries and are not usually subject to layoff.

Earnings

Earnings vary widely by industry, geographical area, and skill level. According to a survey of workplaces in 160 metropolitan areas, general maintenance mechanics had median earnings of about $9.37 an hour in 1992, with the middle half earning between $7.85 and $11.05 an hour. Median earnings were about $8.75 an hour in service businesses and about $9.90 an hour in manufacturing businesses. Mechanics earn overtime pay for work in excess of 40 hours per week.

Some general maintenance mechanics are members of unions, including the American Federation of State, County and Municipal Employees and the United Automobile Workers.

Related Occupations

Some of the work of general maintenance mechanics is similar to that of carpenters, plumbers, industrial machinery mechanics, electricians, and air-conditioning, refrigeration, and heating mechanics.

Sources of Additional Information

Information about job opportunities may be obtained from local employers and local offices of the Job Service.

Productions Occupations

Blue-Collar Worker Supervisors

Nature of the Work

For the millions of workers who assemble manufactured goods, service electronics equipment, build office buildings, load trucks, or perform thousands of other activities, a blue-collar worker supervisor is the boss. These supervisors ensure that workers, equipment, and materials are used properly and efficiently to maximize productivity. They are often responsible for very expensive and complex equipment or systems. Supervisors make sure machinery is set up correctly and schedule or perform repairs and maintenance work.

Supervisors create work schedules, keep production and employee records, monitor employees and ensure that work is done correctly and on time. They organize the workers' activities and make any necessary adjustments to ensure that work continues uninterrupted. Supervisors also train new workers and ensure the existence of a safe working environment.

Blue-collar worker supervisors may have other titles, such as first-line supervisors, foremen, or forewomen. In the textile industry, they may be referred to as second hands; on ships they may be called boatswains. In the construction industry, they can be referred to as superintendents, crew chiefs, or foremen/forewomen depending on the type and size of their employer. Tool pushers or gang pushers are the common terms used to describe blue-collar supervisors in the oil drilling business.

Regardless of industry setting or job title, a supervisor's primary responsibility is to ensure that the work gets done. How supervisors accomplish this task is changing in some organizations. In companies that have restructured their operations for maximum efficiency, supervisors use computers to schedule work flow, monitor the quality of their workers' output, keep track of materials used, update their inventory control system, and perform other supervisory tasks. New management philosophies emphasize fewer levels of management and greater employee power and decision making. In the past, supervisors used their power and authority to direct the efforts of their subordinates; increasingly, supervisors are assuming the role of a facilitator for groups of workers, aiding in group decision making and conflict resolution.

Blue-collar worker supervisors have many interpersonal tasks related to their job as well. They inform workers about company plans and policies; recommend good performers for wage increases, awards, or promotions; and deal with poor performers by outlining expectations, counseling workers in proper methods, issuing warnings, or recommending disciplinary action. They also meet on a regular basis with their managers, reporting any problems and discussing possible solutions. Supervisors also meet among themselves to discuss goals, company operations, and performance. In companies with labor unions, supervisors must follow all provisions of labor management contracts.

Working Conditions

Many blue-collar worker supervisors work in a shop environment. They may be on their feet much of the time overseeing the work of subordinates and may be subjected to the noise and grime of machinery. Other supervisors, such as those in construction and oil exploration and production, may work outdoors and are subject to all kinds of weather conditions.

Supervisors may be on the job before other workers arrive and stay after they leave. Some supervisors work in plants that operate around the clock and may work any one of three shifts as well as weekends and holidays. In some cases, supervisors work all three shifts on a rotating basis; in others, shift assignments are made on the basis of seniority.

Employment

Blue-collar worker supervisors held about 1,757,000 jobs in 1992. Although salaried supervisors are found in almost all industries, 4 of every 10 worked in manufacturing, supervising the production of industrial machinery, motor vehicles, appliances, and thousands of other products. One of every eight worked in the construction industry and one of every nine worked in wholesale and retail trade establishments. Others were employed in public utilities, repair shops, transportation, and government agencies. Employment is distributed in much the same way as the population, and jobs are located in all cities and towns.

Training, Other Qualifications, and Advancement

When choosing supervisors, employers generally look for experience, job knowledge, organizational skills, and leadership qualities. Employers emphasize the ability to motivate employees, maintain high morale and command respect. In addition, employers desire well-rounded applicants who are able to deal with different situations and different types of people. Communication and interpersonal skills are extremely important to most employers.

Although completion of high school is often the minimum educational requirement for supervisors, and many supervisors still rise through the ranks, employers are increasingly hiring college graduates with technical degrees. While work experience creates the advantage of knowing how jobs should be done and what problems may arise, individuals without advanced education need further technical and administrative training. Large companies generally offer better opportunities than smaller companies for promotion to blue-collar worker supervisory positions.

In high-technology industries, such as aerospace and electronics, employers require a bachelor's degree or technical school background. Employers in the manufacturing sector generally prefer a background in engineering, mathematics, science, business administration, or industrial relations.

In most manufacturing companies, a business or engineering master's degree or in-house training is needed to advance to jobs such as department head or production manager. Supervisors in the construction industry may use the experience and skills they gain to become contractors, although a degree in construction management or engineering is required for advancement to project manager, operations manager, or general superintendent. Supervisors in repair shops may open their own business.

Job Outlook

Employment of blue-collar worker supervisors is expected to grow more slowly than the average for all occupations through 2005. However, many openings will arise from the need to replace workers who transfer to other occupations or leave the labor force.

Job prospects vary by industry. In manufacturing, employment of supervisors is expected to decline slightly as the trend continues for supervisors to supervise more workers. This reflects the increasing use of computers to meet supervisory responsibilities such as scheduling, as well as the effects of worker empowerment programs that relieve supervisors of some of the more time-consuming tasks. In construction and most other nonmanufacturing industries, employment of blue-collar worker supervisors is expected to rise along with the employment of the workers they supervise.

Because of their skill and seniority, blue-collar worker supervisors are often protected from layoffs during a recession. However, some in the highly cyclical construction industry may be laid off when construction activity declines.

Earnings

Median weekly earnings for blue-collar worker supervisors were about $590 in 1992. The middle 50 percent earned between $434 and $790. The lowest 10 percent earned less than $323, and the highest 10 percent earned over $1,010. Most supervisors earn significantly more than their subordinates. While most blue-collar workers are paid by the hour, most supervisors receive an annual salary. Some supervisors receive extra pay when they work overtime.

Related Occupations

Other workers with supervisory duties include those who supervise professional, technical, sales, clerical, and service workers. Some of these are retail store or department managers, sales managers, clerical supervisors, bank officers, head tellers, hotel managers, postmasters, head cooks, head nurses, and surveyors.

Sources of Additional Information

For information on educational programs for blue-collar worker supervisors, contact:

❏ American Management Association, 135 West 50th St., New York, NY 10020;

❏ National Management Association, 2210 Arbor Blvd., Dayton, OH 45439; or

❏ American Institute of Constructors, 9887 North Gandy St., St. Petersburg, FL 33702.

Transportation and Material Movers Occupations

Truckdrivers

Nature of the Work

Nearly all goods are transported by truck during some of their journey from producers to consumers. Goods may also be shipped between terminals or warehouses in different cities by train, ship, or plane. But truckdrivers usually make the initial pickup from factories, consolidate cargo at terminals for intercity shipment, and deliver goods from terminals to stores and homes.

Before leaving the terminal or warehouse, truckdrivers check their trucks for fuel and oil. They also inspect the trucks they will drive to make sure the brakes, windshield wipers, and lights are working and see that a fire extinguisher, flares, and other safety equipment are aboard and in working order. Drivers adjust mirrors so that both sides of the truck are visible from the driver's seat, and make sure the cargo has been loaded properly so it will not shift during the trip. Drivers report to the dispatcher any equipment that does not work or is missing, or cargo that is not loaded properly.

Once underway, drivers must be alert to prevent accidents and to drive their trucks efficiently. Because drivers of large tractor-trailers sit higher than cars, pickups, and vans, they can see farther down the road. They seek traffic lanes that allow them to move at a steady speed, and, when going downhill, they may increase speed slightly to gain momentum for a hill ahead.

Long-distance runs vary widely. On short turnarounds, truckdrivers deliver a load to a nearby city, pick up another loaded trailer, and drive it back to their home base the same day. Other runs take an entire day, and drivers remain away from home overnight. On longer runs, drivers may haul loads from city to city for a week or more before returning home. Some companies use two drivers on very long runs. One drives while the other sleeps in a berth behind the cab. Sleeper runs may last for days, or even weeks, usually with the truck stopping only for fuel, food, loading, and unloading.

Some long-distance drivers who have regular runs transport freight to the same city on a regular basis. Because shippers request varying amounts of service to different cities every day, many drivers have unscheduled runs. Dispatchers tell these drivers when to report for work and where to haul the freight.

After long-distance truckdrivers reach their destination or complete their operating shift, they are required by the U.S. Department of Transportation to complete reports about the trip and the condition of the truck and to give a detailed report of any accident. In addition, on-duty drivers are subject to periodic alcohol and drug tests.

Long-distance truckdrivers spend most of their working time behind the wheel but may be required to unload their cargo. Drivers hauling specialty cargo often load or unload their trucks because they may be the only one at the destination familiar with this procedure. Auto-transport drivers, for example, drive and position the cars on the trailers and head ramps and remove them at the final destination. When picking up or delivering furniture, drivers of long-distance moving vans hire local workers to help them load or unload.

When local truckdrivers receive assignments from the dispatcher to make deliveries, pickups, or both, they also get delivery forms. Before the drivers arrive for work, material handlers generally have loaded the trucks and arranged the items in order of delivery to minimize handling of the merchandise.

At the customer's place of business, local truckdrivers generally load or unload the merchandise. If there are heavy loads or many deliveries to make during the day, drivers may have helpers. Customers must sign receipts for goods and drivers may receive money for material delivered. At the end of the day, they turn in receipts, money, and records of deliveries made and report any mechanical problems their trucks may have.

The work of local truckdrivers varies, depending on the product they transport. Produce truckers usually pick up a loaded truck in the early morning and spend the rest of the day delivering produce to many different grocery stores. Lumber truckdrivers, on the other hand, make several trips from the lumber yard to one or more construction sites. Gasoline tank truckdrivers attach the hoses and operate the pumps on their trucks to transfer the gasoline to gas stations' storage tanks.

Some local truckdrivers have sales and customer relations responsibilities. These drivers called driver-sales workers or route drivers are primarily responsible for delivering their firm's products, but they also represent the company. Their reaction to customer complaints and requests for special services can make the difference between a large order and losing a customer. Route drivers may also use their selling ability to increase sales and to gain additional customers.

The duties of driver-sales workers vary according to the industry in which they are employed, the policies of their particular company, and the amount of emphasis which is placed on their sales responsibilities. Most have wholesale routes— they deliver to businesses and stores rather than homes. A few distribute various foods, or pick up and deliver drycleaning to households, but these retail routes are now rare.

Wholesale bakery driver-sales workers, for example, deliver and arrange bread, cakes, rolls, and other baked goods on display racks in grocery stores. Paying close attention to the items that are selling well and those just sitting on the shelves, they estimate the amount and variety of baked goods that will be sold. They may recommend changes in a store's order or may encourage the manager to stock new bakery products. From time to time, they try to get the business of new stores along their route.

Driver-sales workers employed by laundries that rent linens, towels, work clothes, and other items visit businesses regularly to replace soiled laundry. Vending machine driver-sales workers service machines in factories, schools, and other buildings. They check items remaining in the machines, replace stock, and remove money deposited in the cash boxes. They also examine each vending machines to see that merchandise and change are dispensed properly, make minor repairs, and clean machines.

After completing their routes, driver-sales workers order items for the next day which they think customers are likely to buy, based primarily on what products have been selling well, the weather, time of year, and any customer feedback. Trucking companies employed nearly one-third of all truckdrivers.

Working Conditions

Truckdriving has become less physically demanding because most trucks now have more comfortable seats, better ventilation, and improved cab designs. However, driving for many hours at a stretch, unloading cargo, and making many deliveries can be tiring, and driving in bad weather, heavy traffic, or mountains can be nerve-racking. Local truckdrivers, unlike long-distance drivers, can usually return home in the evening. Some self-employed long distance truckdrivers who own and operate their trucks spend more than 240 days a year away from home.

Local truckdrivers frequently work 48 hours or more a week. Many who handle food for chain grocery stores, produce markets, or bakeries drive at night or early in the morning. Although most drivers have a regular route, some have different routes each day. Many local truckdrivers—particularly driver-sales workers—load and unload their own trucks, which require considerable lifting, carrying, and walking.

The U.S. Department of Transportation governs work hours and other matters of trucking companies engaged in interstate commerce. For example, a long-distance driver cannot be on duty for more than 60 hours in any 7-day period and cannot drive more than 10 hours following at least 8 consecutive hours off duty. Many drivers, particularly on long runs, work close to the maximum hours permitted. Drivers on long runs may face boredom, loneliness, and fatigue. Although many drivers work during the day, travel at night and on holidays and weekends is frequently necessary in order to avoid traffic delays and deliver cargo on time.

Employment

Truckdrivers held 2,720,000 jobs in 1992. Jobs are concentrated in and around large cities. Drivers are employed in almost all communities, however. Trucking companies employed nearly one-third of all truckdrivers, and another one-third worked for companies engaged in wholesale or retail trade, such as auto parts stores, oil companies, lumber yards, or distributors of food and grocery products. The rest were scattered throughout the economy, including government agencies. Fewer than 1 out of every 10 truckdrivers is self-employed. Of these, a significant number are owner-operators, who either operate independently, serving a variety of businesses, or lease their services and their trucks to a trucking company.

Training, Other Qualifications, and Advancement

Qualifications and standards for truckdrivers are established by state and federal regulations. States must meet federal standards, and some states have more stringent regulations. All truckdrivers must have a driver's license issued by the state in which they live, and most employers strongly prefer a good driving record. All drivers of trucks designed to carry at least 26,000 pounds—which includes most tractor-trailers as well as bigger straight trucks—are required to obtain a special commercial driver's license (CDL) from the state in which they live. In many states a regular driver's license is sufficient for driving light trucks and vans. All truckdrivers who operate trucks that carry hazardous materials must also obtain a CDL.

To qualify for a CDL, applicants must pass a knowledge test and demonstrate that they can operate a commercial truck safely. A national database permanently records all driving violations incurred by people who hold commercial licenses, so drivers whose commercial license is suspended or revoked in one state may not be issued a new one in another state. Trainees must be accompanied by a driver with a CDL until they get their own CDL. Information on how to apply for a CDL may be obtained from state motor vehicle administrations.

The U.S. Department of Transportation establishes minimum qualifications for truckdrivers who are engaged in interstate commerce. A driver must be at least 21 years old and pass a physical examination, which the employer usually pays for. Good hearing, 20/40 vision with or without glasses or corrective lenses, normal use of arms and legs (unless a waiver is obtained), and normal blood pressure are the main physical requirements. People with epilepsy or diabetes controlled by insulin are not permitted to be interstate truckdrivers, and drivers may not use any controlled substances unless prescribed by a licensed physician. In addition, drivers must take a written examination on the Motor Carrier Safety Regulations of the U.S. Department of Transportation.

Many trucking operations have higher standards than those described. Many firms require that drivers be at least 25 years old, able to lift heavy objects, and have three to five years of experience driving trucks. Many prefer to hire high school graduates and require annual physical examinations. Federal regulations require employers to test their drivers for alcohol and drug use as a condition of employment, and require periodic random tests while on duty.

Because drivers often deal directly with the company's customers, they must get along well with people. For jobs as driver-sales workers, an ability to speak well and a neat appearance are particularly important, as are self-confidence, initiative, and tact. For all truckdriver jobs, employers look for responsible, self-motivated individuals because drivers must work with little supervision.

Driver-training courses are a desirable method of preparing for truckdriving jobs and for obtaining a commercial driver's license. High school driver-training courses are an asset, and courses in automotive mechanics may help drivers make minor roadside repairs. Many private and public technical-vocational schools offer tractor-trailer driver training programs. Students learn to inspect the trucks and freight, to maneuver large vehicles on crowded streets and in highway traffic, and to comply with federal, state, and local regulations. Some programs provide only a limited amount of actual driving experience, and completion of a program does not assure a job. People interested in attending one of these schools should check with local trucking companies to make sure the school's training is acceptable or they should seek a school certified by the Professional Truck Driver Institute of America as providing training that meets Federal Highway Administration guidelines for training tractor-trailer drivers.

Training given to new drivers by employers is usually informal and may consist of only a few hours of instruction from an experienced driver, sometimes on the new employee's own time. New drivers may also ride with and observe experienced drivers before being assigned their own runs. Additional training may be given if they are to drive a special type of truck or if they are handling hazardous materials. Some companies give one to two days of classroom instruction which covers general duties, the operation and loading of a truck, company policies, and the preparation of delivery forms and company records. Driver-sales workers also receive training on the various types of products they carry so they will be more effective sales workers and better able to handle customer requests.

Very few people enter truckdriving directly from school; most truckdrivers previously held jobs in other occupations. Consideration is given to driving experience in the Armed Forces. In some instances, a person may also start as a truckdriver's helper, driving part of the day and helping to unload and load freight. When driving vacancies occur, senior helpers are usually promoted.

New drivers sometimes start on panel or other small straight-trucks. As they gain experience and show good driving skills, they may advance to larger and heavier trucks, and finally to tractor-trailers. Although most new truckdrivers are assigned immediately to regular driving jobs, some start as extra drivers, who substitute for regular drivers who are ill or on vacation. They receive a regular assignment when an opening occurs.

Advancement of truckdrivers is generally limited to driving runs that provide increased earnings or preferred schedules and working conditions. For the most part, a local truckdriver may advance to driving heavy or special types of trucks, or transfer to long-distance truckdriving. Working for companies that also employ long-distance drivers is the best way to advance to these positions. A few truckdrivers may advance to dispatcher, manager, or to traffic work, such as planning delivery schedules.

Some long-distance truckers purchase a truck and go into business for themselves. Although many of these owner-operators are successful, others fail to cover expenses and eventually lose their trucks. Owner-operators should have good business sense as well as truckdriving experience. Courses in accounting, business, and business arithmetic are helpful, and knowledge of truck mechanics can enable owner-operators to perform their own routine maintenance and minor repairs.

Job Outlook

Opportunities should be favorable for people who are interested in truckdriving. This is one of the occupations which has the largest number of job openings each year. Although thousands of openings will be created by growth in demand for drivers, the majority will occur as experienced drivers transfer to other fields of work or retire or leave the labor force for other reasons. In addition, truckdriver jobs vary greatly in terms of earnings, weekly work hours, number of nights that must be spent on the road, and the quality of equipment operated. Because truckdriving does not require education beyond high school, competition is expected for jobs with the most attractive earnings and working conditions.

Employment of truckdrivers is expected to increase about as fast as the average for all occupations through 2005 as the economy grows and the amount of freight carried by trucks increases. However, increased integration of truck and railroad long-distance freight transportation should continue to somewhat slow the growth of truckdriver jobs. Trailers are increasingly expected to be carried between distant regions on trains, and delivered and picked up by trucks. Perishable goods should continue to be shipped long distance by truck.

Average growth of local and long-distance truckdriver employment should outweigh the slow growth in driver-sales worker jobs. The number of truckdrivers with sales responsibilities is expected to increase slowly because companies are increasingly splitting their responsibilities among other workers, shifting sales, ordering, and customer service tasks to sales and office staffs, and using regular truckdrivers to make deliveries to customers.

Job opportunities may vary from year to year because the amount of freight moved by trucks fluctuates with the economy. Many new truckdrivers are hired when the economy and the volume of freight are expanding, but fewer when these decline. During economic slowdowns, some truckdrivers are laid off and others have decreased earnings because of reduced hours or miles driven. Independent owner-operators are particularly vulnerable to slowdowns. Truckdrivers employed in industries such as wholesale food distribution, which is usually not affected much by recessions, are less likely to be laid off.

Earnings

As a rule, local truckdrivers are paid by the hour and receive extra pay for working overtime, usually after 40 hours. Long-distance drivers are generally paid primarily by the mile, and their rate per mile can vary greatly from employer to employer; their earnings increase with mileage driven, seniority, and the size and type of truck. Most driver-sales workers receive a commission based on their sales in addition to an hourly wage.

In 1992, truckdrivers had average straight-time hourly earnings of $12.92. Depending on the size of the truck, average hourly earnings were as follows:

Medium trucks	$13.50
Tractor-trailers	$12.94
Heavy straight trucks	$11.91
Light trucks	$8.51

Drivers employed by trucking companies had the highest earnings, averaging about $14.55 an hour in 1992. Truckdrivers in the Northeast and West had the highest earnings; those in the South had the lowest.

Most long-distance truckdrivers operate tractor-trailers, and their earnings vary widely, from as little as $20,000 to more than $40,000 annually. Most self-employed truckdrivers are primarily engaged in long-distance hauling. After deducting their living expenses and the costs associated with operating their trucks, earnings of $20,000 to $25,000 a year are common.

Many truckdrivers are members of the International Brotherhood of Teamsters. Some truckdrivers employed by companies outside the trucking industry are members of unions that represent the plant workers of the companies for which they work.

Related Occupations

Other driving occupations include ambulance driver, bus driver, chauffeur, and taxi driver.

Sources of Additional Information

Information on truck driver employment opportunities is available from local trucking companies and local offices of the state employment service. Information on career opportunities in truckdriving may be obtained from:

❏ American Trucking Associations, Inc., 2200 Mill Rd., Alexandria, VA 22314.

The Professional Truck Driver Institute of America, a non-profit organization established by the trucking industry, manufacturers, and others, certifies truckdriver training programs that meet industry standards. The Institute has available for $4 *A Checklist for Quality Programs in Tractor Trailer Driver Training*, a do-it-yourself guide for evaluating the quality of a truckdriver training program. This publication, as well as a free list of certified tractor-trailer driver training programs, may be obtained from:

❏ Professional Truck Driver Institute of America, 8788 Elk Grove Blvd., Suite 20, Elk Grove, CA 95624.

Career Planning and Job Seeking Techniques

Section Three

I've spent much of the past 20 years of my professional life learning about career planning and job search methods. My original interest was in helping people find jobs in less time and in helping them find better jobs. In a broad sense, that is or should be the real task of career counseling—helping people develop job seeking skills. While a lot of complexity is involved in these tasks, I have also found some elements of simplicity:

1. If you are going to work, you might as well define what it is you really want to do and are good at; and,

2. If you are looking for a job, you might as well use techniques that will reduce the time it takes to find one and that will help you get a better job than otherwise.

This section covers these topics and more. While I have written much more detailed works on career planning and job seeking, I present the basics in this section. In fact, this section is based on one of my earlier books titled *The Quick Job Search*, and it is available separately. However, I have added more details here that are not included in the previous edition.

Interestingly enough, after reading this chapter and doing its activities, you will have spent more time on planning your career than most people. And you will know far more about how to go about finding a job than the average job seeker. I believe there is enough information here to make a difference for most people. My intent is to give you some things to think about and reveal some useful techniques you might not have already considered. While you may want to know more, I hope this is enough to get you started.

THE
QUICK
JOB SEARCH

THE QUICK JOB SEARCH—TIPS TO MAKE GOOD CAREER DECISIONS AND GET A JOB IN LESS TIME

INTRODUCTION

While this book will teach you techniques to find a better job in less time, job seeking requires you to act, not just learn. So, in going through this book, consider what you can do to put the techniques to work for you. Do the activities. Create a daily plan. Get more interviews. Today, not tomorrow. You see, the sooner and harder you get to work on your job search, the shorter it is likely to be.

Changing Jobs and Careers Is Often Healthy

Most of us were told from an early age that each career move must be up—involving more money, responsibility, and prestige. Yet research indicates people change careers for many other reasons as well.

In a survey conducted by the Gallup Organization for the National Occupational Information Coordinating Committee, 44 percent of the working adults surveyed expected to be in a different job within three years. This is a very high turnover rate, yet only 41 percent had a definite plan to follow in mapping out their careers.

Logical, ordered careers are found more often with increasing levels of education. For example, while 25 percent of the high school dropouts took the only job available, this was true for only 8 percent of those with at least some college. But you should not assume this means that such occupational stability is healthy. Many adult developmental psychologists believe occupational change is not only normal but may even be necessary for sound adult growth and development. It is common, even normal, to reconsider occupational roles during your twenties, thirties,

and forties—even in the absence of economic pressure to do so.

One viewpoint is that a healthy occupational change is one that allows some previously undeveloped aspect of yourself to emerge. The change may be as natural as from clerk to supervisor; or as drastic as from professional musician to airline pilot. Although risk is always a factor when change is involved, reasonable risks are healthy and can raise self-esteem.

BUT NOT JUST ANY JOB SHOULD DO—NOR ANY JOB SEARCH

Whether you are seeking similar work in another setting or changing careers, you need a workable plan to find the right job. This small book will give you the information you need to help you find a good job quickly.

While the techniques are presented here briefly, they are based on my years of experience in helping people find good jobs (not just any job) and to find jobs in less time. The career decision-making section will help you consider the major issues you need to make a good decision about the job you want. The job-seeking skills are ones that have been proven to reduce the amount of time required to find a good job.

Of course, more thorough books have been written on job-seeking techniques and you may want to look into buying one or more of the better ones to obtain additional information. (A list of such books is included in the last few pages of this book.) But, short as this book is, it DOES present the basic skills to find a good job in less time. The techniques work.

THE SIX STEPS FOR A QUICK AND SUCCESSFUL JOB SEARCH

You can't just read about getting a job. The best way to get a job is to go out and get interviews! And the best way to get interviews is to make a job out of getting a job.

After many years of experience, I have identified just six basic things you need to do that make a big difference in your job search. Each will be covered in this book.

▼

THE SIX STEPS FOR A QUICK JOB SEARCH

1. *Know your skills.*
2. *Have a clear job objective.*
3. *Know where and how to look for job leads.*
4. *Spend at least 25 hours a week looking.*
5. *Get two interviews a day.*
6. *Follow up on all contacts.*

Identify Your Key Skills

One survey of employers found that 90 percent of the people they interviewed did not present the skills they had to do the job they sought. They could not answer the basic question, "Why should I hire you?"

Knowing your skills is essential to do well in an interview. This same knowledge is important in deciding what type of job you will enjoy and do well. For these reasons, I consider identifying your skills an essential part of a successful career plan or job search.

THE THREE TYPES OF SKILLS

Most people think of "skills" as job-related skills such as using a computer. But we all have other types of skills that are also important for success on a job—and that are very important to employers. The triangle below presents skills in three groups, and I think that this is a very useful way to consider skills for our purposes.

THE SKILLS TRIAD

Let's review these three types of skills and identify those that are most important to you.

SELF-MANAGEMENT SKILLS

Write down three things about yourself that you think make you a good worker.

> ✔
> ### YOUR "GOOD WORKER" TRAITS
> 1. _____
> 2. _____
> 3. _____

The things you just wrote down are among the most important things for an employer to know about you! They have to do with your basic personality—your ability to adapt to a new environment. They are some of the most important things to emphasize in an interview, yet most job seekers don't realize their importance—and don't mention them.

Review the Self-Management Skills Checklist and put a checkmark beside any skills you have. The Key Self-Management Skills are skills that employers find particularly important. If one or more of the Key Self-Management Skills apply to you, mentioning them in an interview can help you greatly.

> ✔
> ### SELF-MANAGEMENT SKILLS CHECKLIST
>
> #### KEY SELF-MANAGEMENT SKILLS
> ___ accept supervision   ___ hard worker
> ___ get along with coworkers   ___ honest
> ___ get things done on time   ___ productive
> ___ good attendance   ___ punctual
>
> #### OTHER SELF-MANAGEMENT SKILLS
> ___ able to coordinate   ___ friendly
> ___ ambitious   ___ good-natured
> ___ assertive   ___ helpful
> ___ capable   ___ humble
> ___ cheerful   ___ imaginative
> ___ competent   ___ independent
> ___ complete assignments   ___ industrious
> ___ conscientious   ___ informal
> ___ creative   ___ intelligent
> ___ dependable   ___ intuitive
> ___ discreet   ___ learn quickly
> ___ eager   ___ loyal
> ___ efficient   ___ mature
> ___ energetic   ___ methodical
> ___ enthusiastic   ___ modest
> ___ expressive   ___ motivated
> ___ flexible   ___ natural

___formal
___open-minded
___optimistic
___original
___patient
___persistent
___physically strong
___practice new skills
___reliable
___resourceful
___responsible
___self-confident

___sense of humor
___sincere
___solve problems
___spontaneous
___steady
___tactful
___take pride in work
___tenacious
___thrifty
___trustworthy
___versatile
___well-organized

OTHER SELF-MANAGEMENT SKILLS YOU HAVE:

_____

_____

_____

After you are done with the list, circle the five skills you feel are most important and list them in the box below.

▼

Note: Some people find it helpful to now complete the "Essential Job Search Data Worksheet" provided later in this book. It organizes skills and accomplishments from previous jobs and other life experiences.

YOUR TOP 5 SELF-MANAGEMENT SKILLS

1. _____
2. _____
3. _____
4. _____
5. _____

TRANSFERABLE SKILLS

We all have skills that can transfer from one job or career to another. For example, the ability to organize events could be used in a variety of jobs and may be essential for success in certain occupations. Your mission should be to find a job that requires the skills you have and enjoy using.

In the following list, put a checkmark beside the skills you have. You may have used them in a previous job or in some nonwork setting.

TRANSFERABLE SKILLS CHECKLIST

KEY TRANSFERABLE SKILLS

___instruct others
___manage money, budget
___manage people
___meet deadlines
___meet the public

___negotiate
___organize/manage projects
___public speaking
___written communication skills

SKILLS WORKING WITH THINGS

___assemble things
___build things
___construct/repair
___drive, operate vehicles
___good with hands

___observe/inspect
___operate tools, machines
___repair things
___use complex equipment

SKILLS WORKING WITH DATA

___analyze data
___audit records
___budget
___calculate/compute
___check for accuracy
___classify things
___compare
___compile
___count
___detail-oriented

___evaluate
___investigate
___keep financial records
___locate information
___manage money
___observe/inspect
___record facts
___research
___synthesize
___take inventory

SKILLS WORKING WITH PEOPLE

___administer
___advise
___care for
___coach
___confront others
___counsel people
___demonstrate
___diplomatic
___help others
___instruct
___interview people
___kind
___listen
___negotiate

___outgoing
___patient
___perceptive
___persuade
___pleasant
___sensitive
___sociable
___supervise
___tactful
___tolerant
___tough
___trusting
___understanding

SKILLS WORKING WITH WORDS, IDEAS

___articulate
___communicate verbally
___correspond with others
___create new ideas
___design
___edit
___ingenious

___inventive
___library research
___logical
___public speaking
___remember information
___write clearly

LEADERSHIP SKILLS

___arrange social functions   ___mediate problems
___competitive   ___motivate people
___decisive   ___negotiate agreements
___delegate   ___plan events
___direct others   ___results-oriented
___explain things to others   ___risk-taker
___influence others   ___run meetings
___initiate new tasks   ___self-confident
___make decisions   ___self-motivate
___manage or direct others   ___solve problems

CREATIVE/ARTISTIC SKILLS

___artistic   ___expressive
___dance, body movement   ___perform, act
___drawing, art   ___present artistic ideas

OTHER SIMILAR SKILLS YOU HAVE:

_____

_____

_____

_____

_____

When you are finished, identify the five transferable skills you feel are most important for you to use in your next job and list them in the box below.

YOUR TOP 5 TRANSFERABLE SKILLS

1. _____
2. _____
3. _____
4. _____
5. _____

JOB-RELATED SKILLS

Job content or job-related skills are those you need to do a particular job. A carpenter, for example, needs to know how to use various tools and be familiar with a variety of tasks related to that job.

You may already have a good idea of the type of job that you want. If so, it may be fairly simple for you to identify your job-related skills to emphasize in an interview. But I recommend that you complete at least two other things in this book first:

1. Complete the material that helps you define your job objective more clearly. Doing so will help you clarify just what sort of a job you want and allow you to better select those skills that best support it.

2. Complete the Essential Job Search Data Worksheet that appears later in this book (page 22). It will give you lots of specific skills and accomplishments to consider.

Once you have done these two things, come back and complete the box below. Include the job-related skills you have that you would most like to use in your next job.

YOUR TOP 5 JOB-RELATED SKILLS

1. _____
2. _____
3. _____
4. _____
5. _____

BEGIN BY DEFINING YOUR IDEAL JOB (YOU CAN COMPROMISE LATER . . .)

Too many people look for a job without having a good idea of exactly what they are looking for. Before you go out looking for "a" job, I suggest that you first define exactly what it is you really want—"the" job. Most people think a job objective is the same as a job title, but it isn't. You need to consider other elements of what makes a job satisfying for you. Then, later, you can decide what that job is called and what industry it might be in.

THE EIGHT FACTORS TO CONSIDER IN DEFINING THE IDEAL JOB FOR YOU

Following are eight factors to consider when defining your ideal job. Once you know what you want, your task then becomes finding a job that is as close to your ideal job as you can find.

1. WHAT SKILLS DO YOU WANT TO USE?

From the previous skills lists, select the top five skills that you enjoy using and most want to use in your next job.

1. _____
2. _____
3. _____
4. _____
5. _____

2. What Type of Special Knowledge Do You Have?

Perhaps you know how to fix radios, keep accounting records, or cook food. Write down the things you know about from schooling, training, hobbies, family experiences, and other sources. One or more of them could make you a very special applicant in the right setting.

_____

_____

_____

_____

3. With What Type of People Do You Prefer to Work?

Do you like to work with aggressive hardworking folks, creative types, or what?

_____

_____

_____

_____

4. What Type of Work Environment Do You Prefer?

Do you want to work inside, outside, in a quiet place, a busy place, a clean place, have a window with a nice view, or what? List those things that are important to you.

_____

_____

_____

_____

5. Where Do You Want Your Next Job to Be Located—In What City or Region?

Near a bus line? Close to a child care center? If you are open to live or work anywhere, what would your ideal community be like?

_____

_____

_____

_____

6. How Much Money Do You Hope to Make in Your Next Job?

Many people will take less money if the job is great in other ways—or to survive. Think about the minimum you would take as well as what you would eventually like to earn. Your next job will probably be somewhere between.

_____

_____

_____

7. How Much Responsibility Are You Willing to Accept?

Usually, the more money you want to make, the more responsibility you must accept. Do you want to work by yourself, be part of a group, or be in charge? If so, at what level?

_____

_____

_____

_____

8. What Things Are Important or Have Meaning to You?

Do you have values that you would prefer to include as a basis of the work you do? For example, some people want to work to help others, clean up our environment, build things, make machines work, gain power or prestige, or care for animals or plants. Think about what is important to you and how you might include this in your next job.

_____

_____

_____

_____

Your Ideal Job

Use the points above and on previous pages to help you define your ideal job. Think about each one and select the points that are most important to you. Don't worry about a job title yet, just focus on the most important things to include from the previous questions to define your ideal job.

My Ideal Job Objective:

_____

_____

_____

_____

_____

_____

_____

_____

_____

SETTING A SPECIFIC JOB OBJECTIVE

Whether or not you have a good idea of the type of job you want, it is important to know more about various job options. About 85 percent of all workers work in one of the 250 jobs in the list that follows.

A very simple but effective way for exploring job alternatives is to simply go through this list and check those about which you want to learn more. Descriptions for all of them can be found in books titled the *Occupational Outlook Handbook* and *America's Top 300 Jobs*. I encourage you to learn more about the jobs that interest you.

If you need help figuring out what type of job to look for, remember that most areas have free or low-cost career counseling and testing services. Contact local government agencies and schools for referrals.

THE TOP 250 JOBS IN OUR WORKFORCE

EXECUTIVE, ADMINISTRATIVE, AND MANAGERIAL OCCUPATIONS

- Accountants and auditors
- Administrative services managers
- Budget analysts
- Construction and building inspectors
- Construction contractors and managers
- Cost estimators
- Education administrators
- Employment interviewers
- Engineering, science, and data processing managers
- Financial managers
- Funeral directors
- General managers and top executives
- Government chief executives and legislators
- Health services managers
- Hotel managers and assistants
- Industrial production managers
- Inspectors and compliance officers, except construction
- Loan officers and counselors
- Management analysts and consultants
- Marketing, advertising, and public relations managers
- Personnel, training, and labor relations specialists and managers
- Property and real estate managers
- Purchasers and buyers
- Restaurant and food service managers
- Retail managers
- Underwriters

PROFESSIONAL SPECIALTY OCCUPATIONS

ENGINEERS

- Aerospace engineers
- Chemical engineers
- Civil engineers
- Electrical and electronics engineers
- Industrial engineers
- Mechanical engineers
- Metallurgical, ceramic, and materials engineers
- Mining engineers
- Nuclear engineers
- Petroleum engineers

ARCHITECTS AND SURVEYORS

- Architects
- Landscape architects
- Surveyors

COMPUTER, MATHEMATICAL, AND OPERATIONS RESEARCH OCCUPATIONS

- Actuaries
- Computer scientists and systems analysts
- Mathematicians
- Operations research analysts
- Statisticians

LIFE SCIENTISTS

- Agricultural scientists
- Biological scientists
- Foresters and conservation scientists

PHYSICAL SCIENTISTS

- Chemists
- Geologists and geophysicists
- Meteorologists
- Physicists and astronomers

LAWYERS AND JUDGES

SOCIAL SCIENTISTS AND URBAN PLANNERS

- Economists and marketing research analysts
- Psychologists
- Sociologists
- Urban and regional planners

SOCIAL AND RECREATION WORKERS

- Human services workers
- Recreation workers
- Social workers

RELIGIOUS WORKERS

- Protestant ministers
- Rabbis
- Roman Catholic priests

TEACHERS, LIBRARIANS, AND COUNSELORS

- Adult education teachers
- Archivists and curators
- College and university faculty
- Counselors
- Librarians
- School teachers - kindergarten, elementary, and secondary

HEALTH DIAGNOSING PRACTITIONERS

- Chiropractors
- Dentists
- Optometrists
- Physicians
- Podiatrists
- Veterinarians

HEALTH ASSESSMENT AND TREATING OCCUPATIONS

- Dietitians and nutritionists
- Occupational therapists

Pharmacists

Physical therapists

Physician assistants

Recreational therapists

Registered nurses

Respiratory therapists

Speech-language pathologists and audiologists

COMMUNICATIONS OCCUPATIONS

Public relations specialists

Radio and television announcers and newscasters

Reporters and correspondents

Writers and editors

VISUAL ARTS OCCUPATIONS

Designers

Photographers and camera operators

Visual artists

PERFORMING ARTS OCCUPATIONS

Actors, directors, and producers

Dancers and choreographers

Musicians

TECHNICIANS AND RELATED SUPPORT OCCUPATIONS

HEALTH TECHNOLOGISTS AND TECHNICIANS

Cardiovascular technologists and technicians

Clinical laboratory technologists and technicians

Dental hygienists

Dispensing opticians

EEG technologists

Emergency medical technicians

Licensed practical nurses

Medical record technicians

Nuclear medicine technologists

Radiologic technologists

Surgical technicians

TECHNOLOGISTS, EXCEPT HEALTH

Aircraft pilots

Air traffic controllers

Broadcast technicians

Computer programmers

Drafters

Engineering technicians

Library technicians

Paralegals

Science technicians

MARKETING AND SALES OCCUPATIONS

Cashiers

Counter and rental clerks

Insurance agents and brokers

Manufacturers' and wholesale sales representatives

Real estate agents, brokers, and appraisers

Retail sales workers

Securities and financial services sales representatives

Services sales representatives

Travel agents

ADMINISTRATIVE SUPPORT OCCUPATIONS, INCLUDING CLERICAL

Adjusters, investigators, and collectors

Bank tellers

Billing clerks

Bookkeeping, accounting, and auditing clerks

Brokerage clerks and statement clerks

Clerical supervisors and managers

Computer and peripheral equipment operators

Credit clerks and authorizers

Dispatchers

File clerks

General office clerks

Hotel and motel clerks

Information clerks

Interviewing and new accounts clerks

Library assistants and bookmobile drivers

Mail clerks and messengers

Material recording, scheduling, dispatching, and distributing workers

Order clerks

Payroll and timekeeping clerks

Personnel clerks

Postal clerks and mail carriers

Receptionists

Record clerks

Reservation and transportation ticket agents and travel clerks

Secretaries

Stenographers and court reporters

Stock clerks

Teacher aides

Telephone operators

Traffic, shipping, and receiving clerks

Typists, word processors, and data entry keyers

SERVICE OCCUPATIONS

PROTECTIVE SERVICE OCCUPATIONS

Correction officers

Firefighters

Guards

Police, detectives, and special agents

FOOD AND BEVERAGE PREPARATION AND SERVICE OCCUPATIONS

Chefs, cooks, and other kitchen workers

Food and beverage service workers

HEALTH SERVICE OCCUPATIONS

Dental assistants

Medical assistants

Nursing aides and psychiatric aides

PERSONAL SERVICE AND BUILDING AND GROUNDS SERVICE OCCUPATIONS

Animal caretakers, except farm

Barbers and cosmetologists

Flight attendants

Gardeners and groundskeepers

Homemaker-home health aides

Janitors and cleaners

Preschool workers

Private household workers

AGRICULTURE, FORESTRY, FISHING, AND RELATED OCCUPATIONS

Farm operators and managers

Fishers, hunters, and trappers

Forestry and logging workers

MECHANICS, INSTALLERS, AND REPAIRERS

Aircraft mechanics and engine specialists

Automotive body repairers

Automotive mechanics

Commercial and industrial electronic equipment repairers

Communications equipment mechanics

Computer and office machine repairers

Diesel mechanics

Electronic equipment repairers

Electronic home entertainment equipment repairers

Elevator installers and repairers

Farm equipment mechanics

General maintenance mechanics

Heating, air-conditioning, and refrigeration mechanics

Home appliance and power tool repairers

Industrial machinery repairers

Line installers and cable splicers

Millwrights

Mobile heavy equipment mechanics

Motorcycle, boat, and small-engine mechanics

Musical instrument repairers and tuners

Telephone installers and repairers

Vending machine servicers and repairers

CONSTRUCTION TRADES AND EXTRACTIVE OCCUPATIONS

Bricklayers and stonemasons

Carpenters

Carpet installers

Concrete masons and terrazzo workers

Drywall workers and lathers

Electricians

Glaziers

Insulation workers

Painters and paperhangers

Plasterers

Plumbers and pipefitters

Roofers

Roustabouts

Sheetmetal workers

Structural and reinforcing ironworkers

Tilesetters

PRODUCTION OCCUPATIONS

ASSEMBLERS

Precision assemblers

BLUE-COLLAR WORKER SUPERVISORS

FOOD PROCESSING OCCUPATIONS

Butchers and meat, poultry, and fish cutters

INSPECTORS, TESTERS, AND GRADERS

METALWORKING AND PLASTICS-WORKING OCCUPATIONS

Boilermakers

Jewelers

Machinists and tool programmers

Metalworking and plastics-working machine operators

Tool and die makers

Welders, cutters, and welding machine operators

PLANT AND SYSTEMS OPERATORS

Electric power generating plant operators and power distributors and dispatchers

Stationary engineers

Water and wastewater treatment plant operators

PRINTING OCCUPATIONS

Bindery workers

Prepress workers

Printing press operators

TEXTILE, APPAREL, AND FURNISHINGS OCCUPATIONS

Apparel workers

Shoe and leather workers and repairers

Textile machinery operators

Upholsterers

WOODWORKING OCCUPATIONS

MISCELLANEOUS PRODUCTION OCCUPATIONS

Dental laboratory technicians

Ophthalmic laboratory technicians

Painting and coating machine operators

Photographic process workers

TRANSPORTATION AND MATERIAL MOVING OCCUPATIONS

Bus drivers

Material moving equipment operators

Rail transportation workers

Taxi drivers and chauffeurs

Truck drivers

Water transportation workers

HANDLERS, EQUIPMENT CLEANERS, HELPERS, AND LABORERS

JOB OPPORTUNITIES IN THE ARMED FORCES

Job Search Methods That Help You Get a Better Job in Less Time

One survey found that 85 percent of all employers don't advertise at all. They hire people they already know, people who find out about the jobs through word of mouth, or people who simply happen to be in the right place at the right time. This is sometimes just luck, but this book will teach you ways to increase your "luck" in finding job openings.

TRADITIONAL JOB SEARCH METHODS ARE NOT VERY EFFECTIVE

Most job seekers don't know how ineffective some traditional job hunting techniques tend to be.

HOW PEOPLE FIND JOBS

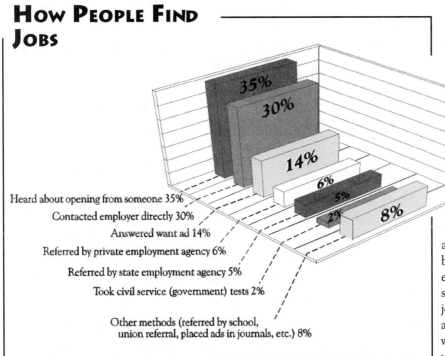

Heard about opening from someone 35%
Contacted employer directly 30%
Answered want ad 14%
Referred by private employment agency 6%
Referred by state employment agency 5%
Took civil service (government) tests 2%

Other methods (referred by school,
union referral, placed ads in journals, etc.) 8%

The chart above shows that fewer than 15 percent of all job seekers get jobs from reading the want ads. Let's take a quick look at want ads and other traditional job search methods.

Help Wanted Ads: As you should remember, only about 15 percent of all people get their jobs through the want ads. Everyone who reads the paper knows about these job openings so competition for advertised jobs is fierce. Still, some people do get jobs this way, so go ahead and apply. Just be sure to spend most of your time using more effective methods.

The State Employment Service: Each state has a network of local offices to administer unemployment compensation and provide job leads and other services. These services are provided without charge to you or employers. Names vary by state, so it may be called "Job Service," "Department of Labor," "Unemployment Office," or another name.

Nationally, only about 5 percent of all job seekers get their jobs here and these organizations typically know of only one-tenth (or fewer) of the actual job openings in a region. Still, it is worth a weekly visit. If you ask for the same counselor, you might impress the person enough to remember you and refer you for the better openings.

You should also realize that some of the state employment services provide substantial help in the form of job search workshops and other resources. Look into it, the price is right.

Private Employment Agencies: Recent studies have found that private agencies work reasonably well for those who use them. But there are cautions to consider. For one thing, these agencies work best for entry-level positions or for those with specialized skills that are in demand. Most people who use a private agency usually find their jobs using some other source and their success record is quite modest.

Private agencies also charge a fee either to you (as high as 20 percent of your annual salary!) or to the employer. Most of them call employers asking if they have any openings, something you could do yourself.

Unless you have skills that are in high demand, you may do better on your own—and save money. At the least, you should rely on a private agency as only one of the techniques you use and not depend on them too heavily.

Temporary Agencies: These can be a source of quick but temporary jobs to bring in some income as well as give you experience in a variety of settings— something that can help you land full-time jobs later. More and more employers are also using them as a way to evaluate workers for permanent jobs. So consider using these agencies if it makes sense to do so but make certain that you continue an active search for a full-time job as you do.

Sending Out Resumes: *One survey found that you would have to mail more than 500 unsolicited resumes to get one interview!* A much better approach is to contact the person who might hire you by phone to set up an interview directly, then send a resume. If you insist on sending out unsolicited resumes, do this on weekends—save your "prime time" for more effective job search techniques.

Filling Out Applications: Most applications are used to screen you out. Larger organizations may require them, but remember that your task is to get an interview, not fill out an application. If you do complete them, make them neat, error-free, and do not include anything that could get you screened out. If necessary, leave a problematic section blank. It can always be explained after you get an interview.

Personnel Departments: Hardly anyone gets hired by interviewers in a personnel department. Their job is to screen you and refer the "best" applicants to the person who would actually supervise you. You may need to cooperate with them, but it is often better to go directly to the person who is most likely to supervise you—even if no job opening exists at the moment. And remember that most organizations don't even have a personnel office, only the larger ones!

THE TWO JOB SEARCH METHODS THAT WORK BEST

Two-thirds of all people get their jobs using informal methods. These jobs are often not advertised and are part of the "hidden" job market. How do **you** find them?

There are two basic informal job search methods: networking with people you know (which I call warm contacts), and making direct contacts with an employer (which I call cold contacts). They are both based on the most important job search rule of all.

▼

THE MOST IMPORTANT JOB SEARCH RULE: DON'T WAIT UNTIL THE JOB IS OPEN BEFORE CONTACTING THE EMPLOYER!

Most jobs are filled by someone the employer meets before the job is formally "open." So the trick is to meet people who can hire you before a job is available! Instead of saying, "Do you have any jobs open?" say, "I realize you may not have any openings now, but I would still like to talk to you about the possibility of future openings."

DEVELOP A NETWORK OF CONTACTS IN FIVE EASY STEPS

One study found that 40 percent of all people found their jobs through a lead provided by a friend, a relative, or an acquaintance. Developing new contacts is called "networking" and here's how it works:

1. Make lists of people you know. Develop a list of anyone with whom you are friendly, then make a separate list of all your relatives. These two lists alone often add up to 25-100 people or more. Next, think of other groups of people with whom you have something in common, such as former coworkers or classmates; members of your social or sports groups; members of your professional association; former employers; and members of your religious group. You may not know many of these people personally, but most will help you if you ask them.

2. Contact them in a systematic way. Each of these people is a contact for you. Obviously, some lists and some people on those lists will be more helpful than others, but almost any one of them could help you find a job lead.

3. Present yourself well. Begin with your friends and relatives. Call them and tell them you are looking for a job and need their help. Be as clear as possible about what you are looking for and what skills and qualifications you have. Look at the sample JIST Card and phone script later in this book for presentation ideas.

4. Ask them for leads. It is possible that they will know of a job opening just right for you. If so, get the details and get right on it! More likely, however, they will not, so here are three questions you should ask.

▼

THE THREE MAGIC NETWORKING QUESTIONS

1. *Do you know of any openings for a person with my skills?* If the answer is no (which it usually is), then ask:
2. *Do you know of someone else who might know of such an opening?* If your contact does, get that name and ask for another one. If he or she doesn't, ask:
3. *Do you know of anyone who might know of someone else who might?* Another good way to ask this is, "Do you know someone who knows lots of people?" If all else fails, this will usually get you a name.

5. Contact these referrals and ask them the same questions. For each original contact, you can extend your network of acquaintances by hundreds of people. Eventually, one of these people will hire you or refer you to someone who will! This process is called networking and it does work if you are persistent.

CONTACT EMPLOYERS DIRECTLY

It takes more courage, but contacting an employer directly is a very effective job search technique. I call these cold contacts because you don't have an existing connection with these contacts. Following are two basic techniques for making cold contacts.

USE THE "YELLOW PAGES" TO FIND POTENTIAL EMPLOYERS

One effective cold contact technique uses the *Yellow Pages*. You can begin by looking at the index and asking for each entry, "Would an organization of this kind need a person with my skills?" If the answer is "yes" then that type of organization or business is a possible target. You can also rate "yes" entries based on your interest, giving an A to those that seem very interesting, a B to those you are not sure of, and a C to those that don't seem interesting at all.

Next, select a type of organization that got a "yes" response (such as "hotels") and turn to the section of the *Yellow Pages* where they are listed. Then call the organizations listed and ask to speak to the person who is most likely to hire or supervise you. A sample telephone script is included later in this book to give you ideas about what to say.

DROP IN WITHOUT AN APPOINTMENT

You can also simply walk in to many potential employers' organizations and ask to speak to the person in charge. This is particularly effective in small businesses, but it works surprisingly well in larger ones, too. Remember, you want an interview even if there are no openings now. If your timing is inconvenient, ask for a better time to come back for an interview.

Most Jobs Are with Small Employers

About 70 percent of all people now work in small businesses—those with 250 or fewer employees. While the largest corporations have reduced the number of employees, small businesses have been creating as many as 80 percent of the new jobs. There are many opportunities to obtain training and promotions in smaller organizations, too. Many do not even have a personnel department, so nontraditional job search techniques are particularly effective with them.

JIST Cards—an Effective "Mini Resume"

JIST Cards are a job search tool that get results. Typed, printed, or even neatly written on a 3-by-5-inch card, a JIST Card contains the essential information most employers want to know. Look at the sample cards that follow:

JIST Cards are an effective job search tool! Give them to friends and to each of your network contacts. Attach one to your resume. Enclose one in your thank-you notes before or after an interview. Leave one with employers as a "business card." Use them in many creative ways. Even though they can be typed or even handwritten, it is best to have 100 or more printed so you can put lots of them in circulation. Thousands of job seekers have used them, and they get results!

Use the Phone to Get Job Leads

Once you have created your JIST Card, it is easy to create a telephone contact "script" based on it. Adapt the basic script to call people you know or your *Yellow Pages* leads. Select *Yellow Pages* index categories that might use a person with your skills and get the numbers of specific organizations in that category. Then ask for the person who is most likely to supervise you and present your phone script.

Sandy Zaremba

Home: (219) 232-7608   **Message:** (219) 234-7465
Position: General Office/Clerical

Over two years work experience plus one year of training in office practices. Type 55 wpm, trained in word processing operations, post general ledger, handle payables, receivables, and most accounting tasks. Responsible for daily deposits averaging $5,000. Good interpersonal skills. Can meet strict deadlines and handle pressure well.

Willing to work any hours

Organized, honest, reliable, and hardworking

Chris Vorhees

Home: (602) 253-9678
Leave Message: (602) 257-6643

OBJECTIVE: Electronics—installation, maintenance, and sales

SKILLS: Four years work experience plus two years advanced training in electronics. A.S. degree in Electronics Engineering Technology. Managed a $300,000/yr. business while going to school full time, with grades in the top 25%. Familiar with all major electronic diagnostic and repair equipment. Hands-on experience with medical, consumer, communications, and industrial electronics equipment and applications. Good problem-solving and communication skills. Customer service oriented.

Willing to do what it takes to get the job done.

While it doesn't work every time, most people, with practice, can get one or more interviews in an hour by making these "cold" calls. Here is a phone script based on a JIST card:

"Hello, my name is Pam Nykanen. I am interested in a position in hotel management. I have four years experience in sales, catering, and accounting with a 300-room hotel. I also have an associate degree in Hotel Management plus one year of experience with the Bradey Culinary Institute. During my employment, I helped double revenues from meetings and conferences and increased bar revenues by 46 percent. I have good problem-solving skills and am good with people. I am also well-organized, hardworking, and detail-oriented. When can I come in for an interview?"

While this example assumes you are calling someone you don't know, the script can be easily modified for presentation to warm contacts, including referrals. Using the script for making cold calls takes courage, but it does work for most people.

Make Your Job Search a Full-Time Job

On the average, job seekers spend fewer than 15 hours a week actually looking for work. The average length of unemployment varies from three or more months, with some being out of work far longer (older workers and higher earners are two groups who take longer). I believe there is a connection.

Based on many years of experience, I can say that the more time you spend on your job search each week, the less time you are likely to remain unemployed. Of course, using more effective job search methods also helps. Those who follow my advice have proven, over and over, that they get jobs in less than half the average time and they often get better jobs too. Time management is the key.

SPEND AT LEAST 25 HOURS A WEEK LOOKING FOR A JOB

If you are unemployed and looking for a full-time job, you should look for a job on a full-time basis. It just makes sense to do so, although many do not due to discouragement, lack of good techniques, and lack of structure. Most job seekers have no idea what they are going to do next Thursday—they don't have a plan. The most important thing is to decide how many hours you can commit to your job search and stay with it. You should spend a minimum of 25 hours a week on hard-core job search activities with no goofing around. Let me walk you through a simple but effective process to help you organize your job search schedule.

> Write here how many hours you are willing to spend each week looking for a job: _____

DECIDE ON WHICH DAYS YOU WILL LOOK FOR WORK

Answering the questions below requires you to have a schedule and a plan, just like you had when you were working, right?

> Which days of the week will you spend looking for a job? _____
>
> How many hours will you look each day? _____
>
> At what time will you begin and end your job search on each of these days? _____
> _____

CREATE A SPECIFIC DAILY SCHEDULE

Having a specific daily job search schedule is very important because most job seekers find it hard to stay productive each day. You already know which job search methods are most effective and you should plan on spending most of your time using those methods. The sample daily schedule that follows has been very effective for people who have used it and it will give you ideas for your own. Although you are welcome to create your own daily schedule, I urge you to consider one similar to this one. Why? Because it works.

A DAILY SCHEDULE THAT WORKS

7:00 - 8:00 a.m.	Get up, shower, dress, eat breakfast.
8:00 - 8:15 a.m.	Organize work space; review schedule for interviews or follow-ups; update schedule.
8:15 - 9:00 a.m.	Review old leads for follow-up; develop new leads (want ads, *Yellow Pages*, networking lists, etc.).
9:00 - 10:00 a.m.	Make phone calls, set up interviews.
10:00 - 10:15 a.m.	Take a break!
10:15 - 11:00 a.m.	Make more calls.
11:00 - 12:00 p.m.	Make follow-up calls as needed.
12:00 - 1:00 p.m.	Lunch break.
1:00 - 5:00 p.m.	Go on interviews; call cold contacts in the field; research for upcoming interviews at the library.

DO IT NOW: GET A SCHEDULE BOOK AND WRITE DOWN YOUR JOB SEARCH SCHEDULE

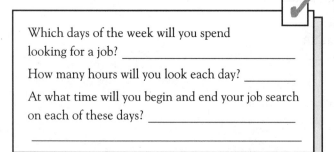

A good daily planner is a cheap investment because cutting your unemployment time by just a few hours will pay for it. I like and use the "Two Page Per Day Original" provided by Day-Timers, Inc. (215-266-9000) because it provides lots of room for notes. It costs about $25 but most stationery stores have others at various prices, although getting an inferior system is unwise.

This is important: If you are not accustomed to using a daily schedule book or planner, promise yourself that you will get a good one tomorrow. Choose one that allows plenty of space for each day's plan on an hourly basis plus room for daily "to do" listings. Write in your daily schedule in advance, then add interviews as they come. Get used to carrying it with you and use it!

Redefine What "Counts" as an Interview, Then Get Two a Day

The average job seeker gets about five interviews a month—fewer than two interviews a week. Yet many job seekers using the techniques I suggest routinely get two interviews a day. But to accomplish this, you must redefine what an interview is.

> **THE NEW DEFINITION OF AN INTERVIEW:** *An interview is any face-to-face contact with someone who has the authority to hire or supervise a person with your skills—even if they don't have an opening at the time you interview.*

With this definition, it is *much* easier to get interviews. You can now interview with all kinds of potential employers, not only those who have a job opening. Many job seekers use the *Yellow Pages* to get two interviews with just one hour of calls by using the telephone contact script discussed earlier. Others simply drop in on potential employers and ask for an unscheduled interview—and they get them. And getting names of others to contact from those you know—networking—is quite effective if you persist.

Getting two interviews a day equals 10 a week and 40 a month. That's 800 percent more interviews than the average job seeker gets. Who do you think will get a job offer quicker? So set out each day to get at least two interviews. It's quite possible to do now that you know how.

How to Answer Tough Interview Questions

Interviews are where the job search action happens. You have to get them, then you have to do well in them. If you have done your homework, you are getting interviews for jobs that will maximize your skills. That is a good start, but your ability to communicate your skills in the interview makes an enormous difference. This is where, according to employer surveys, most job seekers have problems. They don't effectively communicate the skills they have to do the job and they answer one or more problem questions poorly.

While thousands of problem interview questions are possible, I have listed just 10 that, if you can answer them well, will prepare you for most interviews.

> **THE TOP 10 PROBLEM QUESTIONS**
> 1. Why don't you tell me about yourself?
> 2. Why should I hire you?
> 3. What are your major strengths?
> 4. What are your major weaknesses?
> 5. What sort of pay do you expect to receive?
> 6. How does your previous experience relate to the jobs we have here?
> 7. What are your plans for the future?
> 8. What will your former employer (or references) say about you?
> 9. Why are you looking for this type of position and why here?
> 10. Why don't you tell me about your personal situation?

I don't have the space here to give thorough answers to all of these questions and there are potentially hundreds more. Instead, let me suggest several techniques that I have developed which you can use to answer almost any interview question.

A TRADITIONAL INTERVIEW IS NOT A FRIENDLY EXCHANGE

Before I present the techniques for answering interview questions, it is important to understand what is going on. In a traditional interview situation, there is a job opening and you are one of several (or one of a hundred) applicants. In this setting, the employer's task is to eliminate all but one applicant.

Assuming that you got as far as an interview, the interviewer's questions are designed to elicit information that can be used to screen you out. If you are wise, you know that your task is to avoid getting screened out. It's not an open and honest interaction, is it?

This illustrates yet another advantage of nontraditional job search techniques: the ability to talk to an employer before an opening exists. This eliminates the stress of a traditional interview. Employers are not trying to screen you out and you are not trying to keep them from finding out stuff about you.

Having said that, knowing a technique for answering questions that might be asked in a traditional interview is good preparation for whatever you might run into during your job search . . .

THE THREE-STEP PROCESS FOR ANSWERING INTERVIEW QUESTIONS

I know this might seem too simple, but the Three-Step Process is easy to remember. Its simplicity allows you to evaluate a question and create a good answer. The technique is based on sound principles and has worked for thousands of people, so consider trying it.

STEP 1. UNDERSTAND WHAT IS REALLY BEING ASKED.

Most questions are really designed to find out about your self-management skills and personality. While they are rarely this blunt, the employer's *real* question is often:

- ✓ Can I depend on you?
- ✓ Are you easy to get along with?
- ✓ Are you a good worker?
- ✓ Do you have the experience and training to do the job if we hire you?
- ✓ Are you likely to stay on the job for a reasonable period of time and be productive?

Ultimately, if the employer is not convinced that you will stay and be a good worker, it won't matter if you have the best credentials—her or she won't hire you.

STEP 2. ANSWER THE QUESTION BRIEFLY.

Acknowledge the facts, but . . .

- ✓ Present them as an advantage, not a disadvantage.

There are lots of examples in which a specific interview question will encourage you to provide negative information. The classic is the "What are your major weaknesses?" question that I included in my top 10 problem questions list. Obviously, this is a trick question and many people are just not prepared for it. A good response might be to mention something that is not all that damaging such as "I have been told that I am a perfectionist, sometimes not delegating as effectively as I might." But your answer is not complete until you continue.

STEP 3. ANSWER THE REAL CONCERN BY PRESENTING YOUR RELATED SKILLS.

- ✓ Base your answer on the key skills that you have identified and that are needed in this job.
- ✓ Give examples to support your skills statements.

For example, an employer might say to a recent graduate, "We were looking for someone with more experience in this field. Why should we consider you?" Here is one possible answer: "I'm sure there are people who have more experience, but I *do* have more than six years of work experience including three years of advanced training and hands-on experience using the latest methods and techniques. Because my training is recent, I am open to new ideas and am used to working hard and learning quickly."

In the example I presented in Step 2 (about your need to delegate), a good skills statement might be, "I have been working on this problem and have learned to be more willing to let my staff do things, making sure that they have good training and supervision. I've found that their performance improves and it frees me up to do other things."

Whatever your situation, learn to use it to your advantage. It is essential to communicate your skills during

an interview and The Three-Step Process gives you a technique that can dramatically improve your responses. It works!

INTERVIEW DRESS AND GROOMING RULE

If you make a negative first impression, you won't get a second chance to make a good one. So do everything possible to make a good impression.

A GOOD RULE FOR DRESSING FOR AN INTERVIEW IS:

Dress like you think the boss will dress—*only neater.*

Dress for success! If necessary, get help selecting an interview outfit from someone who dresses well. Pay close attention to your grooming, too. Written things like correspondence and resumes must be neat and errorless because they create an impression as well.

Follow Up on All Contacts

People who follow up with potential employers and with others in their network get jobs faster than those who do not.

FOUR RULES FOR EFFECTIVE FOLLOW-UP

1. Send a thank-you note to every person who helps you in your job search.
2. Send the thank-you note within 24 hours after you speak with the person.
3. Enclose JIST Cards with thank-you notes and all other correspondence.
4. Develop a system to keep following up with "good" contacts.

THANK-YOU NOTES MAKE A DIFFERENCE

Thank-you notes can be handwritten or typed on quality paper and matching envelopes. Keep them simple, neat, and errorless. Following is a sample:

April 16, 19XX

2234 Riverwood Ave.
Philadelphia, PA 17963

Ms. Sandra Kijek
Henderson & Associates, Inc.
1801 Washington Blvd., Suite 1201
Philadelphia, PA 17963

Dear Ms. Kijek:

Thank you for sharing your time with me so generously today. I really appreciated seeing your state-of-the-art computer equipment.

Your advice has already proved helpful. I have an appointment to meet with Mr. Robert Hopper on Friday as you anticipated.

Please consider referring me to others if you think of someone else who might need a person with my skills.

Sincerely,

William Richardson

William Richardson

USE JOB LEAD CARDS TO ORGANIZE YOUR CONTACTS

Use a simple 3-by-5-inch card to keep essential information on each person in your network. Buy a 3-by-5-inch card file box and tabs for each day of the month. File the cards under the date you want to contact the person, and the rest is easy. I've found that staying in touch with a good contact every other week can pay off big. Here's a sample card to give you ideas to create your own:

ORGANIZATION: *Mutual Health Insurance*

CONTACT PERSON: *Anna Tomey*   PHONE: *317-355-0216*

SOURCE OF LEAD: *Aunt Ruth*

NOTES: *4/10 Called. Anna on vacation. Call back 4/15. 4/15 Interview set 4/20 at 1:30. 4/20 Anna showed me around. They use the same computers we used in school! (Friendly people) Sent thank-you note and JIST Card. Call back 5/1. 5/1 Second interview 5/8 at 9 a.m.!*

Resumes: Write a Simple One Now, and a "Better" One Later

You have already learned that sending out resumes and waiting for responses is not an effective job seeking technique. However, many employers *will* ask you for them, and they are a useful tool in your job search. If you feel that you need a resume, I suggest that you begin with a simple one that you can complete quickly. I've seen too many people spend weeks working on their resume while they could have been out getting interviews instead. If you want a "better" resume, you can work on it on weekends and evenings. So let's begin with the basics.

BASIC TIPS TO CREATE A SUPERIOR RESUME

The following tips make sense for any resume format.

Write it yourself. It's OK to look at other resumes for ideas, but write yours yourself. It will force you to organize your thoughts and background.

Make it errorless. One spelling or grammar error will create a negative impressionist (see what I mean?). Get someone else to review your final draft for any errors. Then review it again because these rascals have a way of slipping in.

Make it look good. Poor copy quality, cheap paper, bad type quality, or anything else that creates a poor physical appearance will turn off employers to even the best resume content. Get professional help with design and printing if necessary. Many resume writers and print shops have desktop publishing services and can do it all for you.

Be brief, be relevant. Many good resumes fit on one page and few justify more than two. Include only the most important points. Use short sentences and action words. If it doesn't relate to and support the job objective, cut it!

Be honest. Don't overstate your qualifications. If you end up getting a job you can't handle, it will not be to your advantage. Most employers will see right through it and not hire you.

Be positive. Emphasize your accomplishments and results. This is no place to be too humble or to display your faults.

Be specific. Rather than saying "I am good with people," say "I supervised four people in the warehouse and increased productivity by 30 percent." Use numbers whenever possible, such as the number of people served, percent of sales increase, or dollars saved.

You should also know that everyone feels he or she is a resume expert. Whatever you do, someone will tell you it is wrong. For this reason, it is important to understand that a resume is a job search tool. You should never delay or slow down your job search because your resume is not "good enough." The best approach is to create a simple and acceptable resume as soon as possible, then use it. As time permits, create a better one if you feel you must.

CHRONOLOGICAL RESUMES

Most resumes use the chronological format. It is a simple format where the most recent experience is listed first, followed by each previous job. This arrangement works fine for someone with work experience in several similar jobs, but not as well for those with limited experience or for career changers.

Look at the two Judith Jones' resumes. Both use the chronological approach, but notice that the second one includes some improvements over her first. The improved resume is clearly better, but either would be acceptable to most employers.

TIPS FOR WRITING A SIMPLE CHRONOLOGICAL RESUME

Here are some tips for writing a basic chronological resume.

Name. Use your formal name rather than a nickname if it sounds more professional.

Address. Be complete. Include your zip code and avoid abbreviations. If moving is a possibility, use the address of a friend or relative or be certain to include a forwarding address.

Telephone Number. Employers are most likely to try to reach you by phone, so having a reliable way to be reached is very important. Always include your area code because you never know where your resume might travel. If you don't have an answering machine get one, and make sure you leave it on whenever you are not home. Listen to your message to be sure it presents you in a professional way. Also available are a

variety of communication systems: voice mail, professional answering services, beepers, mobile phones, online e-mail programs, etc. If you do provide an alternative phone number or other way to reach you, just make it clear to the caller what to expect.

Job Objective. This is optional for a very basic resume but is still important to include. Notice that Judy is keeping her options open with her objective. Writing "Secretary" or "Clerical" might limit her to lower paying jobs or even prevent her from being considered for jobs she might take.

Education and Training. Include any formal training you've had plus any training that supports the job you seek. If you did not finish a formal degree or program, list what you did complete. Include any special accomplishments.

[Sample of a simple chronological resume.]

Judith J. Jones

115 South Hawthorne Avenue
Chicago, Illinois 46204
(312) 653-9217 (home)
(312) 272-7608 (message)

JOB OBJECTIVE

Desire a position in the office management, secretarial, or clerical area. Prefer a position requiring responsibility and a variety of tasks.

EDUCATION AND TRAINING

Acme Business College, Chicago, Illinois
Graduate of a one-year business/secretarial program, 1996

John Adams High School, South Bend, Indiana
Diploma: Business Education

U.S. Army

Financial procedures, accounting functions. Other: Continuing education classes and workshops in Business Communication, Scheduling Systems, and Customer Relations.

EXPERIENCE

1995-1996 — Returned to school to complete and update my business skills. Learned word processing and other new office techniques.

1992-1995 — Claims Processor, Blue Spear Insurance Co., Chicago, Illinois. Handled customer medical claims, filed, miscellaneous clerical duties.

1990-1992 — Sales Clerk, Judy's Boutique, Chicago, Illinois. Responsible for counter sales, display design, and selected tasks.

1988-1990 — Specialist, U.S. Army. Assigned to various stations as a specialist in finance operations. Promoted prior to honorable discharge.

Previous Jobs — Held part-time and summer jobs throughout high school.

PERSONAL

I am reliable, hardworking, and good with people.

Previous Experience. The standard approach is to list employer, job title, dates employed, and responsibilities. But there are better ways of presenting your experience. Look over the "Improved Chronological Resume" for ideas. The improved version emphasizes results, accomplishments, and performance.

Personal Data. Neither of the sample resumes have the standard height, weight, or marital status included on so many resumes. That information is simply not relevant! If you do include some personal information, put it at the bottom and keep it related to the job you want.

References. There is no need to list references. If employers want them, they will ask. If your references are particularly good, it's okay to say so.

Include those things that relate to doing well in the job you seek now. Even "small" things count. Maybe your attendance was perfect, you met a tight deadline, did the work of others during vacations, etc. Be specific and include numbers—even if you have to estimate them.

Job Titles. Many job titles don't accurately reflect the job you did. For example, your job title may have been "Cashier" but you also opened the store, trained new staff, and covered for the boss on vacations. Perhaps "Head Cashier and Assistant Manager" would be more accurate. Check with your previous employer if you are not sure.

Promotions. If you were promoted or got good evaluations, say so. A promotion to a more responsible job can be handled as a separate job if this makes sense.

TIPS FOR AN IMPROVED CHRONOLOGICAL RESUME

Once you have a simple, errorless, and eye-pleasing resume, get on with your job search. There is no reason to delay! But you may want to create a better one in your spare time (evenings or weekends). If you do, here are some additional tips.

Job Objective. Job objectives often limit the type of jobs for which you will be considered. Instead, think of the type of work you want to do and can do well and describe it in more general terms. Instead of writing "Restaurant Manager," write "Managing a small to mid-sized business" if that is what you are qualified to do.

Education and Training. New graduates should emphasize their recent training and education more than those with five years or so of recent and related work experience. Think about any special accomplishments while in school and include these if they relate to the job. Did you work full time while in school? Did you do particularly well in work-related classes, get an award, or participate in sports?

Skills and Accomplishments. Employers are interested in what you accomplished and did well.

[Sample of an improved chronological resume.]

Judith J. Jones

115 South Hawthorne Avenue
Chicago, Illinois 46204
(312) 653-9217 (home)
(312) 272-7608 (message)

JOB OBJECTIVE

Seeking position requiring excellent management and secretarial skills in an office environment. Position should require a variety of tasks including typing, word processing, accounting/bookkeeping functions, and customer contact.

EDUCATION AND TRAINING

Acme Business College, Chicago, Illinois.
Completed one-year program in Professional Secretarial and Office Management. Grades in top 30 percent of my class. Courses: word processing, accounting theory and systems, time management, basic supervision, and others.

John Adams High School, South Bend, Indiana.
Graduated with emphasis on business and secretarial courses. Won shorthand contest.

Other: Continuing education at my own expense (Business Communications, Customer Relations, Computer Applications, other courses).

EXPERIENCE

1995-1996 — Returned to business school to update skills. Advanced course work in accounting and office management. Learned to operate word processing and PC-based accounting and spreadsheet software. Gained operating knowledge of computers.

1992-1995 — Claims Processor, Blue Spear Insurance Company, Chicago, Illinois. Handled 50 complex medical insurance claims per day — 18 percent above department average. Received two merit raises for performance.

1990-1992 — Assistant Manager, Judy's Boutique, Chicago, Illinois. Managed sales, financial records, inventory, purchasing, correspondence, and related tasks during owner's absence. Supervised four employees. Sales increased 15 percent during my tenure.

1988-1990 — Finance Specialist (E4), U.S. Army. Responsible for the systematic processing of 500 invoices per day from commercial vendors. Trained and supervised eight employees. Devised internal system allowing 15 percent increase in invoices processed with a decrease in personnel.

1984-1988 — Various part-time and summer jobs through high school. Learned to deal with customers, meet deadlines, work hard, and other skills.

SPECIAL SKILLS AND ABILITIES

Type 80 words per minute and can operate most office equipment. Good communication and math skills. Accept supervision, able to supervise others. Excellent attendance record.

Problem Areas. Employers look for any sign of instability or lack of reliability. It is very expensive to hire and train someone who won't stay or who won't work out. Gaps in employment, jobs held for short periods of time, or a lack of direction in the jobs you've held are all things that employers are concerned about. If you have any legitimate explanation, use it. For example:

"1994—Continued my education at . . ."
"1995—Traveled extensively throughout the United States."
"1995 to present—Self-employed barn painter and widget maker."
"1995—Had first child, took year off before returning to work."

Use entire years or even seasons of years to avoid displaying a shorter gap you can't explain easily: "Spring 1994—Fall 1995" will not show you as unemployed from October to November, 1995, for example.

Remember that a resume can get you screened out, but it is up to you to get the interview and the job. So, cut out *anything* that is negative in your resume!

SKILLS AND COMBINATION RESUMES

The functional or "skills" resume emphasizes your most important *skills*, supported by specific examples of how you have used them. This approach allows you to use any part of your life history to support your ability to do the job you seek.

While the skills resume can be very effective, it does require more work to create. And some employers don't like them because they can hide a job seeker's faults (such as job gaps, lack of formal education, or no related work experience) better than a chronological resume.

Still, a skills resume may make sense for you. Look over the sample resumes for ideas. Notice that one resume includes elements of a skills *and* a chronological resume. This is called a "combination" resume—an approach that makes sense if your previous job history or education and training is positive.

[Sample of a simple skills resume.]

ALAN ATWOOD
3231 East Harbor Road
Woodland Hills, California 91367
Home: (818) 447-2111   Message (818) 547-8201

Objective: A responsible position in retail sales

Areas of Accomplishment:

Customer Service
- Communicate well with all age groups.
- Able to interpret customer concerns to help them find the items they want.
- Received 6 Employee of the Month awards in 3 years.

Merchandise Display
- Developed display skills via in-house training and experience.
- Received Outstanding Trainee Award for Christmas toy display.
- Dress mannequins, arrange table displays, and organize sale merchandise.

Stock Control and Marketing
- Maintained and marked stock during department manager's 6-week illness.
- Developed more efficient record-keeping procedures.

Additional Skills
- Operate cash register, IBM compatible hardware, calculators, and electronic typewriters.
- Punctual, honest, reliable, and a hard-working self-starter.

Experience:
Harper's Department Store
Woodland Hills, California
1995 to Present

Education:
Central High School
Woodland Hills, California
3.6/4.0 Grade Point Average
Honor Graduate in Distributive Education

Two years retail sales training in Distributive Education. Also courses in Business Writing, Accounting, Typing, and Word Processing.

[Sample skills resume for someone with substantial experience—but using only one page. Note that no dates are included.]

Ann McLaughlin

Career Objective	Challenging position in programming or related areas which would best utilize expertise in the business environment. This position should have many opportunities for an aggressive, dedicated individual with leadership abilities to advance.
Programming Skills	Include functional program design relating to business issues including payroll, inventory and database management, sales, marketing, accounting, and loan amortization reports. In conjunction with design would be coding, implementation, debugging, and file maintenance. Familiar with distributed network systems including PC's and Mac's and working knowledge of DOS, UNIX, COBOL, BASIC, RPG, and FORTRAN. Also familiar with mainframe environments including DEC, Prime, and IBM, including tape and disk file access, organization, and maintenance.
Areas of Expertise	Interpersonal communication strengths, public relations capabilities, innovative problem-solving and analytical talents.
Sales	A total of nine years experience in sales and sales management. Sold security products to distributors and burglar alarm dealers. Increased company's sales from $16,000 to over $70,000 per month. Creatively organized sales programs and marketing concepts. Trained sales personnel in prospecting techniques while also training service personnel in proper installation of burglar alarms. Result: 90% of all new business was generated through referrals from existing customers.
Management	Managed burglar alarm company for four years while increasing profits yearly. Supervised office, sales, and installation personnel. Supervised and delegated work to assistants in accounting functions and inventory control. Worked as assistant credit manager, responsible for over $2 million per month in sales. Handled semiannual inventory of five branch stores totaling millions of dollars and supervised 120 people.
Accounting	Balanced all books and prepared tax forms for burglar alarm company. Eight years experience in credit and collections, with emphasis on collections. Collection rates were over 98% each year, and was able to collect a bad debt in excess of $250,000 deemed "uncollectible" by company.
Education	School of Computer Technology, Pittsburgh, PA Business Applications Programming/TECH EXEC- 3.97 GPA Robert Morris College, Pittsburgh, PA Associate degree in Accounting, Minor in Management

2306 Cincinnati Street, Kingsford, PA 15171 (412) 437-6217
Message: (412) 464-1273

[Sample combination resume emphasizing skills and accomplishments within jobs. Note that each position within a company is listed.]

THOMAS P. MARRIN
80 Harrison Avenue
Baldwin L.I., New York 11563
Answering Service: (716) 223-4705

OBJECTIVE:

A middle/upper-level management position with responsibilities including problem solving, planning, organizing, and budget management.

EDUCATION:

University of Notre Dame, B.S. in Business Administration. Course emphasis on accounting, supervision, and marketing. Upper 25% of class. Additional training: Advanced training in time management, organization behavior, and cost control.

MILITARY:

U.S. Army — 2nd Infantry Division, 1985 to 1989, 1st Lieutenant and platoon leader — stationed in Korea and Ft. Knox, Kentucky. Supervised an annual budget of nearly $4 million and equipment valued at over $40 million. Responsible for training, scheduling, and activities of as many as 40 people. Received several commendations. Honorable discharge.

BUSINESS EXPERIENCE:

Wills Express Transit Co., Inc. — Mineola, New York

Promoted to Vice President, Corporate Equipment — 1994 to Present
Controlled purchase, maintenance, and disposal of 1100 trailers and 65 company cars with $6.7 million operating and $8.0 million capital expense responsibilities.

- Scheduled trailer purchases, six divisions.
- Operated 2.3% under planned maintenance budget in company's second best profit year while operating revenues declined 2.5%.
- Originated schedule to correlate drivers' needs with available trailers.
- Developed systematic Purchase and Disposal Plan for company car fleet.
- Restructured Company Car Policy, saving 15% on per car cost.

Promoted to Asst. Vice President, Corporate Operations — 1993 to 1994
Coordinated activities of six sections of Corporate Operations with an operating budget over $10 million.

- Directed implementation of zero-base budgeting.
- Developed and prepared Executive Officer Analyses detailing achievable cost reduction measures. Resulted in cost reduction of over $600,000 in first two years.
- Designed policy and procedure for special equipment leasing program during peak seasons. Cut capital purchases by over $1 million.

Manager of Communications — 1991 to 1993
Directed and managed $1.4 million communication network involving 650 phones, 150 WATS lines, 3 switchboards, 1 teletype machine, 5 employees.

- Installed computerized WATS Control System. Optimized utilization of WATS lines and pinpointed personal abuse. Achieved payback earlier than originally projected.
- Devised procedures that allowed simultaneous 20% increase in WATS calls and a $75,000/year savings.

Hayfield Publishing Company, Hempstead, New York

Communications Administrator — 1989 to 1991

Managed daily operations of a large Communications Center. Reduced costs and improved services.

THE QUICK JOB SEARCH REVIEW

There are a few thoughts I want to emphasize in closing my brief review of job seeking skills:

1. Approach your job search as if it were a job itself.

2. Get organized and spend at least 25 hours per week actively looking.

3. Follow up on all the leads you generate and send out lots of thank-you notes and JIST Cards.

4. If you want to get a good job quickly, you must get lots of interviews!

5. Pay attention to all the details, then be yourself in the interview. Remember that employers are people, too. They will hire someone who they feel will do the job well, be reliable, and fit easily into the work environment.

6. When you want the job, tell the employer that you want the job and why. You need to have a good answer to the question "Why should I hire you?" It's that simple.

ESSENTIAL JOB SEARCH DATA WORKSHEET

Completing this worksheet will help you create your resume, fill out applications, and answer interview questions. Take it with you as a reference as you look for a job. Use an erasable pen or pencil so you can make changes. In all sections, emphasize skills and accomplishments that best support your ability to do the job you want. Use extra sheets as needed.

KEY ACCOMPLISHMENTS

List three accomplishments that best prove your ability to do well in the kind of job you want.

1. _____

2. _____

3. _____

EDUCATION/TRAINING

Name of high school(s)/years attended: _____

_____

Subjects related to job objective: _____

_____

Extracurricular activities/Hobbies/Leisure activities:

_____

Accomplishments/Things you did well: _____

_____

Schools you attended after high school, years attended, degrees/certificates earned: _____

_____

Courses related to job objective: _____

_____

Extracurricular activities/Hobbies/Leisure activities:

_____

Accomplishments/Things you did well: _____

_____

Military training, on-the-job, or informal training, such as from a hobby; dates of training; type of certificate earned: _____

_____

Specific things you can do as a result: _____

_____

WORK AND VOLUNTEER HISTORY

List your most recent job first, followed by each previous job. Include military experience and unpaid work here too, if it makes sense to do so. Use additional sheets to cover *all* your significant jobs or unpaid experiences.

Whenever possible, provide numbers to support what you did: number of people served over one or more years, number of transactions processed, percentage of sales increase, total inventory value you were responsible for, payroll of the staff you supervised, total budget you were responsible for, etc. As much as possible, mention results using numbers because they can be impressive when mentioned in an interview or resume.

Job #1 _____

Name of Organization: _____

Address: _____

Phone Number: _____

Dates Employed: _____

Job Title(s): _____

Supervisor's Name: _____

Details of any raises or promotions: _____

Machinery or equipment you handled: _____

Special skills this job required: _____

List what you accomplished or did well: _____

Job #2 _____

Name of Organization: _____

Address: _____

Phone Number: _____

Dates Employed: _____

Job Title(s): _____

Supervisor's Name: _____

Details of any raises or promotions: _____

Machinery or equipment you handled: _____

Special skills this job required: _____

List what you accomplished or did well: _____

Job #3 _____

Name of Organization: _____

Address: _____

Phone Number: _____

Dates Employed: _____

Job Title(s): _____

Supervisor's Name: _____

Details of any raises or promotions: _____

Machinery or equipment you handled: _____

_____

_____

Special skills this job required: _____

_____

_____

List what you accomplished or did well: _____

_____

_____

_____

REFERENCES

Contact your references and let them know what type of job you want and why you are qualified. Be sure to review what they will say about you. Because some employers will not give out references by phone or in person, have previous employers write a letter of reference for you in advance. If you worry about a bad reference from a previous employer, negotiate what they will say about you or get written references from other people you worked with there. When creating your list of references, be sure to include your reference's name and job title, where he or she works, a business address and phone number, how that person knows you, and what your reference will say about you.

The following material is based on content from a book titled Job Strategies for Professionals *written by a team of authors from the U.S. Employment Service for use by the unemployed. (published by JIST)*

Some Tips for Coping with Job Loss

Being out of work is not fun for most people and is devastating to some. It may help you to know that you are not alone in this experience and I've included some information here on what to expect and some suggestions for getting through it.

SOME PROBLEMS YOU MAY EXPERIENCE

Here are some feelings and experiences that you may have after losing your job.

Loss of professional identity: Most of us identify strongly with our careers and unemployment can often lead to a loss of self-esteem. Being employed garners respect in the community and in the family. When a job is lost, part of your sense of self may be lost as well.

Loss of a network: The loss may be worse when your social life has been strongly linked to the job. Many ongoing "work friendships" are suddenly halted. Old friends and colleagues often don't call because they feel awkward or don't know what to say. Many don't want to be reminded of what could happen to them.

Emotional unpreparedness: If you have never before been unemployed you may not be emotionally prepared for it and devastated when it happens. It is natural and appropriate to feel this way. You might notice that some people you know don't take their job loss as hard as you have taken it. Studies show that those who change jobs frequently, or who are in occupations prone to cyclic unemployment, suffer far less emotional impact after job loss than those who have been steadily employed and who are unprepared for cutbacks.

ADJUSTING

You can often adjust to job loss by understanding its psychology. There have been a lot of studies done on how to deal with loss. Psychologists have found that people often have an easier time dealing with loss if they know what feelings they might experience during the "grieving process." Grief doesn't usually overwhelm us all at once; it usually is experienced in stages. The stages of loss or grief may include:

Shock - you may not be fully aware of what has happened.

Denial - usually comes next; you cannot believe that the loss is true.

Relief - you may feel a burden has lifted and opportunity awaits.

Anger - often follows; you blame (often without cause) those you think might be responsible, including yourself.

Depression - may set in some time later, when you realize the reality of the loss.

Acceptance - the final stage of the process; you come to terms with the loss and get the energy and desire to move beyond it. The "acceptance" stage is the best place to be when starting a job search, but you might not have the luxury of waiting until this point to begin your search.

Knowing that a normal person will experience some predictable "grieving" reactions can help you deal with your loss in a constructive way. The faster you can begin an active search for a new job, the better off you will be.

KEEP HEALTHY

Unemployment is a stressful time for most people and it is important to keep healthy and fit. Try to:

✓ **Eat properly.** How you look and your sense of self-esteem can be affected by your eating habits. It is very easy to snack on junk food when you're home all day. Take time to plan your meals and snacks so they are well-balanced and nutritious. Eating properly will help you maintain the good attitude you need during your job search.

✓ **Exercise.** Include some form of exercise as part of your daily activities. Regular exercise reduces stress and depression and can help you get through those tough days.

✓ **Allow time for fun.** When you're planning your time, be sure to build fun and relaxation into your plans. You are allowed to enjoy life even if you are unemployed. Keep a list of activities or tasks that you want to accomplish such as volunteer work, repairs around the house, or hobbies. When free time occurs, you can refer to the list and have lots of things to do.

FAMILY ISSUES

Unemployment is a stressful time for the entire family. For them, your unemployment means the loss of income and the fear of an uncertain future, and they are also worried about your happiness. Here are some ways you can interact with your family to get through this tough time.

✓ **Do not attempt to "shoulder" your problems alone.** Be open with family members even though it may be hard. Discussions about your job search and the feelings you have allow your family to work as a group and support one another.

✓ **Talk to your family.** Let them know your plans and activities. Share with them how you will be spending your time.

✓ **Listen to your family.** Find out their concerns and suggestions. Maybe there are ways they can assist you.

✓ **Build family spirit.** You will need a great deal of support from your family in the months ahead, but they will also need yours.

✓ **Seek outside help.** Join a family support group. Many community centers, mental health agencies, and colleges have support groups for the unemployed and their families. These groups can provide a place to let off steam and share frustrations. They can also be a place to get ideas on how to survive this difficult period. More information about support groups is presented later in this chapter.

HELPING CHILDREN

If you have children, realize that they can be deeply affected by a parent's unemployment. It is important for them to know what has happened and how it will affect the family. However, try not to overburden them with the responsibility of too many emotional or financial details.

✓ **Keep an open dialogue with your children.** Letting them know what is really going on is vital. Children have a way of imagining the worst so the facts can actually be far less devastating than what they envision.

✓ **Make sure your children know it's not anyone's fault.** Children may not understand about job loss and may think that *you* did something wrong to cause it. Or they may feel that somehow *they* are responsible or financially burdensome. They need reassurance in these matters, regardless of their age.

✓ **Children need to feel they are helping.** They want to help and having them do something like taking a cut in allowance, deferring expensive purchases, or getting an after-school job can make them feel as if they are part of the team.

Some experts suggest that it can be useful to alert the school counselor to your unemployment so that they can watch the children for problems at school before the problems become serious.

COPING WITH STRESS

Here are some coping mechanisms that can help you deal with the stress of being unemployed.

✓ **Write down what seems to be causing the stress.** Identify the "stressors," then think of possible ways to handle each one. Can some demands be altered, lessened, or postponed? Can you live with any of them just as they are? Are there some that you might be able to deal with more effectively?

✓ **Set priorities.** Deal with the most pressing needs or changes first. You cannot handle everything at once.

✓ **Establish a workable schedule.** When you set a schedule for yourself, make sure it is one that can be achieved. As you perform your tasks, you will feel a sense of control and accomplishment.

✓ **Reduce stress.** Learn relaxation techniques or other stress-reduction techniques. This can be as simple as sitting in a chair, closing your eyes, taking a deep breath and breathing out slowly while imagining all the tension going out with your breath. There are a number of other methods, including listening to relaxation tapes, which may help you cope with stress more effectively. Check the additional source material books that offer instruction on these techniques—many of these are available at your public library.

✓ **Avoid isolation.** Keep in touch with your friends, even former coworkers, if you can do that comfortably. Unemployed people often feel a sense of isolation and loneliness. See your friends, talk with them, socialize with them. You are the same person you were before unemployment. The same goes for the activities that you have enjoyed in the past. Evaluate them. Which can you afford to continue? If you find that your old hobbies or activities can't be part of your new budget, maybe you can substitute new activities that are less costly.

✓ **Join a support group.** No matter how understanding or caring your family or friends might be, they may not be able to understand all that you're going through, and you might be able to find help and understanding at a job seeking support group.

These groups consist of people who are going through the same experiences and emotions as you. Many groups also share tips on job opportunities, as well as feedback on ways to deal more effectively in the job search process. *The National Business Employment Weekly,* available at major newsstands, lists support groups throughout the country. Local churches, YMCAs, YWCAs, and libraries often list or facilitate support groups. A list of self-help organizations—some of which cover the unemployed—is available from the National Self-Help Clearinghouse, 25 West 43rd St., Room 620, New York, NY 10036. The cost is $3, plus a self-addressed, stamped envelope.

Forty Plus is a national nonprofit organization and an excellent source of information about clubs around the country and on issues concerning older employees and the job search process. The address is 15 Park Row, New York, NY 10038. Their telephone number is (212) 233-6086.

KEEPING YOUR SPIRITS UP

Here are some ways you can build your self-esteem and avoid depression.

✓ **List your positives.** Make a list of your positive qualities and your successes. This list is always easier to make when you are feeling good about yourself. Perhaps you can enlist the assistance of a close friend or caring relative, or wait for a sunnier moment.

✓ **Replay your positives.** Once you have made this list, replay the positives in your mind frequently. Associate the replay with an activity you do often; for example, you might review the list in your mind every time you go to the refrigerator!

✓ **Use the list before performing difficult tasks.** Review the list when you are feeling down or to give you energy before you attempt some difficult task.

✓ **Recall successes.** Take time every day to recall a success.

✓ **Use realistic standards.** Avoid the trap of evaluating yourself using impossible standards that come from others. You are in a particular phase of your life; don't dwell on what you think society regards as success. Remind yourself that success will again be yours.

✓ **Know your strengths and weaknesses.** What things do you do well? What skills do you have? Do you need to learn new skills? Everyone has limitations. What are yours? Are there certain job duties that are just not right for you and that you might want to avoid? Balance your limitations against your strong skills so that you don't let the negatives eat at your self-esteem. Incorporate this knowledge into your planning.

✓ **Picture success.** Practice visualizing positive results or outcomes and view them in your mind before the event. Play out the scene in your imagination and picture yourself as successful in whatever you're about to attempt.

✓ **Build success.** Make a "to do" list. Include small, achievable tasks. Divide the tasks on your list and make a list for every day so you will have some "successes" daily.

✓ **Surround yourself with positive people.** Socialize with family and friends who are supportive. You want to be around people who will "pick you up," not "knock you down." You know who your fans are. Try to find time to be around them. It can really make you feel good.

✓ **Volunteer.** Give something of yourself to others through volunteer work. Volunteering will help you feel more worthwhile and may actually give you new skills.

OVERCOMING DEPRESSION

Are you depressed? As hard as it is to be out of work, it also can be a new beginning. A new direction may emerge that will change your life in positive ways. This may be a good time to reevaluate your attitudes and outlook.

✓ **Live in the present.** The past is over and you cannot change it. Learn from your mistakes and use that knowledge to plan for the future; then let the past go. Don't dwell on it or relive it over and over. Don't be overpowered by guilt.

✓ **Take responsibility for yourself.** Try not to complain or blame others. Save your energy for activities that result in positive experiences.

✓ **Learn to accept what you cannot change.** However, realize that in most situations, you do have some control. Your reactions and your behavior are in your control and will often influence the outcome of events.

✓ **Keep the job search under your own command.** This will give you a sense of control and prevent you from giving up and waiting for something to happen. Enlist everyone's aid in your job search, but make sure you do most of the work.

✓ **Talk things out with people you trust.** Admit how you feel. For example, if you realize you're angry, find a positive way to vent it, perhaps through exercise.

✓ **Face your fears.** Try to pinpoint them. "Naming the enemy" is the best strategy for relieving the vague feeling of anxiety. By facing what you actually fear you can see if your fears are realistic or not.

✓ **Think creatively.** Stay flexible, take risks, and don't be afraid of failure. Try not to take rejection personally. Think of it as information that will help you later in your search. Take criticism as a way to learn more about yourself. Keep plugging away at the job search despite those inevitable setbacks. Most importantly, forget magic. What lies ahead is hard work!

SOURCES OF PROFESSIONAL HELP

If your depression won't go away, or leads you to self-destructive behaviors such as abuse of alcohol or drugs, you may consider asking a professional for help. Many people who have never sought professional assistance before find that in a time of crisis it really helps to have someone listen and give needed aid. Consult your local mental health clinics, social services agencies, religious organizations, or professional counselors for help for yourself and family members who are affected by your unemployment. Your health insurance may cover some assistance or, if you do not have insurance, counseling is often available on a "sliding scale" fee based on income.

MANAGING YOUR FINANCES WHILE OUT OF WORK

As you already know, being unemployed has financial consequences. While the best solution to this is to get a good job in as short a time as possible, you do need to manage your money differently during the time between jobs. Following are some things to think about.

APPLY FOR BENEFITS WITHOUT DELAY

Don't be embarrassed to apply for unemployment benefits as soon as possible, even if you're not sure you are eligible. This program is to help you make a transition between jobs and you helped pay for it by your previous employment. Depending on how long you have worked, you can collect benefits for up to 26 weeks and sometimes even longer. Contact your state labor department or employment security agency for further information. Their addresses and telephone numbers are listed in your phone book.

PREPARE NOW TO STRETCH YOUR MONEY

Being out of work means lower income and the need to control your expenses. Don't avoid doing this because the more you plan, the better you can control your finances.

EXAMINE YOUR INCOME AND EXPENSES

Create a budget and look for ways to cut expenses. The Monthly Income and Expense Worksheet can help you isolate income and expense categories, but your own budget may be considerably more detailed. I've included two columns for each expense category. Enter in the "Normal" column what you have been spending in that category during the time you were employed. Enter in the "Could Reduce To" column a lower number that you will spend by cutting expenses in that category.

TIPS ON CONSERVING YOUR CASH

While unemployed, it is likely that your expenses will exceed your income and it is essential that you be aggressive in managing your money. Your objective here is very clear: you want to conserve as much cash as possible early on so you can have some for essentials later. Here are some suggestions.

✓ **Begin cutting all nonessential expenses right away.** Don't put this off! There is no way to know how long you will be out of work and the faster you deal with the financial issues, the better.

✓ **Discuss the situation with other family members.** Ask them to get involved by helping you identify expenses they can cut.

✓ **Look for sources of additional income.** Can you paint houses on weekends? Pick up a temporary job or consulting assignment? Deliver newspapers in the early morning? Can a family member get a job to help out? Any new income will help and the sooner the better.

✓ **Contact your creditors.** Even if you can make full payments for awhile, work out interest-only or reduced amount payments as soon as possible. When I was unemployed, I went to my creditors right away and asked them to help. They were very cooperative and most are, if you are reasonable with them.

✓ **Register with your local consumer credit counseling organization.** Many areas have free consumer credit counseling organizations that can help you get a handle on your finances and encourage your creditors to cooperate.

✓ **Review your assets.** Make a list of all your assets and their current value. Money in checking, savings, and other

---

MONTHLY INCOME AND EXPENSE WORKSHEET

INCOME

Unemployment benefits	_____	Interest/Dividends	_____
Spouse's income	_____	Other income	_____
Severance pay	_____	**TOTALS**	_____

EXPENSES

	NORMAL	COULD REDUCE TO		NORMAL	COULD REDUCE TO
Mortgage/rent:	_____	_____		_____	_____
maintenance/ repairs	_____	_____	**Health insurance:**	_____	_____
Utilities:			Other medical/ dental expenses	_____	_____
electric	_____	_____	**Tuition:**	_____	_____
gas/oil heat	_____	_____	other school costs	_____	_____
water/sewer	_____	_____	**Clothing:**	_____	_____
telephone	_____	_____	**Entertainment:**	_____	_____
Food:	_____	_____	**Taxes:**	_____	_____
restaurants	_____	_____	**Job hunting costs:**	_____	_____
Car payment:	_____	_____	**Other expenses:**	_____	_____
fuel	_____	_____		_____	_____
maintenance/ repairs	_____	_____		_____	_____
insurance	_____	_____		_____	_____
Other loan payments:				_____	_____
_____	_____	_____	**TOTALS**	_____	_____

---

accounts is the most available, but you may have additional assets in pension programs, life insurance, and stocks that could be converted to cash if needed. You may also have an extra car that could be sold, equity in your home that could be borrowed against, and other assets that could be sold or used if needed.

✓ **Reduce credit card purchases.** Try to pay for things in cash to save on interest charges and prevent overspending. Be disciplined, you can always use your credit cards later if you are getting desperate for food and other basics.

✓ **Consider cashing in some "luxury" assets.** For example, sell a car or boat you rarely use to generate cash and to save on insurance and maintenance costs.

✓ **Comparison shop** for home/auto/life insurance and other expenses to lower costs.

✓ **Deduct job hunting expenses from your taxes.** Some job hunting expenses may be tax deductible as a "miscellaneous deduction" on your federal income tax return. Keep receipts for employment agency fees, resume expenses, and transportation expenses. If you find work in another city and you must relocate, some moving expenses are tax deductible. Contact an accountant or the IRS for more information.

REVIEW YOUR HEALTH COVERAGE

You already know that it is dangerous to go without health insurance, so there is no need to lecture you on this, but here are some tips.

✓ **You can probably maintain coverage at your own expense.** Under the COBRA law, if you worked for an employer that provided medical coverage and had 20 or more employees you may continue your health coverage. However, you must tell your former employer within 60 days of leaving the job.

✓ **Contact professional organizations to which you belong.** They may provide group coverage for their members at low rates.

✓ **Speak to an insurance broker.** If necessary, arrange for health coverage on your own or join a local health maintenance organization (HMO).

✓ **Practice preventive medicine.** The best way to save money on medical bills is to stay healthy. Try not to ignore minor ills. If they persist, phone or visit your doctor.

✓ **Investigate local clinics.** Many local clinics provide services based on a sliding scale. These clinics often provide quality health care at affordable prices. In an emergency, most hospitals will provide you with services on a sliding scale and most areas usually have one or more hospitals funded locally to provide services to those who can't afford them.

Researching Sources of Job Leads and Other Information

If you have been to a large bookstore lately, you may have noticed that there are many, many books in the "career" section. Each year, there are more and more books published on this topic and, unfortunately, most of them are not very good. From among all the books and other sources of information available, I have selected resources that I believe are of particular importance to you in your job search. Of course, I have included many of the books I have written and/or that are published by JIST—it seemed only fair. Most are available through a bookstore or good library.

INFORMATION ON OCCUPATIONS AND INDUSTRIES

Occupational Outlook Handbook (OOH). Published every two years by the U.S. Department of Labor's Bureau of Labor Statistics. Provides excellent descriptions of 250 of the most popular jobs, covering about 85 percent of the workforce. Well-written descriptions provide information on skills required, working conditions, duties, qualifications, pay, and advancement potential. Very helpful for preparing for interviews by identifying key skills to emphasize. (U.S. Department of Labor, JIST publishes a reprint)

America's Top 300 Jobs. This is a version of the *OOH* that is available from bookstores or in the circulation department of your library. Because the *OOH* itself is typically in the reference section of a library, this version, which can often be checked out, can allow you to access the same information at your leisure. (JIST)

Career Guide to America's Top Industries. Provides trends and other information on more than 40 major industries and summary data on many others. Excellent for getting information on an industry prior to an interview. Includes details on employment projections, advancement opportunities, major trends, and a complete narrative description of each industry. (JIST)

Complete Guide for Occupational Exploration (CGOE). This book lists more than 12,000 job titles in a format that makes it easy to use as a tool for exploring career alternatives or other jobs you may seek based on current skills. Jobs with similar characteristics are grouped together. Each group's description includes details on skills required, nature of work, and other information. The CGOE also cross-references to other standard reference sources for additional information on the jobs it lists. (JIST)

Enhanced Guide for Occupational Exploration (EGOE). Uses the same organizational structure as the *CGOE* but includes brief descriptions of about 2,800 jobs. Useful for career exploration, identifying skills used in previous jobs, researching new job targets, and preparing for interviews. (JIST)

Dictionary of Occupational Titles (DOT). Provides descriptions for more than 12,000 jobs, covering virtually all jobs in our economy. This is the only book of its kind and can be used to identify jobs in different fields that use skills similar to those you have acquired in your past jobs, identify key skills to emphasize in interviews, and much more. It provides brief descriptions for each job and additional coded information. (U.S. Department of Labor, JIST publishes a reprint)

The Top Job Series. Each book in the *America's Top Jobs* series, has a specific emphasis. Each provides thorough descriptions for the top jobs in a specific area, career planning and job search tips, plus details on growth projections, education required, and other data on 500 additional jobs. (JIST)

America's 50 Fastest Growing Jobs
America's Federal Jobs
America's Top Office, Management, and Sales Jobs
America's Top Medical and Human Services Jobs
America's Top Military Careers
America's Top Technical and Trade Jobs
America's Top Jobs for College Graduates

Dictionary of Occupational Terms—A Guide to the Special Language and Jargon of Hundreds of Careers by Nancy Shields. An interesting reference book that will answer most of your questions on more than 3,000 terms. (JIST)

SOURCES OF INFORMATION ON SPECIFIC ORGANIZATIONS

After you have a good idea of the industries, fields of work, and geographical areas in which you want to concentrate your job search, the next step is to locate companies that might employ people in your field. A large number of publications are available that contain lists of companies by industry, location, size, and other defining characteristics. A few of them are discussed below.

The Job Hunter's Guide to 100 Great American Cities (Brattle Communications). Rather than concentrating on a particular locale, this guide gives the principal-area employers for 100 of America's largest cities.

Macrae's State Industrial Directories. Published for 15 Northeastern states. Similar volumes are produced for other parts of the country by other publishers. Each book lists thousands of companies, concentrating almost exclusively on those that produce products, rather than services.

National Business Telephone Directory (Gale Research). An alphabetical listing of companies across the United States with their addresses and phone numbers. It includes many smaller firms (20 employees minimum).

Thomas Register. Lists more than 100,000 companies across the country. Contains listings by company name, type of product made, and brand name of product produced. Catalogs provided by many of the companies also are included.

America's Fastest Growing Employers (Bob Adams Inc., Holbrook, MA). Lists more than 700 of the fastest growing companies in the country.

The Hidden Job Market: A Guide to America's 2000 Little-Known Fastest Growing High-Tech Companies (Peterson's Guides). Concentrates on high-tech companies with good growth potential.

Dun & Bradstreet Million Dollar Directory. Provides information on 180,000 of the largest companies in the country. Gives the type of business, number of employees, and sales volume for each. It also lists the company's top executives.

Standard & Poor's Register of Corporations, Directors and Executives. Information similar to that in Dun & Bradstreet's directory. Also contains a listing of the parent companies of subsidiaries and the interlocking affiliations of directors.

The Career Guide—Dun's Employment Opportunities Directory. Aimed specifically at the professional job seeker. Lists more than 5,000 major U.S. companies which plan to recruit in the coming year. Lists personnel directors and gives information about firms' career opportunities and benefits packages.

There are many directories that give information about firms in a particular industry. A few samples are listed below:

The Blue Book of Building and Construction
Directory of Advertising Agencies
Directory of Computer Dealers
McFadden American Bank Directory

The Chamber of Commerce and local business associations may also publish directories listing companies within a specific geographic area. These are available in libraries or by writing to the individual associations. And, of course, the *Yellow Pages* provide local listings of governmental and business organizations for every section of the country.

PROFESSIONAL AND TRADE ASSOCIATIONS

These associations offer another excellent avenue for getting information about where the type of work you want to do might be found. These associations:

✓ Help you identify areas where growth is occurring.

✓ Provide the names of firms that might employ people in a specific type of work.

✓ Can identify the best information sources for developments within the field.

✓ Can provide more information on leads in small firms than directories.

✓ Publish newsletters or journals that provide information on companies needing increased staff in the near future.

Some publications that list trade and professional associations are:

Encyclopedia of Associations (Gale Research). A listing of more than 22,000 professional, trade, and other nonprofit organizations in the United States.

Career Guide to Professional Associations (Garrett Park Press). Describes more than 2,500 professional associations. The information is more specifically oriented to the job seeker than is the *Encyclopedia of Associations*. A word of caution, this guide has not been updated since 1980 and some of the information may not be current.

NEWSPAPERS

Newspapers not only contain want ads but lots of other useful employment information. Articles about new or expanding companies can be valuable leads for new job possibilities.

If relocating is a possibility, look at newspapers from other areas. They can serve as a source of job leads as well as indicate some idea of the job market. The major out-of-town newspapers are sold in most large cities and are also available in many public libraries.

Some newspapers such as *The New York Times, The Chicago Tribune,* and *The Financial Times* are national in scope. *The National Business Employment Weekly,* published by *The Wall Street Journal,* contains much information of interest to professional job seekers.

NETWORKING

Networking is another excellent way of gathering information about a particular field. It is one of the best ways of discovering the existence of smaller companies which often are not listed in directories.

SOURCES OF ADDITIONAL INFORMATION ON CAREER PLANNING, JOB SEEKING, RESUMES, AND CAREER SUCCESS

JOB SEEKING AND INTERVIEW TECHNIQUES

The Very Quick Job Search: Get a Good Job in Less Time by J. Michael Farr (Revised 1996). This is my most thorough job search book and it includes lots of information on career planning and, of course, job seeking. This is the book I would recommend to a friend who was out of work if I had to recommend just one book. (JIST)

The Quick Interview & Salary Negotiation Book— Dramatically Improve Your Interviewing Skills and Pay in a Matter of Hours by J. Michael Farr. While this is a substantial book with lots of information, I've arranged it so that you can read the first section and go out and do better in interviews later that day. (JIST)

Getting the Job You Really Want by J. Michael Farr. This one provides career planning and job search methods in a workbook format that includes lots of worksheets as well as the needed narrative. It has sold more than 150,000 copies and counting. (JIST)

Career Satisfaction and Success—A Guide to Job and Personal Freedom by Bernard Haldane. This is a complete revision of a "classic" by an author many consider to be one of the founders of the modern career planning movement. It's not a job search book as much as a job success book. Contains solid information. (JIST)

Using the Internet in Your Job Search by Fred Jandt and Mary Nemnich. For new or more experienced users of online computer services, this book gives you lots of good information on finding job opportunities on the "net." (JIST)

The PIE Method for Career Success—A Unique Way to Find Your Ideal Job by Daniel Porot. The author is one of Europe's major career consultants and this book presents his powerful career planning and job seeking concepts in a visual and memorable way. (JIST)

Job Strategies for Professionals by U.S. Employment Service. Job search advice for the millions of professionals and managers who have lost their jobs. (JIST)

What Color Is Your Parachute? by Richard N. Bolles. It is the bestselling career planning book of all time and the author continues to improve it. (Ten Speed Press)

The Complete Job Search Handbook: All the Skills You Need to Get Any Job, and Have a Good Time Doing It by Howard Figler. A very good book. (Henry Holt)

Who's Hiring Who? by Richard Lathrop. Another good book. (Ten Speed Press)

Job Hunters Sourcebook: Where to Find Employment Leads and Other Job Search Sources by Michelle LeCompte. (Gale Research)

Sweaty Palms Revised: The Neglected Art of Being Interviewed by Anthony Medley. (Ten Speed Press)

Dare to Change Your Job and Your Life by Carole Kanchier. Practical and motivating guidance on achieving career and personal growth and satisfaction. (JIST)

RESUMES AND COVER LETTERS

The Quick Resume & Cover Letter Book—Write and Use an Effective Resume in Only One Day by J. Michael Farr. Starting with an "instant" resume worksheet and basic formats that you can complete in an hour or so, this book then takes you on a tour of everything you ever wanted to know about resumes and, more importantly, how to use them in your job search. (JIST)

The Resume Solution—How to Write (and Use) a Resume That Gets Results by David Swanson. Lots of good advice and examples for creating superior resumes. Very strong on resume design and layout and provides a step-by-step approach that is very easy to follow. (JIST)

Gallery of Best Resumes by David F. Noble. Advice and over 200 examples from professional resume writers. Lots of variety in content and design, an excellent resource. I consider it to be the best resume "library" since all the resumes are organized into useful categories. (JIST)

Using WordPerfect in Your Job Search by David F. Noble. A unique and thorough book that reviews how to use

WordPerfect to create effective resumes, correspondence, and other job search documents. (JIST)

The Perfect Resume by Tom Jackson. (Doubleday)

Dynamite Cover Letters by Ron and Caryl Krannich. (Impact Publications)

Dynamite Resumes by Ron and Caryl Krannich. A good book. (Impact Publications)

The Damn Good Resume Guide by Yana Parker. Lots of good examples and advice. (Ten Speed Press)

EDUCATION, SELF-EMPLOYMENT, AND STARTING A BUSINESS

Mind Your Own Business—Getting Started as an Entrepreneur by LaVerne Ludden and Bonnie Maitlen. A good book for those considering their own business, with lots of good advice. (JIST)

Directory of Franchise Opportunities by U.S. Department of Commerce and LaVerne Ludden. Lists 1,500 franchise opportunities and information on selecting and financing a start-up. (JIST)

The Career Connection for College Education—A Guide to College Education and Related Career Opportunities by Fred Rowe. Covers about 100 college majors and their related careers. (JIST)

The Career Connection for Technical Education—A Guide to Technical Training and Related Career Opportunities by Fred Rowe. Describes more than 60 technical education majors and the careers to which they lead. (JIST)

COMPUTER SOFTWARE

Any good software store will carry programs to help you write a resume, organize your job leads and contacts, and create your correspondence. Some packages are also designed to provide "career counseling," occupational information, or advice on your job search. Some of these programs are good and some are not. If such programs interest you, consider them—but remember that few people get job offers while playing with their computers. You **do** have to get interviews …

IN CLOSING

Few people will get a job offer because someone knocks on their door and offers one. The craft of job seeking does involve some luck, but you are far more likely to get lucky if you are out getting interviews. Structure your job search as if it were a full-time job and try not to get discouraged. There are lots of jobs out there and someone needs what you can do—your job is to find them.

I hope this little book helps, though you should consider learning more. Career planning and job seeking skills are, I believe, adult survival skills for our new economy. Good luck!

Mike Farr

Additional Information on Trends, Earnings, and Other Fascinating Details on All Major Occupations and Industries

Section Four

This section consists of a series of five appendices. Each contains information that may be of interest to you in considering job alternatives, additional education, or self-employment. While tables of numbers and data are not fun to "read" they do provide a variety of valuable information that can help you in a variety of ways. I have provided a brief overview at the beginning of each appendix. They include the following:

Appendix A: Employment Projections for the 250 Most Popular Jobs, Where 85% of All People Work

Provides basic information on the 250 largest jobs.

Appendix B: Employment Projections, Earnings, and Education Required for the 500 Largest Occupations

Another long appendix that provides details on about 500 jobs. While some of this information is similar to that provided in Appendix A, it also provides additional information and covers additional jobs.

Appendix C: Over 500 Jobs Organized By Training And Education Required

Organizes jobs within clusters based on the level of education or training typically required.

Appendix D: Employment Trends by Industry

There are two tables in this appendix. The first provides information on projected employment growth for several hundred major industries and the second provides brief comments regarding the trends within major industries.

Appendix E: Projections for Self-Employed Workers

Provides brief information on employment and trends for the occupations with the highest numbers of self-employed workers.

Employment Projections for the 250 Most Popular Jobs, Where 85 Percent of All People Work

Appendix A

The information in this appendix was obtained from the *Occupational Outlook Quarterly*, Volume 38, Number 1, published by the U.S. Department of Labor.

This is a long appendix but it provides some interesting information that is not easily obtained elsewhere. It covers 250 of the most important jobs in our economy and arranges them into clusters of similar jobs. This arrangement allows you to find jobs that are related to your interests, training, or experiences, and learn of their prospects for growth as well as the reasons for these trends.

Descriptions for many of these jobs can be found in this book and those that are not covered can be found in the *Occupational Outlook Handbook* or in *America's Top 300 Jobs*. Both are available through most libraries or bookstores or can be ordered from the form in the back of this book.

The chart lists jobs within major occupational clusters such as Executive, Administrative and Managerial; Professional Specialty; Technicians and Related Support Occupations; and others. This arrangement can help you better see the opportunities within major fields you have already trained for, as well as those in other fields that may interest you.

As I have mentioned before, be careful in interpreting the information in the chart that follows. Your local labor market may be considerably different from the national average. This information should only be a starting point for your exploration of careers. It provides outlook information in a format that allows you to easily compare job prospects in different fields, but employment prospects should never be your sole reason for choosing a career. Matching your goals and abilities to the work done on the job and the education required is an important part of choosing a career. Where you want to live and how much money you want to earn are also important.

Here are some comments that will help you interpret the chart:

1. **Occupational groupings:** The names of the 12 major occupational clusters used in the *Occupational Outlook Handbook* are printed in ALL CAPITAL LETTERS. Subgroup names are indented slightly and the names of individual occupations are indented further.

2. **Estimated employment:** This number is an estimate of the number of people employed in each occupation during 1992, the latest figures available at the time this information was gathered.

3. **Percent change of employment:** This is an estimate of the percentage of growth projected for each occupation from 1992 through 2005.

4. **Numerical change in employment:** This presents the projected increase in the number of people working in that occupation between 1992 and 2005.

5. **Employment prospects:** These comments provide information on the trends projected for each occupation as compared to the overall employment. The comments also often provide some information on the amount of competition a jobseeker might expect in this occupation. The following chart contains additional information regarding some of the terms used in this section.

Regarding employment trends:

If the statement about growth reads...	Then employment is projected to...
Much faster than average	Increase 41% or more
Faster than average	Increase 27 to 40%
About as fast as average	Increase 14 to 26%
Little change or more slowly than average	Increase 0 to 13%
Decline	Decrease 1% or more

About opportunities and competition for jobs:

If the statement about opportunities reads...	Then job openings compared to job seekers may be...
Excellent	Much more numerous
Very good	More numerous
Good or favorable	About the same
May face competition	Fewer
May face keen competition	Much fewer

The 1992-2005 Job Outlook in Brief

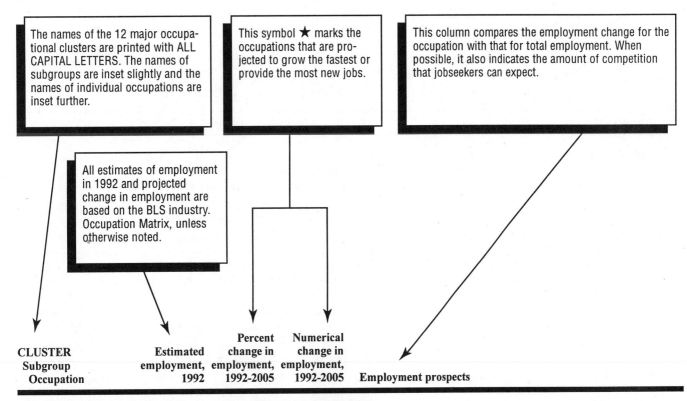

The names of the 12 major occupational clusters are printed with ALL CAPITAL LETTERS. The names of subgroups are inset slightly and the names of individual occupations are inset further.

This symbol ★ marks the occupations that are projected to grow the fastest or provide the most new jobs.

This column compares the employment change for the occupation with that for total employment. When possible, it also indicates the amount of competition that jobseekers can expect.

All estimates of employment in 1992 and projected change in employment are based on the BLS industry. Occupation Matrix, unless otherwise noted.

CLUSTER Subgroup Occupation	Estimated employment, 1992	Percent change in employment, 1992-2005	Numerical change in employment, 1992-2005	Employment prospects
EXECUTIVE, ADMINISTRATIVE, AND MANAGERIAL OCCUPATIONS				
Accountants and auditors	939,000	32	304,000	Faster than average employment growth will be spurred by increases in the number of businesses and the complexity of financial information. In addition to, setting up books and preparing taxes, more accountants and auditors will be needed to tailor financial information and advise management individully. Those with a bachelor's or higher degree in accounting, particularly CPA's, should have good job pportunities; however, competition will remain keen for prestigious jobs with major accounting and business firms.
Administrative services managers	226,000	13	30,000	Slower than average employment growth will result from corporate restructuring and contracting of administrative services in an effort to cut costs. However, demand for these managers will increase in management services, management consulting, and facilities support services firms to which these services are contracted. The ample supply of competent, experienced workers seeking advancement will result in competition for these jobs.

CLUSTER Subgroup Occupation	Estimated employment, 1992	Percent change in employment, 1992-2005	Numerical change in employment, 1992-2005	Employment prospects
Budget analysts	67,000	20	13,000	Average employment growth is expected for budget analysts. Businesses and governments seeking to increase their efficiency will create a strong demand for these workers. However, computer-induced productivity gains will offset some of the demand. The large number of qualified applicants will contribute to competition for positions. Jobseekers with at least a 4-year college degree, some experience, and familiarity with financial software packages will have the best opportunities.
Construction and building inspectors	66,000	30	20,000	Faster than average employment growth will stem from increases in the amount and complexity of construction projects, rising concern for public safety, and improved quality. Job prospects will be best for experienced craft workers who have some college education or certification.
Construction contractors and managers	180,000	47 ★	85,000	Much faster than average growth should result from increases in the size and complexity of construction and increased spending on the Nation's infrastructure—highways, bridges, dams, schools, subways, airports, and water and sewage systems. Particularly favorable prospects are expected for experienced construction managers with a bachelor's or higher degree in construction science with an emphasis on construction management.
Cost estimators	163,000	30	49,000	Employment is expected to increase faster than average as more estimators will be needed to project the cost of construction and manufacturing projects. In construction, job prospects should be best for those workers who have substantial experience in construction or a degree in construction management, engineering, or architectural drafting. In manufacturing, experienced people with degrees in engineering, science, mathematics, business administration, or economics and who have computer expertise should have the best job prospects.
Education administrators	351,000	23	81,000	Employment is expected to grow about as fast as average as school enrollments rise, services provided to students grow, efforts to improve the quality of education continue, and institutions comply with government regulations. However, stiff competition is expected. Candidates who have doctorate degrees and are willing to relocate should have the best job prospects.
Employment interviewers	79,000	22	17,000	Average growth is expected. Most new jobs will be with temporary help or personnel supply firms; little growth is expected in State Job Service offices. Job opportunities will be best for college graduates.
Engineering, science, and data processing managers	337,000	32	106,000	Employment, which is expected to increase faster than average, is closely elated to the growth of the occupations these workers supervise and to changes in the industries in which they are found. Underlying much of the growth of managers in science land engineering are competitive pressures and advancing technologies, which force companies to update

CLUSTER Subgroup Occupation	Estimated employment, 1992	Percent change in employment, 1992-2005	Numerical change in employment, 1992-2005	Employment prospects
Engineering, science, and data processing managers	337,000	32	106,000	and improve products more frequently. Employment of data processing managers will increase rapidly due to the expansion of the computer and data processing services industry and the increased employment of computer systems analysts.
Financial managers	701,000	25	174,000	Average employment growth is expected. The need for skilled financial management will increase due to the demands of global trade, the proliferation of complex financial instruments, and changing laws and regulations; however, many firms are reducing their ranks of middle managers in an effort to be more efficient, thus preventing dramatic employment growth. Like other managerial occupations, the number of applicants for financial management jobs is expected to exceed the number of job openings, resulting in competition for jobs.
Funeral directors	27,000	18	4,700	Average employment growth is expected, as demand for funeral services rises with the number of deaths. Employment opportunities are expected to be excellent because the number of graduates in mortuary science is likely to continue to be less than the number of job openings in the field.
General managers and top executives	2,871,000	13	380,000 ☆	Slower than average employment growth is expected as companies estructure managerial hierarchies to cut costs. Projected employment growth varies widely by industry; for example, employment in the services industries will rise faster than average while that in manufacturing declines. Competition will remain keen for these top managerial jobs.
Government chief executives and legislators	73,000	3	2,200	Little employment growth is expected because few, if any, new governments are likely to form and the number of chief executives and legislators in existing governments rarely changes. Small increases will occur as growing communities become independent and elect a chief executive and legislators. A few positions will arise as cities and counties without managers hire them and as unpaid positions-which are not counted as employment-are converted to paid positions. Generally, there is less competition in smaller jurisdictions than in larger ones.
Health services managers	302,000	45 ☆	135,000	Much faster than average growth is expected as the health care industry expands and diversifies. Most new jobs will be in hospitals, offices and clinics of physicians, nursing facilities, and home health care.
Hotel managers and assistants	99,000	23	23,000	Job growth is expected to be about as fast as average with growth in business and vacation travel and foreign tourism. People with college degrees in hotel or restaurant management will have the best opportunities.
Industrial production managers	203,000	2	4,800	Little change in employment is expected as the trend toward smaller management staffs and the lack of growth in the employment of production workers limit demand. Opportunities should be best for MBA's with undergraduate engineering degrees and college graduates with degrees in industrial engineering or business administration.

CLUSTER Subgroup Occupation	Estimated employment, 1992	Percent change in employment, 1992-2005	Numerical change in employment, 1992-2005	Employment prospects
Inspectors and compliance officers, except construction	155,000	27	41,000	Faster than average growth is expected due to growing public demand for a safer environment and higher quality products. Employment growth in government will stem from the expansion of regulatory and compliance programs; in private industry, from increasing self-enforcement, particularly among franchise dealerships, which are growing rapidly.
Loan officers and counselors	172,000	40	68,000	Faster than average employment growth is expected as the population and economy grow, increasing the number of applications for commercial, consumer, and mortgage loans. Growth in the variety and complexity of loans and the importance of loan officers to the success of banks and other lending institutions should also assure rapid employment growth. College graduates and those with banking and lending experience should have the best job prospects.
Management analysts and consultants	208,000	43 ⭐	89,000	Much faster than average employment growth is projected because of the tendency for businesses to rely on outside experts for many functions previously carried out internally. Demand also will be driven by the need for firms to improve performance, expand markets, incorporate new technologies, cope with government regulations, and adapt to a changing labor force. Despite projected rapid employment growth, jobseekers will face keen competition.
Marketing, advertising, and public relations managers	432,000	36	156,000	Faster than average growth is expected due to increasingly intense domestic and global competition. Many of these highly coveted jobs will be sought by other managers and other experienced people, resulting in substantial competition. College graduates with extensive experience, a high level of creativity, and strong communication skills should have the best job opportunities.
Personnel, training, and labor relations specialists and managers	474,000	32	150,000	Faster than average growth is expected. Greater resources will be devoted to job-specific training programs in response to the growing complexity of many jobs, the aging of the workforce, and technological advances that can leave employees with obsolete skills. In addition, legislation and court rulings setting standards in occupational safety and health; equal employment opportunity; wages; and health, pension, family leave, and other benefits will spur job growth. The job market is likely to remain competitive in view of the abundant supply of qualified college graduates and experienced workers.
Property and real estate managers	243,000	35	85,000	Faster than average employment growth is expected to result from increases in the number of office buildings, retail properties, and apartment and condominium complexes requiring management. Opportunities should be best for people with college degrees in business administration and related fields.
Purchasers and buyers	624,000	8	49,000	Employment is expected to grow more slowly than average as demand is restricted by the consolidation of buying departments resulting from mergers, changes in the way purchases are made, and increases in the use of automated systems.

CLUSTER Subgroup Occupation	Estimated employment, 1992	Percent change in employment, 1992-2005	Numerical change in employment, 1992-2005	Employment prospects
Restaurant and food service managers	496,000	46 ⭐	227,000	Job growth is expected to be much faster than average. Population growth, rising personal incomes, and increased leisure time will continue to produce growth in the number of eating and drinking establishments and, therefore, of managers. People with college degrees in restaurant or institutional food service management will have the best opportunities.
Retail managers	1,070,000[1]	15	162,000	Employment is expected to increase about as fast as average as an increase in the number of retail establishments is offset by labor-saving innovations, such as computerized registers and inventory control systems. Competition is expected for jobs that offer the highest earnings or best working conditions. Candidates with retail experience will have the best opportunities.
Underwriters	100,000	24	24,000	Jobs should increase about as fast as average. Demand for more life, property, and casualty insurance should rise because of population growth—especially of people in their forties and fifties, the age groups that tend to be most concerned about liability and financial security.

PROFESSIONAL SPECIALTY OCCUPATIONS

CLUSTER Subgroup Occupation	Estimated employment, 1992	Percent change in employment, 1992-2005	Numerical change in employment, 1992-2005	Employment prospects
Engineers	1,354,000[2]	23	306,000	Employment is expected to grow as fast as average because of rising investment in plant and equipment to increase productivity and expand the output of goods and services. Job opportunities in engineering have been good for a number of years, and this trend is expected to continue. However, many jobs in engineering are related to national defense. Defense expenditures will decline, so the job outlook for engineers will not be as strong as in the 1980s, when defense expenditures were increasing.
Aerospace engineers	66,000	14	9,200	Employment growth is expected to be about as fast as average, due to declining purchases of military aircraft and only slow growth of the commercial aircraft industry. Keen competition is expected.
Chemical engineers	52,000	19	10,000	Employment growth is expected to be as fast as average. Although employment in the chemical manufacturing industry is expected to grow very little, the relatively small number of chemical engineering graduates should find favorable job opportunities. The production of industrial chemicals, biotechnology, and materials science may provide better opportunities than other segments of the chemical manufacturing industry.
Civil engineers	173,000	24	41,000	Employment is expected to increase about as fast as average, spurred by population growth and an expanding economy. More civil engineers will be needed to design and construct higher capacity transportation, water supply, and pollution control systems and large buildings; the repair or replacement of existing roads, bridges, and other public structures will also stimulate demand.

CLUSTER Subgroup Occupation	Estimated employment, 1992	Percent change in employment, 1992-2005	Numerical change in employment, 1992-2005	Employment prospects
Electrical and electronics engineers	370,000	24	90,000	Average growth is expected, with the fastest growth anticipated outside manufacturing. Increased demand for computers and communications equipment is expected to account for much of the projected employment growth. However, layoffs of electrical engineers could result from cutbacks in defense spending.
Industrial engineers	119,000	17	20,000	Employment is expected to grow about as fast as average due to industrial growth, the increased complexity of business operations, and the rising use of automation in factories and offices. The function of industrial engineers-to improve products and productivity-should keep their services in demand and job opportunities favorable.
Mechanical engineers	227,000	20	46,000	Employment is expected to increase about as fast as average. Even in manufacturing, which is expected to decline overall, the employment of mechanical engineers should increase because industrial machinery and processes are becoming increasingly complex. Although many mechanical engineering jobs are in defense-related industries and reductions will probably continue in these industries, rapid growth in other industries should make job opportunities favorable overall.
Metallurgical, ceramic, and materials engineers	19,000	28	5,400	Employment is expected to increase faster than average. Research testing, engineering, and architectural services should provide significant numbers of job openings.
Mining engineers	3,600	3	(^{3})	Little change in employment is expected. The small number of new graduates, however, is expected to find favorable job opportunities.
Nuclear engineers	17,000	1	(^{3})	Although employment is expected to change little, opportunities should be good because the number of people graduating with degrees in nuclear engineering is likely to be low and in rough balance with the number of job openings.
Petroleum engineers	14,000	-2	(^{3})	Employment is expected to decline unless oil and gas prices rise enough to increase exploration in this country, which is unlikely. Even without job growth, opportunities for petroleum engineers should be good because the number of degrees granted in petroleum engineering is low.

Architects and Surveyors

Architects	96,000	26	25,000	Employment is expected to grow as fast as average as new construction spurs demand. Competition for jobs will be keen, however, particularly during recessions. Architects familiar with computer aided design technology may have better opportunities, especially when the job market is tight.
Landscape architects	19,000	26	5,000	Average employment growth is expected, in keeping with anticipated growth in construction. Landscape architects will be needed to design and develop land surrounding new construction, convert open space into recreation areas and parks, and refurbish existing sites.

CLUSTER Subgroup Occupation	Estimated employment, 1992	Percent change in employment, 1992-2005	Numerical change in employment, 1992-2005	Employment prospects
Surveyors	99,000	13	13,000	Jobs are expected to increase more slowly than average. Job growth will not keep pace with construction activity because new technology makes workers more productive. Growth will fluctuate from year, to year because construction is sensitive to swings in the Nation's economy. Opportunities should be best for people with at least a bachelor's degree.

Computer, Mathematical, and Operations Research Occupations

CLUSTER Subgroup Occupation	Estimated employment, 1992	Percent change in employment, 1992-2005	Numerical change in employment, 1992-2005	Employment prospects
Actuaries	15,000	29	4,300	Despite expected faster than average employment growth, especially for consulting actuaries, the number of job openings will be low because of the small size of this occupation. Relatively high potential earnings make the occupation attractive to many who have a mathematical aptitude, thereby increasing competition.
Computer scientists and systems analysts	666,000	111 ★	737,000 ★	Employment is expected to grow much faster than average as organizations demand technological advances to maximize the efficiency of their computer systems and increasingly recognize the need to design computer networks that will facilitate the sharing of information. Individuals with advanced degrees in computer science should enjoy very favorable job prospects. Those with a bachelor's degree in computer science, computer engineering, information science, or information systems also should have good prospects for employment.
Mathematicians	16,000	8	1,200	Expected slowdowns in research and development will result in slower than average employment growth. Job opportunities will be best for those whose educational background includes both mathematics and a related discipline, such as computer programming, operations research, or engineering.
Operations research analysts	45,000	61 ★	27,000	Employment is expected to grow much faster than average due to the increasing importance of quantitative analysis in decision-making and the increasing availability of computing resources. Much of the expected growth will be in the transportation, manufacturing, finance, and services industries. Job opportunities will be best for those who hold a master's or Ph.D.
Statisticians	16,000	9	1,500	The number of jobs for statisticians is expected to grow more slowly than average. Workers with a bachelor's degree in statisticsand a strong background in mathematics, engineering, or physical or computer science will have the best prospects for finding jobs.

Life Scientists

CLUSTER Subgroup Occupation	Estimated employment, 1992	Percent change in employment, 1992-2005	Numerical change in employment, 1992-2005	Employment prospects
Agricultural scientists	29,000	14	4,200	Overall, average employment growth is expected for agricultural scientists. Continued interest in the environment and in improved food products and processing techniques will spur demand for soil scientists and food technologists. Animal and plant scientists with a background in molecular biology, microbiology, genetics, or biotechnology also should have

CLUSTER Subgroup Occupation	Estimated employment, 1992	Percent change in employment, 1992-2005	Numerical change in employment, 1992-2005	Employment prospects
Agricultural scientists	29,000	14	4,200	good opportunities. However, budget cuts may limit funding for basic research, creating keen competition for these jobs.
Biological and medical scientists	117,000	27	31,000	Efforts to clean up and preserve the environment, use biological methods to develop and produce goods, and expand health-related research will fuel demand for biological and medical scientists, leading to faster than average employment growth. Nevertheless, budget tightening may slow funding of government research grants, creating competition for positions.
Foresters and conservation scientists	35,000	12	4,300	Slower than average employment growth is expected for foresters and conservation scientists, partly due to budgetary constraints in the Federal Government, where employment is concentrated. Opportunities will be better in private industry and State and local governments, where demand will increase in response to a growing emphasis on environmental protection and responsible land management.

Physical Scientists

CLUSTER Subgroup Occupation	Estimated employment, 1992	Percent change in employment, 1992-2005	Numerical change in employment, 1992-2005	Employment prospects
Chemists	92,000	21	20,000	Average employment growth is expected. Demand for new consumer goods such as better pharmaceuticals, personal care products, and specialty chemicals designed to address specific problems will counterbalance the slower growth expected in other types of research and development.
Geologists and geophysicists	48,000	22	11,000	Average employment growth is expected. Although employment prospects are uncertain in the petroleum industry, demand for these professionals in environmental protection and reclamation is expected to be strong.
Meteorologists	6,100	24	1,500	Average employment growth will result both from hiring by the National Weather Service to improve short-term and local-area weather forecasts and from the growth of private environmental, weather, and consulting firms.
Physicists and astronomers	21,000	-3	-700	Small employment declines will result from the expected reduction of civilian and defense-related research.
Lawyers and judges	716,000	28	197,000	Jobs for lawyers are expected to increase faster than average in response to growth in population and business activity. Employment of judges is expected to increase more slowly than average as public concern about crime is tempered by tight government budgets. Keen competition for job openings is expected for both occupations.

Social Scientists and Urban Planners

CLUSTER Subgroup Occupation	Estimated employment, 1992	Percent change in employment, 1992-2005	Numerical change in employment, 1992-2005	Employment prospects
Social scientists and urban planners	258,000	37	95,000	Faster than average growth is expected due to rising concern over the environment, crime, communicable diseases, mental illness; the growing elderly and homeless populations; the increasingly competitive global economy; and a wide range of other issues. Job prospects are best for those with advanced degrees and are generally better in disciplines which offer

CLUSTER Subgroup Occupation	Estimated employment, 1992	Percent change in employment, 1992-2005	Numerical change in employment, 1992-2005	Employment prospects
Social scientists and urban planners	258,000	37	95,000	many opportunities in nonacademic settings. Competition may ease for academic jobs due to an expected wave of retirements among college and university faculty.
Economists and marketing research analysts	51,000	25	13,000	Average growth is expected due to the increasingly complex and competitive global economy and increased reliance on quantitative methods of analyzng business trends, forecasting sales, and planning. Graduates with related work experience or an advanced degree should have the best job opportunities. Training in quantitative techniques and their application to economic modeling, forecasting, and marketing research provide applicants with the most marketable skills.
Psychologists	143,000	48 ⭐	69,000	Much faster than average growth is expected for several reasons: Increased emphasis on mental health maintenance in conjunction with the treatment of physical illness; public concern for the development of human resources, including the growing elderly population; increased testing and counseling of children; interest in rehabilitation of prisoners; and development of programs to combat substance abuse, crime, marital strife, and other problems plaguing society. Opportunities are best for candidates with a doctoral degree in applied specialties. Graduates with a master's degree may encounter competition for the limited number of jobs for which they qualify, while bachelor's degree holders can expect very few opportunities directly related to psychology.
Sociologists	(4)	(4)	(4)	Job growth will stem from increasing demand for research in such fields as demography, criminology, and gerontology and from the need to evaluate and administer social and welfare programs. Sociologists well-trained in quantitative research methods and practical rather than theoretical sociology should have the widest choice of jobs. Ph.D.'s have the best opportunities for academic positions and will find that nonacademic opportunities also are expanding. People with a master's degree face keen competition for academic positions but will be able to enter sociological practice.
Urban and regional planners	28,000	23	6,400	Average growth will stem from the importance of planning in several fields. Those with certification or a master's degree from an accredited planning program, or a master's degree in civil engineering or landscape architecture coupled with training in transportation or environmental planning have the best job prospects. Graduates with an accredited bachelor's degree in planning have relatively good job prospects.

Social and Recreation Workers

CLUSTER Subgroup Occupation	Estimated employment, 1992	Percent change in employment, 1992-2005	Numerical change in employment, 1992-2005	Employment prospects
Human services workers	189,000	136 ⭐	256,000	Jobs are expected to increase much faster than average due to the expansion of facilities and programs for the elderly and disabled and the provision of more services for families in crisis. Opportunities for qualified people should be excellent due to high job turnover, relatively low pay, and the demanding nature of the work.

CLUSTER Subgroup Occupation	Estimated employment, 1992	Percent change in employment, 1992-2005	Numerical change in employment, 1992-2005	Employment prospects
Social workers	484,000	40	191,000	Faster than average job growth is expected in response to the increased needs of the elderly, mentally ill, and disabled as well as individuals and families in crisis. Some of the need will be met through greater use of human services workers to assist social workers. Competition for social worker jobs is expected in some areas.
Recreation workers	204,000	38	78,000	Employment is expected to grow faster than average in response to population growth, increased interest in health and fitness, and rising demand for organized recreational activities. Competition is expected for full-time career positions, but opportunities for seasonal and part-time work should be good.
Religious Workers				
Protestant ministers	290,000[5]	([6])	([6])	Competition is expected to continue due to the slow growth of church membership and the large number of men and women attracted to the profession. Graduates of theological schools should have the best opportunities.
Rabbis	3,900[5]	([6])	([6])	Job opportunities are expected to be generally favorable in the four major branches of Judaism. Present unmet needs for rabbis, together with the many rabbis approaching retirement age, should insure. that the relatively constant numbers of people completing rabbinical training should have good job prospects.
Roman Catholic priests	53,000[5]	([6])	([6])	Opportunities are expected to continue to be very favorable due to a shortage of priests. The number of men becoming priests in recent years has not been, and will not be, enough to meet needs even if seminary enrollments continue their recent slow increase, especially in light of the growing numbers of priests reaching retirement age.
Teachers, Librarians, and Counselors				
Adult education teachers	540,000	32	172,000	Employment is expected to grow faster than average as the demand for adult education programs continues to rise. To keep abreast of changes in their fields and advances in technology, an increasing number of adults are taking courses to advance their careers, upgrade their skills, and enrich their lives. Opportunities will be best in computer technology, automotive mechanics, medical technology, and other fields that offer attractive, and often higher paying, jobs outside of teaching.
Archivists and curators	19,000	18	3,500	Average employment growth is expected. More archivists will be needed as institutions put more emphasis on establishing archives and organizing records. Museums and botanical and zoological gardens, where curators are concentrated, are expected to grow in response to increased interest in science, art, history, and technology. However, competition for jobs is expected to be keen. Graduates with highly specialized training and practical work experience have the best opportunities.

CLUSTER Subgroup Occupation	Estimated employment, 1992	Percent change in employment, 1992-2005	Numerical change in employment, 1992-2005	Employment prospects
College and university faculty	812,000	26	214,000	Employment is expected to increase about as fast as average as enrollment in higher education increases. In addition, retirements should begin increasing in the late 1990s, resulting in improved opportunities for college faculty posi tions and tenure. Fewer faculty members should have to take part-time or short-term appointments. Job prospects will continue to be better in such fields as business, engineering, health science, computer science, physical sciences, and mathematics than in other specialties, largely because very attractive nonacademic jobs will be available for many potential faculty members in these fields.
Counselors	154,000	32	50,000	Employment is expected to grow faster than average in response to increasing demand for school, rehabilitation, mental health, and employment counselors. Opportunities should increase significantly by the end of the decade as a large number of counselors reach retirement age.
Librarians	141,000	12	17,000	Employment is expected to grow more slowly than average, continuing the trend of the 1980s. Budgetary constraints in school, public, and college libraries and the increasing use of computerized information storage and retrieval systems will dampen demand. Opportunities will be best in nontraditional settings—information brokers, private corporations, and consulting firms. Willingness to relocate will greatly enhance job prospects.
School teachers— kindergarten, elementary, and secondary	3,255,000	34	1,113,000 ⭐	Faster than average employment growth is expected; however, projected growth varies among individual teaching occupations. Employment of special education teachers is expected to increase much faster than average due to legislation emphasizing training and employment for individuals with disabilities; technological advances resulting in more survivors of accidents and illnesses; and growing public interest in individuals with special needs. Employment of secondary school teachers is expected to grow faster than average, while average employment growth is projected for kindergarten and elementary school teachers, reflecting population trends and corresponding student enrollment. Job prospects generally are better in cities and rural areas than in suburbs. Mathematics, science, and special education teachers remain in short supply in may locales.
Health Diagnosing Occupations				
Chiropractors	46,000	36	16,000	Employment is expected to grow faster than average because of rapid growth in the older population, with its increased likelihood of physiological problems. Greater public awareness of the profession also will encourage growth. Replacement needs are low because chiropractors generally remain in the profession until they retire.

CLUSTER Subgroup Occupation	Estimated employment, 1992	Percent change in employment, 1992-2005	Numerical change in employment, 1992-2005	Employment prospects
Dentists	183,000	5	9,500	Employment is expected to grow more slowly than average despite growing demand. Dentists will absorb the increase in demand for services by working more hours and hiring more dental hygienists and dental assistants to handle routine services. Demand for dental care should grow substantially: The baby-boom generation will seek more care as it ages; the elderly will require more care than their predecessors because they are more likely to retain their teeth; and the younger generation will need preventive checkups.
Optometrists	31,000	16	4,800	Employment is expected to grow as fast as average in order to meet the needs of a population that is larger, older, and more aware of the need for proper eye care. Replacement needs are low because optometrists generally remain in the profession until they retire.
Physicians	556,000	35	195,000	Employment is expected to grow faster than average due to a growing and aging population and technological improvements that encourage expansion of the health care industry. Job prospects are good for primary, geriatric, and preventive care specialists. Some shortages have been reported in general surgery and psychiatry and in some rural and low income areas. Replacement needs are low because physicians generally remain in the profession until they retire.
Podiatrists	15,000	37	5,500	Employment is expected to grow faster than average due to the rising demand for pediatric services, especially by older people. Establishing a new pediatric practice will be toughest in areas surrounding the seven colleges of pediatric medicine since podiatrists are concentrated in these locations. Replacement needs are low because podiatrists generally remain in the profession until they retire.
Veterinarians	44,000	33	14,000	Employment is expected to grow faster than average due to an increase in the number of pets and greater willingness of pet owners to pay for more intensive care. The outlook will be particularly good for veterinarians with specialty training in toxicology, laboratory animal medicine, and pathology.

Health Assessment and Treating Occupations

CLUSTER Subgroup Occupation	Estimated employment, 1992	Percent change in employment, 1992-2005	Numerical change in employment, 1992-2005	Employment prospects
Dietitians and nutritionists	50,000	26	13,000	Employment is expected to grow about as fast as average because of increasing emphasis on nutrition in nursing homes, hospitals, physicians' offices, and social service programs.
Occupational therapists	40,000	60 ★	24,000	Employment is expected to grow much faster than average due to strong growth in rehabilitative services. Medical advances now make it possible for more patients with critical problems to survive and need therapy. Also, as the baby-boom generation moves into middle age, the incidence of heart attack and stroke will increase. The rapidly growing population 75 years of age and above and disabled children entering special education programs will spur further demand.

CLUSTER Subgroup Occupation	Estimated employment, 1992	Percent change in employment, 1992-2005	Numerical change in employment, 1992-2005	Employment prospects
Pharmacists	163,000	29	47,000	Spurred by the pharmaceutical needs of a larger and older population and greater use of medication, employment is expected to grow faster than average.
Physical therapists	90,000	88 ★	79,000	Employment is expected to grow much faster than average. Growth will occur as new technologies save more trauma victims and permit more disabled people to be treated, who then will need therapy. Demand also will come from an aging population that is more likely to have heart attacks, strokes, and other debilitating conditions. Younger, people will also need therapy as medical advances save the lives of more newborns with birth defects.
Physician assistants	58,000	34	20,000	Employment is expected to grow faster than average due to expansion of the health services industry and increased emphasis on cost containment and primary care. Job prospects will be excellent, especially in rural and low income areas that have difficulty attracting physicians.
Recreational therapists	30,000	40	12,000	Employment is expected to grow faster than average, because of expansion in long-term care, physical and psychiatric rehabilitation, and services for the disabled. The growing number of older people is expected to spur job growth for activity directorsin nursing homes, retirement communities, adult daycare programs, and social service agencies. Continued growth is expected in community residential facilities as well as in daycare programs for people with disabilities. Job prospects are expected to be best for those with clinical experience.
Registered nurses	1,835,000	42 ★	765,000 ★	Much faster than average growth is expected due to overall growth in health care and medical technology. Job prospects will be good, especially as emphasis on primary care grows. Many job openings will also result from the need to replace experienced nurses who leave this large occupation.
Respiratory therapists	74,000	48 ★	36,000	Employment is expected to grow much faster than average because of the substantial growth in the middle-aged and elderly population. An older population is more likely to suffer from cardiopulmonary diseases such as pneumonia, chronic bronchitis, emphysema, and heart disease. Rapid growth in the number of patients with AIDS also will boost demand since lung disease often accompanies AIDS. Because medical advances will allow more premature infants to survive, job opportunities are expected to be highly favorable for those with neonatal care skills.
Speech-language pathologists and audiologists	73,000	51 ★	37,000	Much faster than average overall growth is expected because of the increased number of older people and the entrance of the baby-boomers into an age bracket when the possibility of stroke-induced hearing and speech loss increases. Increased emphasis on early detection and prevention will also spur growth.

CLUSTER Subgroup Occupation	Estimated employment, 1992	Percent change in employment, 1992-2005	Numerical change in employment, 1992-2005	Employment prospects
Communications Occupations				
Public relations specialists	98,000	26	26,000	Average growth will stem from the recognition by organizations of all sizes of the need for good public relations in an increasingly competitive business environment. Keen competition for public relations jobs will likely continue among recent college graduates with a degree in communications as the number of applicants is expected to exceed the number of job openings.
Radio and television announcers and newscasters	56,000	25	14,000	Employment is expected to grow about as fast as average as new radio and television stations are licensed and the number of cable television systems continues to grow. Competition will be very keen because the broadcasting field attracts many more jobseekers than there are jobs. Radio stations are more inclined than are television stations to hire beginners.
Reporters and correspondents	58,000	26	15,000	Employment is expected to grow about as fast as average. Competition on large metropolitan newspapers and broadcast stations and on national magazines will continue to be keen. Small town and suburban newspapers will continue to offer better opportunities for beginners. Talented writers who can handle highly specialized scientific or technical subjects have an advantage.
Writers and editors	283,000	23	66,000	Employment is expected to increase about as fast as average. Employment of salaried writers and editors by newspapers, periodicals, book publishers, nonprofit organizations, and advertising and public relations agencies is expected to increase with growing demand for their publications. Demand for technical writers is expected to increase because of the continuing expansion of scientific and technical information.
Visual Arts Occupations				
Designers	302,000	19	57,000	Employment is expected to grow about as fast as average. Designers in most fields can expect to face competition throughout their careers as a result of the abundant supply of talented, well-educated individuals attracted to this occupation. Job opportunities should be best in floral design due to its relatively low pay and limited advancement opportunities. Opportunities also should be good for qualified people in some specialized fields, such as furniture design.
Photographers and camera operators	118,000	25	29,000	Average employment growth will stem from increasing use of visual images in education, communication, entertainment, marketing, and research and development and as businesses make greater use of videos for training films, business meetings, sales campaigns, and public relations work. However, competition will be keen for what is generally regarded as an exciting field.

CLUSTER Subgroup Occupation	Estimated employment, 1992	Percent change in employment, 1992-2005	Numerical change in employment, 1992-2005	Employment prospects
Visual artists	273,000	23	63,000	Average employment growth is expected for both graphic designers and fine artists,. Despite demands by advertising agencies, publishing firms, and other businesses for creative and ingenious designs, graphic designers can expect competition for employment. Competition for jobs also will continue to be keen among fine artists, who often create art to satisfy their need for self-expression and display their works in museums, art galleries, and homes.

Performing Arts Occupations

Actors, directors, and producers	129,000	54 ⭐	69,000	Much faster than average job growth is expected. Keen competition is expected for jobs because large numbers of people are attracted to these careers, which do not require formal preparation. Only a relatively few people will find regular employment.
Dancers and choreographers	18,000	25	4,600	Jobs are expected to increase about as fast as average due to the public's continued interest in dance. Very keen competition is expected for job openings, and only the most talented will find regular employment.
Musicians	236,000	25	59,000	Jobs are expected to grow about as fast as average due to the continued demand for live and recorded musical entertainment. Competition for jobs will be keen, and even many talented individuals will not be able to make a living solely as musicians. Opportunities will be best for people with an ability to play several instruments and a variety of types of music.

TECHNICIANS AND RELATED SUPPORT OCCUPATIONS

Health Technologists and Technicians

Cardiovascular technologists and technicians	31,000	9	2,600	Overall employment is expected to grow more slowly than average, but technicians and technologists will experience different patterns of employment change. Employment of EKG technicians is expected to decline as hospitals train nurses and other personnel to perform basic EKG procedures. Employment of cardiology technologists is expected to grow faster than average as the population ages because older people have a higher incidence of heart problems.
Clinical laboratory technologists and technicians	268,000	26	71,000	Employment is expected to grow about as fast as average, with demand stimulated by the growth f the older population and its accompanying medical problems. Technological advances will have opposite effects on employment: New, more powerful tests encourage more testing, but automation and simpler tests make each worker more productive. The fastest growth is expected in independent medical laboratories. Rapid growth also is expected in the offices and clinics of physicians. Hospitals will experience only slow growth as they continue to send laboratories a greater share of their testing.

CLUSTER Subgroup Occupation	Estimated employment, 1992	Percent change in employment, 1992-2005	Numerical change in employment, 1992-2005	Employment prospects
Dental hygienists	108,000	43 ⭐	46,000	Employment should grow much faster than average because of increased demand for dental care. Demand will arise from population growth, greater retention of natural teeth by middle-aged and elderly people, and rising incomes. Also, dentists are likely to hire more hygienists as their workloads increase.
Dispensing opticians	63,000	36	22,000	Employment is expected to grow faster than average in response to rising demand for corrective lenses as the population grows and ages. Replacement needs will be significant. This occupation employs many young people; and, like many other occupations in retail trade, many people transfer to other fields.
EEG technologists	6,300	54 ⭐	3,400	Employment is expected to grow much faster than average, reflecting the increased number of neurodiagnostic tests performed. More testing will occur as new tests and procedures are developed and as the aging population requires more medical care.
Emergency medical technicians	114,000	36	41,000	Employment is expected to grow faster than average because of the increasing number of older people, who are more likely to need emergency services. Most job openings will occur because of this occupation's high turnover.
Licensed practical nurses	659,000	40	261,000	Employment is expected to grow faster than average in response to general demand and the long-term-care needs of a rapidly growing elderly population. Job prospects should remain excellent unless the number of people completing LPN training increases substantially.
Medical record technicians	76,000	61 ⭐	47,000	Employment is expected to grow much faster than average. Demand will rise from rapid growth in the number of medical tests, treatments, and procedures and the increasing scrutiny of medical records by third-party payers, courts, and consumers.
Nuclear medicine technologists	12,000	50 ⭐	6,100	Employment is expected to grow much faster than average. Substantial growth in the number of middle-aged and older people will spur demand for nuclear medicine tests. Technological innovations should increase the uses of nuclear medicine, further strengthening demand.
Radiologic technologists	162,000	63 ⭐	102,000	Employment is expected to grow much faster than average. New generations of diagnostic imaging equipment should increase demand. Also, more treatment of cancer is anticipated due to the aging of the population and the improved ability to detect malignancies.
Surgical technologists	44,000	42	19,000	Much faster than average growth is expected as a growing population and technological advances increase the number of surgical procedures performed. Growth will be fastest in clinics and offices of physicians due to increased outpatient surgery; however, most jobs will be in hospitals.

CLUSTER Subgroup Occupation	Estimated employment, 1992	Percent change in employment, 1992-2005	Numerical change in employment, 1992-2005	Employment prospects
Technicians Except Health				
Aircraft pilots	85,000	35	30,000 those with the prospects.	Despite faster than average employment growth, pilots should face considerable competition for jobs because the glamour, prestige, and high pay associated with the occupation attract many applicants. Pilots who have logged the greatest number of flying hours using the most sophisticated equipment and most FAA licenses generally have the best
Air traffic controllers	23,000	10	2,300	Employment growth is expected to be slower than average as productivity gains stemming from laborsaving air traffic control equipment offset some of the demand generated by more aircraft flying. Competition for jobs is expected to remain keen because the occupation's relatively high pay and liberal retirement plan attract many applicants.
Broadcast technicians	35,000	4	1,400	Employment in radio and television broadcasting is expected to grow ore slowly than average because of laborsaving technologies. Employment in the motion picture industry will grow faster than average as more movies are made. Job prospects are expected to remain competitive because of the large number of people attracted to this relatively small field.
Computer programmers	555,000	30	169,000	Employment is expected to grow faster than average as organizations seek new applications for computers and improvement to the software already in use. Employment is not expected to grow as rapidly as in the past, however, because new software and techniques have simplified or eliminated some programming tasks. Job opportunities should be particularly plentiful in data processing services firms, software houses, and computer consulting businesses.
Drafters	314,000	11	35,000	Despite increasing demands by industry for drafting services, productivity gains due to advances in computer-aided drafting technology are expected to result in slower than average employment growth.
Engineering technicians	695,000	19	132,000	Average employment growth is expected. Overall, the drive to improve manufacturing facilities and product designs will provide good employment opportunities; however, the outlook varies with the area of specialization and industry; technicians whose jobs are defense related may experience fewer opportunities because of cutbacks.
Library technicians	71,000	25	18,000	Average employment growth will be spurred by increasing automation. Computerized information systems have simplified certain tasks, such as descriptive cataloging, which can now be handled by technicians instead of librarians. However, budgetary constraints may dampen employment growth in school, public, and college and university libraries. Willingness to relocate enhances one's job prospects.

CLUSTER Subgroup Occupation	Estimated employment, 1992	Percent change in employment, 1992-2005	Numerical change in employment, 1992-2005	Employment prospects
Paralegals	95,000	86 ★	81,000	Employment is expected to grow much faster than average as law firms and other employers of legal workers restructure tasks to make, greater use of paralegals. However, keen competition for jobs should continue as the large number of people graduating from paralegal training programs exceeds job growth.
Science technicians	244,000	25	61,000	Average employment growth is expected because of the growth of scientific research and development and the production of technical products. Job opportunities will be best for individuals who have training or experience on the equip ment currently in use in industrial and government laboratories.

MARKETING AND SALES OCCUPATIONS

CLUSTER Subgroup Occupation	Estimated employment, 1992	Percent change in employment, 1992-2005	Numerical change in employment, 1992-2005	Employment prospects
Cashiers	2,747,000	24	669,900 ★	Average growth is expected, spurred by a growing population's expanding demand for goods and services. As in the past, replacement needs will create a significant number of job openings because the occupation is large and turnover is much higher than average.
Counter and rental clerks	242,000	36	88,000	Faster than average employment growth is expected due to rising demand for laundry and dry cleaning, automobile rental, amusement and recreation, and equipment rental and leasing services. Part-time employment opportunities should be especially plentiful.
Insurance agents and brokers	415,000	15	62,000	Employment is expected to increase about as fast as average as increasing productivity moderates growth in response to the rising volume of sales of insurance and other financial products. Opportunities will be best for ambitious people who enjoy sales work and develop expertise in a wide range of insurance and financial services. Many beginners abandon this highly competitive business because they are unable to establish a sufficiently large clientele.
Manufacturers' and wholesale sales representatives	1,613,000	5	78,000	Employment growth is expected to be slower than average as more firms rely on technology such as electronic data interchange, point-of-sale inventory systems, and expert system software and as more large companies begin to negotiate directly with suppliers, bypassing sales representatives entirely.
Real estate agents, brokers, and appraisers	397,000	16	63,000	Average employment growth is expected as a result of the growing volume of sales of residential and commercial property. Because turnover is high, real estate sales positions should be relatively easy to obtain.
Retail sales workers	4,086,000	21	877,000 ★	Employment is expected to increase about as fast as average due to anticipated growth in retail trade. As in the past, replacement needs will generate an exceptionally large number of sales jobs because the occupation is large and turnover is much higher than average.

CLUSTER Subgroup Occupation	Estimated employment, 1992	Percent change in employment, 1992-2005	Numerical change in employment, 1992-2005	Employment prospects
Securities and financial services sales representatives	200,000	33	65,000	Employment is expected to grow faster than average as economic growth, rising personal incomes, and greater inherited wealth increase the funds available for investment and as banks and other financial institutions offer an increasing array of financial services. Due to the highly competitive nature of securities sales work, many beginners leave the field because they are unable to establish a sufficient clientele. Job prospects should be best for mature individuals with successful sales experience.
Services sales representatives	488,000	38	185,000	Faster than average growth is expected in response to the growth of the services industries. However, employment will not keep pace with industry growth due to downsizing and the use of technologies-such s voice mail, cellular telephones, and laptop computers-that increase productivity. Prospective services sales representatives with a college background or a proven sales record should have the best job opportunities.
Travel agents	115,000	66 ⭐	76,000	Employment is expected to grow much faster than average due to a sharp increase in business and vacation travel.

ADMINISTRATIVE SUPPORT OCCUPATIONS INCLUDING CLERICAL

CLUSTER Subgroup Occupation	Estimated employment, 1992	Percent change in employment, 1992-2005	Numerical change in employment, 1992-2005	Employment prospects
Adjusters, investigators, and collectors	1,185,000	31	367,000 ⭐	Job growth is expected to be about as fast as average as a result of increases in the population, the economy, and the volume of insurance sales. Bill and account collectors and insurance adjusters and examiners will grow the most rapidly.
Bank tellers	525,000	-4	-24,000	Employment is projected to decline. Overexpansion and competition from large nonbank corporations will result in closings, mergers, and consolidations in the banking industry, where employment of tellers is highly concentrated. Further, teller employment could be adversely affected by new technologies if they are widely adopted by banks. Nevertheless, qualified applicants should have good prospects because the number of job openings is large.
Clerical supervisors and managers	1,267,000	24	301,000	Employment is expected to increase as fast as average. These workers will not be affected as dramatically by office automation as other administrative support workers, although automation may limit growth in some areas. Job openings will be numerous due to replacement needs.
Computer and peripheral equipment operators	296,000	-41	-122,000	Employment is expected to decline sharply as data centers become increasingly automated and as more computing is done with personal computers.
Credit clerks and authorizers	218,000	24	53,000	Average employment growth is expected as the number of real estate, retail sales, and other transactions requiring credit increases.
General office clerks	2,688,000	24	654,000 ⭐	Average employment growth is anticipated as more small businesses place a single office worker in charge of all

CLUSTER Subgroup Occupation	Estimated employment, 1992	Percent change in employment, 1992-2005	Numerical change in employment, 1992-2005	Employment prospects
General office clerks	2,688,000	24	654,000 ⭐	clerical duties. Opportunities should be quite favorable because high turnover in this very large occupation produces many job openings.
Information clerks	1,333,000	32	429,000	Faster than average growth is expected due to economic growth and general business expansion. Replacement needs will create large numbers of job openings. Many opportunities for part-time work will be available.
Hotel and motel desk clerks	122,000	40	50,000	Faster than average growth is expected due to the expansion of the number of hotels, motels, and other lodging establishments. Job opportunities should be relatively good because turnover is very high. Opportunities for part-time work should continue to be plentiful.
Interviewing and new accounts clerks	175,000	19	34,000	Overall employment is expected to increase about as fast as average. Employment of interviewing clerks is expected to grow faster than average in the health services industry and much faster than average in personnel supply services as more firms contract for the services of these clerks. New accounts clerks can anticipate slower than average employment growth, reflecting slow growth among commercial banks and savings and loan institutions.
Receptionists	904,000	34	305,000	Faster than average growth is expected due to strong growth in the services sector of the economy. Job opportunities should be plentiful due to high turnover. Because many receptionists also perform secretarial duties, good typing and computer skills, coupled with strong interpersonal and communications skills, enhance one's job prospects.
Reservation and transportation ticket agents and travel clerks	131,000	30	39,000	Faster than average growth is expected due to expansion of both business and pleasure travel. Most applicants are likely to encounter considerable competition because the supply of qualified applicants far outstrips demand. Airline jobs, in particular, attract many applicants because of the travel benefits and glamour associated with the industry.
Mail clerks and messengers	271,000	10	26,000	Jobs are expected to increase more slowly than average as the increasing automation of mail handling somewhat offsets the growing volume of internal mail, parcels, and other written information that must be handled and delivered. High turnover should result in plentiful job openings.
Material recording, scheduling, dispatching and distributing occupations	3,558,000	13	455,000	Overall employment is expected to grow more slowly than average. The volume of business transactions will increase as the economy grows, but automation will enable workers to be more productive, holding down employment growth somewhat. Job prospects for individual occupations vary.
Dispatchers	222,000	21	46,000	Employment is expected to grow about as fast as average due to the growing need for the various services dispatchers provide.

CLUSTER Subgroup Occupation	Estimated employment, 1992	Percent change in employment, 1992-2005	Numerical change in employment, 1992-2005	Employment prospects
Stock clerks	1,969,000	10	187,000	Even though employment is expected to grow more slowly than average, job prospects should be favorable. This occupation is very large, and many job openings will occur each year to replace workers who transfer to other jobs or leave the labor force. Growing use of computers for inventory control and automated equipment are expected to hold down demand, especially in manufacturing and in wholesale trade, industries whose operations are most easily automated.
Traffic, shipping, and receiving clerks	824,000	18	147,000	Employment is expected to increase about as fast as average. Employment growth will be affected by automation, as all but the smallest firms move to hold down labor costs by using computers to store and retrieve shipping and receiving records. However, certain functions cannot be automated.
Postal clerks and mail carriers	361,000	(7)	1,600	Little change is expected in overall employment. Employment of postal clerks is expected to decline due to the implementation of productivity-increasing automated equipment. Postal mail carrier employment is expected to change little, the result of the conflicting factors of increased mail volume and the growing use of automated sorting equipment. Competition for jobs will be keen as the number of applicants continues to far exceed the number of job openings.
Record clerks	3,573,000	6	204,000	Slower than average employment growth is expected as automation makes these workers more productive. However, opportunities will be plentiful for full-time, part-time, and seasonal employment due to above average turnover in this large occupation.
Billing clerks	409,000	3	12,000	Little change in employment is expected as computers are increasingly used to manage account information and as more advanced equipment replaces billing machines.
Bookkeeping, accounting, and auditing clerks	2,112,000	3	73,000	Little change in employment is expected. Although a growing economy will result in more financial transactions, continuing automation will increase productivity and limit employment growth. However, employment opportunities should be plentiful due to the size of the occupation and relatively high turnover.
Brokerage clerks and statement clerks	88,000	7	5,900	Slower than average employment growth is expected as further automatic. and changes in business practices reduce demand for these workers.
File clerks	257,000	19	48,000	Average employment growth is expected as recordkeeping requirements continue to rise. Demand will be strongest in the rapidly growing health sector. Job opportunities should be plentiful due to high turnover.
Library assistants and bookmobile drivers	114,000	18	20,000	Average employment growth is expected due to growth in local government and schools. Job prospects should be favorable, especially for part-time work.

CLUSTER Subgroup Occupation	Estimated employment, 1992	Percent change in employment, 1992-2005	Numerical change in employment, 1992-2005	Employment prospects
Order clerks	300,000	4	13,000	Little change in employment is expected as office automation continues to increase the productivity of these workers. However, job opportunities should be plentiful, especially for outside order clerks who deal directly with the public.
Payroll and timekeeping clerks	165,000	(^{8})	(^{9})	Employment is expected to change little as continuing automation of payroll and timekeeping make these workers more productive.
Personnel clerks	128,000	25	32,000	Average employment growth is expected. Despite an increasing workload, rising productivity through automation will moderate demand.
Secretaries	3,324,000	12	386,000 ⭐	Overall employment is expected to grow more slowly than average, in spite of projected rapid growth for legal and medical secretaries. Employment gains resulting from an increase in the amount of office work and the assumption of new responsibilities by secretaries will be tempered by productivity gains made possible by automation. Job prospects should continue to be excellent, however, for well qualified secretaries.
Stenographers and court reporters	115,000	-2	-1,700	Employment is expected to decline as decreases in stenographer jobs more than offset growth in transcriptionist and court reporter jobs. Widespread use of dictation machines should continue to greatly reduce the need for stenographers, but medical transcriptionist jobs should increase as health services grows. Growing use of video recordings of court proceedings should dampen growth of court reporters.
Teacher aides	885,000	43 ⭐	381,000 ⭐	Employment is expected to grow much faster than average in response to the rising number of special education classes, restructuring of schools, and increasing number of students who speak English as a second language.
Telephone operators	314,000	-28	-89,000	Employment is expected to decline due to automatic switching systems, voice message systems, and voice recognition technology.
Typists, word processors, and datae entry keyers	1,238,000	-4	-46,000	Employment is expected to decline, primarily due to new technologies that allow more data to be collected at the point of its origin or transmitted electronically. Job prospects will be best for those with a broad knowledge of office technology.

SERVICE OCCUPATIONS

Protective Service Occupations

Correction officers	282,000	70 ⭐	197,000	Employment is expected to increase much faster than average as correctional facilities expand and additional officers are hired to supervise and counsel a growing number of inmates. The large number, of job openings from both rapid growth and replacement needs will ensure highly favorable employment prospects.

CLUSTER Subgroup Occupation	Estimated employment, 1992	Percent change in employment, 1992-2005	Numerical change in employment, 1992-2005	Employment prospects
Firefighting occupations	305,000	16	50,000	Average employment growth is expected as the Nation's population grows and fire protection needs increase. Keen competition is expected in most areas; the best opportunities are likely to be found in smaller communities with expanding populations.
Guards	803,000	51 ★	408,000 ★	Much faster than average employment growth is expected due to increasing concern about crime, vandalism, and terrorism. Job opportunities should be plentiful, although some competition is expected for in-house guard jobs, who generally have higher salaries, more benefits, better job security, and greater potential for advancement. Opportunities will be best for those who work for contract security agencies.
Police, detectives, and special agents	700,000	13	92,000	Employment is expected to increase more slowly than average. Job growth resulting from increases in the population and the need for police protection will be restrained by tight government budgets. Keen competition is likely for most jobs.

Food and Beverage Preparation and Service Occupations

CLUSTER Subgroup Occupation	Estimated employment, 1992	Percent change in employment, 1992-2005	Numerical change in employment, 1992-2005	Employment prospects
Chefs, cooks, and other kitchen workers	3,092,000	38	1,190,000 ★	Job growth is expected to be faster than average as the population and economy both grow and as fewer meals are prepared at home. High turnover should result in plentiful job openings.
Food and beverage service workers	4,365,000	26	1,124,000 ★	Employment is expected to grow about as fast as average in response to growth in the population and economy. Job openings should continue to be plentiful due to high turnover.

Health Service Occupations

CLUSTER Subgroup Occupation	Estimated employment, 1992	Percent change in employment, 1992-2005	Numerical change in employment, 1992-2005	Employment prospects
Dental assistants	183,000	39	72,000	Employment is expected to grow faster than average. Population growth, higher incomes, and greater retention of natural teeth by middle-aged and older people will fuel demand for dental services. Also, dentists are expected to hire more assistants to perform routine tasks.
Medical assistants	181,000	71 ★	128,000	Much faster than average growth is anticipated due to expansion of the health services industry. In view of the high turnover in the occupation and the preference of many physicians for trained personnel, job prospects should be excellent for medical assistants with formal training or experience.
Nursing aides and psychiatric aides	1,389,000	44 ★	616,000 ★	Overall employment is projected to grow much faster than average. Employment of nursing aides will also grow much faster than average as a result of the expansion of nursing and personal care facilities. Employment of psychiatric aides is expected to grow faster than average to meet the needs of very old people and those suffering from acute psychiatric and substance abuse problems. Replacement needs will be high because of relatively high turnover in this occupation. Job prospects are expected to be very good.

CLUSTER Subgroup Occupation	Estimated employment, 1992	Percent change in employment, 1992-2005	Numerical change in employment, 1992-2005	Employment prospects
Personal Service and Cleaning Occupations				
Animal caretakers, except farm	103,000	40	41,000	Employment is expected to grow faster than average due to a significant increase in the number of dogs and cats who need care. The best prospects should be for graduates of training programs in veterinary technology.
Barbers and cosmetologists	746,000	32	239,000	Population growth and rising incomes will produce faster than average employment growth. Most of this growth will be in cosmetology, reflecting shifting consumer preferences toward personalized styling in full-service salons. Job prospects will be best for those specializing in nail and skin care. Part-time employment will continue to account for a significant share of the job growth.
Flight attendants	93,000	51 ★	47,000	Employment is expected to grow much faster than average as the number of airline passengers continues to increase. Competition for jobs is expected to remain very keen. Applicants with at least 2 years of college and experience in dealing with the public have the best prospects.
Gardeners and groundskeepers	884,000	35	311,000 ★	Faster than average employment growth is expected in response to increasing demand for gardening and landscaping services. Employment opportunities should be plentiful.
Homemaker-home health aides	475,000	136 ★	645,000 ★	Much faster than average growth is expected to result from a substantial increase in the elderly population, greater efforts to care for the chronically ill at home, and development of in-home medical technologies. Job opportunities are excellent.
Janitors and cleaners and cleaning supervisors	3,018,000	20	600,000 ★	Employment is expected to grow about as fast as average as the number of office buildings, apartment houses, schools, hospitals, and other buildings increases. The occupation is easy to enter, turnover is high, and part-time and temporary jobs are plentiful.
Preschool workers	941,000	65 ★	611,000 ★	Employment is projected to increase much faster than average, reflecting a shift in the kind of childcare arrangements parents choose and a rise in labor force participation among women ages 20 to 44. Job openings should be plentiful because many preschool workers leave the occupation each year for other, often better paying, jobs, family responsibilities, or other reasons. Qualified people should have little trouble finding and keeping a job.
Private household workers	869,000	-33	-286,000	Employment is expected to decline. The severely limited supply of people willing to work in this field has given rise to childcare and household cleaning service firms, which adversely affects employment in this occupation. Nevertheless, job opportunities should be excellent.

CLUSTER Subgroup Occupation	Estimated employment, 1992	Percent change in employment, 1992-2005	Numerical change in employment, 1992-2005	Employment prospects

AGRICULTURE, FORESTRY, FISHING, AND RELATED OCCUPATIONS

Farm operators and managers	1,218,000	-17	-204,000	Employment is expected to decline as farms become larger, more productive, and fewer in number. Nevertheless, replacement needs will result in many job openings.
Fishers, hunters, and trappers	60,000	5	3,000	Slower than average growth is expected due to stock depletion. Many operations currently are at or beyond maximum sustainable yield, limiting potential for occupational growth. Employment growth of fishers will also be restrained by improvements in fishing vessels and gear.
Forestry and logging occupations	131,000	2	3,200	Little change in overall employment is expected. Despite an increase in demand for lumber and wood products, improvements in logging equipment will cause employment of timber and logging workers to decline. Employment of forestry and conservation workers is expected to increase moderately as environmental concerns help spur demand. However, these jobs are sought by many people, and applicants are expected to face competition.

MECHANICS, INSTALLERS, AND REPAIRERS

Aircraft mechanics and engine specialists	131,000	13	17,000	Slower than average employment growth is expected as productivity gains resulting from greater se of automated inventory control and modular systems speed repairs and parts replacement. Job prospects are likely to be best in general aviation.
Automotive body repairers	202,000	30	61,000	Employment is expected to increase faster than average due to a rise in the number of motor vehicles and the popularity of lighter weight cars, which are more easily damaged in collisions and more difficult to repair. Opportunities should be best for people with formal training in automotive body repair or mechanics.
Automotive mechanics	739,000	23	168,000	Employment is expected to increase about as fast as average as the need to service and repair an increasing number of motor vehicles is offset by improvements in their reliability. Most new jobs will be in automotive repair shops and automobile dealerships as fewer gasoline service stations provide repair services. Opportunities should be best for people who complete formal automotive mechanic training programs.
Diesel mechanics	263,000	24	64,000	Employment is expected to increase about as fast as average as freight transportation by truck increases. Opportunities should be best for people who complete formal diesel mechanic training programs.
Electronic equipment repairers	398,000	-4	-15,000	Overall employment is expected to decline due to improvements in product reliability and ease of service; in addition, lower prices will cause consumers to purchase new equipment rather than have old items repaired.

CLUSTER Subgroup Occupation	Estimated employment, 1992	Percent change in employment, 1992-2005	Numerical change in employment, 1992-2005	Employment prospects
Commercial and industrial electronic equipment repairers	68,000	7	5,000	Overall employment is expected to grow more slowly than average. Employment in nondefense industries is expected to grow about as fast as average as firms install more electronic equipment. Because of cuts in the defense budget, employment is expected to decline significantly in the Federal Government.
Communications equipment repairers	108,000	-38	-41,000	Employment is expected to decline sharply. Decreased labor requirements due to improved technology have already used layoffs.
Computer and office machine repairers	143,000	30	43,000	Overall employment is expected to grow faster than average. Employment of computer repairers is expected to grow much faster than average as the amount of computer equipment in use increases. Employment of other office machine repairers is expected to grow more slowly than average due to slow growth in the amount of that equipment.
Electronic home entertainment equipment repairers	39,000	-5	-2,100	Employment is expected to decline. Improvements in reliability and ease of service should reduce service requirements, even though more equipment is expected to be in use. Nevertheless, opportunities should be good because many repairers transfer to higher paying jobs that also require knowledge of electronics.
Telephone installers and repairers	40,000	-50	-20,000	Employment is expected to decline significantly due to technological improvements, such as prewired jacks and modular telephones. Also, fewer phones will be worth repairing as prices continue to decline.
Elevator installers and repairers	22,000	18	3,900	Average growth will occur as the construction of buildings with elevators and escalators increases and as the stock of equipment needing maintenance grows. In addition, demand will be spurred by the need to modernize older equipment. Job prospects will be best for people with postsecondary training in electronics.
Farm equipment mechanics	47,000	13	6,000	Employment is expected to increase more slowly than average. Farmland consolidation and more efficient farm practices will hold down demand, but the tendency of farmers to make fewer of their own repairs will increase it. Opportunities should be best for people who complete formal training in farm equipment repair or diesel mechanics.
General maintenance mechanics	1,145,000	28	319,000 ⭐	Faster than average growth is expected as the number of office and apartment buildings, stores, schools, hospitals, hotels, and factories increases. Although construction of these facilities is expected to slow down, many opportunities will arise because of the high turnover in this large occupation.
Heating, air-conditioning, and refrigeration technicians	212,000	29	62,000	Employment is expected to increase faster than average. Demand for new residential, commercial, and industrial climate control systems, as well as the need to maintain existing systems, should create very favorable job prospects.

CLUSTER Subgroup Occupation	Estimated employment, 1992	Percent change in employment, 1992-2005	Numerical change in employment, 1992-2005	Employment prospects
Home appliance and power tool repairers	74,000	([10])	([11])	Little change in employment is expected as the increasing number of appliances in use will be offset by their greater reliability and durability. Job prospects will be best for people who have a strong background in electronics.
Industrial machinery repairers	477,000	-3	-15,000	Employment is expected to decline as more firms introduce automated production equipment that requires less maintenance than existing machines. Because maintenance and repair of machinery are crucial regardless of the level of production, industrial machinery repairers generally are less subject to layoffs than other workers.
Line installers and cable splicers	273,000	-11	-31,000	Overall employment is expected to decline. Employment of telephone and cable TV line installers and repairers is expected to decline sharply as the conversion to fiber optics is completed and as maintenance requirements are reduced. Employment of electrical power line installers is expected to grow more slowly than average.
Millwrights	73,000	9	6,400	Slower than average employment growth is expected. Millwrights continue to be needed to maintain and repair existing machinery, to dismantle old machinery, and to install and maintain new equipment.
Mobile heavy equipment mechanics	96,000	4	3,900	Employment is expected to grow more slowly than average, matching the slow growth in the amount of mobile heavy equipment in operation. Opportunities should be best for people who complete formal training programs in diesel or heavy equipment mechanics.
Motorcycle, boat, and small-engine mechanics	46,000	15	6,900	Overall employment is expected to grow about as fast as average as rising incomes enable consumers to buy more boats and outdoor power equipment. Opportunities should be best for people who complete formal training programs.
Musical instrument repairers and tuners	12,000	9	1,100	Employment is expected to increase more slowly than average, because the number of students playing instruments should grow only slowly. However, moderate growth is expected in the number of professional musicians.
Vending machine servicers and repairers	20,000	([12])	([13])	change in employment is expected because an increase in the number of vending machines in use is offset by the greater reliability of new equipment.

CONSTRUCTION TRADES AND EXTRACTIVE OCCUPATIONS

Bricklayers and stonemasons	139,000	26	36,000	Average, employment growth is expected as population and business growth create a need for new factories, schools, hospitals, offices, and other structures and as brick is increasingly used for decorative work and for building exteriors.
Carpenters	990,000	20	197,000	Average employment growth is expected in response to demand for new housing, commercial buildings, and industrial plants and the need to renovate and modernize existing struc-

CLUSTER Subgroup Occupation	Estimated employment, 1992	Percent change in employment, 1992-2005	Numerical change in employment, 1992-2005	Employment prospects
Carpenters	990,000	20	197,000	tures. The demand for carpenters will be offset somewhat by expected productivity gains resulting from the increased use of prefabricated components and better tools. Employment opportunities should be plentiful.
Carpet installers	62,000	22	13,000	Average employment growth is expected in response to the continuing need to renovate and refurbish existing structures and growing demand for carpet in new industrial plants, schools, hospitals, and other structures.
Concrete masons and terrazzo workers	100,000	13	13,000	Despite strong demand for concrete and terrazzo, productivity gains from improved materials, equipment, and tools will result in slower than average growth.
Drywall workers and lathers	121,000	37	44,000	Faster than average employment growth is expected as the level of new construction and renovation increases. Many job opportunities will be available because of replacement needs.
Electricians	518,000	19	100,000	Average employment growth will stem from the need to install and maintain electrical devices and wiring in homes, factories, offices, and other structures. Installation of the wiring for computers, telecommunications equipment, and other advanced technologies should also create job opportunities for electricians
Glaziers	39,000	30	12,000	Faster than average employment growth is expected due to the increase in new construction, the need to modernize and repair existing structures, and the increased popularity of glass as a building material.
Insulation workers	57,000	40	22,000	Employment is expected to grow faster than average, reflecting the demand for insulation for new construction and renovation, as well as the demand for asbestos removal in existing structures. Job opportunities should be plentiful because growth will be rapid and turnover is the highest of all construction occupations.
Painters and paperhangers	440,000	29	128,000	Faster than average employment growth is expected as construction activity increases and the number of buildings in need of repainting grows. Job prospects should be quite favorable.
Plasterers	32,000	16	5,200	Employment is expected to grow as fast as average due to growing appreciation for the durability and attractiveness of troweled finishes and the need to repair plaster surfaces in older buildings.
Plumbers and pipefitters	351,000	8	27,000	Slower than average employment growth will result from rising productivity because the growing use of plastic pipe and fittings, more efficient sprinkler systems, and other labor-saving technologies will offset much of the increasing demand for plumbing services.
Roofers	127,000	22	28,000	Average employment growth is expected due to increases in new construction and the need to repair or replace roofs on existing, buildings. Employment will not keep pace with

CLUSTER Subgroup Occupation	Estimated employment, 1992	Percent change in employment, 1992-2005	Numerical change in employment, 1992-2005	Employment prospects
Roofers	127,000	22	28,000	demand because of productivity increases brought about by advances in materials, technology, and tools. Because of high turnover, employment opportunities are expected to be plentiful.
Roustabouts	33,000	-33	-11,000	Employment is expected to decline as a result of reduced exploration and falling production in the domestic oil industry. Opportunities will be very limited.
Sheet-metal workers	91,000	37	34,000	Employment is expected to grow faster than average as more factories, shopping malls, homes, and other structures using sheet metal are built. Additional job opportunities will be created as more efficient air-conditioning and heating systems are installed in existing buildings.
Structural and reinforcing ironworkers	66,000	22	15,000	Average employment growth is expected due to the rising levels of industrial and commercial construction, as well as the rehabilitation and maintenance of an increasing number of older buildings, factories, power plants, highways, and bridges. Job openings for ironworkers are usually more abundant during the spring and summer, when construction activity increases.
Tilesetters	30,000	25	7,400	Rising levels of construction activity and the increased popularity of tile as a building material should ensure average employment growth. Job opportunities will not be as plentiful as in other construction occupations because the occupation is small and turnover is relatively low.

PRODUCTION OCCUPATIONS

Assemblers

CLUSTER Subgroup Occupation	Estimated employment, 1992	Percent change in employment, 1992-2005	Numerical change in employment, 1992-2005	Employment prospects
Precision assemblers	334,000	-6	-18,000	Employment is expected to decline, with increasing automation offsetting any increase in employment that would have occurred due to industrial growth. However, opportunities depend on the industries in which the jobs are located. For instance, keen competition **is** expected for assembly jobs in the aerospace and electronics manufacturing industry. Other industries may provide more opportunities.
Blue-collar worker supervisors	1,757,000	12	217,000	Overall employment is expected to increase more slowly than average. Job creation varies by industry, with employment expected to decline slightly in manufacturing and increase in construction and most other nonmanufacturing industries.

Food Processing Occupations

CLUSTER Subgroup Occupation	Estimated employment, 1992	Percent change in employment, 1992-2005	Numerical change in employment, 1992-2005	Employment prospects
Butchers and meat, poultry, and fish cutters	349,000	3	11,000	Employment is expected to increase more slowly than average as meat cutting and processing shift from the store to the factory. Although consumption of meat, poultry, and fish will continue to increase, growth of lesser skilled factory machine cutter jobs will just barely offset the decline of skilled retail meatcutters.

CLUSTER Subgroup Occupation	Estimated employment, 1992	Percent change in employment, 1992-2005	Numerical change in employment, 1992-2005	Employment prospects
Inspectors, testers, and graders	625,000	-10	-65,000	Employment is expected to decline. Manufacturers are increasingly using automated inspection systems and assigning inspection, testing, and grading duties to production workers. There may be competition for job openings.

Metalworking and Plastics-Working Occupations

CLUSTER Subgroup Occupation	Estimated employment, 1992	Percent change in employment, 1992-2005	Numerical change in employment, 1992-2005	Employment prospects
Boilermakers	26,000	-4	-1,100	Employment is expected to decline due to the trend toward repairing rather than replacing old boilers, the use of smaller boilers requiring less on-site assembly, the automation of production technologies, and the increased use of imported boilers. There may be competition for job openings.
Jewelers	30,000	19	5,700	Average growth is expected. Job opportunities for jewelers depend largely on jewelry sales and on demand for jewelry repair services. Jewelry sales are expected to remain strong. Opportunities should be good for graduates from jeweler training programs. The outlook will be best in jewelry stores and repair shops; competition is expected for jobs in jewelry manufacturing.
Machinists and tool programmers	359,000	-1	-3,400	Employment is expected to decline slightly. Nevertheless, job opportunities will be good because, in recent years, employers have reported difficulties in attracting workers to machining and tool programming occupations.
Metalworking and plastics-working machine operators	1,378,000	-3	-43,000	Overall employment is expected to decline, although machine operators in the plastics industry should fare better than their machine operators counterparts in metalworking. Increasing productivity from automation and growing international competition are combining to dampen the demand for machine operators. Workers able to operate a variety of machines, particularly computer controlled equipment, have the brightest prospects.
Tool and die makers	138,000	-7	-9,400	Employment is expected to decline because of increased automation and imports of finished goods. However, jobseekers with appropriate skills should find excellent opportunities because the number of tool and die makers receiving training is not expected to be, as great as the number of retiring tool and die makers.
Welders, cutters, and welding machine operators	403,000	7	30,000	With automated welding systems taking the place of some workers, employment is expected to increase more slowly than average. Manual welders, especially those with a wide variety of skills, still will be needed for maintenance, repair, and other work that cannot be automated.

Plant and Systems Operators

CLUSTER Subgroup Occupation	Estimated employment, 1992	Percent change in employment, 1992-2005	Numerical change in employment, 1992-2005	Employment prospects
Electric power generating plant operators and power distributors and dispatchers	43,000	10	4,200	Employment is expected to grow more slowly than average. Construction of power plant capacity is expected to be moderate because of overbuilding in the past. The increasing use of automatic controls and more efficient equipment should further offset the need for new plant construction. Keen competition is expected for jobs.

CLUSTER Subgroup Occupation	Estimated employment, 1992	Percent change in employment, 1992-2005	Numerical change in employment, 1992-2005	Employment prospects
Stationary engineers	31,000	5	1,600	Employment is expected to grow more slowly than average as automated and computerized equipment limits the number of engineers needed. Job opportunities will be best for those with apprenticeship training or vocational school courses in computerized controls and instrumentation.
Water and wastewater treatment plant operators	86,000	18	16,000	Employment is expected to grow as fast as average as population and economic growth spur the construction of new plants and the expansion of existing water and wastewater treatment services. Job opportunities should be good.

Printing Occupations

CLUSTER Subgroup Occupation	Estimated employment, 1992	Percent change in employment, 1992-2005	Numerical change in employment, 1992-2005	Employment prospects
Prepress workers	167,000	13	22,000	Employment is expected to increase more slowly than average. The increased use of computers in typesetting and page layout should restrain job growth despite rising demand for printed materials.
Printing press operators	241,000	20	47,000	Job growth is expected to be about as fast as average as needs for printed materials grow. Employment of offset, gravure, and flexographic press operators will grow, while letterpress operator jobs will decline.
Bindery workers	76,000	16	12,000	Employment is expected to increase about as fast as average in response to the growing volume of printed materials that must be bound. Needs for lesser skilled workers will decline as bookbinding machinery becomes more efficient and complex.

Textile, Apparel, and Furnishings Occupations

CLUSTER Subgroup Occupation	Estimated employment, 1992	Percent change in employment, 1992-2005	Numerical change in employment, 1992-2005	Employment prospects
Apparel workers	986,000	-19	-183,000	Employment is expected to decline due to increases in imports, offshore assembly, and automation. However, replacement needs will result in some job openings.
Shoe and leather workers and repairers	22,000	-20	-4,300	Employment is expected to decline, primarily because inexpensive imports have made shoe replacement a reasonable alternative to shoe repair for many.
Textile machinery operators	284,000	-17	-47,000	Employment declines are expected as a result of greater use of automated machinery and changing business practices. However, there will still be job opportunities stemming from the need to replace workers who leave their jobs.
Upholsterers	60,000	11	6,700	Employment is expected to increase more slowly than average as growth in jobs in furniture manufacturing is offset somewhat by declining employment in reupholstery shops. Opportunities for skilled upholsterers should be good.
Woodworking occupations	341,000	8	28,000	Employment is expected to grow more slowly than average, largely reflecting increasing productivity due to technological advances and stiffer international competition. Opportunities should be favorable for woodworkers who specialize in moldings, cabinets, stairs, and windows.

CLUSTER Subgroup Occupation	Estimated employment, 1992	Percent change in employment, 1992-2005	Numerical change in employment, 1992-2005	Employment prospects
Miscellaneous Production Occupations				
Dental laboratory technicians	48,000	3	1,500	Little change in employment is expected. The fluoridation of drinking water and greater emphasis on preventive dental care since the early 1960s have improved the overall dental health of the population. Instead of full or partial dentures, most people will need only a bridge or crown.
Ophthalmic laboratory technicians	19,000	22	4,100	Average growth is expected in response to rising demand for corrective lenses and fashionable glasses.
Painting and coating machine operators	151,000	1	1,800	Little change in overall employment is expected as technological improvements raise productivity. Employment of painting and coating machine operators should fall slightly in manufacturing, due to the expanding use of industrial robots, and increase modestly in nonmanufacturing industries.
Photographic process workers	63,000	20	13,000	Average growth will stem from the increasing volume of film to be processed, as long as film remains the mainstay of photographic processing. Digital cameras have the potential to displace photographic process machine operators but are not likely to affect demand for precision photographic process workers.
TRANSPORTATION AND MATERIAL MOVING OCCUPATIONS				
Busdrivers	562,000	21	119,000	Overall employment is expected to grow about as fast as average. Job opportunities will be best for school busdrivers due to increased enrollments. Local and intercity busdriving jobs that offer the best working conditions and the highest earnings are expected to attract the most competition.
Material moving equipment operators	983,000	13	129,000	Employment is expected to grow more slowly than average. Equipment improvements, including the growing automation of material handling in factories and warehouses, are expected to restrain the growth of this occupation. However, many job opportunities will arise from the need to replace the many experienced workers who leave this large occupation each year.
Rail transportation workers	116,000	21	25,000	Overall employment is expected to grow about as fast as average as an increase in freight shipped by railroad is offset by more efficient operations and laborsaving innovations. Employment of subway and streetcar operators should grow much faster than average due to the rapid expansion of urban rail systems.
Taxidrivers and chauffeurs	120,000	18	22,000	Employment is expected to grow about as fast as average as local and urban travel increases. Competition is expected for jobs that offer the highest earnings or best working conditions.

CLUSTER Subgroup Occupation	Estimated employment, 1992	Percent change in employment, 1992-2005	Numerical change in employment, 1992-2005	Employment prospects
Truckdrivers	2,720,000	26	708,000 ★	Employment is expected to grow about as fast as average. Job opportunities in this large occupation should be plentiful because of the growing demand for truck transportation services and the need to replace drivers who leave the occupation. However, competition is expected for jobs that offer the highest earnings or best working conditions.
Water transportation occupations	54,000	-5	-2,500	Employment is expected to decline due to foreign competition and technological innovations that allow fewer workers to operate a vessel.
HANDLERS, EQUIPMENT CLEANERS, HELPERS, AND LABORERS	4,451,000	17	776,000	Average growth is expected overall, reflecting growth of the industries that employ these workers and rising employment of the skilled workers whom they assist. Projected growth varies widely by occupation. While the employment of service station attendants will decline, that of parking lot attendants will grow faster than average. Overall job openings should be numerous because this occupational group is very large and turnover is relatively high.
THE ARMED FORCES	1,808,000[14]	-14	-254,000	Diminishing threats to U.S. security have led to reductions in military forces. Further reductions are planned through 1997, after which the level of military forces should remain relatively constant. In spite of this, job opportunities should be good in all branches of the Armed Forces because people of prime recruiting age will account for a smaller share of the total population than in the past. Opportunities for enlisted personnel are very limited for those without a high school diploma. Competition for officer positions has always been keen and will continue to be so.

[1] *Includes wage and salary employment only.*
[2] *Total exceeds the sum of the individual estimates because not all branches are covered separately.*
[3] *Less than 500.*
[4] *Estimates not available*
[5] *Includes only those who served congregations.*
[6] *Estimates not available.*
[7] *Less than 1.*
[8] *Less than 1.*
[9] *Less than 500.*
[10] *Less than 1.*
[11] *Less than 500.*
[12] *Less than 1.*
[13] *Less than 500.*
[14] *Source: U.S. Department of Defense.*

Employment Projections, Earnings, and Education Required for the 500 Largest Occupations

Appendix B

Editor's Comments:

When considering various career or job options, most people want to know some basic information such as, "How much will this job pay?" or "What are the future opportunities in this career?"

While there is more to consider in making a career choice than the answers to these questions, much of the basic information people ask about when making career decisions has been assembled in this appendix.

This is a very long appendix and I really don't expect you to *read* it. The information it presents on each job spreads across two pages and includes details many people want to know when considering career alternatives. One way to use it is to locate clusters of jobs that interest you and look at the jobs within those categories or clusters. You may find jobs that you want to learn more about that you had not previously considered. Make note of those jobs. If descriptions of them are not included in this book, you should find them (or similar jobs) described in the current edition of the *Occupational Outlook Handbook* or in *America's Top 300 Jobs* available at most libraries or bookstores.

Note that one of the columns indicates the source of training most often required for each job. Appendix C organizes jobs into groupings based on training required and allows you to quickly identify jobs within occupational groupings and education or training requirements.

The information in this appendix comes from the U.S. Department of Labor's Bulletin 2451, *Occupational Projections and Training Data*, and I have included the introductory material as it appears in the original publication.

Chapter I. Selected Occupational Data, 1992 and Projected 2005

Several years ago BLS recognized that the statistical measures used to present occupational information often are difficult to interpret. Consequently, the Bureau initiated changes designed to help users determine whether data depicted favorable or unfavorable circumstances. This technique was adopted with the 1988 edition of *Occupational Projections and Training Data (OPTD)* and continued through the 1992 edition. It presented tables containing rankings among occupations of characteristics that are most often compared when looking for career information: Projections of numeric and percentage changes in employment, the number of openings due to growth and replacement needs, unemployment rates, median earnings, and the proportion of part-time employees.

Tables in the 1988 through 1992 publications that used alphabetic designations to present rankings of occupational data did facilitate data comparisons, but were not without limitations. Occupational coverage was incomplete—only about two-fifths of the detailed occupations in the national industry-occupation matrix that could be matched with CPS data were included. Also, the rankings and data about all industry-occupation matrix occupations appeared in separate tables, thus requiring users to search a second location to get comparative information. Finally, the ranking tables and the data table contained different categories of information and caused confusion. For example, significant sources of formal training were identified only in the ranking tables.

Table 1 overcomes the limitations of previous efforts to facilitate data comparisons. Current and projected employment, employment change, and self-employment data are presented for all national industry-occupation matrix occupations. For most categories, rankings are presented that designate the relative magnitude of data for each detailed occupation. Rankings that provide relative information about worker characteristics based on Current Population Survey data appear for all occupations, but specific data are not presented because of concerns about the comparability of data from the OES and CPS surveys. In addition, table 1 identifies significant sources of work related and postsecondary school training for all detailed occupations.

Data sources

Table 1 presents information from two sources: 1) the National Industry-Occupation Matrix and 2) the Current Population Survey. The industry-occupation matrix is predominantly based on data about wage and salary occupational employment collected from establishments as part of the Occupational Employment Statistics surveys. This survey counts jobs. Individuals who hold more than one job are counted at each place they work. The CPS is a monthly survey of about 60,000 households that obtains demographic and labor force information about individuals. Employment information from the CPS counts individuals, not jobs. To develop total employment estimates, data on self-employed and unpaid family workers are derived from the CPS and combined with OES data on wage and salary employment.

Occupational data in the industry-occupation matrix are not strictly comparable with those in the CPS because of differences in occupational classification systems and differences in concepts and methods used in the surveys. Information about worker characteristics that is based on CPS data is applied to industry-occupation matrix occupations based on judgments identifying the most comparable CPS occupations. Comparisons based on CPS occupations with fewer than 50,000 workers in 1992 and some other occupations for which the data appeared unreliable were excluded; data for CPS proxy occupations were substituted. Where possible, larger, closely related

CPS occupations were chosen as proxies. For example, data for purchasing agents and buyers, n.e.c., were used to represent purchasing agents and buyers, farm products. When no detailed occupation could be identified, a summary occupation group was used. For example, data about all therapists was substituted for that of inhalation therapists.

Data presented

The source of the data for each variable and a brief discussion of its potential use is presented below. For most data categories rankings are presented that identify the relative magnitude of variables in terms of the distribution of employment. For example, 1992 employment and projected 1992-2005 percent change in employment data were assembled for each occupation. Each occupation's employment as a percent of 1992 total employment was calculated. The occupations were sorted by employment change in descending order and the cumulative percent of 1992 employment for each was determined. Occupations within the group comprising less than 25 percent of total employment are designated VH for a Very High (VH) growth rate. Similarly, occupations sorted by descending order of employment change comprising 25-50 percent of employment receive the designation H for High; 50-75 percent, L for Low; and 75-100 percent, VL for Very Low. Occupations were sorted by other data elements and rankings determined in the same manner.

Employment, 1992 and 2005. (Source: Bureau of Labor Statistics, national industry-occupation matrices for 1992 and 2005.) Employment information is a useful starting point for assessing opportunities because large occupations generally have more openings than small ones regardless of growth or replacement rates.

Employment change, 1992-2005, numeric. (Source: Bureau of Labor Statistics, national industry-occupation matrices for 1992 and 2005.) Information on numerical change provides an absolute measure of projected job gains or losses.

Employment change, 1992-2005, percent. (Source: Bureau of Labor Statistics, national industry-occupation matrices for 1992 and 2005.) The percent change in employment measures the rate of change. When an occupation grows rapidly, this usually indicates favorable prospects for employment. Moreover, the strong demand for workers in a rapidly growing occupation improves chances for advancement and mobility. A modest percentage increase in employment growth can result in many more job openings in a large occupation than in a small occupation that is growing rapidly.

Percent self-employed. (Source: Bureau of Labor Statistics, national industry-occupation matrices for 1992 and 2005.) Knowledge of the percentage of workers who work for themselves may be important to individuals who are interested in creating and managing their own business.

Job openings due to growth plus total replacement needs. (Source: Bureau of Labor Statistics, this publication.) Growth is calculated from national industry-occupation matrices for 1992-2005. Total replacement needs are calculated from 1990-91 CPS data and are described in the 1992 edition of this publication. Data from CPS proxy occupations are used to estimate replacement needs for some matrix occupations. These data provide the broadest measure of opportunities and identify the total number of employees needed annually to enter an occupation.

Job openings due to growth plus net replacement needs. (Source: Bureau of Labor Statistics, this publication.) Growth is calculated from national industry-occupation matrices for 1992-2005. Net replacement needs are calculated from CPS data and are described in the 1992 edition of this publication but have been revised to include

1986-91 and 1987-92 information in making the estimates. Data from CPS proxy occupations are used to estimate replacement needs for some matrix occupations. These data estimate the number of new entrants needed annually for an occupation and, if training is required, measure minimum training needs.

Weekly earnings. (Source: 1992 Current Population Survey, annual average data for wage and salary employees who usually worked full time.) Median earnings of full-time workers are used to compare earnings among occupations. Data from CPS proxy occupations are used to estimate earnings for some matrix occupations.

Unemployment rate. (Source: 1988-92 Current Population Survey annual average data.) Some occupations are more susceptible to the factors that result in unemployment: Seasonality, fluctuations in economic conditions, and individual business failures. A high unemployment rate indicates that individuals in that occupation are more likely to become unemployed than those in one with a low rate. The average unemployment rate over the 1988-92 period was used to reduce sampling variations for small occupations and to reduce the influence of economic fluctuations. Data from CPS proxy occupations are used to estimate unemployment rates for some matrix occupations.

Part-time. (Source: 1992 Current Population Survey, annual average data.) Knowledge of the proportion of workers who work fewer than 35 hours per week may be important to individuals who prefer part-time work so that they can manage other responsibilities, such as attending school or taking care of a family. Data from CPS proxy occupations are used to estimate the proportion of part-time workers for some matrix occupations.

Significant sources of training. (Source: Bureau of Labor Statistics, this publication.) Many jobs require workers to have specialized skills or training beyond that generally acquired in high school. Sources of training vary and in many occupations individuals acquire skills from more than one source. Significant sources of the education or training needed to prepare for each detailed occupation beyond any obtained in secondary schools are shown and the *most significant* is identified by the entry "MS". Other *significant* sources are identified by an "S". An asterisk indicates the source was not significant. For many occupations, no work related or postsecondary school training was significant.

Three postsecondary training categories are identified: Work related; some postsecondary school; and bachelor's degree or higher. Definitions for the categories are:
• *Work related.* Training that results in specialized job skills or knowledge that employees must possess. Such skills may be acquired in a formal employer program with scheduled hours of attendance or an established curriculum, from extensive work experience, as well as from hobbies or other activities that are independent of current or past employment activities.
• *Some postsecondary school.* This category includes training acquired in vocational programs offered through publicly or privately supported postsecondary schools, as well as 1- or 2-year academic or job oriented technical training courses in community colleges or technical institutes. Excluded is postsecondary school training that is part of 4-year college degree programs. Two-year programs generally lead to an associate's degree. One-year programs generally lead to a certificate of completion. Vocational programs generally do not provide college credits.
• *Bachelor's degree or higher.* Training obtained in a program leading to a bachelor's degree or higher.

The level of significance, "MS" for "Most significant" or "S" for "Significant," was designated by staff in the Bureau's Office of Employment Projections. They based their judgment on sources of train-

ing that individuals reported they needed to get their current job.[1] Their judgments were also based on research done while preparing the *Occupational Outlook Handbook.*

Using ranked information

Table 1 consolidates 1992 and 2005 projected employment data and for that reason alone is a convenient reference. Table 1 greatly facilitates comparisons of occupational data. It contains rankings of information about current and projected employment, projected job openings, earnings, unemployment rates, and the proportion of workers on part-time schedules. Except for the unemployment and part-time categories, a high rating should be interpreted as indicating a favorable assessment. A high rating for the unemployment rate is considered undesirable. Unemployment rates in construction occupations, however, are inflated by the nature of the industry and distort comparisons. Individuals in these occupations typically incur periods of unemployment after completing a project and before starting work at a new job site.

The rating for the part-time category also should not be used routinely in assessing the desirability of employment because it can be interpreted differently depending on the perspective of the user. For example, high school students may consider a large proportion of part-time workers desirable because they normally prefer not to work full time. A recent college graduate or anyone seeking full-time employment may reach the opposite conclusion.

The information presented in table 1 has many potential uses because interests in occupational information are so varied. At times, users may want to know how a particular occupation of interest, cashiers, for example, compares with others. As shown in the index, information about cashiers begins on page 12. The "VH" (very high) rankings in table 1 for the increase in the number of jobs and for both categories of jobs openings, point out that many jobs are available, certainly a favorable situation. The "VL" (very low) ranking for earnings and "VH" (very high) for unemployment, however, are unfavorable in comparison with other occupations, and these characteristics detract from the desirability of employment in the occupation. Table 1 also shows that specialized trianing is not required.

Users may wish to identify occupations with favorable characteristics that job seekers can pursue through a specific type of training. For example, a student may be interested in a scientific or engineering occupation but does not care to obtain a 4-year college degree. In another instance a planner may wish to ensure that training programs provided by junior colleges in the area are consistent with the needs of the national labor market. In this case, the planner could examine information for occupations having some postsecondary school training identified as the most significant. Users seeking to identify occupations within training categories may use tables 2-5 in chapter II which list the occupations in each training category and highlights those occupations with above average earnings. Occupations in tables 2-5 are presented in alphabetical order within the major occupational groups.

Although table 1 contains a great deal of information useful for career guidance, information about occupational comparisons should be used as an aid, not an end. After using the table to identify occupations with favorable prospects, additional information should be obtained from other sources such as the *Occupational Outlook Handbook* and local sources, if available. Consideration should be given to individual aptitudes and preferences, and alternative sources of training available in the local area should be investigated.

---

[1]Sources of training needed by individuals to qualify for their current job is reported in *How Workers Get Their Training: A 1991 Update,* Bulletin 2407 (Bureau of Labor Statistics, August 1992), table A-1, pp. 53-59

Table 1. Occupational employment and job openings data, 1992-2005, and worker characteristics, 1992

(Numbers in thousands)

1992 Matrix Occupation	Employment		Employment change, 1992-2005				Per-cent self-empl-oyed, 1992	Annual average job openings due to growth and total replacement needs, 1992-2005	
			Numeric		Percent				
	1992	2005	Number	Rank	Number	Rank		Number	Rank
Total, all occupations	121,099	147,482	26,383	-	21.8	-	8.3	24,423	-
Executive, administrative, and managerial occupations	12,066	15,195	3,129	-	25.9	-	11.6	1,376	-
Managerial and administrative occupations	8,411	10,427	2,016	-	24.0	-	13.2	860	-
Administrative services managers	226	256	30	VL	13.1	L	0.0	20	VL
Communication, transportation, and utilities operations managers	144	158	14	VL	10.0	VL	0.0	12	VL
Construction managers	180	265	85	L	47.0	VH	1.1	23	VL
Education administrators	351	432	81	L	23.2	H	8.8	37	VL
Engineering, mathematical, and natural science managers	337	444	106	L	31.5	H	0.0	38	VL
Financial managers	701	875	174	H	24.8	H	1.1	66	L
Food service and lodging managers	532	764	232	H	43.5	VH	36.3	67	L
Funeral directors and morticians	27	32	5	VL	17.6	L	18.7	3	VL
General managers and top executives	2,871	3,251	380	H	13.2	L	0.0	259	H
Government chief executives and legislators	73	76	2	VL	3.1	VL	0.0	4	VL
Industrial production managers	203	208	5	VL	2.4	VL	0.0	16	VL
Marketing, advertising, and public relations managers	432	588	156	L	36.1	VH	1.6	56	L
Personnel, training, and labor relations managers	193	241	48	L	25.2	H	0.5	20	VL
Property and real estate managers	243	328	85	L	35.0	VH	37.0	33	VL
Purchasing managers	221	252	31	VL	13.9	L	0.0	13	VL
All other managers and administrators	1,676	2,258	582	VH	34.7	VH	46.1	194	H
Management support occupations	3,654	4,767	1,113	-	30.5	-	7.8	516	-
Accountants and auditors	939	1,243	304	H	32.3	H	10.8	138	L
Budget analysts	67	81	13	VL	20.1	L	0.0	9	VL
Claims examiners, property and casualty insurance ...	33	42	9	VL	26.1	H	0.0	5	VL
Construction and building inspectors	66	86	20	VL	29.8	H	3.0	6	VL
Cost estimators	163	211	49	L	29.8	H	0.0	24	VL
Credit analysts	33	35	1	VL	3.7	VL	0.0	4	VL
Employment interviewers, private or public employment service	79	96	17	VL	21.8	H	0.0	9	VL
Inspectors and compliance officers, except construction	155	196	42	L	27.0	H	1.9	14	VL
Loan officers and counselors	171	239	68	L	40.0	VH	0.0	27	VL
Management analysts	208	297	89	L	42.7	VH	40.8	43	L
Personnel, training, and labor relations specialists	281	383	102	L	36.1	VH	3.2	37	VL
Purchasing agents, except wholesale, retail, and farm products	222	216	-6	VL	-2.7	VL	2.3	20	VL
Tax examiners, collectors, and revenue agents	64	75	10	VL	16.2	L	0.0	5	VL
Underwriters	100	124	24	VL	24.1	H	0.0	14	VL
Wholesale and retail buyers, except farm products	180	204	24	VL	13.3	L	12.8	26	VL
All other management support workers	892	1,240	348	H	39.0	VH	6.4	136	L
Professional specialty occupations	16,592	22,801	6,209	-	37.4	-	9.2	2,290	-
Engineers	1,354	1,660	306	-	22.6	-	2.1	83	-
Aeronautical and astronautical engineers	66	75	9	VL	14.1	L	0.0	5	VL
Chemical engineers	52	62	10	VL	19.4	L	1.9	2	VL

NOTE: Rankings are based on all detailed occupations in the National Industry-Occupation Matrix. Codes for desrcribing the ranked variables are: VH = Very high, H = High, L = Low, VL = Very low. Codes used to identify sources of training are: MS = Most significant, S = Significant, * = not significant. A dash indicates data are not applicable.

Table 1. Occupational employment and job openings data, 1992-2005, and worker characteristics, 1992

(Numbers in thousands)

Annual average job openings due to growth and net replacement needs, 1992-2005		Ranking of selected occupational characteristics			Significant sources of training			1992 Matrix Occupation
Number	Rank	Weekly earnings	Unemployment rate	Part-time	Work related	Some secondary school	Bachelor's degree or higher	
4,667	-	-	-	-	-	-	-	**Total, all occupations**
440	-	-	-	-	-	-	-	**Executive, administrative, and managerial occupations**
297	-	-	-	-	-	-	-	Managerial and administrative occupations
6	VL	VH	VL	VL	*	*	MS	Administrative services managers
3	VL	VH	VL	VL	*	*	MS	Communication, transportation, and utilities operations managers
9	L	VH	VL	VL	MS	*	S	Construction managers
15	L	VH	VL	L	*	*	MS	Education administrators
14	L	VH	VL	VL	*	*	MS	Engineering, mathematical, and natural science managers
24	L	VH	L	VL	*	*	MS	Financial managers
26	L	H	VL	L	MS	*	S	Food service and lodging managers
1	VL	VH	VL	VL	*	MS	*	Funeral directors and morticians
75	VH	VH	VL	VL	*	*	MS	General managers and top executives
2	VL	VH	VL	VL	*	*	MS	Government chief executives and legislators
4	VL	VH	VL	VL	S	*	MS	Industrial production managers
20	L	VH	L	VL	*	*	MS	Marketing, advertising, and public relations managers
9	VL	VH	VL	VL	*	*	MS	Personnel, training, and labor relations managers
10	L	H	VL	H	S	*	MS	Property and real estate managers
7	VL	VH	VL	VL	S	*	MS	Purchasing managers
72	VH	VH	VL	VL	*	*	MS	All other managers and administrators
143	-	-	-	-	-	-	-	Management support occupations
37	H	VH	VL	L	*	*	MS	Accountants and auditors
2	VL	VH	VL	VL	*	*	MS	Budget analysts
1	VL	H	VL	VL	MS	*	S	Claims examiners, property and casualty insurance
3	VL	VH	VL	VL	MS	S	*	Construction and building inspectors
6	VL	H	L	L	MS	*	S	Cost estimators
1	VL	VH	VL	VL	*	*	MS	Credit analysts
3	VL	VH	L	L	*	*	MS	Employment interviewers, private or public employment service
6	VL	VH	VL	VL	S	*	MS	Inspectors and compliance officers, except construction
8	VL	VH	VL	VL	*	*	MS	Loan officers and counselors
9	L	VH	VL	H	*	*	MS	Management analysts
12	L	VH	L	L	*	*	MS	Personnel, training, and labor relations specialists
4	VL	H	L	VL	S	*	MS	Purchasing agents, except wholesale, retail, and farm products
2	VL	VH	VL	VL	*	*	MS	Tax examiners, collectors, and revenue agents
4	VL	VH	VL	L	S	*	MS	Underwriters
7	VL	H	L	L	*	*	*	Wholesale and retail buyers, except farm products
41	H	VH	VL	L	*	*	MS	All other management support workers
753	-	-	-	-	-	-	-	**Professional specialty occupations**
52	-	-	-	-	-	-	-	Engineers
2	VL	VH	VL	VL	*	*	MS	Aeronautical and astronautical engineers
2	VL	VH	VL	VL	*	*	MS	Chemical engineers

NOTE: Rankings are based on all detailed occupations in the National Industry-Occupation Matrix. Codes for desrcribing the ranked variables are: VH = Very high, H = High, L = Low, VL = Very low. Codes used to identify sources of training are: MS = Most significant, S = Significant, * = not significant. A dash indicates data are not applicable.

Table 1. Occupational employment and job openings data, 1992-2005, and worker characteristics, 1992 — Continued

(Numbers in thousands)

1992 Matrix Occupation	Employment		Employment change, 1992-2005				Per-cent self-empl-oyed, 1992	Annual average job openings due to growth and total replacement needs, 1992-2005	
			Numeric		Percent				
	1992	2005	Number	Rank	Number	Rank		Number	Rank
Civil engineers, including traffic engineers	173	214	41	L	23.6	H	2.9	15	VL
Electrical and electronics engineers	370	459	90	L	24.2	H	1.6	21	VL
Industrial engineers, except safety engineers	119	138	20	VL	16.8	L	0.8	5	VL
Mechanical engineers	227	273	46	L	20.3	L	2.2	14	VL
Metallurgists and metallurgical, ceramic, and materials engineers	19	24	5	VL	28.3	H	0.0	1	VL
Mining engineers, including mine safety engineers	4	4	0	VL	3.1	VL	0.0	0	VL
Nuclear engineers	17	17	0	VL	0.5	VL	0.0	1	VL
Petroleum engineers	14	14	0	VL	-2.4	VL	7.0	1	VL
All other engineers	295	380	85	L	29.0	H	3.4	20	VL
Architects and surveyors	214	257	43	-	20.2	-	21.0	27	-
Architects, except landscape and marine	96	121	25	VL	26.3	H	33.5	12	VL
Landscape architects	19	24	5	VL	26.3	H	15.8	2	VL
Surveyors	99	112	13	VL	13.2	L	10.1	12	VL
Life scientists	182	222	40	-	21.9	-	6.6	14	-
Agricultural and food scientists	29	33	4	VL	14.4	L	17.3	2	VL
Biological scientists	78	97	19	VL	25.0	H	2.6	6	VL
Foresters and conservation scientists	35	40	4	VL	12.2	VL	2.8	2	VL
Medical scientists	39	51	12	VL	30.8	H	10.3	3	VL
All other life scientists	1	2	0	VL	7.8	VL	0.0	0	VL
Computer, mathematical, and operations research occupations	758	1,530	772	-	101.8	-	4.4	135	-
Actuaries	15	19	4	VL	29.4	H	0.0	1	VL
Computer systems analysts, engineers, and scientists	666	1,403	737	-	110.7	-	4.8	125	-
Computer engineers and scientists	211	447	236	H	111.9	VH	3.8	40	L
Systems analysts	455	956	501	VH	110.1	VH	5.3	85	L
Statisticians	16	18	2	VL	9.3	VL	0.0	1	VL
Mathematicians and all other mathematical scientists	16	18	1	VL	7.6	VL	0.0	1	VL
Operations research analysts	45	72	27	VL	61.4	VH	2.2	6	VL
Physical scientists	197	243	45	-	22.9	-	3.0	17	-
Chemists	92	112	20	VL	21.2	L	0.0	10	VL
Geologists, geophysicists, and oceanographers	48	59	11	VL	22.2	H	10.4	2	VL
Meteorologists	6	8	1	VL	24.4	H	0.0	1	VL
Physicists and astronomers	21	20	-1	VL	-3.2	VL	0.0	1	VL
All other physical scientists	30	45	14	VL	46.2	VH	3.3	3	VL
Social scientists	258	353	95	-	37.0	-	32.6	34	-
Economists	51	64	13	VL	25.3	H	27.3	12	VL
Psychologists	143	212	69	L	48.0	VH	46.7	14	VL
Urban and regional planners	28	34	6	VL	23.2	H	0.0	4	VL
All other social scientists	35	42	7	VL	20.3	L	8.5	4	VL
Social, recreational, and religious workers	1,130	1,731	601	-	53.2	-	3.8	174	-
Clergy	189	245	56	L	29.8	H	16.9	16	VL
Directors, religious activities and education	64	83	19	VL	29.9	H	1.6	9	VL
Human services workers	189	445	256	H	135.9	VH	0.0	51	L
Recreation workers	204	282	78	L	38.1	VH	0.0	32	VL

NOTE: Rankings are based on all detailed occupations in the National Industry-Occupation Matrix. Codes for desrcribing the ranked variables are: VH = Very high, H = High, L = Low, VL = Very low. Codes used to identify sources of training are: MS = Most significant, S = Significant, * = not significant. A dash indicates data are not applicable.

Table 1. Occupational employment and job openings data, 1992-2005, and worker characteristics, 1992 — Continued

(Numbers in thousands)

Annual average job openings due to growth and net replacement needs, 1992-2005		Ranking of selected occupational characteristics			Significant sources of training			1992 Matrix Occupation
Number	Rank	Weekly earnings	Unemployment rate	Part-time	Work related	Some secondary school	Bachelor's degree or higher	
7	VL	VH	VL	VL	*	*	MS	Civil engineers, including traffic engineers
15	L	VH	VL	VL	*	*	MS	Electrical and electronics engineers
5	VL	VH	L	VL	*	*	MS	Industrial engineers, except safety engineers
8	VL	VH	VL	VL	*	*	MS	Mechanical engineers
1	VL	VH	VL	VL	*	*	MS	Metallurgists and metallurgical, ceramic, and materials engineers
0	VL	VH	VL	VL	*	*	MS	Mining engineers, including mine safety engineers
0	VL	VH	VL	VL	*	*	MS	Nuclear engineers
0	VL	VH	VL	VL	*	*	MS	Petroleum engineers
11	L	VH	VL	VL	*	*	MS	All other engineers
7	-	-	-	-	-	-	-	Architects and surveyors
3	VL	VH	L	L	*	*	MS	Architects, except landscape and marine
1	VL	VH	L	L	*	*	MS	Landscape architects
3	VL	H	H	L	*	MS	S	Surveyors
8	-	-	-	-	-	-	-	Life scientists
1	VL	VH	VL	VL	*	*	MS	Agricultural and food scientists
4	VL	VH	VL	VL	*	*	MS	Biological scientists
1	VL	VH	VL	VL	*	*	MS	Foresters and conservation scientists
2	VL	VH	VL	VL	*	*	MS	Medical scientists
0	VL	VH	VL	VL	*	*	MS	All other life scientists
65	-	-	-	-	-	-	-	Computer, mathematical, and operations research occupations
1	VL	VH	VL	VL	*	*	MS	Actuaries
61	-	-	-	-	-	-	-	Computer systems analysts, engineers, and scientists
20	L	VH	VL	VL	*	*	MS	Computer engineers and scientists
42	H	VH	VL	VL	*	*	MS	Systems analysts
0	VL	VH	VL	VL	*	*	MS	Statisticians
0	VL	VH	VL	VL	*	*	MS	Mathematicians and all other mathematical scientists
3	VL	VH	VL	VL	*	*	MS	Operations research analysts
8	-	-	-	-	-	-	-	Physical scientists
4	VL	VH	VL	VL	*	*	MS	Chemists
2	VL	VH	L	VL	*	*	MS	Geologists, geophysicists, and oceanographers
0	VL	VH	VL	VL	*	*	MS	Meteorologists
1	VL	VH	VL	VL	*	*	MS	Physicists and astronomers
2	VL	VH	VL	VL	*	*	MS	All other physical scientists
11	-	-	-	-	-	-	-	Social scientists
2	VL	VH	L	L	*	*	MS	Economists
6	VL	VH	VL	H	*	*	MS	Psychologists
1	VL	VH	VL	L	*	*	MS	Urban and regional planners
1	VL	VH	VL	L	*	*	MS	All other social scientists
59	-	-	-	-	-	-	-	Social, recreational, and religious workers
7	VL	H	VL	L	*	*	MS	Clergy
2	VL	H	VL	L	*	*	MS	Directors, religious activities and education
22	L	H	L	L	*	*	*	Human services workers
8	VL	H	VL	L	*	*	MS	Recreation workers

NOTE: Rankings are based on all detailed occupations in the National Industry-Occupation Matrix. Codes for desrcribing the ranked variables are: VH = Very high, H = High, L = Low, VL = Very low. Codes used to identify sources of training are: MS = Most significant, S = Significant, * = not significant. A dash indicates data are not applicable.

Table 1. Occupational employment and job openings data, 1992-2005, and worker characteristics, 1992 — Continued

(Numbers in thousands)

1992 Matrix Occupation	Employment		Employment change, 1992-2005				Per-cent self-empl-oyed, 1992	Annual average job openings due to growth and total replacement needs, 1992-2005	
			Numeric		Percent				
	1992	2005	Number	Rank	Number	Rank		Number	Rank
Social workers	484	676	191	H	39.5	VH	2.1	67	L
Lawyers and judicial workers	716	913	197	-	27.5	-	30.3	48	-
Judges, magistrates, and other judicial workers	90	92	2	VL	2.3	VL	0.0	4	VL
Lawyers	626	821	195	H	31.1	H	34.7	43	L
Teachers, librarians, and counselors	5,984	8,010	2,026	-	33.9	-	2.5	1,017	-
Teachers, elementary	1,456	1,767	311	H	21.3	L	0.0	176	H
Teachers, preschool and kindergarten	434	669	236	H	54.3	VH	2.1	85	L
Teachers, special education	358	625	267	H	74.4	VH	0.0	51	L
Teachers, secondary school	1,263	1,724	462	VH	36.6	VH	0.0	165	H
College and university faculty	812	1,026	214	H	26.4	H	0.0	132	L
Other teachers and instructors	817	1,082	265	-	32.5	-	14.6	230	-
Farm and home management advisors	16	16	0	VL	-3.0	VL	0.0	4	VL
Instructors and coaches, sports and physical training	260	355	94	L	36.2	VH	0.0	75	L
Adult and vocational education teachers	540	712	172	-	31.8	-	22.0	151	-
Instructors, adult (nonvocational) education ...	235	296	60	L	25.7	H	50.6	63	L
Teachers and instructors, vocational education and training	305	416	111	L	36.5	VH	0.0	88	L
All other teachers and instructors	530	731	201	H	37.9	VH	3.4	134	L
Librarians, archivists, curators, and related workers ...	160	181	21	-	13.0	-	0.0	19	-
Curators, archivists, museum technicians, and restorers	19	23	3	VL	18.2	L	0.0	2	VL
Librarians, professional	141	158	17	VL	12.3	VL	0.0	17	VL
Counselors	154	204	50	L	32.2	H	1.9	25	VL
Health diagnosing occupations	875	1,120	246	-	28.1	-	32.0	49	-
Chiropractors	46	62	16	VL	35.8	VH	60.9	3	VL
Dentists	183	192	9	VL	5.2	VL	50.9	6	VL
Optometrists	31	36	5	VL	15.7	L	32.5	1	VL
Physicians	556	751	195	H	35.0	VH	22.7	35	VL
Podiatrists	15	20	5	VL	37.4	VH	47.7	1	VL
Veterinarians and veterinary inspectors	44	58	14	VL	32.7	H	36.3	3	VL
Health assessment and treating occupations ...	2,436	3,482	1,046	-	42.9	-	2.5	261	-
Dietitians and nutritionists	50	63	13	VL	26.3	H	8.0	4	VL
Pharmacists	163	211	47	L	29.0	H	6.1	15	VL
Physician assistants	58	78	20	VL	33.8	H	0.0	6	VL
Registered nurses	1,835	2,601	765	VH	41.7	VH	0.8	186	H
Therapists	329	530	201	-	60.9	-	9.7	51	-
Occupational therapists	40	64	24	VL	59.6	VH	15.0	6	VL
Physical therapists	90	170	79	L	88.0	VH	13.3	17	VL
Recreational therapists	30	42	12	VL	39.8	VH	13.2	4	VL
Respiratory therapists	74	109	36	L	48.3	VH	1.4	10	VL
Speech-language pathologists and audiologists	73	110	37	L	51.3	VH	9.6	10	VL
All other therapists	23	36	13	VL	55.6	VH	8.7	3	VL
Writers, artists, and entertainers	1,606	2,012	406	-	25.3	-	34.4	266	-
Artists and commercial artists	273	335	63	L	22.9	H	60.9	46	L
Athletes, coaches, umpires, and related workers	36	41	5	VL	13.1	L	30.6	7	VL

NOTE: Rankings are based on all detailed occupations in the National Industry-Occupation Matrix. Codes for desrcribing the ranked variables are: VH = Very high, H = High, L = Low, VL = Very low. Codes used to identify sources of training are: MS = Most significant, S = Significant, * = not significant. A dash indicates data are not applicable.

Table 1. Occupational employment and job openings data, 1992-2005, and worker characteristics, 1992 — Continued

(Numbers in thousands)

Annual average job openings due to growth and net replacement needs, 1992-2005		Ranking of selected occupational characteristics			Significant sources of training			1992 Matrix Occupation
Number	Rank	Weekly earnings	Unemployment rate	Part-time	Work related	Some secondary school	Bachelor's degree or higher	
20	L	H	L	L	*	*	MS	Social workers
25	-	-	-	-	-	-	-	Lawyers and judicial workers
2	VL	VH	VL	VL	*	*	MS	Judges, magistrates, and other judicial workers
24	L	VH	VL	VL	*	*	MS	Lawyers
261	-	-	-	-	-	-	-	Teachers, librarians, and counselors
52	H	VH	VL	L	*	*	MS	Teachers, elementary
22	L	L	L	VH	*	*	MS	Teachers, preschool and kindergarten
25	L	H	VL	L	*	*	MS	Teachers, special education
66	H	VH	VL	L	*	*	MS	Teachers, secondary school
39	H	VH	VL	VH	*	*	MS	College and university faculty
24	-	-	-	-	-	-	-	Other teachers and instructors
0	VL	H	L	VH	*	*	MS	Farm and home management advisors
8	VL	H	L	VH	*	*	MS	Instructors and coaches, sports and physical training
16	-	-	-	-	-	-	-	Adult and vocational education teachers
6	VL	H	L	VH	*	*	MS	Instructors, adult (nonvocational) education
10	L	H	L	VH	*	*	MS	Teachers and instructors, vocational education and training
22	L	VH	VL	VH	*	*	MS	All other teachers and instructors
5	-	-	-	-	-	-	-	Librarians, archivists, curators, and related workers
1	VL	VH	VL	H	*	*	MS	Curators, archivists, museum technicians, and restorers
4	VL	VH	VL	H	*	*	MS	Librarians, professional
6	VL	VH	VL	L	*	*	MS	Counselors
35	-	-	-	-	-	-	-	Health diagnosing occupations
2	VL	VH	VL	L	*	*	MS	Chiropractors
5	VL	VH	VL	L	*	*	MS	Dentists
1	VL	VH	VL	L	*	*	MS	Optometrists
25	L	VH	VL	VL	*	*	MS	Physicians
1	VL	VH	VL	L	*	*	MS	Podiatrists
2	VL	VH	VL	L	*	*	MS	Veterinarians and veterinary inspectors
118	-	-	-	-	-	-	-	Health assessment and treating occupations
2	VL	H	VL	H	*	*	MS	Dietitians and nutritionists
6	VL	VH	VL	H	*	*	MS	Pharmacists
2	VL	VH	VL	H	*	S	MS	Physician assistants
86	VH	VH	VL	H	*	MS	S	Registered nurses
21	-	-	-	-	-	-	-	Therapists
2	VL	VH	VL	H	*	*	MS	Occupational therapists
8	VL	VH	VL	H	*	*	MS	Physical therapists
1	VL	VH	VL	H	*	*	MS	Recreational therapists
4	VL	VH	VL	H	*	MS	S	Respiratory therapists
4	VL	VH	VL	H	*	*	MS	Speech-language pathologists and audiologists
1	VL	VH	VL	H	*	*	MS	All other therapists
58	-	-	-	-	-	-	-	Writers, artists, and entertainers
9	L	H	L	H	*	*	MS	Artists and commercial artists
1	VL	H	H	H	MS	*	*	Athletes, coaches, umpires, and related workers

NOTE: Rankings are based on all detailed occupations in the National Industry-Occupation Matrix. Codes for desrcribing the ranked variables are: VH = Very high, H = High, L = Low, VL = Very low. Codes used to identify sources of training are: MS = Most significant, S = Significant, * = not significant. A dash indicates data are not applicable.

Table 1. Occupational employment and job openings data, 1992-2005, and worker characteristics, 1992 — Continued

(Numbers in thousands)

1992 Matrix Occupation	Employment		Employment change, 1992-2005				Per-cent self-empl-oyed, 1992	Annual average job openings due to growth and total replacement needs, 1992-2005	
			Numeric		Percent				
	1992	2005	Number	Rank	Number	Rank		Number	Rank
Dancers and choreographers	18	23	5	VL	24.8	H	16.3	3	VL
Designers	302	359	57	-	18.7	-	35.7	47	-
Designers, except interior designers	236	285	49	L	20.6	L	33.0	37	VL
Interior designers	66	74	8	VL	12.2	VL	45.3	10	VL
Musicians	236	294	59	L	24.9	H	36.1	45	L
Photographers and camera operators	118	147	29	-	24.7	-	39.8	19	-
Camera operators, television, motion picture, video	11	13	2	VL	23.0	H	9.4	2	VL
Photographers	107	134	27	VL	24.9	H	42.8	17	VL
Producers, directors, actors, and entertainers	129	198	69	L	53.5	VH	20.9	28	VL
Public relations specialists and publicity writers	98	123	26	VL	26.3	H	6.2	17	VL
Radio and TV announcers and newscasters	56	70	14	VL	25.1	H	0.0	3	VL
Reporters and correspondents	58	73	15	VL	26.1	H	12.1	8	VL
Writers and editors, including technical writers	283	348	66	L	23.2	H	32.9	43	L
All other professional workers	883	1,269	386	H	43.8	VH	1.2	166	H
Technicians and related support occupations	4,282	5,664	1,383	-	32.3	-	2.3	562	-
Health technicians and technologists	2,028	2,848	821	-	40.5	-	1.4	261	-
Cardiology technologists	14	19	5	VL	35.0	VH	0.0	2	VL
Clinical lab technologists and technicians	268	339	71	L	26.5	H	0.4	27	VL
Dental hygienists	108	154	46	L	42.7	VH	0.0	15	VL
EEG technologists	6	10	3	VL	53.8	VH	0.0	1	VL
EKG technicians	16	14	-2	VL	-14.4	VL	0.0	1	VL
Emergency medical technicians	114	155	41	L	35.9	VH	0.0	15	VL
Licensed practical nurses	659	920	261	H	39.7	VH	0.8	83	L
Medical records technicians	76	123	47	L	61.5	VH	0.0	12	VL
Nuclear medicine technologists	12	18	6	VL	50.1	VH	0.0	1	VL
Opticians, dispensing and measuring	63	86	22	VL	35.7	VH	6.3	9	VL
Psychiatric technicians	72	90	19	VL	26.0	H	0.0	16	VL
Radiologic technologists and technicians	162	264	102	L	62.7	VH	0.6	16	VL
Surgical technologists	44	62	19	VL	42.4	VH	0.0	6	VL
All other health professionals and paraprofessionals	413	595	181	H	43.9	VH	4.1	56	L
Engineering and science technicians and technologists	1,253	1,482	229	-	18.3	-	2.1	165	-
Engineering technicians	695	827	132	-	19.0	-	1.4	85	-
Electrical and electronic technicians/technologists	323	396	74	L	22.8	H	1.2	36	VL
All other engineering technicians and technologists	372	431	59	L	15.8	L	1.6	49	L
Drafters	314	350	35	L	11.3	VL	3.8	52	L
Science and mathematics technicians	244	305	61	L	25.0	H	1.6	28	VL
Technicians, except health and engineering and science	1,001	1,334	333	-	33.3	-	4.4	137	-
Aircraft pilots and flight engineers	85	115	30	VL	35.2	VH	3.5	9	VL
Air traffic controllers	23	25	2	VL	9.9	VL	0.0	3	VL
Broadcast technicians	35	37	1	VL	4.0	VL	5.6	4	VL
Computer programmers	555	723	169	H	30.4	H	2.9	73	L
Legal assistants and technicians, except clerical	192	299	107	-	56.0	-	5.7	32	-
Paralegals	95	176	81	L	86.1	VH	1.1	21	VL
Title examiners and searchers	29	35	6	VL	19.1	L	23.9	4	VL
All other legal assistants, including law clerks	68	88	20	VL	30.0	H	4.4	7	VL
Programmers, numerical, tool, and process control	7	8	1	VL	8.1	VL	0.0	1	VL

NOTE: Rankings are based on all detailed occupations in the National Industry-Occupation Matrix. Codes for desrcribing the ranked variables are: VH = Very high, H = High, L = Low, VL = Very low. Codes used to identify sources of training are: MS = Most significant, S = Significant, * = not significant. A dash indicates data are not applicable.

Table 1. Occupational employment and job openings data, 1992-2005, and worker characteristics, 1992 — Continued

(Numbers in thousands)

Annual average job openings due to growth and net replacement needs, 1992-2005		Ranking of selected occupational characteristics			Significant sources of training			1992 Matrix Occupation
Number	Rank	Weekly earnings	Unemployment rate	Part-time	Work related	Some secondary school	Bachelor's degree or higher	
1	VL	H	L	H	MS	*	*	Dancers and choreographers
9	-	-	-	-	-	-	-	Designers
7	VL	VH	L	H	*	*	MS	Designers, except interior designers
2	VL	VH	L	H	*	*	MS	Interior designers
8	VL	H	L	VH	MS	*	*	Musicians
5	-	-	-	-	-	-	-	Photographers and camera operators
0	VL	L	L	H	*	*	*	Camera operators, television, motion picture, video
4	VL	L	L	H	*	*	*	Photographers
8	VL	H	L	H	MS	*	*	Producers, directors, actors, and entertainers
4	VL	H	L	H	*	*	MS	Public relations specialists and publicity writers
3	VL	H	H	H	*	*	MS	Radio and TV announcers and newscasters
2	VL	VH	VL	L	*	*	MS	Reporters and correspondents
9	VL	VH	L	H	*	*	MS	Writers and editors, including technical writers
45	H	VH	L	H	*	*	MS	All other professional workers
182	-	-	-	-	-	-	-	**Technicians and related support occupations**
94	-	-	-	-	-	-	-	Health technicians and technologists
1	VL	H	VL	H	*	MS	*	Cardiology technologists
10	L	H	VL	H	*	S	MS	Clinical lab technologists and technicians
5	VL	H	VL	H	*	MS	S	Dental hygienists
0	VL	H	VL	H	*	MS	*	EEG technologists
0	VL	H	VL	H	*	*	*	EKG technicians
5	VL	H	VL	H	*	MS	*	Emergency medical technicians
30	L	H	VL	H	*	MS	*	Licensed practical nurses
5	VL	H	VL	H	S	MS	*	Medical records technicians
1	VL	H	VL	H	*	MS	S	Nuclear medicine technologists
3	VL	L	H	VL	MS	S	*	Opticians, dispensing and measuring
2	VL	VL	H	H	*	MS	*	Psychiatric technicians
10	L	H	VL	H	*	MS	S	Radiologic technologists and technicians
2	VL	H	VL	H	*	MS	*	Surgical technologists
20	L	H	VL	H	*	MS	*	All other health professionals and paraprofessionals
43	-	-	-	-	-	-	-	Engineering and science technicians and technologists
22	-	-	-	-	-	-	-	Engineering technicians
10	L	VH	L	VL	*	MS	*	Electrical and electronic technicians/technologists
12	L	H	L	L	*	MS	*	All other engineering technicians and technologists
11	L	H	H	L	*	MS	*	Drafters
10	L	H	L	L	*	MS	*	Science and mathematics technicians
46	-	-	-	-	-	-	-	Technicians, except health and engineering and science
5	VL	VH	VL	H	MS	S	S	Aircraft pilots and flight engineers
1	VL	VH	L	L	MS	*	*	Air traffic controllers
1	VL	VH	L	L	*	MS	*	Broadcast technicians
26	L	VH	VL	VL	*	S	MS	Computer programmers
10	-	-	-	-	-	-	-	Legal assistants and technicians, except clerical
7	VL	H	L	L	*	MS	*	Paralegals
1	VL	H	L	L	*	*	*	Title examiners and searchers
2	VL	VH	VL	L	*	*	MS	All other legal assistants, including law clerks
0	VL	VH	L	L	MS	*	*	Programmers, numerical, tool, and process control

NOTE: Rankings are based on all detailed occupations in the National Industry-Occupation Matrix. Codes for desrcribing the ranked variables are: VH = Very high, H = High, L = Low, VL = Very low. Codes used to identify sources of training are: MS = Most significant, S = Significant, * = not significant. A dash indicates data are not applicable.

Table 1. Occupational employment and job openings data, 1992-2005, and worker characteristics, 1992 — Continued

(Numbers in thousands)

1992 Matrix Occupation	Employment		Employment change, 1992-2005				Percent self-empl-oyed, 1992	Annual average job openings due to growth and total replacement needs, 1992-2005	
			Numeric		Percent				
	1992	2005	Number	Rank	Number	Rank		Number	Rank
Technical assistants, library	71	89	18	VL	25.0	H	0.0	11	VL
All other technicians	33	37	5	VL	15.1	L	36.9	4	VL
Marketing and sales occupations	12,993	15,664	2,671	-	20.6	-	13.8	3,473	-
Cashiers	2,747	3,417	670	VH	24.4	H	1.0	1,044	VH
Counter and rental clerks	242	331	88	L	36.3	VH	4.1	94	L
Insurance sales workers	415	477	62	L	15.0	L	33.0	40	L
Marketing and sales worker supervisors	2,036	2,443	407	H	20.0	L	36.8	276	H
Real estate agents, brokers, and appraisers	397	461	63	-	15.9	-	63.4	68	-
Brokers, real estate	69	83	14	VL	20.4	L	63.9	12	VL
Real estate appraisers	45	63	17	VL	38.1	VH	24.3	9	VL
Sales agents, real estate	283	315	32	VL	11.3	VL	69.6	47	L
Salespersons, retail	3,660	4,446	786	VH	21.5	L	5.3	1,232	VH
Securities and financial services sales workers	200	265	65	L	32.8	H	24.0	31	VL
Travel agents	115	191	76	L	65.7	VH	12.1	46	L
All other sales and related workers	3,181	3,634	452	VH	14.2	L	11.3	642	VH
Administrative support occupations, including clerical	22,349	25,406	3,057	-	13.7	-	1.4	4,632	-
Adjusters, investigators, and collectors	1,152	1,510	358	-	31.1	-	1.1	244	-
Adjustment clerks	352	445	93	L	26.5	H	0.0	67	L
Bill and account collectors	235	328	94	L	40.0	VH	2.1	64	L
Insurance claims and policy processing occupations ..	434	583	149	-	34.4	-	1.2	89	-
Insurance adjusters, examiners, and investigators	147	220	72	L	49.1	VH	3.4	25	VL
Insurance claims clerks	116	158	43	L	37.0	VH	0.0	18	VL
Insurance policy processing clerks	171	205	34	VL	19.8	L	0.0	46	L
Welfare eligibility workers and interviewers	93	109	16	VL	16.8	L	0.0	16	VL
All other adjusters and investigators	38	44	7	VL	17.2	L	7.9	7	VL
Communications equipment operators	327	234	-93	-	-28.4	-	0.0	39	-
Telephone operators	314	225	-89	-	-28.3	-	0.0	37	-
Central office operators	48	24	-24	VL	-50.3	VL	0.0	5	VL
Directory assistance operators	27	13	-14	VL	-50.6	VL	0.0	3	VL
Switchboard operators	239	188	-51	VL	-21.3	VL	0.0	29	VL
All other communications equipment operators	13	9	-4	VL	-32.9	VL	0.0	2	VL
Computer operators and peripheral equipment operators	296	173	-122	-	-41.4	-	2.0	36	-
Computer operators, except peripheral equipment	266	161	-104	VL	-39.3	VL	2.3	33	VL
Peripheral EDP equipment operators	30	12	-18	VL	-60.2	VL	0.0	3	VL
Information clerks	1,333	1,762	429	-	32.2	-	1.4	443	-
Hotel desk clerks	122	172	50	L	41.3	VH	0.0	52	L
Interviewing clerks, except personnel and social welfare	71	95	24	VL	34.4	H	2.8	22	VL
New accounts clerks, banking	105	114	10	VL	9.3	VL	0.0	27	VL
Receptionists and information clerks	904	1,210	305	H	33.8	H	1.9	300	H
Reservation and transportation ticket agents and travel clerks	131	171	40	L	30.1	H	0.0	43	L
Mail clerks and messengers	271	298	26	-	9.6	-	2.6	64	-

NOTE: Rankings are based on all detailed occupations in the National Industry-Occupation Matrix. Codes for desrcribing the ranked variables are: VH = Very high, H = High, L = Low, VL = Very low. Codes used to identify sources of training are: MS = Most significant, S = Significant, * = not significant. A dash indicates data are not applicable.

Table 1. Occupational employment and job openings data, 1992-2005, and worker characteristics, 1992 — Continued

(Numbers in thousands)

Annual average job openings due to growth and net replacement needs, 1992-2005		Ranking of selected occupational characteristics			Significant sources of training			1992 Matrix Occupation
Number	Rank	Weekly earnings	Unemployment rate	Part-time	Work related	Some secondary school	Bachelor's degree or higher	
3	VL	VH	L	L	*	MS	*	Technical assistants, library
1	VL	VH	L	L	*	MS	*	All other technicians
536	-	-	-	-	-	-	-	**Marketing and sales occupations**
143	VH	VL	VH	VH	*	*	*	Cashiers
11	L	VL	H	VH	*	*	*	Counter and rental clerks
14	L	VH	VL	L	MS	*	*	Insurance sales workers
65	H	H	L	VL	*	*	*	Marketing and sales worker supervisors
11	-	-	-	-	-	-	-	Real estate agents, brokers, and appraisers
2	VL	H	VL	L	*	MS	*	Brokers, real estate
2	VL	H	VL	L	*	MS	*	Real estate appraisers
7	VL	H	VL	L	*	MS	*	Sales agents, real estate
167	VH	VL	H	VH	*	*	*	Salespersons, retail
8	VL	VH	VL	L	*	*	MS	Securities and financial services sales workers
8	VL	L	H	VH	*	MS	*	Travel agents
110	VH	H	L	H	MS	*	*	All other sales and related workers
694	-	-	-	-	-	-	-	**Administrative support occupations, including clerical**
40	-	-	-	-	-	-	-	Adjusters, investigators, and collectors
10	L	L	L	L	*	*	*	Adjustment clerks
9	L	L	H	L	*	*	*	Bill and account collectors
17	-	-	-	-	-	*	-	Insurance claims and policy processing occupations
7	VL	H	VL	VL	MS	*	*	Insurance adjusters, examiners, and investigators
4	VL	H	VL	VL	*	*	*	Insurance claims clerks
7	VL	L	L	H	*	*	*	Insurance policy processing clerks
3	VL	L	L	L	*	*	*	Welfare eligibility workers and interviewers
1	VL	L	L	L	*	*	*	All other adjusters and investigators
8	-	-	-	-	-	-	-	Communications equipment operators
8	-	-	-	-	-	-	-	Telephone operators
1	VL	L	H	H	MS	*	*	Central office operators
1	VL	L	H	H	MS	*	*	Directory assistance operators
6	VL	L	H	H	MS	*	*	Switchboard operators
0	VL	L	H	H	*	*	*	All other communications equipment operators
7	-	-	-	-	-	-	-	Computer operators and peripheral equipment operators
7	VL	L	L	L	*	MS	*	Computer operators, except peripheral equipment
1	VL	L	L	L	*	*	*	Peripheral EDP equipment operators
57	-	-	-	-	-	-	-	Information clerks
8	VL	L	H	VH	*	*	*	Hotel desk clerks
4	VL	L	VH	H	*	*	*	Interviewing clerks, except personnel and social welfare
4	VL	L	VH	H	*	*	*	New accounts clerks, banking
37	H	L	H	VH	*	*	*	Receptionists and information clerks
5	VL	L	H	VH	MS	*	*	Reservation and transportation ticket agents and travel clerks
8	-	-	-	-	-	-	-	Mail clerks and messengers

NOTE: Rankings are based on all detailed occupations in the National Industry-Occupation Matrix. Codes for desrcribing the ranked variables are: VH = Very high, H = High, L = Low, VL = Very low. Codes used to identify sources of training are: MS = Most significant, S = Significant, * = not significant. A dash indicates data are not applicable.

Table 1. Occupational employment and job openings data, 1992-2005, and worker characteristics, 1992 — Continued

(Numbers in thousands)

1992 Matrix Occupation	Employment		Employment change, 1992-2005				Per-cent self-empl-oyed, 1992	Annual average job openings due to growth and total replacement needs, 1992-2005	
			Numeric		Percent				
	1992	2005	Number	Rank	Number	Rank		Number	Rank
Mail clerks, except mail machine operators and postal service	132	155	24	VL	17.9	L	0.8	39	VL
Messengers	140	142	2	VL	1.7	VL	4.3	26	VL
Postal clerks and mail carriers	361	362	2	-	0.4	-	0.0	11	-
Postal mail carriers	297	300	3	VL	0.9	VL	0.0	6	VL
Postal service clerks	64	63	-1	VL	-1.6	VL	0.0	5	VL
Material recording, scheduling, dispatching, and distributing occupations	3,588	4,043	455	-	12.7	-	0.3	742	-
Dispatchers	222	268	46	-	20.9	-	1.4	30	-
Dispatchers, except police, fire, and ambulance	146	181	34	VL	23.3	H	1.4	20	VL
Dispatchers, police, fire, and ambulance	75	87	12	VL	16.3	L	1.3	10	VL
Meter readers, utilities	49	49	0	VL	0.3	VL	0.0	9	VL
Order fillers, wholesale and retail sales	187	216	30	VL	15.8	L	0.0	36	VL
Procurement clerks	61	54	-7	VL	-10.9	VL	0.0	11	VL
Production, planning, and expediting clerks	239	272	32	VL	13.4	L	0.8	42	L
Stock clerks	1,782	1,940	158	L	8.8	VL	0.1	371	VH
Traffic, shipping, and receiving clerks	824	971	147	L	17.8	L	0.1	189	H
Weighers, measurers, checkers, and samplers, recordkeeping	46	54	8	VL	17.2	L	2.2	13	VL
All other material recording, scheduling, and distribution workers	178	219	41	L	23.2	H	0.0	42	L
Records processing occupations	3,621	3,834	213	-	5.9	-	4.2	687	-
Advertising clerks	17	23	6	VL	37.5	VH	0.0	4	VL
Brokerage clerks	57	69	12	VL	20.9	L	0.0	16	VL
Correspondence clerks	31	34	2	VL	7.0	VL	0.0	6	VL
File clerks	257	305	48	L	18.9	L	0.4	99	L
Financial records processing occupations	2,686	2,770	84	-	3.1	-	5.6	456	-
Billing, cost, and rate clerks	315	355	39	L	12.4	VL	1.0	72	L
Billing, posting, and calculating machine operators	93	66	-28	VL	-29.5	VL	1.1	21	VL
Bookkeeping, accounting, and auditing clerks	2,112	2,186	73	L	3.5	VL	6.8	342	H
Payroll and timekeeping clerks	165	164	-1	VL	-0.4	VL	1.2	22	VL
Library assistants and bookmobile drivers	114	135	20	VL	17.8	L	0.0	34	VL
Order clerks, materials, merchandise, and service	300	313	13	VL	4.4	VL	0.3	52	L
Personnel clerks, except payroll and timekeeping	128	160	32	VL	25.2	H	0.0	15	VL
Statement clerks	31	25	-6	VL	-19.9	VL	3.3	6	VL
Secretaries, stenographers, and typists	4,228	4,488	259	-	6.1	-	1.8	692	-
Secretaries	3,324	3,710	386	-	11.6	-	1.2	514	-
Legal secretaries	280	439	160	H	57.1	VH	0.0	62	L
Medical secretaries	235	341	106	L	45.2	VH	0.0	48	L
Secretaries, except legal and medical	2,810	2,930	120	L	4.3	VL	1.4	404	VH
Stenographers	115	113	-2	VL	-1.5	VL	14.8	16	VL
Typists and word processors	789	664	-125	VL	-15.8	VL	2.2	162	H
Other clerical and administrative support workers	7,172	8,702	1,530	-	21.3	-	0.4	1,675	-
Bank tellers	525	502	-24	VL	-4.5	VL	0.0	116	L
Clerical supervisors and managers	1,267	1,568	301	H	23.8	H	0.1	139	L
Court clerks	50	61	12	VL	23.9	H	0.0	9	VL

NOTE: Rankings are based on all detailed occupations in the National Industry-Occupation Matrix. Codes for desrcribing the ranked variables are: VH = Very high, H = High, L = Low, VL = Very low. Codes used to identify sources of training are: MS = Most significant, S = Significant, * = not significant. A dash indicates data are not applicable.

Table 1. Occupational employment and job openings data, 1992-2005, and worker characteristics, 1992 — Continued

(Numbers in thousands)

Annual average job openings due to growth and net replacement needs, 1992-2005		Ranking of selected occupational characteristics			Significant sources of training			1992 Matrix Occupation
Number	Rank	Weekly earnings	Unem-ployment rate	Part-time	Work related	Some secondary school	Bachelor's degree or higher	
6	VL	VL	H	H	*	*	*	Mail clerks, except mail machine operators and postal service
3	VL	L	H	VH	*	*	*	Messengers
8	-	-	-	-	-	-	-	Postal clerks and mail carriers
6	VL	VH	VL	L	MS	*	*	Postal mail carriers
2	VL	VH	L	L	MS	*	*	Postal service clerks
104	-	-	-	-	-	-	-	Material recording, scheduling, dispatching, and distributing occupations
7	-	-	-	-	-	-	-	Dispatchers
5	VL	H	L	L	*	*	*	Dispatchers, except police, fire, and ambulance
2	VL	H	L	L	MS	*	*	Dispatchers, police, fire, and ambulance
1	VL	L	H	L	*	*	*	Meter readers, utilities
6	VL	H	L	L	*	*	*	Order fillers, wholesale and retail sales
1	VL	L	H	L	*	*	*	Procurement clerks
8	VL	H	L	L	*	*	*	Production, planning, and expediting clerks
51	H	L	H	L	*	*	*	Stock clerks
22	L	L	H	L	*	*	*	Traffic, shipping, and receiving clerks
2	VL	L	H	L	*	*	*	Weighers, measurers, checkers, and samplers, recordkeeping
7	VL	L	H	L	*	*	*	All other material recording, scheduling, and distribution workers
97	-	-	-	-	-	-	-	Records processing occupations
1	VL	H	L	L	*	*	*	Advertising clerks
2	VL	L	L	H	*	*	*	Brokerage clerks
1	VL	H	L	L	*	*	*	Correspondence clerks
12	L	VL	VH	VH	*	*	*	File clerks
63	-	-	-	-	*	-	-	Financial records processing occupations
11	L	L	L	L	*	*	*	Billing, cost, and rate clerks
3	VL	H	L	L	*	*	*	Billing, posting, and calculating machine operators
45	H	L	L	H	*	*	*	Bookkeeping, accounting, and auditing clerks
4	VL	L	L	H	*	*	*	Payroll and timekeeping clerks
5	VL	L	L	VH	*	*	*	Library assistants and bookmobile drivers
7	VL	H	L	L	*	*	*	Order clerks, materials, merchandise, and service
5	VL	H	L	L	*	*	*	Personnel clerks, except payroll and timekeeping
1	VL	L	L	H	*	*	*	Statement clerks
118	-	-	-	-	-	-	-	Secretaries, stenographers, and typists
102	-	-	-	-	-	-	-	Secretaries
18	L	L	L	H	*	MS	*	Legal secretaries
13	L	L	L	H	*	MS	*	Medical secretaries
70	H	L	L	H	*	*	*	Secretaries, except legal and medical
2	VL	L	L	H	*	MS	*	Stenographers
13	L	L	H	H	*	*	*	Typists and word processors
246	-	-	-	-	-	-	-	Other clerical and administrative support workers
21	L	VL	L	VH	MS	*	*	Bank tellers
53	H	H	VL	VL	MS	S	*	Clerical supervisors and managers
1	VL	H	L	H	*	*	*	Court clerks

NOTE: Rankings are based on all detailed occupations in the National Industry-Occupation Matrix. Codes for desrcribing the ranked variables are: VH = Very high, H = High, L = Low, VL = Very low. Codes used to identify sources of training are: MS = Most significant, S = Significant, * = not significant. A dash indicates data are not applicable.

Table 1. Occupational employment and job openings data, 1992-2005, and worker characteristics, 1992 — Continued

(Numbers in thousands)

1992 Matrix Occupation	Employment		Employment change, 1992-2005				Per-cent self-empl-oyed, 1992	Annual average job openings due to growth and total replacement needs, 1992-2005	
			Numeric		Percent				
	1992	2005	Number	Rank	Number	Rank		Number	Rank
Credit authorizers, credit checkers, and loan and credit clerks	218	272	53	-	24.4	-	0.0	45	-
Credit authorizers	19	23	5	VL	24.1	H	0.0	4	VL
Credit checkers	41	48	7	VL	17.5	L	0.0	7	VL
Loan and credit clerks	142	179	37	L	26.1	H	0.0	31	VL
Loan interviewers	17	22	4	VL	26.3	H	0.0	4	VL
Customer service representatives, utilities	127	151	24	VL	19.1	L	0.0	25	VL
Data entry keyers, except composing	432	515	83	L	19.2	L	0.7	126	L
Data entry keyers, composing	16	12	-4	VL	-26.4	VL	0.0	4	VL
Duplicating, mail, and other office machine operators	162	183	21	VL	13.1	L	0.6	49	L
General office clerks	2,688	3,342	654	VH	24.3	H	0.5	702	VH
Municipal clerks	22	26	4	VL	16.7	L	0.0	4	VL
Proofreaders and copy markers	27	28	2	VL	6.2	VL	3.7	6	VL
Real estate clerks	24	35	11	VL	44.1	VH	0.0	7	VL
Statistical clerks	74	69	-4	VL	-5.7	VL	0.0	5	VL
Teacher aides and educational assistants	885	1,266	381	H	43.1	VH	0.0	338	H
All other clerical and administrative support workers ...	655	671	16	VL	2.4	VL	2.0	100	L
Service occupations	19,358	25,820	6,461	-	33.4	-	5.6	6,441	-
Cleaning and building service occupations, except private household	3,284	3,913	629	-	19.2	-	4.3	856	-
Institutional cleaning supervisors	156	208	52	L	33.7	H	2.6	21	VL
Janitors and cleaners, including maids and housekeeping cleaners	2,862	3,410	548	VH	19.1	L	4.4	768	VH
Pest controllers and assistants	49	51	2	VL	4.6	VL	10.2	12	VL
All other cleaning and building service workers	217	244	27	VL	12.3	VL	2.8	55	L
Food preparation and service occupations	7,669	10,060	2,391	-	31.2	-	0.9	3,276	-
Chefs, cooks, and other kitchen workers	3,092	4,282	1,190	-	38.5	-	1.5	1,349	-
Cooks, except short order	1,155	1,564	409	-	35.4	-	3.2	411	-
Bakers, bread and pastry	146	216	69	L	47.3	VH	2.1	56	L
Cooks, institution or cafeteria	406	470	64	L	15.7	L	0.0	127	L
Cooks, restaurant	602	879	276	H	45.8	VH	5.6	228	H
Cooks, short order and fast food	714	971	257	H	36.0	VH	1.1	255	H
Food preparation workers	1,223	1,748	524	VH	42.9	VH	0.1	684	VH
Food and beverage service occupations	4,365	5,489	1,124	-	25.8	-	0.5	1,840	-
Bartenders	382	350	-32	VL	-8.3	VL	2.9	105	L
Dining room and cafeteria attendants and bar helpers	441	572	131	L	29.8	H	0.0	172	H
Food counter, fountain, and related workers	1,564	1,872	308	H	19.7	L	0.1	778	VH
Hosts and hostesses, restaurant, lounge, or coffee shop	222	301	79	L	35.6	VH	1.4	69	L
Waiters and waitresses	1,756	2,394	637	VH	36.3	VH	0.4	716	VH
All other food preparation and service workers	212	289	77	L	36.2	VH	0.9	87	L
Health service occupations	2,041	3,073	1,032	-	50.6	-	1.4	520	-
Ambulance drivers and attendants, except EMTs	15	18	3	VL	16.7	L	0.0	3	VL
Dental assistants	183	254	72	L	39.3	VH	0.0	42	L
Medical assistants	181	308	128	L	70.5	VH	0.0	31	VL
Nursing aides and psychiatric aides	1,389	2,006	616	-	44.4	-	2.1	361	-
Nursing aides, orderlies, and attendants	1,308	1,903	594	VH	45.4	VH	2.2	343	H

NOTE: Rankings are based on all detailed occupations in the National Industry-Occupation Matrix. Codes for desrcribing the ranked variables are: VH = Very high, H = High, L = Low, VL = Very low. Codes used to identify sources of training are: MS = Most significant, S = Significant, * = not significant. A dash indicates data are not applicable.

Table 1. Occupational employment and job openings data, 1992-2005, and worker characteristics, 1992 — Continued

(Numbers in thousands)

Annual average job openings due to growth and net replacement needs, 1992-2005		Ranking of selected occupational characteristics			Significant sources of training			1992 Matrix Occupation
Number	Rank	Weekly earnings	Unem-ployment rate	Part-time	Work related	Some secondary school	Bachelor's degree or higher	
7	-	-	-	-	-	-	-	Credit authorizers, credit checkers, and loan and credit clerks
0	VL	H	L	L	*	*	*	Credit authorizers
1	VL	L	L	L	*	*	*	Credit checkers
5	VL	L	H	L	*	*	*	Loan and credit clerks
1	VL	L	H	L	*	*	*	Loan interviewers
4	VL	H	L	L	MS	*	*	Customer service representatives, utilities
10	L	L	H	H	*	*	*	Data entry keyers, except composing
0	VL	L	H	H	*	*	*	Data entry keyers, composing
8	VL	H	H	L	*	*	*	Duplicating, mail, and other office machine operators
95	VH	L	H	H	*	*	*	General office clerks
0	VL	H	L	H	*	*	*	Municipal clerks
1	VL	L	H	H	*	*	*	Proofreaders and copy markers
1	VL	L	H	H	*	*	*	Real estate clerks
1	VL	H	L	L	*	*	*	Statistical clerks
39	H	VL	L	VH	*	MS	*	Teacher aides and educational assistants
6	VL	H	L	H	*	*	*	All other clerical and administrative support workers
973	-	-	-	-	-	-	-	**Service occupations**
107	-	-	-	-	-	-	-	Cleaning and building service occupations, except private household
8	VL	L	L	L	MS	*	*	Institutional cleaning supervisors
92	VH	VL	VH	VH	*	*	*	Janitors and cleaners, including maids and housekeeping cleaners
1	VL	VL	VH	VH	MS	*	*	Pest controllers and assistants
6	VL	VL	VH	VH	*	*	*	All other cleaning and building service workers
427	-	-	-	-	-	-	-	Food preparation and service occupations
164	-	-	-	-	-	-	-	Chefs, cooks, and other kitchen workers
57	-	-	-	-	-	-	-	Cooks, except short order
9	VL	VL	VH	VH	*	*	*	Bakers, bread and pastry
14	L	VL	VH	VH	*	*	*	Cooks, institution or cafeteria
35	H	VL	VH	VH	*	*	*	Cooks, restaurant
35	H	VL	VH	VH	*	*	*	Cooks, short order and fast food
72	VH	VL	VH	VH	*	*	*	Food preparation workers
251	-	-	-	-	-	-	-	Food and beverage service occupations
12	L	VL	VH	VH	*	*	*	Bartenders
28	L	VL	VH	VH	*	*	*	Dining room and cafeteria attendants and bar helpers
79	VH	VL	VH	VH	*	*	*	Food counter, fountain, and related workers
9	L	L	H	VH	*	*	*	Hosts and hostesses, restaurant, lounge, or coffee shop
122	VH	VL	H	VH	*	*	*	Waiters and waitresses
12	L	VL	VH	VH	*	*	*	All other food preparation and service workers
106	-	-	-	-	-	-	-	Health service occupations
0	VL	L	H	VH	MS	*	*	Ambulance drivers and attendants, except EMTs
10	L	L	L	VH	*	MS	*	Dental assistants
12	L	H	VL	H	MS	S	*	Medical assistants
64	-	-	-	-	-	-	-	Nursing aides and psychiatric aides
62	H	VL	H	H	MS	*	*	Nursing aides, orderlies, and attendants

NOTE: Rankings are based on all detailed occupations in the National Industry-Occupation Matrix. Codes for desrcribing the ranked variables are: VH = Very high, H = High, L = Low, VL = Very low. Codes used to identify sources of training are: MS = Most significant, S = Significant, * = not significant. A dash indicates data are not applicable.

Table 1. Occupational employment and job openings data, 1992-2005, and worker characteristics, 1992 — Continued

(Numbers in thousands)

1992 Matrix Occupation	Employment		Employment change, 1992-2005				Percent self-employed, 1992	Annual average job openings due to growth and total replacement needs, 1992-2005	
			Numeric		Percent				
	1992	2005	Number	Rank	Number	Rank		Number	Rank
Psychiatric aides	81	103	22	VL	27.5	H	0.0	19	VL
Occupational therapy assistants and aides	12	21	9	VL	78.1	VH	0.0	3	VL
Pharmacy assistants	54	76	22	VL	41.9	VH	0.0	9	VL
Physical and corrective therapy assistants and aides	61	118	57	L	92.7	VH	0.0	21	VL
All other health service workers	147	273	125	L	85.3	VH	0.0	49	L
Personal service occupations	2,295	3,804	1,509	-	65.7	-	33.4	806	-
Amusement and recreation attendants	207	303	96	L	46.1	VH	1.4	97	L
Baggage porters and bellhops	34	50	16	VL	45.9	VH	0.0	12	VL
Barbers	71	69	-1	VL	-1.7	VL	79.4	4	VL
Child care workers	684	1,135	450	VH	65.8	VH	57.3	350	VH
Cosmetologists and related workers	676	915	240	-	35.5	-	46.6	122	-
Hairdressers, hairstylists, and cosmetologists	628	846	218	H	34.7	VH	47.8	113	L
Manicurists	35	55	19	VL	54.1	VH	42.4	7	VL
Shampooers	12	15	3	VL	24.2	H	0.0	2	VL
Flight attendants	93	140	47	L	51.0	VH	0.0	11	VL
Homemaker-home health aides	475	1,120	645	-	135.9	-	0.0	187	-
Home health aides	347	827	479	VH	138.1	VH	0.0	145	H
Personal and home care aides	127	293	166	H	129.8	VH	0.0	41	L
Ushers, lobby attendants, and ticket takers	56	72	16	VL	29.3	H	0.0	24	VL
Private household workers	869	583	-286	-	-32.9	-	0.1	239	-
Child care workers, private household	350	227	-123	VL	-35.1	VL	0.0	151	H
Cleaners and servants, private household	483	326	-157	VL	-32.5	VL	0.2	82	L
Cooks, private household	9	7	-2	VL	-18.3	VL	0.0	2	VL
Housekeepers and butlers	27	22	-5	VL	-17.5	VL	0.0	5	VL
Protective service occupations	3,200	4,386	1,187	-	37.1	-	2.1	743	-
Firefighting occupations	305	354	50	-	16.3	-	0.0	14	-
Fire fighters	229	267	38	L	16.6	L	0.0	13	VL
Fire fighting and prevention supervisors	62	72	10	VL	16.1	L	0.0	3	VL
Fire inspection occupations	14	15	2	VL	13.2	L	0.0	1	VL
Law enforcement occupations	982	1,271	289	-	29.4	-	0.0	76	-
Correction officers	282	479	197	H	69.9	VH	0.0	48	L
Police and detectives	700	792	92	-	13.1	-	0.0	30	-
Police and detective supervisors	97	109	12	VL	12.6	L	0.0	5	VL
Police detectives and investigators	70	76	6	VL	8.0	VL	0.0	3	VL
Police patrol officers	411	468	57	L	13.9	L	0.0	17	VL
Sheriffs and deputy sheriffs	84	95	12	VL	13.9	L	0.0	3	VL
Other law enforcement occupations	38	43	5	VL	14.4	L	0.0	4	VL
Other protective service workers	1,034	1,529	495	-	47.9	-	1.1	357	-
Detectives, except public	59	100	41	L	70.2	VH	17.1	21	VL
Guards	803	1,211	408	H	50.8	VH	0.1	261	H
Crossing guards	57	69	12	VL	20.4	L	0.0	17	VL
All other protective service workers	115	149	34	L	29.7	H	0.0	57	L
All other service workers	879	1,232	353	H	40.2	VH	6.4	296	H
Agriculture, forestry, fishing, and related occupations	3,530	3,650	120	-	3.4	-	39.4	768	-
Animal caretakers, except farm	103	143	41	L	39.8	VH	15.6	28	VL
Farm occupations	921	832	-88	-	-9.6	-	3.6	218	-

NOTE: Rankings are based on all detailed occupations in the National Industry-Occupation Matrix. Codes for desrcribing the ranked variables are: VH = Very high, H = High, L = Low, VL = Very low. Codes used to identify sources of training are: MS = Most significant, S = Significant, * = not significant. A dash indicates data are not applicable.

Table 1. Occupational employment and job openings data, 1992-2005, and worker characteristics, 1992 — Continued

(Numbers in thousands)

Annual average job openings due to growth and net replacement needs, 1992-2005		Ranking of selected occupational characteristics			Significant sources of training			1992 Matrix Occupation
Number	Rank	Weekly earnings	Unemployment rate	Part-time	Work related	Some secondary school	Bachelor's degree or higher	
3	VL	VL	H	H	*	*	*	Psychiatric aides
1	VL	L	VL	H	*	MS	*	Occupational therapy assistants and aides
2	VL	L	VL	H	*	MS	*	Pharmacy assistants
5	VL	L	H	VH	*	MS	*	Physical and corrective therapy assistants and aides
11	L	L	H	VH	*	*	*	All other health service workers
148	-	-	-	-	-	-	-	Personal service occupations
13	L	VL	VH	VH	*	*	*	Amusement and recreation attendants
2	VL	VL	H	VH	*	*	*	Baggage porters and bellhops
2	VL	VL	VL	VH	*	MS	*	Barbers
39	H	VL	H	VH	*	*	*	Child care workers
28	-	-	-	-	-	-	-	Cosmetologists and related workers
26	L	VL	L	VH	*	MS	*	Hairdressers, hairstylists, and cosmetologists
2	VL	VL	L	VH	*	MS	*	Manicurists
0	VL	VL	L	VH	*	*	*	Shampooers
6	VL	H	L	VH	MS	*	*	Flight attendants
55	-	-	-	-	-	-	-	Homemaker-home health aides
41	H	VL	H	H	MS	*	*	Home health aides
14	L	VL	H	VH	MS	*	*	Personal and home care aides
3	VL	VL	VH	VH	*	*	*	Ushers, lobby attendants, and ticket takers
20	-	-	-	-	-	-	-	Private household workers
13	L	VL	H	VH	*	*	*	Child care workers, private household
6	VL	VL	H	VH	*	*	*	Cleaners and servants, private household
0	VL	VL	H	VH	*	*	*	Cooks, private household
0	VL	VL	H	VH	*	*	*	Housekeepers and butlers
165	-	-	-	-	-	-	-	Protective service occupations
14	-	-	-	-	-	-	-	Firefighting occupations
11	L	VH	VL	VL	MS	*	*	Fire fighters
3	VL	VH	VL	VL	MS	S	*	Fire fighting and prevention supervisors
1	VL	VH	VL	VL	MS	*	*	Fire inspection occupations
48	-	-	-	-	-	-	-	Law enforcement occupations
18	L	H	VL	VL	MS	*	*	Correction officers
30	-	-	-	-	-	-	-	Police and detectives
5	VL	VH	VL	VL	MS	S	*	Police and detective supervisors
3	VL	VH	VL	VL	MS	*	*	Police detectives and investigators
19	L	VH	VL	VL	MS	*	*	Police patrol officers
2	VL	H	VL	VL	MS	*	*	Sheriffs and deputy sheriffs
1	VL	H	L	VL	MS	*	*	Other law enforcement occupations
62	-	-	-	-	-	-	-	Other protective service workers
4	VL	L	H	H	*	*	*	Detectives, except public
46	H	L	H	H	*	*	*	Guards
2	VL	L	H	H	*	*	*	Crossing guards
9	L	VL	VH	VH	*	*	*	All other protective service workers
41	H	VL	H	VH	*	*	*	All other service workers
94	-	-	-	-	-	-	-	**Agriculture, forestry, fishing, and related occupations**
5	VL	VL	H	VH	*	*	*	Animal caretakers, except farm
28	-	-	-	-	-	-	-	Farm occupations

NOTE: Rankings are based on all detailed occupations in the National Industry-Occupation Matrix. Codes for desrcribing the ranked variables are: VH = Very high, H = High, L = Low, VL = Very low. Codes used to identify sources of training are: MS = Most significant, S = Significant, * = not significant. A dash indicates data are not applicable.

Table 1.   Occupational employment and job openings data, 1992-2005, and worker characteristics, 1992 — Continued

(Numbers in thousands)

1992 Matrix Occupation	Employment		Employment change, 1992-2005				Per-cent self-empl-oyed, 1992	Annual average job openings due to growth and total replacement needs, 1992-2005	
			Numeric		Percent				
	1992	2005	Number	Rank	Number	Rank		Number	Rank
Farm workers	849	716	-133	VL	-15.6	VL	3.7	192	H
Nursery workers	72	116	44	L	62.0	VH	2.8	26	VL
Farm operators and managers	1,218	1,014	-204	-	-16.7	-	88.8	96	-
Farmers	1,088	857	-231	VL	-21.2	VL	99.4	82	L
Farm managers	130	157	27	VL	21.1	L	0.0	15	VL
Fishers, hunters, and trappers	60	64	3	-	5.0	-	56.2	3	-
Captains and other officers, fishing vessels	8	9	1	VL	7.4	VL	37.1	0	VL
Fishers, hunters, and trappers	52	55	2	VL	4.7	VL	59.2	3	VL
Forestry and logging occupations	131	134	3	-	2.5	-	25.9	27	-
Forest and conservation workers	35	43	8	VL	22.4	H	8.5	9	VL
Timber cutting and logging occupations	96	91	-5	-	-4.8	-	32.3	18	-
Fallers and buckers	33	29	-4	VL	-11.2	VL	58.3	6	VL
Logging tractor operators	26	27	1	VL	4.0	VL	0.0	4	VL
Log handling equipment operators	15	15	-1	VL	-3.9	VL	19.6	3	VL
All other timber cutting and related logging workers ..	22	20	-1	VL	-6.6	VL	41.0	4	VL
Gardeners and groundskeepers, except farm	884	1,195	311	H	35.2	VH	20.2	343	VH
Supervisors, farming, forestry, and agricultural related occupations	71	83	12	VL	16.6	L	12.6	8	VL
All other agricultural, forestry, fishing, and related workers	142	184	42	L	29.2	H	2.8	44	L
Precision production, craft, and repair occupations	13,580	15,380	1,800	-	13.3	-	13.3	1,747	-
Blue collar worker supervisors	1,757	1,974	217	H	12.4	VL	9.6	155	H
Construction trades	3,510	4,295	786	-	22.4	-	27.7	579	-
Bricklayers and stone masons	139	174	36	L	25.7	H	29.6	29	VL
Carpenters	978	1,176	198	H	20.2	L	40.9	182	H
Carpet installers	62	75	13	VL	21.6	H	64.9	7	VL
Ceiling tile installers and acoustical carpenters	12	12	0	VL	-1.5	VL	0.0	2	VL
Concrete and terrazzo finishers	100	113	13	VL	13.4	L	6.0	3	VL
Drywall installers and finishers	121	165	44	L	36.9	VH	25.7	33	VL
Electricians	518	618	100	L	19.3	L	11.4	42	L
Glaziers	39	51	12	VL	30.2	H	7.6	7	VL
Hard tile setters	30	37	7	VL	25.2	H	54.1	5	VL
Highway maintenance workers	168	217	49	L	29.0	H	0.0	22	VL
Insulation workers	57	79	22	VL	39.8	VH	3.5	22	VL
Painters and paperhangers, construction and maintenance	440	569	128	L	29.2	H	50.2	79	L
Paving, surfacing, and tamping equipment operators	72	107	35	L	47.7	VH	1.4	15	VL
Pipelayers and pipelaying fitters	48	61	13	VL	26.4	H	0.0	6	VL
Plasterers	32	37	5	VL	16.3	L	28.3	5	VL
Plumbers, pipefitters, and steamfitters	351	378	27	VL	7.8	VL	17.1	46	L
Roofers	127	155	28	VL	21.7	H	39.3	41	L
Structural and reinforcing metal workers ..	66	81	15	VL	22.4	H	3.0	13	VL
All other construction trades workers	150	190	40	L	26.3	H	20.6	20	VL
Extractive and related workers, including blasters	231	226	-6	-	-2.4	-	2.6	43	-
Oil and gas extraction occupations	69	48	-21	-	-31.0	-	2.9	11	-
Roustabouts	33	22	-11	VL	-33.2	VL	0.0	5	VL

NOTE: Rankings are based on all detailed occupations in the National Industry-Occupation Matrix. Codes for desrcribing the ranked variables are: VH = Very high, H = High, L = Low, VL = Very low. Codes used to identify sources of training are: MS = Most significant, S = Significant, * = not significant. A dash indicates data are not applicable.

Table 1. Occupational employment and job openings data, 1992-2005, and worker characteristics, 1992 — Continued

(Numbers in thousands)

Annual average job openings due to growth and net replacement needs, 1992-2005		Ranking of selected occupational characteristics			Significant sources of training			1992 Matrix Occupation
Number	Rank	Weekly earnings	Unem-ployment rate	Part-time	Work related	Some secondary school	Bachelor's degree or higher	
23	L	VL	VH	H	*	*	*	Farm workers
5	VL	VL	VH	H	*	*	*	Nursery workers
14	-	-	-	-	-	-	-	Farm operators and managers
10	L	L	VL	L	*	*	*	Farmers
4	VL	L	VL	L	*	*	*	Farm managers
1	-	-	-	-	-	-	-	Fishers, hunters, and trappers
0	VL	L	VH	L	*	*	*	Captains and other officers, fishing vessels
1	VL	L	VH	L	*	*	*	Fishers, hunters, and trappers
4	-	-	-	-	-	-	-	Forestry and logging occupations
2	VL	VL	VH	H	*	*	*	Forest and conservation workers
2	-	-	-	-	-	-	-	Timber cutting and logging occupations
1	VL	VL	VH	H	*	*	*	Fallers and buckers
1	VL	L	H	VL	*	*	*	Logging tractor operators
0	VL	VL	VH	H	*	*	*	Log handling equipment operators
1	VL	VL	VH	H	*	*	*	All other timber cutting and related logging workers
33	H	VL	VH	VH	*	*	*	Gardeners and groundskeepers, except farm
2	VL	L	VL	L	*	*	*	Supervisors, farming, forestry, and agricultural related occupations
7	VL	VL	VH	H	*	*	*	All other agricultural, forestry, fishing, and related workers
470	-	-	-	-	-	-	-	**Precision production, craft, and repair occupations**
63	H	VH	L	VL	MS	*	S	Blue collar worker supervisors
135	-	-	-	-	-	-	-	Construction trades
6	VL	H	VH	L	MS	*	*	Bricklayers and stone masons
36	H	H	VH	L	MS	*	*	Carpenters
3	VL	L	H	H	*	*	*	Carpet installers
0	VL	H	VH	L	*	*	*	Ceiling tile installers and acoustical carpenters
4	VL	H	VH	L	MS	*	*	Concrete and terrazzo finishers
7	VL	H	VH	L	MS	*	*	Drywall installers and finishers
18	L	H	H	VL	MS	S	*	Electricians
2	VL	H	VH	L	MS	*	*	Glaziers
1	VL	H	VH	L	MS	*	*	Hard tile setters
6	VL	H	VH	L	*	*	*	Highway maintenance workers
4	VL	H	VH	VL	*	*	*	Insulation workers
20	L	H	VH	L	MS	*	*	Painters and paperhangers, construction and maintenance
4	VL	H	VH	L	MS	*	*	Paving, surfacing, and tamping equipment operators
2	VL	H	VH	L	MS	*	*	Pipelayers and pipelaying fitters
1	VL	H	VH	L	MS	*	*	Plasterers
10	L	H	VH	VL	MS	*	*	Plumbers, pipefitters, and steamfitters
4	VL	H	VH	H	*	*	*	Roofers
3	VL	H	VH	L	MS	*	*	Structural and reinforcing metal workers
5	VL	H	VH	L	*	*	*	All other construction trades workers
4	-	-	-	-	-	-	-	Extractive and related workers, including blasters
1	-	-	-	-	-	-	-	Oil and gas extraction occupations
0	VL	VH	VH	VL	*	*	*	Roustabouts

NOTE: Rankings are based on all detailed occupations in the National Industry-Occupation Matrix. Codes for desrcribing the ranked variables are: VH = Very high, H = High, L = Low, VL = Very low. Codes used to identify sources of training are: MS = Most significant, S = Significant, * = not significant. A dash indicates data are not applicable.

**Table 1. Occupational employment and job openings data, 1992-2005, and worker characteristics, 1992
— Continued**

(Numbers in thousands)

1992 Matrix Occupation	Employment		Employment change, 1992-2005				Per-cent self-empl-oyed, 1992	Annual average job openings due to growth and total replacement needs, 1992-2005	
			Numeric		Percent				
	1992	2005	Number	Rank	Number	Rank		Number	Rank
All other oil and gas extraction occupations	36	26	-10	VL	-28.9	VL	5.5	6	VL
Mining, quarrying, and tunneling occupations	21	19	-3	VL	-12.4	VL	0.0	4	VL
All other extraction and related workers	141	159	18	VL	13.1	L	2.8	28	VL
Mechanics, installers, and repairers	4,819	5,581	762	-	15.8	-	9.4	600	-
Communications equipment mechanics, installers, and repairers	108	68	-41	-	-37.6	-	2.8	3	-
Central office and PBX installers and repairers	70	45	-25	VL	-35.6	VL	0.0	1	VL
Frame wirers, central office	11	3	-8	VL	-75.3	VL	0.0	0	VL
Radio mechanics	9	8	-1	VL	-10.8	VL	0.0	1	VL
Signal or track switch maintainers	3	1	-2	VL	-74.6	VL	0.0	0	VL
All other communications equipment mechanics, installers, and repairers	15	11	-4	VL	-29.6	VL	19.8	2	VL
Electrical and electronic equipment mechanics, installers, and repairers	545	535	-10	-	-1.7	-	5.9	36	-
Data processing equipment repairers	83	120	38	L	45.5	VH	7.3	10	VL
Electrical powerline installers and repairers	108	117	9	VL	8.5	VL	0.0	7	VL
Electronic home entertainment equipment repairers	39	37	-2	VL	-5.4	VL	31.0	5	VL
Electronics repairers, commercial and industrial equipment	68	73	5	VL	7.4	VL	16.1	10	VL
Station installers and repairers, telephone	40	20	-20	VL	-50.3	VL	0.0	1	VL
Telephone and cable TV line installers and repairers	165	125	-40	VL	-24.4	VL	0.0	4	VL
All other electrical and electronic equipment mechanics, installers, and repairers	42	43	1	VL	2.5	VL	7.1	4	VL
Machinery and related mechanics, installers, and repairers	1,696	2,005	310	-	18.3	-	3.7	230	-
Industrial machinery mechanics	477	462	-15	VL	-3.2	VL	4.2	35	VL
Maintenance repairers, general utility	1,145	1,464	319	H	27.8	H	3.6	185	H
Millwrights	73	79	6	VL	8.7	VL	2.7	10	VL
Vehicle and mobile equipment mechanics and repairers	1,524	1,850	326	-	21.4	-	18.3	213	-
Aircraft mechanics and engine specialists	131	148	17	-	12.7	-	2.3	8	-
Aircraft engine specialists	26	28	2	VL	8.4	VL	7.6	1	VL
Aircraft mechanics	105	120	15	VL	13.8	L	0.9	6	VL
Automotive body and related repairers	202	263	61	L	30.2	H	24.3	31	VL
Automotive mechanics	739	907	168	H	22.7	H	25.2	123	L
Bus and truck mechanics and diesel engine specialists	263	327	64	L	24.4	H	6.5	25	VL
Farm equipment mechanics	47	53	6	VL	12.8	L	10.7	7	VL
Mobile heavy equipment mechanics	96	100	4	VL	4.0	VL	5.2	13	VL
Motorcycle, boat, and small engine mechanics	46	53	7	-	14.9	-	30.4	6	-
Motorcycle repairers	11	10	0	VL	-3.7	VL	27.9	1	VL
Small engine specialists	35	43	7	VL	20.5	L	31.1	5	VL
Other mechanics, installers, and repairers	946	1,123	176	-	18.6	-	8.1	118	-
Bicycle repairers	14	20	6	VL	45.3	VH	22.1	3	VL
Camera and photographic equipment repairers	8	9	1	VL	15.5	L	65.7	1	VL
Coin and vending machine servicers and repairers ...	20	20	0	VL	-0.2	VL	0.0	2	VL

NOTE: Rankings are based on all detailed occupations in the National Industry-Occupation Matrix. Codes for desrcribing the ranked variables are: VH = Very high, H = High, L = Low, VL = Very low. Codes used to identify sources of training are: MS = Most significant, S = Significant, * = not significant. A dash indicates data are not applicable.

Table 1. Occupational employment and job openings data, 1992-2005, and worker characteristics, 1992 — Continued

(Numbers in thousands)

Annual average job openings due to growth and net replacement needs, 1992-2005		Ranking of selected occupational characteristics			Significant sources of training			1992 Matrix Occupation
Number	Rank	Weekly earnings	Unemployment rate	Part-time	Work related	Some secondary school	Bachelor's degree or higher	
0	VL	VH	VH	VL	*	*	*	All other oil and gas extraction occupations
0	VL	VH	VH	VL	MS	*	*	Mining, quarrying, and tunneling occupations
3	VL	VH	VH	VL	*	*	*	All other extraction and related workers
175	-	-	-	-	-	-	-	Mechanics, installers, and repairers
2	-	-	-	-	-	-	-	Communications equipment mechanics, installers, and repairers
1	VL	VH	VL	VL	MS	*	*	Central office and PBX installers and repairers
0	VL	VH	VL	VL	MS	*	*	Frame wirers, central office
0	VL	H	L	L	*	*	*	Radio mechanics
0	VL	VH	L	VL	MS	*	*	Signal or track switch maintainers
0	VL	H	L	L	MS	*	*	All other communications equipment mechanics, installers, and repairers
16	-	-	-	-	-	-	-	Electrical and electronic equipment mechanics, installers, and repairers
4	VL	VH	L	VL	*	MS	*	Data processing equipment repairers
4	VL	VH	L	VL	MS	*	*	Electrical powerline installers and repairers
1	VL	H	L	L	*	MS	*	Electronic home entertainment equipment repairers
2	VL	H	L	L	*	MS	*	Electronics repairers, commercial and industrial equipment
1	VL	VH	VL	VL	MS	*	*	Station installers and repairers, telephone
4	VL	VH	VL	VL	MS	*	*	Telephone and cable TV line installers and repairers
1	VL	VH	H	VL	*	*	*	All other electrical and electronic equipment mechanics, installers, and repairers
57	-	-	-	-	-	-	-	Machinery and related mechanics, installers, and repairers
11	L	H	L	VL	MS	*	*	Industrial machinery mechanics
43	H	H	H	L	*	*	*	Maintenance repairers, general utility
3	VL	VH	H	VL	MS	S	*	Millwrights
66	-	-	-	-	-	-	-	Vehicle and mobile equipment mechanics and repairers
4	-	-	-	-	-	-	-	Aircraft mechanics and engine specialists
1	VL	VH	L	VL	S	MS	*	Aircraft engine specialists
3	VL	VH	L	VL	S	MS	*	Aircraft mechanics
9	L	L	H	VL	MS	S	*	Automotive body and related repairers
34	H	H	H	VL	MS	S	*	Automotive mechanics
12	L	H	L	VL	MS	S	*	Bus and truck mechanics and diesel engine specialists
2	VL	H	H	VL	MS	S	*	Farm equipment mechanics
3	VL	H	H	VL	MS	S	*	Mobile heavy equipment mechanics
2	-	-	-	-	-	-	-	Motorcycle, boat, and small engine mechanics
0	VL	H	H	VL	MS	S	*	Motorcycle repairers
2	VL	H	H	VL	MS	S	*	Small engine specialists
34	-	-	-	-	-	-	-	Other mechanics, installers, and repairers
1	VL	H	H	L	*	*	*	Bicycle repairers
0	VL	H	H	L	MS	S	*	Camera and photographic equipment repairers
0	VL	H	H	L	MS	*	*	Coin and vending machine servicers and repairers

NOTE: Rankings are based on all detailed occupations in the National Industry-Occupation Matrix. Codes for desrcribing the ranked variables are: VH = Very high, H = High, L = Low, VL = Very low. Codes used to identify sources of training are: MS = Most significant, S = Significant, * = not significant. A dash indicates data are not applicable.

Table 1. Occupational employment and job openings data, 1992-2005, and worker characteristics, 1992 — Continued

(Numbers in thousands)

1992 Matrix Occupation	Employment		Employment change, 1992-2005				Per-cent self-empl-oyed, 1992	Annual average job openings due to growth and total replacement needs, 1992-2005	
			Numeric		Percent				
	1992	2005	Number	Rank	Number	Rank		Number	Rank
Electric meter installers and repairers	13	13	-1	VL	-5.6	VL	0.0	1	VL
Electromedical and biomedical equipment repairers	10	13	4	VL	36.8	VH	0.0	2	VL
Elevator installers and repairers	22	25	4	VL	18.1	L	0.0	2	VL
Heat, air conditioning, and refrigeration mechanics and installers	212	274	62	L	29.4	H	12.8	20	VL
Home appliance and power tool repairers	74	74	0	VL	-0.1	VL	13.5	5	VL
Locksmiths and safe repairers	18	22	3	VL	18.5	L	27.1	2	VL
Musical instrument repairers and tuners	12	13	1	VL	9.0	VL	66.2	1	VL
Office machine and cash register servicers	60	65	5	VL	8.1	VL	3.3	1	VL
Precision instrument repairers	45	48	3	VL	6.9	VL	2.2	4	VL
Riggers	12	12	0	VL	1.1	VL	0.0	2	VL
Tire repairers and changers	80	95	15	VL	18.3	L	1.2	35	VL
Watchmakers	9	7	-2	VL	-22.6	VL	63.9	1	VL
All other mechanics, installers, and repairers	338	413	75	L	22.1	H	2.7	35	VL
Production occupations, precision	2,956	2,965	9	-	0.3	-	7.1	353	-
Assemblers, precision	334	316	-18	-	-5.5	-	0.3	40	-
Aircraft assemblers, precision	26	27	1	VL	4.2	VL	0.0	2	VL
Electrical and electronic equipment assemblers, precision	150	129	-21	VL	-13.8	VL	0.7	21	VL
Electromechanical equipment assemblers, precision	48	42	-6	VL	-13.4	VL	0.0	7	VL
Fitters, structural metal, precision	15	14	0	VL	-1.4	VL	0.0	1	VL
Machine builders and other precision machine assemblers	57	59	2	VL	4.0	VL	0.0	5	VL
All other precision assemblers	40	45	6	VL	14.0	L	0.0	4	VL
Food workers, precision	305	279	-26	-	-8.5	-	4.9	47	-
Bakers, manufacturing	43	45	2	VL	5.8	VL	18.7	8	VL
Butchers and meatcutters	222	191	-31	VL	-13.9	VL	1.8	33	VL
All other precision food and tobacco workers	40	43	2	VL	6.0	VL	7.5	7	VL
Inspectors, testers, and graders, precision	625	559	-65	VL	-10.5	VL	0.3	80	L
Metal workers, precision	854	880	26	-	3.1	-	3.6	84	-
Boilermakers	26	25	-1	VL	-4.2	VL	23.0	2	VL
Jewelers and silversmiths	30	35	6	VL	19.1	L	37.0	3	VL
Machinists	352	348	-4	VL	-1.1	VL	0.6	26	VL
Sheet metal workers and duct installers	208	244	36	L	17.5	L	1.0	40	L
Shipfitters	13	11	-2	VL	-18.0	VL	0.0	1	VL
Tool and die makers	138	128	-9	VL	-6.8	VL	2.2	5	VL
All other precision metal workers	88	89	1	VL	1.3	VL	8.0	7	VL
Printing workers, precision	151	176	25	-	16.6	-	4.0	22	-
Bookbinders	8	9	1	VL	14.1	L	25.8	1	VL
Prepress printing workers, precision	130	143	13	-	9.8	-	2.3	17	-
Compositors and typesetters, precision	11	8	-3	VL	-26.5	VL	27.8	1	VL
Job printers	15	10	-5	VL	-35.0	VL	0.0	1	VL
Paste-up workers	22	18	-4	VL	-18.7	VL	0.0	2	VL
Electronic pagination systems workers	18	32	14	VL	77.9	VH	0.0	4	VL
Photoengravers	7	8	1	VL	20.6	L	0.0	1	VL
Camera operators	14	15	1	VL	7.2	VL	0.0	2	VL
Strippers, printing	30	38	8	VL	25.3	H	0.0	5	VL

NOTE: Rankings are based on all detailed occupations in the National Industry-Occupation Matrix. Codes for desrcribing the ranked variables are: VH = Very high, H = High, L = Low, VL = Very low. Codes used to identify sources of training are: MS = Most significant, S = Significant, * = not significant. A dash indicates data are not applicable.

Table 1. Occupational employment and job openings data, 1992-2005, and worker characteristics, 1992 — Continued

(Numbers in thousands)

Annual average job openings due to growth and net replacement needs, 1992-2005		Ranking of selected occupational characteristics			Significant sources of training			1992 Matrix Occupation
Number	Rank	Weekly earnings	Unemployment rate	Part-time	Work related	Some secondary school	Bachelor's degree or higher	
0	VL	H	H	L	MS	*	*	Electric meter installers and repairers
0	VL	H	H	L	MS	*	*	Electromedical and biomedical equipment repairers
1	VL	H	H	L	MS	*	*	Elevator installers and repairers
								Heat, air conditioning, and refrigeration mechanics and installers
8	VL	H	H	VL	MS	S	*	
2	VL	VH	L	VL	MS	*	*	Home appliance and power tool repairers
1	VL	H	H	L	MS	*	*	Locksmiths and safe repairers
0	VL	H	H	L	MS	*	*	Musical instrument repairers and tuners
3	VL	H	L	L	MS	S	*	Office machine and cash register servicers
1	VL	H	H	L	MS	*	*	Precision instrument repairers
0	VL	H	H	L	*	*	*	Riggers
4	VL	VL	VH	H	*	*	*	Tire repairers and changers
0	VL	H	H	L	MS	*	*	Watchmakers
12	L	H	L	VL	*	*	*	All other mechanics, installers, and repairers
81	-	-	-	-	-	-	-	Production occupations, precision
8	-	-	-	-	-	-	-	Assemblers, precision
1	VL	H	H	VL	MS	*	*	Aircraft assemblers, precision
								Electrical and electronic equipment assemblers, precision
3	VL	L	VH	VL	MS	*	*	
1	VL	L	VH	VL	MS	*	*	Electromechanical equipment assemblers, precision
0	VL	H	H	VL	MS	*	*	Fitters, structural metal, precision
								Machine builders and other precision machine assemblers
1	VL	H	H	VL	MS	*	*	
1	VL	H	H	VL	MS	*	*	All other precision assemblers
8	-	-	-	-	-	-	-	Food workers, precision
1	VL	VL	H	H	MS	*	*	Bakers, manufacturing
6	VL	L	H	L	MS	*	`	Butchers and meatcutters
1	VL	L	H	L	*	*	*	All other precision food and tobacco workers
14	L	L	H	VL	*	*	-	Inspectors, testers, and graders, precision
23	-	-	-	-	-	*	-	Metal workers, precision
1	VL	H	H	VL	MS	*	*	Boilermakers
1	VL	H	H	VL	*	MS	*	Jewelers and silversmiths
8	VL	H	H	VL	MS	*	*	Machinists
8	VL	H	H	VL	MS	*	*	Sheet metal workers and duct installers
0	VL	H	H	VL	MS	*	*	Shipfitters
4	VL	VH	VL	VL	MS	*	*	Tool and die makers
2	VL	H	H	VL	MS	*	*	All other precision metal workers
6	-	-	-	-	-	-	-	Printing workers, precision
0	VL	L	H	VL	*	*	*	Bookbinders
5	-	-	-	-	-	-	-	Prepress printing workers, precision
0	VL	H	L	VL	MS	S	*	Compositors and typesetters, precision
0	VL	H	H	VL	MS	*	*	Job printers
0	VL	H	L	VL	MS	S	*	Paste-up workers
1	VL	H	L	VL	MS	*	*	Electronic pagination systems workers
0	VL	H	H	VL	MS	*	*	Photoengravers
0	VL	H	H	VL	MS	*	*	Camera operators
1	VL	H	H	VL	MS	*	*	Strippers, printing

NOTE: Rankings are based on all detailed occupations in the National Industry-Occupation Matrix. Codes for desrcribing the ranked variables are: VH = Very high, H = High, L = Low, VL = Very low. Codes used to identify sources of training are: MS = Most significant, S = Significant, * = not significant. A dash indicates data are not applicable.

Table 1. Occupational employment and job openings data, 1992-2005, and worker characteristics, 1992 — Continued

(Numbers in thousands)

1992 Matrix Occupation	Employment		Employment change, 1992-2005				Per-cent self-empl-oyed, 1992	Annual average job openings due to growth and total replacement needs, 1992-2005	
			Numeric		Percent				
	1992	2005	Number	Rank	Number	Rank		Number	Rank
Platemakers	13	14	1	VL	7.0	VL	0.0	2	VL
All other printing workers, precision	13	24	11	VL	85.1	VH	7.6	3	VL
Textile, apparel, and furnishings workers, precision	266	260	-6	-	-2.3	-	36.4	31	-
Custom tailors and sewers	113	109	-4	VL	-3.7	VL	61.2	11	VL
Patternmakers and layout workers, fabric and apparel	18	15	-3	VL	-18.0	VL	0.0	2	VL
Shoe and leather workers and repairers, precision ...	22	17	-4	VL	-19.6	VL	18.4	2	VL
Upholsterers	60	67	7	VL	11.2	VL	33.2	6	VL
All other precision textile, apparel, and furnishings workers	54	52	-1	VL	-2.0	VL	7.5	10	VL
Woodworkers, precision	220	272	52	-	23.6	-	18.2	21	-
Cabinetmakers and bench carpenters	114	141	28	VL	24.5	H	22.0	6	VL
Furniture finishers	37	43	7	VL	18.0	L	30.1	8	VL
Wood machinists	46	60	13	VL	28.7	H	0.0	2	VL
All other precision woodworkers	24	28	4	VL	18.1	L	16.8	5	VL
Other precision workers	201	222	21	-	10.5	-	8.5	28	-
Dental lab technicians, precision	48	50	2	VL	3.1	VL	14.5	4	VL
Optical goods workers, precision	19	23	4	VL	21.7	H	0.0	2	VL
Photographic process workers, precision	14	18	4	VL	26.1	H	35.4	3	VL
All other precision workers	120	132	12	VL	9.8	VL	4.2	19	VL
Plant and system occupations	308	340	32	-	10.4	-	0.0	17	-
Chemical plant and system operators	39	40	0	VL	1.0	VL	0.0	2	VL
Electric power generating plant operators, distributors, and dispatchers	43	47	4	-	9.9	-	0.0	2	-
Power distributors and dispatchers	17	17	0	VL	0.2	VL	0.0	1	VL
Power generating and reactor plant operators	26	30	4	VL	16.1	L	0.0	2	VL
Gas and petroleum plant and system occupations	31	30	-2	VL	-5.3	VL	0.0	1	VL
Stationary engineers	31	33	2	VL	5.1	VL	0.0	1	VL
Water and liquid waste treatment plant and system operators	86	102	16	VL	18.4	L	0.0	6	VL
All other plant and system operators	78	89	12	VL	15.0	L	0.0	5	VL
Operators, fabricators, and laborers	16,349	17,902	1,553	-	9.5	-	3.8	3,133	-
Machine setters, set-up operators, operators, and tenders	4,676	4,326	-350	-	-7.5	-	1.9	677	-
Numerical control machine tool operators and tenders, metal and plastic	73	87	14	VL	19.9	L	0.0	12	VL
Combination machine tool setters, set-up operators, operators, and tenders	102	126	24	VL	24.0	H	0.0	17	VL
Machine tool cut and form setters, operators, and tenders, metal and plastic	674	586	-89	-	-13.1	-	0.4	73	-
Drilling and boring machine tool setters and set-up operators, metal and plastic	44	38	-5	VL	-12.2	VL	0.0	5	VL
Grinding machine setters and set-up operators, metal and plastic	65	58	-7	VL	-10.9	VL	3.1	9	VL
Lathe and turning machine tool setters and set-up operators, metal and plastic	69	58	-11	VL	-15.6	VL	0.0	8	VL

NOTE: Rankings are based on all detailed occupations in the National Industry-Occupation Matrix. Codes for desrcribing the ranked variables are: VH = Very high, H = High, L = Low, VL = Very low. Codes used to identify sources of training are: MS = Most significant, S = Significant, * = not significant. A dash indicates data are not applicable.

Table 1. Occupational employment and job openings data, 1992-2005, and worker characteristics, 1992 — Continued

(Numbers in thousands)

Annual average job openings due to growth and net replacement needs, 1992-2005		Ranking of selected occupational characteristics			Significant sources of training			1992 Matrix Occupation
Number	Rank	Weekly earnings	Unem-ployment rate	Part-time	Work related	Some secondary school	Bachelor's degree or higher	
0	VL	H	H	VL	MS	*	*	Platemakers
1	VL	H	H	VL	*	*	*	All other printing workers, precision
6	-	-	-	-	-	-	-	Textile, apparel, and furnishings workers, precision
2	VL	VL	H	VH	MS	*	*	Custom tailors and sewers
0	VL	VL	H	H	MS	*	*	Patternmakers and layout workers, fabric and apparel
0	VL	VL	H	H	MS	*	*	Shoe and leather workers and repairers, precision
2	VL	VL	H	H	MS	*	*	Upholsterers
1	VL	VL	VH	H	MS	*	*	All other precision textile, apparel, and furnishings workers
9	-	-	-	-	-	-	-	Woodworkers, precision
5	VL	L	H	L	MS	*	*	Cabinetmakers and bench carpenters
1	VL	L	H	L	MS	*	*	Furniture finishers
2	VL	L	H	L	MS	*	*	Wood machinists
1	VL	L	H	L	MS	*	*	All other precision woodworkers
7	-	-	-	-	-	-	-	Other precision workers
2	VL	L	L	VL	*	MS	*	Dental lab technicians, precision
1	VL	L	H	VL	*	*	*	Optical goods workers, precision
1	VL	L	H	H	MS	*	*	Photographic process workers, precision
4	VL	L	H	VL	*	*	*	All other precision workers
11	-	-	-	-	-	-	-	Plant and system occupations
1	VL	VH	VL	VL	MS	*	*	Chemical plant and system operators
1	-	-	-	-	-	-	-	Electric power generating plant operators, distributors, and dispatchers
0	VL	VH	VL	VL	MS	*	*	Power distributors and dispatchers
1	VL	VH	VL	VL	MS	*	*	Power generating and reactor plant operators
1	VL	VH	VL	VL	MS	*	*	Gas and petroleum plant and system occupations
1	VL	VH	L	VL	MS	*	*	Stationary engineers
3	VL	VH	VL	VL	MS	*	*	Water and liquid waste treatment plant and system operators
3	VL	VH	VL	VL	*	*	*	All other plant and system operators
525	-	-	-	-	-	-	-	**Operators, fabricators, and laborers**
123	-	-	-	-	-	-	-	Machine setters, set-up operators, operators, and tenders
2	VL	H	H	VL	MS	*	*	Numerical control machine tool operators and tenders, metal and plastic
4	VL	H	H	VL	*	*	*	Combination machine tool setters, set-up operators, and tenders
14	-	-	-	-	-	-	-	Machine tool cut and form setters, operators, and tenders, metal and plastic
1	VL	H	H	VL	*	*	*	Drilling and boring machine tool setters and set-up operators, metal and plastic
1	VL	L	VH	VL	*	*	*	Grinding machine setters and set-up operators, metal and plastic
1	VL	H	H	VL	*	*	*	Lathe and turning machine tool setters and set-up operators, metal and plastic

NOTE: Rankings are based on all detailed occupations in the National Industry-Occupation Matrix. Codes for desrcribing the ranked variables are: VH = Very high, H = High, L = Low, VL = Very low. Codes used to identify sources of training are: MS = Most significant, S = Significant, * = not significant. A dash indicates data are not applicable.

Table 1. Occupational employment and job openings data, 1992-2005, and worker characteristics, 1992 — Continued

(Numbers in thousands)

1992 Matrix Occupation	Employment		Employment change, 1992-2005				Per-cent self-empl-oyed, 1992	Annual average job openings due to growth and total replacement needs, 1992-2005	
			Numeric		Percent				
	1992	2005	Number	Rank	Number	Rank		Number	Rank
Machine forming operators and tenders, metal and plastic	155	123	-32	VL	-20.8	VL	0.0	11	VL
Machine tool cutting operators and tenders, metal and plastic	114	95	-19	VL	-16.7	VL	0.0	13	VL
Punching machine setters and set-up operators, metal and plastic	45	38	-7	VL	-16.6	VL	0.0	5	VL
All other machine tool cutting and forming etc.	182	176	-7	VL	-3.6	VL	0.5	21	VL
Metal fabricating machine setters, operators, and related workers	151	134	-17	-	-11.4	-	0.0	17	-
Metal fabricators, structural metal products	45	45	0	VL	0.4	VL	0.0	6	VL
Soldering and brazing machine operators and tenders	9	8	-1	VL	-10.5	VL	0.0	1	VL
Welding machine setters, operators, and tenders	97	80	-17	VL	-17.0	VL	0.0	10	VL
Metal and plastic processing machine setters, operators, and related workers	399	402	3	-	0.7	-	0.3	45	-
Electrolytic plating machine operators and tenders, setters and set-up operators, metal and plastic	42	41	-1	VL	-1.9	VL	2.4	6	VL
Foundry mold assembly and shakeout workers	9	9	0	VL	3.4	VL	0.0	1	VL
Furnace operators and tenders	20	19	-1	VL	-6.4	VL	0.0	2	VL
Heaters, metal and plastic	3	3	0	VL	-3.9	VL	0.0	0	VL
Heating equipment setters and set-up operators, metal and plastic	6	5	-1	VL	-13.2	VL	0.0	1	VL
Heat treating machine operators and tenders, metal and plastic	19	16	-3	VL	-13.7	VL	0.0	3	VL
Metal molding machine operators and tenders, setters and set-up operators	38	34	-4	VL	-11.2	VL	0.0	3	VL
Nonelectrolytic plating machine operators and tenders, setters and set-up operators, metal and plastic	7	7	-1	VL	-8.8	VL	0.0	1	VL
Plastic molding machine operators and tenders, setters and set-up operators	150	161	11	VL	7.1	VL	0.0	14	VL
All other metal and plastic machine setters, operators, and related workers	104	106	2	VL	2.4	VL	0.0	15	VL
Printing, binding, and related workers	375	444	69	-	18.3	-	3.5	46	-
Bindery machine operators and set-up operators	68	79	11	VL	16.3	L	0.0	10	VL
Prepress printing workers, production	24	22	-2	-	-8.5	-	0.0	3	-
Photoengraving and lithographic machine operators and tenders	5	5	0	VL	10.7	VL	0.0	1	VL
Typesetting and composing machine operators and tenders	20	17	-3	VL	-13.1	VL	0.0	2	VL
Printing press operators	217	255	38	-	17.6	-	6.0	24	-
Letterpress operators	13	11	-2	VL	-15.0	VL	0.0	1	VL
Offset lithographic press operators	79	108	29	VL	37.2	VH	7.6	10	VL
Printing press machine setters, operators and tenders	110	118	8	VL	7.3	VL	0.0	11	VL
All other printing press setters and set-up operators	14	17	3	VL	19.1	L	48.5	2	VL

NOTE: Rankings are based on all detailed occupations in the National Industry-Occupation Matrix. Codes for desrcribing the ranked variables are: VH = Very high, H = High, L = Low, VL = Very low. Codes used to identify sources of training are: MS = Most significant, S = Significant, * = not significant. A dash indicates data are not applicable.

Table 1. Occupational employment and job openings data, 1992-2005, and worker characteristics, 1992 — Continued

(Numbers in thousands)

Annual average job openings due to growth and net replacement needs, 1992-2005		Ranking of selected occupational characteristics			Significant sources of training			1992 Matrix Occupation
Number	Rank	Weekly earnings	Unem-ployment rate	Part-time	Work related	Some secondary school	Bachelor's degree or higher	
4	VL	L	VH	VL	*	*	*	Machine forming operators and tenders, metal and plastic
2	VL	H	VH	VL	*	*	*	Machine tool cutting operators and tenders, metal and plastic
1	VL	L	VH	VL	*	*	*	Punching machine setters and set-up operators, metal and plastic
4	VL	L	VH	VL	*	*	*	All other machine tool cutting and forming etc.
4	-	-	-	-	-	-	-	Metal fabricating machine setters, operators, and related workers
1	VL	H	H	VL	*	*	*	Metal fabricators, structural metal products
0	VL	L	VH	L	*	*	*	Soldering and brazing machine operators and tenders
3	VL	H	VH	VL	*	*	*	Welding machine setters, operators, and tenders
12	-	-	-	-	-	-	-	Metal and plastic processing machine setters, operators, and related workers
1	VL	L	VH	VL	*	*	*	Electrolytic plating machine operators and tenders, setters and set-up operators, metal and plastic
0	VL	L	VH	VL	*	*	*	Foundry mold assembly and shakeout workers
0	VL	H	H	VL	*	*	*	Furnace operators and tenders
0	VL	L	VH	VL	*	*	*	Heaters, metal and plastic
0	VL	L	VH	VL	*	*	*	Heating equipment setters and set-up operators, metal and plastic
1	VL	L	VH	VL	*	*	*	Heat treating machine operators and tenders, metal and plastic
1	VL	L	VH	VL	*	*	*	Metal molding machine operators and tenders, setters and set-up operators
0	VL	L	VH	VL	*	*	*	Nonelectrolytic plating machine operators and tenders, setters and set-up operators, metal and plastic
5	VL	L	VH	VL	*	*	*	Plastic molding machine operators and tenders, setters and set-up operators
3	VL	L	VH	VL	*	*	*	All other metal and plastic machine setters, operators, and related workers
14	-	-	-	-	-	-	-	Printing, binding, and related workers
3	VL	H	H	VL	*	*	*	Bindery machine operators and set-up operators
1	-	-	-	-	-	-	-	Prepress printing workers, production
0	VL	H	H	VL	MS	*	*	Photoengraving and lithographic machine operators and tenders
0	VL	H	L	VL	MS	*	*	Typesetting and composing machine operators and tenders
7	-	-	-	-	-	-	-	Printing press operators
0	VL	H	H	VL	*	*	*	Letterpress operators
4	VL	H	H	VL	*	*	*	Offset lithographic press operators
3	VL	H	H	VL	*	*	*	Printing press machine setters, operators and tenders
1	VL	H	H	VL	*	*	*	All other printing press setters and set-up operators

NOTE: Rankings are based on all detailed occupations in the National Industry-Occupation Matrix. Codes for desrcibing the ranked variables are: VH = Very high, H = High, L = Low, VL = Very low. Codes used to identify sources of training are: MS = Most significant, S = Significant, * = not significant. A dash indicates data are not applicable.

Table 1. Occupational employment and job openings data, 1992-2005, and worker characteristics, 1992 — Continued

(Numbers in thousands)

1992 Matrix Occupation	Employment		Employment change, 1992-2005				Per-cent self-empl-oyed, 1992	Annual average job openings due to growth and total replacement needs, 1992-2005	
			Numeric		Percent				
	1992	2005	Number	Rank	Number	Rank		Number	Rank
Screen printing machine setters and set-up operators	25	34	9	VL	36.7	VH	0.0	3	VL
All other printing, binding, and related workers	41	54	12	VL	30.3	H	0.0	6	VL
Textile and related setters, operators, and related workers	1,041	829	-212	-	-20.3	-	1.7	182	-
Extruding and forming machine operators and tenders, synthetic or glass fibers	23	21	-2	VL	-9.5	VL	0.0	2	VL
Pressing machine operators and tenders, textile, garment, and related materials	78	86	8	VL	10.3	VL	0.0	21	VL
Sewing machine operators, garment	556	393	-162	VL	-29.2	VL	2.2	96	L
Sewing machine operators, non-garment	124	114	-10	VL	-8.1	VL	2.4	24	VL
Textile bleaching and dyeing machine operators and tenders	29	26	-3	VL	-10.8	VL	3.4	3	VL
Textile draw-out and winding machine operators and tenders	192	157	-35	VL	-18.3	VL	0.0	30	VL
Textile machine setters and set-up operators	39	32	-7	VL	-17.1	VL	5.1	6	VL
Woodworking machine setters, operators, and other related workers	121	96	-24	-	-20.0	-	7.5	18	-
Head sawyers and sawing machine operators and tenders, setters and set-up operators	59	46	-13	VL	-22.3	VL	3.4	8	VL
Woodworking machine operators and tenders, setters and set-up operators	62	51	-11	VL	-17.8	VL	11.3	10	VL
Other machine setters, set-up operators, operators, and tenders	1,741	1,622	-119	-	-6.8	-	2.7	267	-
Boiler operators and tenders, low pressure	18	16	-1	VL	-7.9	VL	0.0	1	VL
Cement and gluing machine operators and tenders	35	28	-7	VL	-20.2	VL	0.0	5	VL
Chemical equipment controllers, operators and tenders	77	76	-1	VL	-1.5	VL	0.0	10	VL
Cooking and roasting machine operators and tenders, food and tobacco	28	32	4	VL	13.4	L	0.0	4	VL
Crushing and mixing machine operators and tenders	133	117	-16	VL	-12.1	VL	1.5	20	VL
Cutting and slicing machine setters, operators and tenders	94	73	-21	VL	-22.6	VL	5.3	10	VL
Dairy processing equipment operators, including setters	15	17	1	VL	8.9	VL	6.5	2	VL
Electronic semiconductor processors	32	33	1	VL	4.3	VL	0.0	4	VL
Extruding and forming machine setters, operators and tenders	99	101	2	VL	1.7	VL	0.0	16	VL
Furnace, kiln, or kettle operators and tenders	27	25	-2	VL	-5.9	VL	0.0	2	VL
Laundry and drycleaning machine operators and tenders, except pressing	162	237	75	L	46.1	VH	11.1	36	VL
Motion picture projectionists	9	7	-2	VL	-25.8	VL	0.0	1	VL
Packaging and filling machine operators and tenders	319	248	-71	VL	-22.3	VL	0.0	59	L
Painting and coating machine operators	151	152	2	-	1.2	-	8.0	22	-

NOTE: Rankings are based on all detailed occupations in the National Industry-Occupation Matrix. Codes for desrcribing the ranked variables are: VH = Very high, H = High, L = Low, VL = Very low. Codes used to identify sources of training are: MS = Most significant, S = Significant, * = not significant. A dash indicates data are not applicable.

Table 1. Occupational employment and job openings data, 1992-2005, and worker characteristics, 1992 — Continued

(Numbers in thousands)

Annual average job openings due to growth and net replacement needs, 1992-2005		Ranking of selected occupational characteristics			Significant sources of training			1992 Matrix Occupation
Number	Rank	Weekly earnings	Unem-ployment rate	Part-time	Work related	Some secondary school	Bachelor's degree or higher	
1	VL	H	H	VL	*	*	*	Screen printing machine setters and set-up operators
2	VL	H	H	VL	*	*	*	All other printing, binding, and related workers
23	-	-	-	-	-	-	-	Textile and related setters, operators, and related workers
1	VL	VL	VH	VL	*	*	*	Extruding and forming machine operators and tenders, synthetic or glass fibers
3	VL	VL	VH	H	*	*	*	Pressing machine operators and tenders, textile, garment, and related materials
12	L	VL	VH	L	*	*	*	Sewing machine operators, garment
3	VL	VL	VH	L	*	*	*	Sewing machine operators, non-garment
1	VL	VL	VH	VL	*	*	*	Textile bleaching and dyeing machine operators and tenders
4	VL	VL	VH	L	*	*	*	Textile draw-out and winding machine operators and tenders
1	VL	VL	VH	L	*	*	*	Textile machine setters and set-up operators
3	-	-	-	-	-	-	-	Woodworking machine setters, operators, and other related workers
2	VL	L	VH	L	*	*	*	Head sawyers and sawing machine operators and tenders, setters and set-up operators
2	VL	L	VH	L	*	*	*	Woodworking machine operators and tenders, setters and set-up operators
48	-	-	-	-	-	-	-	Other machine setters, set-up operators, operators, and tenders
1	VL	VH	L	VL	*	*	*	Boiler operators and tenders, low pressure
1	VL	L	VH	VL	*	*	*	Cement and gluing machine operators and tenders
2	VL	H	L	VL	*	*	*	Chemical equipment controllers, operators and tenders
1	VL	L	H	VL	*	*	*	Cooking and roasting machine operators and tenders, food and tobacco
3	VL	L	VH	VL	*	*	*	Crushing and mixing machine operators and tenders
2	VL	L	VH	L	*	*	*	Cutting and slicing machine setters, operators and tenders
1	VL	H	L	VL	*	*	*	Dairy processing equipment operators, including setters
1	VL	L	H	VL	*	*	*	Electronic semiconductor processors
3	VL	L	VH	VL	*	*	*	Extruding and forming machine setters, operators and tenders
0	VL	H	H	VL	*	*	*	Furnace, kiln, or kettle operators and tenders
9	VL	VL	VH	H	*	*	*	Laundry and drycleaning machine operators and tenders, except pressing
0	VL	L	VH	VL	*	*	*	Motion picture projectionists
6	VL	VL	VH	VL	*	*	*	Packaging and filling machine operators and tenders
4	-	-	-	-	-	-	-	Painting and coating machine operators

NOTE: Rankings are based on all detailed occupations in the National Industry-Occupation Matrix. Codes for desrcribing the ranked variables are: VH = Very high, H = High, L = Low, VL = Very low. Codes used to identify sources of training are: MS = Most significant, S = Significant, * = not significant. A dash indicates data are not applicable.

Table 1. Occupational employment and job openings data, 1992-2005, and worker characteristics, 1992 — Continued

(Numbers in thousands)

1992 Matrix Occupation	Employment		Employment change, 1992-2005				Per-cent self-empl-oyed, 1992	Annual average job openings due to growth and total replacement needs, 1992-2005	
			Numeric		Percent				
	1992	2005	Number	Rank	Number	Rank		Number	Rank
Coating, painting, and spraying machine operators, tenders, setters, and set-up operators	107	107	0	VL	0.4	VL	0.0	15	VL
Painters, transportation equipment	44	45	1	VL	2.9	VL	27.2	6	VL
Paper goods machine setters and set-up operators	50	64	13	VL	26.4	H	0.0	9	VL
Photographic processing machine operators and tenders	49	59	9	VL	18.8	L	0.0	10	VL
Separating and still machine operators and tenders	21	14	-7	VL	-32.8	VL	0.0	2	VL
Shoe sewing machine operators and tenders	16	10	-6	VL	-38.4	VL	0.0	3	VL
Tire building machine operators	14	11	-3	VL	-22.3	VL	0.0	1	VL
All other machine operators, tenders, setters, and set-up operators	390	302	-88	VL	-22.6	VL	2.3	47	L
Hand workers, including assemblers and fabricators	2,528	2,630	102	-	4.0	-	4.2	424	-
Cannery workers	73	82	10	VL	13.1	L	0.0	17	VL
Coil winders, tapers, and finishers	20	14	-7	VL	-32.4	VL	0.0	3	VL
Cutters and trimmers, hand	49	44	-5	VL	-10.2	VL	0.0	7	VL
Electrical and electronic assemblers	210	187	-23	VL	-11.1	VL	0.0	33	VL
Grinders and polishers, hand	71	72	1	VL	1.6	VL	0.0	11	VL
Machine assemblers	49	49	0	VL	-0.6	VL	0.0	8	VL
Meat, poultry, and fish cutters and trimmers, hand	127	169	42	L	32.9	H	0.0	26	VL
Metal pourers and casters, basic shapes	10	9	-1	VL	-6.8	VL	0.0	1	VL
Painting, coating, and decorating workers, hand	29	37	8	VL	28.0	H	13.8	6	VL
Portable machine cutters	10	6	-4	VL	-40.1	VL	0.0	1	VL
Pressers, hand	16	15	-1	VL	-6.6	VL	0.0	2	VL
Sewers, hand	23	22	-1	VL	-4.6	VL	35.4	2	VL
Solderers and brazers	21	23	2	VL	8.1	VL	0.0	4	VL
Welders and cutters	306	352	46	L	15.2	L	8.8	41	L
All other assemblers and fabricators	1,113	1,007	-107	VL	-9.6	VL	2.5	177	H
All other hand workers	400	542	142	L	35.6	VH	9.5	83	L
Transportation and material moving machine and vehicle operators	4,694	5,719	1,025	-	21.8	-	7.3	723	-
Motor vehicle operators	3,429	4,285	856	-	25.0	-	8.7	574	-
Bus drivers	562	681	119	-	21.2	-	1.1	111	-
Bus drivers	167	177	10	VL	5.9	VL	3.6	29	VL
Bus drivers, school	395	504	109	L	27.6	H	0.0	82	L
Taxi drivers and chauffeurs	120	142	22	VL	18.3	L	40.9	30	VL
Truck drivers	2,720	3,428	708	-	26.0	-	9.0	427	-
Driver/sales workers	329	389	60	L	18.1	L	6.1	54	L
Truck drivers light and heavy	2,391	3,039	648	VH	27.1	H	9.4	373	VH
All other motor vehicle operators	27	34	7	VL	26.5	H	0.0	5	VL
Rail transportation workers	116	141	25	-	21.4	-	0.0	6	-
Locomotive engineers	19	21	2	VL	8.3	VL	0.0	1	VL
Railroad brake, signal, and switch operators	35	38	3	VL	7.7	VL	0.0	1	VL
Railroad conductors and yardmasters	29	37	8	VL	27.9	H	0.0	2	VL
Rail yard engineers, dinkey operators, and hostlers	9	9	1	VL	6.3	VL	0.0	0	VL
Subway and streetcar operators	22	35	13	VL	57.2	VH	0.0	2	VL
All other rail vehicle operators	2	1	-1	VL	-51.7	VL	0.0	0	VL
Water transportation and related workers	134	144	10	-	7.7	-	2.2	19	-

NOTE: Rankings are based on all detailed occupations in the National Industry-Occupation Matrix. Codes for desrcribing the ranked variables are: VH = Very high, H = High, L = Low, VL = Very low. Codes used to identify sources of training are: MS = Most significant, S = Significant, * = not significant. A dash indicates data are not applicable.

Table 1. Occupational employment and job openings data, 1992-2005, and worker characteristics, 1992 — Continued

(Numbers in thousands)

Annual average job openings due to growth and net replacement needs, 1992-2005		Ranking of selected occupational characteristics			Significant sources of training			1992 Matrix Occupation
Number	Rank	Weekly earnings	Unem-ployment rate	Part-time	Work related	Some secondary school	Bachelor's degree or higher	
3	VL	L	VH	VL	*	*	*	Coating, painting, and spraying machine operators, tenders, setters, and set-up operators
1	VL	L	VH	VL	*	*	*	Painters, transportation equipment
2	VL	L	VH	VL	*	*	*	Paper goods machine setters and set-up operators
2	VL	L	H	H	*	*	*	Photographic processing machine operators and tenders
1	VL	H	L	VL	*	*	*	Separating and still machine operators and tenders
0	VL	VL	VH	VL	*	*	*	Shoe sewing machine operators and tenders
0	VL	L	H	VL	*	*	*	Tire building machine operators
8	VL	L	H	VL	*	*	*	All other machine operators, tenders, setters, and set-up operators
68	-	-	-	-	-	-	-	Hand workers, including assemblers and fabricators
2	VL	VL	VH	VL	*	*	*	Cannery workers
0	VL	L	VH	L	*	*	*	Coil winders, tapers, and finishers
1	VL	L	VH	L	*	*	*	Cutters and trimmers, hand
4	VL	L	VH	L	*	*	*	Electrical and electronic assemblers
2	VL	L	VH	L	*	*	*	Grinders and polishers, hand
1	VL	L	VH	L	*	*	*	Machine assemblers
6	VL	L	VH	L	*	*	*	Meat, poultry, and fish cutters and trimmers, hand
0	VL	L	VH	L	*	*	*	Metal pourers and casters, basic shapes
1	VL	L	VH	L	*	*	*	Painting, coating, and decorating workers, hand
0	VL	L	VH	L	*	*	*	Portable machine cutters
0	VL	L	VH	L	*	*	*	Pressers, hand
0	VL	VL	H	VH	*	*	*	Sewers, hand
1	VL	L	VH	L	*	*	*	Solderers and brazers
12	L	H	VH	VL	MS	*	*	Welders and cutters
19	L	L	VH	L	*	*	*	All other assemblers and fabricators
19	L	L	VH	L	*	*	*	All other hand workers
159	-	-	-	-	-	-	-	Transportation and material moving machine and vehicle operators
124	-	-	-	-	-	-	-	Motor vehicle operators
17	-	-	-	-	-	-	-	Bus drivers
3	VL	L	L	VH	MS	*	*	Bus drivers
14	L	L	L	VH	MS	*	*	Bus drivers, school
3	VL	L	H	H	*	*	*	Taxi drivers and chauffeurs
103	-	-	-	-	-	-	-	Truck drivers
13	L	H	L	L	*	*	*	Driver/sales workers
90	VH	H	H	L	MS	*	*	Truck drivers light and heavy
1	VL	H	H	L	*	*	*	All other motor vehicle operators
3	-	-	-	-	-	-	-	Rail transportation workers
0	VL	VH	L	VL	MS	*	*	Locomotive engineers
1	VL	VH	L	VL	MS	*	*	Railroad brake, signal, and switch operators
1	VL	VH	L	VL	MS	*	*	Railroad conductors and yardmasters
0	VL	VH	L	VL	MS	*	*	Rail yard engineers, dinkey operators, and hostlers
1	VL	VH	L	VL	MS	*	*	Subway and streetcar operators
0	VL	VH	L	VL	MS	*	*	All other rail vehicle operators
3	-	-	-	-	-	-	-	Water transportation and related workers

NOTE: Rankings are based on all detailed occupations in the National Industry-Occupation Matrix. Codes for desrcribing the ranked variables are: VH = Very high, H = High, L = Low, VL = Very low. Codes used to identify sources of training are: MS = Most significant, S = Significant, * = not significant. A dash indicates data are not applicable.

Table 1. Occupational employment and job openings data, 1992-2005, and worker characteristics, 1992 — Continued

(Numbers in thousands)

1992 Matrix Occupation	Employment		Employment change, 1992-2005				Per-cent self-empl-oyed, 1992	Annual average job openings due to growth and total replacement needs, 1992-2005	
			Numeric		Percent				
	1992	2005	Number	Rank	Number	Rank		Number	Rank
Able seamen, ordinary seamen, and marine oilers ...	22	21	-1	VL	-5.4	VL	0.0	2	VL
Captains and pilots, ship	16	16	0	VL	-0.5	VL	6.2	1	VL
Mates, ship, boat, and barge	7	7	0	VL	-6.6	VL	0.0	1	VL
Ship engineers	9	8	-1	VL	-9.0	VL	11.4	1	VL
All other transportation and related workers	79	92	13	VL	16.1	L	1.3	14	VL
Material moving equipment operators	983	1,111	129	-	13.1	-	3.8	122	-
Crane and tower operators	46	53	7	VL	16.0	L	0.0	8	VL
Excavation and loading machine operators	72	86	14	VL	20.1	L	18.1	4	VL
Grader, dozer, and scraper operators	102	123	21	VL	20.5	L	6.8	12	VL
Hoist and winch operators	12	13	1	VL	6.2	VL	8.4	1	VL
Industrial truck and tractor operators	413	442	29	VL	7.0	VL	0.7	67	L
Operating engineers	136	159	23	VL	17.2	L	5.1	13	VL
All other material moving equipment operators	201	234	33	VL	16.3	L	3.0	17	VL
All other transportation and material moving equipment operators	32	38	5	VL	16.4	L	3.1	3	VL
Helpers, laborers, and material movers, hand	4,451	5,227	776	-	17.4	-	1.8	1,309	-
Freight, stock, and material movers, hand	845	955	111	L	13.1	L	2.0	288	H
Hand packers and packagers	685	770	85	L	12.4	VL	0.3	189	H
Helpers, construction trades	452	530	79	L	17.4	L	0.9	124	L
Machine feeders and offbearers	255	256	2	VL	0.7	VL	0.0	30	VL
Parking lot attendants	63	85	22	VL	35.3	VH	0.0	13	VL
Refuse collectors	121	134	13	VL	10.5	VL	1.6	18	VL
Service station attendants	190	180	-10	VL	-5.3	VL	2.1	71	L
Vehicle washers and equipment cleaners	219	271	52	L	23.7	H	7.7	93	L
All other helpers, laborers, and material movers, hand	1,621	2,044	423	VH	26.1	H	2.0	482	VH

NOTE: Rankings are based on all detailed occupations in the National Industry-Occupation Matrix. Codes for desrcribing the ranked variables are: VH = Very high, H = High, L = Low, VL = Very low. Codes used to identify sources of training are: MS = Most significant, S = Significant, * = not significant. A dash indicates data are not applicable.

Table 1. Occupational employment and job openings data, 1992-2005, and worker characteristics, 1992 — Continued

(Numbers in thousands)

Annual average job openings due to growth and net replacement needs, 1992-2005		Ranking of selected occupational characteristics			Significant sources of training			1992 Matrix Occupation
Number	Rank	Weekly earnings	Unemployment rate	Part-time	Work related	Some secondary school	Bachelor's degree or higher	
0	VL	VH	H	VL	*	*	*	Able seamen, ordinary seamen, and marine oilers
0	VL	VH	H	VL	MS	*	*	Captains and pilots, ship
0	VL	VH	H	VL	*	*	*	Mates, ship, boat, and barge
0	VL	VH	H	VL	MS	*	*	Ship engineers
2	VL	H	H	L	*	*	*	All other transportation and related workers
28	-	-	-	-	-	-	-	Material moving equipment operators
2	VL	VH	H	VL	MS	*	*	Crane and tower operators
3	VL	H	VH	VL	MS	*	*	Excavation and loading machine operators
4	VL	H	VH	VL	MS	*	*	Grader, dozer, and scraper operators
0	VL	H	VH	VL	*	*	*	Hoist and winch operators
11	L	L	H	VL	*	*	*	Industrial truck and tractor operators
4	VL	H	VH	VL	*	*	*	Operating engineers
5	VL	L	VH	VL	*	*	*	All other material moving equipment operators
1	VL	L	VH	VL	*	*	*	All other transportation and material moving equipment operators
176	-	-	-	-	-	-	-	Helpers, laborers, and material movers, hand
35	H	VL	VH	VH	*	*	*	Freight, stock, and material movers, hand
21	L	VL	VH	H	*	*	*	Hand packers and packagers
21	L	VL	VH	H	*	*	*	Helpers, construction trades
8	VL	L	VH	L	*	*	*	Machine feeders and offbearers
3	VL	H	H	L	*	*	*	Parking lot attendants
3	VL	L	H	L	*	*	*	Refuse collectors
7	VL	VL	VH	H	*	*	*	Service station attendants
7	VL	VL	VH	H	*	*	*	Vehicle washers and equipment cleaners
70	H	L	VH	L	*	*	*	All other helpers, laborers, and material movers, hand

NOTE: Rankings are based on all detailed occupations in the National Industry-Occupation Matrix. Codes for desrcribing the ranked variables are: VH = Very high, H = High, L = Low, VL = Very low. Codes used to identify sources of training are: MS = Most significant, S = Significant, * = not significant. A dash indicates data are not applicable.

Over 500 Jobs Organized by Training and Education Required

Editor's Comments:

This appendix organizes the jobs presented in Appendix B into groupings based on four levels of training or education. This is a very useful series of tables for identifying jobs available within clusters that interest you. The jobs listed are *typically* available to those with varying levels of education or training.

For example, let's say that you are interested in the Executive, Administrative, and Managerial Occupations job cluster. Let's also assume that you have some college and are considering going on to get additional training or education to widen your opportunities. Browsing through the jobs available at various levels of education will give you an idea of the relative opportunities and the types of jobs that become available as you increase your education or training. Note that Appendix B provides additional information on each of the jobs listed in the tables that follow. It is a good place to start learning more about jobs that interest you.

The information in this appendix comes from the U.S. Department of Labor's Bulletin 2451, *Occupational Projections and Training Data*, and the introductory narrative is as it appears in that publication. The "Table 1" it refers to is included in this book as Appendix B.

Chapter II. Training Profiles

Besides providing information about individual occupations, the data and rankings in table 1 permit analyses by types of training. The training groups are: Work related or postsecondary school training generally is not significant, work related, some postsecondary school, and bachelor's degree or higher. Occupations in table 1 for which no training source was identified as being most significant comprise the group, "work related or postsecondary school training generally is not significant." The other groups are those used in table 1 to identify the most significant source of postsecondary training.

Overall, the training groups compare information about the 121 million employees in the 512 detailed occupations identified in the 1992 National Industry-Occupation Matrix. Significant differences exist in the number of employees in each group. The largest—work related or postsecondary school training generally is not significant—contains 61.1 million employees while the smallest—some postsecondary school training—has only 8.9 million. With 25.2 million and 25.8 million employees respectively, the work related and bachelor's degree or higher training programs are about the same size.

In the discussions that follow, lower than average (LA) represents the combination of persons in occupations ranked very low (VL) or low (L) in table 1 for the characteristic being examined; higher than average (HA) is the combination of persons in occupations ranked high(H) or very high (VH). For all characteristics within each training group the number of employees is the same. Their distribution within the lower than average and higher than average categories, however, usually will vary.

Tables 2-5 present the occupations within each training group; occupations with above average earnings are displayed with bold type. Data for CPS proxy occupations have been used to estimate job openings, weekly earnings, the unemployment rate and the percent of parttime workers (see "data sources" section of chapter 1).

Work related or postsecondary school training generally is not significant

Jobs for which work related or postsecondary training generally was not significant was by far the largest of the four training groups. It encompassed 61.1 million employees in 221 occupations—50.4 percent of total employment in 1992. Most persons in this group worked in clerical, sales, service, or operative and laborer occupations that generally need neither postsecondary

school training nor specialized job skills (see table 2). The presence of many occupations with the largest number of employees—for example, cashiers, secretaries, janitors and cleaners, and waiters and waitresses—is the reason the group encompasses 50.4 percent of total employment but only 43.2 percent of the occupations.

The majority of workers in this group are in occupations with lower than average projected increases in employment and projected employment growth rates, but as shown in text table 1, that majority is not dominant; significant numbers are in occupations with higher than average increases and growth rates.

	Lower than average (thousands)	Higher than average (thousands)
Projected increase in employment....	34,120	26,963
Projected percent increase in employment.....................................	37,909	23,174
Job openings due to growth plus total replacement needs.........................	21,708	39,375
Job openings due to growth plus net replacement needs.........................	26,760	34,323
Weekly earnings of full-time workers	52,343	8,740
Unemployment rate	13,163	47,920
Percent working parttime..................	22,395	38,688

Despite the fact that the majority of workers in this group reside in occupations with lower than average projected employment increases and growth rates, the majority are in occupations with higher than average estimates for both categories of projected job openings. Job openings occur because of employment increases and the need to replace workers who leave. Because workers in this group have not invested time or money in acquiring training, they are more likely than workers with training to transfer to different occupations or stop working and, as a result, replacement rates are higher. Higher replacement rates and the inordinately large size of some occupations results in a disproportionate number of job openings due to replacement needs that puts many occupations in the higher than average category.

The most striking characteristic of occupations for which work related or postsecondary school training generally is not significant is the sharp contrast in the distributions of employment by earnings. Six out of 7 employees (52.3 million) are in occupations with lower than average earnings. The number with lower than average earnings is so large that it comprises a majority not only for this training group but for all workers with below average earnings—the majority of workers in each of the other training groups enjoy above average earnings.

While not as extreme as the distribution for earnings, the concentration of workers in this group in occupations with above average unemployment rates also is striking. At 47.9 million, 4 out of 5 employees in occupations for which no postsecondary training is significant, are in occupations with above average unemployment rates. These workers also constitute a majority of workers in all training groups employed in occupations with above average unemployment rates

The 38.7 million workers in occupations with higher than average proportions of part-time workers was almost double those in occupations with lower than average proportions. This may indicate difficulty in acquiring steady, higher paying jobs rather than a preference for reduced hours of work.

Work related training

Work related training is acquired in a formal employer program with scheduled hours of attendance or an established curriculum, from extensive work experience, as well as from hobbies or other activities that are independent of current or past employment activities. It results in specialized job skills or knowledge and is the most significant source of training for 142 occupations representing 25.2 million employees—20.8 percent of total employment. Many occupations in the precision production, craft and repair group that require specialized skills are included in this training group (See table 3).

A small majority of workers exists in occupations with higher than average projected employment increases and in occupations with lower than average projected employment growth rates, but differences are small. Majorities exist in the lower than average group for both categories of job openings, but in both cases the differences are less than 2 to 1.

In contrast, the distribution of workers within the earnings category exhibits major differences. Over four times as many workers are in occupations with higher than average earnings as those with less than average (20.5 million compared to 4.8 million) and indicates that specialized skills yield an earnings premium.

	Lower than average (thousands)	Higher than average (thousands)
Projected increase in employment	12,337	12,910
Projected percent increase in employment.................................	14,262	10,985
Job openings due to growth plus total replacement needs........................	15,285	9,962
Job openings due to growth plus net replacement needs........................	13,279	11,968
Weekly earnings of full-time workers	4,763	20,484
Unemployment rate	13,446	11,801
Percent working parttime..................	17,586	7,661

Nearly equal numbers of employees work in occupations with higher or lower than average unemployment rates (11.8 million Vs. 13.4 million). (See text table 2.) The distribution indicates that high unemployment rates characterize some occupations, construction trades, for example.

Part time work is not the rule for this group. The number working in occupations with lower than average proportions employed part time (17.6 million) exceeds those in occupations with higher than average proportions (7.7 million) by 2 to 1.

Some postsecondary school training

Postsecondary school training, but less than a bachelor's degree encompasses the smallest group of employees for the training groups presented. It is the most significant source of training for 8.9 million workers —7.4 percent of 1992 employment—in 46 occupations. Occupations in this group include many technicians and technologists, as well as large numbers in repairer occupations (table 4).

The number of workers in occupations with higher than average projected employment increases is about the same as those with lower than average increases (4.7 million compared to 4.2 million). (See text table 3.)

	Lower than average (thousands)	Higher than average (thousands)
Projected increase in employment	4,237	4,700
Projected percent increase in employment.................................	2,000	6,937
Job openings due to growth plus total replacement needs........................	6,217	2,721
Job openings due to growth plus net replacement needs........................	6,217	2,721
Weekly earnings of full-time workers	3,058	5,879
Unemployment rate	8,246	691
Percent working parttime..................	2,675	6,262

A much different distribution pattern, however, exists for projected growth rates. Over three times as many employees work in occupations with higher than average growth rates than with lower than average emphasizing that a sizable majority of workers are in occupations with faster than average growth rates. The distribution of employees within the projected annual job openings due to growth and total replacement needs, and those due to growth and net replacement needs show a minority of workers with above average opportunities in spite of anticipated rapid growth. The results are not inconsistent; they indicate fewer job openings may result in occupations with higher than average growth rates if occupations are smaller and/or they have lower replacement needs because persons are less likely to leave.

A significant majority of workers—by a ratio of about 2 to 1—are employed in occupations with above average earnings or in occupations with a higher than average proportion of part-time workers. While the distribution is unequal, the difference in the distribution of workers in the earnings category is not as extreme as for the other training categories. The fact that 11 times as many employees work in occupations with lower than average unemployment rates than in those with a higher than average rates (8.3 million Vs. 0.7 million) indicates that occupations in this group typically offer stable employment opportunities.

Bachelor's degree or higher program

Included in the 4-year or longer college training group are 25.8 million workers—21.3 percent of total employment—distributed among 103 occupations. Most are managerial and executive occupations, or professional specialty occupations that include engineers, scientists, medical practitioners, and teachers (text table 4 and table 5).

	Lower than average (thousands)	Higher than average (thousands)
Projected increase in employment	10,129	15,703
Projected percent increase in employment..................................	7,108	18,724
Job openings due to growth plus total replacement needs.........................	17,683	8,149
Job openings due to growth plus net replacement needs.........................	14,585	11,247
Weekly earnings of full-time workers	434	25,398
Unemployment rate	25,776	56
Percent working parttime...................	19,796	6,036

Workers in occupations with higher than average projected increases in employment (15.7 million) and projected growth rates (18.7 million) constitute a clear majority in each case. With a ratio of over 2 to 1, the majority for occupations with higher than average growth rates is more impressive. The number of workers in these higher than average categories for projected employment increases and projected growth rates is large. It should be noted, however, that there are more workers in these categories among occupations for which work related or postsecondary school training generally is not significant. The latter group is over twice the size of the bachelor's degree or higher training group.

As with every training group except "work related or postsecondary school training generally is not significant," a minority of employees are in occupations with above average job openings due to growth and total replacement needs and above average job openings due to growth and net replacement needs. Occupations in this group tend to be smaller, thus higher growth rates result in smaller employment increases than in occupations with no significant postsecondary training. Also, workers are more likely than those in the group, "work related or postsecondary school training generally is not significant," to remain in the occupation. As a result, replacement rates are lower, and job openings due to replacement needs are lower.

Dramatic insights are revealed by the distribution of workers in occupations having above average earnings and unemployment rates. Virtually all of the workers in these occupations experience above average earnings—25.4 million of 25.8 million. Only one occupation recorded below average earnings. The distribution of workers in occupations with above average unemployment rates is different, but equally dramatic. Virtually none of the employees in this training group—only 56,000 employees in one occupation—work in occupations with higher than average unemployment rates.

The distribution of workers employed in occupations with lower than average proportions of part-time workers was less striking than that for earnings or part-time employment. However, this clearly established that workers in this group are much less likely to work part time than full time, 6.0 million and 19.8 million, respectively. Employees in this group probably work part time by choice rather than because they are unable to locate a full-time job.

Table 2. Occupations for which work related or postsecondary school training generally is not significant

EXECUTIVE, ADMINISTRATIVE, AND MANAGERIAL OCCUPATIONS

Wholesale and retail buyers, except farm products

PROFESSIONAL SPECIALTY OCCUPATIONS

Camera operators, television, motion picture, video
Human services workers
Photographers

TECHNICIANS AND RELATED SUPPORT OCCUPATIONS

EKG technicians
Title examiners and searchers

MARKETING AND SALES OCCUPATIONS

Cashiers
Counter and rental clerks
Marketing and sales worker supervisors
Salespersons, retail

ADMINISTRATIVE SUPPORT OCCUPATIONS, INCLUDING CLERICAL

Adjustment clerks
Advertising clerks
Bill and account collectors
Billing, cost, and rate clerks
Billing, posting, and calculating machine operators
Bookkeeping, accounting, and auditing clerks
Brokerage clerks
Correspondence clerks
Court clerks
Credit authorizers
Credit checkers
Data entry keyers, except composing
Data entry keyers, composing
Dispatchers, except police, fire, and ambulance
Duplicating, mail, and other office machine operators
File clerks
General office clerks
Hotel desk clerks
Insurance claims clerks
Insurance policy processing clerks
Interviewing clerks, except personnel and social welfare
Library assistants and bookmobile drivers
Loan and credit clerks
Loan interviewers
Mail clerks, except mail machine operators and
Messengers
Meter readers, utilities
Municipal clerks
New accounts clerks, banking
Order clerks, materials, merchandise, and service
Order fillers, wholesale and retail sales
Payroll and timekeeping clerks
Peripheral EDP equipment operators
Personnel clerks, except payroll and timekeeping
    postal service
Procurement clerks
Production, planning, and expediting clerks

Proofreaders and copy markers
Real estate clerks
Receptionists and information clerks
Secretaries, except legal and medical
Statement clerks
Statistical clerks
Stock clerks
Traffic, shipping, and receiving clerks
Typists and word processors
Weighers, measurers, checkers, and samplers, recordkeeping
Welfare eligibility workers and interviewers

SERVICE OCCUPATIONS

Amusement and recreation attendants
Baggage porters and bellhops
Bakers, bread and pastry
Bartenders
Child care workers
Child care workers, private household
Cleaners and servants, private household
Cooks, institution or cafeteria
Cooks, restaurant
Cooks, short order and fast food
Cooks, private household
Crossing guards
Detectives, except public
Dining room and cafeteria attendants and bar helpers
Food counter, fountain, and related workers
Food preparation workers
Guards
Hosts and hostesses, restaurant, lounge, or coffee shop
Housekeepers and butlers
Janitors and cleaners, including maids and housekeeping   cleaners
Psychiatric aides
Shampooers
Ushers, lobby attendants, and ticket takers
Waiters and waitresses

AGRICULTURE, FORESTRY, FISHING, AND RELATED OCCUPATIONS

Animal caretakers, except farm
Captains and other officers, fishing vessels
Fallers and buckers
Farm managers
Farm workers
Farmers
Fishers, hunters, and trappers
Forest and conservation workers
Gardeners and groundskeepers, except farm
Log handling equipment operators
Logging tractor operators
Nursery workers
Supervisors, farming, forestry, and agricutural related occupations
Bicycle repairers
Bookbinders
Carpet installers

PRECISION PRODUCTION, CRAFT, AND REPAIR OCCUPATIONS

Ceiling tile installers and acoustical carpenters

Table 2. Occupations for which work related or postsecondary school training generally is not significant—Continued

PRECISION PRODUCTION, CRAFT, AND REPAIR OCCUPATIONS—CONTINUED

Highway maintenance workers
Inspectors, testers, and graders, precision
Insulation workers
Maintenance repairers, general utility
Optical goods workers, precision
Radio mechanics
Riggers
Roofers
Roustabouts
Tire repairers and changers

OPERATORS, FABRICATORS, AND LABORERS

Able seamen, ordinary seamen, and marine oilers
Bindery machine operators and set-up operators
Boiler operators and tenders, low pressure
Cannery workers
Cement and gluing machine operators and tenders
Chemical equipment controllers, operators and tenders
Coating, painting, and spraying machine operators, tenders, setters, and set-up operators
Coil winders, tapers, and finishers
Combination machine tool setters, set-up operators, operators, and tenders
Cooking and roasting machine operators and tenders, food and tobacco
Crushing and mixing machine operators and tenders
Cutters and trimmers, hand
Cutting and slicing machine setters, operators and tenders
Dairy processing equipment operators, including setters
Drilling and boring machine tool setters and set-up operators, metal and plastic
Driver/sales workers
Electrical and electronic assemblers
Electrolytic plating machine operators and tenders, setters and set-up operators, metal and plastic
Electronic semiconductor processors
Extruding and forming machine operators and tenders, synthetic or glass fibers
Extruding and forming machine setters, operators and tenders
Foundry mold assembly and shakeout workers
Freight, stock, and material movers, hand
Furnace, kiln, or kettle operators and tenders
Furnace operators and tenders
Grinders and polishers, hand
Grinding machine setters and set-up operators, metal and plastic
Hand packers and packagers
Head sawyers and sawing machine operators and tenders, setters and set-up operators
Heat treating machine operators and tenders, metal and plastic
Heaters, metal and plastic
Heating equipment setters and set-up operators, metal and plastic
Helpers, construction trades

Hoist and winch operators
Industrial truck and tractor operators
Lathe and turning machine tool setters and set-up operators, metal and plastic
Laundry and drycleaning machine operators and tenders, except pressing
Letterpress operators
Machine assemblers
Machine feeders and offbearers
Machine forming operators and tenders, metal and plastic
Machine tool cutting operators and tenders, metal and plastic
Mates, ship, boat, and barge
Meat, poultry, and fish cutters and trimmers, hand
Metal fabricators, structural metal products
Metal molding machine operators and tenders, setters and set-up operators
Metal pourers and casters, basic shapes
Motion picture projectionists
Nonelectrolytic plating machine operators and tenders, setters and set-up operators
Offset lithographic press operators
Operating engineers
Packaging and filling machine operators and tenders
Painters, transportation equipment
Painting, coating, and decorating workers, hand
Paper goods machine setters and set-up operators
Parking lot attendants
Photographic processing machine operators and tenders
Plastic molding machine operators and tenders, setters and set-up operators
Portable machine cutters
Pressers, hand
Pressing machine operators and tenders, textile, garment, and related materials
Printing press machine setters, operators and tenders
Punching machine setters and set-up operators, metal and plastic
Refuse collectors
Screen printing machine setters and set-up operators
Separating and still machine operators and tenders
Service station attendants
Sewers, hand
Sewing machine operators, garment
Sewing machine operators, non-garment
Shoe sewing machine operators and tenders
Solderers and brazers
Soldering and brazing machine operators and tenders
Taxi drivers and chauffeurs
Textile bleaching and dyeing machine operators and tenders
Textile draw-out and winding machine operators and tenders
Textile machine setters and set-up operators
Tire building machine operators
Vehicle washers and equipment cleaners
Welding machine setters, operators, and tenders
Woodworking machine operators and tenders, setters and set-up operators

Note: Occupations with above average usual weekly earnings appear in bold type. CPS proxy occupations may have been used to estimate earnings.

Individual occupations are listed in alphabetical order within each major occupational group.

Table 3. Occupations for which work related training is most significant

EXECUTIVE, ADMINISTRATIVE, AND MANAGERIAL OCCUPATIONS

Claims examiners, property and casualty insurance
Construction and building inspectors
Construction managers
Cost estimators
Food service and lodging managers

PROFESSIONAL SPECIALTY OCCUPATIONS

Athletes, coaches, umpires, and related workers
Dancers and choreographers
Musicians
Producers, directors, actors, and entertainers

TECHNICIANS AND RELATED SUPPORT OCCUPATIONS

Air traffic controllers
Aircraft pilots and flight engineers
Opticians, dispensing and measuring
Programmers, numerical, tool, and process control

MARKETING AND SALES OCCUPATIONS

Insurance sales workers

ADMINISTRATIVE SUPPORT OCCUPATIONS, INCLUDING CLERICAL

Ambulance drivers and attendants, except EMTs
Bank tellers
Central office operators
Clerical supervisors and managers
Correction officers
Customer service representatives, utilities
Directory assistance operators
Dispatchers, police, fire, and ambulance
Fire fighters
Fire fighting and prevention supervisors
Fire inspection occupations
Flight attendants
Home health aides
Institutional cleaning supervisors
Insurance adjusters, examiners, and investigators
Medical assistants
Nursing aides, orderlies, and attendants
Other law enforcement occupations
Personal and home care aides
Pest controllers and assistants
Police and detective supervisors
Police detectives and investigators
Police patrol officers
Postal mail carriers
Postal service clerks
Reservation and transportation ticket agents and travel clerks
Sheriffs and deputy sheriffs
Switchboard operators

PRECISION PRODUCTION, CRAFT, AND REPAIR OCCUPATIONS

Automotive body and related repairers

Automotive mechanics
Bakers, manufacturing

Blue collar worker supervisors
Boilermakers
Bricklayers and stone masons
Bus and truck mechanics and diesel engine specialists
Butchers and meatcutters
Cabinetmakers and bench carpenters
Camera and photographic equipment repairers
Camera operators
Carpenters
Central office and PBX installers and repairers
Chemical plant and system operators
Coin and vending machine servicers and repairers
Compositors and typesetters, precision
Concrete and terrazzo finishers
Custom tailors and sewers
Drywall installers and finishers
Electric meter installers and repairers
Electrical and electronic equipment assemblers, precision
Electrical powerline installers and repairers
Electricians
Electromechanical equipment assemblers, precision
Electromedical and biomedical equipment repairers
Electronic pagination systems workers
Elevator installers and repairers
Farm equipment mechanics
Fitters, structural metal, precision
Frame wirers, central office
Furniture finishers
Gas and petroleum plant and system occupations
Glaziers
Hard tile setters
Heat, air conditioning, and refrigeration mechanics and installers
Home appliance and power tool repairers
Industrial machinery mechanics
Job printers
Locksmiths and safe repairers
Machine builders and other precision machine assemblers
Machinists
Millwrights
Mining, quarrying, and tunneling occupations
Mobile heavy equipment mechanics
Motorcycle repairers
Musical instrument repairers and tuners
Office machine and cash register servicers
Painters and paperhangers, construction and maintenance
Paste-up workers
Patternmakers and layout workers, fabric and apparel
Paving, surfacing, and tamping equipment operators
Photoengravers
Photographic process workers, precision
Pipelayers and pipelaying fitters
Plasterers
Platemakers
Plumbers, pipefitters, and steamfitters
Power distributors and dispatchers
Power generating and reactor plant operators
Precision instrument repairers
Sheet metal workers and duct installers
Shipfitters

Table 3. Occupations for which work related training is most significant—Continued

PRECISION PRODUCTION, CRAFT, AND REPAIR OCCUPATIONS—Continued	Captains and pilots, ship

PRECISION PRODUCTION, CRAFT, AND REPAIR OCCUPATIONS—Continued

Shoe and leather workers and repairers, precision
Signal or track switch maintainers
Small engine specialists
Station installers and repairers, telephone
Stationary engineers
Strippers, printing
Structural and reinforcing metal workers
Telephone and cable TV line installers and repairers
Tool and die makers
Upholsterers
Watchmakers
Water and liquid waste treatment plant and system operators

OPERATORS, FABRICATORS, AND LABORERS

Bus drivers
Bus drivers, school

Captains and pilots, ship
Crane and tower operators
Excavation and loading machine operators
Grader, dozer, and scraper operators
Locomotive engineers
Numerical control machine tool operators and tenders, metal and plastic
Photoengraving and lithographic machine operators and tenders
Rail yard engineers, dinkey operators, and hostlers
Railroad brake, signal, and switch operators
Railroad conductors and yardmasters
Ship engineers
Subway and streetcar operators
Truck drivers light and heavy
Typesetting and composing machine operators and tenders
Welders and cutters

Note: Occupations with above average usual weekly earnings appear in bold type. CPS proxy occupations may have been used to estimate earnings.

Individual occupations are listed in alphabetical order within each major occupational group.

Table 4. Occupations for which some postsecondary school training is most significant

EXECUTIVE, ADMINISTRATIVE AND MANAGERIAL OCCUPATIONS
Funeral directors and morticians

PROFESSIONAL SPECIALTY OCCUPATIONS
Registered nurses
Respiratory therapists
Surveyors

TECHNICIANS AND RELATED SUPPORT OCCUPATIONS
Broadcast technicians
Cardiology technologists
Dental hygienists
Drafters
EEG technologists
Electrical and electronic technicians/technologists
Emergency medical technicians
Licensed practical nurses
Medical records technicians
Nuclear medicine technologists
Paralegals
Psychiatric technicians
Radiologic technologists and technicians
Science and mathematics technicians
Surgical technologists
Technical assistants, library

MARKETING AND SALES OCCUPATIONS
Brokers, real estate
Real estate appraisers

Sales agents, real estate
Travel agents

ADMINISTRATIVE SUPPORT OCCUPATIONS, INCLUDING CLERICAL
Computer operators, except peripheral equipment
Legal secretaries
Medical secretaries
Stenographers
Teacher aides and educational assistants

SERVICE OCCUPATIONS
Barbers
Dental assistants
Hairdressers, hairstylists, and cosmetologists
Manicurists
Occupational therapy assistants and aides
Pharmacy assistants
Physical and corrective therapy assistants and aides

PRECISION PRODUCTION, CRAFT, AND REPAIR OCCUPATIONS
Aircraft engine specialists
Aircraft mechanics
Data processing equipment repairers
Dental lab technicians, precision
Electronic home entertainment equipment repairers
Electronics repairers, commercial and industrial equipment
Jewelers and silversmiths

Note: Occupations with above average usual weekly earnings appear in bold type. CPS proxy occupations may have been used to estimate earnings.

Individual occupations are listed in alphabetical order within each major occupational group.

Table 5. Occupations for which training in a bachelor's degree or higher program is most significant

EXECUTIVE, ADMINISTRATIVE, AND MANAGERIAL OCCUPATIONS

Accountants and auditors
Administrative services managers
Budget analysts
Communication, transportation, and utilities operations managers
Credit analysts
Education administrators
Employment interviewers, private or public employment service
Engineering, mathematical, and natural science managers
Financial managers
General managers and top executives
Government chief executives and legislators
Industrial production managers
Inspectors and compliance officers, except construction
Loan officers and counselors
Management analysts
Marketing, advertising, and public relations managers
Personnel, training, and labor relations managers
Personnel, training, and labor relations specialists
Property and real estate managers
Purchasing agents, except wholesale, retail, and farm products
Purchasing managers
Tax examiners, collectors, and revenue agents
Underwriters

PROFESSIONAL SPECIALTY OCCUPATIONS

Actuaries
Aeronautical and astronautical engineers
Agricultural and food scientists
Architects, except landscape and marine
Artists and commercial artists
Biological scientists
Chemical engineers
Chemists
Chiropractors
Civil engineers, including traffic engineers
Clergy
College and university faculty
Computer engineers and scientists
Counselors
Curators, archivists, museum technicians, and restorers
Dentists
Designers, except interior designers
Dietitians and nutritionists
Directors, religious activities and education
Economists
Electrical and electronics engineers
Farm and home management advisors
Foresters and conservation scientists

Geologists, geophysicists, and oceanographers
Industrial engineers, except safety engineers
Instructors, adult (nonvocational) education
Instructors and coaches, sports and physical training
Interior designers
Judges, magistrates, and other judicial workers
Landscape architects
Lawyers
Librarians, professional
Mathematicians and all other mathematical scientists
Mechanical engineers
Medical scientists
Metallurgists and metallurgical, ceramic, and materials engineers
Meteorologists
Mining engineers, including mine safety engineers
Nuclear engineers
Occupational therapists
Operations research analysts
Optometrists
Petroleum engineers
Pharmacists
Physical therapists
Physician assistants
Physicians
Physicists and astronomers
Podiatrists
Psychologists
Public relations specialists and publicity writers
Radio and TV announcers and newscasters
Recreation workers
Recreational therapists
Reporters and correspondents
Social workers
Speech-language pathologists and audiologists
Statisticians
Systems analysts
Teachers, elementary
Teachers, preschool and kindergarten
Teachers, special education
Teachers, secondary school
Teachers and instructors, vocational education and training
Urban and regional planners
Veterinarians and veterinary inspectors
Writers and editors, including technical writers

TECHNICIANS AND RELATED SUPPORT OCCUPATIONS

Clinical lab technologists and technicians
Computer programmers

MARKETING AND SALES OCCUPATIONS

Securities and financial services sales workers

Note: Occupations with above average usual weekly earnings appear in bold type. CPS proxy occupations may have been used to estimate earnings.

Individual occupations are listed in alphabetical order within each major occupational group.

Employment Trends by Industry

Appendix D

Editor's Comments:

While much of the data in this book provides information on specific jobs and clusters of jobs, this appendix provides information on major industries. While learning more about industries may not seem that important to you, it is one of the things I urge you to consider in your career planning. For example, some industries will pay substantially more for the same type of work than another industry will. Other industries may offer better benefits or more job security than another. While these issues are not the only ones to consider in making career plans, considering your options in various industries can be worth your time.

There are two tables in this appendix. The first provides information on projected employment growth for several hundred major industries. Another table provides brief comments regarding the trends within major industries. You may find both tables helpful in determining growth trends for a particular industry that either you are considering for the future or are currently employed—or both. If you want to learn more about a specific industry, look for a book title *The Career Guide to America's Top Industries*. It provides helpful and readable information on major trends within more than 40 industries, including details that are important in making career or job-related decisions.

As with all the information in this book, please note that the figures in this appendix are projected national trends and there will be many variations within regions and even specific companies and organizations within the same industry. There will be opportunities for the talented and the well-prepared, even in industries that are declining in the numbers of people they employ.

Table 5.   Employment by industry, 1979, 1992, and projected 2005

Standard Industrial Classification	Industry description	Employment (in thousands)					Annual growth rate[1]	
		1979	1992	2005			Employment, 1992–2005 (moderate scenerio)	Output, 1992–2005
				Low	Moderate	High		
	Nonfarm wage and salary[2]	89,491	107,888	124,931	132,960	138,944	1.6	(3)
10–14	Mining..................................	958	631	510	562	690	− .9	0.4
10	Metal mining	101	53	57	64	67	1.4	2.3
12	Coal mining	259	126	85	90	96	−2.5	3.1
131,132	Crude petroleum, natural gas, and gas liquids	198	187	138	164	197	−1.0	−1.3
138	Oil and gas field services	276	164	130	136	214	−1.4	− .7
14	Nonmetallic minerals, except fuels	124	102	101	107	118	.4	2.2
15,16,17	Construction	4,463	4,471	5,407	5,632	6,643	1.8	1.8
20–39	Manufacturing.........................	21,040	18,040	15,981	17,523	18,866	− .2	2.4
24,25,32–39	Durable manufacturing	12,730	10,237	8,738	9,673	10,788	− .4	2.7
24	Lumber and wood products	782	674	699	690	832	.2	1.9
241	Logging	89	78	65	68	78	−1.0	1.5
242	Sawmills and planing mills	237	179	160	167	196	− .5	1.6
24,31,4,9	Millwork and structural wood members, n.e.c...............	157	190	249	250	317	2.2	3.1
2435,6	Veneer and plywood	77	49	38	39	48	−1.7	1.7
244,9	Wood containers and miscellaneous wood products..................	140	123	107	115	127	− .5	2.1
2451	Mobile homes	58	40	32	33	44	−1.6	−1.1
2452	Prefabricated wood buildings	26	16	18	18	24	1.0	1.7
25	Furniture and fixtures	498	476	479	523	561	.7	1.9
251	Household furniture	329	270	265	283	294	.4	2.0
254	Partitions and fixtures	65	75	82	90	103	1.4	2.4
252,3,9	Office and miscellaneous furniture and fixtures	104	132	133	150	165	1.0	1.7
32	Stone, clay, and glass products	674	512	409	437	492	−1.2	1.1
321,2,3	Glass and glass products	199	152	114	124	129	−1.6	.9
324,327	Cement, concrete, gypsum, and plaster products	249	204	166	174	207	−1.2	1.3
325,6,8,9	Stone, clay, and miscellaneous mineral products[4].................	226	156	129	140	156	− .8	1.1
33	Primary metal industries..............	1,254	693	556	618	680	− .9	1.2
331	Blast furnaces and basic steel products........................	571	250	201	224	247	− .9	1.4
332	Iron and steel foundries.............	241	120	88	97	108	−1.6	.1
333	Primary nonferrous metals	73	43	36	40	43	− .6	1.4
334,9	Miscellaneous primary and secondary metals	51	41	38	42	46	.2	3.2
335	Nonferrous rolling and drawing	220	162	120	133	148	−1.5	.5
336	Nonferrous foundries..............	100	77	74	81	89	.4	2.1
34	Fabricated metal products	1,713	1,322	1,101	1,196	1,327	− .8	1.2
341	Metal cans and shipping containers ...	80	45	30	31	32	−2.8	1.0
342	Cutlery, handtools, and hardware	184	123	98	106	116	−1.1	1.6
343	Plumbing and nonelectric heating equipment	77	56	49	50	59	− .9	.9
344	Fabricated structural metal products ...	516	390	311	331	383	−1.2	.7
345	Screw machine products, bolts, rivets, etc.	116	90	76	85	92	− .4	1.9
3462,3	Forgings	63	36	32	35	37	− .2	1.1
3465	Automotive stampings..............	118	98	103	113	120	1.1	1.7
3466,9	Stampings, except automotive	121	83	53	59	64	−2.6	.1
347	Metal services, n.e.c.	107	115	127	142	159	1.7	4.1
3482,3484	Small arms and small arms ammunition	29	20	14	15	15	−2.1	.1
3483,3489	Ammunition and ordnance, except small arms	35	46	26	27	27	−4.0	−1.0
349	Miscellaneous fabricated metal products......................	269	222	183	203	222	− .7	.7
35	Industrial machinery and equipment	2,508	1,922	1,638	1,868	2,160	− .2	4.6
351	Engines and turbines	145	87	61	69	76	−1.8	.7
352	Farm and garden machinery	182	93	81	91	103	− .2	2.5
3531	Construction machinery	161	73	63	71	81	− .2	3.2
3532,3	Mining and oil field machinery	120	55	52	59	62	.5	.6

See footnotes at end of table.

Table 5.   Continued—Employment by industry, 1979, 1992, and projected 2005

Standard Industrial Classification	Industry description	Employment (in thousands)					Annual growth rate[1]	
				2005			Employment, 1992–2005 (moderate scenerio)	Output, 1992–2005
		1979	1992	Low	Moderate	High		
3534,5,6,7	Materials handling machinery and equipment[4]	101	75	75	84	97	.9	2.3
354	Metalworking machinery	395	302	290	332	377	.7	1.8
355	Special industry machinery	193	148	109	126	147	−1.2	2.0
356	General industrial machinery	304	236	208	238	273	.1	2.0
3571,2,5,7	Computer equipment[4]	318	353	195	237	312	−3.0	8.1
3578,9	Office and accounting machines[4]	68	38	21	27	36	−2.7	1.6
358	Refrigeration and service industry machinery	189	173	169	184	205	.5	3.0
359	Industrial machinery, n.e.c.	332	290	315	351	391	1.5	2.8
36	Electronic and other electric equipment ..	1,793	1,526	1,185	1,354	1,537	− .9	3.3
361	Electric distributing equipment	120	83	60	68	81	−1.5	.9
362	Electrical industrial apparatus	242	158	104	119	137	−2.1	1.3
363	Household appliances	177	116	89	94	97	−1.6	2.2
364	Electric lighting and wiring equipment ..	227	174	138	155	176	− .9	1.0
365	Household audio and video equipment .	115	82	60	63	65	−2.1	3.2
3661	Telephone and telegraph apparatus[4] ..	171	108	68	81	93	−2.3	1.4
3663,9	Broadcasting and communications equipment[4,5]	128	128	104	116	130	− .8	4.4
3674	Semiconductors and related devices ..	201	218	188	224	264	.2	5.6
3671,2,5–9	Miscellaneous electronic components[4] .	309	307	255	300	348	− .2	3.5
3691,4	Storage batteries and engine electrical parts	118	89	77	85	90	− .3	2.5
3692,5,9	Electrical equipment and supplies, n.e.c.[4,5]	77	62	43	49	56	−1.8	3.3
37	Transportation equipment	2,059	1,822	1,610	1,765	1,891	− .2	2.3
371	Motor vehicles and equipment	990	809	686	759	817	− .5	2.6
3711	Motor vehicles and car bodies	463	314	213	241	256	−2.0	2.6
3714	Motor vehicle parts and accessories ...	441	417	379	413	447	− .1	2.4
3713,5,6	Truck and bus bodies, trailers, and motor homes	86	77	94	105	114	2.4	4.8
3721	Aircraft	333	332	274	302	330	− .7	1.2
3724,3764	Aircraft and missile engines	163	149	133	146	156	− .2	3.0
3728,3769	Aircraft and missile parts and equipment, n.e.c.	120	170	236	255	275	3.2	4.2
3761	Guided missiles and space vehicles ...	81	105	69	73	74	−2.8	− .3
3731	Ship building and repairing	173	124	74	77	78	−3.6	−2.3
3732	Boat building and repairing	53	45	53	59	61	2.0	5.9
374	Railroad equipment	74	28	34	38	43	2.5	3.4
375,9	Miscellaneous transportation equipment	74	60	51	56	57	− .5	1.3
38	Instruments and related products	1,006	925	796	887	969	− .3	3.4
381	Search and navigation equipment[4]	227	228	161	177	198	−1.9	2.1
382,387	Measuring and controlling devices, watches[4]	431	300	226	255	282	−1.2	3.7
385	Ophthalmic goods	45	38	34	40	41	.4	3.3
3841–3	Medical instruments and supplies	144	216	269	295	317	2.4	6.1
3844–5	X–ray and other electromedical apparatus[4,5]	26	48	51	58	66	1.5	3.7
386	Photographic equipment and supplies .	134	95	55	62	65	−3.2	1.3
39	Miscellaneous manufacturing industries	445	363	294	334	340	− .6	1.9
391	Jewelry, silverware, and plated ware ..	61	50	41	47	49	− .4	1.0
394	Toys and sporting goods	121	107	81	95	95	− .9	2.2
393,5,6,9	Manufactured products, n.e.c.[4]	263	207	172	192	195	− .6	1.9
20–23,26–31	Nondurable manufacturing	8,310	7,804	7,243	7,851	8,079	.0	1.9
20	Food and kindred products	1,733	1,655	1,589	1,648	1,660	.0	1.5
201	Meat products	358	434	475	496	500	1.0	1.3
2 2	Dairy products	180	152	127	134	135	−1.0	1.0
203	Preserved fruits and vegetables	250	246	252	261	263	.4	1.9
204,7	Grain mill products, fats and oils	189	156	133	139	141	− .9	2.6
205	Bakery products	237	207	183	192	193	− .6	1.0
206	Sugar and confectionery products	113	104	89	91	92	−1.0	.7
2082,3,4,5	Alcoholic beverages	86	66	52	53	54	−1.7	.7

See footnotes at end of table.

Table 5.   Continued—Employment by industry, 1979, 1992, and projected 2005

Standard Industrial Classification	Industry description	Employment (in thousands)					Annual growth rate[1]	
		1979	1992	2005			Employment, 1992–2005 (moderate scenerio)	Output, 1992–2005
				Low	Moderate	High		
2086,7	Soft drinks and flavorings	153	109	81	84	84	−2.0	1.3
209	Miscellaneous foods and kindred products	165	180	197	198	199	.7	1.3
21	Tobacco manufactures	70	49	35	37	39	−2.1	.7
22	Textile mill products	885	671	510	571	585	−1.2	1.2
221,2,3,4,6,8	Weaving, finishing, yarn, and thread mills	528	360	255	287	291	−1.7	.7
225	Knitting mills	231	202	152	173	173	−1.2	.4
227	Carpets and rugs................	61	59	65	68	75	1.1	3.3
229	Miscellaneous textile goods	66	51	39	43	45	−1.4	2.2
23	Apparel and other textile products	1,304	1,005	651	760	765	−2.1	.7
231–8	Apparel	1,115	807	467	556	556	−2.8	.0
239	Miscellaneous fabricated textile products .	189	198	184	205	210	.2	2.6
26	Paper and allied products............	697	687	672	729	752	.4	2.5
261,2,3	Pulp, paper, and paperboard mills	262	239	204	224	227	−.5	2.5
265	Paperboard containers and boxes	214	211	215	231	241	.7	2.2
267	Converted paper products, except containers	221	238	253	274	285	1.1	2.8
27	Printing and publishing	1,235	1,504	1,621	1,751	1,810	1.2	2.9
271	Newspapers	420	451	477	513	532	1.0	1.9
272	Periodicals....................	82	123	135	146	152	1.3	3.2
273	Books	102	118	130	146	151	1.7	3.2
274	Miscellaneous publishing	46	80	108	117	121	3.0	3.9
275,6	Commercial printing and business forms .	451	577	612	656	676	1.0	3.0
277	Greeting card publishing	24	26	27	30	31	1.0	3.3
278	Blankbooks and bookbinding	63	69	71	78	79	1.0	3.2
279	Printing trade services	47	59	61	65	68	.8	3.2
28	Chemicals and allied products	1,109	1,083	1,006	1,090	1,132	.1	2.3
281,6	Industrial chemicals................	333	290	234	255	265	−1.0	1.7
282	Plastics materials and synthetics	212	173	144	158	167	−.7	2.5
283	Drugs........................	193	256	277	297	300	1.1	2.9
284	Soap, cleaners, and toilet goods	140	154	153	167	173	.7	2.3
285	Paints and allied products	69	58	52	56	62	−.4	2.4
287	Agricultural chemicals	70	58	42	45	45	−2.0	1.3
289	Miscellaneous chemical products	93	93	105	113	120	1.5	3.9
29	Petroleum and coal products	210	159	118	128	137	−1.6	.8
291	Petroleum refining	165	120	84	92	98	−2.0	.6
295,9	Miscellaneous petroleum and coal products......................	45	39	34	36	40	−.5	2.8
30	Rubber and miscellaneous plastics products	821	872	979	1,066	1,125	1.6	3.5
301	Tires and inner tubes	127	82	59	64	67	−1.8	.2
302,5,6	Rubber products, plastic hose and footwear......................	208	171	142	158	160	−.6	2.3
308	Miscellaneous plastics products, n.e.c..	486	619	778	843	898	2.4	4.2
31	Leather and leather products	246	119	63	71	73	−3.9	−2.2
313,4	Footwear except rubber and plastic ...	161	69	33	39	41	−4.4	−2.5
311,5,6,7,9	Luggage, handbags, and leather products, n.e.c.	85	51	30	33	33	−3.4	−2.1
40–42,44–49	Transportation, communications, utilities	5,136	5,709	5,909	6,497	6,763	1.0	2.3
40–42,44–47	Transportation	3,019	3,486	3,866	4,310	4,507	1.6	2.8
40	Railroad transportation	556	254	233	252	270	−.1	2.4
41	Local and interurban passenger transit ..	263	359	332	383	386	.5	1.7
42	Trucking and warehousing	1,339	1,606	1,866	2,019	2,130	1.8	2.3
44	Water transportation	214	173	132	154	171	−.9	1.9
45	Air transportation	438	729	835	967	996	2.2	4.0
46	Pipelines, except natural gas	20	19	17	18	19	−.2	1.2
47	Transportation services	189	346	452	516	535	3.1	3.5
472	Passenger transportation arrangement[4] ..	92	183	260	300	307	3.9	2.5
473,4,8	Miscellaneous transportation services[4] ..	96	163	192	216	229	2.2	4.2
48	Communications	1,309	1,268	1,030	1,116	1,142	−1.0	2.7
481,2,9	Communications, except broadcasting[4] ..	1,095	912	660	724	742	−1.8	3.1
483,4	Radio and television broadcasting, cable TV[4]	214	355	370	392	400	.8	1.4
49	Electric, gas, and sanitary services	807	955	1,013	1,072	1,115	.9	1.1
491,pt.493	Electric utilities including combined services	493	553	554	582	606	.4	1.5

See footnotes at end of table.

Standard Industrial Classification	Industry description	Employment (in thousands)					Annual growth rate[1]	
		1979	1992	2005			Employment, 1992–2005 (moderate scenario)	Output, 1992–2005
				Low	Moderate	High		
492, pt.493	Gas utilities including combined services .	220	205	184	190	205	– .6	– .9
494,5,6,7,pt.493	Water and sanitation including combined services	94	197	274	299	304	3.3	3.7
50,5	Wholesale trade	5,221	6,045	6,641	7,191	7,761	1.3	2.9
52–59	Retail trade	14,972	19,346	22,254	23,777	24,336	1.6	2.2
52–57,59	Retail trade, excluding eating and drinking places	10,459	12,744	13,926	14,999	15,511	1.3	2.4
58	Eating and drinking places	4,513	6,602	8,329	8,778	8,825	2.2	1.4
60–67	Finance, insurance, and real estate	4,975	6,571	7,585	7,969	8,078	1.5	2.2
60	Depository institutions[4]	1,890	2,103	2,107	2,195	2,201	.3	2.9
61,7	Nondepository; holding and investment offices[4]	276	615	921	949	957	3.4	4.5
62	Security and commodity brokers	204	439	528	570	575	2.0	4.0
63	Insurance carriers	1,200	1,480	1,549	1,660	1,661	.9	1.7
64	Insurance agents, brokers, and service	443	652	906	971	972	3.1	3.3
65	Real estate	963	1,282	1,574	1,624	1,712	1.8	2.6
70–87,89	Services[2]	16,779	28,422	39,808	41,788	42,766	3.0	3.5
70	Hotels and other lodging places	1,060	1,572	2,136	2,209	2,281	2.6	4.1
72	Personal services	821	1,111	1,352	1,382	1,388	1.7	2.0
721,5	Laundry, cleaning, and shoe repair[4]	367	418	458	475	476	1.0	1.7
722,9	Personal services, n.e.c.[4]	98	216	286	292	294	2.3	2.1
723,4	Beauty and barber shops	318	392	510	516	518	2.1	2.5
726	Funeral service and crematories	69	85	98	99	100	1.2	1.0
73	Business services	2,410	5,313	7,799	8,370	8,664	3.6	4.7
731	Advertising	146	226	268	288	299	1.9	2.4
734	Services to buildings	487	805	937	1,000	1,029	1.7	3.9
735	Miscellaneous equipment rental and leasing[4]	—	205	298	325	343	3.6	3.9
736	Personnel supply services	508	1,649	2,408	2,581	2,656	3.5	2.8
737	Computer and data processing services .	271	831	1,507	1,626	1,697	5.3	5.9
7381,2	Detective, guard, and security services[4] .	—	505	658	716	742	2.7	2.4
7334,5,6;7384	Photocopying, commercial art, photofinishing[4]	—	190	274	291	302	3.4	4.3
732;7331,8; 7383,9	Business services, n.e.c.[4]	—	903	1,450	1,543	1,597	4.2	5.5
75	Auto repair, services, and garages	575	878	1,229	1,293	1,401	3.0	2.3
751	Automotive rentals, without drivers[4]	118	159	206	222	236	2.6	4.1
752,3,4	Automobile parking, repair, and services .	457	719	1,023	1,071	1,165	3.1	1.9
76	Miscellaneous repair shops	282	345	421	449	467	2.0	2.4
762	Electrical repair shops	84	108	131	140	143	2.0	2.4
763,4	Watch, clock, jewelry, and furniture repair	29	27	27	29	30	.7	.2
769	Miscellaneous repair shops and related services	169	210	262	280	295	2.2	2.6
78	Motion pictures	228	404	476	499	511	1.6	2.3
781–3	Motion pictures	228	279	374	392	401	2.6	2.8
784	Video tape rental	—	125	103	110	107	–1.2	–1.3
79	Amusement and recreation services	751	1,169	1,595	1,626	1,646	2.6	3.2
792	Producers, orchestras, and entertainers .	84	143	194	201	208	2.6	2.0
793	Bowling centers	102	88	84	85	86	– .2	– .2
794	Commercial sports	70	113	133	135	138	1.4	.9
791,9	Amusement and recreation services, n.e.c.	494	826	1,184	1,205	1,215	3.0	4.1
80	Health services	4,993	8,523	11,998	12,539	12,632	3.0	3.3
801,2,3,4	Offices of health practitioners	1,200	2,387	3,468	3,617	3,667	3.2	2.9
805	Nursing and personal care facilities	951	1,543	2,215	2,306	2,330	3.1	3.4
806	Hospitals, private	2,608	3,760	4,801	5,039	5,048	2.3	3.4
807,8,9	Health services, n.e.c.	234	833	1,514	1,577	1,587	5.0	3.9
81	Legal services	460	915	1,280	1,355	1,380	3.1	3.4
82	Educational services	1,090	1,700	2,047	2,162	2,174	1.9	2.8
821	Elementary and secondary schools	259	467	616	616	618	2.2	3.0
822	Colleges and universities	717	1,025	1,124	1,236	1,245	1.5	2.7
823–9	Libraries, vocational, and other schools ..	114	208	307	310	312	3.1	2.9
83	Social services	1,081	1,958	3,584	3,691	3,715	5.0	5.1
832,9	Individual and miscellaneous social services	390	703	1,129	1,162	1,167	3.9	5.1

See footnotes at end of table.

Table 5.   Continued—Employment by industry, 1979, 1992, and projected 2005

Standard Industrial Classification	Industry description	Employment (in thousands)					Annual growth rate[1]	
		1979	1992	2005			Employment, 1992–2005 (moderate scenerio)	Output, 1992–2005
				Low	Moderate	High		
833	Job training and related services	187	271	401	418	421	3.4	3.7
835	Child day care services	303	449	757	777	780	4.3	2.8
836	Residential care	201	535	1,297	1,335	1,348	7.3	7.8
84,86,8733	Museums, zoos, and membership organizations	1,652	2,164	2,601	2,674	2,703	1.6	4.1
84;865,9;8733	Museums and noncommercial organizations, n.e.c.	201	298	383	393	399	2.2	5.9
861,2	Business and professional associations. .	117	156	190	200	203	1.9	1.9
863,4	Labor, civic, and social organizations. . . .	453	559	648	661	669	1.3	1.4
866	Religious organizations[5]	882	1,151	1,380	1,420	1,432	1.6	4.8
87(less 8733), 89	Engineering, management, and services, n.e.c.	1,341	2,370	3,290	3,538	3,804	3.1	3.4
871	Engineering and architectural services . .	515	746	928	1,001	1,173	2.3	2.4
8731,2,4	Research and testing services	235	417	522	553	564	2.2	3.3
874	Management and public relations	273	655	1,026	1,110	1,153	4.1	5.5
872,89	Accounting, auditing, and services, n.e.c.	318	553	816	876	914	3.6	2.2
	Government	15,947	18,653	20,836	22,021	23,041	1.3	1.5
	Federal Government	2,773	2,969	2,628	2,815	2,950	− .4	.6
	Federal enterprises	876	985	826	915	984	− .6	2.7
	U.S. Postal Service	661	792	674	751	807	− .4	3.2
	Federal electric utilities	52	28	18	19	21	−2.7	.4
	Federal Government enterprises, n.e.c.	163	165	135	144	156	−1.0	1.8
	Federal general government	1,897	1,984	1,802	1,901	1,966	− .3	− .2
	State and local government	13,174	15,683	18,208	19,206	20,091	1.6	2.0
	State and local enterprises	733	938	1,007	1,137	1,223	1.5	1.9
	Local government passenger transit . . .	130	204	214	254	271	1.7	1.1
	State and local electric utilities	63	81	81	88	96	.6	1.0
	State and local government enterprises, n.e.c.	540	653	712	795	856	1.5	2.2
	State and local general government	12,441	14,745	17,201	18,069	18,868	1.6	2.0
	State and local government hospitals . .	1,108	1,090	1,190	1,250	1,305	1.1	.7
	State government education	1,378	1,797	2,191	2,301	2,403	1.9	2.4
	Local government education	5,107	6,222	7,627	8,012	8,366	2.0	2.7
	State and local general government, n.e.c.	4,847	5,637	6,193	6,506	6,793	1.1	1.3
01,02,07,08,09	Agriculture[6]	3,398	3,295	3,221	3,325	3,535	.1	1.6
pt.01,pt.02	Livestock and livestock products	1,268	1,117	959	993	1,049	− .9	1.1
pt.01,pt.02	Other agricultural products	1,506	1,088	827	846	897	−1.9	1.8
7	Agricultural services	547	984	1,304	1,351	1,442	2.5	3.1
8	Forestry	21	38	49	52	61	2.4	2.5
9	Fishing, hunting, and trapping	57	69	81	83	86	1.4	.1
88	Private households	1,264	1,116	777	802	853	−2.5	−1.0
	Nonagricultural self-employed and unpaid family[7]	7,210	8,794	10,078	10,397	11,098	1.3	(³)
	Total[8]	101,363	121,093	139,007	147,483	154,430	1.5	2.4

[1] Rates are based on moderate scenario.

[2] Excludes SIC 074,5,8 (agricultural services) and 99 (nonclassifiable establishments). The data therefore are not exactly comparable with data published in *Employment and Earnings*.

[3] Comparable estimate of output growth is not available.

[4] Current Employment Statistics (CES) figures are not available for 1979 for this industry (or for at least one component in a group of industries). Estimates were produced by the Bureau's Office of Employment Projections for the purpose of these projections.

[5] Does not meet usual publication criteria of Current Employment Statistics program.

[6] Excludes government wage and salary workers, and includes private SIC 08, 09 (forestry and fisheries).

[7] Excludes SIC 08, 09 (forestry and fisheries).

[8] Wage and salary data are from the Current Employment Statistics (payroll) survey, which counts jobs, whereas self-employed, unpaid family worker, agricultural, and private household data are from the Current Population Survey (household survey), which counts workers. These totals for 1979 and 1992, therefore, differ from the official employment estimates of the Bureau of Labor Statistics.

NOTE: Dash indicates data not available.

SOURCE: Historical output data are from the Bureau of Economic Analysis, U.S. Department of Commerce.

n.e.c. = not elsewhere classified.

Table 1. Specific industry assumptions

Industry	Assumptions
Livestock and livestock products	This industry sells to the meat products and to the diary products industries as well as directly to consumers. A slowing from past growth is noted here as population growth slows and as per capita meat consumption continues to decline due to rising health consciousness.
Other agricultural products	This industry sells to processed food industries and has experienced heavy demand from the grain mill products industry. The grain mill products industry is itself growing rapidly as a result increasing consumer demand from health-conscious individuals, and also because of burgeoning exports. Growth in both exports and imports is expected to continue, particularly with the ratification of NAFTA. Exports of grains and oilseed to Mexico can be expected to jump sharply as vegetable and fruit growers feel increased import pressure from that country.
Agricultural services	Increased demand for landscaping and lawn and garden services is expected to continue, both from individual homeowners and from the owners of large building complexes. This industry also sells to the forestry industry, but this component of demand is expected to grow only moderately as forestry demand slows in the coming 15 years. Veterinary services are also an important component of this industry and are expected to grow only slightly above present levels. This will lead to virtually no growth in the self-employed portion of the industry.
Forestry	Output is expected to increase from the low level of 1990. This industry sells primarily to construction industries and to foreign markets, both of which are projected to recover from the 1990 low point. However, due to slower growth in construction and increased environmental pressures, the growth rate is not expected to reach that attained in the 1960-90 period. The level of output is expected barely to reach the 1987 historical high, even by 2005.
Fishing, hunting, and trapping	This industry sells fresh fish to consumers; it is considered a growth industry because of the health considerations associated with fish. One of the largest intermediate consumers of this industry's output is the eating and drinking places industry, which is expected to continue to grow rapidly through 2005. Import shares are not expected to increase markedly, due to the extension of territorial fishing limits to 200 miles offshore.
Coal mining	The volume of coal exports is expected to continue to expand through 2005. Production assumptions are based on Department of Energy forecasts of domestic demand and modest increases in import shares.
Crude petroleum, natural gas, and gas liquids	Higher prices, more efficient energy use, and advances in the production and transmission of electricity, will keep petroleum demand at moderate levels. Foreign sources are projected to supply an increasing proportion of demand; domestic production is projected to decline. These assumptions are based on Department of Energy forecasts.
Oil and gas field services	Due to a projected decline in domestic production and a rise in the foreign supply of oil and gas, this industry, which provides services to exploration establishments, is expected to continue to decline in the future. Continued relatively low oil price growth will reinforce this effect as secondary and tertiary recovery techniques continue to be uneconomic. Production and foreign supply are based on U.S. Department of Energy forecasts.
Nonmetallic minerals, except fuels	Construction activity has a large indirect effect on the demand for output of this industry. Slowdowns projected for construction are offset, to some extent, by an accelerating demand from the agricultural chemicals industry.
New nonfarm housing	Single- and multi-family housing construction will slow from rates of early 1980's because of the expected slowdown in new household formation.
New industrial buildings	Moderate growth is projected for new factory construction due to the need to modernize existing facilities.
New commercial buildings	Office and other commercial buildings are not expected to recover from the recent overproduction of the 1980's and the resulting high vacancy rates, at least through 2005.
New education buildings	After years of little growth, new school construction will accelerate, reflecting growth in the school-age population.

Table 1. Specific industry assumptions—Continued

Industry	Assumptions
Primary nonferrous metals	Continuing increases in the efficiency of domestic mills, along with the stabilization of world prices, will result in stable growth. Output is consumed mainly by the auto and construction industries; almost 20 percent is supplied by imports. The aluminum industry is expected to grow but not the copper industry. Due to the general slowdown in construction growth and the continuing substitution of PVC pipe for copper in new plumbing installations, copper industry growth is expected to be stagnant.
Miscellaneous primary and secondary metals	The machinery-producing and automotive industries purchase the output of this industry. As these industries grow, so too will miscellaneous metals demand.
Nonferrous foundries	Flat productivity is expected in this industry following big improvements in the 1980's.
Metal cans and shipping containers	Growth will slow as many processors of foods and other materials continue to substitute plastics for metal cans in response to a demand for microwave- and freezer-proof containers. However, reclycing programs and environmental concerns about the over use of plastics are expected to prevent this industry from going into an absolute decline.
Plumbing and nonelectric heating equipment	Almost all output of this industry is consumed by the construction industry, so projected growth depends on what is happening in construction.
Fabricated structural metal products	Growth of construction determines the growth of this industry. A small amount of output is purchased by the defense indusrty, a declining sector of the economy over the projection period.
Screw machine products, and bolts, nuts, screws, rivets and washers	This industry will continue to grow due to increasing demand for capital equipment, a heavy user of these types of goods. The airline, auto, and petroleum refining industries also purchase these products. Imports are projected to raise their market share.
Stampings, except automotive	Growth is expected in intermediate demand for computer cases. Technological advances and diffusion are likely to come slowly because much of this industry consists of small-job shops.
Metal services, n.e.c.	Productivity growth is limited by product diversity and the large number of small firms in the industry.
Small arms and small arms ammunition	Strong export growth will offset decreased defense spending and slowing growth in personal consumption.
Ammunition and ordnance, except small arms	Defense spending cutbacks will lead to output declines.
Miscellaneous fabricated metal products	Slow growth because output is linked heavily to construction activity.
Engines and turbines	Imports are expected to improve their market share. Offsetting this is strong growth projected for exports.
Farm and garden machinery	Demand is expected to increase moderately as a result of spending by farms and by the real estate sector on equipment. Exports are also expected to show moderately strong growth in this industry.
Construction machinery	Demand in this industry is expected to be strong despite the slowdown in new construction due to infrastructure maintenance and repair and also because of growing exports.
Mining and oil field machinery	Export growth is quite strong and is expected to continue. Environmental concerns and generally lower energy prices have led to sharp slowdowns in domestic petroleum exploration, but oil exploration abroad is expected to continue to be strong.
Material handling machinery and equipment	This sector will continue to be stimulated by increasing factory automation and the attendant spending for this type of equipment.
Metalworking machinery	Domestic output is expected to grow modestly because of intense international competition. The import share of output will likely continue to increase.

Table 1. Specific Industry assumptions—Continued

Industry	Assumptions
New hospitals and institutions	Slight increases are expected in nursing home and health clinic facilities.
New water supply and sewer facilities	Increasing population and environmental pressures are expected to increase demand for sewage treatment plants, waste disposal facilities, and clean water projects.
New Roads	Replacement of aging bridges and highways and a growing emphasis on improved infrastructure will lead to continued growth of road construction.
Logging	The highest output level was attained in 1987, a level not expected to be reached by 2005. Moderate growth in paper products industries and slow growth in residential construction and exports are expected to lead to increased demand at a slower pace than in the past. Substitution of new materials for wood in all kinds of construction will keep projected output from attaining the 1987 level. Environmental concerns will lead to much less strip cutting and a more intensive use of present land.
Sawmills and planing mills	Slow growth in residential construction (mainly from additions and alterations) and healthy growth in exports and paper, partially offset by strong growth in imports, will lead to moderate growth in this industry.
Millwork and structural wood members, n.e.c.	The structure of this industry does not permit for much automation beyond what is already in place. This industry sells primarily to the new residential construction sector and to repairers/remodelers. Output growth is projected to slow to grow less rapidly than in the past.
Veneer and plywood	Most of the output of this industry is sold to the residential construction industry which is expected to have a lower growth rate in the coming 15 years. A healthy growth in imports will also dampen domestic growth.
Wood containers and miscellaneous wood products	This industry will grow slowly over the projection period, largely because of its dependence on residential construction as a prime customer. Output is also consumed by the wholesale trade and auto industries which will provide growth.
Prefabricated wood buildings	All output is consumed by the construction industry, which allows for very little growth in the projection period.
Household furniture	The outlook for household furniture is positive since the older and higher income baby boom groups tend to favor higher quality goods. International trading patterns are expected to undergo a transformation, particularly as NAFTA comes into play. Production of less expensive furniture may migrate to low wage countries. Both exports and imports of household furniture will continue to grow during the projection period.
Partitions and fixtures	Growth will moderate due to a slowdown in office and shopping center construction, the major components of construction purchasing this industry's output.
Office and miscellaneous furniture and fixtures	The increase in demand is due to more rapid investment growth and relatively strong growth in school construction. No significant technological advances are expected for this industry.
Glass and glass products	A continued decline in the use of glass for packaging foods and beverages is projected.
Cement, concrete, gypsum, and plaster products	All output is consumed by new construction and maintenance and repair construction. It also goes to industries like utilities and real estate which purchase large amounts of maintenance and repair construction. Growth will primarily reflect the weighted mix of growth in these industries.
Blast furnaces and basic steel products	Only slight growth is projected for this industry. Imports will continue to hold about the same share of the market and will constitute mainly semifinished steel, to be processed in U.S. finishing mills.
Iron and steel foundries	Almost 30 percent of this industry's output is sold to the auto industry, with smaller amounts taken by construction. The substitution of plastics and ceramics in autos will reduce the use of steel in the projection period.

Table 1. Specific industry assumptions—Continued

Industry	Assumptions
Special industry machinery	The food, paper, printing, and textile industries buy investment goods from this industry. Imports, however, are expected to make strong inroads in this industry's markets, but sales to foreign markets are also likely to grow at a healthy rate.
Computer equipment	Technological advances in the personal computer market are expected to continue to make systems more capable and easier to use. All industries are projected to have strong investment demand for computer equipment. Computer-aided design, flexible manufacturing systems, and computer-integrated manufacturing will affect all areas of manufacturing. Both exports and imports are expected to have strong gains. However, starting in 1991, the U.S. computer industry has posted its first-ever negative trade balance. It is assumed that much of production and assembly of this equipment will be done overseas. Imports are expected to continue to exceed exports through 2005.
Electrical distribution equipment	This industry's output is consumed by the railroad, computer, construction, and capital goods producing industries. Imports are projected to account for about 30 percent of demand by 2005, resulting in no growth and falling employment.
Electrical industrial apparatus	Most of the demand for the products of this industry are from mature markets—mainly appliances and industrial machinery and equipment. As a result, there is little potential for rapid growth in output and employment levels are projected to fall. Export growth is projected to match import growth.
Household appliances	Appliances will have more microprocessors replacing electromechanical controls. Productivity improvements are likely to displace many hand assembly steps, and many products can be standardized and the production process mechanized. The industry could use robots and other automation methods. Imports are expected to grow as a share, but will not dominate. The prospect of demand for household appliances is more positive because of demographic trends: The older and higher income baby boom groups tend to favor higher quality goods with advanced features.
Household audio and video equipment	The consumer electronics market is projected to continue the trend of very high levels of demand. Consumers will upgrade their existing systems by purchasing such items as a second video casette recorder, wider screen television sets, and compact disc players. High definition television will likely become available in the United States by 2005. It is assumed that much of the production and assembly of this equipment will be done overseas; the domestic industry will concentrate on management and research and development. Growth in high-priced stereo equipment in motor vehicles will also help to fuel growth in this industry.
Telephone and telegraph apparatus	The communications sector buys investment goods from this industry. Slight growth will be derived from upgrade demands that are due to technology advances. Specific improvements are expected in wireless telephones and cellular technology, faxes and modems, and fiber optic cable technologies in network systems.
Broadcasting and communications equipment	Increases in civilian requirements will offset decreases in defense demand. Future growth will be attributable to private sector purchases of satellites, fiber optic systems, and equipment related to telecommunications. The impact of high definition television will begin to be felt by 2005.
Semiconductors and related devices	More equipment and instruments will have electronic components. There are some limits to growth as this industry matures and imports rise, but domestic production will still expand rapidly. Increased demand will be driven by growth chiefly in the computers and telecommunication sectors.
Miscellaneous electronic components	Strong long-term growth is projected due to strong demand for computers, communications equipment, and electronic automotive products. The expansion in component exports is expected because of the continued dynamic growth in Asian markets. In addition, NAFTA contains a tariff reduction package, which may further stimulate trade with Canada and Mexico. However, the electronic component industry is also facing potentially heavy competition from other countries in the world market place.
Storage batteries and engine electrical parts	Autos and personal consumption together account for the lion's share of demand for the output of this industry. As auto demand slows, so too will production in this industry, resulting in only moderate growth.

Table 1. Specific industry assumptions—Continued

Industry	Assumptions
Motor vehicles and car bodies	The growth of the driving age population is slowing but the aging of the population will result in a tendency toward larger, higher-valued cars. With the ratification of NAFTA, U.S. producers are expected to benefit from greatly improved access to the Mexican market, where growth in new car consumption is expanding rapidly.
Aircraft	Defense purchases of aircraft is expected to decline sharply over the projection period. Commercial demand will remain strong, but increased competition from abroad means slower export growth and faster import growth, leading to generally slower domestic production growth in this sector.
Aircraft and missile engines	Reduced defense spending will lower demand. However, export growth is expected to be very strong.
Aircraft and missile parts and equipment	Reduced defense spending will lower demand. However, export growth is expected to be very strong.
Guided missiles and space vehicles	Reduced defense spending will lower demand. However, export growth is expected to be very strong.
Ship building and repairing	Defense demand is expected to decline sharply while commercial demand for ships is expected to remain quite low, leading to continued declines for this sector.
Boat building and repairing	Modest recoveries are expected in both consumer and business markets during the coming 13 years, more than offsetting defense purchase declines. Part of the reason for the strong slowdowns during the 1990's and, conversely, for the moderate pickup in growth expected in the coming period, is the enactment and subsequent cancellation of the luxury tax.
Miscellaneous transportation equipment	Individuals are expected to continue to purchase recreational transportation equipment such as travel tailers and recreational vehicles in moderately growing numbers. Defense purchases of tanks and tank components will, however, decrease. The defense component of the industry is quite small, though, and these cutbacks should not materially affect expected growth.
Measuring and controlling devices; watches	Demand will be dependent on investment, especially by public utilities, and on exports. More instruments and equipment will incorporate automatic sensors. Continued growth of imported watches will lead to a further decline in the domestic industry.
Ophthalmic goods	Personal consumption will grow due to an aging population requiring more vision care.
Medical instruments and supplies	Demand will increase because of high investment by health services. Consumer demand is also expected to show strong growth because of the expanding elderly population. The aging of the population in the United States and abroad and the increase in diseases prevalent among the elderly, will continue to spur technological innovation.
X ray and other electromedical apparatus	The health industries buy investment goods from this sector; and demand is assumed to be especially strong because of rapid growth in health services and advances in biotechnology.
Photographic equipment and supplies	Demand will increase due to the capital needs of the trade and service sectors and also due to consumer expenditures. Advances in technology will lead to continued purchases of new equipment and they will become inputs into the medical sectors.
Jewelry, silverware, and plated ware	Rising income levels will drive demand for higher priced jewelry, especially since the repeal of the luxury tax. Growth of imported goods will continue to occur at the expense of domestic production.
Toys and sporting goods	Domestic output will continue to grow at historical rates despite the accelerating growth of imports.
Manufactured products, n.e.c.	Healthy growth is expected by the half of output purchased by consumers (Personal Consumptions Expenditures—PCE), while the half of output used as inputs by other industries is projected to grow at a rate in line with overall GDP.

Table 1. Specific industry assumptions—Continued

Industry	Assumptions
Meat products	Slow growth of meat products is due to slower population growth and less meat consumption. Poultry will increasingly replace pork and beef for health reasons, thought not at the rates predicted by some health authorities. Productivity will continue to increase, but at a much slower rate because mechanization and assembly line speed are reaching limits.
Dairy products	Slow growth is expected for the part of output that is demanded by consumers—i.e., PCE—and as inputs into other products; both areas are projected to grow at an annual rate of 1 percent. Health concerns expected to lead a movement to low-fat products.
Preserved fruits and vegetables	Demand is expected to be very strong for dried or frozen specialties but weak for canned goods.
Grain mill products and fats and oils	Health concerns will boost demand for grain products. Exports will provide a source of growth as the rest of the world expands economically and raises its standard of living and diet.
Bakery products	Slower population growth and a more health conscious population will lead to slow growth in demand for the output of this industry.
Sugar and confectionery products	Health concerns will lead to a relative decrease in the use of sugar as an ingredient in prepared foods.
Alcoholic beverages	Consumers are expected to continue to drink fewer alcoholic beverages per capita. As the population ages, the movement toward wine and away from beer will continue.
Soft drinks and flavorings	The slower growth of the teenage population will limit demand for soft drinks. Some increase expected as consumers substitute soft drinks for alcoholic beverages.
Tobacco manufactures	Health concerns and anti-smoking campaigns will cause domestic sales of tobacco to continue to decline. Overall output will increase, however, because strong export growth will outweigh domestic declines.
Weaving, finishing, yarn, and thread mills	Automated production technologies will become more widespread; this industry already is heavily mechanized.
Knitting mills	This industry is already heavily automated; domestic producers are very competitive with importers.
Carpets and rugs	This industry sells to consumers and construction and other industries as inputs in about equal shares. Export trade is a small part. Demand growth is expected from consumers and the construction industry.
Miscellaneous textile goods	Ninety percent of this industry's output is consumed as inputs by other industries, such as furniture and apparel, the demand of which drives this industry.
Apparel	Consumer demand will grow faster than the population due to rising income levels. However, more of this demand will be met by imports, with domestic production growing very little.
Pulp, paper, and paperboard mills	The output of this industry is entirely consumed as inputs to other industries. Continued growth of the paper products and printing and the publishing industries will lead to growth. The industry is expected to continue to enjoy strong productivity growth.
Paperboard containers and boxes	Because the output of this industry is consumed by virtually every other sector in the economy, it is projected to grow at the same rate as GDP.
Converted paper products except containers	About 60 percent of the output of this industry is consumed by other industries as inputs to their production processes. Of the remainder, most is purchased by consumers. Healthy growth is expected, in part, due to strong exports.
Newspapers	Output will grow again because the increasingly elderly population reads more newspapers. Productivity will receive moderate benefits from computerization.

Table 1. Specific industry assumptions—Continued

Industry	Assumptions
Miscellaneous publishing	Production will be high due to the growth of catalogs, directories, newsletters, technical manuals, and other types of miscellaneous publishing.
Commercial printing and business forms	Desktop publishing software is not expected to hurt this industry. Rather, the ease with which material can be set up for printing will allow for some growth in this sector from persons who would not in the past have turned to a commercial printing service.
Industrial chemicals	Disposal of toxic wastes will be troublesome for the industry, possibly leading to some slowdowns in growth.
Plastics materials and synthetics	Output grows as plastics and composites continue to substitute for metals.
Drugs	Strong long-term growth is projected due to a strong demand for established drugs, a vast array of new products, and an expanding elderly population. Biotechnology advances are expected to contribute to the number of products available. Strong export growth is assumed.
Agricultural chemicals	Imports will continue to increase. Economic liberalization in eastern Europe should open new opportunities for U.S. companies as countries in that region develop their agricultural sectors. However, growing concerns about environmental and health issues are among challenges that this industry will face.
Petroleum refining	Industries will continue energy conservation measures in an attempt to control costs. Vehicles will become more energy efficient and the use of coal for electric generation will increase. Production projections are based on data developed by the U.S. Department of Energy.
Miscellaneous petroleum and coal products	Output in this industry is consumed by the construction industry, mainly for highways, and is driven primarily by assumptions regarding government spending in this area.
Tires and inner tubes	The move to long-life radial tires is now complete and only modest growth is expected in the coming 13 years as auto demand slows.
Miscellaneous plastic products, n.e.c.	Substitution of plastics for metal and glass, and its almost exclusive use as inputs by a wide range of other industries, will continue to spur growth.
Footwear, except rubber and plastic	The industry continues to be one of declining production and increasing imports. Over 85 percent of demand for footwear is expected to be met through imports, resulting in continued declines projected for domestic output.
Luggage, handbags, and leather products, n.e.c.	Output will decline as imports are expected to continue their increase.
Railroad transportation	The potential for high-speed rail passenger service and increased concerns over traffic congestion and air pollution will provide favorable conditions for railroad transportation. Rail freight will hold a steady share of the transportation sector.
Local and interurban passenger transit	Both public transit and contracted school bus transportation are expected to continue recent growth trends.
Trucking and warehousing	This industry is projected to grow faster than the total economy due to increases in exports, just-in-time inventory controls, and smaller plus more dispersed specialized industries, which are expected to shift more demand to trucking.
Water transportation	A continued relative decline in shipping as means of transporting goods to market is expected.
Air transportation	The demand for air travel is expected to continue to grow rapidly. Significant increases in consumer demand reflect growth in income and the impact of airline deregulation on the fare structure. Exports of air travel will continue to dominate imports due to the relatively cheap fares offered by U.S. airlines.

Table 1. Specific industry assumptions—Continued

Industry	Assumptions
Pipelines, except natural gas	The output of this industry is consumed as inputs to a wide variety of other industries but mainly by the petroleum refining industry, which has slow projected growth.
Passenger transportation arrangement	While growth will continue to be substantial, the increasing use of technologies such as video-conferencing and electronic document sharing will cause a decrease in business travel and therefore slower projected growth than that of the past two decades.
Communications, except broadcasting	Telephone services are expected to show rapid growth with new applications and extensions of current technology. Productivity growth will be high.
Radio and television broadcasting; cable TV	Despite advances in cable TV offerings, this industry will not sustain the rapid growth of the past, particularly as the cable TV market approaches saturation. In addition, there will be a considerable blurring in the future as to which of the communications industries will actually be providing expanded cable and other communications services.
Electric utilities, including combined services	The shift away from oil and natural gas in home heating and towards electric heat pumps is expected to continue. Demand for electric utilities is expected to grow slightly due to general growth of the economy despite continued conservation of energy.
Gas utilities, including combined services	Continued energy conservation measures will decrease the relative use of natural gas by most industries and by individual homes.
Water and sanitation, including combined services	This industry is expected to grow due to general growth of the economy and to increasing demand for waste disposal and the recycling of refuse.
Wholesale trade	Growth is projected to slow from its recent high rates but still exceeds that of GDP. Exports are expected to take up the slack from deliveries to PCE and in selling inputs to industries.
Retail trade, except eating and drinking places	Grocery stores will be faced with increasing pressures to raise productivity, but at the same time they will offer more labor-intensive services (salad bars, prepared foods, deli's, etc.), and more grocery stores will extend hours. Tele- and computer-shopping is not assumed to have a major impact on retailers through 2005.
Eating and drinking places	Demand for fast-food will slow as the population ages. The increasing popularity of microwave ovens and the availability of prepared meals from grocery and specialty stores will also help to explain the slowdown in food-away-from-home sales. Full-service restaurants are expected to grow, as is contracting for food service operations by hospitals, schools, and other institutions.
Depository institutions	Persons consume 60 percent of the output of this industry, which is produced primarily by commercial banks. The gradual slowing in annual output growth rates from 1960 is expected to continue. Consolidation through mergers will result in substantial productivity gains that allows fewer employees to produce this increased output.
Nondepository institutions; holding and investment offices	The output of this industry is split between persons and as inputs to other industries about equally. Demand from both these sources at double the rate of GDP growth insures healthy growth here. It is expected that some demand will shift here from place of depository institutions.
Security and commodity brokers	Personal spending on brokerage charges and investment counseling has undergone tremendous growth recently. Growth is expected to continue, although the projected growth rate is not expected to match that of recent years. As the baby boomers age, demand for financial planning advice will increase. Other growth will come from expanding pension funds, college endowments, and retirement programs such as IRA and Keogh; under deregulation, brokerage firms can offer more financial and credit services.
Insurance carriers	Increasing demand is assumed for specialized insurance, such as accident and health or fire and casualty, which is not easily standardized. Work force may have to increase because of the demand for new commercial coverage such as product liability, prepaid legal, or pollution liability. Competition from noninsurance firms, such as banks and department stores, and from foreign companies may take away some of the insurance industry's business. However, this should be partially offset by expansion of insurance firms into other financial services.

Table 1. Specific industry assumptions—Continued

Industry	Assumptions
Real estate	The output here is sold 30 percent to consumers and 70 percent to industries as inputs. Demand on the part of both is projected to grow at the rate of GDP resulting in this industry doing likewise.
Hotels and other lodging places	Personal expenditures are expected to outstrip business expenditures as more discretionary income and more senior citizens lead to increased vacation expenditures. In addition, increased productivity will cut employment growth because of more demand for budget lodging places.
Personal services, n.e.c.	Fueled by higher income levels, demand for personal services will continue to grow, particularly given an expected array of new services.
Services to buildings	Slower growth and flat productivity is projected because contracting out of services is nearly reaching its limits.
Personnel supply services	Businesses will increase their expenditures, especially for temporary help services. The market for temporaries will expand to include more nurses, engineers, and accountants for jobs of longer duration. Continued contracting for facilities management on the part of government is also assumed.
Computer and data processing services	Business expenditures will increase as firms attempt to find the right software to fill their needs, and as specialized software is designed and developed. Strong government demand assumed.
Detective, guard, and security services	Business and government will continue to increase their expenditures for these services. However, as the industry matures, guard services are not expected to grow as rapidly as in the past. Some additional growth will come from the sale and operation of security systems.
Photocopying, commercial art, photofinishing	Productivity is expected to increase in the projection period as digital photograhy and digital processing techniques revolutionize this industry. Personal consumption is expected to grow strongly as individuals convert to the new digital cameras.
Business services, n.e.c.	Business expenditures on miscellaneous services are expected to increase as the number of services expands. In addition, services such as direct mail, paralegal services, and driving services will expand.
Automotive rentals, without drivers	Productivity will increase sharply due to the expected increasing use of computerized reservations systems.
Electrical repair shops	Growth in this industry is entirely to continued growth from the consumer sector, primarily for electronics equipment repairs.
Video tape rental	It is expected that the vigorous expansion in the 1980's will come to an end due to innovations in cable TV offerings.
Motion pictures	Output will be stimulated by increased business use of videos for training, and increased personal consumption of videos.
Producers, orchestras, and entertainers	Output will be stimulated by rising personal incomes and the increased programming required for cable television.
Offices of health practitioners	More health services will be performed in group practice centers, particularly HMO's.
Nursing and personal care facilities	Fueling the demand for nursing homes and skilled-care nursing facilities will be strong growth in the elderly population, especially those over age 85.
Hospitals, private	Growth will occur as the demand for health care grows with expanded insurance coverage and as hospitals expand outpatient facilities. Partially offsetting this growth will be cost-containment pressures and new technologies that permit more procedures to be performed in doctors' offices and other outpatient facilities.
Health services, n.e.c.	Continued greater reliance on outpatient and home health care, more contracting out of medical laboratory work, and general growth of demand for health services will result in growth in this industry.

Table 1. Specific industry assumptions—Continued

Industry	Assumptions
Legal services	Increased litigation and the trend toward more specialized services and regional expansion of law firms will boost output at a slightly slower rate than historically. Increased productivity due to computers will require fewer employees. Use of computers will increase productivity.
Elementary and secondary schools	State and local government spending will increase due to general growth in the school age population. Within the industry, secondary school enrollments will grow faster than those in elementary schools, reflecting growth in the population of 14-17-year-olds versus 5-13-year-olds.
Colleges and universities	Continued enrollment increases, particularly of part-time and older students, will drive growth in this industry. Increases in foreign students' expenditures in the U.S.(exports) are also expected to continue.
Libraries, vocational, and other schools	Vocational programs will grow due to increased efforts to train individuals who do not go to college.
Individual and miscellaneous social services	Growth will be driven by health insurance reimbursements for counseling services and increased use of senior services, such as adult day care.
Job training and related services	The recent emphasis on job training for the physically impaired will drive this industry.
Child day care services	Growth will occur as the number of children under age 5 increases, as more mothers enter the work force, and as care continues to shift from home-based baby-sitting, such as from unpaid relatives, to the commercial sector.
Residential care	This sector will be affected by the shift away from hospital care. Strong growth is expected for drug and alcohol rehabilitation centers and elderly residential care.
Engineering and architectural services	Spending will increase as demand for engineering services increases with growth in private construction industries and government-funded infrastructure.
Research and testing services	Continued demand by other industries for these services will be offset somewhat by lower defense spending.
Management and public relations	Government agencies and businesses will continue spending for specialized services, such as financial, personnel, and information systems and for managerial and consulting services.
Accounting, auditing, and services, n.e.c.	The growing complexity of tax laws, accounting procedures, and reporting requirements will cause continued expenditures by business and government for these services.
Private households	Demand for housekeeping and babysitting will grow, but will be met more by contract firms than by private individuals.
U.S. Postal Service	The increased use of electronic communications and alternate carriers will slow the grwoth in demand for these services.
Federal general government	With the general downsizing of the Federal Executive Branch, especially in defense, employment will decline.
Local government passenger transit	Output will grow in this industry as subway and light rail construction are more and more used by cities to alleviate downtown congestion.
State and local government hospitals	Spending will increase although more slowly than in the past and more slowly than private hospitals as cost-containment measures are introduced.
State government education	Increasing emphasis on education and general population growth will raise demand for public colleges and universities.
Local government education	An increasing emphasis on education and more rapid secondary school age population growth will drive demand for elementary and secondary schools.

Projections for Self-Employed Workers

Appendix E

Editor's Comments:

If you are considering self-employment as an option, this appendix will provide you with some information that you may find helpful. It lists occupations that have larger numbers of people who are self-employed along with projections for growth and other details. While this is not nearly enough information on which to base a decision, it will show you the many options for self-employment that others have found.

JIST Works, Inc., publishes several books that may be of help if you are considering self-employment as an option, including *Mind Your Own Business!* and *Franchise Opportunities Handbook*. There are also many books and other resource materials on this topic at libraries, bookstores, the Small Business Administration, and many other sources.

Table 6.   **Occupations with 50,000 or more self-employed workers, actual 1992 and projected to 2005**

[Numbers in thousands]

Occupation	1992			2005			Change in self-employed, 1992–2005	
	Total employment	Self-employed	Percent of total employment	Total employment	Self-employed	Percent of total employment	Number	Percent
Total, all occupations	121,099	10,009	8	147,482	11,501	8	1,492	15
Executive, administrative, and managerial occupations	12,066	1,395	12	15,195	1,916	13	521	37
Managerial and administrative occupations	8,411	1,110	13	10,427	1,562	15	452	41
Food service and lodging managers	532	193	36	764	270	35	77	40
Property and real estate managers	243	90	37	328	100	30	10	11
Management support occupations ..	3,654	285	8	4,767	354	7	69	24
Accountants and auditors	939	101	11	1,243	110	9	9	9
Management analysts	208	85	41	297	125	42	40	47
Professional specialty occupations	16,592	1,522	9	22,801	1,793	8	271	18
Social scientists	258	84	33	353	120	34	36	43
Psychologists	143	67	47	212	100	47	33	49
Lawyers and judicial workers	716	217	30	913	234	26	17	8
Lawyers	626	217	35	821	234	29	17	8
Teachers, librarians, and counselors .	5,984	149	2	8,010	178	2	29	19
Other teachers and instructors	817	119	15	1,082	136	13	17	14
Adult and vocational education teachers	540	119	22	712	136	19	17	14
Instructors, adult (nonvocational) education ...	235	119	51	296	136	46	17	14
Health diagnosing occupations	875	280	32	1,120	305	27	25	9
Dentists	183	93	51	192	98	51	5	5
Physicians	556	126	23	751	135	18	9	7
Health assessment and treating occupations	2,436	60	2	3,482	78	2	18	30
Writers, artists, and entertainers	1,606	553	34	2,012	637	32	84	15
Artists and commercial artists	273	166	61	335	196	58	30	18
Designers	302	108	36	359	114	32	6	6
Designers, except interior designers	236	78	33	285	81	28	3	4
Musicians....................	236	85	36	294	95	32	10	12
Writers and editors, including technical writers	283	93	33	348	105	30	12	13
Technicians and related support occupations	4,282	98	2	5,664	131	2	33	34
Marketing and sales occupations	12,993	1,791	14	15,664	1,890	12	100	6
Insurance sales workers	415	137	33	477	147	31	10	7
Marketing and sales worker supervisors	2,036	750	37	2,443	782	32	32	4
Real estate agents, brokers, and appraisers	397	252	63	461	272	59	20	8
Sales agents, real estate	283	197	70	315	210	67	13	7
Salespersons, retail	3,660	193	5	4,446	201	5	8	4
Administrative support occupations, including clerical	22,349	313	1	25,406	318	1	5	2
Records processing occupations	3,621	153	4	3,834	153	4	0	0
Financial records processing occupations	2,686	150	6	2,770	150	5	0	0
Bookkeeping, accounting, and auditing clerks	2,112	144	7	2,186	144	7	0	0
Secretaries, stenographers, and typists....................	4,228	74	2	4,488	80	2	6	8
Service occupations	19,358	1,076	6	25,820	1,542	6	466	43
Cleaning and building service occupations, except private household	3,284	142	4	3,913	227	6	85	60
Janitors and cleaners, including maids and housekeeping cleaners	2,862	127	4	3,410	210	6	83	65

Table 6.   Continued—Occupations with 50,000 or more self-employed workers, actual 1992 and projected to 2005

[Numbers in thousands]

Occupation	1992			2005			Change in self-employed, 1992–2005	
	Total employment	Self-employed	Percent of total employment	Total employment	Self-employed	Percent of total employment	Number	Percent
Food preparation and service occupations	7,669	71	1	10,060	80	1	9	13
Personal service occupations	2,295	766	33	3,804	1,099	29	333	43
Barbers	71	56	79	69	56	81	0	0
Child care workers	684	392	57	1,135	630	56	238	61
Cosmetologists and related workers	676	315	47	915	410	45	95	30
Hairdressers, hairstylists, and cosmetologists	628	300	48	846	390	46	90	30
Protective service occupations	2,320	11	0	3,154	16	1	5	45
Agriculture, forestry, fishing, and related occupations	3,530	1,390	39	3,650	1,238	34	−152	−11
Farm operators and managers	1,218	1,081	89	1,014	850	84	−231	−21
Farmers	1,088	1,081	99	857	850	99	−231	−21
Gardeners and groundskeepers, except farm	884	179	20	1,195	255	21	76	42
Precision production, craft, and repair occupations	13,580	1,809	13	15,380	2,042	13	233	13
Blue-collar worker supervisors	1,757	168	10	1,974	190	10	22	13
Construction trades	3,510	972	28	4,295	1,175	27	203	21
Carpenters	978	400	41	1,176	475	40	75	19
Electricians	518	59	11	618	72	12	13	22
Painters and paperhangers, construction and maintenance	440	221	50	569	295	52	74	33
Plumbers, pipefitters, and steamfitters	351	60	17	378	64	17	4	7
Roofers	127	50	39	155	61	39	11	22
Mechanics, installers, and repairers	4,819	454	9	5,581	470	8	16	4
Machinery and related mechanics, installers, and repairers	1,696	63	4	2,005	70	3	7	11
Vehicle and mobile equipment mechanics and repairers	1,524	279	18	1,850	286	15	7	3
Automotive mechanics	739	186	25	907	200	22	14	8
Other mechanics, installers, and repairers	946	77	8	1,123	77	7	0	0
Production occupations, precision	2,956	209	7	2,965	201	7	−8	−4
Textile, apparel, and furnishings workers, precision	266	97	36	260	88	34	−9	−9
Custom tailors and sewers	113	69	61	109	63	58	−6	−9
Operators, fabricators, and laborers	16,349	615	4	17,902	630	4	16	3
Machine setters, set–up operators, operators, and tenders	4,676	91	2	4,326	86	2	−6	−6
Hand workers, including assemblers and fabricators	2,528	105	4	2,630	115	4	10	10
Transportation and material moving machine and vehicle operators	4,694	341	7	5,719	349	6	8	2
Motor vehicle operators	3,429	300	9	4,285	310	7	10	3
Truck drivers	2,720	245	9	3,428	248	7	3	1
Truck drivers light and heavy	2,391	225	9	3,039	225	7	0	0
Helpers, laborers, and material movers, hand	4,451	78	2	5,227	81	2	3	4

More Good Books from JIST Works, Inc.

The Quick Interview and Salary Negotiation Book
Dramatically Improve Your Interviewing Skills and Pay in a Matter of Hours
by J. Michael Farr

More than 80 percent of job applicants do a poor job of presenting their skills in job interviews. Even more people are baffled by "problem questions" such as these:

✓ What salary are you expecting?
✓ Why should I hire you?
✓ What is your major weakness?

The simple yet powerful three-step process explained in this book unravels the secret of answering these and other difficult interview questions. This valuable book contains features that will enable readers to quickly improve their interviewing skills, including development of a powerful "skills language." A series of practical, proven techniques for getting more interviews is included as well as dress and grooming tips.

Other information
■ "If you have an important interview later today" Section designed to be read in one hour or less
■ Includes basic and advanced techniques
■ Contains many specific examples
■ Provides advice on how to avoid being screened out

7-1/2 x 9-1/2, Paper 400 pp.
ISBN 1-56370-162-6
$12.95
Order Code J1626

- -

The Quick Resume & Cover Letter Book
Write and Use an Effective Resume in Only One Day
by J. Michael Farr

7-1/2 x 9-1/2, Paper, 320 pp.
ISBN 1-56370-141-3
$9.95
Order code RCLQG

First title in JIST's new *Quick Guides* series, by a best-selling author whose job search books have sold more than one million copies! Contains an "Instant Resume Worksheet" that enables job seekers to put together a basic, acceptable resume in less than one day. Provides helpful advice on creating job objectives, identifying skills, dealing with special situations, and getting a job. No matter what your employment history, read this book to discover how your resume can emphasize your strengths and diminish your weaknesses.

Other information
■ Contains more than 60 sample resumes and cover letters
■ Logical structure makes information easy to locate
■ Includes crucial career planning and job search sections
■ Gives tips on using computers to develop superior resumes
■ Advice on writing cover letters, thank-you notes, and other correspondence

Look for these and other fine books from
JIST Works, Inc. at your full service bookstore
or call us for additional information